INTERCULTURAL COMMUNICATION

INTERCULTURAL COMMUNICATION

A Global Reader

Editor
Fred E. Jandt
California State University, San Bernardino

SAGE Publications
International Educational and Professional Publisher
Thousand Oaks ▪ London ▪ New Delhi

For information:

Sage Publications, Inc.
2455 Teller Road
Thousand Oaks, California 91320
E-mail: order@sagepub.com

Sage Publications Ltd.
6 Bonhill Street
London EC2A 4PU
United Kingdom

Sage Publications India Pvt. Ltd.
B-42, Panchsheel Enclave
Post Box 4109
New Delhi 110 017 India

Printed in the United States of America

Library of Congress Cataloging-in-Publication Data

Intercultural communication : a global reader / edited by Fred E. Jandt.
 p. cm.
Includes bibliographical references and index.
ISBN 0-7619-2899-5 (cloth)
 1. Intercultural communication. I. Jandt, Fred Edmund.
HM1211.I5624 2004
306—dc21

           2003011332

Printed on acid-free paper

04 05 06 07 08 09 10 9 8 7 6 5 4 3 2 1

Acquiring Editor:	Todd R. Armstrong
Editorial Assistant:	Veronica Novak
Developmental Editor:	Alicia Carter
Production Editor:	Claudia A. Hoffman
Typesetter:	C&M Digitals (P) Ltd.
Cover Designer:	Ravi Balasuriya

Contents

About the Author

Fred E. Jandt was born of second-generation German immigrants in the multicultural south-central region of Texas. His doctorate in communication is from Bowling Green State University. He has taught and been a student of intercultural communication for more than 30 years, developing his experience through travel and international training and research projects.

While Professor of Communication at State University of New York at Brockport, his reputation as a teacher led to this appointment as SUNY's first director of faculty development. He is currently Professor of Communication at California State University, San Bernardino, and recently was a visiting professor at Victoria University of Wellington in New Zealand.

He has extensive experience in the areas of intercultural and international communication, negotiation and mediation, and computer-mediated communication. He is known for his book *Win-Win Negotiating* (1985), which has been translated into seven languages. The focus of his interest is on the overlap of conflict and culture studies. He edited with Paul B. Pedersen *Constructive Conflict Management: Asia-Pacific Cases* (1996).

To the Reader

I have had the opportunities on occasion to teach intercultural communication classes outside of the U.S. On one such occasion, the textbook for the course had been chosen in advance by members of the local university faculty. Their logic was to select a reader that was popularly used in the U.S. As the class progressed, I found myself becoming more and more uncomfortable with that selection because of the students' reactions. The students took offense to the textbook because they found it U.S.-centric—most of the readings seemed to reflect only U.S. views of the world, of research questions, and of research methodologies. I became increasingly aware that textbooks written by U.S. authors and published by U.S. publishers can be U.S.-centric. Textbooks are only one small example of what some perceive as U.S. global dominance.

As I developed this book of readings, I had two objectives. The first was to include researchers from as many parts of the world as possible. This book of readings includes authors from Australia, Canada, China, Egypt, France, Germany, Hong Kong, India, Iran, Japan, Korea, Mali, the Netherlands, New Zealand, Nigeria, Norway, Singapore, Taiwan, Thailand, the United Kingdom, and the United States. Sage, as perhaps the most international of the communication book publishers, has the unique resources to support this approach.

The second objective comes out of a concern with the concept of othering. This concept is developed in my reading with Dolores Tanno in this volume. Generally, it is a concern that researchers not impose research questions and research methodologies on others, that is, that peoples speak in their own voices. For examples, Thais investigate conflict resolution strategies in Thai organizations and a Maori writes about Maori language education. I did not design this volume to include readings where outside researchers speak for others. Consistent with this objective, rather than convert spellings to those preferred in the U.S., I have retained spellings as they appeared in the original publications.

Instructors using editions of my textbook, *An Introduction to Intercultural Communication: Identities in a Global Community*, have written me on occasion with questions about classes that are largely homogeneous and students who have had little international experience. I chose the readings in this collection to introduce students not only to intercultural communication constructs and theories but also to global issues. Lalita Rajasingham, the author of "The Impact of Universities on Globalisation" in this volume, suggested that, instead of "think globally, act locally," in today's technological world it is "act globally, think locally." It is our world stage, but that does not mean we must lose our local identities to perform there.

—Fred E. Jandt

ix

PART I

Cultural Values

What is meant by the word *culture*? There is no easy answer. In 1952, Alfred Kroeber and Clyde Kluckhohn published a list of 160 different definitions of the word: We could define culture from a historical perspective, that is, the traditions that are passed on to future generations; we could define culture from a behavioral perspective, that is, the learned, shared ways of behaving in life; we could define culture from a symbolic perspective, that is, the arbitrarily assigned meanings that are shared by a society. We could also define culture from a structural perspective, that is, patterns and interrelated ideas, symbols, or behaviors. Finally, we could define culture from a normative perspective, that is, the ideals, values, and rules for living.

From all these perspectives, we acknowledge culture to be learned rather than biologically inherited and to involve arbitrarily assigned, symbolic meanings. Human ability to assign arbitrary meanings is what, at base, distinguishes one culture from another. The readings in this first section address culture from structural and normative perspectives to examine the values that guide behavior within a cultural group.

Claude Lévi-Strauss was born in 1908 in Belgium and studied at the University of Paris. For a time in the 1930s, he was a professor at the University of Sao Paulo, making several expeditions into central Brazil. His belief that the characteristics of humans are everywhere identical was found after countless visits to North and South American Indian tribes. The method he used to study the social organization of these tribes is called *structuralism*, which he defined as "the search for unsuspected harmonies." Lévi-Strauss derived structuralism from a school of linguistics whose focus was not on the meaning of the word but the patterns that the words form. He is also known for his structural analysis of mythology. He was interested in explaining why myths around the world seem so similar. Perhaps he was most recognized for his refusal to see Western civilization as privileged and unique and for his insistence that the savage mind is equal to the civilized mind. This reader begins with excerpts from Lévi-Strauss's writings as a voice for cultural diversity.

Geert Hofstede was born in 1928 at Haarlem, the Netherlands. His formal education included an internship as an assistant ship's engineer on a voyage to Indonesia. He founded and managed the Personnel Research Department of IBM Europe. Later he was co-founder and first director of IRIC, the Institute for Research on Intercultural Cooperation in the Netherlands, and professor of organizational anthropology and international management at Maastricht University, also in the Netherlands. Hofstede was partly responsible for IBM's International Employee Opinion

Research Programme. Over a 6-year period, he and his colleagues collected and analyzed more than 100,000 questionnaires completed by matched groups of IBM employees in 72 countries around the world. The influence of his work is evidenced by his being the most cited non-American in the field of management in the U.S. Social Science Citation Index. In the reading "Business Cultures," Hofstede briefly describes what we commonly refer to as *Hofstede's cultural dimensions.*

Hofstede's dimensions have become the basis of extensive research projects. In "Human Factors on the Flight Deck: The Influence of National Culture," Ashleigh C. Merritt and Robert L. Helmreich used Hofstede's dimensions to study group processes among pilots and flight attendants working on national airlines.

Cultural values permeate all aspects of culture, and we frequently study them when we examine how conflicts within a culture develop and evolve. In "Conflict Management in Thai Organizations," Rujira Rojjanaprapayon and his graduate students Porntipha Chiemprapha and Achaya Kanchanakul explore the characteristics of conflict management within the context of Thai cultural values. And in

"An Examination of Taoist and Buddhist Perspectives on Interpersonal Conflicts, Emotions, and Adversities," Rueyling Chuang explores Taoist and Buddhist teachings as basis for fundamental Asian cultural values. And finally, in a well done and extensive study, Jung-huel Becky Yeh and Ling Chen examine value orientations, behavioral variations to arguing, and perceptions of being argumentative in Taiwan, Hong Kong, and mainland China.

Jonathan J. H. Zhu and Zhou He report the results of a study of adult Internet users in Beijing and Guangzhou and value orientations of Communism, materialism, and postmaterialism.

In 1831, the 26-year-old aristocrat Alexis de Tocqueville toured the U.S. His pioneering ethnographic work *Democracy in America* continues to enlighten readers with its insights into U.S. cultural values. His work is an example of *etic knowledge,* that is, theoretical and normative information about a culture learned by an outsider. In the final reading in this section, M. Gene Aldridge offers his individual and personal insight in understanding contemporary U.S. His observations are an example of *emic knowledge,* that is, what is learned about a culture from an insider.

Reading 1.1

Race, History, and Culture

CLAUDE LÉVI-STRAUSS

A culture's chance of uniting the complex body of inventions of all sorts which we describe as a civilization depends on the number and diversity of the other cultures with which it is working out a common strategy.

RACE AND HISTORY[1]

The development of human life is not everywhere the same but rather takes form in an extraordinary diversity of societies and civilizations. This intellectual, aesthetic and sociological diversity is in no way the outcome of the biological differences, in certain observable features, between different groups of men; it is simply a parallel phenomenon in a different sphere. But, at the same time, we must note two important respects in which there is a sharp distinction. First, the order of magnitude is different. There are many more human cultures than human races, since the first are to be counted in thousands and the second in single units. . . . Second, in contrast to the diversity of races, where interest is confined to their historical origin or their distribution over the face of the world, the diversity of cultures gives rise to many problems; it may be wondered whether it is an advantage or a disadvantage for human kind. . . .

Last and most important, the nature of this diversity must be investigated even at the risk of allowing the racial prejudices whose biological foundation has so lately been destroyed to develop again on new grounds. . . . We cannot therefore claim to have formulated a convincing denial of the inequality of the human *races,* so long as we fail to consider the problem of the inequality—or diversity—of human *cultures,* which is in fact—however unjustifiably—closely associated with it in the public mind. . . .

COLLABORATION BETWEEN CULTURES

A culture's chance of uniting the complex body of inventions of all sort which we describe as a civilization depends on the number and diversity of the other cultures with which it is working out, generally involuntarily, a common strategy. Number and diversity: a comparison of the Old World with the New on the eve of the latter's discovery [in 1492] provides a good illustration of the need for these two factors.

Europe at the beginning of the Renaissance was the meeting-place and melting pot of the most diverse influences: the Greek, Roman, Germanic and Anglo-Saxon traditions

---

Reprinted with permission from the *UNESCO Courier*, March 1996, Claude Lévi-Strauss.

combined with the influences of Arabia and China. Pre-Columbian America enjoyed no fewer cultural contacts, quantitatively speaking, as the various American cultures maintained relations with one another and the two Americas together represent a whole new hemisphere. But, while the cultures which were cross-fertilizing each other in Europe had resulted from differentiation dating back several tens of thousands of years, those on the more recently occupied American continent had had less time to develop divergencies; the picture they offered was relatively homogeneous. Thus, although it would not be true to say that the cultural standard of Mexico or Peru was [in 1492] inferior to that of Europe at the time of the discovery (we have in fact seen that, in some respects, it was superior), the various aspects of culture were possibly less well organized in relation to each other.... Their organization, less flexible and diversified, probably explains their collapse before a handful of conquerors. And the underlying reason for this may be sought in the fact that the partners to the American cultural "coalition" were less dissimilar from one another than their counterparts in the Old World.

No society is therefore essentially and intrinsically cumulative. Cumulative history is not the prerogative of certain races or certain cultures, marking them off from the rest. It is the result of their *conduct* rather than their *nature*. It represents a certain "way of life" of cultures which depends on their capacity to "go along together." In this sense, it may be said that cumulative history is the type of history characteristic of grouped societies—social super-organisms—while stationary history (supporting it to exist) would be the distinguishing feature of an inferior form of social life, the isolated society.

The one real calamity, the one fatal flaw which can afflict a human group and prevent it from achieving fulfillment is to be alone.

We can thus see how clumsy and intellectually unsatisfactory the generally accepted efforts to defend the contributions of various human races and cultures to civilization often are. We list features, we sift questions of origin, we allot first places. However well-intentioned they may be, these efforts serve no purpose for, in three respects, they miss their aim.

In the first place, there can never be any certainty about a particular culture's credit for an invention or discovery.... In the second place, all cultural contributions can be divided into two groups. On the one hand we have isolated acquisitions or features, whose importance is evident but which are also somewhat limited.... At the other end of the scale (with a whole series of intermediates, of course), there are systematized contributions, representing the peculiar form in which each society has chosen to express and satisfy the generality of human aspirations. There is no denying the originality and particularity of these patterns, but, as they all represent the exclusive choice of a single group, it is difficult to see how one civilization can hope to benefit from the way of life of another, unless it is prepared to renounce its own individuality. Attempted compromises are, in fact, likely to produce only two results: either the disorganization and collapse of the pattern of one of the groups; or a new combination, which then, however, represents the emergence of a third pattern, and cannot be assimilated to either of the others. The question with which we are concerned, indeed, is not to discover whether or not a society can derive benefit from the way of life of its neighbours, but whether, and if so to what extent, it can succeed in understanding or even in knowing them....

WORLD CIVILIZATION

Finally, wherever a contribution is made, there must be a recipient. But, while there are in fact real cultures which can be localized in time and space, and which may be said to have "contributed" and to be continuing their contributions, what can this "world civilization" be, which is supposed to be the recipient of all these contributions? It is not a civilization distinct from all the others, and yet real in the same sense that they are. . . . [It is] an abstract conception, to which we attribute a moral or logical significance—moral, if we are thinking of an aim to be pursued by existing societies; logical, if we are using the one term to cover the common features which analysis may reveal in the different cultures. In both cases, we must not shut our eyes to the fact that the concept of world civilization is very sketchy and imperfect, and that its intellectual and emotional content is tenuous. To attempt to assess cultural contributions with all the weight of countless centuries behind them . . . by reference to the sole yardstick of a world civilization which is still a hollow shell, would be greatly to impoverish them, draining away their life-blood and leaving nothing but the bare bones behind.

. . . The true contribution of a culture consists not in the list of inventions which it has personally produced, but in its difference from others. The sense of gratitude and respect which each single member of a given culture can and should feel towards all others can only be based on the conviction that the other cultures differ from his own in countless ways. . . .

We have taken the notion of world civilization as a sort of limiting concept or as an epitome of a highly complex process. If our arguments are valid, there is not, and never can be, a world civilization in the absolute sense in which that term is often used, since civilization implies, and indeed consists in, the coexistence of cultures exhibiting the maximum possible diversities. A world civilization could, in fact, represent no more than a worldwide coalition of cultures, each of which would preserve its own originality.

RACE AND CULTURE[2]

[In 1952] in a booklet written for UNESCO, I suggested the concept of "coalition" to explain why isolated cultures could not hope to create single-handed the conditions necessary for a truly cumulative history. To achieve this, I said, different cultures must, voluntarily or involuntarily combine their respective stakes in the great game of history, to increase their chances of making that long run of winning plays by which history progresses. Geneticists are at present [1971] putting forward very similar views on biological evolution, in pointing out that a genome is in reality a system within which certain genes function as regulators and others act in concert on a single characteristic (or the contrary, if several characteristics depend on a single gene). What is true of the individual genome is also true of a population, in which the combination of a number of genetic inheritances—in which until recently a "racial type" would have been identified—must always be such as to allow the establishment of an optimum equilibrium and improve the group's chances of survival. In this sense, it might be said that in the history of populations, genetic recombination plays a part comparable to that played by cultural recombination in the evolution of the ways of life, techniques, knowledge and beliefs by which different societies are distinguished. . . .

THE NATURE-CULTURE DEBATE

[But] one fact cannot be too strongly emphasized: while selection makes it possible for living species to adapt to their natural environment or to resist its changes more effectively, in the case of man this environment ceases to be natural in any real sense. Its characteristics arise from technical, economic, social and psychological conditions which, through the operation of culture, create a particular environment for each human group. We can go a step further, and consider whether the relation between organic evolution and cultural evolution is not merely analogical, but also complementary. . . .

In the dawn of humanity, biological evolution perhaps selected such pre-cultural traits as upright posture, manual dexterity, sociability, the capacity to think in symbols, speech and the ability to communicate. But once a culture existed, these traits were consolidated and propagated by cultural factors. When cultures became specialized, it was again cultural factors which consolidated and encouraged other traits, such as resistance to heat or cold for those societies which had willy-nilly to adapt themselves to extreme climatic conditions; aggressive or contemplative dispositions, technical ingenuity etc. None of these traits, as perceived at a cultural level, can clearly be attributed to a genetic basis, although we cannot exclude the possibility that such a connexion—even if partial, remote and indirect—may sometimes exist. In that case, it would be true to say that every culture selects genetic aptitudes which then, by reflex action, influence those cultures by which they were at first stimulated.

AN IDEOLOGICAL COVER

By pushing back the earliest beginnings of humanity to an ever more remote past—according to recent estimates, some millions of years ago—physical anthropology has undermined one of the principal bases for racialist theory, since the number of unknowable factors concerned thus increases much more rapidly than the number of landmarks available to stake out the paths followed by our earliest ancestors in the course of their evolution.

Geneticists delivered even more decisive blows to these theories when they replaced the concept of type by that of population and the concept of race by that of the genetic stock, and again when they demonstrated that there is a gulf between hereditary differences attributable

to a single gene—which are of little significance from the point of view of race, since they probably always have an adaptive value—and those attributable to the combined action of several, which makes it virtually impossible to determine them. . . .

Only in the last ten years have we begun to understand that we were discussing the problem of the relation between organic and cultural evolution in terms which Auguste Comte would have described as metaphysical. Human evolution is not a by-product of biological evolution, but neither is it completely distinct from it. A synthesis of these two traditional points of view is now possible, provided that biologists are not content with answers not based on fact, or with dogmatic explanations, and realize both the help they can give each other and their respective limitations.

The unsatisfactory nature of the traditional solutions to the problem perhaps explains why the ideological struggle against racialism has proved so ineffective on a practical level. There is nothing to indicate that racial prejudice is declining and plenty of evidence to suggest that, after brief periods of localized quiescence, it is reappearing everywhere with increased intensity. It is for this reason that UNESCO feels called upon to renew from time to time a battle whose outcome appears uncertain, to say the least.

But can we be so sure that the racial form taken by intolerance results primarily from false beliefs held by this or that people about the dependence of culture on organic evolution? Are these ideas not simply an ideological cover for a more real form of antagonism, based on the will to subjugate and on relations of power? This was certainly the case in the past, but, even supposing that these relations of power become less marked, will not racial differentiation continue to serve as a pretext for the growing difficulty of living together, unconsciously felt by mankind, which is undergoing a demographic explosion and which . . . is beginning to hate itself, warned by a mysterious prescience that its numbers are becoming too great for all its members to enjoy freely open space and pure, non-polluted air?

Racial prejudice is at its most intense when it concerns human groups confined to a territory so cramped and a share of natural resources so meager that these peoples lack dignity in their own eyes as well as in those of their more powerful neighbours. But does not humanity today, on the whole, tend to expropriate itself and, on a planet that has grown too small, reconstitute, to its own cost, a situation comparable to that inflicted by some of its representatives on the unfortunate American or Oceanic tribes? Finally, what would happen to the ideological struggle against racial prejudice, if it were shown to be universally true—as some experiments conducted by psychologists suggest—that if subjects of any origin whatever are divided into groups, which are placed in a competitive situation, each group will develop feelings of bias and injustice towards its rivals?

Minority groups appearing in various parts of the world today, such as the hippies, are not distinguished from the bulk of the population by race, but only by their way of life, morality, hair style and dress; are the feelings of repugnance and sometimes hostility they inspire in most of their fellows substantially different from racial hatred? Would we therefore be making genuine progress if we confined ourselves to dissipating the particular prejudices on which racial hatred—in the strict sense of the term—can be said to be based?

THE MIRAGE OF UNIVERSAL ENTENTE

In any case, the contribution ethnologists can make to the solution of the race problem would be derisory; nor is it certain that psychologists and educators could do any better, so strong is the evidence—as we see from the evidence of the so-called primitive peoples—that mutual tolerance presupposes two conditions which in contemporary society are further than ever from being realized: one is relative quality; the other is adequate physical separation. . . .

No doubt we cherish the hope that one day equality and fraternity will reign among men without impairing their diversity. But if humanity is not to resign itself to becoming a sterile consumer of the values it created in the past and of those alone . . . , it will have to relearn the fact that all true creation implies a certain deafness to outside values, even to the extent of rejecting or denying them. For one individual cannot at the same time merge into the spirit of another, identify with another and still maintain his own identity. Integral communication with another, if fully realized, sooner or later dooms the creative originality of both. The great creative epochs in history were those in which communication had become adequate for distance individuals to stimulate each other, but not frequent or rapid enough for those obstacles, indispensable between groups, to be reduced to the point at which diversity becomes leveled out and nullified by excessively facile interchange.

Convinced that cultural and organic evolution are inextricably linked, [biologists and ethnologists] know, of course, that a return to the past is impossible, but they know, too, that the course humanity is at present following is building up tensions to such a degree that racial hatred is a mere foretaste of the greater intolerance that may hold sway tomorrow, without even the pretext of ethnic differences. To forestall the dangers threatening us today and those, still more formidable, that we shall have to face tomorrow, we must accept mere ignorance or prejudice: we can only hope for a change in the course of history, which is even more difficult to bring about than progress in the march of ideas.

NOTES

1.   Extract from *Race and History,* first published in *The Race Question in Modern Science,* Paris, UNESCO, 1952.

2.   Extract from "Race and Culture," published in UNESCO's *International Social Science Journal,* Vol. XXIII, No. 4, 1971.

Claude Lévi-Strauss is a French social anthropologist and university teacher whose work has exerted considerable influence on the development of contemporary social sciences.

Reading 1.2

Business Cultures

GEERT HOFSTEDE

EVERY ORGANIZATION HAS ITS SYMBOLS, RITUALS, AND HEROES

Management means getting things done through (other) people. This is true the world over. In order to achieve this, one has to know the people involved. Understanding people means understanding their background, from which their present and future behaviour can be predicted.

Their background has provided them with a certain culture, the word *culture* being used in the sense of "the collective programming of the mind which distinguishes the members of one category of people from another." The "category of people" may be a nation, a region or an ethnic group, women or men (gender culture), old or young (age group and generation culture), a social class, a profession or occupation (occupational culture), a type of business, a work organization or part of it (organizational culture), or even a family.

Culture is composed of many elements which may be classified in four categories: symbols, heroes, rituals and values.

Symbols are words, objects and gestures which derive their meaning from convention.

At the level of national cultures, symbols include the entire area of language. At the level of organizational culture, symbols include abbreviations, slang, modes of address, dress codes and status symbols, all recognized by insiders only.

Heroes are real or imaginary people, dead or alive, who serve as models for behaviour within a culture. Selection processes are often based on hero models of "the ideal employee" or "the ideal manager." Founders of organizations sometimes become mythical heroes later on, and incredible deeds are ascribed to them.

Rituals are collective activities that are technically superfluous but, within a particular culture, socially essential. In organizations they include not only celebrations but also many formal activities defended on apparently rational grounds: meetings, the writing of memos, and planning systems, plus the informal ways in which formal activities are performed: who can afford to be late for what meeting, who speaks to whom, and so on.

Values represent the deepest level of a culture. They are broad feelings, often unconscious and not open to discussion, about what is good and what is bad, clean or dirty, beautiful or ugly, rational or irrational, normal or abnormal, natural or paradoxical, decent or indecent. These feelings are present in the majority of the members of the culture, or at least in those persons who occupy pivotal positions.

Nationality (and gender as well) is an involuntary attribute; we are born within a family, within a nation, and are subject to the mental programming of its culture from birth. Here we acquire most of our basic values. Occupational choice is partly voluntary (dependent on the society and family); it leads to choice of schools, and at school we are socialized to the values and the practices of our chosen occupation.

When we enter a work environment, we are usually young or not-so-young adults, with most of our values firmly entrenched, but we will become socialized to the practices of our new work environment. National cultures, therefore, differ mostly at the level of basic values, while occupational and, even more, organizational cultures differ more superficially (in their symbols, heroes and rituals).

NATIONAL CULTURE DIFFERENCES

Results from a number of research projects have led me to classify national cultures along five dimensions. The first four were found by comparing the values of employees and managers in fifty-three different national subsidiaries of the IBM Corporation. They have been labeled:

1. *Power distance,* or the degree of inequality among people which the population of a county considers as normal: from relatively equal to extremely unequal.
2. *Individualism,* or the degree to which people in a country have learned to act as individuals rather than as members of cohesive groups: from collectivist to individualist.
3. *Masculinity,* or the degree to which "masculine" values like assertiveness, performance, success and competition prevail over "feminine" values like the quality of life, maintaining warm personal relationships, service, caring, and solidarity: from tender to tough.
4. *Uncertainty avoidance,* or the degree to which people in a country prefer structured over unstructured situations: from relatively flexible to extremely rigid.

The table . . . lists for twenty-five out of the fifty-three countries studied the scores for these dimensions (the table also contains a fifth dimension that will be explained later). All scores are relative: the scales have been

Table 1   Score for 25 Countries on Five Dimensions of National Values

Country	Power Distance		Individualism		Masculinity		Uncertainty Avoidance		Long-term Orientation	
	Index (PDI)	Rank	Index (IDV)	Rank	Index (MAS)	Rank	Index (UAI)	Rank	Index (LTO)	Rank
Austria	11	53	55	18	79	2	70	24-25		
Belgium	65	20	75	8	54	22	94	5-6		
Brazil	69	14	38	26-27	49	27	76	21-22	65	5
Denmark	18	51	74	9	16	50	23	51		
Finland	33	46	63	17	26	47	59	31-32		
France	68	15-16	71	10-11	43	35-36	86	10-15		
Germany	35	42-44	67	15	66	9-10	65	29	31	11-12
Greece	60	27-28	35	30	57	18-19	112	1		
Hong Kong	68	15-16	25	37	57	18-19	29	49-50	96	1
India	77	10-11	48	21	56	20-21	40	45	61	6
Ireland	28	49	70	12	68	7-8	35	47-48		
Israel	13	52	54	19	47	29	81	19		
Italy	50	34	76	7	70	4-5	75	23		
Japan	54	33	46	22-23	95	1	92	7	80	3
Mexico	81	5-6	30	32	69	6	82	18		
Netherlands	38	40	80	4-5	14	51	53	35	44	9
Norway	31	47-48	69	13	8	52	50	38		
Portugal	63	24-25	27	33-35	31	45	104	2		
Spain	57	31	51	20	42	37-38	86	10-15		
Sweden	31	47-48	71	10-11	5	52	29	49-50	33	10
Switzerland	34	45	68	14	70	4-5	58	33		
Taiwan	58	29-30	17	44	45	32-33	69	26	87	2
Turkey	66	18-19	37	28	45	31-33	85	16-17		
United Kingdom	35	42-44	89	3	66	9-10	35	47-48	25	15-16
U.S.A.	40	38	91	1	62	15	46	43	29	14

Note: Ranks: 1 = highest; 53 = lowest. For LT Orientation, 20 = lowest.

chosen so that the distance between the lowest and highest scoring country on each dimension is about 100 points.

The table shows that European countries vary widely on all four dimensions. Power distances are large in France and Portugal; collectivism prevails over individualism in Portugal and Greece; Austria and Italy are very masculine, while Sweden and the Netherlands are very feminine; Belgium and France are uncertainty-avoiding, while Denmark and the United States easily accept uncertainty.

All these differences affect ways of management in these countries. Large power distances favour centralization, while small power distances favour decentralization. Collectivism favours group rewards and family enterprises, while individualism favours easy job-hopping and individual rewards. Masculinity favours competition and survival of the fittest while femininity favours solidarity and sympathy for the weak. Uncertainty avoidance favours strict rules and principles, while its opposite favours opportunism and tolerance of deviant behaviour.

THE FIFTH DIMENSION

In subsequent research, a fifth dimension of national culture differences has been found. Professor Michael H. Bond of the Chinese University of Hong Kong studied value differences among students in twenty-three different countries using a questionnaire originally designed in the Chinese language by Chinese scholars. Analysis of the data produced four dimensions, three of them very similar to three of the IBM dimensions (all except uncertainty avoidance), the fourth entirely new and very meaningful.

This fifth dimension was called "long-term orientation" (LTO) as against "short-term orientation." Values positively rated in LTO are thrift and perseverance; values negatively related are respect for tradition, and fulfilling social expectations, "keeping up with the Joneses."

The last column in the table lists the LTO scores by country, this time based on the data collected by Bond. The highest scores on the fifth dimension are all found in East Asian countries: Hong Kong, Taiwan, Japan. As these are also the countries with the world's fastest rates of economic growth in the past twenty-five years, we can say that long-term orientation is strongly related to recent economic growth.

Not only values and practices, but even theories are products of culturally determined socialization. This has far-reaching consequences for management training in a multi-cultural organization. Not only our techniques but even the categories in which we think may be unfit for a different environment.

ORGANIZATIONAL CULTURES

Research data on differences in organizational cultures within a given country were collected in 1985 and 1986 in twenty work organizations or parts of organizations in Denmark and the Netherlands. The units studied varied from a toy company to two municipal police forces.

Analysis of the data showed large differences between units in symbols, heroes and rituals (we labeled the three together "practices"), but only modest differences in values. Different organizations within the same countries can maintain very different practices on the basis of fairly similar employee values.

Six independent dimensions made it possible to describe the larger part of the variety in organizational practices:

1. *Process-oriented* as opposed to *results-oriented* units, the former being dominated by technical and bureaucratic routines, the latter by a concern for outcomes. This dimension was associated with the degree of homogeneity of the unit's culture: in results-oriented units, everybody perceived their practices in about the same way; in process-oriented units, there were vast differences in perception within the unit. We consider the homogeneity of a culture as a measure of its "strength"; strong cultures are more results-oriented than weak ones, and vice versa.

2. *Job-oriented* as opposed to *employee-oriented* units. Job-oriented cultures assume responsibility for the employees' job performance only, and nothing more; employee-oriented cultures assume a broader responsibility for their members' well-being. A unit's position on this dimension seems to be largely the result of historical factors, such as the philosophy of its founder(s) and the presence or absence in its recent history of economic crises with collective layoffs.

3. *Professional* as opposed to *parochial* units. In the former, the (usually highly educated) members identify primarily with their profession; in the latter, the members derive their identity from the organization for which they work.

4. *Open systems* as opposed to *closed systems*. This dimension refers to the style of internal and external communication, and to the ease with which outsiders and newcomers are admitted.

5. *Tight internal control* as opposed to *loose internal control*. This dimension deals with the degree of formality and punctuality within the organization. It is partly a function of the unit's technology: banks and pharmaceutical companies can be expected to show tight control, research laboratories and advertising agencies loose control; but even with the same technology, units still differ on this dimension.

6. A *pragmatic* as opposed to a *normative* way of dealing with the environment, in particular with customers. Service units should be found towards the pragmatic (flexible) side, units involved in the application of legal rules towards the normative (rigid) side, but reality does not always correspond to this pattern.

According to this research, what a person has to learn when (s)he joins a work organization is mainly a matter of practices. Employee values have been developed in the family and the school; they play a role in the selection and self-selection process for the job. The workplace can only change people's values to a limited extent. In the popular literature, organization cultures are often presented as a matter of values. The confusion arises because this literature does not distinguish between the values of the founders and leaders and those of the bulk of employees.

Founders and leaders, on the basis of *their* values, create the symbols, the heroes and the rituals that constitute the daily practices of the organization's members. However, members only to a limited extent have to adapt their personal values to the organization's needs. A work organization, as a rule, is not a "total institution" like a prison or mental hospital. Organizational cultures according to our data reside at a more superficial level of mental programming than the things learned previously in the family and at a school. In spite of their more superficial nature, organizational cultures are still hard to change because they have developed into collective habits. Changing them is a top management task that should be based on a strategy and a cost-benefit analysis. Here again there is no single formula for success.

All statements in this article should be seen as only "statistically" true: they are common trends, but individuals may differ from them. Within each country there is a wide range of individuals, and this fact too should be taken into account in order to manage successfully. However, an insight into cultural differences will prevent us from attributing to an individual's personality forms of behaviour which are normal in his or her country, and from trying to apply supposedly universal success formulas to people who are not universal.

Geert Hofstede of the Netherlands taught organizational anthropology and international management at the University of Limburg, Maastricht, before becoming the first director of the Institute for Research on International Co-operation.

Reading 1.3

Human Factors on the Flight Deck

The Influence of National Culture

ASHLEIGH C. MERRITT
ROBERT L. HELMREICH

*NASA / University of Texas / FAA
Aerospace Crew Research Project*

Commercial aviation accident statistics from 1959 through 1989 indicate that flight crew actions, rather than technical failures, have been causal in more than 70% of worldwide hull loss accidents (Helmreich & Foushee, 1993). With such chilling statistics regarding human error, the aviation industry worldwide has expanded its human factors training beyond the human-machine interface to embrace social psychological areas such as communication, leadership/followership, performance under stress, interpersonal relations, and decision making (see Wiener, Kanki, & Helmreich, 1993). Evidence suggests that these areas are all influenced by national culture (Berry, Poortinga, Segall, & Dasen, 1992; Bond, 1988; Hofstede, 1991).

The actions of flight crews are best understood within a systems perspective (Maurino, 1993). This approach suggests that behavior on the flight deck is influenced by many factors, including individual skills and group performance, organizational priorities, regulatory environment, and national culture. An example may elucidate these multiple influences. On January 25, 1990, Avianca Flight 052, flown by a Colombian crew, crashed after running out of fuel following a missed approach to New York's John F. Kennedy Airport. A total of 73 people died in the accident. The information provided by the cockpit recorder indicates that there was little discussion between the captain and the first and second officers regarding the worsening situation.

Reprinted with permission from Ashleigh C. Merritt and Robert L. Helmreich, *Journal of Cross-Cultural Psychology*, Volume 27, Issue 1, pp. 175–24. © 1996 Western Washington University. Reprinted by permission of Sage Publications, Inc.

Authors' Note: Portions of this study were presented at the seventh annual Symposium of Aviation Psychology, Columbus, Ohio, April 1993. The research reported here was supported partly by NASA-Ames Research Center, Cooperative Agreement NCC2–286, and by FAA Grant 92-G-017 (principal investigator, Robert L. Helmreich).

The first officer failed to notify air traffic control (ATC) of an emergency until it was too late and also failed to alert the captain to the seriousness of the situation. The captain, although continuously asking the first officer to repeat information provided by ATC, did not actually elicit suggestions from the crew, nor were any suggestions forthcoming. None of the sparse communications associated with the fuel state indicated a discussion of actual status, and none addressed contingency planning.

A comprehensive systems analysis of the accident has implicated many causal factors in the crash, from individual and group process issues such as ineffective leadership and poor crew communication, to organizational and regulatory factors such as outdated manuals and vague safety procedures, to cultural influences such as the interface between the American air traffic controllers and the Colombian crew, to the interactions between the captain and junior officers (Helmreich, 1994). Understanding the effects of national culture on attitudes and behavior has always been important in global aviation. It is becoming increasingly important as international mergers become more commonplace, as more airlines employ personnel from diverse backgrounds, and as training programs designed in one country are implemented in other countries.

In the present study, we "revisited" data that had been collected as part of an ongoing research and training project with pilots and flight attendants from the United States and Asia; however, this time we paid particular attention to national culture and its influence. Following the suggestions of other authors who had studied national culture in aviation (Johnston, 1993; Redding & Ogilvie, 1984), we focused our attention on individualism-collectivism and power distance, as presented by Hofstede (1980, 1991).

In an exhaustive study of work values in more than 40 countries, Hofstede identified four dimensions of cultural variation in work values. The dimension of individualism-collectivism, the extent to which the individual's behavior is defined and influenced by others, has probably received the most attention (Berry et al., 1992; Schwartz, 1990). Individualists consider the implications of their behavior within a narrowly defined area of personal costs and benefits, and they value independence and self-sufficiency, preferring individual achievement and recognition to group rewards. Self-reliance is a strength, whereas seeking help implies weakness, and mistakes are evaluated by personal standards (Hui & Triandis, 1986; Triandis, McCusker, & Hui, 1990). There is some speculation that extreme forms of individualism are associated with higher crime rates, suicide, and stress-related diseases (Triandis et al., 1986; Triandis, Bontempo, Villareal, Asai, & Lucca, 1988).

Under conditions of low accountability, individualists tend to perform better on their own than they do as part of a group, a phenomenon known as social loafing (Earley, 1993; Latane, Williams, & Harkins, 1979). In comparison, collectivists consider the implications of their behavior in a wider framework of concern for others, particularly members of their in-group. They conform, obey, and are unquestioningly loyal to their in-group to maintain in-group harmony and the social order. Because place and position are determined by group membership, which is often outside the influence of the individual, there is a stronger belief in fate. Resources, responsibilities, and outcomes are shared with other in-group members (Bond & Hwang, 1986; Hui & Triandis, 1986). There is a motivating sense of shame not to disgrace the other group members with one's weakness or failure (Bond, 1991). Regardless of the level of accountability, collectivists tend to perform better as part of their in-group than they do on their own or with out-group members, the reverse of the social loafing phenomenon, sometimes referred to as social striving (Gabrenya, Latane, & Wang, 1981; Gabrenya,

Wang, & Latane, 1985; Earley, 1989, 1993). There is speculation that collectivism, and its personality correlate allocentrism, are associated with lower stress (Triandis et al., 1988). Reasons include greater social support from one's in-group, fewer self-attributions for failure (a corollary of fatalistic thinking), and an emphasis on stability and harmony that reduces the incidence of confrontations. Most Asian and Latin American countries are collectivist, whereas the United States and other Western countries are more individualist.

A second dimension identified by Hofstede was power distance, the extent to which the less powerful members of institutions and organizations within a country *expect and accept* that power is distributed unequally. This value can be seen in the decision-making style of the superior, ranging from participative to autocratic, and the (un)willingness of subordinates to disagree with their superior. Hofstede notes that in countries with low-power distance, there are occupational differences in the perception of power distance, with those in lower status occupations perceiving greater power distance than those in higher status occupations (Hofstede, 1991). In countries characterized by high power distance, no such occupational differences are apparent. The United States is considered to be a moderate power distance culture, whereas Asian cultures have higher power distance scores (Hofstede, 1980).

Table 1 lists the individualism and power distance index scores calculated on a scale of 0 to 100 by Hofstede (1991) for the countries represented in this study. The numbers serve to highlight similarities and differences among the eight countries, most notably the distance between the United States and other countries, particularly for individualism. An instrument that was designed to assess attitudes toward performance on the flight deck, the Cockpit Management Attitudes Questionnaire (CMAQ; Helmreich, 1984; also

Table 1   Individualism and Power Distance Index Scores from Hofstede (1991)

Country	Individualism	Power Distance
United States	91	40
Japan	46	54
Philippines	32	94
Hong Kong	25	68
Singapore	20	74
Thailand	20	64
Korea	18	60
Taiwan	17	58

see Gregorich, Helmreich, & Wilhelm, 1990), was used in this study. The questionnaire uses a 5-point Likert scale *(strongly disagree* to *strongly agree)* and includes items about the importance of briefings and debriefings; communication styles; decision making in emergencies; coordination issues; the role of the captain; attitudes toward authority; the importance of monitoring performance in self and others; and the effects on performance of personal problems, fatigue, and working with less experienced crew members. The items are listed in the Appendix. The attitudes measured by the CMAQ have been validated as predictive of effective and ineffective crew performance (Helmreich, Foushee, Benson, & Russini, 1986). Used with U.S. flight crews, three factors consistently emerge from analyses of the CMAQ (Gregorich et al., 1990); they are named communication and coordination, command responsibility, and recognition of stressor effects.

The CMAQ was not originally designed for cross-cultural use. Preliminary work with aviation personnel from Asian countries has indicated that the CMAQ's three-factor structure is not replicable, suggesting that the imposed etic (Berry, 1980) of the U.S. factor structure is not applicable in other cultures. However, given the questionnaire's content areas—leadership/followership, crew

coordination, interpersonal communication, and stress—it should nonetheless be possible to elicit differences at the cultural level if those differences are permitted to emerge without prior, culturally derived constraints.

A methodological strategy that avoids such imposed constraints is individual differences multidimensional scaling (INDSCAL; Takane, Young, & De Leeuw, 1976). The utility of INDSCAL over other analyses such as factor analysis, and the reason it has been recommended for use in cross-cultural studies (Hui & Triandis, 1983, 1985), is that it allows for the possibility of individual differences in how the test material is conceptualized in terms of its underlying dimensions. With countries or groups being the unit of analysis, the individual differences that emerge discriminate at the group level. For example, if all groups are homogeneous in their attitudes, then we can expect an approximately equal use of each dimension by each group, as revealed by approximately equal subject weights. If, however, groups differ in the underlying way with which they conceptualize the items, then added dimensions may be needed to capture idiosyncratic patterns, and subject weights will vary. Another feature of INDSCAL that makes it suitable for cross-cultural analysis is the matrix-conditional option that is available in some statistical software packages. By specifying this option, responses are standardized within each group before comparative analyses are made. This option effectively removes acquiescence and/or other response biases at the group level. A final practical advantage of the INDSCAL procedure is that it requires considerably fewer subjects than does factor analysis or other multivariate procedures because convergence on a stable solution is dependent on the number of stimuli and dimensions selected rather than the number of subjects (Davison, 1983).

We selected subjects for the study by four criteria. The first and perhaps most salient criterion for inclusion in the study was a concern for cultural distinctness. To that end, we matched the highly individualist United States with some collectivist countries from Asia. Second, we included pilots and flight attendants because both groups are conceptualized as being part of the flight crew in current crew resource management research (Helmreich & Foushee, 1993). In line with Hofstede's (1980) recommendation for a narrow sample strategy, pilots and flight attendants provide an excellent subject group for cross-cultural study. Working within the same highly regulated worldwide industry, pilots and flight attendants perform very similar tasks in very similar work environments regardless of national boundaries. Job differences within occupation are therefore minimized across cultures, with the result that attitudinal differences that emerge at the national level can be confidently attributed to differences in national culture.

Also, the two occupations, although co-occurring and interacting in the same work environment, are really very different in task demands and status. First, the status (and income) of the pilot is typically much higher than that of the flight attendant; this allows for occupational contrasts while holding other effects constant (e.g., organizational, regulatory, cultural). Second, the task demands of the two occupations attract different personalities. Historically in the United States, the pilot stereotype has been heroically self-reliant, white scarf blowing in the wind, the "strong, silent type" (Helmreich & Foushee, 1993). Using the terminology of Triandis and his colleagues (Triandis et al., 1986; Triandis, Leung, Villareal, & Clark, 1985; Triandis et al., 1990), the typical U.S. pilot is idiocentric. In a culture that is already highly individualistic, the pilot occupation has tended to attract the self-reliant and independent, suggesting an additive interaction among culture, occupation, and personality. The stereotypical flight attendant, on the other hand, is seen as socially nurturant, showing concern for and

taking care of others. Using both pilots and flight attendants in the sample, within-culture comparisons as well as the broader between-culture comparisons can be made.

A third criterion for inclusion in the study was a recognition and response to the confounding of the two occupations with gender. To date, we have not been able to find an airline that has a sufficient number of female pilots to allow gender-based comparisons. There are, however, sufficient numbers of male flight attendants in U.S. airlines. Consequently, for this study we included three flight attendant groups from the United States—two groups from the same regional base (one all male, the other all female) and one group sampled to reflect the gender mix at another base (approximately 85% female). This separation was not possible with the Asian flight attendant groups; the number of males per group did not exceed 20 (or 15%) in any group.

The fourth and final criterion for subject selection was a concern with organizational effects. Just as Hofstede (1980) used IBM employees based in different countries, we used Asian-based flight attendants who worked for the same U.S. international airline as did the U.S. pilots and flight attendants.

The Taiwanese and Philippine pilots were employed by their own national carriers. This variation allows for some limited tracking of attitudinal similarities and differences that may be attributable to organizational membership rather than national culture. Selecting the subjects by these four criteria, and using INDSCAL for the statistical analysis, a number of issues can be investigated. Our primary interest is in testing the cross-cultural sensitivity of the CMAQ. We know that the three-factor structure derived with U.S. flight crews is not replicable in many overseas carriers. However, we believe that the content of the questionnaire group processes on the flight deck is culturally influenced.

Therefore, an analysis such as INDSCAL that allows for individual variations in interpretation

may be able to elicit cross-cultural differences in attitudes regarding optimal behavior on the flight deck.

Second, we were curious about the occupational differences. Hofstede's work was based on employees in a large multinational organization, particularly the sale and service personnel, and the data were collected more than 20 years ago. Studies since then have typically used students (e.g., Chinese Culture Connection, 1987; Hofstede & Bond, 1984; Triandis et al., 1986) or management personnel (e.g., Earley, 1993; Ronen & Shenkar, 1985). It is possible that the pilot profession, with its emphasis on modernization and technological advancement, may act to neutralize the effects of national culture, as suggested by Yamamori and Mito (1993). If that is the case, then the three pilot groups can be expected to have similar views regarding optimal behavior on the flight deck. If modernization does not have such a potent effect (e.g., Bond & King, 1985; Yang, 1988), then the pilot groups will hold views more in common with their national groups than with their professional counterparts.

Another expectation concerns an observation made by Hofstede (1991). In reviewing power distance and occupational differences, Hofstede noted greater differences among occupations in the perception of power distance in low power distance cultures. If correct, then greater differences in the perception of power distance can be expected between the flight attendants and pilots in the United States, whereas perceptions of higher power distance will be similarly shared by pilots and flight attendants of the Asian countries.

METHOD

Subjects

Choosing flight attendants and pilots, both Asians and Americans, 12 groups were selected for the study from the archives of the NASA/University of Texas/FAA Aerospace

Crew Research Project. The 1,800 subjects were grouped as follows. From the United States, there were 200 pilots (5 female), 200 flight attendants (170 female) from a West Coast base, 185 male flight attendants from a large Midwest base, and 200 female flight attendants from the same Midwest base. From Asia, there were 136 Philippine pilots and 269 Chinese pilots (all male) and the following numbers of flight attendants: from Thailand, $n = 95$ (all female); from Hong Kong, $n = 118$ (15 male); from Japan, $n = 141$ (12 male); from Korea, $n = 44$ (2 male); from Singapore, $n = 80$ (8 male); and from Taiwan, $n = 132$ (20 male). The Philippine and Taiwanese pilots were employed by their national carriers and had an average of 17 years or more of flying experience. All other groups were employed by the same U.S. international carrier. The U.S. pilots and the U.S. flight attendants had an average of 10 years or more of flying experience, whereas the Asian flight attendants had an average of 2 to 3 years of total flying experience.

Instruments and Procedure

The CMAQ (Helmreich, 1984), or the shorter 20-item version (Gregorich et al., 1990), was administered to all subjects. Subjects completed the questionnaire before attending a training course in crew resource management. The U.S. pilots were tested in 1989, the Philippine pilots were tested in 1991, and all other groups were tested in 1992.

Analysis

INDSCAL (Takane et al., 1976) was used to determine the underlying dimensions that respondents were using to rate the items and the extent to which different groups employed different dimensions. To prepare the data for analysis, the reverse-scored items were recoded such that high scores reflected positive attitudes for all items. Next, the data from

each of the 12 groups were transformed via the Proximities routine in SPSS-X (SPSS, Inc., 1988) into a dissimilarities matrix using squared Euclidian distances. Using this measure, items that were given very similar ratings by individuals within a group were conceptualized as being close together and were assigned small distance measures, whereas items that were rated very differently were seen as being farther apart and were assigned larger distance measures. With the data from each group reduced to a single matrix, initial differences in sample size were eliminated, thereby ensuring equal contribution to the final solution by the 12 groups.

The 12 matrices were then entered into the INDSCAL program and, because there is no statistical test that determines a "correct" number of dimensions in INDSCAL, two-, three-, and four-dimensional solutions were requested. MacCallum's (1981) equations were used to establish fit to the data, and all solutions provided a satisfactory fit (ratios of expected to obtained stress of 1.7:1.0 or better); the three-dimensional solution, in which 90% of the variance in the distances was accounted for by the disparities, was chosen for interpretation in this article. The two- and four-dimensional solutions are referenced later in the article to support the overall interpretation of the data.

RESULTS

The results are reported in two parts. First, there is a description and interpretation of the three-dimensional solution for the 20 CMAQ items. Second, the subject weights are used to interpret the extent to which different groups employed the different dimensions.

Dimensions

The INDSCAL analysis provided Cartesian coordinates for the 20 CMAQ items for the three dimensions, thereby providing a three-dimensional "map" of the results. The

following strategy was used to define the dimensions. The items that grouped together at the extremes of each dimension were isolated.

Item means were used to establish whether the items were associated with the *agree* or *disagree* end of the spectrum, and the wording of reverse-scored items was noted. The items were then used to define the pattern of responses that distinguished the dimension. The CMAQ items are concerned with the role of the captain, the importance of communication and coordination and the process(es) by which they can be achieved, and the effects of external and internal stressors on performance. The three dimensions that emerged from the INDSCAL analysis varied in the relative importance assigned to these content areas, each producing a slightly different pattern of responses. The defining characteristics of the dimensions are described in the following subsections. In each case, we summarize or paraphrase the items that were located at the extremes of the dimension in such a way as to describe a high endorsement of the dimension. Following each description, we synthesize the material and draw an interpretation. Using Hofstede's cultural dimensions as a guide, we argue that dimension 1, with its emphasis on group-based performance and absolute authority, reflects collectivism and high power distance, whereas dimension 3, with its greater egalitarianism and individual responsibility, reflects individualism and lower power distance. Dimension 2 represents moderate power distance and individualism.

Dimension 1: Collectivism and High Power Distance

Characteristics. Good communication and crew coordination are perceived as important. This is achieved via preflight briefings, the verbalizing of plans, and the captain's coordination of cockpit and cabin crew. There is also a belief that the captain should take charge and fly the plane in nonstandard situations because successful flight deck management is due primarily to the captain's flying skills. Personal problems, fatigue, and emergencies are not considered a hindrance to crew member performance.

Interpretation. In dimension 1, the captain is clearly the *unquestioned* leader. It is the captain's job to communicate his or her plans to the crew both before and during the flight and to coordinate the crew's activities. In return for this clearly communicated top-down direction, the crewmembers are unquestioningly loyal and believe that they can overcome any personal or situational adversity to ensure that the captain *and* the other crewmembers are not let down. Group harmony is maintained through conformity with the captain's wishes, and questions are not asked for fear of disrupting that harmony (losing face). There is the expectation that information will be disseminated from the top down and not require assertive, potentially face-threatening inquiries.

The belief that personal problems can be left behind may be attributed to in-group loyalty. It would be selfish (self before group) to bring personal issues to work because it would be subverting the group goals with personal concerns. There may also be a sense of shame that prevents admitting any impairment to performance caused by stressors such as fatigue. Alternately, the social striving phenomenon, with its origins in social support, may in fact operate to reduce the impact of stressors in a group situation.

Dimension 2: Individualism and Moderate Power Distance

Characteristics. As with dimension 1, good communication and crew coordination are perceived as important. This is achieved via preflight briefings, the verbalizing of plans, the captain's coordination of cockpit and cabin crew, *and* the captain's encouragement of questions from other crew members. There is a belief that crew members should not question the captain's actions and that the captain should always take charge in nonstandard situations. There is also the belief that it is not important to admit one's own stress or problems to others.

Interpretation. The second dimension overlaps the first with its emphasis on communication and coordination, and it adds a degree of assertion and individualism. The captain is still unquestioned and is expected to take charge in nonstandard situations, yet a good captain is also seen as someone who invites questions from the crew. This consultative approach suggests a lower power distance between the captain and the crew than is the case in the first dimension.

This second dimension also suggests that there is less disclosure among crew members about their problems and therefore less team interdependence. Stress is perceived as a personal issue, and the implications are considered for self only. There is little recognition that one's performance can affect other crewmembers' performance. Crewmembers are working more as individuals with specific jobs to do than they are as an interconnected team.

Dimension 3: Individualism and Low Power Distance

Characteristics. In some ways, dimension 3 is almost the reverse of dimension 1. There is the attitude that the captain's authority is not absolute and that crew members are not invulnerable. There is greater recognition that one's performance can be affected by emergencies, personal problems, and/or the performance of less capable crew members. There is also less reliance on the total authority of the captain, with the belief that there *are* circumstances in which the first officer should assume command and that successful flight deck

management is *more* than simply a function of the captain's flying skills. Although good communication and coordination are seen as important, there is less perceived need for pre-flight briefings, the verbalizing of plans, or the coordination of cockpit and cabin crew.

Interpretation. The third dimension stresses more self-reliance and more personal responsibility for success and failure. The prevailing attitude is that as long as all know their jobs and do them, there will be no problems. There is therefore little need for cross-communication, with the added assumption that if one wants to know something, then one asks.

Consistent with lower power distance is the attitude that the captain's authority is not absolute and that subordinates are free to question decisions. Consistent with individualism is both the expectation of assertion and the personal but not public acknowledgment of stress; the information is not shared with others because the individual does not feel reliant on or connected to others.

As a check on the interpretation of these dimensions, we can predict the pattern of subject weights that accompany the group solution. In particular, one can expect dimension 1 to be used primarily by Asian subjects and dimension 3 to be used primarily by American subjects.

Subject Weights

The INDSCAL solution provided subject weights for each of the 12 groups on each of the three dimensions. Subject weights indicate the extent to which each group employed each dimension in rating the 20 CMAQ items.

Subject weights can range from 0 to 1, with higher numbers representing greater use of the dimension. Subject weights are constrained such that the sum of the squares of the subject weights across the dimensions for each subject represents the full accounting of the subject's

Table 2   Group Subject Weights for the
                 Three-Dimensional Solution

		Dimension	
Group	*1*	*2*	*3*
United States			
Pilots	.36	.19	.86
Flight attendants			
Male, Midwest	.63	.68	.21
Female, Midwest	.59	.75	.11
Mixed, West Coast	.44	.85	.08
Asia			
Pilots			
Philippines	.83	.23	.23
Taiwan	.96	.00	.00
Flight attendants			
Thailand	.95	.00	.01
Hong Kong	.97	.08	.04
Japan	.91	.14	.04
Korea	.85	.17	.10
Singapore	.91	.27	.06
Taiwan	.97	.12	.03

equally explained by all the dimensions, then subject weights will be approximately equal. On the other hand, if a greater part of the subject's ratings can be accounted for by one dimension with a high subject weight, then the other dimensions must carry lower weights.

Table 2 shows the subject weights for the 12 groups on each of three dimensions. Note that the eight Asian groups have loadings of .83 or higher on dimension 1 and .27 or lower on dimensions 2 and 3. Note also that U.S. pilots have a loading of .86 on dimension 3 and loadings of .36 or lower on dimensions 1 and 2. These weights are consistent with the interpretation of dimension 1 as a collectivist/ high power distance dimension and dimension 3 as an individualist/low power distance dimension. Dimension 2 belongs almost exclusively to the three U.S. flight attendant groups with loadings of .68 to .85. Note how the analysis was able to explicate differences between occupations and regions of the United States with subject weight differences as large as .78. Within the eight Asian groups, the largest difference between any two subject weights on any dimension was only .27.

ratings by the solution (similar to *R*2). This number also ranges from 0 to 1, and in the present solution the average sum of squares of subject weights was .9. This summing constraint means that if a subject's ratings are

Figure 1, by plotting the subject weights for the 12 groups for the three dimensions, shows

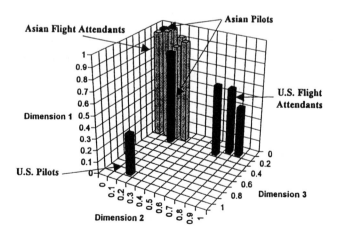

Figure 1   Subject Weights for the 12 Groups Plotted on the Three Dimensions.

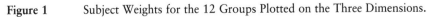

graphically the tight clustering of the Asian groups and the clear distinction made between American pilots and flight attendants in their attitudes toward flight management.

Inspection of the alternate, two-dimensional INDSCAL solution, interestingly, revealed an attitudinal split, not between the Asians and the Americans but between the U.S. pilots and all other groups. A four-dimensional solution was necessary before any distinction could be made among the eight Asian groups; Asian pilots were shown to have subject weights different from those of Asian flight attendants in this solution.

DISCUSSION

The INDSCAL analysis has demonstrated that the CMAQ is sensitive to national culture. The distinct and idiosyncratic subject weights support the interpretation of the dimensions. The first dimension of collectivism and high power distance, which was endorsed primarily by the eight Asian groups, valued top-down communication and coordination, a preference for autocratic leadership, a willingness to monitor others' performance, and a disregard for stress. The second dimension was endorsed by the three U.S. flight attendant groups. It also valued top-down communication and coordination but showed a preference for consultative leadership and a reluctance to monitor performance or admit stress. The third dimension of individualism and low power distance was endorsed by the U.S. pilots and valued self-reliance, participative leadership, and less regard for communication and coordination.

The CMAQ asks subjects what they consider to be optimal behavior on the flight deck. It is interesting to note that three different styles of leadership/followership are endorsed. Although there may be a universal concept of the effective leader as being both task (performance) and relationship (maintenance) oriented (Bond, 1991; Misumi, 1985; Sinha,

1981; Stogdill & Coons, 1957), it appears that the specifics of that behavior will vary cross-culturally (Smith & Tayeb, 1988).

Figure 1 shows the tight attitudinal clustering of the Asian groups relative to the U.S. groups. This pattern can be explained by a number of complementary findings. First, the similarity of the Asian attitudes may be due to stronger in-group norms in collectivist cultures (Triandis et al., 1988). In cultures here conflict with in-group members is avoided at all costs and the social order is maintained through conformity, there is a need for behavior to be more proscribed and predictable and more rule bound to avoid social transgressions (Barnlund & Yoshioka, 1990; Bond & Hwang, 1986; Tang & Kirkbride, 1986). The Asian pilots and flight attendants show a greater conformity in their attitudes than do the U.S. pilots and flight attendants.

Second, the observation by Hofstede regarding power distance was replicated, thereby providing a rationale for the separation between the U.S. occupational groups. All three flight attendant groups in the low power distance U.S. culture preferred a captain who encouraged their questions but who nonetheless took charge in emergencies. The U.S. pilots, on the other hand, preferred a more participative and interactive leadership. These differences in power distance were not observed in the Asian groups; Asian flight attendants and pilots both preferred an autocratic and communicative captain.

Further support for the separation of the two U.S. occupations is suggested by the strong congruence of occupation and national culture for U.S. pilots. The within-culture attitudinal differences between the idiocentric pilots and the more socially oriented flight attendants may also be contributing to the groups' separation.

Third, the structure of the subject weights and the dimensions demonstrates that modernization does not have a differential effect

on the Asian pilots; their attitudes are closer to those of the Asian flight attendants than they are to their occupational counterparts, the U.S. pilots. Also, the limited test of gender differences and organizational effects revealed that national culture and occupational subcultures take precedence over gender and organizational distinctions. The all-male group of flight attendants was clustered with the other flight attendant groups in the United States, the male pilots were clustered with the female flight attendants in Asia, and, despite being employed by the same U.S. airline, flight attendants aligned with their national counterparts rather than their organizational counterparts.

Finally, there is an equally plausible explanation for the tight clustering of the eight Asian groups and the spread of the U.S. groups that cannot be discounted and that can be traced to the origin of the CMAQ. The CMAQ was originally designed by American researchers and psychometrically refined for American pilots. The items in the questionnaire, although general in nature, still reflect the ubiquitous Western bias because the items were written by researchers from and for the one Western culture. As the product of American minds, the CMAQ can detect subtle within-culture differences in the United States, as we have seen in the present analysis. But the questionnaire lacks any fine understanding of other cultures as such, and so it fails to ask the questions that might be able to detect important differences.

From the analysis of the CMAQ using American and Asian pilots and flight attendants, we conclude that results of cross-cultural analyses using the CMAQ will most likely be able to detect subtle differences in cultures similar to the United States while perhaps capturing only the grossest of differences in other cultures. An expanded, more culturally sensitive questionnaire is needed for cross-cultural research in aviation.

FUTURE DIRECTIONS: RESEARCH AND TRAINING

We are very interested in cross-cultural differences in flight attitudes, and we have developed a new questionnaire, the Flight Management Attitudes Questionnaire (FMAQ; Helmreich, Merritt, Sherman, Gregorich, & Wiener, 1993), that we hope will capture those differences. The 82-item FMAQ contains items from the original CMAQ (so that longitudinal analysis can continue), previously validated items that capture cross-cultural differences in broad work-based values (taken from Hofstede's Value Survey Module [1982 version], with permission), items suggested by Bond and his Chinese colleagues (Chinese Culture Connection, 1987), and more specific items written expressly for the aviation environment. These items will be asked of pilots and flight attendants and, in some cases, management. There is also a subscale that rates attitudes toward cockpit automation that will be asked of the pilots and for which we also anticipate cultural differences. Data collection has begun on this project with participant airlines from Europe, the Pacific region, South and North America, and Asia, and efforts are under way to enlist as many countries as possible to ensure a truly global study.

Recognition that the causes of aviation accidents rest largely in interpersonal issues has led to the worldwide initiation of training programs in aviation human factors, known generically as crew resource management (CRM; Cooper, White, & Lauber, 1980; Helmreich & Foushee, 1993). CRM programs attempt to optimize performance on the flight deck by addressing group process factors such as interpersonal relations, leadership style, and communication patterns. The ideal outcomes of CRM are more effective communications, situational awareness leading to improved decision making, workload distribution that avoids overload, and realistic expectations

regarding performance—all contributing to increased flight safety. Most programs have been adaptations of U.S. approaches, and many have not been sensitive to cultural issues (Johnston, 1993). From a cultural perspective, CRM represents low power distance (free exchange of information among the crew) and collectivism (recognition and acceptance of crew interdependence), a rare cultural combination (Hofstede, 1991). With the recognition that the principles of CRM do not align completely with existing national cultures, there comes the realization that CRM training needs will differ as a function of the culture. It is our hope that information gathered from this project will be used in the refinement of CRM curricula to reflect cultural influences.

All cultures contain strengths that can be used in CRM training. For example, when CRM was introduced in the United States, the highly individualist U.S. pilots were asked to forgo their romantic image of the solo flyer/ hero and to value more working as a team. Their willingness to be assertive—a manifestation of the individualist culture—was exploited in the training to help achieve a low power distance cockpit. By comparison, collectivist cultures, such as those found in Asia and Latin America, already value team interdependence and communication. However, given the high power distance norms, free and open exchange of information in the cockpit may be difficult. Formalizing the communication between officers via checklists may be one way to facilitate the desired end goal without disrupting the high power distance norms.

Ultimately, the ideal training program will be designed in conjunction with members of the host culture and will include cultural mediators (Bochner, 1981) who may help to focus cultural differences. Training will be successful only if it can resonate to the national culture. And only members of a culture can predict to what extent deviations from the culture will be tolerated. As an example, assertiveness by junior officers may be too great a deviation from the cultural norm in China to be tolerated, just as the concept of shared rewards or group sacrifice may be inconceivable to American pilots.

This study has focused on the impact of national culture on the attitudes of flight personnel regarding appropriate behavior on the flight deck. Even with a culturally biased instrument, the influence of national culture can be seen in the systematic variation of flight crew attitudes toward appropriate flight management behavior. With the increasing globalization of the aviation industry, efforts must be made to understand these differences more completely.

APPENDIX

The 20 Items From the Cockpit Management Attitudes Questionnaire

1. The captain should take physical control and fly the aircraft in emergency and non-standard situations.
2. Captains should encourage crew member questions during normal flight operations and in emergencies.
3. Even when fatigued, I perform effectively during critical times in a flight.
4. Pilots should be aware of and sensitive to the personal problems of other crew members.
5. I let other crew members know when my workload is becoming (or about to become) excessive.
6. My decision-making ability is as good in emergencies as it is in routine flying situations.
7. A debriefing and critique of procedures and decisions after each flight is an important part of developing and maintaining effective crew coordination.
8. The pilot flying the aircraft should verbalize plans for procedures or maneuvers and should be sure that the information is understood and acknowledged by the other crew members.

9. The preflight briefing is important for safety and for effective crew management.

10. The captain's responsibilities include coordination between cockpit and cabin crew.

11. Successful flight deck management is primarily a function of the captain's flying proficiency.

12. Crew members should not question the decisions or actions of the captain except when they threaten the safety of the flight.

13. My performance is not adversely affected by working with an inexperienced or a less capable crew member.

14. Crew members should monitor each other for signs of stress or fatigue.

15. A truly professional crew member can leave personal problems behind when flying.

16. There are no circumstances (except total incapacitation) where the first officer should assume command of the aircraft.

17. Crew members should feel obligated to mention their own psychological stress or physical problems to other flight crew personnel before or during a flight.

18. Good communications and crew coordination are as important as technical proficiency for the safety of the flight.

19. Effective crew coordination requires crew members to take into account the personalities of other crew members.

20. Crew members should avoid disagreeing with others because conflicts create tension and reduce crew effectiveness.

REFERENCES

Barnlund, D. C., & Yoshioka, M. (1990). Apologies: Japanese and American styles. *International Journal of Intercultural Relations, 14,* 193–206.

Berry, J. W. (1980). Introduction to methodology. In H. C. Triandis & J.W. Berry (Eds.), *Handbook of cross-cultural psychology* (Vol. 2, pp. 1–28). Boston: Allyn & Bacon.

Berry, J. W., Poortinga, Y. H., Segall, M. H., & Dasen, P. R. (1992). *Cross-Cultural psychology: Research and applications.* Cambridge, UK: Cambridge University Press.

Bochner, S. (1981). *The mediating person: Bridges between cultures.* Boston: G. K. Hall.

Bond, M. H. (Ed.). (1988*). The cross-cultural challenge to social psychology* (Vol. 11, Cross-Cultural Research and Methodology Series). Newbury Park, CA: Sage.

Bond, M. H. (1991). *Beyond the Chinese face: Insights from psychology.* Hong Kong: Oxford University Press.

Bond, M. H., & Hwang, K. K. (1986). The social psychology of Chinese people. In M. H. Bond (Ed.), *The psychology of the Chinese people* (pp. 219–266). Hong Kong: Oxford University Press.

Bond, M. H., & King, A. Y. C. (1985). Coping with the threat of Westernization in Hong Kong. *International Journal of Intercultural Relations, 9,* 351–364.

Chinese Culture Connection. (1987). Chinese values and the search for culture-free dimensions of culture. *Journal of Cross–Cultural Psychology, 18,* 143–164.

Cooper, G. E., White, M. D., & Lauber, J. K. (Eds.). (1980). *Resource management on the flightdeck: Proceedings of a NASA/industry workshop* (NASA CP-2120). Moffett Field, CA: NASA-Ames Research Center.

Davison, M. L. (1983) *Multidimensional scaling.* New York: Wiley.

Earley, P. C. (1983). Social loafing and collectivism. *Administrative Science Quarterly, 34,* 565–581.

Earley, P. C. (1993). East meets West meets Mideast: Further explorations of collectivistic and individualistic work groups. *Academy of Management Journal, 36,* 319–348.

Gabrenya, W. K., Jr., Latane, B., & Wang, Y. (1981, August). *Social loafing among Chinese overseas and U.S. students.* Paper presented at the Second Asian Conference of the International Association for Cross-Cultural Psychology, Taipei, Taiwan.

Gabrenya, W. K., Jr., Wang, Y., & Latane, B. (1985). Social loafing on an optimizing task: Cross-cultural differences among Chinese and Americans. *Journal of Cross-Cultural Psychology, 16,* 223–242.

Gregorich, S., Helmreich, R. L., & Wilhelm, J. (1990). The structure of cockpit management attitudes. *Journal of Applied Psychology, 75,* 682–690.

Helmreich, R. L. (1984). Cockpit management attitudes. *Human Factors, 26,* 63–72.

Helmreich, R. L. (1994). Anatomy of a system accident: The crash of Avianca Flight 052. *International Journal of Aviation Psychology, 4,* 265–284.

Helmreich, R. L., & Foushee, H. C. (1993). Why crew resource management? Empirical and theoretical bases of human factors training in aviation. In E. L. Wiener, B. G. Kanki, & R. L. Helmreich (Eds.), *Cockpit resource management* (pp. 3–45). San Diego: Academic Press.

Helmreich, R. L., Foushee, H. C., Benson, R., & Russini, W. (1986). Cockpit management attitudes: Exploring the attitude-performance linkage. *Aviation, Space, and Environmental Medicine, 57,* 1198–1200.

Helmreich, R. L., Merritt, A. C., Sherman, P., Gregorich, S., & Wiener, E. (1993). *The Flight Management Attitude Questionnaire* (NASA/University of Texas/FAA Technical Report 93–4). Austin, TX: NASA/University of Texas/FAA Aerospace Crew Research Project.

Hofstede, G. (1980). *Culture's consequences: International differences in work-related values.* Beverly Hills, CA: Sage.

Hofstede, G. (1991). *Cultures and organizations: Software of the mind.* Maidenhead, UK: McGraw-Hill.

Hofstede, G., & Bond, M. (1984). Hofstede's culture dimensions: An independent validation using Rokeach's Value Survey. *Journal of Cross-Cultural Psychology, 15,* 417–433.

Hui, C. H., & Triandis, H. C. (1983). Multistrategy approach to cross-cultural research: The case of locus of control. *Journal of Cross-Cultural Psychology, 14,* 65–83.

Hui, C. H., & Triandis, H. C. (1985). Measurement in cross-cultural psychology: A review and comparison of strategies. *Journal of Cross-Cultural Psychology, 16,* 131–152.

Hui, C.H., & Triandis, H. C. (1986). Individualism-collectivism: A study of cross-cultural researchers. *Journal of Cross-Cultural Psychology, 17,* 222–248.

Johnston, N. (1993). CRM: Cross-cultural perspectives. In E. L. Wiener, B. G. Kanki, & R. L. Helmreich (Eds.), *Cockpit resource management* (pp. 367–398). San Diego: Academic Press.

Latane, B., Williams, K., & Harkins, S. (1979). Many hands make light work: The causes and consequences of social loafing. *Journal of Personality and Social Psychology, 37,* 822–832.

MacCallum, R. (1981). Evaluating goodness of fit in nonmetric multidimensional scaling by ALSCAL. *Applied Psychological Measurement, 5,* 377–382.

Maurino, D. (1993). Cross-cultural perspectives in human factors training: The lessons from the ICAO Human Factors Programme. In R. S. Jenson & D. Neumeister (Eds.), *Proceedings of the Seventh International Symposium on Aviation Psychology* (pp. 606–611). Columbus: Ohio State University, Department of Aviation.

Misumi, J. (1985). *The behavioral science of leadership.* Ann Arbor: University of Michigan Press.

Redding, S. G., & Ogilvie, J. G. (1984). Cultural effects on cockpit communications in civilian aircraft. In *Flight Safety Foundation Conference, Zurich.* Washington, DC: Flight Safety Foundation.

Ronen, S., & Shenkar, O. (1985). Clustering countries on attitudinal dimensions: A review and synthesis. *Academy of Management Review, 10,* 435–454.

Schwartz, S. (1990). Individualism-collectivism: Critique and proposed refinements. *Journal of Cross-Cultural Psychology, 21,* 139–157.

Sinha, J. B. P. (1981). *The nurturant task manager: A model of the effective executive.* Atlantic Highlands, NJ: Humanities Press.

Smith, P., & Tayeb, M. (1988). Organisation structure and processes. In M. H. Bond (Ed.), *The cross-cultural challenge to social psychology* (Vol. 11, pp. 153–164, Cross-Cultural Research and Methodology Series). Newbury Park, CA: Sage.

Stogdill, R. M., & Coons, A. E. (1957). *Leader behavior* (Monograph 88). Columbus: Ohio State University, Bureau of Business Research.

SPSS, Inc. (1988). *SPSS-X user's guide* (3rd ed.). Chicago: Author.

Takane, Y., Young, F. W., & De Leeuw, J. (1976). Nonmetric individual differences multidimensional scaling: An alternating least squares method with optimal scaling features. *Psychometrika, 42*, 7–67.

Tang, S., & Kirkbride, P. (1986). Developing conflict management skills in Hong Kong: An analysis of some cross-cultural implications. *Management Education and Development, 17*, 287–301.

Triandis, H. C., Betancourt, H., Bond, M. H., Leung, K., Brenes, A., Georgas, J., Hui, C. H., Marin, G., Setiadi, B., Sinha, J., Verma, J., Spangenberg, J., Touzard, H., & Montmollin, G. (1986). The measurement of etic aspects of individualism and collectivism across cultures. *Australian Journal of Psychology, 38*, 257–267.

Triandis, H. C., Bontempo, R., Villareal, M. J., Asai, M., & Lucca, N. (1988). Individualism and collectivism: Cross-cultural perspectives on self-ingroup relationships. *Journal of Personality and Social Psychology, 54*, 323–338.

Triandis, H. C., Leung, K., Villareal, M., & Clark, F. L. (1985). Allocentric vs. idiocentric tendencies: Convergent and discriminant validation. *Journal of Research in Personality, 13*, 395–415.

Triandis, H. C., McCusker, C., & Hui, C. H. (1990). Multimethod probes of individualism and collectivism. *Journal of Personality and Social Psychology, 59*, 1006–1020.

Wiener, E. L., Kanki, B. G., & Helmreich, R. L. (Eds.). (1993). *Cockpit resource management*. San Diego: Academic Press.

Yamamori, H., & Mito, T. (1993). Keeping CRM is keeping the flight safe. In E. L. Wiener, B. G. Kanki, & R. L. Helmreich (Eds.), *Cockpit resource management* (pp. 399–420). San Diego: Academic Press.

Yang, K. S. (1988). Will societal modernization eventually eliminate cross-cultural psychological differences? In M. H. Bond (Ed.), *The cross-cultural challenge to social psychology* (Vol. 11, pp. 67–85, Cross-Cultural Research and Methodology Series). Newbury Park, CA: Sage.

Ashleigh C. Merritt is a doctoral candidate in psychology at the University of Texas at Austin. A native of Brisbane, Australia, she is completing a dissertation with Robert Helmreich investigating the influence of national culture on the attitudes and values of flight crews in civil aviation from Asia, Latin America, Europe, and the United States.

Robert L. Helmreich, Ph.D., is Professor of Psychology at the University of Texas at Austin. His research focuses on individual and group determinants of behavior and performance, including the influence of organizational and national culture. He is coeditor of *Cockpit Resource Management* (Academic Press, 1993) and director of the NASA/University of Texas/FAA Aerospace Crew Research Project. He is also Visiting Professor at the University of Basel/Kantonsspital (Switzerland), conducting research into group dynamics in the operating room.

Reading 1.4

Conflict Management in Thai Organizations

RUJIRA ROJJANAPRAPAYON
PORNTIPHA CHIEMPRAPHA
ACHAYA KANCHANAKUL

INTRODUCTION

Conflict is seen as inevitable in organizations. It can be both destructive and constructive depending on how it is perceived and handled. Conflict has been an interesting topic in the Western perspectives for decades; many Western scholars have focused their attention on conflict management in organizations. The findings of their works generally seem applicable to only Western organizational context, but they may not be applicable to non-Western context, particularly Thai organizations.

This study was aimed at exploring characteristics of conflict management in Thailand. In investigating how Thai informants managed conflicts in organizations, the researchers attempted to classify and clarify conflict management styles in Thai organizations. The findings of this study became examples of conflict management styles in Thai organizations and should urge Thai and non-Thai employers to be sensitive to and have an awareness of conflict management strategies in Thai context. In

this study, the researchers attempted to answer the following two research questions:

RQ. 1 What conflict management styles do Thai organizational members use when having conflict in horizontal interactions or among peers or colleagues?

RQ. 2 What conflict management styles do Thai organizational members use when having conflict in vertical interactions or between subordinates and superiors?

LITERATURE REVIEW

There are three areas of previous studies to be reviewed. They are: (1) Thai social values and characteristics, (2) conflict management in Western perspective, and (3) conflict management in Thai perspective.

Thai Social Values and Characteristics

Several scholars (e.g., Komin, 1995; Kosalakood, 1998; Rochanapruk, 1999;

Reprinted with permission from *NIDA Language and Communication Journal, 5*(5), January, 2001, pp. 63–77.

Editor's Note: This reading was revised by Rujira Rojjanaprapayon in December 2002.

Rojjanaprapayon, 1997) found that Thai values and characteristics affect how Thais behave in organizations and perceive conflicts in organizational and non-organizational contexts; these Thai values and characteristics include: (1) avoiding interpersonal conflict, (2) smooth relationships, (3) indirectness and politeness, (4) consciousness of social hierarchy, and (5) face-saving. For example, Rochanapruk asserts that face-saving strategies are always used in organizations regarding employee relations and negotiations, while Rojjanaprapayon found that in general most Thais avoid conflicts in order to maintain social harmony and personal relations and that indirectness in communication is specifically employed for this purpose.

Conflict Management in Western Perspective

Several studies on conflict and conflict management in superior-subordinate relationships and conflict management among peers exist in the West. Putnam and Poole (1989) found that subordinates prefer to avoid or to compromise when placed in a conflict situation with their superiors. Putnam and Wilson (1982, as cited in Putnam & Poole, 1989) add that "managers prefer forcing strategies with subordinates, confronting and smoothing styles with superiors, and smoothing and avoiding behaviors with peers" (p. 558). However, Putnam and Poole argue, based on some other studies, that managers may employ confronting with subordinates, smoothing with superiors, and compromise with peers or colleagues (p. 558).

Morrill and Thomas (1992) argue that, regarding conflict among peers or colleagues, the peers or colleagues with weak ties seem to rely on third parties who can facilitate their communication leading to conflict settlement, if they do not obtain satisfaction from covert means. They further find that if those peers or colleagues have more invested in their social ties, they are more likely to seek mutually accommodating solutions by using negotiation or more aggressive forms of confrontation.

Van de Vliert, Euwema, and Huismans (1995) discuss the notion of conflict management effectiveness. They assert that the degree of effectiveness depends on the practice of "the aggregation of various degrees of several modes of conflict handling, rather than one dominant and isolated mode of conflict handling" (p. 277).

Conflict Management in Thai Perspective

Roongrengsuke and Chansuthus (1998) assert that typically a collaborative approach to conflict management is preferred among Thai business professionals in all three dimensions—among peers or colleagues, with subordinates, and with superiors (p. 218). Also, they found that, in Thai context, the most common strategy used for managing conflict is having a mediator who is a mutually respected third party.

Komin (1995) claims that Thais in general do not like conflict; they feel uneasy about it, had better avoid conflict and find ways to handle it indirectly. Komin also found that when dealing with conflict, most Thais respectively employ the following styles: integrative or collaboration, compromising, avoiding, and dominating. This raises a notion that in reality Thais do not frequently handle conflicts by using "avoidance" as expected, as Komin argues, "the high rate on femininity and collectivism does not lead to the prediction of avoidance and accommodation conflict handling styles as expected" (p. 23). This could mean that conflict should be avoided at all costs, but avoiding is not a best strategy when conflict really has occurred.

RESEARCH METHODOLOGY

Participants

Three female participants were intentionally selected for this study. These three participants were working at three different organizations and ranged from 32–48 years of age. Participant A was a marketing manager and owner of a medium-sized manufacturing organization. Participant B was a personnel manager of a small-sized Internet services provider organization. Participant C was a senior personnel staff member of a small-sized trading organization.

They were selected to participate in this study for three reasons. Firstly, they represented different types of business organizations—manufacturing, services, and trading. Secondly, they represented different management levels. Participant A was a business owner and on the level of top management. Participant B was a personnel manager and on the middle level of management. Participant C was a senior personnel staff member and on the lower level of management. Finally, these three were selected because of the convenience and availability.

Research Tools and Types of Data

There were two types of data gathered: those from preliminary questions and those from in-depth interviews.

Preliminary Questions

Preliminary questions were employed to collect the personal data of the participants before the in-depth interviews. They were comprised of two aspects: personal information and organizational profile. Firstly, twelve questions regarding personal information were asked to get information in 12 areas. They are: (1) name, (2) company, (3) position, (4) gender, (5) age, (6) educational background, (7) experience

prior to working for the present organization, (8) years of working with the present organization, (9) years of working in the present position, (10) job descriptions and responsibilities, (11) number of employees under the informants' supervision, (12) number of males and females under the informants' supervision. Secondly, four questions were asked to get their organizations' profile. The researchers put more emphasis on the types of organizations, the number of employees, products, and departments.

In-depth Interviews

In-depth interviews were conducted to elicit the data concerning the perceptions and experience of the participants about conflict and conflict management in Thai organizations. The semi-structured interview questions were employed. The questions were grouped into three categories: (1) individual perspectives of conflict and conflict management, (2) conflict and conflict management between the same-level dyads (peers/colleagues), and (3) conflict and conflict management between superiors and subordinates. The questions were adapted and developed from two previous studies: (1) Morrill and Thomas's study (1992) "Organizational conflict management as disputing process: The problem of social escalation," and (2) Jehn's study (1997) "A qualitative analysis of conflict types and dimensions in organization groups."

Data Collection Process

Data were collected in January and February 2000 from the three selected female participants from three Thai organizations. The participants were asked to provide their personal information in the question list (the preliminary questions) at their convenience. After that, each participant contacted the researchers for the interviews; the semi-structured interview

questions were administered. The interviews were all conducted and recorded in Thai. The recorded data were then transcribed and translated into English. The researchers also took notes during the interview sessions.

Questions were asked in three major categories: (1) individual perspectives on conflict and conflict management in Thai organizations, (2) conflict and conflict management between the same-level dyads (peers/colleagues), and (3) conflict and conflict management between the superiors and the subordinates. The details are reported below.

Individual Perspectives on Conflict and Conflict Management in Thai Organizations

The content of the data includes the participants' perceptions of organizational conflict, types of conflict, causes of conflict, and levels of aggressiveness caused by organizational conflicts. These data were used as additional information in interpreting data in two other categories.

- Perceptions of Organizational Conflict

This part was about how the participants perceived organizational conflict. For examples, the participants viewed the conflict as negative, positive, constructive, or destructive.

- Types of Conflict

The participants were asked about the types of conflict such as task-oriented conflict, relationship-oriented conflict, or personalized conflict arising in their organizations. Moreover, they were asked whether task-oriented conflict could turn into relationship conflict or vice versa.

- Causes of Conflict

The participants were first asked to recall some samples of conflict situations. Then, they were asked to report what were the causes of such conflict such as overlapping responsibilities, different organizational goals, or limited resources.

- Levels of Aggressiveness

The participants were asked whether the conflict caused violence or not. Furthermore, they were also asked whether any violent behavior would emerge because of conflict in their organizations.

Conflict and Conflict Management between the Same-Level Dyads (Peers/Colleagues)

The data concerning conflict and conflict management between the same-level dyads corresponded to RQ.1. The data in this part were divided into two main aspects: (1) conflict and conflict management between the same-level dyads under the participants' supervision and (2) conflict and conflict management between the participants and their peers or colleagues.

- Conflict and conflict management between the same-level dyads under the informants' supervision

In this part, the participants (as the superior) were asked to recall some conflict situations between their subordinates and to describe what the conflict was about and whether or not it affected the individuals' relationship, the tasks, or other employees. In addition, the participants were requested to identify the conflict management styles their subordinates used when having conflict with their same-level peers and comment on whether or not such styles were effective.

- Conflict and conflict management between the participants and their peers or colleagues

In this part, the participants were asked to recall some conflict situations between the participants (as a peer) and their same-level peers and to describe what the conflict was about and whether or not it affected the relationship of the participants and their peers, the tasks, or other employees. In addition, the participants were requested to identify the conflict management styles they and the other disputant(s) used when conflicting with each other and comment on whether or not such styles were effective.

Conflict and Conflict Management
between Superiors and Subordinates

The data concerning conflict and conflict management between superiors and subordinates corresponded to RQ.2. The data in this part were divided into two main aspects: (1) conflict and conflict management between the participants (as subordinates) and their supervisor(s) and (2) conflict and conflict management between the participants (as supervisors) and their subordinates.

- Conflict and conflict management between the participants (subordinates) and their supervisor(s)

In this part, the participants were asked to recall some conflict situations between the participants and their supervisors and to describe what the conflict was about and whether or not it affected the relationship of the participants and their supervisors, the tasks, or other employees. In addition, the participants had to identify the conflict management styles they and their supervisors used when conflicting with each other and comment on whether or not such styles were effective.

- Conflict and conflict management between the participants (as supervisors) and their subordinates

In this part, the participants were asked to recall some conflict situations between the participants (as a supervisor) and their subordinates and to describe what the conflict was about and whether or not it affected the relationship of the participants and their subordinates, the tasks, or other employees. In addition, the participants had to identify the conflict management styles they and their subordinates used when conflicting with each other and comment on whether or not such styles were effective.

FINDINGS
AND DISCUSSIONS

After the data were obtained, listed, and organized, the findings have emerged. Then,

discussions of the findings are presented. There are four dimensions on findings and discussions: (1) individual perceptions about organizational conflict, (2) conflict and conflict management between the same-level dyads, (3) conflict and conflict management between the participants and their superiors, and (4) other factors and characteristics related to Thai conflict management. Dimensions II and III also are presented as the answers for RQ.1 and RQ.2 of this study.

Dimension I: Individual
Perceptions about Organizational Conflict

Regarding the individual perceptions about organizational conflict, participants A and B agreed that the conflict could be perceived as both constructive and destructive to the organization. On the contrary, participant C commented that conflict in the organization was very destructive.

In terms of types of conflict, all participants agreed that conflict was initially task-oriented but could be transformed into relationship-oriented. Participant A stated that interdepartmental conflict could easily change into relationship conflict. Also, participant C said that conflict within a department could lead to relationship conflict. With respect to the causes of conflict, all participants stated that the highly interdependent work (workflow) and the different perceptions of individuals about their inputs and outcomes caused the conflict.

With regard to the levels of aggressiveness of conflict in organizations, all participants agreed that physically violent behavior was never reported to them. However, the opponents would raise their voices when having conflict. Moreover, several factors including sex difference, levels of education, and the positions of the disputants affected the level of aggressiveness.

Dimension II: Conflict and Conflict Management between the Same-Level Dyads (Peers/Colleagues) and Characteristics

Regarding the conflict and conflict management between the same-level dyads, all participants agreed that this kind of conflict was caused by workflow and the discrepancy between the inputs and outcomes of individuals. In terms of effects of this conflict, the participants stated that the conflict affected the individuals' relationship on tasks and on other employees, respectively.

For the conflict management styles, the disputants frequently employed three styles; they were third party intervention, avoidance, and confrontation. Also, the disputants occasionally used forcing, covert retaliation, accommodating, and compromising in dealing with conflict.

In many cases, the most effective conflict management style was third party intervention. Compromising was effective in maintaining the relationship of the disputants, while forcing could efficiently improve work progress but did not help much in personal relationship of the individuals.

Specifically, among the weakly tied peers, the four most frequently used conflict management styles were found to be confrontation, third party intervention, avoidance, and covert behaviors. Many weakly tied dyads reportedly confronted and directly faced another disputant when conflict was about only business or work issues, but they avoided the other disputant when it was about personal issues. Confrontation and avoiding were employed at the very first phase of conflict. When the weakly tied dyads found that the conflict was not solved by these two strategies, the disputants asked a third party to settle the solutions for them. In other words, third party intervention was used when the disputants were aware that the conflict had become more serious or when other strategies had failed to handle the problem. This finding is consistent with Roongrengsuke and Chansuthus's study (1998), which claims that when conflict occurs, the most common strategy used is having a mediator who is a mutually respected third party.

The weakly tied peers reportedly also used covert behavior (such as gossiping and talking behind one's back) and then third party intervention. This finding supports Morrill and Thomas's claim (1992) that "interpersonal problems among weakly tied peers are likely to be contained at the grievance stage using covert behaviors or to be socially escalated to disputes involving a third party" (p. 400).

On the other hand, the findings of conflict management among strongly tied peers have revealed that the disputants used confrontation and compromise, together with avoidance, to handle the conflict. Regarding the compromising strategy, one participant reported that she used it because she was concerned about maintaining her relationship with her peers but not concerned about the work accomplishment. This finding supports Roongrengsuke and Chansuthus's claim (1998) that Thais are likely to value maintaining a good relationship more than completing tasks and Komin's finding (1995) that compromise is often used as an effective means to save face, and to keep the surface harmony (p. 11).

It is also noteworthy that, when conflict was concerning work matters only, all same-level disputants, regardless how close they were, confronted the other disputant; however, when conflict was concerning personal or social relationships, they reportedly avoided face-to-face interactions with the other disputant. These findings are consistent with Rojjanaprapayon's claim (1997) that Thais are expected to display indirect, contextual, and feminine communication features in order to avoid social and personal conflicts at all costs (p. 61). Similarly, the findings reflect Kosalakood's finding (1998) that Thais

usually avoid public confrontation and strong criticism, if possible (p. 5).

Dimension III: Conflict and Conflict Management between the Superiors and the Subordinates and Characteristics

In terms of conflict and conflict management between the participants and their superiors, two participants, B and C, agreed that the kind of conflict was caused by different opinions and working styles. Data from participant A were not presented in this discussion because, as an owner of the business in Thai context, she reportedly had no superiors and did not expect conflicts with her subordinates.

Participants B and C reported that this kind of conflict had no effect on the individuals' relationship, on work, or on other disputants. The conflict management styles commonly employed by the participants and their superiors included confrontation, accommodation, compromise, and forcing. In terms of the effectiveness, these strategies made good progress in work and had no effect on personal relationships.

As a subordinate, participant B, particularly, reported that she effectively employed a combination of confronting, accommodating, forcing, and compromising strategies to deal with her superior. She asserted that she had to consider when to use each strategy, saying:

> At first I told him directly that I did not want to do it {task} his way. Sometimes, I just changed my standpoint to please him, especially when he strongly insisted. But at other times, he recommended me when he realized that I was very assertive in my opinion. In some cases, we had to compromise our solutions. In other words, we changed our roles back and forth.

This finding fits Van de Vliert, Euwema, and Huismans's findings (1995) that "the

effectiveness is a function of conglomerated conflict behaviors rather than one dominant and isolated mode of conflict handling" (p. 277). Van de Vliert et al. further state that "a whole composition of more or less salient reactions that are more or less effective constructive" determines the effectiveness of conflict management (p. 277). Therefore, one must be aware that the use of only one dominant and isolated mode of conflict handling may not be as effective.

In terms of conflict and conflict management between the participants and their subordinates, participant B stated that the misinterpretation of nonverbal cues and the discrepancy between inputs and outcomes were the causes of this kind of conflict. The conflict had an effect on work, on personal relationship, and on other parties.

The conflict management styles frequently employed by participant B, as a supervisor, were confrontation and third party intervention. Her subordinates were likely to use third party intervention, covert retaliation, and confrontation to manage the conflict. The strategies used by participant B and her subordinates were reportedly effective in making work progress. However, the problem in their personal relationship was not solved.

For participant C, the conflict between her and her subordinates was caused by their different working styles, but it had no effect on their relationship or on tasks. Participant C frequently used a forcing strategy to deal with her subordinates, while her subordinates employed an accommodating strategy. These two strategies made good progress in work but were not effective in solving their personal relationship problem.

Apparently, when the participants were the superiors/supervisors, they were likely to use forcing the most, while the participants reportedly preferred accommodation when they were the subordinates. These findings provide support to Putnam and Wilson's claim (1982, as cited in Putnam & Poole, 1989) in two

folds: (1) forcing and confronting are likely to be used by the superiors; and (2) smoothing, avoidance, compromise, and confronting are likely to be used by the subordinates. However, the effectiveness of forcing and accommodation was still doubtful. The participants admitted that the two strategies helped in the accomplishment of work tasks but not in the relationship or the feelings of the disputants.

Also, the participants as the superiors reportedly were in favor of a combination of forcing and confrontation and believed that they were the most effective conflict management style. This seems to be consistent with Van de Vliert, Euwema, and Huismans's claim (1995) that "an increase in problem solving (confrontation) tended to enhance effectiveness, especially if a superior combined it with much forcing vis-à-vis a subordinate" (p. 271).

Dimension IV: Other Factors and Characteristics Related to Thai Conflict Management

Other findings also suggest that several factors were to be taken into consideration when individuals selected the conflict management styles/strategies such as personality, age, closeness of relationship, sex, levels of education, protection from arbitrary action, and their position in the organization and that of the other disputant(s). For example, participant B, as a subordinate, practiced confrontation and assumed that she was close enough to her male supervisor. In contrast, participant C did not use confrontation with her female superior because she was not closely related to her superior, saying, "When I proposed any new ideas to her, she often turned them down or asked me to amend them. I was a bit upset, but I could not express my feeling to her. . . . We were not closely related. . . ."

All participants named third party intervention, emotionless confrontation, and compromise as the most effective conflict management styles. Three reasons why these three strategies are most effective in handling conflict can be discussed. Firstly, these three strategies seek more information about the problem through direct or face-to-face communication, regardless of the level of direct communication. Secondly, because of more information, they are likely to be able to investigate the causes of conflict and create a mutual understanding of the conflict. Lastly, because of the mutual understanding, all parties are likely to be able to establish mutually accepted solutions.

It also is noteworthy that all three participants reported that conflict had to be and could be "solved." They believed that when conflict was "solved," the work could be done and the disputants could maintain friendly relations. This seems to be inconsistent with many scholars' view that conflict may not be "completely solved," but it can only be "managed" and "handled." Pedersen and Jandt (1996) explain that conflict management strategies and conflict resolution are not alike, saying:

> Conflict management brings conflict under control, whereas conflict resolution attempts to terminate the conflict. Conflict management recognizes the importance of positive conflict in relationships and may be a strategy to prevent conflicts from being solved. (p. 4)

Regarding the successfulness of conflict management style, these three participants as organizational members reportedly assessed it in terms of whether or not it could totally eliminate the conflict problem. As a result, the criteria of a "fair" solution and successfulness of conflict styles became in question.

Another notion of conflict management in Thai organizations is whether the skills for constructive conflict management in Thailand have been introduced or well developed. It is still doubtful because studies in this aspect relating to Thai context are still rare. However, an attempt to generalize conflict management from Western perspective to Thai context may result in failure or sound inappropriate and need to be reexamined.

Essentially, conflict issues and conflict management concepts can be contextual and culturally specific. Each conflict case is unique, and there is no absolute guideline or theoretical framework that can be perfectly applied to every single conflict case. At this point, further research on conflict and conflict management in Thailand is certainly encouraged, while the application of conflict management in Western perspective also should be carefully considered.

LIMITATIONS AND RECOMMENDATIONS

In this section, limitations of this study and recommendations for future research are presented. The details are below.

Limitations of the Study

There are five limitations in this present study. The first limitation is that there were only three participants, therefore, qualitative data and a small number of informants; this may affect the generalizability of the study. The second limitation is that all participants in this study were Thai female organizational members. No perspective of Thai male organizational members is included in this study. It is likely that male perspectives will provide different points of views and remarkable notions of conflict and conflict management in Thai organizations.

The third limitation is that the participants were chosen from different positions (top-level management, middle-level management, and lower-level management) and from different types of organizations (manufacturing, services, and trading organizations). Therefore,

no comparison of the same positions and the same kinds of organizations can be made.

The fourth limitation is that this study has put emphasis only on the management perspectives. Therefore, the perspectives on the lower level employees are excluded. The fifth limitation is that this study contains a sensitive matter concerning conflict and conflict management of the employees in organizations. Participants could be affected by "social desirability." Therefore, information could be distorted, biased, and falsified in order to maintain their organizations' reputation.

Future Research Recommendations

In future research, the researchers should take the participants' background into consideration (i.e., sex, age, levels of education, and work experience). The researchers should also put an emphasis on perspectives from other levels of employees. Lastly, the researchers must acquire more participants and these participants must be diverse enough; the participants can be selected from the same-level position of different organizations or at different-level positions of the same organization.

REFERENCES

Jehn, A. K. (1997). A qualitative analysis of conflict types and dimensions in organizational groups. *Administrative Science Quarterly, 42,* 530–557.

Komin, S. (1995). *Cross-cultural management communication in Thailand.* Paper presented at the SEAMEO's RELC Regional Seminar, Singapore.

Kosalakood, A. (1998). *The use of upward compliance gaining strategies in Thai organizations.* Unpublished master's thesis, National Institute of Development Administration, Bangkok, Thailand.

Morrill, C., & Thomas, K. C. (1992). Organizational conflict management as disputing process: The problem of social escalation.

Human Communication Research, *18*, 400–428.

Pedersen, P. B., & Jandt, F. E. (1996). Culturally contextual models for creative conflict management. In F. E. Jandt & P. B. Pedersen (Eds.), *Constructive conflict management* (pp. 3–26). Thousand Oaks, CA: Sage.

Putnam, L. L., & Poole, S. M. (1989). Conflict and negotiation. In F. M. Jablin, L. L. Putnam, K. H. Robert, & L. W. Porter (Eds.), *Handbook of organizational communication: An interdisciplinary perspective* (2nd ed., pp. 549–599). Beverly Hill, CA: Sage.

Rochanapruk, D. (1999). Employee relations and labor union in service industries in Thailand: A management perspective. *NIDA Language and Communication Journal*, *4*, 68–81.

Rojjanaprapayon, W. (1997). *Communication patterns of Thai people in a non-Thai context*. Unpublished doctoral dissertation, Purdue University, Indiana.

Roongrengsuke, S., & Chansuthus, D. (1998). Conflict management in Thailand. In K. Leung & D. Tjosvold (Eds.), *Conflict management in the Asia Pacific: Assumptions and approaches in diverse cultures* (pp. 167–221). Singapore: John Wiley & Sons (Asia).

Van de Vliert, E., Euwema, C. M., & Huismans, E. S. (1995). Managing conflict with a subordinate or a superior: Effectiveness of conglomerated behavior. *Journal of Applied Psychology*, *80*, 271–281.

Rujira Rojjanaprapayon earned his Ph.D. in Communication from Purdue University in 1997 and has taught at several Thai universities. He is currently an Assistant Professor of Speech Communication, University of Minnesota, Morris.

Porntipha Chiemprapha earned her M.A. from National Institute of Development Administration (NIDA). She is currently working at AutoAlliance (Thailand), a Ford and Mazda joint venture.

Achaya Kanchanakul also earned an M.A. from National Institute of Development Administration (NIDA).

Reading 1.5

An Examination of Taoist and Buddhist Perspectives on Interpersonal Conflicts, Emotions, and Adversities

RUEYLING CHUANG

> As stars, a fault of vision, as a lamp,
> A mock show, dew drops, or a bubble,
> A dream, a lightning flash, or cloud,
> So should one view what is conditioned.
>
> —*The Diamond Sutra*
> (trans. Conze, 1958, p. 68)

INTRODUCTION

Recent research has afforded insight into the Chinese value system: facework (Chen & Starosta, 1997); (Hwang, 1997), yuan (Chang & Holt, 1991a), direct versus indirect communication (Fong, 1998; Ma, 1996), and Confucian impact on organizational communication (Chen & Chung, 1994), among many other concepts. Traversing the current research in Chinese communication, one finds that the emerging research on both facework and *guanxi (kuan-hsi)* (Chang & Holt, 1991b) sheds light on the cultural roots of Chinese conflict resolution, although these writers seldom explicate emotionality and approaches to coping with adversities. The existing research on emotions in communication discipline has been derived primarily from Eurocentric perspectives and values (e.g., Lewis & Haviland-Jones, 2000). Additionally, current mainstream studies on spirituality and communication tend to focus on western perspectives (e.g., Ramsey & Blieszner, 2000).

Taoist Chuang Tzu and Buddhist teachings, such as the *Prajnaparamita Heart Sutra* and the *Diamond Sutra,* provide alternative views on emotions and conflict resolution. Taoist and Buddhist thought represent underlying Asian values and the patterned way of ideal thinking and action. For example, Taoists advise individuals to "embrace rather than

Reprinted with permission from *Intercultural Communication Reader* X1–1, 2002, 23–40.

Author's Note: The author is grateful to Otto and Corrina Chang for their invaluable insights on Buddhism.

resist" personal conflicts and to "take no [unnatural] action" in dealing with adversarial situations. As De Bary, Chan, and Watson (1960) noted, the core of Taoism is *"wu"* (nonexistence), which is a pure being that transcends any "forms and names" (p. 240). In a similar vein, the impetus of the *Heart Sutra* and the *Diamond Sutra* is to enlighten individuals to surpass emotional highs and lows and to see them as part of the flow of nature.

The purpose of this paper is to unveil the spiritual and philosophical roots of Chinese communication and their connection to fundamental Asian values. Specifically, the author seeks to examine the Chinese philosophical and spiritual underpinnings of emotionality and conflict resolution. By examining Taoist teachings such as Chuang Tzu and Buddhist sutras, this essay strives to illuminate the extent to which these texts reflect Chinese philosophical ideals as they relate to western preoccupations with resolving conflicts and emotional adversity. To interpret Buddhist and Taoist teachings of spontaneity, *wu-wei* (nonaction), dialectic thinking, *kong/sunyata* (emptiness or selflessness), nonattainment and ebb and flow of life, this paper extrapolates specific passages from the *Heart Sutra,* the *Diamond Sutra,* Lao Tzu's *Tao Te Ching,* and Chuang Tzu. Thematic analyses from these texts and personal observations are utilized to illustrate the essence of Taoist and Buddhist teachings and to ascertain their relevancy to our contemporary life.

VALUES AND RELIGION AS A CULTURAL SYSTEM

In his discussion of the dimensions of culture, Hofstede (2001) noted that values and culture guide our mental software. A value is an implicit or explicit conception of a desirable and preferable mode of conduct or state of existence (Hofstede, 2001; Kluckhohn, 1951;

Rokeach, 1972). Values indicate a broad propensity to favor certain states of affairs or frames of mind. Values are associated with feelings (e.g., like versus dislike) and they deal with judgments such as good versus bad, "paradoxical versus logical," and "irrational versus rational" (Hofstede, 2001, p. 6). Hofstede further delineated three types of values: "those dealing with relationships with (1) other people, (2) things (our nonhuman environment), and (3) our own inner selves and God" (p. 8).

Hofstede's assertions underscore the interconnectedness among values, culture, and religion. Religion is part of a cultural system because it affects culture's social-structural and psychological processes (Geertz, 1973). Through symbols (e.g., scriptures) and rituals (e.g. chanting), religion not only offers models of preferable conduct but also a "synopsis of cosmic order" and "a gloss upon the mundane world of social relationships and psychological events" (Geertz, 1973, p. 124). Religion provides a system of meaning embodied in symbols. Symbols describe cultural values and social order. For example, many Buddhist sutras such as the *Diamond Sutra* reveal the importance of appreciating emptiness (*kong*), understanding impermanence in life, and avoiding extremes (taking the middle paths).

THE CONCEPT OF *YUAN*

Chang and Holt's (1991) study of the concept of *yuan* and the Chinese perspective on social and romantic relationships exemplifies how religion affects an individual's social and psychological interactions. Through an examination of Chinese literature and the Mandarin Chinese language, Chang and Holt found that the Buddhist concept of *yuan* ("dependent origination") plays an important role in describing how the Chinese perceive their interpersonal relationships. *Yuan,* one of the most commonly referred to phrases derived

from Buddhism, is also defined as "secondary causation" (p. 30). It is, as explained by Chang and Holt, a force in dyadic encounters that allows both the present environment and previous deeds (what they call "contextual factors") to determine whether people will or will not be connected with each other. *Yuan* is paired with *yinyuan* (both principal and subsidiary causes or predestined relationship). *Yin* denotes principal cause, while *yuan* refers to secondary causation. The Chinese use the terms *yuan* and *yinyuan* simultaneously to describe relationship development or the lack thereof. It is through *yuan* and *yinyuan* that two individuals serendipitously cross paths. Conversely, lack of *yuan* or due to bad *yinyuan* two people may part ways or are constantly in conflict with each other. Thus, to put it in a cause and effect relationship, destructive *yinyuan* in the past leads to devastating consequences in the present moment.

The concept of *yuan* and *yinyuan* originates from the Sanskrit word *hetupratyaya*. *Yuan* and *yinyuan* and the Chinese rendition of *hetupratyaya*. *Hetu* denotes causes, whereas *pratyaya* means secondary causes. For example, seed is the cause (*hetu*) and rain, water, climate, and the gardener are secondary causes (*pratyaya*). According to Soothill and Hodous (1962), the compilers of *A Dictionary of Chinese Buddhist Terms* (1962), there are twelve causes or links (*yinyuan*) in the chains of the whole range of human existence. They are "old age and death, rebirth, existence, grasping, love, receiving, feeling," and "our six senses," "our six forms of perceptions," and finally "action and ignorance" (p. 186). These twelve causes are closely related to our interpersonal relationships and profoundly affect our emotional highs and lows. Thus, Chinese may see emotional turmoil and profound happiness as the results of these causes. *Yinyuan* can bring a relationship to fruition and it can also exacerbate relationship deterioration because of the seeds planted in a previous life.

For example, instead of trying to force a relationship which is ultimately doomed anyway, Chinese who believe in *yuan* may attribute the failed relationship to a lack of *yuan* or previous bad *yinyuan*.

Though Buddhists understand the importance of *yinyuan* (predestined relationship), they are not to be mistaken for fatalists. Rather, they believe in cosmic order and the law of nature. To be in harmony with nature or a person's life is to follow the law of nature. *Yuan* and *yinyuan* are related to the concept of karma (law of causality) in that a person's suffering or fortune can be caused by his or her previous deeds. The concept of *yuan* and *yinyuan* are cyclical rather than linear. Unlike Western intellectuals who hold dear such traditions as the Cartesian paradigm, the Chinese generally believe that relationships are affected by karma or *yinyuan*, which is predetermined by one's previous deeds. Coincidentally, most Buddhists and Taoists hold similar views on the laws of causality, rhythm of nature, and the nature of human interdependence. The following sections provide a brief summary of the essential Taoist and Buddhist perspectives to illustrate Chinese cultural values.

AN OVERVIEW OF BUDDHIST AND TAOIST PERSPECTIVES

The *Prajnaparamita Heart Sutra* and the *Diamond Sutra* are probably the most commonly recited Buddhist scriptures in Asian and Western Buddhist communities. Sutra can be loosely translated as the Buddhist scriptural narrative or sermon of Buddha. As Conze (1957) stated, among the thirty-eight different books of *Prajnaparamita* (transcendent wisdom in Sanskrit) literature, among the thirty generations of Buddhists in China, Japan, Tibet, and Mongolia, the holiest Buddhist scriptures are the *Diamond Sutra* and the *Heart Sutra*. Both sutras are regarded as the core of Buddhist teachings, especially their

discussions on wisdom and the concept of *sunyata* (emptiness, void, or selflessness). They are also two of Zen Buddhism's most important scriptures and essential teachings. The *Heart Sutra* and the *Diamond Sutra* were composed in India between 100 B.C. and 600 A.D. (Conze, 1957) and the *Prajnaparamita* (perfection of wisdom) literature has been analyzed and expounded for more than 2500 years (Nhat Hanh, 1988), especially in Mahayana Buddhism. *Prajna* means (transcendent) wisdom and *paramita* denotes going beyond (Bokar & Donyo, 1994). Thus, *prajnaparamita* literally means that the understanding of the true nature of transcendent wisdom allows individuals to go beyond the endless reincarnation of this suffering world (samsara). Though Mahayana Buddhism originated in India, it flourished in China. As Takakusu (1956) pointed out, Mahayana Buddhism emphasizes universal salvation. It was fostered in China where "great strides in Buddhist studies were made and the different thought in Mahayana schools were systematized" (p. 9).

The *Heart Sutra* and the *Diamond Sutra* exemplify the essence of Mahayana Buddhism teachings. They are perhaps the most diligently studied and analyzed scriptures in Buddhist monasteries and within Western scholarly circles (Lopez, 1998). Both sutras offer great emotional comfort to Chinese converts, so much so that the chanting of both scriptures have become part of Chinese funeral rituals. It is quite common for the deceased's family to hire Buddhist nuns to chant the *Diamond Sutra* or the *Heart Sutra* at a traditional Chinese Buddhist or religious Taoist funeral. These sutras provide a glimpse of hope for the family members that the deceased may transcend this suffering world (samsara), which continues the endless cycle of birth, death, and reincarnation, to nirvana. The mantra, originated from the *Heart Sutra*—(om) *gate gate pragate prasangate bodhi svaha*

(having gone, having gone, having gone beyond, having completely gone beyond, there is enlightenment)—represents five progressive paths to an exalted state of enlightenment.

Recitation of the aforementioned mantra and the *Heart Sutra* is commonly utilized in exorcism (Lopez, 1996). It is believed that the *Heart Sutra* possesses such profound mythical power that it will repel demons and ward off misfortune. It is important to know, though, that rather than condemn this ritual as a religious superstition, one should see the chanting of the *Diamond Sutra* and the *Heart Sutra* as a communication art, which consoles and uplifts the family members' spirits. The ritual of chanting both sutras is a form of communication which serves to remind individuals to be empathic and to stay in a state of calmness and meditative concentration (*samadhi*). It is said that Buddhism is not just a religion, it is also related to psychology. As one of my friends, whose father just passed on, once said, the chanting of the *Heart Sutra* is actually for the surviving members of the family rather than for the deceased. It offers hope and comfort to the family members amidst their profound loss and grief.

In the *Heart Sutra*, we read "no interdependent origins and no extinction of them (from ignorance to old age and death); no suffering, no origination of suffering, no extinction of suffering; no path; no understanding; no attainment" ([*parentheses original*] trans. Nhat Hanh, 1988, p. 1). The chanting of the *Heart Sutra* or the *Diamond Sutra* presents a form of communication, which lends individuals emotional support and consolation while they are in despair. As Chodron (2000) revealed in her book *When Things Fall Apart,* by adopting the Buddhist perspective (and I add Taoist outlook on life), an individual learns to accept that life is groundless, and filled with difficulties. By letting go, we free ourselves from suffering. Through attunement with our intense emotions such as resentment, depression, sadness, and guilt, we learn to embrace these afflictions and allow ourselves to be healed. Several passages from both scriptures have become common phrases in the Chinese language. For example, one of the widely popularized phrases from the *Heart Sutra*—"Form is emptiness and emptiness is form"—is often quoted in Chinese conversation, regardless of an individual's religious background. The general themes of Buddhism, such as emptiness (*sunyata*) right view, four noble truths, and no attainment, are germane to overcoming calamities in our everyday life.

THE FOUR NOBLE TRUTHS

The Four Noble Truths consist of affliction, response to affliction, containment, and the right track. The Four Noble Truths were upheld by Mahayana Buddhism, which includes offshoots such as Zen Buddhism. One of the important concepts of Buddha's teaching is the inevitability of affliction and adversity. Thus, the first noble truth is *dukkha* (affliction). Birth, old age, sickness, death, grief, lamentation, pain, depression, and agitation are *dukkha* (Brazier, 1998). Brazier (1998) noted that Buddhism is about noble living and not about eliminating calamity. Noble living invokes the existence of hardship. The cause of affliction or adversity is then the second noble truth. In response to *dukkha,* an individual is triggered by a "thirst for self-recreation which is associated with greed" and "sense pleasure, for being and non-being" (p. 185). Looking at the second noble truth, it makes sense as to why people use drugs, alcohol, or any kind of addiction to mask their misery and affliction. The third noble truth is complete extinction, which means to let go of that thirst and unshackle oneself from that thirst. Buddha informed us that "Containment should be understood to be a noble truth—this was the insight, understanding, wisdom, knowledge,

and clarity which arose in me about things untaught" (Brazier, 1998, p. 186).

Finally, after letting go of desire, a person should follow the right path. The fourth noble truth *marga* (the right track) entails the noble eight-limb way, "namely, right view, right thought, right speech, right action, right livelihood, right effort, right mindfulness and right *samadhi* (concentration)" (Brazier, 1998, p. 186). By embarking on the aforementioned Eightfold Path, a person ends his or her suffering and reaches nirvana. Accordingly, Buddha's teaching is to show us how to be enlightened amidst our adversity and emotional turmoil and not be defeated by life's difficulties. Buddha taught us to accept suffering and affective situations, and to "meet affliction and live nobly, so that suffering is not unnecessarily multiplied" (Brazier, 1998, p. 43).

TAO, CONFLICT, AND EMOTIONS

Buddhist teachings of the Four Noble Truths and ways to cope with our profound sadness and sufferings resonate with Taoist views of acceptance and *wu-wei* ("non-action"). One of the essential teachings of philosophical Taoism is the notion of ebb and flow of human existence (Crawford, 1996), which includes conflict, adversity, and emotional upheaval. Crawford (1997) suggested four approaches, originated from Taoist philosophy, to manage interpersonal conflict. They are: "Don't fight, recognize conflict as merely part of a larger whole," realize that conflict can be viewed as a vehicle to solidify relationships, and acknowledge the principle of "exhausting the *yang* to return to the *yin*" (p. 367).

Crawford, by examining Chinese Taoist classics, concluded that conflict and harmony are closely connected. Crawford's first rule of framing interpersonal conflict via Taoist perspectives, "don't fight," cautions us in regard to the downside of being belligerent. To be contentious or readily quarrelsome fuels the fire of conflict. Secondly, Crawford reminded us to see conflict from a larger picture and to identify conflict from a wider and holistic perspective. Thirdly, he suggested that we view conflict as a possible way to strengthen interpersonal ties. Crawford's third observation of Taoist approach to conflict is in sync with other communication scholars who argue that conflict can be positive, exciting, and helpful. For example, Wilmot and Hocker (2001) listed the positive sides of conflict. It can enrich and energize relationships, help to clarify illusive goals, and produce growth opportunity for the conflicting parties. Finally, Crawford's (1997) idea of "exhausting the *yang* to return to the *yin*" embodies the core value of Taoism.

Tao (the way), as a Taoist sees it, is the harmonious cycle between *yin* and *yang*. Everything extreme must swing to the opposing end. As *I Ching* revealed, excessive *yang* is the time *yin* initiates momentum, and vice versa. Thus, Lao Tzu asserted, "All beings bear *yin* and embrace *yang*, with a mellowing energy for harmony" (chap. 42, trans. Cleary, 1991, p. 35). The natural cycle of *yin* and *yang* indicates the importance of avoiding extremes. Individuals are warned that "those who contrive spoil it; those who cling lose it" (chap. 29). Lao Tzu continued to reveal the wisdom of keeping our perspective. As he stated, since things "sometimes go and sometimes follow, Sometimes puff and sometimes blow, Are sometimes strong and sometimes weak, Begin sometime and end sometime; Therefore sages remove extremes, Remove extravagance, Remove arrogance" (chap. 29). Since being strong or weak is part of the cycle, it is then paramount for us to remember that conflict is a natural process and to lose something in an adversarial situation is to gain something in return.

To continue and expand Crawford's (2002) delineation of the philosophical Tao's approach to conflict resolution, he supplied us with the following six ideas: embrace rather than resist, accept things for whatever they are; no expectations, allow things to happen as they go; don't take anything personally; everything changes—the only certainty is uncertainty and nothing stays the same; let other people off the hook; and death is imminent. Crawford's six ideas, derived from Taoist teachings, are beneficial for resolving interpersonal conflicts. In close relationships, we often see divorced couples who waited too long to communicate and when they do express their frustration, it is already too late.

Crawford (2002) advocated that we should embrace our circumstances and confront the conflict with an open mind rather than to resist it. In a dysfunctional relationship a person takes everything in until s/he cannot take it any longer and then explodes. Avoiding afflictive situations or using passive aggressive tactics also can lead to destructive conflict (Wilmot & Hocker, 2001). Along with the idea of acceptance, the principle of "no expectation" is also paramount to maintaining interpersonal relationships. Lao Tzu brought to light the paradoxical nature of letting go. By expecting nothing, and having no expectations, the relationship becomes more fulfilling. In Chapter 55 of *Tao Te Ching,* we read "To hasten the growth of life is ominous. To control the breath by the will is to overstrain it. To be overgrown is to decay" (trans. Wu, p. 113). Only when we cease to weary people, will people then cease to be wearied of us. Crawford's (2002) Taoist idea of "Nothing changes—Nothing stays the same" synchronizes with Buddhism's perspective that nothing is forever. Once we recognize that nothing is permanent, we can elevate ourselves above suffering. As the *Heart Sutra* reveals, once we accept that nothing stays the same and we forgo those "thoughts-coverings" we will not "tremble." Consequently, we can "overcome what can upset" (trans. Conze, 1958, p. 93).

BUDDHISM, TAOISM, AND WESTERN PSYCHOLOGY OF SELF-ACTUALIZATION

Buddhist teachings of an exalted state of enlightenment and the four noble truths bear a strong resemblance to Taoist notions of following the "way," and Western communication aspects of "self-actualization." In Chang and Page's (1991) comparison of Chinese Taoism and Zen Buddhism's view of human potential versus Carl Rogers and Abraham Maslow's theories of self-actualization, they revealed great similarities among the four. The sage manifested in Taoism and the enlightened person in Zen Buddhism resemble the self-actualizing person indicated in Western psychology. Chang and Page argued that both Rogers and Maslow emphasized that self-actualization constitutes the most favorable psychological stage for all human beings. The goal of psychotherapy then is to help individuals develop their full potential for self-actualization. Similarly, Chang and Page observed that both Zen Buddhism and Taoism also are concerned with the development of full human potential.

Taoists, such as Lao Tzu and Chuang Tzu, looked at human existence as an integral part of the great cosmos. What then is Tao or the way? Tao is the belief in which the spontaneous processes created by the phenomenal and natural worlds influence all creation in life and life itself. One of the most important principles of Taoism is to maintain a harmonious relationship with Tao, a state of metaphysical reality, which can be loosely interpreted as a natural law or pattern of human existence. Zen Buddhism, Chang and Page observed, stresses the importance of human naturalness and spontaneity and recognizes the illusory nature of the ego. Here we see the similarities between Taoism and Zen Buddhism in their emphasis on nature (i.e., "the way" or "suchness") and spontaneity. Accordingly, Chang

and Page asserted that the Zen idea of human independence is to participate in each moment of living, achieve full independence in one's thought and action, and not to place oneself in conflict with nature or other people.

SPONTANEITY AND NONACTION

Liu (1998) asserted that *tzu-jan* (spontaneity or natural) and *wu-wei* are "essential notions in Taoism, whose meanings are often thought to be identical" (p. 211). However, Liu argued that spontaneity is the principal value of Taoism while *wu-wei* is the core method to achieve it in social life. In explaining a different meanings for *tzu-jan*, Liu focused on the meaning of "natural, naturalness, spontaneous or spontaneity" (p. 212) or "to be natural" (p. 212). The state of naturalness or "so on its own" implies a harmonious situation, which does not involve conflict, drastic change, external enforcement, or abrupt transformations. "Taken literally, *wu-wei* seems to deny all human behavior and action" (p. 218); however, Liu noted, the overall implication of *wu-wei* is to eradicate or "reduce" human actions.

The following passage exemplifies the Taoist notion of *wu-wei:* "The world is a sacred vessel, which must not be tampered with or grabbed after. To tamper with it is to spoil it, and to grasp it is to lose it" (*Tao The Ching,* chap. 29, trans. Wu, 1997, p. 59). The following excerpt from *Tao Te Ching* also illustrates the importance of *tzu-jan,* that is, to go with the flow and not to apply excessive forces in changing things: "He who fusses over anything spoils it. He who grasps anything loses it. The Sage fusses over nothing and therefore spoils nothing. He grips at nothing and therefore loses nothing" (chap. 64).

Lao Tzu's approach to conflict is very different from popular American sayings such as "Don't just sit there, do something." His advice of letting things go reminds us to keep our perspective in the midst of our quest for perfection. For example, I have friends who pride themselves on being "fussy" and insisting on everything being "neat and tidy." Because of their persistence with being "very picky," they have forgotten to see the whole big picture, have spoiled their harmonious relationship with people around them, and have hindered their own growth. And thus, Lao Tzu cautioned us to keep in mind that there is a natural way that affects our action: "Man follows the ways of the Earth. The Earth follows the ways of Heaven. Heaven follows the ways of Tao. Tao follows its own ways" (chap. 25). In a similar vein, Chuang Tzu also advised us to let go of our own preconceived frame of mind and allow ourselves to embrace the natural cycle of ups and downs, especially in dealing with our physical conditions and afflictive situations. The readers are to be reminded that "Hunger and thirst, cold and heat, being pent in and stopped up, and failing to advance are heaven and earth proceeding on their courses, the off-flow from things as they turn in their cycles; the point is to let oneself flow on with them" (*Chuang Tzu,* chap. 20, trans. Graham, 1986, p. 167).

The aforementioned excerpt reinforces Lao Tzu's and Chuang Tzu's idea of harmonizing with the natural flow of action, letting Tao go on its own course, without excessive strife. Paradoxically, also because of this approach to a conflictual situation, one actually conquers. As Lao Tzu asserted, "It is Heaven's Way to conquer without striving, to get responses without speaking. To induce the people to come without summoning, To act according to plans without haste" (chap. 73). Lao Tzu's teaching of bringing about other people's compliance contradicts the Machiavellian manipulation of power and threat to achieve a person's goal.

Along with the idea of going with the flow and following the natural way, Taoists also advocate *wu-wei*. Both Lao Tzu and Chuang Tzo mentioned in their teachings that the best ruler is a ruler who does not rule. As Chuang Tzu stated, "So if the gentleman is left with no choice but to preside over the world, his best policy is Doing Nothing. Only by Doing Nothing will he find security in the essentials of his nature and destiny" (trans. Graham, 1986, p. 212). It is only because of the leader's adaptation of *wu-wei* that this person actually achieves more. "The doer of the Way every day does less, less, and less until he does nothing at all, and in doing nothing there is nothing that he does not do" (p. 159). The Taoist approach of *wu-wei* seems quite challenging to those who live amidst an era where bigger is better (*a la* SUVs and big houses) and a person is judged on how much he or she achieves. The notion of *wu-wei* accentuates the difference of cultural values from an intercultural communication point of view. For example, Jandt (2001) notes that one of the dominant U.S. cultural patterns is activity orientation. "Activity and work," "efficiency and practicality," and "progress and change" are the prevailing cultural values of the United States (pp. 238–239).

SUNYATA/KONG (*EMPTINESS*)

In his analysis of Tao and conversation, Crawford (1996) revealed that emptiness is one of the major themes of Taoist teaching. The Sanskrit word *sunyata* denotes *kong* in Chinese, and the concept of *sunyata/kong* is widely translated as "emptiness" in English. Interestingly enough, *sunyata* (emptiness) is one of the most essential ideas of Buddhism, so much so that Lopez (1998) entitled his book on the analysis of the *Heart Sutra, Elaborations on Emptiness.* Both Taoist and Buddhist teachings of emptiness have increasingly drawn attention to the field of psychology (Brazier, 1998). Consider the following passage from the *Heart Sutra:* "Form is emptiness and the very emptiness is form; emptiness does not differ from form, form does not differ from emptiness; whatever is form, that is emptiness, whatever is emptiness, that is form, the same is true of feelings, perceptions, impulses and consciousness" (*Heart Sutra*, trans. Conze, 1958, p. 81). The following passage from the *Heart Sutra* captured the essence of Buddhist teachings:

> Therefore in emptiness there is neither form, nor feelings, nor perceptions, nor mental formations, nor consciousness; no eye, or ear, or tongue, or body, or mind; no form, no sound, no smell, no taste, no touch, no object of mind; no realms of elements (from eyes to mind consciousness); no interdependent origins and no extinction of them (from ignorance to old age and death); no suffering, no origination of suffering, no extinction of suffering, no path; no understanding, no attainment. [*parentheses original*] (trans. Nhat Hanh, 1988, p. 1).

Here the *Heart Sutra* teaches us to realize that our emotions, perceptions, and our sense, are a mere illusion and nothing stays permanent. Our feelings and myriad things are like a dream, a magic show, a bubble, a shadow, like the morning dew, and the lightning thunderbolt. They come and go, as part of the natural cycle, as stated in the fourth stanza of lines I quoted from the *Diamond Sutra*. Accordingly, Chuang Tzu reminded us to question our own emotions and perceptions, because the way is invisible and forever changeable and non-changeable: "Whatever you hear is something else. The way is invisible, whatever you see is something else. The way is ineffable, whatever you talk about is something else. Do you know that the shaper of shapes is unshaped? The Way does not fit a name" (p. 163).

(NON)PERCEPTION AND NON-ATTAINMENT

Because our feelings, emotions, and our sense are in the form of emptiness, we should then challenge our perceptions and be mindful about our attachment to things or people. The *Diamond Sutra* revealed that perception of self is indeed no perception. And that "perception of a being, a soul or person," is "indeed no perception" (trans. Conze, 1958, p. 53). Since our perception is unobtainable, so are our thoughts and actions.

And the *Heart Sutra* continued to accentuate the importance of liberating our clinging attachment from things and feelings: "It is because of his nonattainmentness that a Bodhisattva, though having relied on the perfection of wisdom, dwells without thought-coverings. In the absence of thought-coverings, he has not been made to tremble, he has overcome what can upset, and in the end he attains to Nirvana" (trans. Conze, 1958, p. 93). We fall because we try too hard; we lose because we want something too much. We dwell on our thoughts too much and, consequently, we hinder our own progression. Time and time again both Taoism and Buddhism advocate the dialectical nature of human existence. As Lao Tzu simply put it in Chapter 22: "Bend and you will be whole. Curl and you will be straight. Keep empty and you will be filled. Grow old and you will be renewed. Have little and you will gain."

EBB AND FLOW/DIALECTICAL NATURE OF LIFE

Traversing all these essential teachings of Buddhism and philosophical Taoism such as emptiness, non-attainment, non-perception, we found an overarching theme: human interactions are consistent with this dialectical, and sometimes paradoxical, rhythm of life. Just like the ebb and flow of tides, our lived experience is filled with emotional ups and downs. As Lao Tzu eloquently stated:

> Bad fortune is what good fortune leans on,
> Good fortune is what bad fortune hides in,

Who knows the ultimate end of this
process?
Is there no norm of right?
Yet what is normal soon becomes
abnormal,
And what is auspicious soon turns
ominous.
Long indeed have the people been in a
quandary. (chap. 58)

DISCUSSION AND IMPLICATIONS

By examining Taoist and Buddhist scriptures, this paper reveals the general themes of both teachings: four noble truths, self-actualization, *kong* (emptiness), ebb and flow/dialectical nature of life, impermanence and non-attainment. These themes undergird fundamental Asian values, which are pervasive in Northeast Asia and certain parts of Southeast Asia. These ideal cultural values provide guidance for Chinese and Asians' modes of conduct and social/psychological frames of mind. To compare different commentaries and interpretations of these Taoist and Buddhism classics, I used different versions/translations of *Tao Te Ching,* Chuang-Tzu's *Inner Chapters,* the *Heart Sutra,* and the *Diamond Sutra.* These four texts reveal several similarities in their approach to resolving interpersonal conflict, emotions, and adversities. The essence of Taoist and Buddhist teachings, such as *kong/sunyata,* impermanence, and nonattachment, are enunciated in these four texts. Their discussions of diminishing one's ignorance, freeing ourselves from attachments and suffering, and viewing the ups and downs of life as being part of the natural cycle/rhythm, offer valuable suggestions for individuals both in the psychology and communication fields.

   Taoists and Buddhists adopt a similar communicative approach of negation in their discussion of Tao and dharma. Taoists and Buddhists never explicitly discuss what is Tao or dharma, but rather they explain both terms based on what it is not. For example, the beginning of *Tao Te Ching* clearly specifies that if Tao can be talked about then it is not the eternal Tao, and if Tao can be explicitly named then it is not the right name. Accordingly, for Buddhists dharma is not attainment and not permanent. Enlightenment is a state of not clinging to one's desire, perception, emotion, and fixation. Through rhetorical strategies of negation, double negation (e.g., no permanent, no impermanent), and paradox (e.g., grasp then you will lose), Taoist and Buddhist teachings propose a dialectical communication model which is different from the Western model of rational and linear communication.

   The Western concept of logical linear causation or rationality neither explains the complexity of *yuan* or *yinyuan* nor the dialectical relationship between *yin* and *yang.* Buddhist perspectives illuminate ideal moral consciousness (e.g., the eight paths) and Taoist thoughts predispose communicative action (e.g., parsimoniousness, no excessiveness), as contrasted with the Western values and *modus operandi.* Taoist and Buddhist approaches to communication encourage individuals to be flexible and empathic, to think outside the box, and to free oneself from materialism and selfishness which may bring unhappiness and affliction. The Western communication model of goal orientation, compliance-gaining strategies, sender-centered approach, communication competence, and individualism may not account for the Asian view on relational outcome. Contrary to the Western model of the uncertainty reduction theory (Berger & Bradac, 1982; Gudykunst, 1988), which is widely adopted in the fields of interpersonal and intercultural communication, Buddhist and Taoist perspectives encourage individuals to embrace uncertainty and to realize that life is impermanent and constantly in flux. Instead of "reducing" uncertainty, Buddhism and Taoism, through their verbal symbols (i.e., scriptures and texts) and dialectical/ paradoxical reasoning, invite individuals to accept uncertainty and to see calamity as part of life.

Though Taoism and Buddhism caution individuals to be parsimonious and be skeptical about language, nonetheless, they do not discourage communication. Instead, they address the importance of nonverbal communication and keen awareness of one's harmony with the environment and the metaphysical world of one's existence. Taoism and Buddhism shift the primary attention of communication from self to contextual factors, which include cause and effect, human relationships, *yinyuan*, and the law of nature. This paper discusses the transcendental dimensions of self, relationship, and human emotion. It is important to know that, though Taoists and Buddhists adopt dialectical perspectives on human existence, they do not perceive *yin/yang* and permanent/impermanent as mutually exclusive nor the opposite end of contradictions as Western communication scholars such as Baxter (1988) suggested. Instead, Taoists and Buddhists propose a transcendental communication model, which sees yin/yang, win/lose, happiness/suffering, death/ rebirth, and permanent/impermanent as an ongoing complementary cycle. Though both Baxter and Taoists coincidentally highlight the dialectical nature of human relationships, Taoism and Buddhism provide a transcendental dimension to spirituality, which is in sync with the rhythm of nature.

In addition to the elaboration on *yuan* as an exemplary Chinese value, this paper also brings to light the importance of *sunyata* or *kong* in transcendental communication. The concept of *kong* is germane to the essential teachings of Buddhism and Taoism. As illustrated by the *Heart Sutra* and *Diamond Sutra*, the form is empty and the emptiness is form and the law of all conditions is like a dream and flashing light. Though it is important to understand that all our emotions and

sensations are illusionary and ephemeral, it is equally important to be mindful of the true essence of *sunyata* (or *kong* in Chinese). The English translation of emptiness does not quite capture the complexity and multifaceted dimensions of *kong/sunyata*. *Kong* is often mistaken for nothingness or misinterpreted as a passive outlook on life. Rather, *kong,* just like Tao, means impermanence and selflessness, which means that nothing can stand alone and everything relies on interdependence. *Kong* represents one of the essential terminal values (end states) of Buddhism, while eradication of covetousness, hatred, and ignorance exemplifies Buddhists' instrumental values (means to get there). *Yuan,* right view, and state of *kong* are independent. *Yuan* arises from selflessness, and once one empties out his or her fixation and correct one's views, then everything will naturally flow.

Future communication researchers can consider a postmodern approach to Buddhism (Lopez, 1998) and further explicate the connection between philosophical Taoism and interpersonal communication. This paper provides a first attempt to consolidate Buddhist and Taoist texts and apply them in the interpersonal and intercultural contexts, specifically in discussing how Chinese cope with conflict and emotional ups and downs. It adopts the concepts of *yuan, kong wu-wei,* spontaneity and harmony with nature to illustrate underlying Chinese values. Buddhist and Taoist teachings contain an immense amount of knowledge which future researchers can explore, such as illuminating Zen Buddhism's approach to human communication and theorizing transcendental communication.

REFERENCES

Baxter, L. (1988). A dialectical perspective on communication strategies in relationship development. In S. Duck (Ed.), *A handbook of personal relationships* (pp. 257–273). New York: John Wiley & Sons.

Berger, C. R., & Bradac, J. J. (1982). *Language and social knowledge: Uncertainty in interpersonal relations.* London: Edward Arnold.

Bokar, Rinpoche, & Donyo, K. (1994). *Profound wisdom of The Heart Sutra and other teachings.* San Francisco, CA: ClearPoint Press.

Brazier, D. (1998). *The feeling Buddha: A Buddhist psychology of character, adversity and passion.* New York: Fromm International.

Chang, H-C., & Holt, G. R. (1991a). The concept of *yuan* and Chinese interpersonal relationships. In S. Ting-Toomey & F. Korzenny (Eds.), *Cross-cultural interpersonal communication* (pp. 28–57). Newbury Park, CA: Sage.

Chang, H-C., & Holt, G. R. (1991b). More than relationship: Chinese interaction and the principle of guan-hsi. *Communication Quarterly, 39,* 251–271.

Chang, R., & Page, R. C. (1991). Characteristics of the self-actualized person: Visions from the East and West. *Counseling and Values, 36*(1), 2–10.

Chen, G. M., & Chung, J. (1994). The "Five Asian Dragons": Management behaviors and organizational communication. *Communication Quarterly, 42(2),* 93–105.

Chen, G. M., & Starosta, W. J. (1997). Chinese conflict management and resolution: Overview and implications. *Intercultural Communication Studies, 7(1),* 1–16.

Chodron, P. (2000). *When things fall apart.* Boston: Shambhala.

Chung, T. C. (1992). *Zhuangzi speaks: The music of nature* (Trans. by B. Bruya). Princeton, NJ: Princeton University Press.

Chuang-Tzu: The inner chapters. (1986). (A. C. Graham, Trans.) London: Unwin Paperbacks.

Cleary, T. (Trans.). (1991). *The essential Tao: An initiation into the heart of Taoism through the authentic Tao Te Ching and the inner teachings of Chuang-Tzu.* San Francisco: HarperSanFrancisco.

Conze, E. (Trans.). (1958). *Buddhist wisdom books: Containing the Diamond Sutra and the Heart Sutra.* London: George Allen & Unwin.

Crawford, L. (1996). Everyday Tao. *Communication Studies,* 1966 (1&2), 25–34.

Crawford, L. (1997). Conflict and Tao. *The Howard Journal of Communications, 8,* 357–370.

Crawford, L. (2002). Six ideas, interpersonal conflict, and philosophical Taoism. In G. M. Chen & R. Ma (Eds.), *Chinese conflict management and resolutions* (pp.117–126). Westport, CT: Ablex.

De Bary, W. T., Chan, W-T., & Watson, B. (1960). *Sources of Chinese tradition* (vol. 1). New York: Columbia University Press.

Fong, M. (1998). Chinese immigrants' perceptions of semantic dimensions of direct/indirect communication in intercultural compliment interactions with North Americans. *The Howard Journal of Communications, 9,* 245–262.

Geertz, C. (1973). *Interpretation of culture.* New York: Basic Books.

Gudykunst, W. (1988). Uncertainty and anxiety. In Y. Y. Kim & W. Gudykunst (Eds.), *Theories in intercultural communication* (pp. 123–156). Newbury Park, CA: Sage.

Nhat Hanh, T. (1988). *The heart of understanding: Commentaries on the Prajnaparamita Heart Sutra.* Berkeley, CA: Parallax Press.

Hofstede, G. (2001). *Culture's consequences: Comparing values, behaviors, institutions, and organizations across nations.* Thousand Oaks, CA: Sage.

Hwang, K-K. (1997). *Guanxi* and *Mientze:* Conflict resolution in Chinese society. *Intercultural Communication Studies, 7,* 17–42.

Jandt, F. (2001). *Intercultural communication: An introduction* (3rd ed.). Thousand Oaks, CA: Sage.

Jia, W. (1997). Facework as a Chinese conflict-preventive mechanism. *Intercultural Communication Studies, 7,* 43–62.

Kluckhohn, C. (1951). The study of culture. In D. Lerner & H. D. Lassell (Eds.), *The policy sciences* (pp. 86–101). Stanford, CA: Stanford University Press.

Lao Tzu (1997). *Tao Te Ching* (J. C. H. Wu, Trans.). New York: Barnes & Noble.

Lewis, M., & Haviland-Jones, J. M. (Eds.). (2000). *Handbook of emotions.* New York: Guilford.

Liu, X. (1998). Naturalness (*Tzu-jan*), the core value in Taoism: Its ancient meaning and its significance today. In L. Kohn & M. LaFargue (Eds.), *Lao-tzu and the Tao-te-ching* (pp. 211–230). Albany, NY: State University of New York Press.

Lopez, D. (1998). *Elaborations on emptiness.* Princeton, NJ: Princeton University.

Ma, R. (1996). Saying "yes" for "no" and "no" for "yes": A Chinese rule. *Journal of Pragmatics, 25,* 257–266.

Ramsey, J., & Blieszner, R. (2000). Community, affect, and family relations: A cross-cultural study of spiritual resiliency in eight old women. *Journal of Religious Gerontology, 11* (1), 39–64.

Rinpoche, B., & Donyo, K. (1994). *Profound wisdom of The Heart Sutra and other teachings.* San Francisco, CA: ClearPoint Press.

Rokeach, M. (1972). *Beliefs, attitudes and values: A theory of organization and change.* San Francisco: Jossey-Bass.

Soothill, W. E., & Hodous, L. (Eds.). (1962). *A dictionary of Chinese Buddhist terms.* Taipei, Taiwan: Buddhist Culture Service.

Takakusu, J. (1956). *The essentials of Buddhist philosophy.* Westport, CT: Greenwood.

Wilmont, W., & Hocker, J. (2001). *Interpersonal conflict.* New York: McGraw-Hill.

Rueyling Chuang, born in Taiwan, is Assistant Professor of Communication Studies at the California State University, San Bernardino. She is a Buddhist who enjoys meditation and yoga.

Reading 1.6

Cultural Values and Argumentative Orientations for Chinese People in Taiwan, Hong Kong, and Mainland China

JUNG-HUEL BECKY YEH

LING CHEN

With the increasing growth of communication technology and the convenience of transportation, cultural and individual values can hardly remain intact. Carried over from a historical heritage perspective, Chinese people have always struggled between tradition and innovation. Though sharing the same ethnic root, people in Taiwan, mainland China, and Hong Kong not only have experienced different degrees of transitions toward modernization, but also have been governed by different sets of political and ideological systems for several decades.

Though they have been identified as collectivism and high-context cultures (Yum, 1988), the three Chinese societies have been influenced by various political rulings. With the ideological conditioning of communism and the rampant destruction brought about during the Cultural Revolution, young mainland Chinese have been in a dilemma between Mao's teaching and the substantial well-beings that result from materialism and technology. A similar battle is also burgeoning in Hong Kong. In a culture where numerology is revered, the structure and social tendency of this former British colony to PRC rule might be viewed with ambivalence. An island flourished by technology manufacturing and international trade, Taiwan is also searching for a balance between maintaining tradition and devoting itself to modernization. When values of Confucius tradition are shaded by the belief in competition and efficiency, people on this island ponder the continuum of Confucius virtues at the one end and individualism at the other.

In the twenty-first century, there is a tendency to integrate the different divisions into a unified entity versus dividing up an entity into different parts. Before integrating and unifying

From a paper presented at the 2002 International Communication Association Annual Conference, Seoul, Korea.

the different entities into one, people at least need to know the current status of these entities. After a departure from politics and ideology, the best way to explore commonalities and differences is to ask:

RQ1: How do people in the three Chinese societies appraise and perceive Confucian values in the 21st century?

Under the influences and teachings of Confucianism where social harmony, seniority, and hierarchy as well as saving face have been emphasized in daily routines, the social interactions and communication practices in a Chinese culture have provided the foundation for maintaining these concerns. Researchers in cross-cultural communication conceptualize that silence, responses, apologies, self-disclosure, and requests can universally happen in any culture (Gudykunst & Nishida, 1987). However, these communication behaviors react differently to meet the needs of each culture's societal demands and conditions. Consequently, investigations emphasizing communication behaviors and strategies in various cultures have devoted much effort on characterizing communication behaviors that commonly reside in each culture: silence (Hasegawa & Gudykunst, 1998), responses (Bresnahan, Ohashi, Liu, Nebashi, & Liao, 1999), apologies (Barlund & Yoshioka, 1990; Sugimoto, 1997), self-disclosure (Chen, 1995; Goodwin, Nizharadze, Luu, Kosa, & Emelyanova, 1999) and requests (Kim. M., Hunter, Miyahara, Horvath, Bresnahan, & Yoon, 1996; Kim, Shin, & Cai, 1998).

To predict and understand differences in communication behaviors, Kim et al. (1996) contend that social values and norms strongly influence the amount of talk and argument. She exemplifies three Asian cultures that value social harmony more than expressing one's personal inner thoughts and feelings: Japanese, Korean, and Chinese. In the past,

Japan and the U.S. were respectively classified as collectivist/masculine and individualist/feminine cultures. Members in individualist cultures are more affect-oriented (Frymier, Klopf, & Ishii, 1990) and talkative (Gaetz, Klopf & Ishii, 1990) than in collectivist cultures, whereas the Chinese are more "tolerant" of silence and perceive quietness as a way of controlling what goes on (Giles, Coupland, & Wiemann, 1992).

The term "argumentative" is used to refer to the tendency of approaching and avoiding arguing. Infante and Rancer (1996) assert that cultures and belief structures vary in predispositions for aggressive communication. They define that verbal aggressiveness and argumentativeness differ in that verbal aggressiveness attacks the self-concept of others, whereas argumentativeness verbally attacks the positions that other people hold on controversial issues. Scholars contend that the tendency of being argumentative relates to collective cultural values embedded in each culture (Kim, 1999) and cultural beliefs of arguing (Rancer, 1998).

Previous research findings have found individuals who perceive arguing as enjoyable, functional, and pragmatic tend to be high in argumentativeness (Rancer, Kosberg, & Baukus, 1992). No difference, however, is found in verbal aggressiveness and argumentativeness in American, Japanese (Prunty, Klopf, & Ishii, 1990a, 1990b), and Korean cultures. In the same research, the result also indicates that Americans overall are found to be higher in argumentativeness than Asians (Japanese and Koreans). A study conducted by Zhang, Butler, and Pryor (1996) also indicates that Chinese society values less individual assertiveness than the U.S. society does.

Based on previous findings in cross-cultural comparisons, a prominent pattern indicates that individualism societies are inclined to communicate more directly, assertive, and argumentative than collectivism societies. In addition, under the teaching of Confucius disciplines and the concern for maintaining social relationships and harmony, confrontation and arguments are considered as rude and impolite in East Asian cultures (Robinson, 1996; Yum, 1988). On the bipolar continuum of individualism and collectivism, argumentative orientations also reflect the ranking of collectivism. Moreover, as to the perceptions of argumentative behaviors, members in the three societies (Taiwan, Hong Kong, and mainland China) might be influenced or educated by the dominant authority differently. The second research question regarding argumentative behaviors is hence:

RQ2: Will argumentative orientations differ from one another in mainland China, Hong Kong, and Taiwan?

RQ2a: Are the people in these three societies different from one another in approaching an argument?

RQ2b: Are the people in these three societies different from one another in avoiding an argument?

Although a theoretical framework has explained why the daily routines and behaviors operate in a certain way across nations, some researchers still indicate the inadequacy of using I/C (Individualism/Collectivism) to classify the difference between culture dimensions and communication behaviors (Gudykunst, Matsumoto, Ting-Toomey, Nishida, Kim, & Heyman, 1996; Kagitcibasi, 1994; U. Kim, 1994; Triandis, 1994). Gudykunst et al. (1996) and Kim et al. (1996) assume that individuals are influenced by the cultures they are raised in. Consequently, they assert that socialization processes, including the way individuals conceive of themselves (self-construals) and their values, have direct effects on communication behaviors.

Self-construal is conceptualized as a "constellation of thoughts, feelings, and actions concerning one's relationship to others, and the self as distinct from others" (Singelis, 1994, p. 518). Markus and Kitayama (1991) propose that individuals with independent self-construals view themselves as autonomous and invariant, whereas those who with interdependent self-construals perceive themselves as flexible and having a variable self. Individuals with the stronger part of an interdependent self-construal will think that one cannot live without connecting or influencing others. As a result, people with an interdependent self-construal are likely to act as anticipated expectations of social norms or others. Individuals emphasizing independent self-construal usually look at the uniqueness and wholeness of each individual. Though family, friends, or intimate in-group members are naturally important, they are also sources verifying or affirming a person's standards.

The construct of self-construals has been used to link cultural I/C dimension and various communication behaviors, for example, conversation constraints (Kim, 1993, 1996), request strategies (Kim, Shin, & Cai, 1998), conflict styles (Oetzel, 1998; Ting-Toomey, 1988), and decision-making processes in small groups (Oetzel, 1998). In general, the greater an individual's self-construal as being interdependent, the higher correlation there will be of individuals who perceive "not hurting the others' feeling," "minimizing imposition," and/or "avoiding negative evaluation by the hearer" as the primary goals when making requests. Similarly, the greater the level is of the independent construal of self, the greater concern there will be for clarity and effectiveness (Kim et al., 1996). Independent self-construal is correlated positively with dominating or competing styles, and interdependent self-construal is correlated positively with avoiding, obliging, and compromising styles in small group conflicts (Oetzel, 1998).

To more accurately investigate the effects of cultures on communication behaviors,

Gudykunst et al. (1996) and Kim (1999) suggest comparing communicative behaviors by measuring collective values and individual values (e.g., self-construals) as the intermediate variables. Therefore, the final goal of this study intends to understand:

RQ3: How do collective values and individual values relate to argumentative communication?

Previous cross-cultural investigations mostly employ a cultural I/C scale or Rokeach's Value Survey to measure differences between East and West cultures. This study, however, utilizes both the Chinese Values Survey (Chinese Culture Connection, 1987) and 24 items of a self-construal scale (Singelis & Brown, 1995) for several reasons: First, the CVS is derived by Chinese people, reflecting genuine Confucian values and containing values that Western values or scales can hardly include. Second, instead of measuring the degree of individualism and collectivism, CVS represents collective values of Chinese in three societies transformed through different cultural and ideological governing. Third, the self-construal scales may account for value differences at the individual-level, portraying idiosyncratic orientations and tendencies that collective values cannot conclude within each culture. Fourth, both CVS and self-construal scales may help to conceive the influences of Chinese value orientations at the collective and individual levels on argumentative behaviors.

METHOD

Participants

A total of 1528 college students from mainland China (N = 857), Hong Kong (N = 300), and Taiwan (N = 371) participated in this survey. The samples from mainland China are respectively collected from five different cities (Xi'an, Shanghai, Beijing, Chengtu, and Guangzhou) with 48.9% females and 49.5% males. Samples from Taiwan and Hong Kong are collected from more than one university. The average age in mainland China's data is 19.58 years (SD = 5.56 years), Hong Kong is 19.30 years (SD = 7.78) and Taiwan is 20.47 years (SD = 4.36).

Measurement

Each participant was asked to fill out a questionnaire booklet containing four scales: Chinese Value Survey (Chinese Culture Connection, 1987), 24 items of a self-construal scale (Singelis & Brown, 1995), a 30-item assertiveness scale (Lorr & More, 1980), and an argumentativeness scale (Infante & Rancer, 1982). The questionnaire was translated from English to colloquial Chinese, and then back translated into English in order to maintain instrument validity. Similarly, the questionnaire was printed in simplified Chinese characters for samples in mainland China and in traditional characters for Hong Kong and Taiwanese respondents.

Forty of 41 items were mainly adopted from the Chinese Values Survey (CVS) (Chinese Culture Connection, 1987) included fundamental and basic values, such as rites and social rituals (禮), resistance to corruption (廉), having a sense of shame (知恥), filial piety (孝順), and Confucian work dynamism, for example, persistence (毅力) and orderly relationships (尊卑有序). In addition to the 40 items, this study adds one item, loyalty and obligation (義), to exhaustively include four core values of Confucius disciplines—rites and rituals (禮), loyalty and obligation (義), resistance to corruption (廉) and having a sense of shame (恥).

The 24 item-scale of self-construal (Singelis & Brown, 1995) was designed to measure the self-construal of independence and interdependence separately. Each scale uses a 7-point response format. The Argumentativeness Scale (Infante & Rancer, 1982) was adapted to measure the participants' tendency degree of argument approaching and argument avoidance.

RESULTS

Collective and Individual Values

To know how Chinese people perceive Confucian values among three societies, 41 values were submitted to a culture-free factor analysis to reduce data sets. Principal components extraction, varimax rotation, and an eigenvalue greater than 1 were used in the principal components analyses. This data-reduction procedure yielded 5 factors as the best solution, accounting for around 44% of the variance. Reliabilities of the 5 factors are respectively 82%, 78%, 79%, 75%, and 63% (Table 1).[1]

A one-way ANOVA was conducted to compare the differences of each factor in the three societies (Table 2). Forty-one items are also individually examined to understand commonalities and differences in each society. As indicated in Table 2, mainland China is significantly different from Hong Kong and Taiwan in Personal Deeds ($M = 7.36$, $SD = 0.89$, $p < .05$) and Group Integrity ($M = 7.59$, $SD = 0.95$, $p < .05$), but Hong Kong and Taiwan are not significantly different in these two factors. The results also indicate that the three societies have shown a significant difference in Social Traditionalism ($M = 4.94$, $SD = 1.21$ in mainland China; $M = 5.79$, $SD = 1.03$ in Hong Kong, $M = 5.35$, $SD = 1.17$ in Taiwan), but no difference among the three societies in both Personal Behaviors and External Composition.

Among 41 values, only two values indicate commonality among the three societies—rites and social rituals (禮儀) and having a sense of shame (知恥) at the significant level of .05. The other values are either common in two societies, or all different among the three. There are five values significantly different in all three societies: Hard Working (勤勞), Knowledge (學識), Sense of Righteousness (正義感), Non-competitiveness (不重競爭), and Being Conservative (保守). Based on the mean scores of these five values, two ranking patterns emerge among the three societies. For values of Hard Working ($M = 7.44$ in mainland China, $M = 7.11$ in Hong Kong, $M = 6.81$ in Taiwan), Knowledge ($M = 8.01$ in mainland China, $M = 7.48$ in Hong Kong, $M = 7.19$ in Taiwan) and Sense of Righteousness ($M = 7.34$ in mainland China, $M = 6.90$ in Hong Kong, $M = 6.40$ in Taiwan), participants in mainland China rank these values the highest and participants in Taiwan rank them the lowest. In contrast, for items associated with masculinity values, such as non-competitiveness ($M = 3.90$ in mainland China, $M = 5.24$ in Hong Kong, $M = 4.70$ in Taiwan) and being conservative ($M = 3.57$ in mainland China, $M = 4.65$ in Hong Kong, $M = 4.11$ in Taiwan), Hong Kong participants turn out to rank the highest and participants in mainland China are the lowest.

The results of a one-way ANOVA find no difference in the 12-item value of independent self-construal among mainland China ($M = 56.27$, $SD = 7.6$), Hong Kong ($M = 55.47$, $SD = 7.52$), and Taiwan ($M = 56.39$, $SD = 8.28$), but the three societies are very different in the value of interdependent self-construal. In terms of interdependent self-construal values, Taiwan ($M = 60.67$, $SD = 9.10$) is found to be significantly higher than mainland China ($M = 59.23$, $SD = 8.35$) and Hong Kong ($M = 55.47$, $SD = 7.52$).

Argumentative Orientation

The Argumentative Scale is calculated into 3 scores, Argument Approaching, Argument Avoidance, and Argumentative Orientation, in order to examine perceptions of argumentative behaviors and their motives of approaching and avoiding arguments in

Table 1   Factor Analysis of Chinese Value Survey

	Factor Loadings				
	Personal Deeds	Social Traditionalism	Group Integrity	Pro-social Behavior	External Composition
Persistence	0.697	0.133	0.233	8.40E-02	3.46E-03
Patience	0.668	0.09	0.201	0.196	−1.01E-03
Adaptability	0.568	−0.186	0.189	0.118	0.253
Knowledge	0.565	−0.157	0.268	7.295E-02	0.215
Prudence	0.515	0.198	−8.59E-02	0.203	0.24
Steadiness and Stability	0.513	0.232	0.115	0.182	9.14E-02
Courtesy	0.483	7.00E-02	0.296	0.387	0.17
Self-Cultivation	0.482	−2.70E-02	0.275	0.289	0.218
Trustworthy	0.46	−0.181	0.412	0.251	0.143
Thrift	0.437	0.425	0.359	5.58E-02	−0.136
Solidarity	0.399	8.31E-03	0.382	0.268	9.92E-02
Being Conservative	−9.73E-02	0.715	−1.08E-02	0.104	0.17
Having Few Desires	1.512E-02	0.687	0.195	1.539E-02	−1.51E-02
Contentedness	0.117	0.591	−2.16E-02	0.303	8.56E-02
Disinterested	0.114	0.577	1.068E-02	−8.81E-02	0.141
Non-competitiveness	−0.178	0.524	−0.109	0.16	1.736E-02
Chastity in Women	5.28E-02	0.464	0.354	8.97E-02	2.793E-02
Respect for Tradition	0.143	0.455	0.323	−5.73E-02	0.171
Loyalty to Superiors	0.102	0.446	4.89E-02	0.344	0.117
Moderation	0.248	0.44	−0.259	0.311	0.15
Ordering in Relationships and Status	0.121	0.408	−3.83E-02	0.314	0.239
Patriotism	0.203	1.728E-02	0.717	−7.70E-02	8.09E-02
Righteousness	0.212	7.23E-02	0.651	0.162	8.70E-02
Resistance to Corruption	0.396	0.217	0.564	2.598E-02	−0.118
Sincerity	0.398	6.80E-02	0.537	0.228	2.88E-03
Filial Piety	4.08E-02	−7.43E-02	0.461	0.371	0.107
Kindness	0.22	0.124	0.454	0.388	0.133
Having a Sense of Shame	0.376	0.131	0.386	0.252	0.122
Close and Intimate Friends	0.235	−0.177	0.352	0.186	0.285
Harmony with Others	0.154	0.139	0.127	0.653	6.14E-02
Tolerance of Others	0.135	0.135	0.102	0.629	−4.30E-02
Humbleness	0.242	0.235	9.50E-02	0.587	−7.15E-02
Rites and Social Rituals	0.367	3.76E-02	0.137	0.491	0.252
Hard working	0.317	6.12E-02	0.334	0.44	−9.95E-02
Reciprocation of Greetings, Favor or Gifts	0.188	0.108	0.17	0.424	0.399
Wealth	0.184	−0.144	−7.05E-03	1.914E-03	0.619
Protecting One's Face	−6.93E-02	0.352	−2.70E-02	0.139	0.576
Repayment of Good and Evil	6.51E-02	0.199	0.101	−1.08E-02	0.531

Extract: Varimax

Table 2   Multiple Comparisons in Chinese Values

Dependent Variable	(I) Society	(J) Society	Mean Difference (I-J)	Sig.
Personal Deeds (VAI)	1	2	.2529*	0
		3	.3449*	0
	2	1	−.2529*	0
		3	9.21E-02	0.452
	3	1	−0.3449	0
		2	−0.092	0.452
Social Traditionalism (VAII)	1	2	−0.8499	0
		3	−0.4137	0
	2	1	0.8499	0
		3	0.4362	0
	3	1	0.4137	0
		2	−0.4362	0
Group Integrity (VAIII)	1	2	0.5524	0
		3	0.7151	0
	2	1	−0.5524	0
		3	0.1627	0.107
	3	1	−0.7151	0
		2	−0.1627	0.107
Prosocial Behavior (VAIV)	1	2	0.1366	0.168
		3	7.84E-02	0.498
	2	1	−0.1366	0.168
		3	−5.82E-02	0.784
	3	1	−7.84E-02	0.498
		2	5.82E-02	0.784
External Composition (VAV)	1	2	−6.41E-02	0.708
		3	−7.03E-03	0.995
	2	1	6.41E-02	0.708
		3	5.71E-02	0.814
	3	1	7.03E-03	0.995
		2	−5.71E-02	0.814

* The mean difference is significant at the .05 level.

1 = Mainland China; 2 = Hong Kong; 3 = Taiwan.

socialization processes. The result reveals that participants in mainland China perceive arguments to be the most positive ($M = 5.38$, $SD = 1.33$), when compared with the other two societies, consecutively followed by Hong Kong ($M = 5.14$, $SD = .96$) and Taiwan ($M = 4.76$, $SD = 1.03$). Young people in Hong Kong and Taiwan are not significantly different in both argument approaching and argumentative orientations, whereas the youths in mainland China are found to be different from both Hong Kong and Taiwan. Among the three Chinese societies, respondents in mainland China are more inclined to approach arguing than those from Taiwan and Hong Kong. On the other hand, Taiwan respondents ($M = 2.91$, $SD = .56$) have shown to be significantly different from both Hong Kong ($M = 3.09$, $SD = .50$) and mainland China ($M = 3.12$, $SD = .57$) in the lowest tendency of avoiding arguing behaviors.

Table 3   Correlation of 5 values, self-construals, assertiveness, and argumentativeness

	Personal Deeds	Social Traditionalism	Group Integrity	Prosocial Behavior	External Composition	Interdependent Self-construal	Independent Self-construal	Assertiveness	Argumentativeness
Personal Deeds	1	.33**	.71**	.63**	.39**	.33**	.21**	.12**	.07*
Significant (2-tailed)		0	0	0	0	0	0	0	.007
N =	1484	1465	1463	1477	1469	1450	1455	1476	1476
Social Traditionalism	.33**	1	.27**	.41**	.43**	.39**	.16**	-.10**	-.18*
Significant (2-tailed)	0		0	0	0	0	0	0	0
N =	1465	1485	1465	1479	1471	1453	1465	1478	1477
Group Integrity	.71**	.27**	1	.56**	.32**	.38**	.19**	.10**	.09*
Significant (2-tailed)	0	0		0	0	0	0	0	.001
N =	1463	1465	1486	1481	1472	1455	1458	1478	1478
Pro-social Behavior	.63**	.41**	.56**	1	.33**	.37**	.16**	.05*	-.03
Significant (2-tailed)	0	0	0		0	0	0	.038	.22
N =	1477	1479	1481	1504	1487	1469	1475	1496	1496
External Composition	.39**	.43**	.32**	.33**	1	.17**	.16**	.08**	.04
Significant (2-tailed)	0	0	0	0		0	0	.003	.13
N =	1469	1471	1472	1487	1493	1460	1463	1485	1485
Interdependent Self-Construal	.33**	.39**	.38**	.37**	.17**	1	.24**	-.001	-.15*
Significant (2-tailed)	0	0	0	0	0		0	.956	0
N =	1450	1453	1455	1469	1460	1477	1465	1470	1470
Independent Self-Construal	.21**	.16**	.19**	.16**	.16**	.24**	1	.27**	.17*
Significant (2-tailed)	0	0	0	0	0	0		0	0
N =	1455	1465	1458	1475	1463	1465	1482	1478	1478
Assertiveness	.12**	-.10**	.10**	.05*	.08**	-.001	.276**	1	.36*
Significant (2-tailed)	0	0	0	.038	.003	.96	0		0
N =	1467	1477	1478	1496	1485	1470	1478	1504	1502
Argumentativeness	.07**	-.18**	.09**	-.03	.04	-.15	.17**	.36**	1
Significant (2-tailed)	007	0	.001	.22	.127	0	0	0	
N =	1476	1477	1478	1496	1485	1470	1478	1502	1504

Correlations Between Values and Communication Behaviors

The correlation analysis finds weak coefficients between the individual value (self-construal) and cultural values. Pearson correlation coefficients are first used to examine relationships between individual values (self-construal) and collective values (Personal Deeds, Social Traditionalism, Group Integrity, Pro-social Behaviors, and External Composition). The result indicates self-construal (scores in independence minus interdependence) is related to Personal Deeds ($r = -.1$, $p < 0.0001$), Social Traditionalism ($r = -.2$, $p < .0001$), Group Integrity ($r = -.15$, $p < .0001$), and Pro-social Behaviors ($r = -.18$, $p < .0001$), but no significance in External Composition ($r = -.0009$, $p = .7$). In addition, the correlation of interdependent self-construal is found to be stronger related to the five sets of Chinese values than that of independence (Table 3).

A regression analysis was then used to further analyze relations of the individual value to the five sets of cultural values. Though the rejection of the null hypothesis indicates that the five variances of cultural sets are different, parameter estimates show a low correlation of Personal Deeds with self-construal ($p = .136$). Taking away the value set of Personal Deeds, another parameter estimate was operated to measure the relationships of four sets of Social Traditionalism, Group Integrity, Pro-social Behaviors, and External Composition. The result finds that these four sets of values have closer relationships to the individual values (Table 4).

A possibility of multi-collinearity between the five sets of cultural values needs to be checked in addition to examining correlation of the individual values (independent and interdependent of self-construals) and collective cultural values. A collinearity diagnosis of culture values indicates that the sets of Social Traditionalism, Group Integrity, Pro-social Behaviors, and External Composition are linearly independent (none of condition index > 30). In the same analysis, the individual value is shown to be negatively correlated to Social Traditionalism, Group Integrity, and Pro-social Behaviors, but positively related to External Composition, and there are no significant relations with Personal Deeds.

To measure the effects of collective and individual values on argumentative behaviors, this analysis respectively tests the correlation of collective cultural values and individual values to argumentative orientation and assertiveness. Results of a regression analysis show positive relations of individual self-construal, Personal Deeds and External Composition, and that the Traditionalism is negatively related to assertiveness. Similarly, argumentative orientation is positively related to individual self-construal, Group Integrity, and External Composition, but indicates a negative relation to Traditionalism. No relation is found between Personal Deeds and Pro-social Behaviors.

DISCUSSION

The purpose of this study is to explore the current status of Taiwan, Hong Kong, and mainland China in collective cultural and individual values by investigating value orientations in both collective (Confucian values) and individual (self-construal) levels, assertiveness, and argumentative orientations. The results of this study ascertain that: (1) the three Chinese societies have a similar amount of respect for Confucian values in general; (2) mainland China has demonstrated a prominent pattern in perceiving "being argumentative" as a positive and constructive action, and has also shown a strong motivation for argument; (3) the individual value (self-construal) and some of the Confucian values have significant effects

Table 4 Parameter Estimates

Variable	DF	Estimate	Error	Parameter = 0	Prob > |T|
Intercept	1	.92	.1999	4.6	0.0001
Personal Deeds	1	.07	.0386	1.8	0.0693
Social Traditionalism	1	−.15	.0226	−6.7	0.0001
Group Integrity	1	−.12	.033	−3.50	0.0005
Prosocial Behavior	1	−.09	.030	−3.14	0.0017
External Composition	1	.099	.024	4.19	.0001

Means and Standard Deviations in Argumentativeness

	China			Hong Kong			Taiwan		
	N	Mean	SD	N	Mean	SD	N	Mean	SD
Argument Approach	850	3.25	0.63	288	3.02	0.56	365	3.02	0.66
Argument Avoidance	850	3.12	0.58	288	3.1	0.5	366	2.91	0.57
Argumentativeness	850	3.19	0.51	288	3.06	0.41	366	2.96	0.49
Perception to Argue	808	5.38	1.33	286	5.14	0.96	334	4.79	1.03

Means in Behavioral and Perceptual Differences Among Societies

Dependent	Society (I)	Society (J)	Mean	Standard Error	Sig.
Assertiveness	1	2	7.82E-03	0.031	0.968
		3	1.87E-03	0.028	0.998
	2	1	−7.82E-03	0.031	0.968
		3	−5.94E-03	0.035	0.986
	3	1	−1.87E-03	0.028	0.998
		2	5.95E-03	0.035	0.986
Argument Approach	1	2	.2372*	0.042	0
		3	.2318*	0.039	0
	2	1	−.2372*	0.042	0
		3	−5.45E-03	0.049	0.994
	3	1	−.2318*	0.039	0
		2	5.45E-03	0.049	0.994
Argument Avoidance	1	2	2.72E-02	0.038	0.776
		3	.2117*	0.035	0
	2	1	−2.72E-02	0.038	0.776
		3	.1844*	0.044	0
	3	1	−.2117*	0.035	0
		2	−.1844*	0.044	0
Argumentativeness	1	2	.1322*	0.033	0
		3	.2258*	0.031	0
	2	1	−.1322*	0.033	0
		3	9.36E-02	0.038	0.052
	3	1	−.2258*	0.031	0
		2	−9.36E-02	0.038	0.052
Perception to Argument	1	2	.2424*	0.082	0.013
		3	.5907*	0.078	0
	2	1	−.2424*	0.082	0.013
		3	.3483*	0.096	0.002
	3	1	−.5907*	0.078	0
		2	−.3483*	0.096	0.002

*$p < .05$

on being argumentative and assertive. This section will discuss these findings and note the implications of these findings for future cross-cultural research in Chinese societies.

Confucius Values

While people are suspicious about the effects of the Cultural Revolution, Communism, and British colonization on the Chinese value structure, the mean scores of these values demonstrate that the Confucian values still maintain their influences in mainland China and Hong Kong. In the 41-value (CVS) items, the results show that three values—sense of righteousness, non-competitiveness, and conservatism—are distinctive under the .01 level. Overall, people in mainland China value the sense of righteousness the highest, followed by Hong Kong, and Taiwan the lowest. By contrast, for the values that are negatively connoted from the Western perspective, Hong Kong participants indicate valuing non-competitiveness and conservatism as the highest, but mainland China the lowest. The high value placed on non-competitiveness and conservatism by Hong Kong participants, compared to those from Taiwan and mainland China, may force us to re-evaluate the impact of Western colonization on Hong Kong Chinese. Having more frequent contact with Western thoughts and ideals, Hong Kong participants may resist adopting all Western values and carefully watch over their own traditional values. On the other hand, the lowest values on non-competitiveness and conservatism reflect the enthusiasm of pursuing economic prosperity and national modernization for the young generation in mainland China.

When researchers examine correlations of each value item in the Chinese Value Survey, non-competitiveness and conservatism are negatively correlated with some items (though the relations are weak). This result may indicate that people perceive the values of non-competitiveness and being conservative differently ever since the late twentieth century. Being competitive, liberal, and technologically modern, in contrast to remaining harmonious and preserving old traditions, have become the ultimate objectives of normal education in Chinese societies. Chinese people, including our participants in the three societies, can be caught and confused between the stream of tradition and innovation when construing these two items.

Argumentative Behaviors

Based on individualism/collectivism theory, members in a collectivism culture put a higher consideration in maintaining group and social harmony. Findings of this study indicate that participants become more assertive, because of their personal belief, than having group concerns or cultural influences (that is why Group Integrity and Pro-social Behaviors are not correlated with assertiveness). Similarly, participants choose to be argumentative with the higher group and social concerns than with personal beliefs and factors.

In this study the results conclude that traditional Chinese values do not have significant effects on argumentative behaviors. Instead, degrees of independent and interdependent self-contruals have shown to have effects on argumentative behaviors. When concluding that traditional Chinese values have no effect on argumentative behaviors, researchers have started scrutinizing possible reasons for this finding. First, this result can be interpreted that Chinese values either are not related to communicative behaviors or should involve intermediary variables to affect communication behaviors. Second, following the stream of dramatic technological development, human minds have also gone through a dramatic revolution. The correlation of the Chinese Value Survey with Hofstede's (1987) cultural dimensions needs to be replicated fifteen years later in order to validate the

proposition that the values of collectivism are correlated to Chinese Values.

As the results indicate, the three societies do not show significant differences on the independent construal of self, but do so on the interdependent construal. Consistent to previous investigations (Gudykunst et al., 1996; Kim et al., 1996; Park & Levine, 1999), this study again verifies that different cultures may all naturally construe themselves to be more independent than interdependent in relation to others. Taiwanese participants in this study have the highest mean in interdependent construal of self, followed by mainland China and Hong Kong. The mean score of independent self-construal in mainland China is still higher than both Hong Kong and Taiwan. It is worth further investigation to see how the combined independent and interdependent self-construals relate to Chinese values and other communication behaviors.

NOTE

1. Only three loadings are under .40, but none of the items was deleted, because deleting these items did not raise reliability for factors.

REFERENCES

Barnlund, D.C., & Yoshioka, M. (1990). Apologies: Japanese and American styles. *International Journal of Intercultural Relations, 14*, 193–206.

Bresnahan, M.J., Ohashi, R., Liu, W.Y., Nebashi, R. & Liao, C-. (1999). A comparison of response styles in Singapore and Taiwan. *Journal of Cross-Cultural Psychology, 30*, 342–358.

Chen, G-.M. (1995). Differences in self-disclosure patterns among Americans versus Chinese: A comparative study. *Journal of Cross-Cultural Psychology, 26,* 84–91.

Chinese Culture Connection. (1987). Chinese values and the search for culture-free dimensions of culture. *Journal of Cross-Cultural Psychology, 19*, 143–164.

Goodwin, R., Nizharadze, G., Luu, L.A.N., Kosa, E. & Emelyanova, T. (1999). Glasnost and the art of conversation: A multilevel analysis of intimate disclosure across three former Communist cultures. *Journal of Cross-Cultural Psychology, 30*, 72–90.

Frymier, A., Klopf, D., & Ishii, S. (1990). Japanese and Americans compared on the affect orientation construct. *Psychological Reports, 66*, 985–986.

Gaetz, L., Klopf, D., & Ishii, S. (1990). Predispositions toward verbal behavior of Japanese and Americans. Paper presented at the Communication Association of Japan Convention, Tokyo.

Giles, H., Coupland, N., & Wiemann, J.M. (1992). "Talk is cheap . . ." but "my word is my bond": Beliefs about talk. In K. Bolton & H. Kwok (Eds.), *Sociolinguistics today: Eastern and Western perspectives* (pp. 218–243). London: Routledge.

Gudykunst, W.B., Matsumoto, Y., Ting-Toomey S., Nishida, T., Kim, K. & Heyman, S. (1996). The influence of cultural individualism-collectivism, self construals, and individual values on communication styles across cultures. *Human Communication Research, 22*, 1996.

Gudykunst, W.B., & Nishida, T. (1986). Attributional confidence in low- and high-context cultures. *Human Communication Research, 12*, 525–549.

Gudykunst, W.B., & Nishida, T. (1987). The influence of cultural variability on perceptions of communication behavior associated with relationship terms. *Human Communication Research, 13*, 147–166.

Gudykunst, W.B., & Ting-Toomey, S. (1988). *Culture and interpersonal communication.* Newbury Park, CA: Sage.

Gudykunst, W.B., Yoon, Y.-C., & Nishida, T. (1987). The influence of individualism-collectivism on perceptions of communication in ingroup and outgroup relationships. *Communication Monographs, 54*, 295–306.

Hasegawa, T., & Gudykunst, W. (1998). Silence in Japan and the United States. *Journal of Cross-Cultural Psychology, 29*, 668–684.

Infante, D.A., & Rancer, A.S. (1982). A conceptualization and measure of argumentativeness.

Journal of Personality Assessment, 46, 72–80.

Infante, D.A., & Rancer, A.S. (1996). Argumentativeness and verbal aggressiveness: A review of recent theory and research. In B.R. Burleson (Ed.), *Communication yearbook 19* (pp. 319–351). Beverly Hills, CA: Sage.

Kagitcibasi, C. (1994). A critical appraisal of individualism and collectivism: Toward a new formulation. In U. Kim, H.C. Triandis, C. Kagitcibasi, Choi, S.-C., & G. Yoon (Eds.,) *Individualism and collectivism: Theory, method and applications* (pp. 52–65). Newbury, CA: Sage.

Kim, M. (1993). Culture-based interactive constraints in explaining intercultural strategic competence. In R.L. Wiseman & Koester, J. (Eds.), *Intercultural communication competence* (pp. 132–150). Newbury Park, CA: Sage.

Kim, M. (1999). Cross-cultural perspectives on motivations of verbal communication: Review, critique, and a theoretical framework. In M. E. Roloff (Ed.), *Communication Yearbook 22* (pp. 51–89). Sage: Newbury Park, CA.

Kim, M., Hunter, Miyahara, Horvath, Bresnahan & Yoon. (1996). Individual- Vs. culture-level dimensions of individualism and collectivism: Effects on preferred conversation styles. *Communication Monograph, 63,* 29–49.

Kim, M., Shin, Ho-C., & Cai, D. (1998). Cultural influences on the preferred forms of requesting and re-requesting. *Communication Monographs, 65,* 47–66.

Kim, U. (1994). Individualism and collectivism: Conceptual clarification and elaboration. In U. Kim, H.C. Triandis, C. Kagitcibasi, Choi, S.-C., &G. Yoon (Eds.,) *Individualism and collectivism: Theory, method and applications* (pp. 19–40). Newbury, CA: Sage.

Markus, H., & Kitayama, S. (1991). Culture and the self. *Psychological Review, 98,* 224–253.

Ng, S.H., Loong, C.S.F., He, A.P., Liu, J.H., Weatherall, A. (2000). Communication correlates of individualism and collectivism: Talk directed at one or more addressees in family conversations. *Journal of Language and Social Psychology, 19,* 26–45.

Oetzel, J. (1998). Explaining individual communication processes in homogeneous and heterogeneous groups through individualism-collectivism and self-construal. *Human Communication Research, 25,* 202–224.

Prunty, A.M., Klopf, D.W. & Ishii, S. (1990a) Argumentativeness: Japanese and American tendencies to approach and avoid conflict. *Communication Research Reports, 7,* 75–79.

Prunty, A.M., Klopf, D.W., & Ishii, S. (1990b). Japanese and American tendencies to argue. *Psychological Reports, 66,* 802.

Rancer, A. (1998). Argumentativeness. In James C. McCroskey, Daly, J.A., Martin, M.M, & Beatty, M (Eds.), *Communication and Personality: Trait Perspectives* (pp. 149–170). Hampton: New Jersey.

Rancer, A.S., Kosberg, R.L., & Baukus, R.A. (1992). Beliefs about arguing as predictors of trait argumentativeness: Implications for training in argument and conflict management. *Communication Education, 41,* 375–387.

Schwartz, S.H. (1990). Individualism-collectivism: Critique and proposed refinements. *Journal of Cross-Cultural Psychology, 21,* 139–157.

Singelis, T.M. (1994). The measurement of independent and interdependent self-construals. *Personality and Social Psychological Bulletin, 20,* 580–591.

Singelis, T.M., & Brown, W.J. (1995). Culture, self, and collectivist communication: Linking culture to individual behavior. *Human Communication Research, 21,* 354–389.

Sugimoto, N. (1977). A Japan-U.S. comparison of apology styles. *Communication Research, 24,* 249–369.

Ting-Toomey, S. (1988). Intercultural conflict styles: A face negotiation theory. In Y.Y. Kim & W.B. Gudykunst (Eds), *Theories in intercultural communication* (pp. 213–235). Newbury Park, CA: Sage.

Ting-Toomey, S., Gao, G., Trubinsky, P., Yang, Z., Kim, H.S., Lin, S.L., & Nishida, T. (1991). Culture, face maintenance, and styles of handling interpersonal conflict: A study in five cultures. *The International Journal of Conflict Management, 2,* 275–296.

Triandis, H.C. (1989). Triandis, H.C. (1989). Self and social behavior in differing cultural contexts. *Psychological Review, 96*, 269–289.

Triandis, H.C. (1994). Theoretical and methodological approaches to the study of collectivism and individualism. In U. Kim, H.C. Triandis, C. Kagitcibasi, Choi, S.-C., & G. Yoon (Eds.,) *Individualism and collectivism: Theory, method and applications* (pp. 41–51). Newbury, CA: Sage.

Triandis, H.C., Brislin, R.& Hui, C.H. (1988). Cross-cultural training across the individualism-collectivism divide. *International Journal of Intercultural Relations, 12*, 269–289.

Yum, J.O. (1988). The impact of Confucianism on interpersonal relationships and communication patterns in East Asia. *Communication Monographs, 55*, 374–388.

Zhang, Y., Butler, J., & Pryor, B. (1996). Comparison of apprehension about communication in China and the United States. *Perceptual and Motor Skills, 82*, 1168–1170.

Jung-huel Becky Yeh, Ph.D., is in the Department of Speech Communication at Shih Hsin University in Taipei, Taiwan.

Ling Chen was born in P.R. China and completed graduate work in the UK and the U.S.A. Currently she is an associate professor of communication at Hong Kong Baptist University in Hong Kong.

Reading 1.7

Information Accessibility, User Sophistication, and Source Credibility

The Impact of the Internet on Value Orientations in Mainland China

JONATHAN J. H. ZHU

ZHOU HE

INTRODUCTION

The Internet has penetrated China, the most populous nation in the world, at a rapid rate. Of 2,600 adult residents in Beijing and Guangzhou interviewed for this study at the end of 2000, 27% had already adopted the Internet and another 20% were planning to do so in a year or so. While the Internet, as the latest technology of mass media, has enormous potential to bring profound changes to the information environment in China, there are a wide range of constraining forces at work, including governmental control, inadequate infrastructure, economic affordability, cultural perceptions, and language barriers (He & Zhu, in press). Drawing on a theoretical model for analyzing the use and effects of conventional media in China (Zhu, 1995; 1997a; 2001), this paper tests the role of access to the Internet, perceived credibility of the Internet, and sophistication level among Chinese audiences in the formation and change of preferred value orientations. In particular, it examines how the adoption and use of the Internet affect Chinese audiences' identification with three competing value orientations: Communism, Materialism, and Post-materialism.

Value Orientations in Contemporary China

Value orientation refers to an individual's preference for a value system. The preference is a psychological state and a behavioral pattern underlying all domains of beliefs, perceptions, opinions, attitudes, actions, and lifestyle. Thus, value orientation is at the heart of social science research. In societies undergoing a dramatic transition, there are often several major value orientations competing for followers. Our observations of the ideological landscape in China have revealed that Communism, Materialism, and Post-materialism are the major rival value orientations during the country's current tacit

Reprinted with permission from *Journal of Computer Mediated Communication*, 7(2), January, 2002.

transition toward post-Communism (He, 2000b).

Communism was undoubtedly the predominant value orientation for the Chinese populace for decades (Zhu, 1997b). As a value system, Communism, in the simplest operational terms, can be defined as selfless dedication to the well-being of society and mankind.[1] The Chinese Communist Party (CCP) has made the indoctrination of Communism among the populace the ultimate goal of its propaganda efforts, such as promoting Communist models like Lei Feng, a 20-year-old solider who sacrificed his life for the Communist cause (Zhu, 1990). However, Communism has increasingly lost popularity among the public (He, 2000a). The acceptance of Communism involves an internalization process that is a fundamental change and, thus, requires complete congruency with existing values (Kelman, 1958). Starting from the 1980s when the CCP began to embark on economic and structural reforms and improve the standard of living for Chinese citizens, it unexpectedly invited the rise of Materialism as a challenge to Communism.

Materialism can be defined as a persistent pursuit of immediate rewards and physical happiness, which is nothing new to the Chinese people. It had for centuries been the cornerstone of the Chinese cultural tradition that emphasized pragmatism and immediate rewards. Therefore, Materialism remained deeply rooted in individual value systems even when it was under severe attack during the Socialist Revolution (1950s), the Cultural Revolution (1966–1976), and the Socialist Spiritual Civilization Movement (1980s). However, Materialism became a notorious symbol and disappeared almost completely from the public discourse as the CCP launched one campaign after another to divest private ownership, assault self-concern and self-rewarding behaviors, and promote non-materialistic values (e.g., "socialist spiritual civilization"). Materialism returned in the 1980s when the Chinese people

were allowed to seek well-being for themselves. The Communist slogan "Looking Forward" ("Xiang Qian Kan") has since been replaced by the Materialistic motto "Looking For Money" (pronounced also as "Xiang Qian Kan") throughout the nation.

Post-materialism has emerged as a new alternative even though the competition between Communism and Materialism still occupies the center stage of the public discourse. Post-materialism is a way of life that downplays the importance of material rewards and emphasizes harmony with people and nature (Inglehart, 1979). Such a value system is widely considered viable only in post-industrial societies where people's basic needs have long been met. Nevertheless, we have increasingly observed anecdotal signs of Post-materialism among certain segments of the Chinese population. In our previous studies (e.g., Zhu & Rosen, 1993), however, it was difficult to distinguish empirically Post-materialism from Communism in the Chinese context because both were opposed to Materialism.

In the current study, we propose a new line of conceptualization to relate and differentiate the three value orientations along two dimensions (Figure 1). The first dimension draws on Maslow's hierarchy of human needs (1987). Materialism is a direct response to basic needs whereas Communism and Post-materialism deal with higher levels of needs such as well-being of mankind or self-actualization. The second dimension involves individualism versus collectivism. Both Materialism and Post-materialism are individualistically oriented, whereas Communism is collectivist. This two-dimensional conceptualization highlights the diametrically opposing relationship between Communism and Materialism on the one hand, and the overlap between Communism and Post-materialism (in spiritual needs) and between Materialism and Post-materialism (in individualism).

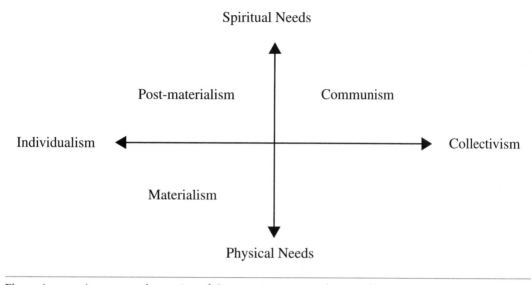

Figure 1 A conceptual mapping of Communism, Materialism, and Post-materialism.

Causal Factors of Value Orientations

A person's value orientation is largely formed during his/her socialization stage. Once formed, the value orientation usually remains stable and enduring. However, for people living in a society that is undergoing dramatic changes, such as China, their value orientations may involve adjustment or conversion as the influx of information and changing realities challenge the existing value system. As Bishop noted more than a decade ago (1989):

> The media and official communication channels are very important in publicizing official demands, and they have been quite influential for relatively short periods, such as during the Cultural Revolution, but this influence seems to be declining. The decline may be due to the growing sophistication of the audience, thanks in part to travel, personal contacts, and a critical view of leadership fostered by the Cultural Revolution and by the educational programs aimed at peasants and workers. (p. 276)

Several observations can be made here. First, CCP propaganda efforts used to be effective. Second, their influence has been on the decline. Third, the decline can be attributed to the increase in audience sophistication. Fourth, increased audience sophistication has resulted from increased access to information. The decline in CCP's credibility has been furthered by improvements in education. Drawing on Bishop's observations and those of others, we have developed an integrated framework for media effects in China (Zhu, 1995; 1997a; 2001). The framework emphasizes the impact of three factors: the individual's access to information, cognitive sophistication, and perceived media credibility.

Information accessibility refers to the extent to which the audience has access to a diversified range of information. In particular, our concern is with the number of alternative sources of information available to the audience in addition to the official media. Previous research on mere exposure has demonstrated that exposure to information alone can make a big difference in knowledge, attitudes, and behavior (Zajonc, 1974). Conversely, as inoculation research has suggested, individuals living in a "germ-free" environment are more likely to be affected by a non-orthodox message when facing such a situation (McGuire, 1964). It is then reasonable to assume that those Chinese audience members who have access to alternative information could differ significantly from those who are only exposed to official messages (Zhao, Zhu, Li & Bleske, 1994).

There is a wide range of alternative information accessible to Chinese audiences, such as direct observations on overseas trips, word-of-mouth from others, international broadcasting, etc. Our previous research has found that Chinese audiences listen to cross-border broadcast programs most intensively during major domestic crises when there is a strong need for accurate information but the official media do not provide it (He & Zhu, 1994). The Internet is the latest, and perhaps most powerful, addition to this arsenal of information. However, one should not be overly optimistic about the impact of new communication technologies, because the Chinese government has always been able to levy heavy penalties for "undesirable" access and utilize sophisticated techniques to block "harmful" information, as in the case of fax machines, satellite broadcasts, and the Internet.

Cognitive sophistication refers to the extent to which an audience is able to make critical judgments and resist propaganda. While almost every scholar would agree that there is a negative relationship between cognitive sophistication and persuasibility, there is no established measure of sophistication. Therefore, educational attainment has traditionally been used as a surrogate for cognitive sophistication. Hovland and his associates were among the first to identify the impact of education on communication effects (Hovland, Lumsdiane & Sheffield, 1949). Hyman and

his associates concluded that, based on their secondary analysis of longitudinal survey data in the United States over a period of 30 years, formal education could have an enduring impact on people's cognitive structure throughout their lives (Hyman, Wright & Reed, 1979). Recent research in cognitive psychology has further suggested that sophistication involves information schema developed from previous knowledge and experience.

Independent of their level of access to alternative information, Chinese audiences have become increasingly sophisticated partly because of a continuous rise in the population's educational level and partly because of their learning from past experience. Students of China have long observed that, while the CCP initially dealt with a naive audience, that advantage has inevitably vanished as time has passed: "It would seem that the Communists are engaged in a "race against time." They must win the hearts of a substantial number of the Chinese before they outstay their welcomes [sic]." (Houn, 1961, p. 2)

Media credibility refers to the perceived believability of media content "beyond any proof of its contentions" (West, 1994, p. 159). Drawing on the classic persuasion research on source credibility (Hovland & Weiss, 1951), media credibility research has shifted the focus from characteristics of information sources, such as competence, expertise, honesty, and likable personality, to characteristics of media behaviors such as objectivity, accuracy, fairness, and lack of bias (Gaziano & McGrath, 1986). Media credibility research is now more concerned about channel effects such as differences between newspapers and television (Newhagen & Nass, 1989). Overall, empirical investigations in the West have found that media credibility is an important ingredient, along with message characteristics and audience characteristics, of effective communication.

Table 1 Hypothesized Effects on Value Orientations

	Materialism vs Communism	*Value Orientations* Post-materialism vs. Communism	Post-materialism vs. Materialism
Independent Variable			
Cognitive Sophistication	+	+	+
Information Access			
Overseas Media & the Internet	+	+	+
Domestic Media	−	−	−
Media Credibility			
Domestic Old and New Media	−	−	−
Overseas Old and New Media	+	+	+

Note: + means the independent variables increase the likelihood of accepting the first value orientation and rejecting the second value orientation; - means the independent variables reduce the likelihood of accepting the first value orientation and rejecting the second value orientation.

We have argued elsewhere that media credibility plays a greater role in China, given the unique structure and functionality of Chinese media system (Zhu, 1997a). Based on a secondary analysis of six surveys conducted in China between 1985 and 1989, we have found unambiguous and consistent evidence that media credibility is the single most significant and strongest predictor of audiences' attitudes and behaviors, among a host of demographic, socioeconomic, and media exposure variables (Zhu, 1997a). The effect size of media credibility also appears to be much greater than what has been found in the West. However, our test of the impact of media credibility was incomplete because there was no measure of access to alternative information in the data used for the secondary analysis.

Hypotheses

Based on the above discussion of Chinese value orientations and the causative factors, we have formulated three hypotheses for empirical testing in a study that includes the Internet as one of the sources of alternative information. Each of the three hypotheses deals with a particular independent variable (i.e., cognitive sophistication, information accessibility, and media credibility), which in turn includes a number of sub-hypotheses for various value orientations (Table 1).

Hypothesis 1: cognitive sophistication has a significant impact on the preference of value orientations, in the following directions:

1a. the more sophisticated, the more likely an individual is to prefer Materialism to Communism;

1b. the more sophisticated, the more likely an individual is to prefer Post-materialism to Communism;

1c. the more sophisticated, the more likely an individual is to prefer Post-materialism to Materialism.

Hypothesis 2: information accessibility has a significant impact on the preferred value orientation, in the following directions:

2a. the more exposure to the domestic media (newspapers, television, and radio), the more likely an individual is to prefer Communism to Materialism;

2b. the more exposure to the alternative media (the Internet and overseas media), the more likely an individual is to prefer Materialism to Communism;

2c. the more exposure to the domestic media (newspapers, television, and radio), the more likely an individual is to prefer Communism to Post-materialism;

2d. the more exposure to the alternative media (the Internet and overseas media), the more likely an individual is to prefer Post-materialism to Communism;

2e. the more exposure to the domestic media (newspapers, television, and radio), the more likely an individual is to prefer Materialism to Post-materialism;

2f. the more exposure to the alternative media (the Internet and overseas media), the more likely an individual is to prefer Post-materialism to Materialism.

Hypothesis 3: perceived media credibility has a significant impact on the preference for value orientation, as follows:

3a. the more credible the domestic media (both conventional and new) are perceived to be, the more likely an individual is to prefer Communism to Materialism;

3b. the more credible the overseas media (both conventional and new) are perceived to be, the more likely an individual is to prefer Materialism to Communism;

3c. the more credible the domestic media (both conventional and new) are perceived to be, the more likely an individual is to prefer Communism to Post-materialism;

3d. the more credible the overseas media (both conventional and new) are perceived to be, the more likely an individual is to prefer Post-materialism to Communism;

3e. the more credible the domestic media (both conventional and new) are perceived to be, the more likely an individual is to prefer Materialism to Post-materialism;

3f. the more credible the overseas media (both conventional and new) are perceived to be, the more likely an individual is to prefer Post-materialism to Materialism.

METHOD

Sampling

The data came from a large-scale survey in two Chinese cities, Beijing and Guangzhou. The two cities, which are among the most developed in China, were chosen because they often serve as barometers of changing trends in China. As we have found in the diffusion of television and telephony in China, the difference in the diffusion of new communication technologies across the country is merely a function of time with major cities leading other localities by a few years (Zhu, 1997c; 1999). Therefore, it is reasonable to believe that the findings from Beijing and Guangzhou will be generalizable to the rest of China in the near future. Of a number of major cities (e.g., Shanghai), we have chosen Beijing and Guangzhou to have an equal representation between the north (by Beijing) and the south (by Guangzhou).

We employed a multi-stage, non-proportional probability sampling (NPPS) procedure to generate a sample of adult residents in Beijing and Guangzhou. At the first stage, we randomly selected 100 residential communities (called Juwei in Chinese) in Beijing and 150 in Guangzhou and collected all residential addresses in the chosen communities to form our sampling frame.[2] At the second stage, 30 households were randomly drawn from each of the chosen communities (or 3,000 households in Beijing and 4,500 in Guangzhou) to form the initial sample. At the final stage, an adult at an age between 18 and 74 was randomly selected for a face-to-face interview from each of the chosen households. Up to five visits were made to each of the chosen households/individuals before an alternative case was used from the initial sample. We commissioned a local marketing research company to carry out the in-house interviews during late November and early December of 2000.

The completed sample consisted of 2,664 adults, with 1,116 from Beijing and 1,548 from Guangzhou, which translates into a sampling error of ±1.9% for the entire sample at the 95% confidence level. As calculated using the RR3 formula of the American Association for Public Opinion Research (2000),[3] the response rate for the entire sample is 50%, which is the average of the 61% in Beijing and the 39% in Guangzhou.

The sample has been weighted to offset the impact of our non-proportional sampling method. We first scaled down the Guangzhou sample by 39% to make it equal to the Beijing sample, which reduced the total sample size to 2,232 with 50% from each city. The resultant sample was then weighted based on the joint distribution of age and sex of the adult population in each city. Compared with the original samples, the weighted sample is more conservative in key statistics (e.g., the proportion of Internet users). All data reported below are based on the weighted sample.

Measurement

Value orientations. We asked in the survey a single question: "What is the most important goal in your life?" Respondents could choose only one answer from a list of three: "To contribute to the state and mankind," "To create comfortable material conditions for myself and my family," and "To realize my personal value." These three answers correspond to the three value orientations we have discussed: Communism, Materialism, and Post-materialism. One may argue that the statement of "To contribute to the state and mankind" is not an idea unique to

Communism but rather the altruism embodied in many religious beliefs or ethical norms. However, from ancient times to the modern day in China, Communism appears to be the only value system that puts such singular emphasis on the idea of altruism. It is also important to note that "value orientation" is a descriptive concept, used to depict an empirical profile of what the public in a society actually thinks, whereas religious beliefs or ethical codes are normative terms, used by social elites to persuade the masses. There is also empirical evidence in our survey suggesting that the acceptance of altruism as measured in the study is highly correlated with other views supportive of Communism.[4]

Audience's cognitive sophistication. In the absence of a standard measure of cognitive sophistication, we have followed Hyman, Wright and Reed's (1979) argument that level of formal education is the best predictor of a person's cognitive structure.

Access to official and alternative information. Two types of alternative information are practically available to the respondents in our sample: the Internet for all users in both Beijing and Guangzhou, and Hong Kong-based television channels for all residents in Guangzhou. Therefore, we have created two dichotomized variables to measure the two sources of information: use of the Internet (user = 1, non-user = 0), and access to Hong Kong television (Guangzhou = 1, Beijing = 0). For comparison, we have also included three measures of exposure to the domestic media: reading newspapers, watching television, and listening to radio, all of which are measured by average hours per day.

Perceived media credibility. Parallel to the measures of information accessibility, we asked the respondents to indicate, on a 5-point scale, how credible they felt ten information sources to be: (i) domestic websites; (ii) domestic ICQ/BBS/Chat rooms; (iii) domestically-originated e-mail news; (iv) domestic newspapers; (v) domestic television; (vi) overseas websites; (vii) overseas ICQ/BBS/Chat rooms; (viii) overseas-originated email news; (ix) overseas newspapers; and (x) overseas television. To simplify the analysis, we later reduced the 10 sources into four categories: (a) the domestic new media (including i, ii, and iii); (b) the domestic traditional media (including iv and v); (c) the overseas new media (including vi, vii, and viii); and (d) the overseas traditional media (ix and x).

Control variables. Four demographic and socio-economic variables, including age, sex, occupation, and family income, have been included in the analysis to offset their contributions to the impact of information access or media credibility on value orientations.

Data Analysis

Because the dependent variable, Value Orientation, is a nominal variable with three categorical values, we have chosen to use multinomial logistic regression (MLR) to examine the simultaneous impact of the independent and control variables on the preference for the three value orientations. Two MLRs have been carried out, with the first for the overall sample including both users and nonusers of the Internet, whereas the second was exclusively for users. While the MLR of the overall sample tests the hypotheses, the MLR of the users' sub-sample provides additional insight into specific impact of Internet use. In addition to the MLR analyses, a discriminant analysis was performed to provide supplementary information about the grouping patterns among the independent variables.

RESULTS

Adoption and Use of the Internet in China

Of the 2,664 respondents in the sample, 27% (30% in Beijing and 24% in Guangzhou) have adopted the Internet. The users have, on average, used the Internet for 2.4 years. They spend an average of about 9 hours per week on the Internet, which is less than watching television (14 hours) but more than reading newspapers (7 hours) or listening to the radio (3 hours). The users spend the largest amount of their online time on search for work- or study-related information, followed by reading online news and participating in online chat or discussions. The activities that attract the least amount of time are using E-mail, searching for personal interest information, and playing online games or other entertainment. The users allocate over 80% of their online time to local websites using the Chinese language, with the remaining time to overseas sites in either Chinese or non-Chinese languages. E-mail appears to be very popular among the Chinese users, with three out of four using it on a regular basis. Participation in online chat or discussions is also fairly popular, with 46% of the users having done so. Chat or discussions on personal hobbies rank at the top, followed by discussions on personal relations, government and politics, and investment.

Compared with users, non-users are significantly older, less educated, and more likely to be female, unemployed or retired, and married. Of various reasons cited for not using the Internet, lack of a computer is ranked first (by 58%), followed by expense of getting online (30%), lack of knowledge (by 24%), lack of interest (22%), home PC not connected (15%), concerns for bad influences on children (15%), and lack of time (12%).

Value Orientations in China

Our data has shown that Materialism is the most popular value orientation in China, attracting 59% in the sample, followed by Post-materialism, selected by 25% of the respondents. The least popular value orientation in today's China appears to be Communism,

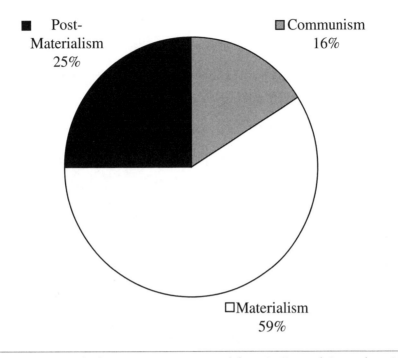

■ Post-
Materialism
25%

☐ Communism
16%

☐ Materialism
59%

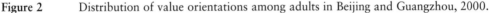

Figure 2   Distribution of value orientations among adults in Beijing and Guangzhou, 2000.

which is subscribed to by 16% of the respondents. Compared with their counterparts in Beijing, respondents in Guangzhou are significantly more oriented toward Materialism (64% vs. 54%), less favorable about Communism (12% vs. 19%) and Post-materialism (23% vs. 27%).

It is instructive to compare the findings with the results from a survey of 1,400 adult residents in Beijing by the Chinese People's University in 1986 (Zhu, 1990). The survey asked respondents to identify a most agreeable statement from a list of six items.[5] Although the wording of these items is not exactly the same as that in our survey, the items represent more or less the same three value orientations, with Communism being the overwhelmingly popular choice (79%), followed by Materialism (12%) and Post-materialism (9%). As compared with our sub-sample from Beijing, the

drastic changes in value orientations, namely a decline in Communism and a rise in both Materialism and Post-materialism, are evident.

**Impact on Value
Orientations (Overall Sample)**

Table 2 reports the unstandardized MLR coefficients. A positive coefficient, when significant, indicates the effects of the corresponding variable on the logarithmic likelihood of an individual's choosing one value orientation (e.g., Materialism) over another (e.g., Communism).

Testing of Hypothesis 1. The evidence is mixed for Hypothesis 1, which predicts significant effects of cognitive sophistication on value orientations. Contrary to H1a, the more-sophisticated a person is, the less likely the person is found to prefer Materialism to

Table 2   Unstandardized Multinomial Logistic Regression Coefficients Predicting Value Orientations

	Materialism vs Communism	Value Orientations Post-materialism vs. Communism	Post-materialism vs. Materialism
Independent Variable			
Cognitive Sophistication	−.347***	−.091	.256***
Information Access			
The Internet	−.156	.022	.178
Domestic TV	−.099[a]	.081	.181*[a]
Hong Kong TV	.153[a]	.128	−.026[a]
Newspapers	.030	−.038	-.068
Radio	.006	.031	.025
Media Credibility			
Domestic Websites	−.609***	−.829***	−.220
Domestic Media	−.045	−.127	−.082
Overseas Websites	.361*	.648***	.286*
Overseas Media	−.083	−.089	−.005
Control Variables			
Age	−.046***	−.077***	−.031***
Sex	−.233	.031	.264*
Family Income	.028	.085*	.057*
Intercept	5.875***	5.211***	−.664
Cox and Snell R^2	.169		
Model Chi-square	357.2		
Degrees of Freedom	26		
Number of Cases	1,928		

Note: *$p < .05$; **$p < .01$; ***$p < .001$.

a. The pair differs at $p < .05$ or beyond.

Communism (b = −.347, $p < .001$). On the other hand, consistent with H1c, the more-sophisticated an individual is, the more likely the person is to prefer Post-materialism to Materialism (b = .256, $p < .001$). Finally, H1b was not supported; there was no significant difference in the choice between Post-materialism and Communism across all levels of cognitive sophistication (b = −.092, $p > .20$).

Testing of Hypothesis 2. Hypothesis 2, which predicts significant effects of information accessibility on value orientations, is largely not supported because exposure to most domestic and overseas media, including the Internet, domestic newspapers, and domestic radio, does not seem to have any significant impact on the choice of value orientations. However, exposure to television represents a different and quite interesting scenario. On the one hand, the more a person watches domestic television, the more likely the person is to prefer Post-materialism to Materialism (b = .181, $p < .05$), which is opposite to what H2e predicts. On the other hand, as tested by interaction terms, the difference between the effects of domestic and Hong Kong television on value orientation is significant for Materialism vs. Communism (b = .252, or −.099 vs. .153, $p < .05$) and Post-materialism vs. Materialism (b = .207, or .181

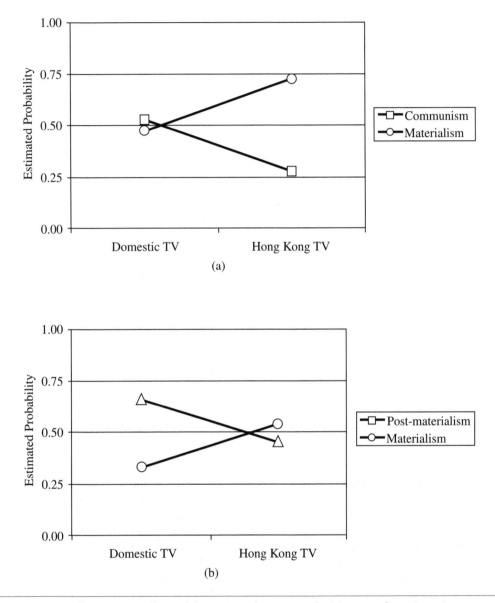

Figure 3   Differentiating effects of domestic and overseas television on value orientations.

vs. -.026, $p < .05$). Figure 3 illustrates the detected interaction effects.

As shown in Figure 3a, exposure to domestic television does not help to differentiate Communism and Materialism whereas exposure to

Hong Kong television leads to a stronger preference for Materialism and a weaker preference for Communism. On the other hand, as shown in Figure 3b, exposure to domestic television results in a stronger preference for

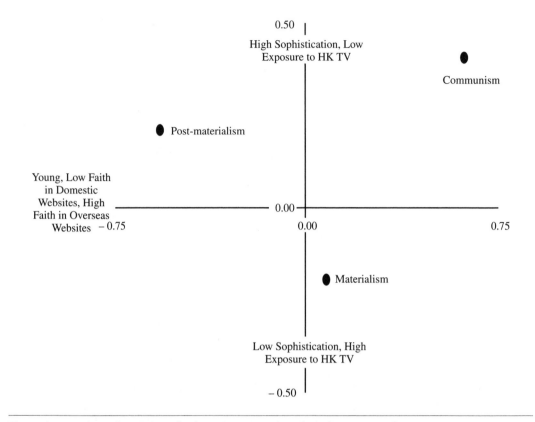

Figure 4   Spatial mapping of value orientations based on discriminant functions.

Post-materialism and a weaker preference for Materialism where exposure to Hong Kong television does not show such a differentiating impact.

Testing of Hypothesis 3. Hypothesis 3, which predicts significant effects of media credibility on value orientations, is generally supported. For example, the more credible a person perceives domestic websites to be, the more likely the person is to prefer Communism to Materialism (b = −.609, $p < .001$), as predicted by H3a, or to prefer Communism to Post-materialism (b = −.829, $p < .001$), as predicted by H3c. Conversely, the more credible a person perceives overseas websites to be, the more likely the person is to

prefer Materialism to Communism (b = .361, $p < .05$), as predicted by H3b; to prefer Post-materialism to Communism (b = .648, $p < .001$), as predicted by H3d; or to prefer Post-materialism to Materialism (b = .286, $p < .05$), as predicted by H3f. Most interesting is the consistent finding that new media (both domestic and overseas) have a significant impact on value orientations, whereas traditional media (both domestic and overseas) do not.

Impact of control variables. Age has been found to have a strong and consistent impact on value orientations, in the predicted direction. Other things being equal, the younger a person is, the more likely he or she is to choose Post-materialism over Materialism or Materialism over Communism. Also as expected, the wealthier the individual, the more likely he or she is to prefer Post-materialism to Communism or Materialism. Equally interesting is that family income has no impact on the choice between Materialism and Communism, which suggests that the difference between the pair is not economically driven. These findings confirm the need to control for demographic and socio-economic characteristics.

Spatial mapping of value orientations. Results from a discriminant analysis helps further elaborate the impact of value orientations. The analysis identifies two discriminant functions that maximize the differences among the three value orientations. Function 1, which has a Wilks's Lambda of .83 ($df = 26$, $p < .001$) and explains 70% of the variance, mainly involves age and media credibility whereas function 2, which has a Wilks's Lambda of .94 ($df = 12$, $p < .001$) and explains 30% of the variance, mainly involves age and media credibility whereas function 2 reflects cognitive sophistication and access to alternative information. The two functions taken together correctly classify 62% of the group members. Figure 4 displays the centroid (i.e., the geometric means) of each value orientation along the two functions.

Function 1 of Figure 4 suggests that the older generations with high trust in domestic websites but low trust in overseas websites are more likely to follow Communism; middle-age generations with medium levels of faith in both domestic and overseas websites are more likely to prefer Materialism; and the younger generations with low confidence in domestic websites but high trust in overseas websites are more likely to adopt Post-materialism. Function 2 shows that the more sophisticated audiences who watch less Hong Kong television are more likely to choose Communism and slightly less likely to pursue Post-materialism, whereas the less sophisticated audiences who watch extensive Hong Kong television are more likely to lean toward Materialism.

In summary, the two functions emerging from the discriminant analysis are largely consistent with the two theoretical dimensions we have previously assumed to underlie the three value orientations (Figure 1). In particular, function 1 corresponds to the individualism vs. collectivism dimension whereas function 2 corresponds to the physical needs vs. spiritual needs dimension.

Impact of the Internet among Users

As mentioned earlier, the analysis above might be too simplistic to capture the impact of the Internet by including both users and nonusers in the same analysis. To find out specific effects of Internet use, we performed a second MLR analysis exclusively for users of the Internet. The new analysis includes not only the same independent and dependent variables as used in the overall sample but also six variables measuring use of the Internet, including (a) reading online news, (b) receiving and sending E-mail messages, (c) participating in chat rooms, ICQ, BBS, and online discussion forums, (d) searching for work-related information, (e) searching for personal interest-related information, and (f) playing games or other online entertainment, all measured in the number of hours spent per week. The results are reported in Table 3.

Because the range of variations in the subsample is necessarily narrower than that in the overall sample, the effect size of almost all independent and control variables as shown in Table 3 is therefore expected to be smaller. We are more interested, however, in the impact of the six online activities. Of 12 non-redundant coefficients, three are significant: online chatting for Materialism vs. Communism and

Table 3   Unstandardized Multinomial Logistic Regression Coefficients Predicting Value
Orientations Among Internet Users

		Value Orientations	
	Materialism vs Communism	Post-materialism vs. Communism	Post-materialism vs. Materialism
Independent Variable			
Cognitive Sophistication	−.255*	−.031	.224*
Information Access			
Internet Use			
Online News	−.063	−.177*	−.054
E-mails	.086	.101	.015
Chat room/ICQ/BBS	.126*	.162*	.036
Search for Work-related Info	.011	−.005	−.015
Search for Personal Info	.035	.089	.054
Games and Entertainment	−.024	−.034	−.009
Newspapers	−.057	−.442****	−.385***
Radio	.082	.144	.062
Domestic TV	.450*	.499*	.049
Hong Kong TV	.273	.479*	.206
Media Credibility			
Domestic Websites	−.672*	−.950*	−.278
Domestic Media	−.186	−.353	−.166
Overseas Websites	.371	.612*	.241
Overseas Media	.000	−.012	−.012
Control Variables			
Age	−.019	−.037***	−.018*
Sex	−.144	−.246	−.102
Family Income	−.009	.001	.010
Intercept	4.620***	5.563***	.943
Cox and Snell R^2	.137		
Model Chi-square	119.1		
Degrees of Freedom	36		
Number of Cases	811		

Note: $*p < .05$; $**p < .01$; $***p < .001$.

Post-materialism vs. Communism, and online news reading for Post-materialism vs. Communism. In particular, the more time a person spends on online chatting, the more likely the person is to prefer Materialism or Post-materialism to Communism (b = .126 and .162, $p < .05$); however, the more time a person spends on reading online news, the more likely for the person to choose Communism over Post-materialism (b = −.117, $p < .05$).

CONCLUSIONS AND DISCUSSION

The current study aims to test the impact of three theoretical constructs, information accessibility, cognitive sophistication, and media credibility, on the preference for rival value orientations: Communism, Materialism, and Post-materialism. This multi-causal, multi-effects research issue has generated more than a dozen hypotheses. As such, we have set up a highly rigorous test that is unlikely to find

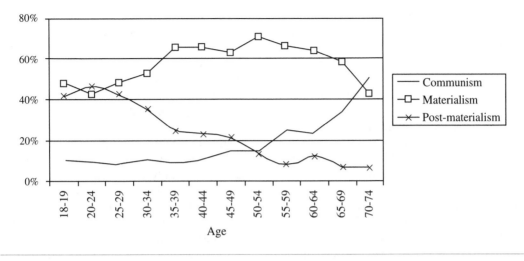

Figure 5   Value orientations by age.

full support in survey-based data. However, we have obtained a number of interesting results that either support previous findings or shed new light.

First of all, our study has revealed that Communism has become the least popular value orientation among Chinese audiences, whereas Post-materialism has already been adopted by a significant portion (about a quarter) of the populace. Compared with similar surveys in the 1980s, this represents both a sharp departure from the past and an unfolding path into the future. Although Materialism has become the prevalent value orientation among the Chinese populace, there is reason to believe that it will gradually fade out from its dominance and shift to Post-materialism. For example, there is an almost imperceptible decline in Post-materialism and increase in Materialism along the age dimension (Figure 5), with Post-materialism being more popular than Materialism among the youngest cohort. All things considered, there are at least three areas that can be pursued along this line of research in the future: (a) cross-validating the measurement of the three value orientations,[6] (b) monitoring the dynamic process of the rise

and fall among the value orientations, and (c) exploring the consequences of the value orientations.

More importantly, our analyses have shown that Chinese audience members' choice among value orientations is influenced by media credibility, cognitive sophistication, and access to alternative information, in that order. These causal factors altogether define a conceptual mapping that not only supports the existence of two dimensions (i.e., collectivism-individualism and basic needs-spiritual needs) underlying Communism, Materialism, and Post-materialism, but also provides substantive meanings that help to interpret the two dimensions. The significance of this two-dimensional conceptualization lies in its ability to relate and differentiate the three value orientations. Otherwise, it would be quite easy to see the diametric clash between Communism and Materialism but rather difficult to conceive the fundamental difference (i.e., collectivism vs. individualism) between Communism and Post-materialism, which we encountered in our previous research (e.g., Zhu & Rosen, 1993), or the common ground (i.e., in individualism) between Materialism and Post-materialism, which is not readily obvious until a third element (e.g., Communism) comes in as a point of comparison.

While the finding that media credibility is the strongest predictor of Chinese audiences' attitudes confirms what has been found in our previous research (Zhu, 1997a), the evidence presented here is more direct and unequivocal because the current study involves a simultaneous test of all key causal factors, whereas media credibility was previously tested in the absence of access to alternative information. A new twist has emerged, unexpectedly, from the current study, that perceived credibility of the new media (i.e., the Internet) is far more important than that of conventional media. More interestingly, the pattern holds for both domestic and overseas media. This may suggest that credibility of the new media is more sensitive to ongoing trends in contemporary China. More research is needed to help us fully understand the nature and implications of this differentiation between the old and new media.

Cognitive sophistication, operationally measured by educational level, presents a mixed picture. It significantly predicts the choice between Post-materialism and Materialism in the expected direction (i.e., the more sophisticated audiences are more likely to prefer Post-materialism to Materialism) in both the overall sample and the sub-sample of Internet users. On the other hand, it has no impact on the choice between Post-materialism and Communism in both the overall sample and the sub-sample of Internet users. Given the assumption that the two value orientations differ primarily along the individualism-collectivism dimension, this finding suggests that cognitive sophistication has nothing to do with self-interest or altruism (i.e., the highly educated are just as selfish, or generous, as the poorly educated, see the parallel lines in Figure 6b). Our original hypothesis (H1b) is too simplistic to accommodate this plausible scenario.

The most challenging question in our findings is that sophistication has a significant and strong impact on the selection between Materialism and Communication but in an opposite direction to what has been hypothesized (H1a). A closer look at Figure 6a reveals that, while the level of Materialism goes down almost linearly as education goes up, the acceptance of Communism stays around the 15–20% level for most of the educational groups. It is only those with a postgraduate degree, accounting for 2% of the sample, whose preference for Communism is significantly higher (36%). Therefore, it appears that the observed impact of sophistication on the choice between Communism and Materialism is primarily a function of the negative relationship between education and Materialism. Still, it does not help explain why sophistication does not have the anticipated negative impact on Communism. One can speculate such possible causes as the overlapping between Communism and altruism that is more popular among better-educated people, or social desirability that may also be more salient to sophisticated respondents. We will further explore these and other possibilities in future research.

Finally, the study has found weak evidence for the impact of the Internet. In our analysis of the overall sample, use of the Internet (a simple, dichotomous measure of yes and no) fails to show any impact on value orientations. When examining the sub-sample of Internet users, we have found only online chatting, out of six online activities, to have some impact. Reading online news is significant in one instance, but in a direction opposite to the hypothesis. While we are puzzled about the general weakness (or lack) of Internet power in the study, it is helpful to recall at least two characteristics of this study. First, our test of Internet impact is in the presence of more than a dozen other variables, which has removed all possible confounding effects from other

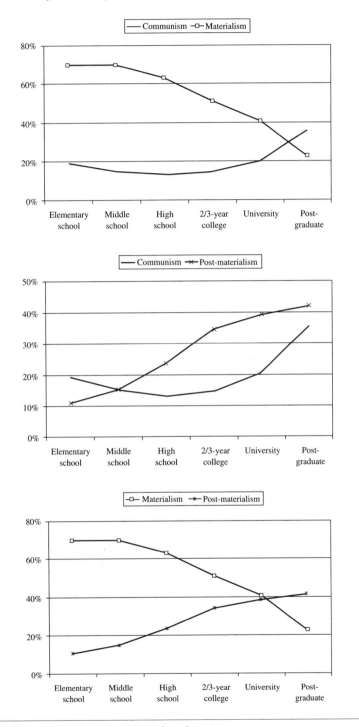

Figure 6   Preference for value orientations by education.

Table 4   Preference for Value Orientations by Education

Value Orientation	Users	Nonusers	Difference
Communism	14%	17%	3%
Materialism	48%	64%	15%
Post-materialism	38%	20%	18%
Total	100%	100%	
Number of Cases	529	1,405	

Note: $\chi^2 = 68.8$, $df = 2$, $p < .001$.

variables. In fact, a bivariate analysis would suggest a strong impact of the Internet on value orientations (Table 4). For example, compared with nonusers, Internet users are less likely to subscribe to Communism (by 3%) and Materialism (by 13%) but far more open to Post-materialism (by 18%). However, these differences vanished when other independent and control variables were included to share the impact on value orientations.

Second, the Internet is still new to Chinese users, two-thirds of whom have adopted the new medium within the past 24 months and will need some time to fully demonstrate the potential impact on them. This possibility will be tested in our follow-up surveys. Of course, informed by media effects research history (e.g., Klapper, 1964), we need to be prepared to find "limited effects" of the Internet in a rigorous test that controls for the impact of all other intervening variables, even a few years down the road when the Internet penetrates most households in China.

NOTES

1. We believe that Communist value orientation differs from the ideology of Communism and Communist polity that involve, among other things, coercive functions and operations of state apparatus.

2. Because this is the first wave of a three-year panel sample, we have intentionally used a larger sample size to offset a possibly higher attrition rate in Guangzhou, based on our previous experience with panel surveys in both cities.

3. The formula defines response rate as the number of completed interviews divided by the number of interviews, non-interviews (refusal and break-off plus non-contacts plus others), and the estimated eligible cases among status unknown cases.

4. For example, 62% of those who selected the altruistic notion "completely agreed" to the statement that "It is necessary to continue learning from the Lei Feng Spirit in the new millennium," as compared with 41% of those who chose Materialism or 37% of those who prefer Post-materialism. Likewise, 33% of those in favor of the altruistic view "completely agreed" to the statement that "In the final analysis, Communism is still superior to Capitalism even though Capitalist countries are currently quite advanced," as compared with 15% of Materialists or 14% of Post-materialists. The difference in both cases is highly significant beyond the .001 level.

5. Of the sample, 30% chose "to contribute to human beings' progress," 26% "to contribute to country's prosperity," 23% "to work hard for my organization's success," 12% "to work hard to make more money," 5% "to compete with nobody, just enjoy my life," and 4% "to study hard to make myself famous." Answers 1, 2, and 3 correspond to Communism, answer 4 to Materialism, and answers 5 and 6 to Post-materialism.

6. As shown in Figure 6, age has already provided some criterion validity to the single measure employed in this study. For example, the younger the respondents are, the more likely they are to accept Post-materialism and reject Communism,

which cannot be simply interpreted as the rise of individualism because young cohorts are also less interested in the individualistically oriented Materialism.

REFERENCES

Bishop, R. (1989). *Qi lai! Mobilizing one billion Chinese: The Chinese communication system.* Ames: Iowa State University Press.

Gaziano, C., & McGrath, K. (1986). Measuring the concept of credibility. *Journalism Quarterly, 63*, pp. 451–462.

He, Z., & Zhu, J. H. (in press). *The ecology of online newspapers: The case of China. Media, Culture and Society.*

He, Z., & Zhu, J. H. (1994). The Voice of America and China: Zeroing in on Tiananmen Square. *Journalism Monographs, 43*, pp. 1–45.

He, Z. (2000a). Chinese party press in a tug of war: A political-economy analysis of the Shenzhen Special Zone Daily. In C. Lee (Ed.) *Money, power and media: Communication patterns in cultural China* (pp. 112–151). Evanston: Northwestern University Press.

He, Z. (2000b). Working with a dying ideology: Dissonance and its reduction in Chinese journalism. *Journalism Studies, 1*, pp. 599–616.

Houn, F. (1961). *To change a nation: Propaganda and indoctrination in Communist China.* New York: The Free Press of Glencoe.

Hovland, C., Lumsdiane, A., & Sheffield, F. (1949). *Experiments on mass communication.* Princeton: Princeton University Press.

Hovland, C., & Weiss, W. (1951). The influence of source credibility on communication effectiveness. *Public Opinion Quarterly, 15*, pp. 635–650.

Hyman, H., Wright, C., & Reed, J. (1979). *The enduring effects of education.* Chicago: The University of Chicago Press.

Inglehart, R. (1979). Value priorities and socioeconomic change. In S. Barnes, et al. (Eds.), *Political action: Mass participation in five Western democracies* (pp. 305–342). Beverly Hills: Sage.

Kelman, H. (1958). Compliance, identification, and internalization: Three processes of attitude change. *Journal of Conflict Resolution, 2*, pp. 51–60.

Klapper, J. (1957). What we know about the effects of mass communication: The brink of hope. *Public Opinion Quarterly, 21*, pp. 453–474.

Maslow, A. (1987). *Motivation and personality.* New York: Harper and Row.

McGuire, W. (1964). Inducing resistance to persuasion: Some contemporary approaches. In L. Berkowitz (Ed.), *Advances in experimental social psychology Vol. 1* (pp. 91–229). New York: Academic Press.

Newhagen, J., & Nass, C. (1989). Differential criteria for evaluating credibility of newspaper and television news. *Journalism Quarterly, 66*, pp. 277–284.

West, M. (1994). Validating a scale for the measurement of credibility: A covariance structure modeling approach. *Journalism Quarterly, 71*, pp. 159–1168.

Zajonc, R. (1974). Attitudinal effects of mere exposure. In S. Himmelfarb & A. Eagly (Eds.), *Readings in attitude change* (pp. 52–80). New York: John Wiley.

Zhao, X., Zhu, J., Li, H., & Bleske, G. (1994). Media effects under a monopoly: The case of Beijing in economic reform. *International Journal of Public Opinion Research, 6*, pp. 95–117.

Zhu, J. H. (2001). Theorization versus indigenization of Chinese communication research: The integrated theory of audiences and media effects as a case study. *Mass Communication Research, 68*, pp. 1–21.

Zhu, J. H. (1999, September). The viability of telephone surveys in China: Telephone coverage rate, survey Response rate and item response rate. Paper presented at the annual conference of the World Association for Public Opinion Research, Paris, France.

Zhu, J. H. (1997a). Antecedents, covariates, and outcomes of media credibility in *China. Mass Communication Review, 24*, pp. 4–17.

Zhu, J. H. (1997b). Political movements, cultural values, and mass media in China: Continuity and change. *Journal of Communication, 47*, pp. 157–164.

Zhu, J. H. (1997c). Growth, competition and survival: Forecasting of Chinese-language television based on the S-curve model. in W. Xie, X. Cai, H. Huang and Z. Shi (Eds.), *Perspectives on Chinese-language television* (pp. 41–50), Guangzhou: Flower City Press.

Zhu, J. H. (1995). Information availability, source credibility, and audience sophistication: Factors conditioning the effects of communist propaganda in China. *Political Communication, 12*, pp. 347–348.

Zhu, J. H. (1990). Information availability, media credibility, and audience sophistication: Factors conditioning the effects of communist propaganda in China. Doctoral dissertation. Bloomington, IN: Indiana University, 1990.

Dissertation Abstract International, 50, p. 5417.

Zhu, J. H., & Rosen, S. (1993). From discontent to protest: Individual-level causes of the 1989 pro-democracy movement in China. *International Journal of Public Opinion Research, 5*, pp. 234–249.

Jonathan J. H. Zhu is Professor in the Department of English and Communication at City University of Hong Kong.

Zhou He is Associate Professor in the Department of English and Communication at City University of Hong Kong.

Reading 1.8

What is the Basis of American Culture?

M. GENE ALDRIDGE

What is it that intercultural communication students cannot afford to miss about the American Culture?

INTRODUCTION AND PURPOSE

Culture is about survival of the human species. Without culture, human beings cannot survive. For example, the Neanderthal human, it is hypothesized, did not survive because of the inability to speak clearly and transmit culture (Ape Man, 1994).[19] Homo sapiens survive, it is hypothesized, because of culture and the ability to speak, therefore, they symbolize and create culture (art and play, tool making, economic organization, social organization,

Reprinted with permission from *Intercultural Communication, Issue 5*, April, 2002.

world view, political organization, language, social control and material culture). It is both a physiological-genetic issue (zoosemiotic) of the changing structure of the mouth and tongue which allowed the homo sapien to do what its relative, the Neanderthal, could not do, namely, to speak with clarity and advance the culture via symbols (anthroposemiotic). Unlike all other animals humankind is composed of both zoosemiotic and anthroposemiotic sign systems. Animals, by contrast, are singularly zoosemiotic (Sebeok, 1968).[18] Human culture is, therefore, unique from Orangutan culture because of speech communication.[14] Speech communication, as defined by Larson and Dance, is as follows: "Uniquely human. The process or the product of the process of the fusion of genetically determined speech with culturally determined language."[1]

Culture, it would seem, provides certain contributions to the survival of humankind that makes survival of the species, homo sapien possible. Cultures die out because they did not provide sufficient vitality for the culture to survive and/or they met with catastrophic conditions that allowed their culture to be overtaken by other cultures. This process, it would seem, is a kind of evolutionary sorting process between cultures that collide with one another.[3] Those principles that lend vitality to one culture can often be inculcated into the values of the next culture. Therefore, to study the value roots or the basis of various cultures via intercultural communication disciplines, might lend predictability to either the survival of a particular culture and/or understanding of its predictable elemental roots. It is theorized here that the cultures that remain most open to change in a way that brings to bear these core values for survivability, are the cultures that have the most to gain with respect to survivability, not only for the particular culture, but maybe for human civilizations as a whole. This produces

a seemingly interesting paradox. How can culture both preserve values (resist change) while using change to enhance the species? This is possible as described by Watzlawick, Weakland and Fisch because of first order changes and second order changes that occur in groups.[15] Human culture is a problem formation and problem resolution process and uses higher order abstractions via speech communication to provide for change. Some cultures can produce superficial change, but do not have the core values which allow them to produce second order change that could advance the culture into survivability. The Cold War produced such a condition for two camps. Osgood is quoted as follows on this issue:

"Our political and military leaders have been virtually unanimous in public assertions that we must go ahead and stay ahead in the armament race; they have been equally unanimous in saying nothing about what happens then. Suppose we achieve the state of ideal mutual deterrence . . . what then? Surely no sane man can envisage our planet spinning on into eternity, divided into two armed camps poised to destroy each other, and call it peace and security! The point is that the policy of mutual deterrence includes no provisions for its own resolution."[20]

Cultures are afflicted similarly. That is, they appear to be making all sorts of changes as measured by cultural traits, but in fact, the core values remain in tact that prevent or enhance the survivability of the culture. Teaching intercultural communication via trait studies alone may be a good measure of first order change, but it may miss the underlying values of the culture that can enhance or limit second order change leading to survivability. It is possible, for example, to have a highly individualistic culture, as defined by Hofstede, but miss the variations in individualistic cultures around the globe which have differing core values that may enhance or limit second order change. This same condition can prevail in collectivistic cultures as well. Asians, like Lee Kuan Yew, promote and posit Confucian value traits for all of Asia that simply do not exist in other cultures like Malaysia (Muslim and Chinese cultures), Thailand, Indonesia (primarily Muslim culture), Japan, or even the Philippines.[22]

His assertion in support of Asian traits and values simply are hollow assertions and do not apply to all of Asia, for example. Lee has been severely criticized by Chris Patton, former Governor of Hong Kong, in the 1999 book *East and West,* for trying to superimpose Confucian value traits on all of Asia as if there was a cultural "systems fit" for countries like India and China, for example.[21] Lee's approach is hollow and will not succeed as a mechanism for uniting all of Asia because the underlying value and traits are primarily Chinese, i.e., Confucian values and do not represent the values in many other Asian cultures. These issues are relevant to a discussion of American values precisely because assertions of this nature about traits confuse the cultural dialogue East to West and do not lead us to a better understanding of Asian values or American values.

Lee, as a Chinese Singaporean Asian, has asserted that American values are different from Asian collective values via Confucian philosophical roots (Lee Kuan Yu, 2000).[22] There are Confucian values that are different from other cultures, but to assert that there is a single set of Asian values begs the question: name them? This kind of trait analysis by Lee is weak because it lacks cultural developmental historical data in support of his assertions. Hong Kong's existence is proof positive that a Chinese city-state can be created that does not have the social engineering and/or the iron fist of leadership associated with it that is the norm for Singapore. Recent visits in Asia and speeches by Mr. Lee clearly demonstrate that

he may not want a democratic, free, and stable city-state of Chinese origin in Asia to compete with his own cultural ideologies about how Chinese or Asians need to be governed.[21] These cultural trait clashes, East to West, miss the underlying values that a developmental approach might bring to understanding the core values of many cultures in each region. For this reason, Lee's musings are instructive for scholars in intercultural communication.

Much discussion is also underway in European cultures about the American culture and its preoccupation with certain values that seem antithetical or at least disruptive to intercultural communication between nations and peoples.[27] Diplomats are discussing the role that both diplomacy and culture (sharing of the performance and visual arts between nations) play in humanizing the political processes between nations as yet another way to enhance intercultural communication (White House Conference on Diplomacy and Culture, November 28, 2000). Many cultures see the U.S. culture as a menace. There are many who believe, according to opinion polls, that America is out to impose its values and culture on others (CSA poll, September, 1998).[27] In fact, many believe that globalization has an American face and this is a danger somehow to other cultures and societies in this process.

This paper examines a key elemental value of the American cultural system and suggests that this value is what attracts people to the culture worldwide. Further, it is hypothesized that this core value is instrumental in assuring second order change for the United States, thus promoting survivability culturally.

DEFINING THE DIFERENCE OF HUMANKIND AND THE DIFFERENCE IT MAKES TO CULTURE

What is human culture? Human culture is the shared learned symbolic knowledge derived from speech communication. The basis and uniqueness of human culture is speech communication as defined herein. That is to say, animal communication is distinguishable from human communication in that humans are symbolic anthroposemiotic sign communicators whereas animals are sign limited by zoosemiotic communication (Sebeok, 1968).[18] Using Sebeok's study of animal communication, Dance and Larson (1972) made a persuasive argument for the idea that speech communication, thus human symbolic communication is the difference of man and the difference it makes. They said, "Symbolic communication is man's alone." (Dance and Larson, 1972, p. 41).[1] How, then, do we define culture?

Culture as defined here is as follows:

> Culture is the shared system of symbolic knowledge and patterns of behavior derived from speech communication, that human individuals carry to provide predictable internal and external psychological stability so as to prevent chaos among human individuals. We learn cultural codes for social life, role expectations, common definitions of situations, and social norms in order to provide predictability and survival of the human species. Human language (spoken and written) is the symbolic glue for human culture. (Aldridge, 1997).[29]

What is uniquely human is our symbolic knowledge that we carry and act upon in our varied cultural settings. Speech communication makes culture possible because it is uniquely human. Gudykunst discusses how the reduction of uncertainty is important to intercultural communication.[16] We want to know the cultural rules or codes so that we can predict mutual group behaviors and reduce the chaos in our lives as we move from culture to culture or even within sub-cultural settings. This allows the human being to share specialized knowledge in group settings and makes it possible for the species to survive without having to carry out all the necessary acts for living and survival because we can communicate the rules symbolically and learn them over time. Sharks have survived a long time because they have built in genetic codes that make it a stealthy hunter, but they are not symbolic animals in the human sense. Pavlov defined human communication as the "second signal system" by using a single vocal/verbal signal.[30] Humans rely on this second signal system, through culture, for survival. Animals do not.

Human beings progressed over time from non or low-symbolic animals to highly symbolic ones. It is the gift that keeps humanity from becoming extinct. In this sense, the function of human speech communication is to provide, by logical necessity, for the vase in which the flowers of culture are grown. Culture's function is to reduce uncertainty by developing, with the use of speech communication, order out of chaos. Culture is predicable social glue. Think about it for a moment. Culture preserves values for future generations to embrace. It provides education which is shared so that the species might become more understanding of the environment, create higher mental processes, and regulate behavior.[1] The newborn infant has the ability to speak, but the child must be taught the language of choice and the rules for the culture in which it resides.

Where those values become irrelevant, culture demonstrates to us that new and better functional ways of survival can be born. Human beings advanced from caves to houses for a reason. Political ideological cultures have emerged as well. What seems functional for societies can also become dysfunctional for humanity too. Hitler's 3rd Reich was not acceptable as a cultural political ideology for the majority of cultures, it was destroyed by other cultures. Locke says, "For I have reason to conclude that he who would get me into his power without my consent would use me as he please when he had fancy to do it; for nobody can desire to have me in his absolute power unless it be to compel me by force to that which is against the right of my freedom, i.e., to make me a slave."[40] That is, cultures can begin to promulgate ideas and values which they believe will lead to the survival of the species, but which in fact do not and further, when they impinge on the freedom of others in doing so makes it impossible because it violates the natural liberty of humankind. Human cultures come and go in this process; a process that is both biological and culturally induced. This is best demonstrated by trying to seek out a Neanderthal and ask him why he is not around any more. Through the strange mix of biology, genetics and language, culture is developed, shared and passed on to new generations of people for the sole purpose of survival.

Intercultural communication is the mechanism (the mixing of cultures and languages via speech communication) by which human beings have compared ways of living, economic order, social order, and values from other cultures. These ideas are compared between, within and among cultural groups. Thus, the American and the European cultures do not always agree on the same values. For example, when it comes to cultural comparisons, like the death penalty, Europeans are astonished that 38 states allow the death penalty in the United States. Europeans see this as American barbarism.[27] In April of 2000, only 30 percent of the French felt that there was anything to admire in the United States. Nonetheless, aside from the political posturing imbedded in these arguments superficial assessments of other cultures can lead to a false understanding of the other culture. Even Americans promote a lack of cultural understanding about Europeans when people, like Steve Forbes, declare Charlemagne a unifier of Europe, when, in fact, Europeans view Charlemagne as a conqueror of cultures.[27]

French bookstores are full of this kind of diatribe about the U.S. culture and its failings as viewed from the Eiffel Tower. The titles are amusing. "No Thanks Uncle Sam," "The World is not Merchandise," "Who is killing France, the American Strategy," "American Totalitarianism" and many more (Daley, 2000).[27] Poking fun at the American culture has been part of the French pastime for many years. Mr. Clinton did not help matters any by declaring through his foreign relations communications that the U.S. is the "indispensable" nation now. But all of this intercultural banter misses the underlying core value of the U.S. culture.

Just what is the basis for the culture of the United States? What is the core value of the culture? What are the fundamental assumptions around which the U.S. culture spins on its axis? What does the U.S. uniquely contribute by way of their cultural heritage that is so appealing to those that migrate to its shores? Is this core cultural value worth some consideration with respect to the advancement of the species, homo sapien? To fully understand these questions a short diversion with respect to human intercultural communication is necessary. First, the case for speech communication as the basis of human culture.

THE PHYSIOLOGICAL AND BIOLOGICAL BASIS FOR SPEECH COMMUNICATION

Without speech communication human beings do not have a culture. Language provides us, through our unique biology of created speech via the larynx, the opportunity to share symbolic ideas like no other creature on earth. We are, therefore, fragile species compared to our other animal friends with whom we share this planet.

Most other species survive exclusively on the basis of built-in instincts that are biologically pre-determined. The sounds a cricket makes, for example. The flight patterns of birds and their migrations are evidence of built-in genetic codes and learned behavior in other species. The long life of the shark as a species is another example. Only the human being communicates, via higher order abstractions, symbolically and then creates cultures (predictability) to increase the probability for survival. While monkeys and some apes, it has been demonstrated, can communicate via sign language, the development of this language falls far short of the capabilities of the human being in terms of symbolic communication. As noted by Linden (1999), animals' use of tools does not necessarily imply insight into their purpose.[14] Imitation is the behavior, but not intentionality as in the case of human communication.

Animal research demonstrates clearly that human communication is distinguishable from animal communication. Dance and Larson (1972) have provided adequate defense on the uniqueness of speech communication behavior.[1] To use Mortimer Adler's phrase, "the difference of man and the difference it makes," is speech communication, our ability to speak and create symbolic language that leads to thought.[2] While we cannot know precisely in time when humankind became "truly human" via speech communication, we can attest to the fact that the moment in time was a radical change (a second order change) and the beginning of human culture. Primitive groups had to find a way in which to educate all members about the rules and values for existence. Culture was that mechanism for human tribes and ethnic groups. An exploration of the anthropology of cultures can provide some understanding here.

THE DEVELOPMENT ANTHROPOLOGY OF CULTURES

Cultures were born because humankind moved from the original African homeland and began migrating around the world. With recent DNA discoveries in Australia that are 40,000 to 60,000 years old, the migration of humans out of Africa becomes much more complicated.[26] This new DNA analysis posits that homo erectus left Africa and homo sapiens developed, most likely in regions of the world. Nonetheless, these peoples moved, first, north to what is now Europe, but then to Asia and on to the North American continent. It is an amazing 2.5 million year story of the survival of a species.

In order to survive, various cultures and species were born and reborn, that is, they learned different ways in which to gather food, hunt and maintain life. Each of the new cultures were adapted and interwoven into humankind's early cultural developments such as language, religion, art, science, and even government or social organization.

Conquests were won and lost between cultures as Thomas Sowell has demonstrated in his work *Conquests and Cultures*.[3] Conquests have produced cultural evolution. What seems quite clear from Sowell's work is that "cultural capital" not genes or race, per se, lead us to cultural evolution. This is important because buried in the cultural capital are cultural values. Eventually the vanquished adapted and adopted many new cultural behaviors and values that led to their own survival. The cultural capital is the result of historical, geographic, and social innovations says Sowell.

> "Cultural resistance is both spontaneous and artificial. The desire to cling to the familiar, or to remain loyal to traditions and to the people in whom those traditions are embodied, are all readily understandable. In addition, however, concerted campaigns to resist new cultures or to retrieve ancestral cultures already abandoned have also been promoted to both political and intellectual leaders."[3]

Ideas, because of technology and cultural diffusion, spread around the world. Ideas, (cultural capital) about liberty and freedom, ideas about scientific knowledge and cultural ways of innovating move like lightning around the world because of language. Music, fast food, and even ways of governing sweep around the world with great speed in the information age. Does this mean that we have a common world culture? Do we want to have, for example, a singular world civilization, with many cultural tribes, as Braudel and Sowell have outlined?[3,4] What humankind does with intercultural communication opportunities may determine the historical, biological and cultural outcomes for humankind. Cultures can both simultaneously deliver first and second order change that leads to survival. In this respect, we are sealers of our own fate and we do not seem to be doing well with respect to advancing these opportunities through our intercultural experiences as we move into the new millennium. We do not seem to be able to get tribes in the Middle East, for example, to manage their cultural clashes. Asian Muslims and Chinese Asians are, yet, another example. The cultural clashes identified by Huntington in 1993 seem to be living out the prediction or at least moving in the direction he proposed.[41]

CULTURE, LANGUAGE, AND CHANGE

Culture provides predictability for humankind. Because human life can be quite inefficient, culture offers us the predictable patterns of behavior that lead to cooperative expectancies. How do we eat food properly? How do we create common measurements upon which we can rely? How do we introduce, greet and sustain relationships with others? In what manner shall we conduct commerce and under what government conditions? Inside international business, rules for conducting business are becoming quite homogenous, e.g., banking,

finance methods, marketing strategies and management of intercultural groups. Each culture provides predictability, thus changing culture can be quite difficult unless the cultural value being changed has been demonstrated to be of less value or no longer useful to a particular group.

Cultures also test new ideas and introduce potential change. The introduction of English, for example, on a worldwide basis for use in business and international trade is threatening to some cultures. Language, too, provides the social bonding and predictability because humans have rules for language and these rules lead us to communicate more efficiently and effectively. It has often been said prescriptively, if you want to learn the heart of the people, you must learn the language. We say this because language helps us understand how to "think" in a particular culture.

Cultures borrow from each other's language in order to provide more precision for their language. English, for example, quite readily adapts words from other cultures like the French laissez faire (hands off) or perestroika (restructuring) from the Russians.[23] On the other hand, the French have people who watch for new words, particularly in the high technology arena, so that they can quickly create French words that can be used instead of English words.

Sometimes, the word as it is found in the original language really communicates the word more effectively and is more easily understood and adopted. Language, Whorf (1956) pointed out, is directly related to the thoughts and actions which cultures develop.[31] Yet, through the study of linguistics we understand that cultural diversity is based upon universal human foundations, i.e., universal human experiences (Sapir-Whorf (1921/1956), Lucy (1992), Silverstein (1976), Langacker (1987).[23,24,31,32,34] Boas (1911/1966) has demonstrated how language structure, via the Native Americans, provides researchers with the insight to understand culture via "other mentalities" of meaning.[25] Goffman (1974) suggests that culture frames our experience and organizes data.[36] Harrison (1985) is convinced that culture and the organizing language of culture can explain "Underdevelopment as a State of Mind."[24]

Language is, therefore, extremely important to the understanding of what I like to call "core meanings" in each culture. In each culture there are "novices" and "knowing" generations. Only that which is communicated between the "knowing" and the "novices" in each culture has the chance for survival of important core meanings that make up the culture. To understand the core meaning of a culture is a dive into the pool of consistent thought and actions of a people (Benedict, 1934).[37] Important and lasting core meanings and values become a part of civilizations because they have endured. . . . they have added to the survival of the human species. These values produce a patterning that is predictable in order to create the "mindfulness" which Gudykunst (1984) understands to be a key element in producing effective intercultural communication.[16] So what happens when we apply these developmental-historical principles and ideas to a specific culture? The following is an analysis of the origins of American cultural values which are often discussed in the developmental history of the United States. Predictability in understanding intercultural communication rests on our ability as researchers to sort these values much like sorting the wheat from the chaff.

AMERICAN CULTURE AND THE IDEA OF SELF-GOVERNMENT

Edward T. Hall (1966) has said that the "hidden dimensions" of language and culture provide interesting insights into understanding the cultural behavior of other groups with whom we may not be familiar.[7] For example,

Thomas Woods, Jr. (2000) points out that the seeds of liberty are found in the behavior of the colonies.[5] The practical nature of the colonies and its commitment to self-government were driving cultural forces that eventually produced the Constitution of the United States of America. Fischer (1989) provides an analysis of the English immigration to the colonies by insisting that the differences between the Virginians and the Puritans of New England were huge and each was very suspicious of the other.[38]

From the beginning, American culture was defining itself against confederations of big government in favor of self-government. The Dominion of New England included Massachusetts, Maine and New Hampshire with a single governor. Andros, in 1686, became Governor and raised taxes, jailed persons who did not abide by his autocratic rule, and by 1688 the colonists had had enough. They revolted and threw the system out. Colonists also threw out Ben Franklin's Albany Plan of Union in 1754. This plan was rejected by all the colonies (Wood, 2000).[5] There is much more evidence to indicate that the early period (1600s), before the American revolution, was filled with cultural emphasis about self-government. The people were quick to rise up against any condition which prevented self-government from dominating their lives, even taxation.

Self-government, then, is one of the cultural dimensions that, when carefully analyzed, appears early in cultural colonial American assumptions. The colonists were suspicious of monarchies, theocracies, and anything that smacked of big government that could usurp the rights of individuals and their liberty. But if we carefully analyze the development of the Constitution of the United States, we find that the underlying value for self-government was the commitment to rights of the individual. . . . what we now call "liberty." Liberty is the freedom from despotic or arbitrary government or any other rule of law that is not grounded in self-government. Using John Locke's own words, "The natural liberty of man is to be free from any superior power on earth . . . The liberty of man in society is to be under no other legislative power but that established by consent. . . . "[40] But what is the underlying cultural value behind self-government? What are the a priori hidden dimensions (values) of the American culture that require Americans to be committed to self-government?

The analysis, leading to the answers for these questions, is interesting. I often have my graduate students in intercultural communication write down answers to the following questions:

1. What is the basis for American cultural principles, values and issues?
2. What is unique, if anything, about the American culture?

What would you list here? My students write about religious freedom, freedom from the tyranny of the state as the American dream, covenantal freedom associated with humility and equality at its core, and national values that allow for immigration of all people to our shores. Many immigrants discuss the ideas about economic freedom to choose their life and their work in a manner that is of their own choosing. But under closer analysis, are these issues really the cultural glue that holds Americans together?

Because my research and travel take me to many cultures, over 100 now, I have often been asked by outsiders to the American culture, what is it that really drives the culture of the United States? They ask, "What would you say is the core value of your culture?" At first, I was stunned by these questions. It wasn't that I did not think they were good questions, but I found that the answer to them was not quickly forthcoming. I told them of our

immigration and that our diversity has helped us. I spoke, too, about the creativity and freedom which go hand in hand with the culture in North America. The interesting structure of the English language was also mentioned, but somehow I was very uneasy with all these answers. I knew these were not the answers which really persuaded the United States to Revolution and Re-Revolution every four years. Here, then, is a descriptive exploration and analysis of a core value within the American culture as explicated by others. Their views are important because in intercultural discussions about the United States we hear these various arguments all the time. The arguments presented are not meant to be exhaustive, rather illustrative of the ideas often presented inside and outside the American culture. The research approach here is historical-developmental as it relates to the analysis. Just what are the various historical-developmental arguments for the basis of the American culture?

COVENANTAL FREEDOM AS THE BASIS FOR AMERICAN CULTURE

Richard Parker of the Kennedy School in Boston (1995) maintains that American culture is neither cultural nor a civilization.[6] Rather, that America is the dream born out of the Protestant Reformation that individuals can find God on their own terms, and without intervention by the church. He believes that America's core is born out of the need to free oneself from both the tyranny of the state and the church. He maintains that it was the community of belief around these ideas that the American culture and state were born. Land availability made all this possible as immigrants flocked to the continent to begin again on new land that was their own. Remember, in Europe the land was owned by the few and these were usually controlled by the monarchies, directly or indirectly, in the 1600s and

1700s. Parker maintains that it was the value of a covenantal freedom which drove the Pilgrims to the Massachusetts shores. Further, he believes our own Civil War was based upon upholding the covenantal freedom couched in the Constitution of the United States.

THE BASIS FOR AMERICAN VALUES AS RELIGIOUS COMMITMENT

Maier (1995) suggests another view of American culture.[8] He is concerned about Americans believing that religion is the basis of American culture because the root word is "cult"(as defined here he means a particular system of religious worship) or a small group of religions that formed the basis for American values. To be sure, the role of religion in America is an interesting one. Maier understands it this way; the foundation for America cannot be religion because the United States could not account for Muslims, Christians, Jews, Buddhists and the many other diverse groups that have come to the nation. His point is that religion cannot, therefore, be the basis for the American culture because it is too limiting, Maier would argue. He asks, what is the concord of love for things held in common (his definition from St. Augustine for civilization) which binds Americans? Americans, he states, are one civilization held together by many cultures. . . . Muslims, Jews, Christians, Buddhists and other ethnic groups.

St. Augustine said, "a people is a multitudinous assemblage of rational beings united by concord regarding love of things held in common" . . . thus, we need to investigate what a people's concord is in order to get at the heart of a civilization.[9] America, according to Maier, is a multi-cultural group with many ethnic groups, bound by a market economy and representing many cultures.

This approach does not help the analysis because it still does not articulate a core value

presupposed by some scholars that religion alone was the basis for foundational America.

AMERICA'S IDENTITY AS A CONFIGURATION OF VALUES AND THEMES

Eisenach (1995) approaches the central idea for the basis of "being American" within the framework of underlying values which link all Americans to an identity.[10] According to Ruth Benedict, identity is a whole or gestalt or configuration which leads to a national identity. This identity is shared by many cultures within American society. We derive who we are by our holistic underlying values. The problem is that when a nation is in trouble it looks for national identity. . . . something upon which all people in the society can share. WWII, for example, pulled everyone together around the idea that Japanese theo-militarism and German Nazi despotism would not stand. American identity was bound around the idea that you went to war to represent and do battle against those that did not support freedom and liberty. That was, for the moment, our national identity. We didn't care where you came from or what culture you represented, if you cared and identified with America's commitment against despotism, then you were one of us.

The difficulty with national identity is that this feeling of national identity is short-lived. It is fleeting. National identities shift as politics and social conditions may dictate. Eisenach also notes that we should look not to culture, but rather causal relationships inside culture to find national identity and core values. He raises interesting questions.

He is right that America is always on the verge of chaos and anarchy because we are consistently revolutionary in the approach to culture; a theme that many in Asia and elsewhere do not often understand clearly. He says that the United States is a configuration of causal ideas that leads to a national identity and suggests that more research is needed to sustain and understand these themes and patterns in history.

While these "identity themes" may contribute to America's national identity, they do not, in and of themselves, provide us with the core cultural principles that remain as the necessary and sufficient cause for American cultural value roots. These are candidate ideas which require further research. By form, then, they leave us in a stew of abstraction in understanding American cultural values.

AMERICAN PROSPERITY AS A CULTURAL ROOT

In an analysis of "Tocqueville Revisited," Handy (2001) suggests that earned wealth, not inherited wealth, is a value that was immediately embraced by American cultural values.[17] He also suggests that by "codifying and legalizing the emerging property" it was possible to move capital and grow into a wealthy culture. Without the legal means, cultures cannot move capital freely or accumulate wealth. Without the legal means, underdeveloped economic cultures fail. The wealthy in the United States are encouraged to display their wealth by helping others. By giving back to the community and to the culture at large, Americans demonstrate that their life meant something and that wealth was earned legally and respectfully. The ability of Americans to believe in a bright future is another value embraced by Handy which he believes fuels America's self-confidence.

While material goods alone do not drive the new forms of cultural capitalism that we see emerging in the United States and in the new global economy, it is clear that services and information now become the new vehicle for the growth of capitalism. For economic growth to occur economists like Romer (1994) believe that capital accumulation and less

spending by governments eventually reaches a cultural dead-end of diminishing returns. Cultures that can promote, via human capital formation, an "institutional environment that supports technological change" will be the masters of growth.[17] He believes that the United States leads the way on this front culturally. Cultures, then, that can master both economic progress while sustaining substantial second order change will be those cultures that move quickly past the competition in the new global economy. These values, inside the American psyche, associated with human capital and knowledge, create a United States that is pivotal in the global economy. But even these sustained economic conditions for amassing human cultural capital cannot occur without another primary value that is even more fundamental to the American culture.

THE NATURAL RIGHTS OF MAN AS A CENTRAL CULTURAL VALUE

All of these candidate value notions raise interesting questions about culture, civilization, national identity, prosperity, economics, and religion. By themselves, however, they do not make the case for a necessary and sufficient cause for a cultural value around which American society spins.

It is the thesis of this paper that John Locke and Thomas Jefferson left America with the enduring value that does sustain the culture and glues people together.[40,11] That core value of America rests on the assertion for the "natural rights" of humankind. The shared feeling of belonging hovers always around individual and natural rights of man as outlined in the Constitution and the Declaration of Independence.

Regardless of America's sub-cultural heritage, this is what draws people to America, not religion, not economics by itself nor even national identity. Even the Puritans wanted to keep everyone out after they came to America.

Left unfettered, they could have been as despotic as the European system from which they came seeking religious freedom. So it would seem that the enduring value of United States culture is not religion, but the individual rights, the natural rights of all humankind. How might this be the case?

National identity and the idea that America is a "civilization" with higher order values in art, science and government seems a bit ethnocentric after only 225 years. On the issue of "civilization" value around technology and science, it is true that America holds a strong advantage, but that advantage is short-lived without the enduring value of natural rights is it not? Besides many other cultures have a strong tradition of science and technology as well. China, for example, can boast a cultural line that extends over 3000 years. It is also true that the Protestant Reformation may have sparked interest in immigrating to North American continent (free land and free religion), but it certainly was but one issue among many historical events that triggered the colonization of America and not a core value as some would like to believe. What good is free land without legal means to hold onto it or the liberty to protect it?

The Civil War, many other scholars have noted, was a defining moment in the history of the American culture. Why was this so? Because the Civil War was a fight over the individual rights of a segment of society, that if left as is, would have negated the core value associated with natural rights. The United States citizens took up arms against each other because this culture could not let stand the evil of slavery. The idea that slavery must go, or else we would be hypocrites in the eyes of other nations and cultures, was understood by President Lincoln. The ideas about slavery and what it meant to be a slave where well documented by John Locke (1690) in his second essay on "Concerning Civil Government." Slavery in the United States created the state of

war which Locke argues about in his Chapter IV on Slavery. . . . . "the natural liberty of man is to be free from any superior power on earth."

Other people flock to American shores because the American culture is trying to perfect the American shared value of "natural rights." American institutional life is reflective of this struggle. The cultural debates about schools, the role of family, the role of religion, and the debates that center on collectivism vs. individualism as a goal for government permeate the American cultural life. On the issue of government's role or the form of social organization that the Americans require, no election in the history of the United States was closer than the one in the year 2000. It is clear that the debate about individualism and collectivism as an emphasis for government will continue, but few debate the issue of natural rights. Rather, the debate is about how human cultural capital can best be mobilized around the value of natural rights; how it will be implemented by the American culture and what role should government play in this development? To understand the United States, then, is to understand how deeply imbedded into the cultural experience is the value of natural rights.

To other cultures in Europe, Asia, Africa and even Latin America, many of these American elections and their debates can be confounding. It looks, superficially, to outsiders like so much chaos. But the core value of natural rights sustains the debate and the culture moves on to debate again in four years. The a priori reason that the debate can continue is imbedded in the core value of natural rights.

When viewed from the perspective of "natural rights" as a core cultural value, ethnic diversity and special rights for special groups becomes a pagan ignorant exercise that only leads to the altar of humility as a error of judgment by political leaders and social philosophers. Like the Europeans, Asians, Africans, and Latin Americans, the United States is a multi-racial and hybrid group. No group today in the world can claim racial purity as did the Nazis. To make natural rights work, means that there can be no "special groups" and any exercise which moves toward creating special needs of special groups, prima facie, defies the root value of natural rights.

Recent studies by some African-American intellectuals in the United States explores the ideas that reflect again, on natural rights, not special rights, as creating the underlying value for all members of the American culture (McWhorter, 2000 and Sowell, 1998).[12,3] Other cultures may wish to take heed in what McWhorter is saying, namely, that special considerations only create less, not more, self-actualization among African Americans in the United States because victimology (studying to be a victim) only continues to drive the insecurity. Competition is the way to build confidence in sub-cultures, not special programs that create the very anti-intellectualism which prevents African Americans from achievement by their own hand. Often academic discussions are held, not with rigorous academic debate, but with "folk tales" that simply are not supportable by rigorous debate. This perpetuates the "cult of separatism" by their own choosing. Based upon liberty, and to ensure that African Americans were not discriminated against, the United States embarked upon a legal overhaul of the culture in the 1960s to ensure that African Americans were not segregated, separated, or discriminated against. This codification of the law was a phenomenal commitment on the part of the American culture to ensure that African Americans had legal redress around the idea of individual liberty. The film with Sean Connery entitled *Finding Forrester* demonstrates the anti-intellectualism point most effectively. Here is a white professor and writer, developing a relationship with an African American young person who suddenly discovers that it is "ok" to "be smart" . . . to be a nerd and to develop self-confidence as an intellectual.

Sub-cultures must be very careful in the United States to not allow the cults and cultural folk tales to overshadow the real value of liberty that drives the culture. Outsiders to the American culture often miss these subtle, but important issues that are at the heart of the liberty-natural rights value. Time does not allow for a full discussion of all these issues, but *Losing the Race: Self-Sabotage in Black America,* (McWhorter, 2000) is a must read for students of intercultural communication because he peels away core value issues for clear debate. Again, this is an example of human capital formation within the American culture that provides second order change around sub-cultural issues. The American experiment continues in earnest debate.

Thomas Jefferson (1826) in his last message before he died on the 50th Anniversary of the Declaration of Independence said it best . . . "the signal of arousing men to burst the chains under which monkish ignorance and superstition (religion) had persuaded them to bind themselves and to assume the blessings and security of self government . . . the form which we have substituted restores the faith in unbounded reason and freedom of opinion . . . and all eyes are open or are opening to the rights of man. . . . "[11]

To be "mindful," as Gudykunst puts it, then, of the American culture is to remember the idea of "natural rights" in the developmental history of the American culture.[16] This, in turn, has produced the reason for self-government. Further research is needed to explore the ideas around historical-developmental research as a tool for intercultural communication researchers, but the mining of the American culture produces a rich ore called natural rights that has value for the study of intercultural communication. Students of intercultural communication would do well to advance this method and apply it to other cultures, for comparative purposes while remembering that it is human capital formation, not race or ethnicity, which drives cultures.

NOTES

1. Dance. Frank E.X. and Larson, Carl E., (1972) *Speech Communication*, Holt Rinehardt and Winston, Inc., New York.

2. Adler, Mortimer, (1973) *The Difference of Man and the Difference it Makes*, Fordam University Press, New York.

3. Sowell, Thomas, (1998) *Conquests and Cultures*, Basic Books, New York.

4. Braudel, Fernand, (1994) *A History of Civilizations*, The Penguin Group, New York.

5. Woods, Thomas E. Jr. (2000) "The Colonial Origins of American Liberty," in *Ideas on Liberty*, September, Vol 50, No. 9, The Economic Foundation for Economic Education, Hudson, New York.

6. Parker, Richard, (1995) "Does America Have a Civilizational or Cultural Identity?" from a speech presented at Tulsa University, 4th International Conference - Global Paradigms: The Impact of Cultures and Trade on Diplomacy, Tulsa, OK.

7. Hall, Edward T. (1966) *Hidden Dimension*, Doubleday, New York.

8. Maier, Charles, (1995) "The Changing Bases of National Identity" from a speech present at Tulsa University, 4th International Conference–Global Paradigms: The Impact of Cultures and Trade on Diplomacy, Tulsa, OK.

9. St. Augustine, "The City of God" in the Great Books of the Western World, Vol. 18, *Encyclopedia Britannica*, 1952.

10. Eisenach, Eldon, (1995) "Does America Have a Civilizational or Cultural Identity?" from a speech presented at Tulsa University, 4th International Conference–Global Paradigms: The Impact of Cultures and Trade on Diplomacy, Tulsa, OK.

11. Jefferson, Thomas, (1826) "Last Letter: Apotheosis of Liberty–To Roger Weightman," Monticello, in Thomas Jefferson, Library of America, 1984, New York, pp. 1516–1517.

12. McWhorter, John H., (2000) *Losing the Race, Self Sabotage in Black America*, The Free Press, New York, NY.

13. Stewart, Edward C. and Bennett, Milton J., (1991) *American Cultural Patterns*, Revised Edition, Intercultural Press, Inc., Yarmouth, Maine.

14. Linden, Eugene, (1999) *The Parrot's Lament, and other tales of animal intrigue, intelligence, and ingenuity*, Plume–Penguin Group, New York.

15. Watzlawick, Paul and Weakland, John, (1974) *Change*, W.W. Norton & Company, Inc., New York.

16. Gudykunst, William B. and Young Yun Kim, (1984) *Communicating with Strangers*, 3rd Ed., McGraw Hill, Boston, MA.

17. Handy, Charles, (2001) Tocqueville Revisited: The Meaning of American Prosperity, *Harvard Business Review*, January, p. 57.

18. Sebeok, Thomas A. (1968) "Goals and Limitations of the Study of Animal Communication," ed. T.A Sebeok, University Press, Bloomington, IN, p. 8.

19. *Ape Man*, (1994) Hosted by Walter Cronkite, a television series, 4 color videocassettes, 50 minutes each, A & E Television Networks, Hearst ABC/NBC, New York.

20. Osgood, Charles E., (1962) *Reciprocal Initiative in The Liberal Papers*, ed. James Roosevelt, Quadrangle Books, Chicago, p. 172.

21. Patton, Chris, (1999) *East and West*, Macmillan–Pan Books, London, p. 146–172.

22. Cheung, Jimmy, (2000) "SAR must prove it can thrive without Western 'meddling' if it wants democracy, says Singaporean statesman," *China Morning Post*, December 9.

23. Gorbachev, Mikhail, (1987) *Perestroka: New Thinking for our Country and the World*, Harper and Row, New York.

24. Harrison, Lawrence E., (1985) *Underdevelopment is a State of Mind*, Madison Books, Lanham, MD.

25. Boas, F. (1966), Introduction, in F. Boas and J.W. Powell, eds., *Handbook of American Indian Languages*, Lincoln: University of Nebraska (original work published in 1911).

26. CNN, "Australian fossil finder disputes age, backs evolution claim," January 10, 2001,

Website: CNN.com/2001/Nature/01/10/Australia. evolution.reut/index.html.

27. Daley, Suzanne (2000), "Europe's Dim View of U.S. Is Evolving Into Frank Hostility," *New York Times*, April 9, Sunday, Foreign Desk.

28. Aldridge, M. Gene, (1997) *Lectures on Intercultural Communication*, Troy State University, Troy, AL.

29. Palov, I.P., (1960) *Conditioned Relfexes: An Investigation of the Physiology Activity of the Cerebral Cortex*, trans. Anrep.ed., Dover Publications, Inc. p. 14.

30. Whorf, B.L., (1956) *Language, thought, and reality*, Cambridge: MIT Press, 1956.

31. Sapir, E., (1921), *Language*, New York: Harcourt Brace.

32. Lucy, J., (1992), *Language diversity and thought*, Cambridge: Cambridge University Press.

33. Silverstein, M., (1976), "Shifters, linguistic categories and cultural description" in K. Basso & H Selby (eds), *Meaning in anthropology*, Albuquerque: University of NM Press.

34. Langlacker, R. W., (1987), *Foundations of cognitive grammar:* Vol 1, Theoretical prerequisites, Stanford, CA: Stanford University Press.

35. Goffman, E.F., (1974), *Frame analysis.* New York: Harper & Row.

36. Benedict, R., (1934), *Patterns of Culture*, Boston: Houghton Mifflin.

37. Fischer, David H., (1989), *Albion's Seed: Four British Folkways in America*, New York: Oxford University Press.

38. Reisman, David, (1961), *The Lonely Crowd*, New Haven, CT: Yale University Press.

39. Locke, John, (1690), "Concerning Civil Government, Second Essay" in *Great Books of the Western World*, Vol 35, Locke, Berkeley, Hume, Chicago: Encyclopedia Britannica, Inc., 1952, pp. 1–85.

40. Huntington, Samuel, (1993) "The Clash of Civilizations," Foreign Affairs, Summer, New York.

––––––––––––––––––

M. Gene Aldridge is President/CEO of the New Mexico Independence Research Institute, Inc., a public policy think tank dedicated to educating the citizens of New Mexico about public policy issues. He holds the rank of Associate Professor and continues to teach. Aldridge has his own international marketing and investment firm, World Marketing, Inc., which has taken him to over 100 countries for lecturing, business and study in the past 28 years. He has authored numerous articles on intercultural communication, international marketing, health care management, marketing international higher education, economics, and developed case studies for project management, finance, marketing and information technology. He is a specialist on the role of taxation in the New Mexico economy. He lectures throughout the world on issues associated with intercultural communication, brand equity, economic development, international marketing, and project management in high technology.

PART II

Language

No one is born knowing a language. Some linguists, such as Noam Chomsky, believe that we are biologically programmed for language learning. Others argue that we develop language skills from clues in the environment; they suggest that, from all the sounds they hear, babies use pitch, stress, pauses, and rhythm to learn where word sounds stop and start. By 6 months of age, babies seem to have begun to ignore the sounds that do not characterize the language they will be speaking. The ability to learn a second language is its highest between birth and 6 years of age and declines after that. Learning a new language as an adult is a struggle compared to the ease in learning our first language. In either case, the language you speak was culturally transmitted. That is, you learned the language of those who raised you, regardless of the language of your biological parents. A language must be learned, and in so doing, the brain is changed forever. Language learning is intrinsic to being human.

Scholars since the 18th century have classified languages by the family-tree model. For example, dozens of languages now spoken by half the world's population all descended from the same ancient language spoken some 8,000 years ago. These languages include Albanian, Armenian, Slavic (Czech, Polish, Russian, etc.), Celtic (Irish, Scots, Welsh, etc.), Germanic (Dutch, English, German, etc.), and the Romance languages (French, Italian, Spanish, etc.), and linguists now call them Indo-European languages.

Linguists Thomas Gamkrelidze and Vyacheslav Ivanov have attempted to reconstruct the vocabulary of Indo-European from the common-sounding words of these languages. This reconstructed vocabulary is called proto-Indo-European. Because they can find many words for domesticated animals and plants, they conclude that the Indo-Europeans were farmers. Because they can find many words for mountains and flowing rivers, they conclude that the Indo-Europeans lived in a hilly terrain. From these and other clues, it is believed that Indo-European originated in an area of Turkey known as Anatolia and, from there, spread throughout Europe and the subcontinent.

In a similar manner, other language families have been identified. Asian languages including Turkic, Mongolic, Japanese, and Korean are grouped together as Altaic languages that share subject-object-verb word order. The origin of Japanese is unclear. Much of Japanese grammar resembles the Altaic languages; however, in its use of prefixes and its sound system with a limited set of consonants and a preference for open syllables, Japanese resembles the Austronesian languages thought to have originated in Taiwan.

Linguists Vladislav Illich-Svitych and Aharon Dolgoposky contend that Indo-European, Altaic, and other languages are derived from an even more ancient language now called Nostratic, or "our language," which may have originated around 13,000 to 10,000 B.C.E. From their reconstruction of the Nostratic language, they believe its speakers were hunter-gatherers because of a lack of words for domesticated plants or farming.

Another scientific area of study gives support for these conclusions. By tracing the developmental history of human genes, geneticists have constructed a family tree of the human race. The groupings on this family tree based on genetic evidence closely resemble the language groupings laid out independently by the linguists.

Although their work has been strongly disputed, biologists Rebecca Cann, Mark Stoneking, and Allan C. Wilson (1987) studied genetic material from women around the world and contend that all humans alive today share genetic material from a woman who lived some 200,000 years ago in sub-Saharan Africa. The origin of language may then lie in sub-Saharan Africa. Some scientists now argue for a single ancestral prehuman species that may have thrived across Africa for almost 1 million years without significant physical change. Climate changes or some other pressure led to the sudden development of several different humanoid species, one of which became the line that led to modern humans who discovered fire and language. Their original African "Eve" conclusion may be supported by linguistic observations. Luigi Cavalli-Sforza and others (1988) have shown that there is considerable similarity between Cann's tree of genetic relationships and the tree of language groups. For example, languages that are most different from other languages today are in Africa. This may suggest that they are older. Africa's Khoisan languages, such as that of the !Kung San for example, use a clicking sound that is denoted in writing with an exclamation point. However, later reanalysis has suggested that

"Eve" could have come from Asia, Europe, or Africa, that there could have been more than one "Eve," and that any common ancestor could easily have lived tens or hundreds of thousands of years earlier.

Linguists are now trying to reconstruct this African group's language, which may be the first human language and is now called proto-World. As they reconstruct the language, they also reconstruct the culture. It may have been a culture before mathematics because linguists believe this language had ones, twos, and many. There may have been the same word for life, breath, and blood. And there appear to have been no words to express emotions.

Would international communication be facilitated if everyone spoke the same language? Universal languages such as Esperanto have no relationship to a culture and can't reflect any individual culture's worldview. A major concern today is the spread of English as the world's dominant language. Any language brings to its speakers a unique worldview. The concern is that as any one language dominates, other languages and worldviews may forever disappear. The readings in this section address this issue.

Peter Mühlhäusler was born in Freiburg, Germany and studied Linguistics at Stellenbosch, Reading, and at the Australian National University. He has carried out field work in Papua New Guinea, Samoa, Torres Straits, Northern Queensland, Northern New South Wales, and outback areas of South Australia. His main teaching interest is pidgin and Creole linguistics. He writes about the interdependencies between language and the rest of the world in "Babel Revisited," and argues for linguistic diversity.

Amadou Hampâté Bâ was born in 1901 in Mali. He worked to bring international recognition for African oral cultures south of the Sahara and for safeguarding them. He published extensive examples of Peul oral tradition. In "Africa: The Power of Speech," he shows how oral tradition creates identity.

In "Mexican American Ethnicity in Biola, CA: An Ethnographic Account of Hard Work, Family, and Religion," Eric Aoki, an assistant professor at Colorado State University, reports an ethnographic study conducted in a small, agricultural community. Through his study of language use, he shows how the role of family and religion serve as unifying forces.

Professor Kil-Ho Kang teaches in the Department of Media and Communication at Korea's Yeungnam University. In "Korean's Politeness Strategies," he describes the ways Koreans politely communicate with conversation partners. Following this reading is a report by Hee-Soo Kim, Greg Hearn, Caroline Hatcher, and Ian Weber from the School of Communication at the Queensland University of Technology on the online communication between Koreans and Australians. Their study offers examples of the ways that both Koreans and Australians symbolically structure their worlds.

In "Language Choice Online: Globalization and Identity in Egypt," Mark Warschauer, Ghada R. El Said, and Ayman Zohry also address the issue of language use on the Internet. English did dominate the Internet's early years. The authors examine how young professionals in Egypt use English and Arabic online and discuss this in relation to broader social trends of language, technology, globalization, and identity.

In New Zealand, there has been a demonstrated demand for Maori language education programs. Surveys of parents report that more than half of Maori families prefer primary and secondary schools in which their children could be taught in both Maori and English. Wally Penetito, who is of Tainui descent (Ngati Haua, Ngati Tamatera, Ngati Raukawa), addresses this issue in "Research and Context for a Theory of Maori Schooling." He is a senior lecturer in education at New Zealand's Victoria University with research interests in Maori education, the sociology of education, and teacher education.

Finally, Crispin Thurlow studies a form a hate speech—homophobic pejoratives used by high school youth in Welsh and English schools. He shows how this language reflects social inequalities and power relations and is a major psychological stress in the lives of young bisexual, gay, and lesbian youth.

Many of the world's 5,000 to 6,000 languages (depending on what is counted as dialect or language) are on the verge of extinction. The losses are due to a variety of reasons: war, genocide, fatal natural disaster, government policies, and the adoption of more dominant languages. More than half of the world's languages are moribund or are no longer learned by children and therefore will disappear. There are examples of a dead language being revived. Hebrew, for example, was once no longer spoken on a daily basis but used only by scholars and in worship. It was revived as a spoken language in the late 19th century in a movement led by Eliezer Ben-Yehuda. With the founding of the state of Israel, Hebrew was taught in Israeli schools and many immigrants shifted to the language. Whether from Russia, Europe, the Middle East, Africa, or the Americas, Jewish immigrants by and large speak Hebrew. Hebrew is now a native language for over 3 million people.

Only about 10% of the world's languages are spoken by more than 100,000 people. It is estimated that 90% of the world's languages will be dead or moribund 100 years from now. The loss of any language means the loss of most of the culture of those who spoke it and the loss of the knowledge that culture had about its world codified in its language.

The readings in this section all show us how culture is shared and revealed through verbal symbols and how it can be said that communication and culture are truly inseparable.

REFERENCES

Cann, R. L., Stoneking, M., & Wilson, A. C. (1987, January 1). Mitochondrial DNA and human evolution. *Nature, 325*, 31–36.

Cavalli-Sforza, L., Menozzi, P., & Piazza, A. (1994). *The history and geography of human genes*. Princeton, NJ: Princeton University Press.

Reading 2.1

Babel Revisited

PETER MÜHLHÄUSLER

Linguistic diversity is a resource whose value has been widely underestimated.

In the biblical story of the Tower of Babel, the descendants of Noah tried to build a tower leading to heaven, but God frowned on their presumption and sabotaged the common language that enabled them to communicate. This story, which portrays linguistic diversity as a divine punishment, has dominated Western thinking about languages for centuries and as a result many people believe that a multiplicity of languages is undesirable.

I believe, on the other hand, that linguistic diversity should not be seen as a problem but as an essential resource and that there is an urgent need to reverse policies and practices that currently threaten thousands of small languages. Unless this is done, the chance to learn from the cumulative insights, successes and errors of a large proportion of the human species will be lost forever.

THE ATTRACTIONS
OF A SINGLE LANGUAGE

There have been many attempts to replace the diversity of human languages with a single language. This goal was vigorously pursued by the philosophers of the European Enlightenment and, in the latter half of the nineteenth century, by the supporters of artificial languages such as Volapük and Esperanto which attracted millions of followers around the globe. Many Esperantists hoped not only that Esperanto would one day become a universal auxiliary language but that at a later stage it would be the world's *only* language.

The idea of the modern nation-state also provides a powerful inspiration for those who are committed to reducing linguistic diversity: A common language is often seen as a necessary binding ingredient for new nations. Only 200 years ago, French was not the mother tongue of the majority of people born in France, whereas today, non-French-speakers living in France belong to a small and shrinking minority. What happened in Western Europe in the past is being repeated nowadays in states such as Indonesia, where Bahasa Indonesia developed from being a small auxiliary language into the country's main language and will soon be the mother tongue of more Indonesians than any other language.

It would be no exaggeration to say that the choice of a single national language is often regarded as a precondition for all modernization. No matter what language is chosen—an introduced language such as English, French,

Mandarin or Russian, or a newly-developed language such as Filipino—a basic requirement is that it should be fully intertranslatable, that is, capable of expressing the concepts and distinctions that are needed in the modern world. But the need for intertranslatable languages has an unfortunate side effect—the destruction of small languages as outmoded and irrelevant.

The processes of streamlining which are taking place in the field of language can be compared to the streamlining of the world's plant and animal species. Both developments have been promoted by people acting with the best of intentions—reducing the cost of communication in the first case and feeding the world's growing population in the second. Regrettably, those people had only a very limited understanding of the nature and function of diversity.

In recent years there has been a growing realization of the importance of biological diversity, and even more recently the voices of those advocating linguistic and cultural diversity have become louder. However, the importance of linguistic diversity has not yet aroused widespread public concern; nor has the notion that "linguistic ecology" needs the same amount of care as natural ecology. There are, however, a number of parallels between the two. First, all present-day diversity is the outcome of processes that took a very long time: millions of years in the case of biodiversity, at least 100,000 years in the case of linguistic diversity. And once genuine diversity is lost, it cannot be easily restored, in spite of progress in bioengineering and linguistic engineering. A second, equally important similarity is that linguistic diversity and diversity in the natural world are both functional. The 10,000 or so languages that exist today reflect necessary adaptations to different social and natural conditions. They are the result of increasing specialization and finely tuned adaptation to the changing world.

ONE WORLD OR MANY?

To understand the nature of this fine-tuning, we need to contrast two theories about the relationship between language and the world. One theory, known as the mapping or labeling view, maintains that we live in one world that consists of many parts and each language provides a different set of labels for the same set of parts. According to this theory, the differences between languages are only superficial and all languages are fully intertranslatable.

The second theory holds that most perceptions of the world and parts of the world are brought into being and sustained by languages. Speakers of different languages, therefore, do not perceive the same world. Instead, different languages emphasize and filter various aspects of a multi-faceted reality in a vast number of ways.

If we accept this theory, each language may be seen as a provisional interpretation of a world so complex that the only hope for understanding it is to approach it from as many different perspectives as possible. If we regard each language as the result of a long history of human endeavour to gain knowledge of the world, we may begin to see why linguistic diversity is an invaluable resource rather than an obstacle to progress.

Different languages communicate different perceptions of reality in a number of ways. These include differences in vocabulary, differences in the grammatical information that is expressed, and differences in the boundary between what is regarded as literal truth and what is regarded as metaphorical.

Virtually all human knowledge depends on having criteria with which to determine similarities and differences. Doctors need to know, for instance, whether or not the red spots on the foreheads of two patients are symptoms of the same disease. Psychologists need to know whether two forms of behaviour are manifestations of the same psychological state, and biologists need to know whether two animals are members of the same species. In most instances, reliable criteria for similarities and differences are difficult to come by and decisions are usually determined by the available lexical resources.

One well-known area is that of colour names. The same area of the colour spectrum may have one name in one language, two names in a second language, and three names in a third. Not making a lexical distinction between, say, green and blue (as in the Welsh *glas*), means not focusing on the difference between the two colours in real life. In the field of plants, there are again considerable differences. Where certain plants are central to a culture, an amazing degree of lexical fine-tuning can occur. Many New Guinea languages, for example, make dozens of distinctions between different types of cordi-lyne leaves, according to whether such leaves are used for dressmaking, decoration, magic or other purposes. Similar fine-tuning can also be observed in the sub-languages spoken by specialist groups in Western societies, for example, the sub-language of motor mechanics, painters, doctors or bankers.

Suddenly to get rid of all these fine distinctions developed by specialists over centuries would greatly impoverish a language such as English, making it incapable of referring to anything except in general terms. Abandoning language diversity could have similar consequences on a global scale. Specialist vocabularies and specialist knowledge, about phenomena as diverse as types of snow, useful plants, types of weather or ways of dealing with children would suddenly be lost.

LANGUAGE AND
THE BREAKDOWNS OF
TRADITIONAL SOCIETIES

One area that offers many examples of differences of this kind is kinship. Anthropological linguists have accumulated a vast amount of evidence as to how different languages focus in different ways on the shared properties and differences among family members. While in English, the word "sister" refers to the female sibling of both males and females, in Tok Pisin of Papua New Guinea, a pidgin language that often reflects a Melanesian interpretation of the world, the word "sister" means sibling of the opposite sex. A brother calls his sister "sister" and a girl calls her brother "sister." In some Aboriginal languages in Australia and other languages in Melanesia, the same word is used to refer to both grandfather and grandchild. In these instances, having the same label usually means getting the same treatment. Such labels reinforce solidarity within the group. For example, giving the same name to members of different generations can be a way of reducing generational conflict. The rather impoverished inventory of words in most modern Western languages may not be sufficient to sustain complex extended family networks, and the replacement of an indigenous language with more distinctions by a Western language with fewer distinctions could be a factor in the breakdown of traditional societies.

Another area in which there are considerable differences between languages is the naming of parts of the body. In many languages, including some spoken in West Africa, the term "hand" covers either the whole arm or the arm up to the elbow. The West African practice of gripping another person's lower arm when "shaking" is a reflection of a different linguistic organization. In my own native Alemannic, the terms "foot" and "leg" are not distinguished lexically, something that caused me considerable confusion when learning High German, where the distinction is made. In Melanesia, dogs are said to have two arms and two legs rather than four legs, and centipedes are perceived as having many arms rather than many legs.

Most of the examples given so far have dealt with the different ways in which languages lexically subdivide a fairly tangible reality—the reality of colour or the reality of plants and people. There are other less tangible realities where perception is even more closely linked to language: for example, the names of emotions or states of mind. The German word *Gemütlichkeit* does not compare neatly with the English word "cosiness," nor is "depression" the same as the outmoded "melancholy." The absence of words for depression or sadness is certain Polynesian languages would seem to correspond to the absence of the associated phenomena.

Language is even more directly involved in the creation of philosophical and religious approaches to the world. It sustains the meaningfulness of ideas such as solipsism, "the view that self is all that exists or can be known" or of elements in systems used to explain the workings of the universe such as "phoneme" in linguistics or "phlogiston" in eighteenth-century science. Death in traditional Polynesian languages is described by a number of words, ranging from initial permanent unconsciousness to the ultimate disintegration of the body. The practice of "reburial" reflects this linguistic distinction.

Another important difference between languages relates to the ways in which they require speakers to make important choices about the people they are addressing. This is well known to English speakers who find that when they learn French the neutral English second person singular pronoun "you" has to translated into "tu" or "vous," depending on the degree of politeness or solidarity being shown towards the person addressed. When using nouns, some languages do not have number distinctions at all, while others like Fijian need to express at all times whether the speaker is talking about one, two, three, a few or more than a few entities. In some New Guinea Highland languages, a sentence such

as, "The pig broke the fence," cannot be said in this kind of neutral manner. Using grammatical endings the speaker has to indicate whether this is a report of what he or she has actually observed or whether it is an inference from indirect evidence such as pig droppings or hearsay.

METAPHORICALLY SPEAKING

The expression of social distinctions, numbers or the credibility of a piece of information can lead to interesting quandaries. One wonders what advertising is like in Aiwo, a language spoken in the Solomon Islands in which all words referring to useless objects have to be given a prefix indicating uselessness. How could one describe a nuclear power station in Aiwo? Would one have to use a prefix indicating the class of entities that are dormant but liable to sudden change?

The influence of certain semantic distinctions may be so strong that it leads languages to interpret reality in very different ways, that may be described as either event-dominated or object-dominated. Many standard European languages can be regarded as object-dominated because of their strong tendency to convert processual verbs into abstract, object-like nouns. For example, the subject matter of linguistics is not perceived as the activity of speaking but as an object termed "language." One of the consequences for this area of enquiry is that, while speaking always involves people, and a spatial, temporal situation, the abstract term *language* suggests an object that can be analysed as something self-contained.

Equally important in Western languages is the very strong presence of causality. Verbs such as "to teach" or "to cure" can be paraphrased as "to cause to learn" and "to cause to get better." However, there is a very different, equally valid way of looking at what goes on in the classroom or in a doctor's practice, as seen in languages such as Wintu, an American

Indian language spoken in California, which favours comitative, or "being with" interpretations. In a Wintu's perception, the doctor takes part in the patient's recovery and the teacher shares the learner's learning progression. It is not at all clear that a causative view of these matters necessarily leads to better teaching or healing practice.

Languages, finally, differ according to the metaphors their speakers live by. Western life tends to be dominated by a small number of metaphors. The saying "time is money," for instance, reinforces cultural practices such as charging by the hour, trying to save money by getting things done more quickly and the view that there are more economical and less economical uses of time. Needless to say, such a metaphor does not occur in non-monetary, traditional societies where work and gain are measured in terms other than quantity of time "spent." Another prominent Western metaphor is that of "rule," the idea that there is an abstract ruler of the universe who has laid down the rules of nature. So deeply entrenched is this metaphor that scientists believe that it is literally true and are convinced they can discover the rules of nature, a belief that has only recently begun to weaken as a consequence of discoveries by chaos theoreticians. Researchers on neural networks are now beginning to question the idea that language learning involves rule and rule systems, a dogma of linguistics for many decades. It is quite likely that metaphors of other cultures not dominated by the idea that the world needs to be governed by rules may produce future breakthroughs in scientific thinking.

Environmental discourse provides a striking example of why learning from different languages may be very important. Western languages have many gaps in their ability to express aspects of the environment. The number of edible plants the average Westerner can name contrasts very unfavourably with the many hundreds of names known to the average speaker of a South American Indian language.

There is now a growing awareness of "green" issues, and "green" vocabulary is on the increase. We have words such as "biodiversity," "recycling" and "lead-free petrol" but not all of these terms are equally suitable for environmental discourse. For instance, the word "resource" suggests that the notion of regeneration is applicable to both renewable and non-renewable resources and the very term "environment" suggests a division between humans and what is around them, an idea that is not widely found in the languages of the world.

The combined propensity of Western languages to emphasize human causativity and control and their object-dominated character suggests that the best course of action is one of establishing control over a small bounded area and not, as other languages would suggest, learning to understand an undivided whole.

Note also the underdifferentiation between different types of control in languages such as English, where the possessive pronoun "my" can be used to express three situations:

A controls B = my child (A's child)

B controls A = my father (A's father)

A and B reciprocally control one another = my partner

In Barrai, a language of Papua New Guinea, these three categories are clearly distinguished by different pronominal forms. Interestingly, to express the notion of "my land" in Barrai, one uses the pronoun for mutual control suggesting interdependence, the need for balance and co-operation between people and the land. Western metaphors of the land are dominated by the distinction between human beings and the non-human world, and the idea that human beings are a privileged species, the rulers or controllers for whose benefit the rest of the world was created. Recent metaphors such as "Spaceship Earth" reinforce the idea that the Earth exists predominantly for the benefit of its human inhabitants, and the idea of environmental management and eco audits is just another version of the old picture of human beings as rulers over the rest of creation.

I would suggest that Westerners are trapped within the limitations imposed on them by their languages and this is one of the principal reasons for the lack of genuine progress in the environmental sciences. This example of environmental discourse illuminates the dangers of monolingualism and monoculturalism and shows how many different interpretations—and many different languages—are necessary to solve the problems facing the world.

Peter Mühlhäusler of Germany taught linguistics at the Technical University of Berlin, Oxford University in the United Kingdom, and the University of Adelaide in Australia.

Reading 2.2

Africa

The Power of Speech

AMADOU HAMPÂTÉ BÂ
TEXTS CHOSEN BY HÉLÈNE HECKMANN

"Listen," says old Africa. "Everything speaks. Everything is speech. Everything around us imparts a mysterious enriching state of being. Learn to listen to silence, and you will discover that it is music."

A LIFE-FORCE

The Bambara tradition of the Komo[1] teaches that the Word, Kuma, is a fundamental force emanating from the Supreme Being himself—Maa Ngala, creator of all things. It is the instrument of creation: "That which Maa Ngala says, is!" proclaims the cantor—the singing priest—of the god Komo.

Reprinted with permission from the *UNESCO Courier*, September, 1993, pp. 20–24, Amadou Hampâté Bâ.

Maa Ngala, it is taught, deposited in Maa the three potentialities of ability, willing and knowing. But all the forces to which he is the heir lie dumb within him. They are static, till speech comes and sets them into motion. Then, vivified by the divine Word, they begin to vibrate. At a first stage they become thoughts, at a second sound, and at a third words.

In the same way, since speech is the externalization of the vibrations of forces, every manifestation of a force in any form whatever is to be regarded as its speech. That is why everything in the universe speaks: everything is speech that has taken on body and shape.

Let me point out, though, that at this level the terms "speaking" and "listening" refer to realities far more vast than those we usually attribute to them. It is said: "The speech of Maa Ngala is seen, is heard, is smelled, is tasted, is touched." It is a total perception, a knowing in which the entire being is engaged.

If speech is strength, that is because it creates a bond of coming-and-going which generates movement and rhythm and therefore life and action. This movement to and fro is symbolized by the weaver's feet going up and down, as we shall see later.

In the image of Maa Ngala's speech, of which it is an echo, human speech sets latent forces into motion. They are activated and aroused by speech—just as a man gets up, or turns, at the sound of his name.

Speech may create peace, as it may destroy it. It is like fire. One ill-advised word may start a war just as one blazing twig may touch off a great conflagration. According to a Malian adage: "What puts a thing into condition [that is, arranges it, disposes it favourably]? Speech. What damages a thing? Speech. What keeps a thing as it is? Speech."

Tradition, then, confers on Kuma, the Word, not only creative power but a double function of saving and destroying. That is why speech, speech above all, is the great active agent in African magic.

But for spoken words to produce their full effect they must be chanted rhythmically, because movement needs rhythm, which is itself based on the secret of numbers. Speech must reproduce the to-and-fro that is the essence of rhythm.

In ritual songs and incantatory formulae, therefore, speech is the materialization of cadence. And if it is considered as having the power to act on spirits, that is because its harmony creates movements, movements which generate forces, those forces then acting on spirits which themselves are powers for action.

THE WEAVER
AND THE BLACKSMITH

In the traditional African society, every artisanal function was linked with an esoteric knowledge transmitted from generation to generation and taking its origin in an initial revelation. The craftsman's work was sacred because it imitated the work of Maa Ngala and supplemented his creation. Bambara tradition, in fact, teaches that creation is not yet finished and that Maa Ngala, in creating our earth, left things there unfinished so that Maa, his interlocutor, might supplement or modify them with a view to leading nature towards its perfection. The craftsman's activity in operation was supposed to repeat the mystery of creation. It therefore focused an occult force which one could not approach without respecting certain ritual conditions.

That is why traditional craftsmen accompany their work with ritual chants or sacramental rhythmic words, and their very gestures are considered a language. In fact the gestures of each craft reproduce in a symbolism proper to each one the mystery of the primal creation, which, as I indicated earlier, was bound up with the power of the Word. It is said:

The smith forges the Word,
The weaver weaves it,
The leather-worker curries it smooth.

Let us take the example of the weaver, whose craft is linked with the symbolism of the creative Word deploying itself in time and space.

A man who is a weaver by caste is the repository of the secrets of the thirty-three pieces that are basic to the loom, each of which has a meaning. Before starting work, the weaver must touch each piece of the loom, pronouncing words or litanies that correspond to the forces of life embodied in them.

The movement of his feet to and fro as they go up and down to work the pedals recalls the original rhythm of the creative Word, linked with the dualism of all things and the law of cycles. His feet are supposed to speak as follows:

Fonyonko! Fonyonko! dualism! dualism!

When one goes up the other goes down.

There is the death of the king and the coronation of the prince, the death of the grandfather and the birth of the grandson. . . .

[In Africa, to say that someone is dead, people use the expression: "His feet are in agreement," in other words "they have ceased moving." "For the wise elders" notes Amadou Hampâté Bâ,[2] "life is movement and movement begins with the contradiction of the limbs. . . . Non-contradiction means death." The shuttle, the throwing of which by each hand evokes a need to "let go," is supposed to say: "Life is a constant toing and froing, a permanent gift of self."]

The gestures of the weaver as he operates his loom [like those of the smith or other traditional craftsmen] are creation in action. His words accompanying his gestures are the very song of Life.

As for the smith, he is the repository of the secret of transmutations. He is pre-eminently the Master of Fire. His origin is mythical and in Bambara tradition he is called the First Son of the Earth.

The elements of the smithy are linked to a sexual symbolism, itself the expression or reflection of a cosmic process of creation.

Thus the two round bellows worked by the smith's assistant are likened to the male's two testicles. The air they are filled with is the substance of life, sent through a kind of tube that represents the phallus into the furnace of the forge, this representing the womb where the transforming fire works.

The traditional smith may enter the smithy only after a ritual purifying bath prepared with a decoction of certain leaves or barks or roots of trees chosen according to the day. Then the smith garbs himself in a special way, since he may not penetrate the forge dressed in just any sort of clothes.

Every morning he purifies the smithy by means of special fumigations based on plants he knows of.

These operations over, cleansed of all outside contacts he has had, the smith is in a sacramental state. He has become pure once again and is equivalent to the primordial smith. Only now can he create in imitation of Maa Ngala, by modifying and fashioning matter.

Before beginning work, he invokes the four mother elements of creation (earth, water, air, fire), which are necessarily represented in the forge: there is always a receptacle filled with *water, fire* in the furnace, *air* sent by the bellows, and a little pile of *earth* beside the forge.

During his work, he pronounces special words as he touches each tool. Taking his anvil, which symbolizes feminine receptivity, he says: "I am not Maa Ngala, I am the representative of Maa Ngala. It is he who creates and not I." Then he takes some water or an egg and presents it to the anvil, saying: "Here is your bride-price."

He takes his hammer, which symbolizes the phallus, and strikes the anvil a few times to sensitize it. Communication established, he can begin work.

The apprentice must not ask questions. He must only look and blow. This is the mute stage of apprenticeship. As he advances in knowledge, he blows in rhythms that are more and more complex, each one having a meaning. During the oral stage of apprenticeship, the master will gradually transmit all his skills to the pupil, training him and correcting him until he acquires mastery. Then, after a liberation ceremony, the new smith may leave his master and set up his own forge. [In most cases he will previously have made a tour of the country to work for other great masters from whom he will have learned not only new techniques but also new practical or occult skills that form part of the great initiatory tradition of the blacksmiths.]

The smith must have knowledge covering a vast sector of life. With his reputation as an occultist, his mastery of the secrets of fire and iron make him the only person entitled to perform circumcision—the grand Master of the Knife in the Komo initiation is always a smith. In addition to all his knowledge of metallurgy, he has a perfect knowledge of the Sons of the womb of the Earth (mineralogy) and the secrets of plants and the bush. He knows what kind of vegetation covers the earth, where it contains a particular metal, and he can detect a lode of gold merely by examining plants and pebbles.

He knows the incantations to the earth and the incantations to plants. Nature being regarded as living and as animated by forces, any act that disturbs it must be accompanied by a ritual behaviour designed to save and safeguard its sacred equilibrium, for everything is connected, everything echoes everything else, every action agitates the life-forces and sets up a chain of consequences the repercussions of which are felt by man.

The craft or the traditional function can be said to sculpt man's being. The whole difference between modern education and oral tradition lies there. What is learned at the Western school, useful as it may be, is not always *lived;* whereas the inherited knowledge of oral tradition is embodied in the entire being.

The instruments or tools of a craft give material form to the sacred word; the apprentice's contact with the craft obliges him to live the word with every gesture he makes.

That is why oral tradition taken as a whole cannot be summed up as transmission of stories or of certain kinds of knowledge. It *generates and forms a particular type of man.* One can say that there is the smiths' civilization, and so on.

Thus the traditional artisan, imitating Maa Ngala, repeating the primal creation by his gestures, used to perform, not work, in the purely economic sense of the word, but a sacred function that brought the fundamental forces of life into play and engaged him in his entire being. In the secrecy of his workshop or his smithy he partook of the renewed mystery of eternal creation.

NOTES

1. One of the great initiation schools of the Mande (Mali).
2. Interview in *Jeune Afrique* magazine, Paris (N° 1095, 30 December 1981).

Amadou Hampâté Bâ, Malian writer, historian, and philosopher won international recognition for his half century of studies of African oral traditions south of the Sahara.

Hélène Heckmann of France, a former staff member of the French Senate, is the literary legatee of the late Amadou Hampâté Bâ and has charge of his manuscript archives.

Reading 2.3

Mexican American Ethnicity in Biola, CA

An Ethnographic Account of Hard Work, Family, and Religion

ERIC AOKI

In exploring the use of "avowed" and "ascribed" ethnic labels used by community members in Biola, California (Martin & Nakayama, 2000, p. 114), this study investigates an understanding of ethnicity by forging connections with interlocutors' cultural ways of life. In a call for refining ethnicity, Methuen (1983) asserts, "the extent to which internal or external factors shape or foster ethnicity has not been fully documented" (p. 210). In this study, ethnicity is made meaningful, not only by historical associations, but also by the management and self-presentation of identities in talk and the communicative conduct of those interlocutors who associate with particular ethnic labels.

Ethnicity, as one facet of identity, is managed and actively constructed in conversation (Otis, 1993). In this article, I argue that locating the use of ethnic labels in talk provides definitive markers to help unpack cultural information from the surrounding discourse that gives meaning to the ethnic label and,

hence, ultimately informs ethnicity. The use of ethnic labels in talk, then, both marks a presentation of ethnic self by the speaker and simultaneously remains open to new constructions with other interlocutors. This simultaneous existence of ethnic identity, marked as both situational and communicatively evolving, is what allows interlocutors to understand one another as ethnic people and not as static or fixed stereotypical entities.

From this ethnographic project, I present three themes (that is, "hard work," "family," and "religion") that inform Mexican American ethnicity in Biola. Although, I walked into the cultural context with a notion that I was interested in issues of family and community, my initial observation and informal/formal chats with community members served to guide my more particularized questions with the interlocutors. Through observations and interviews I came to understand the centrality of issues that the participants enacted and discussed in situ (for example, discourses on hard work, family, and religion). Prior to addressing these three central themes, I, first, review the concepts of ethnicity, culture, and speech codes as used in this study.

REVIEW OF CONCEPTS

In this study, ethnicity[1] is used to refer to the synthesis of common themes of behaviors and perceptions that interlocutors enact and talk about in conjunction with avowed or ascribed ethnic labels of historical connectedness and present-day, cultural group affiliation. J. A. Fishman (1983) explains:

> Ethnicity is a bound (self-perceived and/or ascribed by others, with or without objective justification) to a historically continuous authenticity collectivity. Thus, ethnicity assists individuals in coping with the existential question of "Who am I?" and "What is special about me?" by contextualizing these questions in terms of putative ancestral origins and characteristics. These questions are therefore illuminated in terms of "Who are my own kind of people?" and "What is special about us?" and come to be answered at the level of peopleness *being* . . . peopleness *doing* . . . and peopleness *knowing*. . . . Language is a central component in all three of the above experiential components. (p. 128)

Additionally, Otis (1993) asserts that speakers establish social identities of self and others through both social acts (behaviors) and stances (point of view or attitude). Taking into consideration both of these elements, Otis (1992) discusses indexicality as "a property of speech through which cultural contexts such as social identities [e.g., gender, ethnicity] and social activities [e.g., gossip session, family life] are constituted by particular stances and acts" (p. 335). At one level, using an ethnic label in talk can serve as an explicitly stated, basic, historical descriptor of self (for example, "I'm a Mexican American," "As a Mexican

American"). In addition, Otis (1990) asserts that "language signals or *indexes* sociocultural information at the level of particular communicative events" (p. 292). An example of this would be the interlocutor who code switches at a moment of conversational excitement, nervousness, or other emotional trigger, or the call of the context or both. Such code switching also is a communicative manifestation of ethnicity. Code switching enacts an identity claim without making an explicit statement such as "I am Mexican American." It illuminates the communicative event, as cultural site, with a focus on the dynamics of language use to accomplish particular sociocommunicative ends. I propose that both the historical and constructed descriptors are important when providing accounts of ethnicity.

Finally, Otis (1993) outlines three minimal criteria for determining a connection of social identity to a social interaction. These criteria include shared cultural and linguistic conventions for constructing particular acts and stances; shared economic, political, or other social histories and conventions that associate those acts and stances with the social identity a speaker attempts to project; and whether other interlocutors are able and willing or are otherwise constrained to ratify the speaker's claims to that identity.

Given this conceptualization, ethnicity does not, in and of itself, constitute a culture of a speech community. Rather than working from the premise that a phenomenon such as "Mexican American culture" exists, I use Philipsen's (1992) definition of culture as a "socially constructed and historically transmitted pattern of symbols, meanings, premises, and rules" (p. 7). I believe that this definition, although arguably viewed as liberal in scope, allows for a more distinct and detailed assessment of what constitutes culture systematically, especially when assessing culture via various ethnic labels used by interlocutors in a speech community.

Features such as geography, politics, cultural background, and common language influence the ways of life of people, but those features do not constitute the operationalization of how I define and research culture and ethnicity. I advocate Philipsen's (1997) position that "culture refers to a particular system and not to the geographic or political unit in which it is found" (p. 125). Additionally, Horowitz (1983) advocates an approach that concentrates on systems of speech and other communicative behavior as a site for illuminating culture.

Thus the view of culture espoused in this study is responsive to the premise that people who use different ethnic labels to avow ethnicity can enact the same speech codes—"A speech code, then, is defined here as a system of socially constructed symbols and meanings, premises, and rules, pertaining to communicative conduct" (Philipsen, 1997, p. 126). The primary benefit of this move is to avoid the limitations of assigning a closed system of behaviors to only one ethnic group, for example, claiming that a specific behavior is enacted because he or she is Mexican American.

As the above section suggests, a focus on ethnic labels, discourse, and other communicative conduct provides a means of operationalizing ethnicity.[2] The goal is to avoid the explanation of interactions or communication problems with an essentialized view of members of any ethnic group. Rather, I use ethnic labels in talk, the content of the interlocutors' discourse, and field observations to operationalize the larger issue of ethnicity, as it is expressed and experienced by the people whose spoken life I have studied. The emphasis is placed on terms of identification, cultural patterns, and cultural domains. From this, I forge connections with the communicative patterns and themes of interlocutors who avow particular ethnic labels to ultimately inform a more global conceptualization of their sense of ethnicity. With this careful accounting of ethnic labels, social context, discourse, and other communicative conduct, I argue that assessments of culture and ethnicity can be illuminated while also providing the opportunity for informants to label their own ethnic group affiliations.

METHODOLOGY

Biola, California[3] provides a rich context for understanding ethnic individuals in a diverse society. The community history is one of ethnic people living together in close proximity over several generations. While in Biola, I learned a great deal about the lives, the struggles, and the ethnic themes of Mexican America[4] interlocutors[5] as well as about the community in which they reside.

As an ethnographer in the field, I spent approximately four summers (that is, 1993–1996, June-August) and several winter and spring breaks collecting field observations and conducting formal interviews with 43 informants.[6] In addition to these formal interviews, I conducted countless informal talks with the people of Biola. Although I visited the elementary school and community center, I spent the majority of my time talking with individuals in their homes.

TO BE MEXICAN AMERICAN IN BIOLA[7]

In this study, I present three general themes found in the discourse and communicative behavior of Biola interlocutors of Mexican descent: hard work, family, and religion.[8] Specifically, I assess the discourse of informants who self-identified with any of the Mexican American ethnic labels (for example, Mexican, Hispanic, Chicano/a, and Mexican American) and who discussed these three themes. Additionally, ethnic-other interlocutors also discussed these themes when talking about people who align with these related ethnic labels. In some instances, the ethnic labels were used, explicitly, in conjunction with the topics in the interviews. For example, regarding the label "Mexican" and the topic of work a statement was made: "This *Mexican* people is different than any other kind of people. They just, whatever they happen to make in a week, they spend another week to work for another check for another week." I provide and discuss examples such as this one for each of the three themes. Additionally, I provide examples where the informants who self-identify with or who are associated with the Mexican American related labels discuss the themes. For example, Raul,[9] a self-identified "Mexican American," states how the children of Biola receive "first-hand knowledge of how the farm operates."

The following research question was developed to address generally the connection between the compilation of Mexican American related labels and the thematic topics of interlocutors' discourse and communicative practices:

> RQ1: What general themes emerge from analysis of the discourse and observed communicative practices of speakers in Biola who identify with the related Mexican American ethnic labels (that is, Mexican, Hispanic, Chicano/a, Mexican American, Spanish)?

To understand further the formal talks conducted with the informants, I use Spradley's (1980) "single semantic relationship" (p. 93) cultural tool to organize interlocutor utterances of what it means, generally, to be Mexican American in Biola. In addition, I use observational field notes to draw conclusions about the dynamics and patterns of self, other, family, and community—that is, the themes that help constitute Mexican American ethnicity.

I use the general label "Mexican American" to account for the themes that emerged in the talk and in observations of interlocutors who used or who aligned with the variety of ancestrally and politically oriented ethnic labels "Mexican," "Hispanic," "Mexican American," "Chicano/a," and "Spanish." Here, the goal is to provide a holistic account of Mexican American ethnicity in Biola.

Table 1 displays 25 quoted phrases or utterances spoken by my Biola interlocutors in our conversations. In each case either (a) I have taken the phrase or utterance from a larger passage in which the speaker linked some attribute to someone or some collection of people labeled "Mexican," "Hispanic," "Chicano/a," "Mexican American," "Spanish"; or (b) the speaker's linkage is preserved in the quoted passage. Table 1 presents interlocutor utterances in which attribution or characteristics of Mexican Americans are the semantic focus. For example, "X is an attribution (characteristic) of Y" (Spradley, 1980, p. 93). In this study, more specifically, X is an attribution (characteristic) of *Mexican Americans*. The ethnic label key is used to show that each thematic element (for example, hard work) was brought up in the discourse of interlocutors who used or identified with the labels or who were associated with the particular labels (for examples, M, MA, H). Using a compilation of interlocutors' use of and identification with the related ethnic labels, Table 1 provides a general overview of characterizations of Mexican Americans in Biola.

Although Table 1 presents a variety of thematic elements to explore in detail, in the remainder of this study, I discuss three of the themes displayed in Table I (that is hard work, family as clan, and Catholicism). I concentrate on these three themes because they remain central to the focus of family and community in Biola. These themes also are ones that patterned out in my observations and surfaced frequently in formal and informal discussions. With this in mind, I begin this next section with a discussion of work, "hard work" as many interlocutors have put it, which speaks

Table 1   Characterizations of Mexican Americans in Biola, California

Utterances Taken from the Informant Interviews

— "Hard work" (H, MA); "You work together, this is actually our background"; "Mexican people . . . they work very hard these people" (M, MA); "Farm workers" (M, MA)

— "Family"; [Like a] "clan"; "My family is my whole life"; "Real supportive family" (M, MA, H)

— "Very Catholic Oriented"; "Catholic"; "I was raised a Catholic"; "Catholic movies . . . and have rosaries" (M, MA, S)

— "Not involved" [at the school]; "Lack of involvement" (MA, M, H, C); "Feel that they don't have anything to contribute" [at school] (H)

— "I don't see the, you know, to dream for a future, no, this Mexican people is a different kind of people" (M, MA)

— "Combining the histories of both sides, speaking the language of Spanish as well as English" (C); "Not really fluent in Spanish" (H, C)

— "Listening to Mexican music" (M, MA, H)

— "Born and raised here, they're Americanized"; "People without a country" (C)

— "Kids in gangs" (M, MA); "Kids having kids" (M, H)

— "Mexican American Political Association (MAPA) member and politically active" (C); "Chicano's pulling the Chicano community down" (C)

Key: Mexicans (M), Hispanics (H), Mexican Americans (MA), Chicano/as (C), Spanish (S).

to the life condition of many Mexican Americans in Biola.

Hard Work

The people of this community work in a wide variety of jobs. Although there are individuals in the community who own and operate the local businesses (for example, the grocery stores, mechanic shops, butane service, the local tavern, and the hardware store), none are Mexican American. Mexican American interlocutors, however, do work as teachers and aides at Biola Pershing Elementary School. Others perform service work, including working in restaurants, cleaning offices and homes, and working as nurses or office managers in various neighboring cities (for example, Fresno, Madera, Kerman). Mexican American informants also work in the newly built community center, work factory jobs, and provide the strong backbone for jobs related to the

agricultural needs of this farming area (for example, serving as contractors for the labor force, picking grapes, turning raisin trays, and working at packing sheds).

In this section, I analyze two excerpts from conversations in which the topic of work is linked explicitly with Mexican American ethnicity. Jafar (a self-identified "East Indian") and Virginia (a self-identified "Hispanic" and "Mexican American") discuss, respectively, the condition of the Mexican worker and the generation difference of Mexican men in home and work roles. Additionally, I intersperse comments made by Pablo, Raul, and Romona (respectively, a self-identified "Hispanic" and two "Mexican Americans") where the topic of work was discussed.

Many people in Biola articulate that they understand hard work, that they understand what it means to make sacrifices and that they, as Pablo states, know what it means to "put food on the table." In many ways, this tradition of hard work is something that people take pride in and consider as lessons of life. Raul (midthirties, "Mexican American") indicates that in Biola there is a knowledge that the local agricultural area provides. When asking Raul, specifically, about the perks children enjoy in Biola, he states: "First-hand knowledge of how the farm operates. . . . Most city kids don't see that; they see grapes on the table, but don't understand the meaning of hard labor." Along with the "first-hand knowledge" one might learn in a farming community, many people in Biola echo similar sentiments about the reality of struggle and sacrifice. As another interlocutor stated to me in an informal talk on G Street, "these days it is really hard to make a living."

In the following extended excerpt Jafar (middle-aged, "East Indian," new resident to the community) acknowledges in particular the "Mexican" individuals who work the land in this community and who have lived in the community for up to 20 years. When asking Jafar about any other unique characteristics of the people who live in the small town of Biola, he responds:

> They live in small town life, very easy life. They workin' and just spending for food and all that, these people, I don't see them, you know, to dream for the future, no, this Mexican people is different than any other kind of people. They just, whatever they happen to make in a week, they spend another week to work for another check. . . . They work very hard . . . they look [he points to a customer in the store and rubs hands over his body to emphasize how covered in dirt the man is]. Very troubling. They work very hard these people . . . in this hot weather.

Jafar points out that residents of Biola have lived in the town for upward of 20 years, if not a lifetime. He then described the situation as generally a small town, an "easy life." Despite describing the life as easy, Jafar raises the point

that the "Mexican" people are different because they live from paycheck to paycheck with no hope or dreams for the future.

Through subsequent interviews, I learned that "Mexican" in some cases meant people from Mexico and in other cases meant both resident and nonresident interlocutors of Biola. From the passage above, I asked myself the following question: In Jafar's use of the label "Mexican" and the phrase "they work very hard" was he referring to resident, nonresident, or both groups of "Mexicans"? Although it is not explicitly stated in his commentary, I believe that Jafar uses the ethnic label "Mexican" to mean both residents and nonresident groups. When he states early on in the passage that he has talked to many of them and that many have lived their whole life in Biola, this fact of longevity of residency (that is, upward of 20 years) would apply most specifically to the "Mexicans" of Biola who hold U.S. residency. Additionally, during an informal talk with Jafar, he listed quite a few family names in Biola (local names that I recognized) who have credit accounts at his store. When he made the comment, "They just, whatever they happen to make in a week, they spend another week to work for another check for another week," Jafar was likely speaking from a vantage point of understanding the economic situation of his patrons, the longtime Biola community members who owe him money. Nevertheless, Jafar also is aware that people who are "Mexicans" also come from Mexico. At one point in the interview Jafar clarifies, "From Mexico. Most of them didn't have no papers."

Understanding the emphasis on work as a way of life has implications for not only how one might live but how one may be motivated and able both psychologically and economically to invest into goals for the future. Jafar makes the comment that "I don't see them, you know, to dream for the future." Given that Biola is a majority community of

Mexican Americans, the level of motivation for investment into future goals has potentially serious implications for the sustaining of family and community in this predominantly Mexican American social context.

In Biola, some discourse emphasized how the changing times require that men, women, and family members work. Virginia (middle-aged, "Hispanic" and "Mexican American") says, "I mean, it's just a matter of survival; I mean, you pull together, you work together, this is actually our background." This interlocutor-discussed reality has created changes in their attitudes when dealing with the issue of work and roles. Virginia[10] discusses further the focus on the "work ethnic background" of people like her family and of my family, whom she knows.

> *Virginia:* See, you know why, Eric,[11] you have to remember that you come . . . from a background that's work ethnic [sic] wise, to survive, I mean everybody pulled together at the store . . . At the store, you guys all did. . . . Why should it diminish even further into life, you know, as you get older? Say, even if you do come, it's just the fact that those two people sacrificed a lot for you kids, too.
>
> *Eric:* Oh, I know they did, yeah.
>
> *Virginia:* And I mean the thing is, that you've going to be gone out of their lives pretty soon, you'll probably get married, have your own home, you'll have your own job, but the thing is that, I mean, survival is something that . . . it's just a matter of survival, you pull together, you work together, this is actually our background.

In the above passage, Virginia, by bringing up my family background, establishes a connection that she perceives us to share. She emphasizes how a strong work ethic as an element of survival is such a key factor in what she calls "our background." The question that

remained, however, is, Did Virginia mean our working class background or our ethnic background? Despite Virginia's strong focus on the economics of the work situation ("You pull together, you work together, this is actually our background"), I believe she uses the phrase "our background" to mean ethnicity. Virginia and I are both aware that we share a common ethnic background (that is, we both identify with the labels "Mexican," "Hispanic," and "Mexican American"), we shared a common church (St. Patrick's in Kerman, California), and we share a common second language (Spanish). Because the nexus of race and social class are a heavily travelled intersection for many families in Biola and in larger U.S. society, deciphering race and class elements in the phrase "our background" is a complex one. With regard to this complex nexus, Virginia uses the phrase "work ethnic" (she used this phrase in two separate interviews) in place of the more commonly used expression, "work ethic." Although this is likely a linguistic slip, I find it an interesting and poignant slip that accurately captured the strong connection between Mexican Americans and the theme of working to survive.

With a strong emphasis on hard work being a staple for describing Biola families, there is the question of how this way of life has affected the work roles of individuals across generations. Virginia points out both generation and gender distinctions in the following excerpt:

> Men aren't like women. . . . I mean like for me . . . there's always those things that're going to pop up, come up, things that need attention, things that have to have decisions, ah, and I can't wait for my husband to come out with an idea, whatever, because he's slow. I think, ah, Oh, I hate to use the word, basically, Mexican men, we're talking about my generation, aren't like the new generation, ah, not all men, . . . but they're not very, their values are very different from the women. . . . To me, even just the caring, ah, that total

commitment, a man, a Mexican man will always kind of stand, put himself on the pedestal. He's different, he can do anything he wants. I mean, we're talking about my generation . . . to where women were more conscientious of the needs of the household, the family, the community. I think you see that in a lot of the women that came from my time . . . like myself, I would work the house, teach catechism, sing in the choir. . . . If women can be so active, and come at night and do some of my yard, whatever, why can't men?

Virginia provides a perspective on the tension of gender roles particularly held toward Mexican men of her generation who "aren't like the new generation." She believes that older Mexican men create relational distance by viewing themselves on a pedestal, whereas women more often become the caretakers of both family and community. She emphasizes how Mexican men hold different values of responsibility than that of the women. When I asked Virginia, to give me an example of a couple of values, she provided a focus on "the caring" and "total commitment." Virginia believes that women of her generation have traditionally given a lot of themselves. In another segment of the interview, Virginia mentions that her mother carried on the great "matriarchy" of the family household and kept family life in order. She mentions that after her mother passed on she saw herself as "a very important person in this family." As the conversation continues, Virginia makes clear the distinction of her generation with the "new generation" or the "new people." She indicates how the new generation, more specifically her own adult children, most of whom are men, have taken on responsibilities of home, children, and activities. She also states that their wives have taken on "full-time" work outside of the home. Despite these shifts and extensions of traditional roles, Virginia mentions how her daughter, Maria, "already

knows the role," a role that incorporates a commitment to hard work and an understanding of who must take on that work.

Virginia accounts for the changing times by stating, "I see in the new generation that commitment. . . . There's a lot of good new people that are coming up now in, in your new generation, and I see my children like that." In this statement, Virginia acknowledges me as part of the "new generation" that learned "that commitment" by helping out at the family grocery store. I find Virginia's positive outlook on people of my generation to be interesting commentary. Generally speaking, it is not difficult to hear in U.S. society the discourse that implicates my generation for the loss of commitment, morality, and a strong work ethic. Virginia, however, expresses approval of a feature of the "new generation," that it has embraced a value of gender equity, which from her perspective is a step in a positive direction. Finally, Virginia states that the value of commitment and the equity of gender roles are a contributing factor to a "good new people."

In another informant interview, Ramona (early thirties "Mexican American") provides an alternative view of how the roles of men and women in the workforce as well as at home have changed over the years. To my question about the differences between men and women, she answers:

Oh, well, the parents were so strict. . . . The differences is that the men could do whatever they wanted to do, they were men, they were allowed to, but the ladies couldn't, they had to stick to the house and do the homework. . . . Now, it's different. Sometimes my mom takes off, she tells my dad, "I'm going to go to one of my friend's house," she goes all day long, my dad's here by himself, he's got to cook and do everything, ha ha ha hu hu hu.

Like Virginia, Ramona emphasizes the evolving state of gender roles. Interestingly,

Ramona expresses the historical influence of agriculture on the role of women, but when I asked her about the present day she claimed roles were "different." Following this part of our discussion, Ramona continues by talking about how her brother, who lives in a trailer behind the family house, has taken on domestic duties while his wife works outside the home.

Taking into consideration the formal interviews with informants, my observational field notes, and off-the-record talks, I would not conclude that a reversal of traditional gender roles is in fact typical for the families of Biola, but it is present to some degree in some families. Ramona's point that in earlier generations roles other than secretary and teacher would not have been considered appropriate emphasizes change or the broadening of social roles over time.

For most Biola residents, the focus on hard work still remains a part of the present day picture. In today's economic climate, as is the case with many families in the large U.S. society, the need for dual-parent income, family-based income, governmental subsidy or both is felt by people in Biola. As was reported by most informants and many other community members with whom I spoke on the streets, money and educational achievement are two things that the people of this community struggle to attain. Although some individuals have finished high school, earned college degrees, and made decent and honest livings, Biola is still a community where a primary focus is about making ends meet—or as Pablo, an employee at Biola Pershing Elementary School, states, "putting food on the table and clothes on their backs." (Pablo, a self-identified "Hispanic," used the pronoun "their." This use removes him from, necessarily, being included in the description of this way of life.) When talking informally with people around the community, I consistently heard that they have lived good lives. Despite this characterization,

Biolans are very much aware that their community does not reflect the stereotypical, wholesome picture of the "American Dream." That is, Biolans realize that they live without health services, well-paved streets, big homes, and other amenities that often reflect a life of economic security or the idealized lifestyle of financial luxury.

The focus on "hard work" to "make ends meets" is a characterization that is echoed again and again as one asks about life in Biola. As Jafar indicated earlier, this way of life can be one that is "Very troubling. They work very hard these people." Despite the nuance in work roles based on gender and generation differences, it is important to highlight that the family system remains central to the identity of its members who make up the system. Finally, this way of life is not only troubling with regard to the endless generations of struggle to make ends meet, but also troubling in that a heavy concentration on this element of survival as a life priority means that other family and community issues get shoved to the wayside. When we consider the spectrum of Maslow's Hierarchy of Needs (1954, pp. 80–98), we see that the ability to move beyond the plane of maintaining security and shelter needs and towards higher planes of stability and self-actualization remains in constant tension and a challenge to many. In the next section, the focus on Mexican American ethnicity continues, but the focus shifts from hard work to the theme of the family unit. The following research question was designed to explore the unit of family:

RQ2: What characterizations of family life do speakers, who align with Mexican American and related ethnic labels, provide?

In the remainder of this article, I discuss two prominent themes of family that pertain to the interlocutors who aligned themselves with any of the related Mexican American

Table 2   Characterizations of Mexican American Family Life. Utterances Taken from the Informant Interviews

— "Clan thing"; "Addicted to the presence of family"

— "Real supportive family"; "Supporting each other"; "Communication and people"

— "Spend time with the family"; "Love"; "Love each other"

— [Having parents who are] "positive role models"; "Tendency to be with your parents"; "Parents in denial" [of problems with their kids]

— "You get to be more with your children, more at home and stuff"

— [Attending the] "Roman Catholic Church"; "Church is going to be there"

— "Making ends meet"

ethnic labels. The two themes are the closeness and importance of family (family as clan) and the role of religion (Catholicism) in the family unit.

Family As "Clan"

A lengthy stay in Biola is not needed to understand the influence that family and family life has on interlocutors who align generally with the ethnic label Mexican American. Using Spradley's (1980, p. 93) semantic cultural tool, Table 2 summarizes the semantic space of the attributions or characteristics of Mexican American family life. The Mexican American informants discuss in detail the topic of family and its social importance. As self-identified Mexican Americans, many interlocutors state the primacy of family in their lives. In the section that follows, I provide a chorus of voices that express this view. Then I examine two extended excerpts (a joint interview with Virginia and Maria and another with Ramona) that raise the issue of conflict occurring within the context of family.

When asked about what family means, Mexican American informants provided the following comments:

Veronica (twenties): Family means everything.

Delores (middle-aged): Family is, ah, number one. . . . My family is priority, and I have to have my kids in priority because God gave them to me, and he gave 'em to me for a reason, and that's to take care of them and raise them the best I can. So that's my top priority, is my family.

Raul (midthirties): Family means to me working close together, supporting each other, love each other, no matter how bad they might treat you, kids will always be kids. . . . The bottom line is that families that work together love each other.

Enrique (12): Like, I think family is like to, everybody, to be together, and um, everybody to be happy and have what they need, but not like to, into, want a lot of money and try to take it away from people and hurt people. I think family is better like being a happy family, have their food, and everything, everything that they need to live.

Even Enrique, at the age of 12, is able to articulate the prominent role of the family unit to provide the essentials needed to sustain life. In observing interactions with Enrique and his mother, I was consistently drawn to their strong focus on each other, what I described in my field notes as their "comfortable manner" of being together as family.

Although the family unit (in its diversified makeup) is both a present and a defining characteristic in Biola, this does not mean that communication events are without conflict. In an interview with a mother and daughter, Maria (27 "Hispanic" and "Mexican American") and Virginia (middleaged, "Hispanic" and "Mexican American"), the reality of day-to-day tensions were an issue for discussion. The following conversation took place in the family living room upon Virginia's return from work at the packing shed.

Virginia: You know, right now you think your mom is wrong on a lot of issues like someone I know [looking at Maria]. But . . . wait til she finds out, ah, when she has kids, and then she's going to know, her kids are going to think she's wrong, how funny we outgrow each other. . . . Every generation . . . well, things in general.

Maria: Oh, no. She thought . . . I'm taking a course right now, it's Child and Society . . . and I've been studying Toxic Parents . . . and so, I've just been questioning some of her, ah.

Virginia: Oh, we get into a lot of arguments and we disagree on many things. . . . Maria is so used to being on her own, and she gets very moody. . . . I can tolerate my moods because I know where I'm coming from, but her, who hasn't even lived, you know?

Maria and Virginia raise the concern of how influences from outside the family unit impact familial relations. Virginia believes that the arguments, from her perspective, are because of differences in life experience. Virginia also acknowledges that this issue of change happens with families as kids outgrow their parents and establish a life of independence. As a mother, Virginia is convinced that her role and experience place her in a position to see the bigger picture of life.

Although the strong tie to family for Mexican Americans is typically accounted for in literature, what often has been neglected is the coexistence of the parents' and children's desire each to establish a life of independence. As the conversation continues, Virginia discusses this point of independence in the interview:

It's a beautiful thing, and we want it. Oh God, we want it. We want it . . . we want more money for us, we want more time for us, we want more things for us as we get older . . . and so, you know, you want to sever that, that, what it is? That cord, I mean, you just want to say . . . you're on your own, thank God. But it doesn't work that way. They get married, they get divorced, they come back, and have more problems, and this and that, and there's always that continual, "I want, I need," and those, those needs, yet they don't want it, but then they hate you for it, but they take it, but we don't understand "em, and it's a battle, it's a continual battle, do you understand where I'm coming from?

Because Biola family members place such a high value on caring for their children (regardless of age), it is not uncommon to find families doing the types of things that Virginia points out (that is, taking in adult children after divorce or during other problems). Virginia also articulates the strains that this type of obligation to their kids places on the family. Not only do those obligations prevent the parents from having more money, more time, and more things, but it also adds relational strains because their children end up "hating" their parents because of the tension with independence and dependence that accrues with age and situation. Although I use this conflict excerpt to add depth to the research addressing cultural prominence of *la familia,* I also acknowledge that the excerpt can be interpreted to say something about both gendered communication and intergeneration change within a cultural group of speakers.

As I listened to the stories and observed Mexican American families in Biola, the fact that family members had arguments, that children were scolded, and that problems were discussed became increasingly apparent over my summers in Biola. The following conversation with Ramona (early thirties, Mexican American) provides another example of familial relational concerns:

> *Ramona:* Helping one another, showing appreciation for what, you know, help the other one can give, sometimes, you know, there's, huhhh [sigh], times where I think every one of us has always lived, there's always somebody living at my parents' house because they're down and out. . . . There's one moving out and the other one's staying. . . . That's family, that's what it's all about, helping one another.

> *Eric:* How do you think your parents feel about that?

> *Ramona:* Sometimes they, they want to escape from here, hu hu ha ha. But they enjoy the grandkids to drive them nuts, but they enjoy it, and the message, like my dad said, "If we don't help one another, who will?"

Ramona echoes Virginia's concern that the family is the support system during times of being "down and out" and additionally expressed a sigh that captured the overwhelming nature of this cycle that consumes her parents' time and energy—"Sometimes they, they want to escape from here." Nevertheless, Ramona indicates that family is about support. She also states her father's bottom line of, "If we don't help one another, who will?"

In both good times and rough times, family support remains a constant theme. Given the majority of the informants' strong ties to being

"Mexican" in Biola, it is not surprising that informants described their families in terms of being clanlike. For many Mexican American families in Biola, the family unit influences who one is and who one continues to become. Despite the struggles of making ends meet and keeping relations among family members connected, there is strength in knowing that when all else fails, the family remains always a part of one's life. As Virginia states, "My family is my whole life."

Catholicism

As I walked door to door to see who might speak with me about life in Biola, I noticed not the usual signs found on homes in my parents' neighborhood that read "No Solicitors Allowed," but rather signs with the words, "Somos Catolicos" (We are Catholics). Enough of these signs were present in Biola that I asked Angie, a self-identified "Mexican American," to tell me about the signs. She responded that her family was Catholic:

> We're all involved now . . . I, in the confirmation classes . . . and, real active in the . . . youth part of the Catholic [church], and my sister, going to classes right now, my brother going to class right now to make his First Communion, so, we go to church every Sunday if we can. And, it's a pretty big part of our life.

Angie's point that religion is "a pretty big part of our life" captures the essence of the linguistic form *Somos Catolicos*. That is, SOMOS CATOLICOS—a declension of *ser*, to advertise an unchangeable condition, as opposed to *estar*, the changeable. And SOMOS "we are," because Catholics exist in the plural (Rodriguez, 1992, p. 175).

Other interlocutors, who at the end of interviews identified themselves with the Mexican American ethnic labels, echo the importance of Catholicism and of family/community (the "we" or plural elements of religious involvement). For example, Veronica, a self-identified Chicana, states, "God comes first, We're very Catholic oriented." Jose, a self-identified "Mexican American," says, "Religion is still in the family . . . I was raised Catholic and I've been to Christianity, Baptist, but I always go back to my roots of Catholicism." Maria, a self-identified "Mexican American/Hispanic and Catholic," states, "I don't know if we practice our faith from day to day, mainly other than kind of our. They're built into our belief system, but on Sunday, we know the weekend, we know church is going to be there. It's going to be a part of our plans." Virginia, a self-identified "Mexican American and Catholic," also emphasizes the role of religion in stating, "And, the thing is, it's so strange though cause my kids, Eric, I can tell you, I can count on my hand the times they missed mass." Finally, Delores, a self-identified "Hispanic" and "Catholic," says, "I have to have my kids in priority because God gave them to me, and he gave 'em to me for a reason, and that's to take care of them and raise them the best I can."

In addition to the self-identified Mexican American interlocutors who discussed religion, interlocutors used "our nationality" or used an ethnic label to create a more explicit tie to the role of religion in their lives. In the remaining section, I present four excerpts from Antonia, Virginia, Maria, and Jose. Each of them self-identified with at least one of the five related Mexican American ethnic labels while discussing the topic of religion. Although in the first excerpt Antonia did not use an ethnic label explicitly in the context of the conversation about religion, I include the excerpt to add depth to the discussion of the "we" element of religion as defined by this self-identified "Mexican" woman. In the second excerpt, Virginia makes a semiexplicit connection when discussing the elements of "nationality" and the primary role of the Roman

Catholic Church in her family's life. In the remaining two excerpts, Maria and Jose forge explicit connections between the ethnic label Hispanic and being Catholic, or practicing Catholicism.

There is a strong commitment to practicing religion through celebration and, through this practice, keeping in contact with other families in the community. Antonia (midsixties, "Mexican" and "Spanish") discusses this interactive level of religious community: "We're all friends and we get along together, all of us. . . . Well, we just talk . . . Catholic movies . . . or we get together and have rosaries for someone who's passed away." Although Antonia perceives her community relationships to be friendly, the scope of individuals whom she keeps in contact with is framed within common, religious activity. She points out that this group of individuals comes together to talk, to pray rosaries, and to watch Catholic movies. With a focus on these events, the conversation continued:

> *Antonia:* Rosa shows us movies or talks to us about Catholic church, and if somebody dies, we have a rosary . . . together, and then in December we have for 12 days, a rosary in each house, friends. We go to the house, and . . . we celebrate the Virgin de Guadalupe. . . . They're most of the same people . . . that Rosa . . . has got, I don't know how many years. . . . She was the one who first started having a rosary.

> *Eric:* Can you tell me . . . what do you do? I know you pray the rosary.

> *Antonia:* We pray the rosary and then give us coffee, doughnuts, cookies. We get together, remember about years back . . . our kids, and how they, grown up.

Antonia discusses how religious activity has provided a common context to reminiscing about their children growing up and for praying or engaging in other religious activities. Although the people come together and celebrate their families, it is a focus on prayer that brings them together. Finally, religion functions as a shared cultural event where entry into one's home can be accomplished.

Although traditions such as the celebration of the Virgin of Guadalupe prior to Christmas remain in place for interlocutors in the community, informants talk about the changing ways of practicing religion within the family context across different generations. In the next excerpt, the role of religion in life is one that appears to be tested in much the same way as the tensions associated with family independence/dependence.

Virginia (middle-aged, Hispanic, Mexican American, and "a Person") addresses how one's commitment to religion says something about the changing morals and values in U.S. society. When asking Virginia about raising family as a "vocation" (her word), she states:

> It's a very large commitment. You have to pass on to your children the values and tradition of our nationality, the family life, religion, which is one of the basic things, the most important thing in our life, which is the Roman Catholic Church. I remember, you know, picking up the kids, even when we used to work in those days, it was customary to wear long coats, so if you came in from the field, you washed up a little bit, put on the long coat, put a scarf on, and you get all those kids to the Holy Days of Obligation, you get them to Sundays, and of course that was special. . . . Now my children, of course, don't have their faith as I wish they would, but it's there and it, it'll come back to them.

Virginia acknowledges the importance of ensuring that "values and traditions" are connected to issues of "nationality, family, and religion." She believes that raising family is a vocation that requires commitment and

obligation. She also points to the "Holy Days of Obligation" or religion as one of the most basic and important values in her family's life.

In the next phase of the interview, I ask Virginia about her concern that the children are losing the strength of religion. She replies:

> When they were little, they were made to go to church. . . . It was part of the family life. But now they have that choice to make, to go or not to go. And I can't force them, but I can kind of bring back some of those memories when they used to go. They do baptize their children and everything in the church. . . . I see tradition fading a little. . . . The morals and the values aren't there like they used to be at one time.

Virginia believes that the tradition of religion has faded a bit in her family. She attributes this to her children now having a "choice" in matters of attending church. She also highlights that a change in morals and values has impacted the family tradition.

As the interview continued, I questioned Virginia about the fading of morals and values in society. When I asked if she had any ideas about why this might be the case in today's society, she responds:

> With society there's been so many changes. It's hard for children . . . because you see all these things like abortion, you see war, you see the bomb, you see all these things to where it's kind of scary for the young people, and they're so busy. . . . In these times, two people have to work to support the family, mother and father. . . . There's a lot of baby-sitting done in daycare, and there's that missing link between family. At one time, you never took your kid to the neighbor or someplace else, it was always family, that commitment of family holding that bond. Your old people were always kept with you. They took care of them, just like we did with my mom, until she passed away. We never thought of putting her in a

rest home, so I wonder, what are my kids going to do with me? They love you so much. All the energy, all the sacrifices, everything you put into your children, it comes back 10 times or, if not, more.

Often Virginia's concerns are expressed in a broader scope that imply a general focus on families in today's society rather than, necessarily, as a serious concern of only her family. She mentions that, today, daycare has become the replacement for family. Virginia is not only concerned with the loss of "commitment" to the family bond in the early years, however; she is also concerned as someone who is reaching her older years of life. Virginia reflects, briefly, on the possibility of whether her kids would place her in a rest home. Finally, although Virginia expresses concern for the changing times and the effect that has had on children, on many occasions she refers to the "wonderful people" that make up her family.

In this final phase of the interview with Virginia, I ask her to discuss more specifically her parents and whether they might have wondered about what their children would do with them in the later years. She responds: "I think my mother knowing that she was the great matriarch of our family . . . she held us together. So, when she passed away, we kinda scattered a little bit, because our families are so large now." At another point in the interview, however, Virginia states that since her mother's passing, she views herself as being pushed up to the level of being the "important person in the family." Thus, it is a focus on the many elements (that is, "the values and traditions of our nationality, the family life, religion") that Virginia discusses that provides understanding about the importance of keeping family intact.

Given how articulate Virginia is in acknowledging her role in providing spiritual guidance in her children's lives (for example, watching

them from the choir chamber at church to keep an eye on them at mass) and also believing that the strength of her children's faith, as stated earlier, will "come back to them," it is evident that Virginia's eight children have received a significant amount of influence from her in the areas of religion and family. Finally, as a way of responding to her concerns, Virginia states, "They love you so much. All the energy, all the sacrifices, everything you put into your children, it comes back 10 times or, if not, more."

Virginia's daughter, Maria (27, "Hispanic" and "Mexican American"), discusses the influence of church through the years. She brought the topic of church into the conversation and also acknowledged how it is a staple or constant of family that reflects the traditions of the clan:

> Then, there's always church . . . Church in the family's life. We all used to go to the same church, but now each of us has found our own churches. . . . I'm not speaking of different religions . . . but I'm speaking of pastors, congregations that they've taken a liking to.

The connection between family and religion is supported as a relevant one in Maria's talk. Maria discusses the consistency of Catholicism in her family's life despite the diversity of congregations that family members attend because of preferences of "pastors" and "youth-oriented" activities. This division of churches among the family, however, may be a factor that also influences her mother's attitude that religion has lost some of its strength at the family level. Maria explains to me how the choice to pick one's own congregation is something that changed over time. She explains how the children grew up and took on more independent roles. She discusses in detail how the children moved from being initially in her mother's view at church, to the back of the church, and later on to different congregations. As our conversation continues, I ask about religion being "a pretty defining characteristic" of her family. Maria replies:

> I don't know if we practice our faith from day to day. . . . They're built into our belief system, but on Sunday, we know the weekend, we know church is going to be there. . . . It's going to be a part of our plans. . . . We know we don't do certain things because the church rules against then . . . If you use the bathrooms, you'll notice that there's Catholic magazines and things like that. I guess we're just very outright. . . . We're Hispanic and Catholic, so I guess the Virgin Mary does play a big role.

At one point in the interview, Maria points out that religion was a "constant" in her family's life. Although religion is not something that her family practices each day, explicitly, she confirms that church and religion have been built into their belief system and help to define their actions and home environment. Finally, Maria makes an explicit link between ethnicity and the topic of religion when she states, "we're Hispanic and Catholic, so I guess the Virgin Mary does play a big role."

The influence of church in many of the informant's lives is one that resonates as a significant, but also everyday, foundation of life. When asked about religious icons on their walls, shrines in their bedrooms, crucifixes and crosses hanging over doorways, many informants, like Maria, indicate that those things have always been there and "You just know that they are there." Living out a life of Catholic faith means working to establish strength for life. For many informants, "faith" is what helps them "to keep going in life." Often times, the Roman Catholic Church provides this element of "faith" by providing hope, belief, and guidance for their families. Without this emphasis, or when pulling away from church, informants

discuss the breakdown of morals, values, and standards for living.

A conversation with Jose (middle-aged, "Mexican American") provides a focus of the concerns of pulling away from church, the impact that decision has on the values of his generation, and the problems of the "American" public today:

> Well, religion is still in the family. We've been very diverse . . . experimented by, say, going to different churches and see what things are like, but I always go back to my roots of Catholicism. . . . Hispanic people, I think they're kinda pulling away a little bit now, more nineties, but they [inaudible] together. It's something that they all should return to. It's an important aspect of the family. I think we're slowly pulling away from church and I think that's hurting the public in general today, no morals . . . no guidelines, nobody says that you have to live hard and fast to the rules of the Bible, but it does set some kind of standard in life. . . . I think that's what's hurting America's families today. There's just no morality.

Like Maria, Jose discusses the role of diversity in religion. Unlike Maria, however, the diversity that Jose speaks of is with regard to the different types of religions that he has explored. With regard to religion (Catholicism) and the "Hispanic" people, specifically, Jose provides a prescriptive rule for the role of religion in family life. He advises that returning to a religious foundation is a way of countering the problems of society. Thus, for Jose, it is the lack of setting "some kind of standard in life" that he believes has moral implications for U.S. society. The distancing of the younger generations away from church and family values, however, was a concern often expressed by the older generation of Mexican Americans in Biola. Whether it is expressed as an issue of getting "back to my roots of Catholicism" or getting "all those kids to the Holy Days of Obligation," informants often discussed the importance of having and needing some moral "standards" by which to live.

In the end, a strong work ethic, the strength of family, and the role of religion in matters of la familia, reflect themes that are accounted for in the discursive and communicative practices of Mexican Americans in Biola. Although these three themes do not make up an exhaustive list of issues that affect and illuminate elements of Mexican American ethnicity in this small, rural community, they do represent patterned ways of life for a particular people in a particular place.

CONCLUSION

Work, family, and religion represent three themes that emerged as characteristics of being Mexican American in Biola. Because Biola's people live in an area that thrives on agricultural production, they often take on jobs that are described as "hard work." With their efforts, the people of the community are contributors to the hard labor that aids in the production of food for the U.S. American breadbasket.

The Mexican Americans of the community provided strong support for the value placed on family. Whether family is viewed as a "clan" or as one's "whole life," community members stated again and again how family is a foundation upon which life grows. Additionally, religion binds the strength of the Mexican American family unit. Although some informants acknowledged struggles associated with sustaining church involvement among the younger generation, religion was still discussed as a "constant" in their lives. In many cases, it is "faith" that provides the inspiration for the goodness in their lives despite having financial or other problems.

Although often described by interlocutors as a "small, quiet community," Biola is a community with its share of problems. When the three themes of "hard work," "family," and "religion" are taken holistically into account, it becomes apparent that Mexican Americans of Biola expend great energy in sustaining the family unit. And it is no news to Mexican American interlocutors of Biola that the family system and its traditions and breakdowns of shared core values inherently affects the larger system of community as well as the social relations and ethnic identity of a cultured people in this U.S. American speech community.

NOTES

1. The following is a list of additional authors who contributed to my investigation into issues of ethnicity and identity (see references for full citations): Carbaugh, 1993; Collier, 1994; Goodwin, 1990; Hecht & Ribeau, 1987; Lampe, 1977; Leets, Giles, & Clement, 1996; Marin & Marin, 1991; McCready, 1983; Nakayama, 1994; Oboler, 1995; Strauss, 1959; Tanno, 1994; Thompson, 1989; Valdes & Pino, 1974.

2. Aoki (1994, 1995) are two papers presented at the National Communication Association convention. They served as exploratory projects on indexing cultural identity in talk through the use of ethnographic methods and attending to ethnic labels used in talk.

3. Biola, California, is an "unincorporated community" (Fresno County Public Works & Development Services Department, 1990) located in the agriculturally abundant region of the Central San Joaquin Valley. The community population is estimated to be about 1,100 residents. In 1991, a fire destroyed community logs making current demographic information unavailable. Word-of-mouth estimates from school officials, Chamber of Commerce members, and the local residents, indicate that between 85% and 90% of the community residents are Mexican American, with the remaining population composed of White, East Indian, and one Black and one Hmong family.

4. When speaking generally about this indigenous minority group of the United States, I

use the term "Mexican American" for reasons of practicality through out this paper. Because this study is concerned with allowing for voice when referring to interlocutors specifically, I will respect the ethnic label(s) that each interlocutor uses for reasons of identity. I use quotes for ethnic labels to indicate that they represent actual appellations used by interlocutors of Biola. Quotes also are used to refer to specific ethnic labels used in other research studies. When referring *generally* to various ethnic groups (for example, Mexican Americans, Whites), quotes are not used.

5. I used informant and interlocutor synonymously. Spradley (1979) defines an informant as "first and foremost *native speakers.* . . . Informants are engaged by the ethnographer to speak *in their own language or dialect.* Informants provide a *model for the ethnographer to imitate;* the ethnographer hopes to learn to use the native language in the way the informants do. Finally, informants are a *source of information;* literally, they become teachers for the ethnographer" (p. 25). *Random House Webster's College Dictionary* (1996) defines interlocutor as "a person who takes part in a conversation or dialogue" (p. 703). Interlocutor is a term that captures the essence of Spradley's definition of informant. Also, I was introduced to the term interlocutor in my first course in "Ways of Speaking" at the University of Washington with Dr. Gerry Philipsen. I have since used the term interlocutor to refer to the individuals who take part in my research in the ethnography of communication. As the researcher of the project, I make a distinction, however, in that I consider myself to be an interlocutor but not an informant.

6. Briggs ([1986] 1992) and Lofland and Lofland (1984) provide the methodological framework for conducting the participant observations and field interviews.

7. The general descriptions provided for this community overview come from informal talks, formal interviews, and field notes that used Hymes's "SPEAKING" mnemonic and approach (1962, 1964, 1967, 1972, 1974) as a method of inquiry into the speech community of Biola, California. Philipsen (1992, 1997) also provides grounding for the theoretical and methodological inquiry of this study.

8. This study is focused on the basic units of family and community, particularly with regard to concerns in the United States. When researching these basic units, I believe that different societies may have different conceptions (or labels) for how their social networks are composed and named. I believe it is worth researching how family and community systems are defined by interlocutors in various local contexts. In doing this, my goal is not to say that all local contexts in the United States should be like Biola, but rather that research on various speech communities can potentially enable productive assessments of what works and does not work for the particular people in a particular place. From that, a more universal understanding of family and community systems may come.

9. I have given pseudonyms to the informants of this study. The reason I do this is twofold: (1) the names add a qualitative tone to the informants of the study (rather than the most distant Informant One, Informant Two, and so on, and (2) the use of names makes the read a more fluid one. Additionally, I have only used first names. Because of the small size of this community, and the fact that this study is primarily focused on Mexican American families, first names are slightly more abstract and varied than family names.

10. Because my ethnographic work is concerned with strict content analysis of discourse, the transcripts are presented in simple block style to present both comments provided by the informant/interlocutor and conversational turns between the interlocutor of the community and myself. Occasionally, I have used the symbol "[inaudible]" to represent a word or phrase lapse in the transcription data.

11. The name, Eric, is used to represent and reference the researcher in the transcript data.

REFERENCES

Aoki, E. (1994, November). Indexing cultural identity in talk: A Mexican-American's interview with an interlocutor of the same and different ethnic background. Paper presented at the National Communication Association Convention, New Orleans, LA.

Aoki, E. (1995, November). Indexing ethnicity in talk: How labels can come to mean. Paper presented at the National Communication Association Convention, San Antonio, TX.

Briggs, C. [1986] (1992). *Learning how to ask: A sociolinguistic appraisal of the role of the interview in social science research.* Cambridge: Cambridge University Press.

Carbaugh, D. L. (1993). "Soul" and "self": Soviet and American cultures in conversation. *Quarterly Journal of Speech, 79*, 182–200.

Collier, M. J. (1994). Cultural identity and intercultural communication. In L. A. Samovar & R. E. Porter (Eds.), *Intercultural Communication: A Reader* (8th ed., pp. 36–45). Belmont, CA: Wadsworth.

Fishman, J. A. (1983). Language and ethnicity in bilingual education. In W. C. McCready (Ed.), *Culture, ethnicity, and identity: Current issues in research* (pp. 127–137). New York: Academic.

Fresno County Public Works & Development Services Department. (1990, April 1). Biola: A Fresno county community. Fresno, CA: California Department of Commerce.

Goodwin, M. H. (1990). *He-said-she-said: Talk as social organization among Black children.* Bloomington: Indiana University Press.

Hecht, M. L., & Ribeau, S. (1987). Research note: Afro-American identity labels and communication effectiveness. *Journal of Language and Social Psychology, 6*(3), 319–326.

Horowitz, R. (1983). *Honor and the American dream: Culture and identity in a Chicano community.* New Brunswick, NJ: Rutgers University Press.

Hymes, D. (1962). The ethnography of speaking. In T. Gladwin & W. C. Sturtevant (Eds.), *Anthropology and human behavior* (pp. 13–53). Washington, DC: Anthropological Society of Washington.

Hymes, D. (1964). Introduction: Toward ethnographies of communication. In J. J. Gumperz & D. Hymes (Eds.), *The ethnography of communication, American Anthropologist, 66* (part 2), 1–34.

Hymes, D. (1967). Models of the interaction of language and social setting. *Journal of Social Issues, 23*, 8–28.

Hymes, D. (1972). Models of the interaction of language and social life. In J. J. Gumperz and D. Hymes (Eds.), *Directions in sociolinguistics: The ethnography of communication*, pp. 35–71. New York: Holt, Rinehart & Winston.

Hymes, D. (1974). Ways of speaking. In R. Bauman & J. Sherzer (Eds.), *Explorations in the ethnography of speaking* (pp. 433–451). Cambridge: Cambridge University Press.

Lampe, P. E. (1977). Student acceptability of "Black" and "Chicago" as ethnic labels. *Urban Education, 12*, 223–228.

Leets, L., Giles, H., & Clement, R. (1996). Explicating ethnicity in theory and communication research. *Multilingua, 15*(2), 115–147.

Lofland, J. & Lofland, L. H. (1984). *Analyzing social settings: A guide to qualitative observation and analysis* (2nd ed.). Belmont, CA: Wadsworth.

Marin, G. & Marin, B. V. (1991). *Research with Hispanic populations.* Newbury Park, CA: Sage.

Martin, J. N. & Nakayama, T. K. (2000). *Intercultural communication in contexts* (2nd ed.). Mountain View, CA: Mayfield.

Maslow, A. H. (1954). *Motivation and personality.* New York: Harper & Brothers.

McCready, W. C. (Ed.). (1983). *Culture, ethnicity, and identity: Current issues in research.* New York: Academic Press.

Methuen, J. S. (1983). The role of the family in acculturation and assimilation in America: A psychocultural dimension. In W. C. McCready (Ed.), *Culture, ethnicity, and identity: Current issues in research* (pp. 209–221). New York: Academic Press.

Nakayama, T. (1994). Dis/orienting identities: Asian American, history, and intercultural communication. In A. Gonzalez, M. Houston, & V. Chen (Eds.). *Our voices: Essays in culture, ethnicity, and communication.* Los Angeles, CA: Roxbury.

Oboler, S. (1995). *Ethnic labels, Latino lives: Identity and the politics of (re)presentation in the United States.* Minneapolis: University of Minnesota Press.

Otis, E. (1990). Indexicality and socialization. In J. W. Stigler, R. A. Shweder, & G. Herdt (Eds.), *Cultural psychology: Essays on comparative human development*. Cambridge: Cambridge University Press.

Otis, E. (1992). Indexing gender. In A. Duranti & C. Goodwin (Eds.). *Rethinking context: Language as an interactive phenomenon.* Cambridge: Cambridge University Press.

Otis, E. (1993). Constructing social identity: A language socialization perspective. *Research on Language and Social Interaction, 26,* 287–306.

Philipsen, G. (1992). *Speaking culturally: Explorations in social communication.* Albany: State University of New York Press.

Philipsen, G. (1997). A theory of speech codes. In G. Philipsen & T. Albrechts (Eds.), *Developing communication theories 6* (pp. 119–156). Albany: State University of New York.

Random House Webster's College Dictionary. New York: Random House.

Rodriguez, R. (1992). *Days of obligation: An argument with my Mexican father.* New York, NY: Viking Penguin Press.

Spradley, J. P. (1979). *The ethnographic interview.* New York: Holt, Rinehart & Winston.

Spradley, J. P. (1980). *Participant observation.* New York: Holt, Rinehart & Winston.

Strauss, A. L. (1959). *Mirrors and masks: The search for identity.* Glencoe, IL: The Free Press.

Tanno, D. V. (1994). Names, narratives, and the evolution of ethnic identity. In A. Gonzalez, M. Houston, & V. Chen (Eds.). *Our voices: Essays in culture, ethnicity, and communication.* Los Angeles: CA: Roxbury.

Thompson, R. H. (1989). *Theories of ethnicity: A critical appraisal.* New York: Greenwood.

Valdes, D. T. & Pino, T. (1974). *Ethnic labels in majority minority relations.* University of Washington, Seattle, WA: Marfel Associates.

Eric Aoki is in the department of speech communication at Colorado State University.

Reading 2.4

Korean's Politeness Strategies

KIL-HO KANG

In Korea, politeness is one of the most important virtues. Since Korean culture has emphasized polite speech, Koreans develop various ways in which they politely communicate to their conversational partners. Basically, this study aims to investigate politeness strategies employed by Korean people. In order to find the typologies of politeness strategies useful to Korean society, this study proposes the new conceptualization of politeness. Further, this study addresses some determinants which affect the choice of politeness strategies in Korea society.

Generally, politeness is defined by using the concept of face, since face is the underlying construct of politeness. Face refers to the positive value people claim for their own images to others, while politeness is verbal behaviors which satisfy a hearer's face. This study argues that there are two important types of faces in Korea: normative and displaying face. The former represents a desire to behave suitably along the lines of social norms in a given context, that is, a desire to behave as general people are expected, while the latter refers to a desire to show or display more outstandingly than others. Accordingly, politeness is defined in this study as behaviors which satisfy a hearer's normative and/or displaying face.

The typologies of politeness strategies are proposed on the basis of this new conceptualization of politeness. Specifically, this study argues that there are two politeness strategies in terms of the types of faces (i.e., face-type dimension); normative politeness strategy which satisfy a hearer's normative face and displaying politeness strategy which satisfy a hearer's displaying face and that there are two politeness strategies in terms of how to communicate politely (i.e., perspective dimension); direct politeness strategy which directly enhances a hearer's face and indirect politeness strategy which indirectly enhances a hearer's face by lowering a speaker's own face. As a result, by crossing the face-type dimension by the perspective dimension, four politeness strategies were theoretically proposed; direct/displaying, indirect/displaying, direct/normative, and indirect/normative politeness strategy. In addition, politeness tactics were specified for each politeness strategy.

The important determinants such as social status, sex, age, situational formality, and the third party are identified as influencing the use of politeness strategies in Korea. Finally, this study presents propositions regarding these determinants and suggests future directions of research on politeness phenomena in Korea.

Koreans attempt to keep etiquette when they encounter their communication partners. One of the most important social virtues in Korea is to respect older (or superior/more powerful) people, to deal with younger (or inferior/less powerful) people gently, and to be humble to others. Today, social tradition which emphasizes that politeness is one of the most beautiful social virtues that remains deeply ingrained in Korea. As a matter of fact, Korean people are still willing to praise as polite persons those who behave along such a social norm.

Since Korean society considers politeness as one of the most important social virtues, most of the behaviors which they perform in everyday life are related to politeness. For example, they use polite language forms toward older people, frequently tell white lies, and attempt to avoid words which give emotional hurt to others. Although politeness behaviors are some of the most important social phenomena that frequently appear and exist in society, studies on politeness phenomena have tended to neglect systematic investigation.

The purpose of this study is to examine Korean politeness phenomena from a communication perspective. Specifically, this study will focus on politeness strategies employed by Korean people in social interaction. In order to achieve the goal, this study will attempt the new conceptualization of politeness relevant to Korean society. Then, this study will address the theoretical rationale for categorizing politeness strategies on the basis of the new conceptualization of politeness. Further, politeness tactics contained in politeness strategies will be identified from the data of naturalistic conversations. Finally, important determinants which affect the choice of politeness strategies in Korea will be discussed.

THE CONCEPT OF POLITENESS

What is politeness? Is Western definition of politeness useful to Korean society? Or, although politeness is a universal phenomena, is it likely that differences in the concept of politeness between Korea and Western societies exist since politeness phenomena vary across cultures? If it is true that politeness phenomena vary across cultures, what are the characteristics of politeness phenomena in Korean society? In order to solve these questions, it is necessary to answer what is the conceptual definition of politeness useful to the society.

General Conceptual Definition of Politeness

Let's look at what the general conceptual definition of politeness is. It is important to understand the concept of face in order to identify the concept of politeness, because face is the underlying construct of politeness. Then, what is face?

Students of communication (e.g., Goffman, 1967) including Brown and Levinson (1978, 1987) define face as the positive social images (or values) that persons claim for their public selves. This broad definition of face has two implications. First, face is an image of self that persons want to be known to others. That is, face is a public image that persons desire to be approved by others. Second, face is composed of numerous identities or images. The specific qualities which are perceived as socially desirable vary across situations. For example, I might lose face if I appeared incompetent to my students or disloyal to my wife. Face is socially situated on the basis of what are desirable images in the specific situation.

Generally, politeness refers to verbal and/or nonverbal behaviors which enhance or support other's face. For example, the statement, "you are very brave," is one of the polite expressions to those who desire to acquire a manly image, since a speaker supports a hearer's face (i.e., image) that the hearer desires to obtain through the statement. Since politeness is directly associated to face, verbal behaviors related to politeness vary along the types of faces or images that a society regards as important. Accordingly, politeness phenomena can be comprehended in a society only when the types of faces regarded as important in the society are identified.

To summarize, face is public self-image that a person desires to obtain. Politeness is verbal and/or nonverbal behaviors which enhance or maintain others' faces that they desire to acquire. Put differently, since face is the underlying concept of politeness, the work for understanding the concept of face is prerequisite. In the next section, the conceptualization of politeness useful to our society will be discussed by searching for the types of faces regarded as important and desirable in Korea.

The Conceptualization of Politeness Useful in Korea

In the above, the general conceptual definition of politeness is addressed. This definition of politeness is too broad and ambiguous, it is unlikely to understand and explain politeness phenomena in our society by using this definition. If so, what is the conceptual definition of politeness useful and appropriate to Korea? Since face is the underlying concept of politeness, we need to identify the types of faces that Korean people desire to acquire, i.e., the types of images regarded as important in Korea.

There seem to be two important types of faces that Korean people desire to obtain. The first type of face is "normative face," while the other one is "displaying face." Normative face refers to the desire to show the image that persons follow social and/or cultural norms. Since social or cultural norms are persons' expectancies toward formal behaviors in given communicative situations (Forgas, 1979), normative face can be defined as the desire to keep expectancies toward socially and/or culturally appropriate patterns of behaviors. In other words, normative face is related to the image that people behave along cultural and social norms.

The definition of normative face has three implications. First, normative face is associated with etiquettes which people have to maintain when they encounter each other. Given that normative face is behaviors expected by most people of a community in a given communication situation and that etiquettes are behaviors which people must keep in a given communication situation, etiquettes are behaviors which satisfy other's normative face. Accordingly, behaviors that verbally satisfy other's normative face are verbal behaviors conventionally expected in a society. Similarly, behaviors that do not show etiquettes to others (e.g., rude behaviors) are unconventional behaviors that violate other's expectancies. In this sense, politeness strategies that support other's normative face are conventional behaviors related to etiquettes (i.e., courtesy).

Second, normative face varies across societies or cultures. Since normative face is social and cultural expectancies toward the patterns of behaviors, it is closely associated with norms. Norms are traditional conventions which a society has formed, developed, and modified for a long time. Further, norms differ along social or cultural characteristics. Accordingly, normative face varies across societies or cultures.

Finally, normative face has been learned through people's direct or indirect experiences and lives in their society. Since normative face is relevant to traditional lives and patterns of behaviors in a society, members of the society have learned normative face empirically by living in the society and through having contact with other members in the society. Thus, persons who have lived in a society for a long time explicitly or implicitly know what norms their society has.

On the other hand, displaying face refers to the desire to show a self-image which is superior to others'. This definition emphasizes that displaying face is comparative and relative. Put differently, displaying face can be satisfied by claiming a self-image which is more positive than others'. In this sense, displaying face includes desires to show that persons perform their given roles successfully in communicative situations, that their personalities, beliefs, or behaviors are more desirable than others', and that their competence is superior to others'.

It seems that displaying face exists widely in Korea. As a matter of fact, we can frequently encounter situations in which people desire to display a self-image that is more positive than others'. For example, housewives enjoy praising their husbands, sons, or daughters to others and politicians fight against their opponents due to their causes. Displaying face has deeply penetrated our everyday life. Accordingly, displaying face appears to be one of the useful concepts that are necessary to understand politeness phenomena in Korean society.

To summarize, the concept of politeness useful to Korea can be specified on the basis of normative and displaying face. Given that politeness is behaviors which enhance a hearer's face, politeness is defined as verbal behaviors that satisfy a hearer's normative and/or displaying face. Put differently, polite behaviors to a hearer are to show verbal behaviors culturally or socially expected to the hearer and/or to verbally express that a speaker approves the hearer's self image as more positive than others'. In the next section, the categorization of politeness strategies frequently employed in Korea will be attempted. Prior to identifying politeness strategies used in Korean society, the theoretical framework for categorizing politeness strategies will be addressed.

Politeness Strategies

So far, the conceptualization of politeness useful in Korea has been discussed. As argued above, it is necessary to understand the concept of face regarded as important and desirable in Korean society, since face is an underlying concept of politeness. The types of face that are important in Korea are normative and displaying face. Politeness was defined as verbal behaviors that satisfy a hearer's normative and/or displaying face. In this section, the theoretical rationale for categorizing politeness strategies frequently employed in Korea will be proposed. Then, the implications on the categorization of politeness strategies proposed in this study will be addressed.

Theoretical Rationale for the Categorization of Politeness Strategies

Here, politeness strategies refer to verbal message strategies on politeness. Although politeness behaviors contain verbal and nonverbal behaviors on politeness, only verbal politeness strategies will be introduced in this study since the main purpose of this study is to investigate politeness strategies that emerge in Korean's verbal communication. Therefore, the term, "politeness strategies" in this study refers to verbal message strategies that satisfy or support a hearer's normative and/or displaying face.

Politeness strategies as verbal message strategies can be divided logically into two types on the basis of the conceptualization of politeness proposed in this study. The first type of politeness strategies is the normative politeness strategy which meets a hearer's normative face. Given that a speaker's behaviors that

satisfy the need for a hearer's normative face are associated with etiquettes, the normative politeness strategy is likely to be conventional and ritual message strategies.

The second type of politeness strategies is the displaying politeness strategy. This displaying politeness strategy is verbal message strategies that satisfy a hearer's displaying face. Since the need for displaying face is deeply penetrated into our society and displaying face is a type of face that people principally desire to acquire in our society, the displaying politeness strategies can be regarded as verbal message strategies that approve or accept the hearer's need for displaying face.

In addition, politeness strategies are likely to be categorized in terms of perspectives that messages take. Since a speaker and a hearer participate in a communicative situation, politeness strategies can be divided into two categories. In other words, two polite expressions can be made by taking a speaker's or a hearer's perspective. The first category of politeness strategies is verbal message strategies which take a hearer's perspective. That is, this politeness strategy is verbal messages that directly enhance or satisfy a hearer's normative and/or displaying face. The statement, "you are cool," is an example of this politeness strategy, since this statement directly enhances a hearer's displaying face.

In contrast, the second type of politeness strategies is verbal message strategies that indirectly enhance or satisfy a hearer's normative and displaying face by lowering a speaker's face. Since two or more participants (i.e., a speaker(s) and a hearer(s)) exist in communicative situations, this indirect method for satisfying a hearer's face can be employed. Put differently, when a speaker lowers his/her own face, a hearer can perceive that his/her face is relatively enhanced or satisfied by comparing a hearer's face with a speaker's face. The statement, "I am more foolish than you," is an example of this politeness strategy, since this

Table 1   Four Types of Politeness Strategies

	Displaying	*Normative*
Direct	Type I (direct/displaying)	Type II (direct/normative)
Indirect	Type III (indirect/displaying)	Type IV (indirect/normative)

statement indirectly implicates that a hearer is brighter than a speaker. In sum, politeness strategies can be categorized into strategies that directly enhance a hearer's face and strategies that indirectly enhance a hearer's face by lowering a speaker's own face. In this study, the former will be called direct politeness strategies, while the latter indirect politeness strategies.

As argued above, politeness strategies can be categorized into two politeness strategies with regards to the types of face; that is, normative and displaying politeness strategies. Furthermore, politeness strategies can also be divided into two politeness strategies with regards to whether the content of messages takes a hearer's or a speaker's perspective; that is, direct and indirect politeness strategy. Accordingly, politeness strategies can be categorized into four strategies by crossing two politeness strategies related to the types of faces by two politeness strategies related to the perspective of the content of messages. Put differently, normative and displaying politeness strategies can be categorized into two politeness strategies on the basis of the perspective of the content of messages, respectively. That is, politeness strategies can be divided into four types of strategies: direct/normative, indirect/normative, direct/displaying, and indirect/displaying politeness strategies.

The Implications of the Categorization of Politeness Strategies

In the above section, the categories of politeness strategies deduced from theoretical reasoning were proposed. Here, the implications of these categorizations of politeness strategies will be discussed.

The categorization of politeness strategies proposed in this study has three implications for future studies. First, the categories of politeness strategies proposed in this study are highly likely to be hierarchical in terms of the degree of perceived politeness. Four politeness strategies suggested in this study were categorized on the basis of two dimensions, i.e., the types of faces and perspective. Since both dimensions can be logically ordered with regards to the perceived politeness, these four politeness strategies also are likely to be ordered. Specifically, for the perspective dimension, direct politeness strategy is more polite than indirect politeness strategy. That is because the former shows respect more directly to a hearer than the latter (Lakoff, 1973). Accordingly, the direct politeness strategy is likely to be perceived more politely than the indirect politeness strategy.

For the face-type dimension, it is highly likely that displaying politeness strategy is more polite than normative politeness strategy. Since the normative politeness strategy is related to social norms, it is a kind of obligatory behavior that people have to maintain in communicative situations. In this sense, the normative politeness strategy is passive. On the other hand, the displaying politeness strategy is not associated with obligations nor moral constraints that people should keep. Rather, the displaying politeness strategy is behaviors that a speaker willingly performs. In this sense, the displaying politeness strategy is active. Consequently, a hearer is likely to perceive the normative politeness strategy as formal strategies performed due to social conventions or morality, while he/she may perceive the displaying politeness strategy as message strategies that a speaker performs voluntarily and truly. Thus, the displaying politeness strategy is more likely than the normative politeness strategy to be perceived politely.

To summarize, direct and displaying politeness strategies are more polite than indirect and normative politeness strategies, respectively. From these facts, direct/displaying politeness strategy is expected to be the most polite, indirect/normative politeness strategy the least polite, and direct/normative and indirect/displaying politeness strategies lie in the degree of politeness between direct/displaying and indirect/normative politeness strategies. In order to test this prediction empirically, however, future studies are necessary.

Second, since politeness strategies are verbal message strategies that enhance a hearer's face, the categorization of politeness strategies contributes to the categorization of face strategies which enhance, maintain, or lower a hearer's face. Put differently, although these politeness strategies do not contain face strategies that maintain or lower a hearer's face, the theoretical rationale for categorizing politeness strategies can be applied to the categorization of face strategies. For example, regarding the perspective dimension, those face strategies that lower a hearer's face can be divided into face strategies that directly lower the hearer's face and face strategies that indirectly lower the hearer's face by enhancing a speaker's face. Furthermore, there may be normative and displaying face strategies that lower a hearer's face with regards to the face-type dimension. Accordingly, the theoretical rationale for categorizing politeness strategies proposed in this study is useful to the categorization of face strategies.

Finally, normative and displaying politeness strategies are not mutually exclusive. Since normative face is independent of displaying face, normative and displaying politeness strategies derived from these two types of faces also are independent of each other. Accordingly, it is possible to simultaneously use both normative and displaying politeness strategies. Future studies on this issue seem to be in need.

To summarize, the categories of politeness strategies proposed in this study have three implications. Especially, it is emphasized that these strategies are likely to be hierarchical in the degree of perceived politeness and that the theoretical rationale for categorizing these politeness strategies can be extensively applied to the categorization of face strategies. In the next section, various politeness tactics included in each politeness strategy will be introduced. Specific examples of these politeness tactics will be suggested from the data of naturalistic conversations.

Politeness Tactics

Here, various politeness tactics for each politeness strategy proposed in this study will be introduced. These tactics were identified from naturalistic conversations that Koreans actually perform, on the basis of the conceptualization of politeness and theoretical rationale for categorizing politeness strategies suggested in the above sections. Thus, politeness tactics which this study will introduce can be regarded as politeness tactics frequently employed by Koreans in actual communicative contexts.

Direct/displaying politeness tactics. Politeness tactics for direct/displaying politeness strategy contain "praising," "emphasis on interpersonal relationship," "comparison," "offering causes," and "joke." These five tactics have common features in the sense that these tactics directly satisfy a hearer's displaying face. Besides, these tactics are frequently used by Koreans.

"Praising" is a tactic that satisfies a hearer's displaying face by evaluating the hearer's attitudes, opinions, beliefs, behaviors, and so forth positively. The statement, "that's a good idea" is an example of praising tactic. "Emphasis on interpersonal relationship" is a tactic which emphasizes that a speaker has a positive or friendly relationship with a hearer. The expressions of "between ourselves," "between you and me," or "I trust you" are examples of this tactic. "Comparison" is a tactic which makes a hearer's image more positive than a speaker, a third party, or generalized other(s). The statement, "you are more competent than I" is an example of the comparison tactic. The key point of "offering causes" tactic is that a speaker provides external causes to a hearer who makes a mistake. As a result, these external causes make a hearer's mistake lessened. This tactic is one in which a speaker says what a hearer has to say for the hearer in a situation in which the hearer's face is likely to be lowered or in which a speaker attributes a hearer's mistake to external circumstances in order to prevent the hearer's face from be threatened. For example, a speaker says to a hearer who was late "Is traffic jammed?" Finally, "joke" is a tactic in which a speaker reduces a hearer's threatened face by using popular idioms, slangs, or humorous expressions in situations in which the hearer's face can be lowered.

Indirect/displaying politeness tactics. "Lowering a speaker's own competence," "emphasizing equal or similar qualification," and "criticizing a speaker's own mistakes" tactics are involved in a indirect/displaying strategy. "Lowering a speaker's own competence" is a tactic in which a speaker evaluates his/her own attitudes, beliefs, opinions, behaviors, and so on negatively. In this aspect, this tactic is contrasted with the praising tactic contained in

the direct/displaying strategy. An example of this tactic is the response, "I am not playing guitar very well" in a situation in which a communicative partner praises that he/she plays guitar very well.

A speaker emphasizes that his/her competence or qualification is very similar to a hearer's in the "emphasizing equal or similar qualification" tactic. The statement, "I do not play guitar, either" is an example of this tactic. Finally, "criticizing a speaker's own mistakes" is a tactic in which a speaker criticizes his/her own mistakes or misbehaviors so that he/she may enhance a hearer's displaying face. The statement, "What I said is cruel to you" is an example of this tactic.

Direct/normative politeness tactics. The direct/normative politeness strategy includes "understanding a hearer's position," "agreement," "comforting," and "appreciation" tactics. The reason why these tactics are involved in the direct/normative politeness strategy is that these tactics are conventional expressions frequently employed in our society in order to enhance a hearer's face.

In the "understanding a hearer's position" tactic, a speaker emphasizes that he/she understands a hearer's positions, circumstances, and emotion. The expression, "I understand your feeling, but . . ." is an example of this tactic. In "agreement" tactic, a speaker agrees with a hearer. The statement "yes, I agree" is an example of this tactic. In "comforting" tactic, a speaker attempts to support and comfort a hearer by using conventional expressions. The statement, "anyway, you really did a good job" is an example of this tactic. Finally, "appreciation" is conventional expressions in which a speaker appreciates a hearer. The typical example of this tactic is the expression, "Thank you."

Indirect/normative politeness tactics. There are "apologizing," "conceding," and "being humble" tactics in the indirect/normative politeness strategy. These tactics included in the indirect/normative politeness strategy also are conventional expressions often employed in our society.

As is guessed in the term, "apologizing" is that a speaker talks to a hearer politely by apologizing for the speaker's own mistake. The typical examples are the expressions, "I apologize for it," and "excuse me." In "conceding" tactic, a speaker indirectly concedes or refuses what a hearer urges for the speaker (especially, something profitable to the speaker). For example, when a host urges a guest to help him/herself in a party, the guest replies, "I'm full. I'm very satisfied." The guest's statement is an example of this tactic. Finally, in "being humble" tactic, a speaker is humble in situations in which he/she can boast of what he/she did by using conventional expressions. For example, after a host invites a guest and provides much food and dishes, he said, "I didn't prepare lots of dishes but enjoy dinner." Table 2 summarizes these tactics for four politeness strategies.

Determinants That Influence the Use of Politeness Strategies

In the above sections, the conceptual definition of politeness, the theoretical rationale for categorizing politeness strategies, and politeness tactics employed in Korea have been addressed. Here, the determinants which affect the choice or use of politeness strategies will be explicated. Since it is unlikely that all the determinants will be introduced in this study, however, only important determinants will be indicated.

Social status. Social status is one of the most important factors which influence the use of politeness strategies in Korea. Social status refers to hierarchical position which an individual socially takes. The effect of social status on the choice of politeness strategies is inferred from the fact that social courtesy varies across his/her social status in our society. Specifically, Koreans are expected to be more polite to persons with high social status than persons with low social status, since it is a social moral to show respect to persons with high social status. Accordingly, the following proposition can be established.

> Proposition 1: Koreans will use or choose more direct/displaying politeness strategies to persons with high social status than persons with low social status.

Age. Age also is one of the most important factors that influence the use of politeness strategies in Korea. Since Koreans have learned that they are polite to older persons, age is an important reference for behaviors in daily life. Specifically, Koreans criticize impolite behaviors to older persons that violate "sam-kang-oh-ryun" (this is a traditional manual which specifies three principles and five norms for ethical behaviors). Accordingly, the following proposition can be proposed.

> Proposition 2: Koreans will use or choose more direct/displaying politeness strategies to older persons than to younger persons.

Sex. Sex is expected to affect the use of politeness strategies in Korea. Although the Confucianism of respecting males and despising females has tended to disappear, it still remains in Korean society. The social stereotype in Korea is that females are tender and humble and that males are aggressive. Accordingly, the following proposition can be made.

> Proposition 3: Females will use more direct/displaying politeness strategies than males.

Situational formality and the third party. Situational formality is expected to influence

Table 2   Politeness Tactics for Four Politeness Strategies

(A) Direct/displaying politeness strategy: politeness strategy that directly satisfies a hearer's displaying face
   1. praising – a tactic which evaluates a hearer's attitudes, beliefs, behaviors, and so forth positively (e.g.) "That's a good idea."
   2. emphasis on interpersonal relationship – a tactic which emphasizes that a speaker has a positive or friendly relationship with a hearer (e.g.) "Between you and me, . . ." "I trust you."
   3. comparison – a tactic which makes a hearer's image more positive than a speaker, the third party, or generalized other(s) (e.g.) "You are more competent than I."
   4. offering causes – a tactic in which a speaker provides external causes to a hearer who makes a mistake (e.g.) A speaker says to a hearer who is late "Is a traffic jammed?"
   5. joke – a tactic in which a speaker reduces a hearer's threatened face by using popular idioms, slangs, or humorous expressions

(B) Indirect/displaying politeness strategy: politeness strategy that indirectly enhances a hearer's displaying face by lowering a speaker's face
   1. lowering a speaker's own competence – a tactic in which a speaker evaluates his/her own attitudes, beliefs, opinions, behaviors and so forth negatively (e.g.) In a situation in which a communicative partner praises that he/she plays guitar very well, "I'm not playing guitar very well."
   2. emphasizing equal or similar qualification – a tactic which emphasizes that his/her competence or qualification is very similar to a hearer's (e.g.) "I don't play guitar, either."
   3. criticizing a speaker's own mistakes – a tactic in which a speaker criticizes his/her own mistakes or misbehaviors so that he/she may enhance a hearer's displaying face (e.g.) "What I said is cruel to you."

(C) Direct/normative politeness strategy: politeness strategy that directly satisfies a hearer's normative face
   1. understanding a hearer's position – a tactic in which a speaker emphasizes that he/she understands a hearer's positions, circumstances, and emotion (e.g.) "I understand your feeling, but . . ."
   2. agreement – a tactic in which a speaker agrees with a hearer (e.g.) "Yes, I agree."
   3. comforting – a tactic in which a speaker attempts to support and comfort a hearer by using conventional expressions (e.g.) "Anyway, you really did a good job."
   4. appreciation – a tactic in which a speaker appreciates a hearer by using conventional expressions (e.g.) "Thank you."

(D) Indirect/normative politeness strategy: politeness strategy that indirectly satisfies a hearer's normative face by lowering a speaker's own face
   1. apologizing – a tactic in which a speaker talks to a hearer politely by apologizing for the speaker's own mistake (e.g.) "I apologize for it."
   2. conceding – a tactic in which a speaker indirectly concedes or refuses something profitable that a hearer offers to the speaker (e.g.) When a host urges a guest to help him/herself at a party, the guest replies, "I'm full. I'm satisfied very much."
   3. being humble – a tactic in which a speaker is humble in situations in which he/she can boast of what he/she did by using conventional expressions (e.g.) In a party, a host says to guests, "I didn't provide much food and dishes."

the choice of politeness strategies in Korean society. Situational formality refers to the extent to which a communicative situation is formal or informal. Communication situations can be divided into formal and informal situations on the basis of the degree of situational formality. Public communicative situations such as classes and ceremonies are formal situations, while private situations such as parties and jokes are informal situations. Since formal situations tend to be public situations, the impact of various private factors such as intimacy on communication behaviors are constrained. For example, two intimate professors who work for the same department can hardly behave privately in formal public activities at school. One of our social conventions is to maintain the formality of behavioral patterns in public and formal communication contexts.

In addition, the emergence of the third party tends to make communicative situations more formal. For example, when two professors who are close friends joke in an office and a colleague enters there, two professors stop joking at a moment and make their communicative situation more formal. Accordingly, Koreans are likely to be polite under the existence or emergence of the third party. Based on the above rationales, the following propositions will be established.

> Proposition 4: Koreans will use more direct/ displaying politeness strategies in formal communication situations than in informal communication situations.

> Proposition 5: Koreans will use more direct/ displaying politeness strategies under the circumstance in which the third party exists than under the circumstance in which the third party does not exist.

DISCUSSIONS AND CONCLUSION

The purpose of this study is to investigate politeness strategies employed in Korea. In other words, this study purports to identify politeness strategies frequently used by Koreans. This work is valuable in a sense that it provides the basis for developing theoretical frameworks that explain politeness phenomena in our society.

In order to achieve this purpose of this study, the new conceptualization of politeness was proposed in this study. Specifically, politeness was defined as verbal behaviors in which a speaker satisfies a hearer's normative and/or displaying face. Normative face refers to the desire to keep expectancies on socially and/or culturally appropriate patterns of behaviors, while displaying face refers to the need to show self-image which is superior to others'. Besides, the theoretical rationale for categorizing politeness strategies on the basis of the new conceptualization of politeness was suggested in this study.

The theoretical rationale for categorizing politeness strategies proposed in this study lies in the types of face and perspectives (i.e., how to verbally express the content of messages in order to enhance a hearer's face). Since the concept of politeness is associated with normative and displaying face, politeness strategies can be largely categorized into normative politeness strategies that satisfy a hearer's normative face and displaying politeness strategies that satisfy a hearer's displaying face. Furthermore, since politeness strategies are verbal behaviors that enhance or satisfy a hearer's face, politeness strategies can be divided into direct politeness strategy in which a speaker directly satisfies a hearer's face and indirect politeness strategy in which a speaker indirectly satisfies a hearer's face by lowering the speaker's own face. As a result, by crossing the types of face by perspectives, four politeness strategies were theoretically found in this study: that is, direct/displaying, indirect/ displaying, direct/normative, and indirect/ normative politeness strategies.

One of the implications that the theoretical categorization of politeness strategies has is that these four politeness strategies are likely to be hierarchically ordered with regards to the degree of perceived politeness. In our society, direct and displaying politeness strategies are more likely than indirect and normative politeness strategies to be polite, respectively. If this is the case, direct/displaying politeness strategy is the most polite, indirect/normative politeness strategy is the least polite and indirect/display and direct/normative politeness strategies lie between direct/displaying and indirect/normative politeness strategies. Since this prediction is deduced from theoretical reasoning, however, future studies are necessary for empirically testing this proposition.

Various politeness tactics which are included in each politeness strategy also were found by using naturalistic data of conversations. Direct/displaying politeness strategy contains praising, emphasis on interpersonal relationship, comparison, offering causes, and joke. Indirect/displaying politeness strategy involves lowering a speaker's own competence, emphasizing equal or similar qualification, and criticizing a speaker's own mistakes. Understanding a hearer's position, agreement, comforting, and appreciation tactics are included in direct/normative politeness strategy. Finally, indirect/normative politeness strategy contains apologizing, conceding, and being humble.

Finally, the determinants that affect the use of politeness strategies were indicated in this study. Social status, age, sex, situational formality, and the third party were expected to affect the use of politeness strategies. Besides, the hypothetical propositions on the relationships between the determinants and use of politeness strategies were suggested in this study. Of course, future studies are necessary for empirically testing these propositions.

NOTE

1. A strategy is an abstract behavioral unit and provides general guidelines for action (Berger,

1985). A strategy refers to a sequence of actions or to a family of related actions (Wheeless, Barraclough, & Stewart, 1983). In contrast, a tactic is a more specific act carried out in support of an overarching strategy. In the theory of message behaviors, a tactic refers to a single action, or a single message in the case of communication, while a strategy refers to a sequence of actions.

REFERENCES

Berger, C. R. "Social power and interpersonal communication," In M. Knapp & G. Miller (Eds.), *Handbook of interpersonal communication*. (Beverly Hills, CA: Sage, 1985), pp. 439–499.

Brown, P., & Levinson, S. "Universals in language usage: Politeness phenomena," In E. Goody (Ed.), *Questions and politeness: strategies in social interaction* (Cambridge: Cambridge University Press, 1978), pp. 56–289.

Brown, P., & Levinson, S. *Politeness: some universals in language usage.* (Cambridge: Cambridge University Press, 1987).

Goffman, E. *Interaction rituals: essays on face-to-face behavior.* (NY: Doubleday Anchor Books, 1967).

Forgas, J. *Social episodes: the study of interaction routines.* (London: Academic Press, 1979).

Lakoff, R. "The logic of politeness: or, minding your P's and Q's," CLS, 9, 1973. In C. Colum et al. (Eds.) *Papers from the ninth regional meeting of the Chicago linguistic society.* (Chicago: Chicago linguistic society). pp. 292–305.

Wheeless, L., Barraclough, R., & Stewart, R. "Compliance-gaining and power in persuasion," In R. Bostrom & B. Westley (Eds.), *Communication yearbook, vol. 7,* (Beverly Hills, CA: Sage, 1983). pp. 105–145.

Kil-Ho Kang is Professor and Chair of the Department of Media and Communication at Korea's Yeungnam University.

Reading 2.5

Online Communication Between Australians and Koreans

Learning to Manage Differences That Matter

HEE-SOO KIM
GREG HEARN
CAROLINE HATCHER
IAN WEBER

INTRODUCTION

Most modern firms now have an e-mail system with access to the Internet (Mandeville & Rooney, 1997). This development is changing the nature of business communication in significant ways (Rogers & Albritton, 1995). Many studies of e-mail use within monocultural organizations have also been conducted (Garton & Wellman, 1994; Holmes, 1994; Ross-Flanigan, 1998). These are, however, a number of more subtle ways culture (Straub, 1994), gender (Wajcman, 1991), and hierarchy (Hearn & Mandeville, 1995) are changed by and change these new communication practices. Intercultural and online communication are, too often, studied separately (Lennie, Hearn, Stevenson, Inayatullah & Mandeville, 1996). Intercultural issues need to be given more attention in the on-line environment (Mobley & Wilson, 1998), particularly when many organisations' operations now necessitate intercultural communication.[1] (Jarvenpaa, Knoll & Leidner, 1998).

This paper, therefore, has an explicit focus on e-mail communication between cultures. Initially, we define this domain and show its relationship to the more established research literatures which have investigated e-mail and intercultural communication separately. We show that the general literature on e-mail suggests possible lines of investigation. Most importantly, this literature shows that e-mail communication can be thought of as a socially constructed phenomenon. Research on culture and computerization more generally supports this assertion. This gives the paper a mandate to conduct its exploratory work examining e-mail communication between Korean and Australian businesses.

A well-established research literature examining functionalities and social and

Reprinted with permission from World Communication Association from *World Communication*, Vol. 28, No. 4, 1999, pp. 48–68.

	Monocultural	Intercultural
Online	➼	?
Face-to-face	➼	➼

Figure 1   Research Domains Informing On-line—Intercultural Communication

organization impacts of e-mail already exists (Garton & Wellman, 1994; Holmes, 1994). We would expect a study of e-mail use in intercultural settings to confirm at least some the known findings. For example, e-mail use contributes to locational flexibility, shifts time and space considerations (Holmes, 1994), and is affected by organizational structures and processes (Garton & Wellman, 1994). Though we do not offer a review of this literature here it nevertheless provides insights which are indirectly relevant to theorizing the intercultural-e-mail domain of effects.

For example, e-mail use has been argued to provide fewer cues than face-to-face communication, which may foster status equalization (Garton & Wellman, 1994; Sproull & Keisler, 1991). Given that cultures differ in status (Hofstede, 1994) e-mail may have complicated effects depending on the combination of cultures involved. Also, consensus regarding behaviour is different in e-mail mediated discussion compared to face-to-face (Sproull & Keisler, 1991) and this is also a feature which differentiates cultures.

Although it is tempting to develop contingency formulae predicting variable outcomes, we believe these would be premature. Rather, we would argue that, more generally, e-mail use has been shown to be socially (as well as rationally) constructed (Holmes, 1994; Jackson, 1995).

As such, precise specifications of social outcomes of e-mail use are difficult to generalize (Garton & Wellman, 1994); it is the meaning of the social context rather than specifiable social variables that are at work (Jackson, 1995; Poole & DeSanctis, 1990).

For example, e-mail use has been found to both accelerate & decelerate non-conforming behavious (Garton & Wellman, 1994). Our study is exploratory & seeks to make sense broadly of intercultural context and e-mail use. This research will serve both those who would proceed with variable deductive work (Garton & Wellman, 1994) and those who wish to retain a more holistic view (Jackson, 1995; Orlikowski et al., 1995; Poole & DeSanctis, 1990). Some precedents guide our quest.

Figure 1 depicts the research domains which contextualise this discussion.

Extensive research has been conducted in all domains of Figure 1, except the on-line intercultural domain. While we will refer to research for the established domains where relevant, our primary intention in this paper is to contribute to the development of a research agenda for online-intercultural communication. Some research has already explored the intersection of culture and technology generally.

For example, the different communicative realities of cultural groups affects people's perception of, and attitudes toward, new communication technologies. Culture influences the use of modern communication and information technologies (Allwood & Wang, 1990; Gattiker & Nelligan, 1988; Makrakis, 1992; Marcoulides, 1991; Straub, 1994) and cultural orientations encourage or impede the implementation of the new technologies (Harvey, 1997; Kirlidog, 1996; Narula, 1988; Sewell, 1996).

As well, a number of studies have been undertaken cross-culturally regarding conceptions of information society, including technological change and its impacts (for example, Makrakis, 1992; Wang, 1991; Yuchtman-Yaar & Gottlieb, 1985), and the implementation of other innovative technologies (Harvey, 1997; Sewell, 1996). Those studies illustrate cultural effects on the different understanding of the technology between cultures. For example, Harvey (1997) argues that in the practice of information system design (in this case geographic information systems technology) between a German and a U.S. county, while the techniques used may well be similar, different cultural values of the two countries resulted in completely different designs. In a study that compared Chinese and Swedish students' concepts of computers, Allwood and Wang (1990) found that Chinese students showed more optimism about the effects of computers on society and were more likely to believe that humans and computers shared similar characteristics than did their Swedish counterparts (whose country used computers much more extensively). Allwood and Wang (1990) conclude that the culture and the society in which people live significantly affect their opinions about computers.

Straub (1994) argues that culture has an effect on the predisposition toward and selection of new communication technologies, including e-mail and fax. He conducted a cross-cultural study to examine the effect of culture on communication and information technology diffusion between two Japanese and two U.S. organizations. The study found that the Japanese respondents perceived e-mail to be lower in social presence and to be less useful than did U.S. respondents. The Japanese reported less e-mail use and rated lower productivity benefits of e-mail than the U.S. respondents. The Japanese perceived the fax to be higher in social presence and were more likely to perceive the fax to be more useful than the U.S. respondents. The Japanese rated the productivity benefits of the fax higher than the U.S. respondents did. The study also

reported that responses to traditional media, such as face-to-face and the telephone, illustrated remarkable similarities between two cultures.

Umble (1991) similarly suggests that the implication of a new technology for any social group is shaped by its historical and cultural contexts and is also negotiated while serving specific social purposes. Kinsella (1993) provides a comprehensive comment on social and cultural influences:

> . . . Technologies and attitudes toward technologies are socially constructed within particular contexts and must be analysed in terms specific to those contexts. Different cultures will respond to new technologies in different ways, depending upon cultural values, ontologies, epistemologies, ideologies, power relations, and other social systems. . . . Cultures vary in their degrees of reflexivity regarding processes of social construction. While these processes are masked in all cultures, some are better equipped than others to undertake the self-scrutiny that can foster their emancipation from reified views of technology. Where the status of technological determinism as a "social fact" is not accepted uncritically, cultures can enhance their abilities to control their technological destinies (pp. 11–12).

As Woolgar (1991) argues, attributes of technologies are institutionalised conventional ways, that is, the "distribution of attributes is sanctioned in virtue of conventions for correct/normal usage" (p. 62). Therefore, technologies will be used to meet these same customs and practices of the systems, like any other social resource would be (Poole & DeSanctis, 1990). Similarly, Green and Guinery (1994) argue that a technological object is framed by the discourse within which it is discussed. They use the car as an example of the way in which people in different cultural contexts perceive domestic vehicles. For example, functional and economic agendas, such as fuel economy, top speech, safety or price, appear to influence the way people in the West, who are familiar with these advertising strategies, perceive a car. While in Africa, the use of a car is thoroughly culture-specific.

Hakken (1991) argues that, in the long run, the character of communication and information technology must become informed by a more cultural and social but less technical perspective. The difficult and prolonged adaptation surrounding technology adoption will not be offset through the benefits of the technological innovation (Straub, 1994). Poole and DeSanctis (1990) believe developing theories with an adequate understanding of the contexts of individual and social technology usage is needed in order to explain, in detail, the social aspects of technology and how context becomes involved in its use. A careful examination of the social and cultural impacts of the technology will ease the burdens of cultural change.

This paper therefore examines those organization, social, and cultural issues in intercultural settings, which may constrain or enhance e-mail communication but also may be overridden by the capacity of e-mail. Initially, we briefly examine the common pragmatics of the process, that is why and how people from both cultures use e-mail in these settings. These commonalities are engendered essentially by the inherent logistics of e-mail as a medium. However, a number of cultural differences in e-mail use also emerge that cannot be fully explained by language differences and the pragmatics of business, and which we analyse by examining some of the "core symbols" individuals use to describe their intercultural communication (Collier & Thomas, 1988). Well known formulations of these core symbols (Hall, 1959; Hofstede, 1983, 1994; Lustig & Koester, 1996) provide one useful frame for categorizing the symbols, meanings,

and norms applied as rules for e-mail use by the participants in the study. However, possibly because technology itself asserts an influence that demands accommodation, both cultures—Australian and Korean—need to make adjustments. Thus, we theorise the process of learning to recognize and manage the differences in intercultural communication that arise in an on-line environment.

METHOD

The focus of this study is the contemporary phenomenon of e-mail with a natural setting (Yin, 1994). The study describes e-mail communication as it unfolds through a "holistic, contextual investigation of the subjective and intersubjective processes of interpretation and perspective taking" (Kim & Gudykunst, 1988, 17) in intercultural settings. It also aims to examine the topic area where there are few empirical studies on the issue (Eisenhardt, 1989). Therefore, the study uses a qualitative study methodology, adopting in-depth interviews as a research method, to provide a rich source of data for examining how and why e-mail communication occurs as it does in this intercultural situation.

Twenty telephone interviews were conducted with ten Australians and ten Koreans who were working in Korean companies in Sydney. The Australians and Koreans interacted through e-mail within their company, as well as with a head-office in Korea, and with other overseas branch offices. They used the e-mail facility to transfer information, drawings and specifications, and a range of other documents and to exchange opinions and decisions made about the projects they are working on together. As well, e-mail is used for internal communication between the Australians and Koreans. But e-mail's principle role in the companies is as a tool through which the head office in Korea and overseas branches communicate with each other. The experience of e-mail use. of both Australians and Koreans interviewed varies: Australians (from 1 year to 5 years) and Koreans (from 2 months to 9 years). On average, both groups have 3 years experience of e-mail use with each other.

Qualitative data analysis methods (Eisenhardt, 1989; Guba, 1978; Kaplan, 1986; Patton, 1990; Simon, 1978) were used to classify the data by common concepts and themes to derive similarities and patterns of use. To obtain a possibly complete picture, as Orlikowski, Yates, Okamura, and Fujimoto (1995) suggest, all of the data was analysed together and iteratively.

The role of the researchers is also an important dimension of intercultural research. As Kim and Gudykunst (1988) acknowledge, doing intercultural research requires a good deal of sensitivity to the cultures under study to prevent assumptions based in one culture or the other from dominating the research interpretations. Consequently, the research design was a joint Korean/Australian collaboration with discussions of findings and interpretations carefully monitored from within an Australian and Korean framework. Thus, the interview data were analysed by one of the researchers, a Korean with extensive contact with Australians in an Australian environment. Consequently, a claim of validity can be made in terms of sensitivity to the cultural constructs, norms, and meaning systems of both groups.

Two constraints of the study are worth noting. First, we were unable to obtain access to e-mail transcripts. However, as Collier and Thomas (1988) suggest, an analysis of the experience of those engaged in communication, such as the interviews conducted, does provide an opportunity to identify the "normative" and "constituent" dimensions of a process (p. 111). Second, the richness of the data meant some important issues had to be quarantined for later analysis. In particular, the interaction of gender and culture in this setting has been excluded from this analysis

because it constitutes a complex agenda, which we are treating in a separate paper.

FINDINGS AND DISCUSSION

Initial findings replicated that what is known about e-mail holds true for Koreans and Australians. For example:

1. The timing requirement of the communication task influences the choice of e-mail.
2. The economics of the medium influences the choice of e-mail as a medium.
3. The content of the communication (e.g., strategic or sensitive) influences choice of e-mail.
4. Informal and immediate communication often leads to e-mail choice.
5. E-mail offers accurate and easily retrieved records of communication.

That these findings are consistent with non-culture specific studies of e-mail (Garton & Wellman, 1994; Holmes, 1994; Rogers & Albritton, 1995) suggests that the small sample is not atypical. Thus, these preliminary findings are an important baseline for the main focus of the study which examines cultural differences. The primary focus of this paper, however, is to explore the interaction of two specific cultures in online communication.

Some of the differences between the two cultural groups can clearly be attributed to language differences:

Because Koreans have to communicate with Australians in their second language, there are a lot of restrictions when they express themselves, feelings of unease (Interview 8).

Koreans at my office are reluctant to use e-mail because of English language barriers. When Koreans e-mail in English, messages are shorter than other reports because they are short of expressions (Interview 9):

At the moment it is very difficult for Koreans to feel comfortable to write messages in

English. It not only takes a lot of time but it is also a psychological pressure. In my case, I don't have a great difficulty in writing in English, compared with other Koreans and in cases I need to use e-mail I use it. . . . They have language barriers when Australians and Koreans communicate face-to-face. It takes time to explain things, and sometimes they don't get to the point. If the language barrier is the most significant problem in e-mail use, it would be ideal if e-mail has a translation function which automatically translate messages written in Korean into English. Would it be possible to have such function? (Interview 9).

Language barriers of the sort described above, however, do not adequately explain some of the differences observed. Communication behaviours differ according to cultural differences, such as divergent value assumptions and different expectations and attitudes. Culture includes the use of modern communication and information technologies (Allwood & Wang, 1990; Sewell, 1996), and cultural orientations may encourage or impede the implementation of the new technologies (Harvey, 1997; Kinsella, 1993; Kirlidog, 1996; Narula, 1988; Sewell, 1996; Umble, 1991). Such cultural differences were analysed here by reading the interviews as discursive texts to grasp the "normative patterning" and "symbolic structuring" (Collier & Thomas, 1988) of the interviews. Hofstede's (1983) and Hall's (1959) formulations provide a framework to understand the reflections about contexted interaction between Australians and Koreans in the study.

Exploring the Meanings Systems of Intercultural Communication

An important preliminary step in improving intercultural communication is the development of a substantial knowledge base about the way individual communicators enact their

daily work practices in an intercultural context. Descriptions of the "web of significance," to use Geertz's well worn phrase, in which communicators are caught as they enact their business communication across large geographical distances and outside the frame of the face-to-face interaction, are incomplete without detailed accounts of the rules by which communicators currently make their decisions. The word "rule" is used here, following Collier and Thomas (1988) to mean, not something laid down and formalised, but rather "communicative prescriptions that specify when and how actions are to be peerformed" (p. 108) and may vary in scope and salience according to the context. These rules have also been suggested as providing the basis on which intercultural competence is judged. Therefore, description is useful in providing knowledge about how the new medium of e-mail intersects with the normative prescriptions of different cultural groups and how individuals form and manage their identities during intercultural contact.

Theorising Cultural Difference

Numerous formulations of theories of intercultural communication have been developed. However, given the humanist epistemological and ontological framework within which this study has been developed, Hall's (1959) explanation, elaborated on by Hofstede (1983, 1994), of the differences in communicative style based on what he has called "high" and "low" context cultures, provides a useful tool of analysis. He suggests that low context cultures, such as those of most Western countries, emphasise individual value orientation, line logic, direct verbal interaction, and individualistic nonverbal style. In low context cultures, intentions and meanings are exhibited clearly. In contrast, high context cultures, such as those of most Eastern countries, think highly of group value orientation, spiral logic, indirect verbal interaction, and contextual nonverbal style. High, context cultures place intentions and meanings within the larger shared knowledge of the sociocultural context. This analytical framework is complementary of Hofstede's (1983) delineation of four dimensions of a culture. Cultures are different in the extent to which they perceive status differences and social hierarchies. Hofstede (1983) refers to this as the "power-distance" dimension. This dimension is related to the extent to which societies display degrees of centralization of authority and of autocratic leadership (Hofstede, 1983) or the interpersonal power or influence between bosses and subordinates (Triandis & Albert, 1987, p. 276). Korea and Australia are described as being very contrasting countries in terms of the dimension. Australia can, therefore, be anticipated to display moderately small power-distance, whereas Koreans would have fairly large power-distance.

Hofstede draws on the idea of core symbols that differentiate groups, and has identified these dimensions as power-distance, uncertainty avoidance, masculinity-femininity, and individualism-collectivism. These dimensions can be tracked through exploring the way participants in the interviews represent their cultures, and the normative patterns and symbolic structuring devices they use can be identified. In this study, different cultural styles were reflected in e-mail communications between Australians and Koreans, particularly in terms of power-distance and uncertainty avoidance (Hofstede, 1983). Only these two dimensions of Hofstede's model, power-distance and uncertainty avoidance, will be dealt with in this paper because of their significance to the findings.

Managing Style

Several factors emanating from the research indicate contrasting e-mail communication behaviours between the Australians and Koreans. These factors could be attributed to the high and low context cultural backgrounds (Hall, 1959). Reconfirming Saral's (1979) comments on the differences of Western-Eastern thinking, the data in the current study showed that Australians, in their e-mail communication with Koreans, placed higher value on categorization, classification, logical sequencing and rational relationships, whereas Koreans, like other Easterners, emphasized intuitive thinking and analogical processing. Korean interviewees generally commented that the typical Australian e-mail user tended to be informal and lengthy in the written style. The Koreans tend to believe that they are brief, formal, functional, and precise in their manner of e-mail communication. For example, a Korean made a detailed comment on the different styles between Australians and Koreans:

> Koreans generally write messages including other reports brief and try to put everything in one page. Australians seem to explain everything in detail in order to reduce the possibility of the other party making a subjective judgement due to insufficient information provided. Consequently, a file made by Australian staff is thicker than one by Korean, although it deals with a small issue. In short, we like to make tables and describe things with dot-points where Australians like to describe issues, explaining every detail. Their messages are well structured, for example, paragraphs are well linked, each paragraph has a theme, and sentences in a paragraph play a role. Although their English command is good, Koreans educated in Korea appear to express issues very brief. Maybe we are not trained to express issues in a written form which has a logical structure (Interview 9).

The interviews with Australians communicating with Koreans over e-mail elicited some other observations. Specifically, Koreans looked upon directness of intent in a message as rudeness. For example, an Australian interviewee indicates:

> If you ask—sometimes, you don't feel comfortable after you have interacted with some Korean on e-mail to ask for some information, directly. You might have to send an e-mail initially and then follow it up with specific questions and get answers to that. When you are writing to Australians, you can be more direct. G'day Anthony etc. etc. and they reply back in point form (Interview 7).

The Australian's observation is clearly supported by a Korean counterpart:

> When you e-mail to the Aussies it is pretty much freer, but when you e-mail to Koreans it takes more number of exchanges before you get information. You don't get it immediately. But with an Australian it comes very quick. . . . You have to break ice initially and then ask the questions (Interview 7).

As Lustig and Koester (1996) suggest, in high context cultures, one purpose of interaction is to promote and sustain harmony among the interactants. Therefore, unconstrained and explicit reactions could threaten the "face" or social esteem of others. This situation is in contrast to the e-mail protocol in low context cultures such as Australia, where the purpose of communication is to convey exact meanings, and explicit and direct messages help to achieve this goal. Consequently, the Australians anticipated that directness in approach or in a message would be looked upon as being culturally impolite and initiated culturally acceptable procedures in order to facilitate the e-mail communication in this intercultural setting.

Managing Power

Consistent with Hofstede's index, the study indicated that Australians and Koreans differ in the degree to which they believe that institutional and organizational power should be distributed unequally, and the decisions of the power holders should be challenged or accepted. The Korean e-mail user is very conscious of typical hierarchical and bureaucratic organization structures, power and communication related issues at his or her workplace. Upward communication through e-mail to immediate bosses, departmental managers and other senior staff—both within and outside Korea—tend to be formal, respectful, limited, and indirect in nature, according to the interviewees in the study. They maintain that formality and the show of respect in upward communication is an unwritten law of the organizational culture, as, for example, through the use of appropriate greetings while informing or consulting on issues through e-mail. There were several instances during the interviews that represent these themes:

> It is more serious and you gotta make sure what you put in there is great, and you have to make sure you get your points across and tell people this is the way something must be done. I think basically the writing style and who you are writing to [are important, as well as] you've got to be sure that you are not joking around when writing (Interview 6).

It is more depending on the organisation position, rather than the gender, that makes the e-mail usage different. For example, when a person in a higher position sends e-mail to the subordinate, she/he does not seem to pay attention to those things, such as format or style. They are freer in writing messages. On the contrary when juniors send e-mail to their bosses, they try not to make mistakes and pay attention to content, style, format, and politeness (Interview 3).

Therefore, the specific relationship that ought to be maintained with certain categories of people needs to be considered while communicating to Koreans. Such consideration leads to a lack of directness on the part of Koreans, as an Australian interviewee pointed out:

> When you engage in commercial relationships . . . you have a specific relationship with specific people be they your superior or otherwise, and that has to be given consideration in terms of how you address people, speed with which you come to the point . . . Two Korean people that I talk to make a reference to the weather and then start, so that they are not too direct. And I might advise people that, in certain circumstances, it is nice to share some point like I hope the weather is not too hot for you this time or I hope the peach blossoms are very colourful (Interview 3).
>
> E-mail use seems to have a lot to do with a leader of a team. It depends of the leader to what extent members of a team use e-mail. When the leader encourages or supports the e-mail use or considers the e-mail communication is important, the team members highly use e-mail. Corollary teams, which have leaders who are not enthusiastic about e-mail use, tend to use the telephone and fax (Interview 3).

The Australians interviewed believed that they were far less formal in their style of e-mail communication. However, in the event of intercultural business communication with Koreans, Australians were familiar with recognition of hierarchy by Koreans, as is indicated in the quotation below:

> Well, Koreans are very aware of the seniority structure. So when Koreans make contact with Australians, they are unaware of what their seniority is. You'll probably find that they use more formal kind of speech (Interview 1).

The Australian e-mail users interviewed also felt the need to be careful with matters pertaining to salutation of Korean counterparts. This situation is manifested in the styles of addressing staff, particularly senior managers. For example, an Australian interviewee observed that if he were in a typical Australian organisation, the upward communication via e-mail would be information, and he could address his superior by first name. However, the situation differs in the Korean firm in which he worked. For example, formal communication and "Dear Mr. President" were more acceptable. Another Australian e-mail user also added that he would not address Korean personnel by their first name. This usage is considered to be culturally incongruent with Korean customs:

> . . . It reflects that type of culture. Whereas Australians can be different. If I were in another company and if I had to send a letter to the general manager, I'd probably start the letter with his first name. But here it will be Dear Mr. President or Dear Dr. Chairman. And we are quite aware of the formality required with senior Korean management. You know it does vary from Australian company to Australian company. But the ones I work with you are much more in an informal footing, with senior management. As you get to know each other more, you get very informal (Interview 1).
>
> Probably, with the managing director of a company, one should be very respectful. I haven't done it, but probably Mr. XYZ, Chairman, Korea Zinc, make it like a letter. . . . Sometimes it is used as an official logo. So still formality is preferred (Interview 2).

In particular, the Australians in the study recognized that if they are interacting with Koreans through e-mail, there are perceived strong elements of bureaucracy and a need to adhere to formal upward communication, which is referred to as "Kyul-Jae" in the Korean culture. Often, such communication from the Koreans is used to double check on issues before intimating a final outcome electronically to the Australians. The net result, at least from the Australian perspective in the study, is quite often delays in matters requiring immediate and critical attention, even over e-mail. To an extent, the efficacy of the medium is defeated by time intensive work patterns among Koreans:

> We don't agree with some of the way the Korean engineers do things; it is different to Australia where we are used to making all around decisions more quickly without a lot of reference. Whereas in Korea, everything has to be put through a supervisor before being accepted. Little things like that which take, you know, a little bit of getting used to, but beyond that, there isn't much of a problem (Interview 1).

A major theme that arose from the study was the dichotomy between formal and informal use of communication via e-mail and factors related to these across Korean and Australian cultures:

> Basically it is more formal to communicate through e-mail. However, there are advantages and disadvantages in written communication. Because you can have more time in writing, you can write easily your exact thoughts. But it is sometimes better to talk in person in expressing yourself (Interview 1).
> . . . Communications are more systematic through e-mail compared with telephone, which we use for an instant interaction (Interview 3).
> It's easy to change or correct what you are saying in conversation as you speak with the other person. But when you e-mail, it takes more time because you have to write each paragraph carefully and choose words carefully (Interview 6).
> It would be [a] little different when you talk on the telephone because you can explain or add other relevant information. Written communication technologies, such as e-mail or fax, are mainly used for formal

and official purposes, such as offering the price (Interview 7).

> There are many cases I choose to use e-mail. Not necessarily e-mail all the time but I think written communication is best. When we do business, we often deal with all sorts of problems. When you discuss these on the phone, you get easily emotional. But when you write to send via e-mail or fax, anyhow you become to calm down and think over a matter. Use of internal mail for a daily report at the office is really useful in that sense. We e-mail our daily tasks done and leave a record of everything. While writing the e-mail messages I get reminded of, for example, any discussions I had through the telephone (Interview 7).

The display of respect for seniors through electronic communication and formal use of e-mail for business communication appears to be more of a cultural and organizational norm that personal choice:

> I normally write business messages formal. Particularly when I e-mail to my boss I make it more formal, paying attention to the details. I also try to use more polite expressions. For example, I conclude a message with Yours sincerely or Best regards. Or when I request something, I say can you be able to advise . . . instead of could you tell me . . . (Interview 5).
> Wording is different. I found myself writing e-mail messages more formal polite and elaborate using a number of honorifics, although I could point-form the message (Interview 6).
> When I send e-mail messages directly, not CC, to people in a higher position, I definitely write them very carefully. I pay attention to spellings, wordings, sentence structures and so on. I try to make the message precise, getting to the point. But with people those who I communicate with everyday I don't have time to check spelling mistakes or sentence structures. I don't think it's necessary (Interview 7).

In the instance of an Australian who worked in a Korean firm, the case was largely that upward e-mail communication was formal, irrespective of the fact that the immediate boss could be from either of the two cultures. In another case, an Australian, who had been deputed to the Korean branch of the firm for a few months, observed that the medium was strictly used for the purpose of internal and external business communication, and to that extent was formal.

However, as indicated in the previous section, there was also a change, over time, in e-mail communication in terms of its formality. An Australian respondent suggested that, through a series of e-mail exchanges between colleagues in Korea and Australia, the degree of formality associated with e-mail communication tended to wear off. There were, indeed, some intercultural experimentation and adjustments on the part of Korean e-mail users. Some Koreans were fascinated with cultural aspects of the Australian society, as seen in the informal first name based address of bosses and other staff. A few even requested to be greeted in similar terms:

> It can break down a little and a number of my counterparts in Korea have asked that I call them by their given names rather than their surnames. I was always taken to calling them by their surnames first. And this is another way some informality has been introduced to break down some of the barriers to ensure that we have a good electronic work forum, and it is the same thing on the telephone. A couple of people, with whom I have liaised, prefer to be called in that manner because they think that this is one way to make us feel more at ease. Perhaps they are somewhat fascinated by the tendencies in the West, particularly Australia, to use first names between people in comparable positions (Interview 3).

Some of the interviewees also perceived that frequent periodic communication via other media, such as telephone, between Koreans and Australians helped to initiate a degree of informality. At times, a direct face-to-face conversation could help relieve the formality of ensuing business communication:

> To develop a less formal rapport, a more periodic exchange would help to advance the similiarity and the understanding between the two parties and lead to a less formal, vernacular style between the participating bodies. But in circumstances [where] you don't ever speak to the person, then I guess time and trust and understanding will help to advance those causes (Interview 3).

Learning to Adapt

Although the styles of e-mail communication are disparate between the Australians and Koreans, the interviews clearly indicate mutual adjustments made by the users for the purpose of business. Specifically, the Australians interacting with the Koreans attempt to take on Korean norms and styles of communication with a view to making more sense while discussing business. One of these strategies was to accommodate the uncertainty avoidance dimension identified by Hofstede (1983, 1994). The study indicates that there is a disposition among Australians to make the first move towards such adaptation in intercultural business communication:

> So when I write and request something I try and be like them. Be more direct about how to write (Interview 4).
>
> . . . Australians tend to write a small précis. I think we've changed to the ways of the Koreans. Dot pointing items and highlighting them. So I think we made the change to meet the Koreans "cos it's practical. We both work on the same lines (Interview 1).

Likewise, there are instances where Koreans, who had settled in Australia, exhibited local characteristics of typical communication and lifestyle patterns:

> . . . When I joined up, he was initially in Brisbane. He changed his style, being in Australia and doing things the way Australians do. I speak to him once or twice every month and he sort of says that it is good to be back sort of thing. I think the longer the Koreans stay in Australia, the more Australianised they become rather the Koreanised we become. Would be different if we probably went to Korea (Interview 1).

Another interesting aspect that arose from the study was the change in written communication via e-mail between Koreans and Australians over time. As both Australian and Korean interviewees point out, messages tend to be more open after a few exchanges. The Koreans in the study perceived Australians as being friendly and open right from the start, and growing even more amicable over time. In particular, the Korean senders followed norms of formality and structure, thus adhering more carefully to strong cultural norms with regard to paying basic respect to people while deliberating on business issues:

> You get messages that are more open and once the ice is broken, say, after a couple of exchanges, you do get very quickly to the issues without having to go through the usual. But still the structures hang on. You don't get messages hanging loose. 'Cos I think there must be some formal idea of communicating to people, basic respect or something like that in the mindsets of the people (Interview 7).
>
> I think people change a little bit as they exchange e-mail over time. For example, at first even I didn't write greetings like "how are you?" because we don't know each other. As we exchange e-mail messages a number of times and talk on the telephone several times, I feel a sense of familiarity

with the person. Although the other person hasn't seen me, I feel as if she/he knows me. Although I don't drastically change my style of writing messages, I think I write messages more friendly. It appears to be same with the other party. Although I don't see a big change of working in their messages, formal letters surely have a friendly aspect (Interview 6).

> Koreans make their messages greatly formal. After exchanging a few messages the formality tends to decrease (Interview 11).

However, except for changes in written styles with regard to salutations become more informal, both Koreans and Australians in the study stated that there were few other variations to the above trend for the Koreans, as is indicated below:

> The greeting becomes informal, the contents remains formal (Interview 5).
>
> As we get to know each other through e-mail interactions, messages become more friendly. But it is the greetings that get informal. Business issues or important issues stay the same, formal (Interview 5).
>
> Over time e-mail messages become friendly; no major differences otherwise (Interview 6).
>
> Little change in style over time (Interview 7).
>
> I think the communication itself, including its style, stays the same as you interact via e-mail over time. For example, with Koreans because we exchange business information, we try to make e-mail messages as brief and simple as possible. I think it's best to get to the point in e-mail without being too friendly. First of all, it's a waste of your time if you write messages long or friendly. Also, it doesn't look professional (Interview 7).

The Australians observed, however, that after a few exchanges with their Korean counterparts in business over e-mail, the latter were conditioned to accept directness of message as a matter-of-fact issue. An interviewee states that messages could increasingly become concise, and electronic exchange takes on a more informal mode:

> Yes, sort of . . . we started to employ each other's first names and we got to a stage in a number of relationships, where we didn't have to give any sort of preamble; message could be concise and to the point and over and done with quickly (Interview 3).

Koreans also showed characteristics of a high context culture. Their reactions were reserved, meanings were internalized, and there was a strong emphasis on nonverbal codes. One Australian commented that, from his experience, he believed that it was safer to communicate urgent and important matters to Koreans on a face-to-face basis rather than through e-mail, because seldom the latter seek to clarify matters, even when required. The suggestion was that at least through facial gestures, one could guess if a matter had been understood in its entirety or not:

> More by face-to-face . . . May be in the case of face to face you are 100% sure that there is no misunderstanding. Whereas if it is down on e-mail, they wouldn't come and ask you if there is a misunderstanding. But in face-to-face, they can ask you. . . . I've never been asked by a Korean in a situation that they didn't understand. Who knows if they did or didn't (Interview 4).

Clearly, e-mail offers Korean users another avenue to stay silent and protect their public image. This situation links closely to Hofstede's (1983, 1994) notion of uncertainty avoidance. Given Hofstede's definition, Korean e-mail users feel comfortable with uncertain or unknown situations because it prevents them from being placed in a situation that could result in a loss of face. In other words, Korean users feel less anxious not understanding the meaning of an e-mail message than they would asking Australian counterparts for clarification and thus suffering the possibility of humiliation and embarrassment. By staying silent, they are protecting their public image and that of their organization, even if that means lower productivity.

In relation to the English language issue, Australians interviewed exhibited adaptations to Koreans, which could be a strategy for effective e-mail communication within this intercultural communication setting. The Australian user warns against indiscriminate use of the colloquialisms or slang to prevent distortion of meaning communicated to the less advantaged Korean:

> To avoid using colloquial expressions, as even as these are written down, they may not be understood. And to be—perhaps, shorter sentences, which are quite concise. And to keep messages as brief as possible. Not that they are too long (Interview 3).

However, Australian e-mail users who interacted with Koreans were wary of informal communication in the initial stages. They preferred their messages to look good, structured and formal, and to indicate a sense of respect for the recipient. Australians interviewed suggested the following strategies for e-mail business communication with Koreans:

> I would advise them [Australians who are going to communicate via e-mail] to be pretty careful in the beginning; not to take off the way they would. On the Net, or the other ordinary e-mail networks we have here in Australia, I'd ask them to be a little structured, a little formal and to look good when you send a message, 'cos there must be some sense of respect or presenting oneself even when you send a message electronically and then see how it goes and tackle the issues, as it comes by. And then go informal slowly, switch to the mode you want, you know, speak issues and mix things together,

if the other person starts responding to you. But then you've got to test things initially (Interview 7).

It will depend on the circumstance. If it is to a company or a client, then etiquette might dictate that you do make it more formal. But certainly within the office . . . with the colleagues, I can just say: I'll see you at 10 o'clock and you don't have to give them a formal missive as far as instructions are concerned, whereas if it is going outside the organization you have to bear in mind that the person is likely to be a client and that you show a little more respect, behave a little bit more formally until the rapport is established. Whereas with colleagues perhaps you already have a working relationship and electronic communications is just another dimension in the way you interact with those people (Interview 3).

This follows Hofstede's notion of power-distance; Australians display a moderately small power distance, whereas Koreans show fairly large power distance on Hofstede's index. This suggestion is consistent with the present findings. The Austalians interviewed showed less concern about differences in rank, indicating that superiors and subordinates should have equal rights, prefer two-way communication, and act in a friendly, informal manner by, for example, addressing people by their given name. Koreans, on the other hand, were more concerned about hierarchy and differences in rank, and they also exhibited greater formality in their manner. However, in the work environment as well as the working relationship with a client outside the office, formality took on a significant role in e-mail communication, both within Australian and Korean cultures.

CONCLUSION

The aim of the present study was to gain a general understanding of intercultural communication via e-mail: how different cultures, users, and the technology interact for effective communication. The overall results of this study revealed that the interaction is more complex than direct intercultural communication between Australians and Koreans. Social and cultural issues shaped users' e-mail adaptation. For example, Korean cultural factors such as an hierarchical structural system with its use of a large power distance, affected most aspects of Australians' adaptation. Also, an Australian cultural factor such as strong individualism tended to help Australians persist in their own ways. However, structural issues of efficiency and convenience also mediated the process of the adaptation and presentation of users for effective communication. For example, even though Australians' and Koreans' different cultural backgrounds and lack of similarities inhibited successful exchange, mutual understanding, agreement, and cooperation (such as sharing information or ideas and solving problems via e-mail), they *did* attempt to accommodate and adapt to one another and produce effective on-line communication.

In general, intercultural communication via e-mail offers new challenges to users. Along with the complex task of deciding which media can provide the most effective business practices, users such as those in the study face new challenges. On one hand, it is clear that the categories of, and symbolic structuring by which different groups manage their world culture prescribe certain behaviours and proscribe others. The interviews provided discursive texts that offered many examples of the ways that both Koreans and Australians symbolically structure their worlds. These ranged from simple structures and normative prescriptions such as the layout and formulation of ideas to the more complex tasks of handling business decisions in culturally appropriate ways. Additionally, e-mail users, regardless of their culture, displayed propensities, sensitivities, and the facility to adapt. However, some of the most significant findings of the study are derived from the complex way in which culture and technology intersect. Three of these, in particular, need further exploration: first, the ways in which the Korean and Australian staff adapted to each other's styles and demeanours; second, as a mechanism for freeing up of some bureaucratic patterns of organization; and third, the use of e-mail to handle sensitive issues. Together, these aspects all point to the possibilities that new technologies offer for changing work practices and easing workplace tensions.

Further studies, drawing on the interpretive paradigm, could provide more detailed ways in which the new technologies can contribute to intercultural understanding in a global economy. There is no doubt that an increased understanding of intercultural communication, and technology as integral to its practice, is needed with the internationalisation of business practice. Managing intercultural communication competence is undoubtedly one of the industries that has the potential to dominate the new millennium.

NOTE

1. We use the term "intercultural communication," following Collier and Thomas (1988), "as characterized by contact between persons who identify themselves as distinct from one another in cultural terms" (p. 100).

REFERENCES

Allwood, C. M. & Wang, Z. M. (1990). Conceptions of computers among students in China and Sweden. *Computers in Human Behavior, 6,* 185–199.

Collier, M. J. & Thomas, M. (1988). Cultural identity: An interpretive perspective. In Y. Kim, & W. Gudykunst, (Eds.), *Theories in intercultural communication.* Thousand Oaks: Sage.

Eisenhardt, K. M. (1989). Building theories from case study research. *Academy of Management Review,* 14(4), 532–550.

Garton, L. & Wellman, B. (1994). Social impacts of electronic mail in organizations: A review of the research literature. *Communication Yearbook, 18,* 434–453.

Gattiker, U. E. & Nelligan, T. (1988). Computerized offices in Canada and the United States: Investigating dispositional similarities and differences. *Journal of Organizational Behavior, 9,* 77–96.

Green, L., & Guinery, R. (eds.), (1994). *Framing technology: Society, choice and change.* St Leonards, NSW: Allen & Unwin.

Guba, E. G. (1978). *Toward a methodology of naturalistic inquiry in educational evaluation.* CSE Monograph Series in Evaluation, No. 8, Los Angeles: University of California, L.A., Centre for the Study of Evaluation.

Hakken, D. (1991). Culture-centered computing: Social policy and development of new information technology in England and the United States. *Human Organization, 50* (4), 406–423.

Hall, E. T. (1959). *The Silent Language.* Garden City, NY: Doubleday.

Harvey, F. (1997). National cultural differences in theory and practice. Evaluating Hofstede's national cultural framework. *Information Technology and People, 10* (2), 132–146.

Hearn, G. & Mandeville, T. (1995). The electronic superhighway: Increaed commodification or the democratization of leisure? *Media Information Australia, 75,* 92–101.

Hofstede, G. (1983, Fall). The cultural relativity of organizational practices and theories. *Journal of International Business Studies, 75,* 223–245.

Hofstede, G. (1994). *Cultures and organizations: Intercultural cooperation and its importance for survival.* London: HarperCollins.

Holves, M. E., (1994). Don't blink or you'll miss it: Issues in electronic mail research. *Communication Yearbook, 18,* 454–463.

Jackson, M. H. (1995). The meaning of "communication technology": The technology-context scheme. *Communication Yearbook, 19,* 229–267.

Jarvenpaa, S. L., Knoll, K., & Leidner, D. E. (1998). Is anybody out there? Antecedents of trust in global virtual teams. *Journal of Management Information Systems, 14,* 14–24.

Kaplan, R. S. (1986). The role for empirical research in management accounting. *Accounting, Organizations and Society, 111* (4/5), 429–452.

Kim, Y. & Gudykunst, W. (1988). *Theories in intercultural communication.* Thousand Oaks, CA: Sage.

Kinsella, W. J. (1993). Communication and information technologies: A dialectical model of technology and human agency. *The New Jersey Journal of Communication, 1* (1), 2–18.

Kirligod, M. (1996). Information technology transfer to a developing country: executive information systems in Turkey, *Information Technology and People, 9* (3), 55–84.

Lennie, J., Hearn, G., Stevenson, T., Inayatullah, S., & Mandeville, T. (1996). Bringing multiple perspectives to Australia's communication futures: Beyond the superhighway? *Prometheus, 14* (1), 10–30.

Lustig, R. W., & Koester, J. (1996). *Intercultural competence: Interpersonal communication across cultures.* New York: HarperCollins.

Makrakis, V. (1992). Cross©cultural comparison of gender differences in attitude towards computers in Japan and Sweden. *Scandinavian Journal of Educational Research, 36* (4), 275–287.

Mandeville, T., & Rooney, D. (1997). The government use of e-mail: Impacts on organization and work practice. *The Communication Centre Research Report Series Research Report No. 5,* The Communication Centre, Queensland University of Technology.

Marcoulides, G. A. (1991). An examination of cross-cultural differences toward computers. *Computers in Human Behavior, 7,* 281–289.

Mobley, M., and Wilson, M. (1998). Cultural aspects of internet usage: A preliminary inquiry, *Educational Technology, Research and Development, 46,* 109–112.

Narula, U. (1988). The cultural challenge of communication technology. *American Behavioral Scientist, 32* (2), 194–207.

Orlikowski, W. J., Yates, J., Okaumra, K. & Fujimoto, M. (1995). Shaping electronic communication: The metastructuring of technology in the context of use. *Organization Science, 6* (4), 423–444.

Patton, M. Q. (1990). *Qualitative evaluation and research methods* (2nd edition). Newbury Park: Sage.

Poole, S. M. & DeSanctis, G. (1990). Understanding the use of group decision support systems: The theory of adaptive structuration. In J. Fulk and C. Steinfield (Eds.), *Organizations and communication technology.* Newbury Park, CA: Sage.

Rogers, E. M. & Albritton, M. M. (1995). Interactive communication technologies in business organizations. *The Journal of Business Communication, 32* (2), 177–190.

Ross-Flanigan, N. (1998). The virtues (and vices) of virtual colleagues. *MIT's Technology Review, 101* (2), 52–59.

Saral, T. B. (1979). Intercultural communication theory and research: An overview of challenges and opportunities. *Communication Yearbook, 3,* 395–405.

Sewell, G. (1996). A Japanese "cure" to a British "disease'?: Cultural dimensions to the development of workplace surveillance technologies. *Information Technologies and People, 9* (3), 12–29.

Simon, J. L. (1978). *Basic research methods in social science: The art of empirical investigation.* (2nd ed.). New York: Random House.

Sproull, L. & Kisler, S. (1991). *Connections: New ways of working in the networked organization.* Cambridge: MIT Press.

Straub, D. (1994). The effect of culture on IT diffusion: E-mail and fax in Japan and the United States. *Information Systems Research, 5* (1), 23–47.

Triandis, H. C. & Albert, R. D. (1987). Cross-cultural perspectives. In F. M. Jablin, L. L. Putnam, K. H. Roberts, and L. W. Porter (Eds.), *Handbook of organizational communication: An interdisciplinary perspective.* Newbury Park, CA: Sage.

Umble, D. Z. (1991). *The coming of the telephone to plain country: A study of Amish and Mennonite resistance in Lancaster County.*

Pennsylvania at the turn of the century, Unpublished PhD thesis, University of Pennsylvania.

Wajcman, J. (1991). *Feminism confronts technology*. North Sydney: Allen and Unwin.

Wang, G. (1991). Information society in their mind: A survey of college students in seven nations. *Asian Journal of Communication, 1* (2), 1–18.

Woolgar, S. (1991). Configuring the user. In J. Law (Ed.), *A sociology of monsters: Essays on power, technology and domination*. (57–102). Keele: Sociological Review Monograph.

Yin, R. K. (1994). *Case study research: Design and methods* (2ⁿᵈ ed.). Applied Social Research Methods Series Vol. 5. Thousand Oaks: Sage.

Yuchtman-Yaar, E., & Gottlieb, A. (1985). Technological development and the meaning of work: A cross-cultural perspective, *Human Relations, 38* (7), 603–621.

Hee-Soo Kim, Ph.D. from Queensland University of Technology, is a Research Fellow at the Asian-Australia Institute, The University of New South Wales.

Greg Hearn, Ph.D. from University of Queensland, is an associate professor in the School of Communication at the Queensland University of Technology.

Caroline Hatcher, Ph.D. from Queensland University of Technology, is a Senior Lecturer in the School of Communication at the Queensland University of Technology.

Ian Weber, Ph.D. from Queensland University of Technology, is a Lecturer in the School of Communication at the Queensland University of Technology.

Reading 2.6

Language Choice Online

Globalization and Identity in Egypt

MARK WARSCHAUER

GHADA R. EL SAID

AYMAN ZOHRY

INTRODUCTION

As a major new means of global communication, the Internet is bound to have a great impact on language use. Probably the most feared result, voiced most often in the Internet's early years, was that the Internet would encourage global use of English to such a degree that other languages would be crowded out. And indeed, in the mid-1990s, fully 80% of international Web sites were reported to be in English (Cyberspeech, 1997). Though no recent studies have been done on the number of Web sites in each language, the number of non-English Web sites is by all accounts growing quickly and is expected to overtake the number of English language Web sites shortly if it has not already done so (Crystal, 2001).[1]

In spite of this change, English remains a dominant force within certain Internet realms. A study conducted by the Organization for Economic Co-operation and Development (The Default Language, 1999) found that while some 78% of Web sites in OECD countries were in English, 91% of Web sites on "secure-servers" were in English, and a fully 96% of Web sites on secure servers in the .com domain were in English. This is significant because secure servers (and, especially those in .com) are used for e-commerce. Presumably then, while a growing number of non-commercial sites are in local languages, English remains the dominant language of commercial sites.

The strong presence of English online has caused consternation in many parts of the world. Local opposition to English Internet use has sprung up in many places, most notably France, where a 1994 law mandates that all advertising must be conducted in the French language (Online, 1998) and where the Finance Minister reportedly banned the use in his ministry of English-derived terms such as e-mail or start-up in favor of French terms such as courier electronique or jeune pousse. In

---

*Reprinted with permission from *Journal of Computer Mediated Communication*, Vol. 7(4), July, 2002.

Authors' Note: An earlier version of this chapter was presented at the American Association of Applied Linguistics annual meeting in Vancouver, Canada in March 2000.

other countries, concerns about English use online have sparked new efforts to improve English language instruction (Takahashi, 2000).

Of course the Internet is not only a boon to English but potentially to many other languages as well, especially minority languages that bridge geographically dispersed speakers or which have insufficient resources to make use of more expensive media. There are numerous examples of technology use for indigenous language revitalization (see Warschauer, 1998). The Internet has also proven to be a vehicle for written communication in dialects and languages that previously were used principally for oral communication (see, for example, Warschauer, 2001).

In spite of the concern about the competition between English and other languages online, very little research has been done on the topic, with the notable exception of two studies by Paolillo on language use in a Usenet group (1996) and an IRC channel (2001). These studies highlighted, among other things, the role of code-switching between two languages within a particular group of interlocutors.

This paper goes beyond a particular channel to look more broadly at language choice online by a group of Egyptian Internet users, examining in what circumstances, and why, this group uses English and Arabic in their computer-mediated communication. In the remainder of this paper, we will first provide some background information on language use and Internet use in Egypt, then introduce and discuss the study, and finally analyze the results in terms of broader global trends of language, identity, and globalization.

LANGUAGE CONTEXT

Language use in Egypt is considered as a classic example of diglossia, that is, a situation in which one dialect or language is used in formal or written realms and a second dialect or language is used largely in informal or spoken realms (Ferguson, 1972, p. 244). Diglossia can refer either to the use of two different languages (for example, English and Tagalog in the Philippines) or to the use of two different varieties or dialects of the same language (for example, Standard German and Swiss German in parts of Switzerland).

In Egypt, the two varieties used are both varieties of Arabic rather than different languages. The two varieties used in Egypt are referred to as Classical Arabic and Egyptian Arabic (Haeri, 1997). Actual usage of Classical or Egyptian Arabic in Egypt falls along a continuum, rather than in complete bipolar opposition (Bentahila, 1991; Parkinson, 1992), but since most uses tend toward one pole or the other these two are considered as the main Arabic dialects of Egypt. Classical Arabic is the literary dialect which is used in the Qu'ran; in most print publications including books, magazines, and newspapers; and in formal spoken discourse, including prayer, television news broadcasts, and formal prepared speeches. It is used with relatively little variation throughout the Arab world; Moroccans, Egyptians, Iraqis, and Saudis who know Classical Arabic will be mutually comprehensible in writing or speech.

Egyptian Arabic, also referred to as Egyptian colloquial Arabic (see, for example, Al-Tonis, 1980), is the spoken dialect of the Egyptian people and is used in conversation, songs, films, and television soap operas. As for written forms, it is used in comic strips and, occasionally, in novels and short stories (similarly to how non-standard English dialects might be occasionally used either as a literary device or specifically for the reporting of dialogue and conversation). Both Classical Arabic and Egyptian Arabic use the same Arabic script. Egyptian Arabic is spoken only in Egypt (or by Egyptians elsewhere), but it is understood widely in the Arab world due to the popularity of Egyptian films and songs.

Both Classical Arabic and Egyptian Arabic have their own powerful symbolism for Egyptians. Classical Arabic, as the language of the Qu'ran and the common language of the Arab nation, is central to their identity as members of that nation and of the broader Islamic community. Egyptian Arabic, as the language of daily communication, jokes, song, and cinema, is central to their identity as Egyptians. While virtually all Egyptians are competent speakers of Egyptian, only about half of adults in the country can read and write Classical Arabic (Fandy, 2000). The country's low rate of adult literacy—52.7% according to the United Nations Development Programme (2000)—stems in part from the difficulty that Egyptian children have in mastering a written language that is at large variance from their spoken variety.

Beyond this diglossia of Classical and Egyptian Arabic, many other languages are used in Egypt, including the ancient Coptic language that is sometimes used in Coptic Christian church services (Takla, 2002), African languages are used by refugees, and European languages are used in business and tourism. The use of European languages in Egypt has a long history dating back to periods of French and British colonialism, and the Egyptian elite often preferred to be educated in French or English rather than Arabic (Haeri, 1997). Most recently, though, the use of English has far surpassed that of French and other foreign languages within Egypt. According to a recent study by Schaub (2000), English plays a dual role in Egypt. On the one hand it is the principle foreign language of the general population. English is the first and only mandatory foreign language taught in schools, with obligatory English language instruction starting in fourth grade. Hotel workers, shopkeepers, and street salespeople use English to communicate with foreign visitors and residents, especially in major cities and tourist destinations (Schaub, 2000; Stevens, 1994).

Beyond that though, English serves as a second language of additional communication for a large swath of Egypt's elite. The majority of private schools are considered English language schools, which means that English language instruction begins in kindergarten and that English is a medium of instruction of other specified subjects (i.e., mathematics and science). Recently, the Ministry of Education has also launched experimental language schools within the public school system, and 79 of the 80 launched so far are English medium, with one being French medium (personal interview with Reda Fadel, former Councilor of English, Egyptian Ministry of Education, April 2000). The elite usually continue their post-secondary education in English, studying either abroad (e.g., in the United States or England), at an English-medium university in Egypt (the most established being the American University in Cairo), or in an English-medium department of an Egyptian public university. Medicine, dentistry, veterinary studies, engineering, the natural sciences, and computer sciences all use English as a main medium of instruction, and other disciplines, such as commerce and law, have special English-medium sections which are considered more prestigious and difficult to enter. Graduates from these universities and programs often enter careers in which English continues to be used as a daily medium of communication, such as international business or computer science. Professionals in other elite fields, such as medicine, continue to use English as an additional language through frequent contact with foreigners and through professional activities; for example, the conferences of doctors, dentists, and nurses in Egypt are conducted in English, even without foreigners present, and professional publications of these groups are published in English (see discussion of English as a second language of the Egyptian elite in Haeri, 1997, and in Schaub, 2000).

TECHNOLOGY CONTEXT

The other main contextual factor framing this study is the use of the Internet in Egypt. The Internet was first introduced to Egypt in 1993, when a small university network was established (Information technology in Egypt, 1998). Commercial Internet use began three years later and has developed with more government support and less censorship than in many other Mideast countries, reaching a total of some 440,000 Internet users by 2000 (Dabbagh Information Technology Group, 2000), representing 0.7% of the population. Though the growth of the Internet in Egypt is constrained by economic (i.e., high expense in relation to average income) and infrastructure factors (i.e., low teledensity), the impact of the Internet extends beyond its current limited reach. The Egyptian government is placing great emphasis on information and communication technologies, and Egypt is said to have one of the fastest growing ICT markets in the world. Initiatives to expand Internet access and use abound in the educational system, the business community, and the non-profit sector. Furthermore, those who are already connected disproportionately represent the economic elite, so their influence extends far beyond their somewhat limited numbers, especially in major population centers such as Cairo and Alexandria (Warschauer, 2003).

With this context as a background, an exploratory study was conducted of a group of Internet users in Egypt. The study sought to find out which languages this group of people used in online communications and why.

METHOD

Subjects

The study was carried out among 43 young professionals in Cairo known to be Internet users. The category of "young professionals" was chosen because it represents the first generation of Internet users in Egypt. Young professionals are of course not representative of the overall Egyptian population or even of current Internet users, but they do include among them many of the early adopters of the Internet in Egypt. The young professionals in this study were selected through personal contacts; the subjects may not be representative of all young professionals in Cairo.

"Young professionals" were defined for the purpose of the study as people between the ages of 24 and 36 engaged in introductory or middle level professional and management positions. All 43 of the people in the sample had at least a bachelor's degree and 30 of the group (70%) had a master's or doctorate. Areas of study ranged broadly and included engineering, economics, computer science, and medicine. The sample was fairly evenly balanced for gender, with 23 men and 20 women. A total of 23 of the people in the sample worked in the information technology industry, and included computer engineers, information technology specialists, system engineers, and managers. The remaining 20 worked for a variety of business and research industries and included an environmental researcher, librarians, statisticians, and doctors. Almost all had part of their education in English and part in Arabic.

Instruments

Survey

A written survey was developed that inquired about people's language and literacy practices online. The survey included six questions about personal information (e.g., what is your profession?), four general questions about computer and Internet access and use (e.g., how long have you been using the Internet), eight questions about language use online (e.g., what language[s] do you use in online "real-time" chatting with Egyptians or other Arabic speakers), and eight questions about print literacy practices (e.g., what kind of things do you write regularly and in what language?) The survey was first pilot tested among a small group of people who were not in the final survey, and then finalized and distributed by e-mail to 50 people. Recipients were also asked to include voluntarily examples of any e-mail messages or online chats that illustrated the points covered in the survey.

A total of 43 out of 50 people returned the survey. Eight of the 43 included examples of e-mail messages or online chats, and some of these are included within the analysis.

The survey was non-anonymous, so that the researchers could conduct follow-up interviews. People were asked their name and e-mail address and whether they agreed to be contacted for a follow-up interview. A total of 31 people volunteered to be interviewed.

Interviews

Four people were selected for interviews who, judging by their survey answers, represented a cross-section of language use patterns found in formal and informal Internet communications. Two of the four came in together; the other two came in alone. The interviews were conducted using a semi-structured approach, that is, a set of interview questions were planned ahead of time related to language and literacy practices online, but the interviews diverged as appropriate to explore interesting points that came up. The interviews lasted from 60 to 90 minutes and were tape recorded with the consent of the subjects.

Data Analysis

Survey data was tallied to allow the examination of various types of online communication by language, dialect, and script. In

addition, after the use of Egyptian Arabic was identified as occurring in online communication, a two-tailed Analysis of Variance (ANOVA) was performed to investigate which factors were correlated with online use of Egyptian Arabic (with alpha established at .05).

The interviews were transcribed and the written transcripts were examined by the researchers to identify patterns and illustrative examples of when and why the participants used a particular language, dialect, and script online.

Limitations

Finally, it is important to point out the limitations of this study. The sample size is small and was selected through personal contacts of the researchers, and is thus non-random. The facts that the subjects were personally known by the researchers and that the survey was non-anonymous (to allow for follow-up contact) may have affected people's responses. The survey was not formally tested for reliability. Only 4 of the 43 participants were interviewed, and the interview transcripts were examined for patterns and illustrative examples rather than systematically coded; furthermore, this examination process was not checked for inter-rater reliability. In addition, no systematic attempt was made to assess participants' fluency in English, Classical Arabic, or Egyptian Arabic. For all of these reasons, the results of the study cannot be assumed to be generalizable to other populations beyond this group of subjects. Rather, this study should be considered an exploratory investigation that had the goal of identifying possible issues and trends for further research.

RESULTS

The most interesting results of the survey were in the area of language use online.

Table 1   Language and Script Use

	Formal E-Mail	Informal E-Mail	Online Chat
English	37 (92.5%)	35 (83.3%)	22 (71%)
Classical Arabic (Arabic Script)	4 (10%)	4 (9.5%)	2 (6.5%)
Classical Arabic (Roman Script)	1 (2.5%)	7 (16.7)	3 (9.7%)
Egyptian Arabic (Arabic Script)	0 (0%)	2 (4.8%)	5 (16.1%)
Egyptian Arabic (Roman Script)	4 (10%)	21 (50%)	17 (54.8%)
Total Number of Participants Using this Feature	40	42	31

Basically, Classical Arabic in Arabic Script, the most common form of writing in Egypt, was seldom used by any of the 43 participants in their Internet communications. Rather, online communications featured a new and unusual diglossia-between a foreign language, English, and a Romanized, predominately colloquial form of Arabic that had very limited use for these informants prior to the development of the Internet.

Table 1 shows the number of people who indicated that they used English, Classical Arabic (in either Arabic script or Romanized script), and Egyptian Arabic (in either Arabic script or Romanized script) in their formal e-mail messages, informal e-mail messages, and online chats.[2] English and Romanized Egyptian Arabic are the two main language forms used and will be discussed in turn below.

English Online

Table 2 indicates the number of people who used English, Classical Arabic (in either Arabic or Romanized script), and Egyptian Arabic (in either Arabic or Romanized script) in their online communications. Table 3 displays a simple comparison between English and any form of Arabic (or English and Arabic combined). Both sets of data indicate that English is the dominant language used in online communication among this group of Egyptian young professionals.

The dominance of English is particularly strong in formal e-mail communication, with 82.5% of the participants using only English in that medium (see Table 3). In informal e-mail communication, the situation is more balanced, with a slight majority of the participants code switching between English and Arabic (principally Egyptian Arabic, see Tables 2 and 3). In online chats, the majority also code-switch, with smaller and equal numbers using English or Arabic only (see Table 3). An examination of e-mail messages and online chat transcripts that were submitted indicated that, when English and Arabic were combined in a single message, there tended to be more use of English. In addition, each person who was interviewed indicated that the majority of their Web page reading was also done in English.

The interviews and survey data made it clear that the prominence of English in Internet communication stems from a variety of social, economic, and technological factors that are closely related to the more general role of English in Egyptian society. The following points were stressed by interviewees as to why they use English predominately in online communication:

General dominance of English in the professional milieu. Most of the formal online communication carried out by the young professionals in this study was done within broader environments that strongly emphasized English.

Table 2   Language and Dialect Use

	Formal E-Mail	Informal E-Mail	Online Chat
English	37 (92.5%)	35 (83.3%)	22 (71%)
Classical Arabic	5 (12.5%)	11 (26.2%)	6 (19.5%)
Egyptian Arabic	4 (10%)	21 (50%)	19 (61.2%)
Total Number of Participants Using this Feature	40	42	31

Table 3   English vs. Arabic*

	Formal E-Mail	Informal E-Mail	Online Chat
English only	33 (82.5%)	13 (31%)	6 (20.7%)
Arabic only	5 (12.5%)	7 (16.7%)	6 (20.7%)
English and Arabic	2 (5%)	22 (52.4%)	17 (58.7%)
Total Number of Participants Using this Feature	40	42	29

Note: Includes Egyptian Arabic, Classical Arabic, or both.

For example, one information technology professional explained most of his professional contacts are with software or hardware firms that are branches of international companies. Therefore, even if he is contacting a local branch office in Egypt, he is aware that that branch functions in a broader English language milieu, and he thus directs his professional communications in English. The study indicated that some 75% of the participants do most of their professional writing in English. It is thus certainly not a surprise that their formal e-mail communication is also in English. Similarly, most of the types of business and technical information sought by these young professionals are available on the World Wide Web in English, so they naturally search the Web in that language.

Lack of Arabic software standards. A second reason for a dominance of English is the lack of a common Arabic software standard. The reasons for this are part technical, as computing throughout the world is easier in the "ASCII" code that supports unmodified Roman letters. The larger reason, however, is socio-economic. Countries such as Japan, Taiwan, and Israel have been able to develop common standards for non-Roman computing and telecommunications due to the prominence of a national bourgeoisie within a particular country. Computing leadership within the Arabic world is spread over a number of countries, and the business community in each of these countries—especially in the information and communications technology field—is largely dominated by foreign companies and managers. This is especially true in the oil-rich Gulf countries, which employ huge numbers of foreign managers and technicians. The lack of a single common standard for Arabic language computing, together with the large presence of foreign nationals in the business community, hinders Arabic language computing. For example, one of the participants in the survey had started an online sales business targeted to consumers in Egypt. Though the majority of his customers were Egyptians, information on his pages was available only in English. He explained that most of his customers accessed the Web at their jobs, and they often worked at foreign companies that had not upgraded to Arabic language operating systems (due, in part, to the desire to use a single standard throughout their companies, the headquarters of which were based outside the Arab world). This budding entrepreneur felt that his best chance of building an audience in Egypt would thus be to market his product in English.

Computer and Internet use learned in English environments. Most of the participants stressed that they first learned to use computers and the Internet in English environments, either in their English-medium coursework or in English-dominant work environments. For this reason, they were not experienced typists in Arabic, either using Arabic script or Roman script. Several mentioned that they thus wrote principally in English and only used Arabic where there was a special feeling or sentiment that was difficult to say in English.

Early adopters' fluency in English. The majority of the people in this survey were educated in English and can write English as well as or better than Arabic. This, together with the other reasons listed above, provides another disincentive to switch to Arabic in online communications, especially for formal interaction.

Use of Egyptian Arabic

The other interesting result of the study was the considerable amount of Romanized Egyptian Arabic used by the participants. Romanized Egyptian Arabic was widely used in both informal e-mail communications and online chatting, with many people engaging in code-switching (between English and Egyptian Arabic) and some writing exclusively in Egyptian Arabic.

The emergence of Romanized Egyptian Arabic is especially interesting because it was previously not a widely used language form. As discussed earlier, Egyptian Arabic is principally a means of oral communication. Though it has been written in certain realms, such as comic books, prior to the Internet it appeared mainly in Arabic script, with several unofficial Romanized versions existing principally for the benefit of foreigners (for example, in language instruction books and dictionaries). Broader written uses of Egyptian Arabic in areas such as business, scholarship, and religion are frowned upon by society and by various educational and religious authorities. The use of Egyptian Arabic in online communications represents a major expansion of its written use, especially in a Romanized form, in a new realm in which informality is considered acceptable and in which no authority has stepped forward to discourage its use.

One of the interesting features of this adaptation is the widespread use of the numbers 2, 3, and 7 to represent phonemes that are not easily rendered in the Roman alphabet. The uses of these numbers arose among Internet users and have spread spontaneously and are now widely recognized. The use of two of these numbers is seen in the following informal e-mail, which also provides a good example of code-switching:

Hello Dalia,

7amdellah 3ala el-salama ya Gameel. we alf mabrouk 3alal el-shahada el-kebeera . .

Keep in touch . . I really hope to see you all Soooooooooooooooon (Maybe in Ramadan).

Kol Sana Wentom Tayyebeen.

Waiting to hear from you. . .

Laila

Greetings
Salamt [Greetings]
Ezayek [How are you?]
Akhbarek eih, [What's new?]
Sarcastic Expressions
Ya Fandem !! [Sir (sarcastic)]
Rabena yg3al fe weshek e120bol :) [Let God make it easy for us (sarcastic)]
Food and Holidays
Kahek el Eid [Egyptian sweet only, usually to be eaten after Ramadan]
Fanousse Ramadan [Ramadan Lantern]
Agazet noss el sanna [Mid term vacation]
Religious Expressions
In shaa Allah [God willing]
El hamdoulellah [Thank God]
Besm Allah el Rahman el Raheem [In the name of God the merciful and most compassionate]
As-Salamu alaikum wa rahmatu Allahi wa barakatu [May God give you peace, his mercy and blessing]

Figure 1   Representative expressions in Romanized Egyptian Arabic

Translation:

Hello Dalia,

Thank God for the safe return, my sweet. Congratulations for the big certificate [sarcastic].

Keep in touch . . . I really hope to see you all Soooooooooooooon (Maybe in Ramadan)

Happy Ramadan.

Waiting to hear from you. . . .

Laila

Participants in the study who engaged in code-switching indicated that they most frequently used Egyptian Arabic to express highly personal content that they can't express well in English. Several interviewees explained that they start off in English and switch over to Egyptian Arabic when they feel they need to. Analysis of sample messages indicated that, in bilingual messages, Egyptian Arabic was most often found in greetings, humorous or sarcastic expressions, expressions related to food and holidays, and religious expressions (see Figure 1).

Finally, a means test (using a two-tailed ANOVA) was carried out to investigate further the online use of Egyptian Arabic. Two factors correlated significantly ($p < .05$) with increased use of Egyptian Arabic in online chatting: (1) years of experience using the Internet and (2) working in an information technology profession. The latter is of interest because information technologies professionals in Egypt, in addition to being proficient with computers, are also known for being highly proficient in English (see discussion in Schaub, 2000), a characteristic which extends to this particular group as well, based on the researchers' evaluation following extensive personal communication with the subjects. This suggests that there are other explanations for use of Egyptian Arabic rather than lack of familiarity with English or computers. One possible, though untested, explanation is that the familiarity of the information technology professionals with computers and the Internet has led them to want to experiment more, especially in online chatting. At least within this group of young professionals, use of Egyptian Arabic does not appear to be a crutch used by those with less background in computers and English, but rather an additional communicative tool selected by those with expertise and experience with computers and English.

Other factors, such as gender or amount of education, were not found to correlate with whether people used Egyptian Arabic in online communication.

DISCUSSION

Two interesting findings have emerged from this study: first, that English is the dominant language used online among a particular group of early Internet adopters in Egypt, and secondly, that a previously little used written form of Romanized Egyptian Arabic is also widely used in informal communication by this group. We believe that the possible meaning of these findings is better understood when examined in a broader context of language, technology, and society in Egypt and internationally.

Sociologists have pointed to the current era as marked by a contradiction between global networks and local identities (Barber, 1995; Castells, 1996/2000; Castells, 1997). On the one hand, global flows of capital, finance, markets and media increasingly impinge on our lives, weakening traditional pillars of authority such as the nation-state, the permanent job, and the family (Castells, 1996/2000). On the other hand, this breakdown of traditional authority has caused a reaction as people attempt to defend their cultures and identity from an amorphous globalized control. Thus, we witness the increased power of

transnational corporations, international media, and multilateral institutions such as the World Trade Organization and the International Monetary Fund, and also witness the rise of religious fundamentalists, anarchist groups, and identity movements. Within this matrix, language is a potential medium of both global networks and local identities (Warschauer, 2000a, 2000b). Economic and social globalization, pushed along by the rapid diffusion of the Internet, creates a strong demand for an international lingua franca, thus furthering English's presence as a global language (Crystal, 1997). On the other hand, the same dynamics that gave rise to globalization, and global English, also give rise to a backlash against both, and that gets expressed, in one form, through a strengthened attachment to local dialects and languages. This tension—between Internet-led globalization and an increased need for local culture and language—has pushed Singaporeans to cling closely to their own highly colloquial dialect (Singlish) even as the government pushes them to adapt standard English in order to market their goods more effectively (Warschauer, 2001). It has also given a push to movements in defense of other languages, such as French (Online, 1998). And the Internet can be a convenient medium for both sides of this dynamic. It is not only a medium for global interaction in English, but it also allows for new forms of communication and interaction in local languages. Eritreans living in Italy or the U.S. can chat in their native language and read online newspapers. Hawaiians can produce curricular materials in their indigenous language that would have previously been unaffordable (Warschauer & Donaghy, 1997). And, as seen by the use of numbers to represent Arabic phonemes discussed above, new written forms of language can emerge.

In this context, then it is not surprising that we witness expanded use of both English and

Arabic online among this group of Egyptians, that is, the instrumental use of a global language and the more intimate and personal use of a local one. What is interesting, though, and worthy of further analysis is how the main literacy language of Egypt, Classical Arabic, may be getting squeezed from both above and below by this dynamic.

Niloofar Haeri, a sociolinguist who has written broadly on language and power in Egypt (e.g., Haeri, 1996), argues that the ties of the Egyptian elite to Classical Arabic are not particularly strong (Haeri, 1997). This stems, in her eyes, from a number of factors, including the elite's immersion in private, foreign language education; elite involvement in occupations demanding use of English (e.g., international banking, medicine, and research) or Egyptian Arabic (e.g., movie and stage acting) rather than Classical Arabic (e.g., government clerk positions); and the elite's distance from Islamic fundamentalist movements (which try to defend Classical Arabic as a religious language). It has also been pointed out that the links between the poor and written Classical Arabic as a language of scholarship are weak, since the majority of the poor are illiterate (see discussion in Fandy, 2000). In this context, it is not unlikely that the advent of the Internet could be one factor, together with other socioeconomic changes (e.g., globalization), that contributes toward a shift from the traditional diglossia in Egypt to increased multilingualism, with both English (from "above") and Egyptian Arabic (from "below") encroaching on the traditional dominance of Classical Arabic in written communication. If this were the case, it could be one expression of a strengthening of global (English-language dominant) networks in Egypt, as well as local (Egyptian) identities, with a corresponding weakening of more "traditional" sources of identity, such as (Arab) nationalism. The long-term consequences of such a trend, if it continues, is unclear. On the one hand, the

participants in this study made quite clear that their use of English does not signify an embrace of Western culture or an abandonment of Egyptian identity. In contrast, they tended to describe their use of English in terms of Egypt's long and proud history of being able to absorb the best from a broad array of cultures and make it its own. And they also made clear that their own local language, Egyptian Arabic, is a particularly powerful vehicle for expressing their most personal thoughts and feelings. Their use of Egyptian Arabic online thus represents the appropriation of technology toward a people's own communicative purposes.

On the other hand, the continued encroachment of English on the prestigious realms of language use, in business, commerce, and academia—bolstered now by online communications—could be viewed as a threat to the national language and values. While the informants in this particular study, most of whom have been immersed in an English language environment for years, did not express this concern, press reports indicate that many other Egyptians are worried about the future status of Classical Arabic vis-à-vis English (e.g., Fawzy, 1999; Hassan, 1999; Howeidy, 1999). This could portend a class split, suggested by Haeri (1997), with the elite continuing to gravitate toward English as their prestige language, while the lower-middle class excels in Classical Arabic.

CONCLUSION

As an important new medium of human communication, the Internet is bound to have an important long-term effect on language use. It is too early to tell what that impact will be. The trends discussed in this paper could prove to be temporary, if, for example, the development and diffusion of Arabic language software and operating systems bolsters the use of Classical Arabic and stems the tide of online communication in English or in Romanized

Arabic dialects. However, language use online, in Egypt and elsewhere, will be shaped not just by the technical capacities that technology enables, but also by the social systems that technology encompasses. And, as Castells (1996; 1997) and others (Barber, 1995; Friedman, 1999) have pointed out, the major social dynamic shaping international media and communication in this age of information is the contradiction between global networks and local identities. In that light, it is worthwhile to consider whether the online use of English and Egyptian Arabic by this small group of Egyptian professionals might reflect broader and more enduring social and linguistic shifts.

NOTES

1. The claim, however, of a recent advertising campaign that Chinese will be the dominant language of the Internet by 2007 lacks empirical support.

2. "Formal e-mail messages" refers to those sent for professional or business purposes. "Informal e-mail messages" refers to those sent between friends and acquaintances for personal reasons. Online chat refers to synchronous communication using programs such as ICQ and Yahoo Messenger. The numbers in this figure do not add up to 43 because some people indicated they use more than one language, and others indicated no languages used (if, for example, they never engage in a particular feature, such as online chat).

REFERENCES

Al-Tonis, A. (1980). *Egyptian colloquial Arabic: A structural review.* Cairo: American University in Cairo.

Barber, B. R. (1995). *Jihad vs. McWorld.* New York: Ballantine Books.

Bentahila, A., & Davies, E. (1991). Standards for Arabic: One, two, or many. *Indian Journal of Applied Linguistics, 17,* 69–88.

Castells, M. (1996). *The rise of the network society.* Malden, MA: Blackwell.

Castells, M. (1997). *The power of identity.* Malden, MA: Blackwell.

Crystal, D. (1997). *English as a global language.* Cambridge: Cambridge University Press.

Crystal, D. (2001). *Language and the Internet.* Cambridge: Cambridge University Press.

Cyberspeech. (1997, June 23, 1997). *Time, 149,* 23.

Dabbagh Information Technology Group. (2000). Number of Internet users in Arab countries edges toward 2 million, [Online article]. Available: http://www.dit.net/itnews/newsmar2000/newsmar20.html [2001, March 2].

The Default Language. (1999, May 15). *Economist,* p. 67.

Fandy, M. (2000). Information technology, trust, and social change in the Arab world. *Middle East Journal, 54*(3), 378–394.

Fawzy, H. (1999, September 26). Decision banning use of foreign names a step to preserve mother tongue. *Egyptian Gazette,* p. 7.

Ferguson, C. (1972). Diglossia. In P. Giglioli (Ed.), *Language and social context* (pp. 232–251). Harmondsworth, UK: Penguin.

Friedman, T. (1999). *The Lexus and the olive tree: Understanding globalizations.* New York: Farrar, Straus and Giroux.

Graddol, D. (1997). *The future of English.* London: The British Council.

Haeri, N. (1996). *The sociolinguistic market of Cairo: Gender, class, and education.* London: Kegan Paul International.

Haeri, N. (1997). The reproduction of symbolic capital: Language, state, and class in Egypt. *Current Anthropology, 38*(1), 795–805.

Hassan, F. (1999, October 21–27, 1999). Advocating Arabic. Al-Ahram Weekly, p. 17.

Howeidy, A. (1999, September 23–29). From right to left. *Al Ahram Weekly,* p. 19.

Information technology in Egypt. (1998). Cairo: American Chamber of Commerce in Egypt.

Online. (1998, May 8). *Chronicle of Higher Education,* pp. A27.

Paolillo, J. (1996). Language choice on soc.culture.punjab [Online manuscript]. Retrieved January 10, 2002 from the World Wide Web: http://ella.slis.indiana.edu/~paolillo/research/paolillo.publish.txt

Paolillo, J. (2001). Language variation on Internet Relay Chat: A social network approach. *Journal of Sociolinguistics, 5*(2), 180–213.

Parkinson, D. (1991). Knowing standard Arabic: Testing Egyptians' MSA abilities. *Perspectives on Arabic Linguistics, 5.*

Parkinson, D. (1992). Good Arabic: Ability and ideology in the Egyptian Arabic speech community. *Language Research, 28*(225–253).

Schaub, M. (2000). English in the Arab Republic of Egypt. *World Englishes, 19*(2), 225–238.

Stevens, P. B. (1994). The pragmatics of street hustlers' English in Egypt. *World Englishes, 13*(1), 61–73.

Takahashi, H. (2000). *Dealing with dealing in English: Language skills for Japan's global markets* (Report 7A). Washington, DC: Japan Economic Institutue.

Takla, H. H. (2002). Coptic liturgy: Past, present, and future [Online article]. St. Shenouda the Archimandite Coptic Society. Retrieved June 16, 2002, from the World Wide Web: http://www.stshenouda.com/coptman/colgsurv.pdf

United Nations Development Programme. (2000). Human development report 2000. New York: Oxford University Press.

Warschauer, M. (2003). *Technology and social inclusion: Rethinking the digital divide.* Cambridge: MIT Press.

Warschauer, M. (1998). Technology and indigenous language revitalization: Analyzing the experience of Hawai'i. *Canadian Modern Language Review, 55*(1), 140–161.

Warschauer, M. (2000a). The changing global economy and the future of English teaching. *TESOL Quarterly, 34,* 511–535.

Warschauer, M. (2000b). Language, identity, and the Internet. In B. Kolko & L. Nakamura & G. Rodman (Eds.), *Race in Cyberspace* (pp. 151–170). New York: Routledge.

Warschauer, M. (2001). Singapore's dilemma: Control vs. autonomy in IT-led development. *The Information Society, 17*(4), 305–311.

Warschauer, M., & Donaghy, K. (1997). Leoki: A powerful voice of Hawaiian language revitalization. *Computer Assisted Language Learning, 10*(4), 349–362.

Mark Warschauer is Vice Chair of the Department of Education at the University of California, Irvine, and Associate Professor of Education and of Information & Computer Science.

Ghada R. El Said is a doctoral candidate in the Department of Information Systems and Computing, Brunel University, UK, and is currently the Information Systems Unit Manager on an international development project in Egypt.

Ayman Zohry, Ph.D., of Egypt is president of The Egyptian Society for Population Studies.

Reading 2.7

Research and Context for a Theory of Maori Schooling

WALLY PENETITO

BACKGROUND[1]

The values that underlie virtually everything in the current New Zealand education system are those which owe their allegiance to Western capitalist, secular, conflict-oriented history and philosophy. In Maori terms, these are the main labels that identify Pakeha culture. They have their roots in ancient Greece, in Rome and Jerusalem, in the Renaissance, in the eighteenth century period of Englightenment, in what Weber refers to as the Protestant ethic, in the emergence of the Industrial Revolution, and in the creation of commercial classes. Out of this history comes a genius which Mazrui (1986, p. 263) refers to as "Europe's spirit of organization." Nineteenth century European colonising nations had a great deal of practice in ensuring their cultural, economic and political biases became rapidly embodied in the members of host societies wherever they chose to put down roots (Adams, 1977; Moorehead, 1979; Willinsky, 1998).

From its inception, the education system in New Zealand took on board a set of "values," "ideals" and "standards," more or less coherent with the cultural history of Britain and

Europe, that had evolved over several hundred years. These are essentially the same values for the public and private sectors, although emphasis or priority may vary from one area to another. What these values actually are is a matter of conjecture but again, through Maori eyes, they seem consistently to reflect ideals like the priorities of individualism, self-governance and impersonal bureaucratic administration. These values and ideals revolve around the right to private property, the nuclear family, evidence and due process, and are deeply embedded in middle-class Pakeha society and embodied in the populace at large, defining who we are as New Zealanders.

Most Maori have few problems, if any at all, with these ideals. What they object to, when they do, is the imposition of these ideals on them and the subsequent diminution of their own values. The right of Pakeha to hold fast to these ideals is not challenged, but to incorporate them into all walks of life as though they were universally accepted and approved is considered by Maori to be both Euro-centric and cognito-centric. The education system has played a crucial role in acculturating Maori children and their families into

Reprinted with permission from *McGill Journal of Education* 37 no 1 89–110 Wint 2002.

accepting these ideals as being right and proper for them.

The problem has not been one of simply proselytising one set of ideals until they replace the original. There has also been the accompanying perceived need to quash the "oppositional" set of ideals, to ridicule and even legally prohibit their use, and in so doing to diminish the people and their culture as a whole. The Tohunga Suppression Act (1907),[2] the symbolic acts of violence against using the Maori language (Waitangi Tribunal, 1986), and the driving of Maori away from their traditional marae or institutional base have not been random acts of unthinking bias, prejudice and ethnocentrism, but instead a disturbingly long trail of cultural imperialism and associated institutional racism.

Individualism became opposed to collectivism, self-governance was seen as contradictory to whanau (extended family) autonomy, while the tradition of whitiwhiti korero (the nature of discussion in a meeting house) and runanga (the specific council of leaders) was treated as inferior to the democratic decision-making capability of impersonal bureaucratic administration. Rights to private property could not survive alongside communally-based tenure, while the nuclear family was seen as far more beneficial as an agency for socialisation than the extended family. Responsibility could be tied more easily to biological parents, to increased intimacy for the rearing and supervision of children, and to the private pursuit of well being.[3] The dualism of Western thinking is highly frustrating to Maori. An underlying principle of dualism seems to be manicheanism; the priority of the individual is not just a different preference to the priority of the collective, it is also a better preference. This is the problem of seeing the world made up of "goodies" and "baddies" or, as Popper (1977, pp. 29–30) would have it, a world made up of "open societies" and their "enemies," the latter, presumably, belonging to "closed societies."[4] It is astonishing that scholars such as Popper do not see the basic contradictions in their own claims about "rationalism"; if you cannot or will not be like me, you must be against me.

The early colonists certainly perceived Maori tribalism as being sufficiently developed technologically, aesthetically and in terms of complexity of social organisation to consider Maori worth sharing the land with, but not to the extent of accepting their "beastly communism" (cited in Ministerial Advisory Committee, 1986, pp. 6–7). This perception persists to this day: in fact, the recently released Review of the School of Maori Studies (January 2000)[5] at Victoria University of Wellington has a recommendation that requires the staff and students of the School who undertake research to "respect the 'tapu'" (sacred) nature of tribal knowledge and comply with the protocols of the Human Ethics Committee of the University." The relationship between tribal knowledge and university protocols escapes me when juxtaposed in this way. The two ideas belong in different dimensions. The tribal knowledge that is tapu is not available to university study, which is why it is called tapu knowledge. It is "closed" to the extent that it is not available to everybody, but it is available to those members of the tribe who want it and have the pre-requisite attributes to access it. History has shown that Maori were prepared to allow Pakeha who could demonstrate their knowledge of Maoritanga (Maori knowledge, language and belief) into the very inner sanctum of tapu knowledge. The remarkable nineteenth century ethnographic work of Elsdon Best (1974/1924), in the midst of the Tuhoe tribe, is testimony to the openness of Maori traditional thinking.

UNDERLYING PHILOSOPHICAL ASSUMPTIONS

This article argues the case for increasing the quantity and quality of "Maori" knowledge in all New Zealand schools and through such actions creating a context which empowers Maori students and communities without disempowering or disqualifying any other. The Ministry of Education's Revised National Administrative Guidelines[6] is an appeal for such increases but without the parallel appeal to examine contextual issues.

These issues must include factors like the historical relationship between the school and the Maori communities that are serviced by the school; the social and geographical history of the communities in pre-European times; the history of colonialism embedded in local education; and, most critically, a comparison of assumptions underlying Maori/Pakeha philosophies for (a) knowing about the world and beyond, and (b) knowing about oneself and one's place in the world.

These are fundamental questions about epistemology (what counts as knowledge); they raise questions about metaphysics or first principles and how the universe is structured (cosmology); and they ask what it means to be and exist in the world (ontology). The third branch of philosophical thought asks questions about what we should value, whose values are more important, what is right and wrong, and how we might know the difference (Kincheloe et al., 2000). Closely associated with the philosophical field of epistemology is methodology, and although this is also concerned with how we come to know, it is much more practical in nature. Methodology focuses on how we come to know the world, and the approaches we might use to try to understand our world better (Trochim, 1999).

Theories, policies, practices and strategies to improve Maori education by improving education generally, without addressing the underlying philosophical assumptions such as those mentioned above, are doomed to failure. Planting new regulations and policies without first tilling the soil does little to improve a context which is already barren if not antagonistic

to Maori aspirations. That is the challenge the mainstream New Zealand education system has to face up to. To continue in the same vein as has been the practice since the Native Schools Act 1867 will result in the same "measured" progress for Maori as has occurred up to now. A zero sum ideology is common practice when there is a call to increase, for example, the Maori curriculum base. If we are to schedule more Maori history, what are we to take out of the curriculum? If we must increase the Maori language component, what will it replace?

FRAMING THE PROBLEM

There can be no Maori knowledge production or debate around creating a new schooling context without a rethinking of the sort of research that would be most appropriate to support this, especially given what is known about the relationship between Maori education and the research that has already been done under that rubric. Historically, the education system has carried out research in the field of Maori education but it has mainly addressed problems relevant to the system rather than to Maori. The research methodologies have been grounded in Western philosophic thought, and the outcomes have been mainly accountable to mainstream theories and policies. Maori education has thus been moulded to fit a mainstream framework rather than a Maori one.

None of this is necessarily surprising for two reasons. There will always be a "politics of research" because research is always about power—about whose values will be represented in the project (Stanfield, 1985), about what should count as knowledge (Guba & Lincoln, 1991), about the process for conducting research (Bishop, 1996), about whether and how the research findings will be disseminated (Weiss, 1991), and about who should benefit from the research findings (Smith, L.T., 1999). Maori, as a marginalised ethnic minority, have struggled to find a voice in the world of research. A second reason for the lop-sided representation of research in Maori education is that few Maori, historically, have graduated through the universities with research qualifications in education. From a Maori perspective, this is a highly significant point of view despite the rhetoric of scientific, hypothetico-deductive methodologies espoused by researchers, because most research undertaken by non-Maori has not worked to the advantage of Maori. Indeed, as Tahana (1980) has argued, some of the most influential research in the Maori domain did little more than justify the dominant use of deficit theories when researching Maori.

I will argue that it is critical that we begin to research Maori education in its own terms using its own criteria. The burgeoning of what has been referred to as the modern Maori renaissance (Webster, 1998)[7] represents the ultimate resistance of Maori against the existing system continuing its hegemony over Maori culture through education.

The dramatic response on the part of the education system to the transformations occurring in Maori education represents a failure of nerve. Two recent policy developments are offered as evidence of this uncertainty. Firstly, universal initiatives to "close the gap" in performance between Maori and non-Maori student achievements; and secondly, attempts to secure forms of modified autonomy in governance as in Memoranda of Understanding between the Ministry of Education and tribal/iwi authorities such as Tuhoe, Ngati Porou and Tuwharetoa. If this is not a failure of nerve, then it most certainly represents a new act of faith. Government departments and ministries have never been noted for enthusiastic action on the advice elicited after consultations with Maori groups.

This is not a dismissive, cynical remark but one with which the writer has had recent national experience, through being involved in a comprehensive educational exercise on behalf of the Crown in consultation with Maori parents and communities. The consultation in which I was the contracted project manager involved a team of government officials charged with three tasks. These tasks were: preparing a discussion document to inform parent, professional and community groups about the nature of the problem facing Maori education (continuing disparities in achievement between Maori and non-Maori); conducting face-to-face consultations with mainly Maori community groups (to ascertain how they perceived the problem in Maori education as well as what they thought needed to be done to rectify the problem); and analysing the consultation data and outlining the key components of a long-term strategic plan to implement change.

In a separate but related initiative, a Maori Education Commission set up by the National/New Zealand First Alliance (1998–2001) reviewed recommendations from major reports on Maori education over the last 20 years. The Commission was understandably critical of the general inaction over many of the recommendations made to improve the system's response to policy and practice in Maori education.

Why is this? Demographically speaking, Maori make up approximately 27% of the total 0–4 age group and approximately 23% of the total compulsory school-age students in New Zealand (Ministry of Education, 1999, p. 10). The majority of those at school age attend "mainstream" educational institutions. This has been the pattern since 1910 (Simon, 1998, p. 134), including the peak periods of the 1930s and 1950s when the Native/Maori Schools were at their most numerous. Not too much can be read into this enrollment pattern since issues of access to any school (during the nineteenth and early twentieth centuries) depended on where schools were built. Most Maori throughout the 1930–50 period lived in relatively remote parts of the country. The availability of Maori medium schools (over the last 30 years) has structurally determined to a significant degree the choice of schools for Maori parents who wanted their children to be educated through the Maori language and within a Maori system of values. In terms of schooling achievement and under-achievement, there is nothing that I know of that has changed substantially in this relationship over the last 50 years, yet officials are now slowly engaging with community views about how this problem might be remedied.

I have seen nothing that suggests to me that Maori are seriously contemplating establishing a separate nation state. On the contrary, what they seem to be seeking is "true partnership" in some things (that is, power sharing), "delegated power" in other areas (that is, where Maori have the majority decision-making influence), and "absolute control" in those matters that derive from their ancestral roots. Yet, up to recent times, consultation where officials seemed to have all the authority but little responsibility was the norm.[8]

RESEARCH: CRITICAL SCRUTINY VERSUS EMOTIONAL POLITICS

Some of the key value orientations that differentiate Western research paradigms from ones that see research in Maori education in its own terms need to be explored. The idea of examining variations in value orientations is not new. There are long histories of this type of research in education (Spindler, 1963; Wallace, 1973), but for the purposes of this paper I will restrict myself to those values raised in the review by the Victoria University historian, Professor Emeritus Peter Munz (1999) of Linda Tuhiwai Smith's recent publication, *Decolonising Methodologies— Research and Indigenous Peoples*. In many

ways this article highlights the epistemological, ontological and methodological gaps that persist between Maori and Pakeha thinking about the world we cohabit.

The purpose of Linda Smith's text on *Decolonising Methodologies* (1999) is first and foremost "a concern to develop indigenous peoples as researchers" (p. 17). Her beginning point is to contextualise the research already done on indigenous peoples. The opening four chapters of the book are critiques of the context within which Maori and indigenous peoples have been researched. Chapter one opens with the assertion, "Imperialism frames the indigenous experience" (p. 19) and, despite her quotation from Audre Lorde, "The master's tools will never dismantle the master's house," these are precisely the tools Smith uses so skillfully to challenge the knowledge base and the value orientations of Western research in the fields of Maori and indigenous education.

The themes she explores are the familiar ones of the post-colonial, post-modernist writers such as Franz Fanon, Edward Said and Michel Foucault; contemporary indigenous scholars such as Gregory Cajete and Haunani Kay Trask; and Third World authors like Bhikhu Parekh and Gayatri Chakravorty Spivak. In my view Munz does have some justification in accusing Smith of being "behind the times" in that her critique of "old-fashioned positivism" does not take into account the major contributions of more recent philosophers of science such as Thomas Kuhn, Steve Fuller and especially Karl Popper. These philosophers reject the positivist agenda and its empiricist epistemology in favour of a "critical scrutiny." Following Popper, the crucial role of method is not to confirm, verify or prove scientific theories, but rather to challenge, evaluate and, if possible, refute the "conjectures" normally advanced to explain some state of affairs (Carr & Kemmis, 1986, p. 119). It is this process, according to Munz, that leads to "genuine," "real," "proper," knowledge rather than the knowledge or, more accurately, "stories"/"narratives" that constitute the "social cement" so necessary for community solidarity which, according to Munz, is Smith's project. Proper knowledge, he claims, is subjected to critical scrutiny.

The British comparative educationist, Brian Holmes (1981, p. 50), describes Popper's criterion for the scientific status of a theory as "its falsifiability, or refutability, or testability." The idea sounds plausible, except that terms like these have to be defined and then interpreted. Indigenous peoples' experiences of this process everywhere point to the fact that the act of defining and interpreting is no longer merely a search to extend knowledge, as Munz would have it, if indeed it ever was so. Rather it is a political act in which imperialist or colonialist outcomes are the goals, tacit or otherwise. Anthropological studies like those of Margaret Mead on Samoans, and Percy Smith and Elsdon Best on Maori attest to the vulnerability of objective social science research.

The context Smith describes begins with the "big picture" of nineteenth century European imperialism and colonialism and their manifestation in the social scientific research practices of Pakeha on Maori. These relationships are seen to be paralleled with other "first nations" (indigenous peoples) who have shared the nineteenth century colonial experience. Her thesis is simple and utterly contemporary: despite Western researchers' best intentions, they imposed their perceptions on what they observed and what they heard. None of this is surprising to indigenous peoples, but the pretence that the application of scientific method by Western researchers in some magical way produces "real/genuine/proper" knowledge, to quote from Munz (op. cit.), because it is "knowledge that results from disinterested, critical scrutiny of the evidence," is a leap of faith very similar to the

idea espoused by Maori that "there is no such thing as Maori knowledge; there is only tribal knowledge." Immersed in the Maori relativist position is an absolutist ethical belief: "We are all entitled to our own interpretation of the truth but collectively, through whitiwhiti korero/dialogue there is some hope for there being an agreed ultimate truth or pono. The realization of ultimate truths is dependent on politics." Munz argues that this knowledge is important as "social cement" but is pseudo-science because it remains unexposed to criticism and the critical scrutiny of evidence.

In the final analysis, as Carr & Kemmis (1986, p. 216) maintain, "For any educational research study, what might be called a 'political economy' of knowledge is created: certain persons initiate research work, certain persons do the work, certain products are produced, and certain interests are served by the doing of the work and the use of its products." The politics involved in whitiwhiti korero is a dynamic process which calls into question assumptions underlying what counts as knowledge and what is taken for granted. It is a rigorous process conducted publicly. Quality of outcome is ascertained using criteria like trustworthiness and authenticity rather than the scientific measures of deductive validity and their empirical testability.

Smith's thesis is that indigenous researchers already bring something to the research enterprise: an ontology which is relativist, socially and experientially-based, and supported by a constructivist epistemology where truth linked to context is embedded in the social milieu. The preferred methodology among indigenous researchers is the "passionate participant." Although these are the likely value orientations of the indigenous researcher, Smith does not claim that they ought to replace those of the standard scientific research model. Indeed, it is held (p. 191) that the better prepared indigenous researcher will be informed by at least these two world views on the research enterprise. This leaves us with a very difficult question to answer: how is Maori research articulated in a society where structural dominance has existed for more than a hundred years?

THE CONTEXT FOR
RESEARCH IN MAORI EDUCATION

In the 1840s, Hone Heke, a famous chief of the northern tribes of New Zealand, knew something was askew when he acted in defiance of British arrogance and demonstrated his opposition to the British imposition of sovereignty by repeatedly chopping down the flagpole supporting the British ensign. The New Zealand Wars of 1845–72 left no doubt that Maori were not about to roll over because of the threats of the might of the British war machine. The Kingitanga Movement (modelled on the British sovereignty to protect the sale of Maori land to early settlers) of the late 1850s had already deduced at that time that the only way Maori could survive intact was for them to develop separately, thus their motto, "mana motuhake'—spiritual prestige set apart.

Various prophetic movements through the nineteenth century were clearly aware that Pakeha cultural influence had already made powerful inroads into the Maori psyche. The line from the Taranaki haka (tribal posture dance), "e kore e piri te uku te rino," clay will not stick to iron, was a reminder to their kin to remember they were Maori; the time would come when Western culture (iron) would fall from them and they would return to their Maoritanga (Maori-ness).

By 1928, the anthropologist and university professor Felix Keesing reported a statement attributed to a kaumatua (elder) which went, "ka ngaro te tangata, ka memene ki tawhiti," lost are the people, dispersed and driven far away. The hopelessness of the struggle among Maori to find a place in the new order of things is clearly articulated in this saying.

The complexity of contextual issues around the so-called "Maori education problem" is huge enough in itself to create a form of cognitive inertia, or what Thomas Kuhn (1962) refers to as "paradigm exhaustion." The establishment of a separate Native Schools System in 1867; compulsory schooling of all children between the ages of six and fifteen (extended to include Maori in 1894); policies of equality of educational opportunity (for example, the creation of denominational secondary schools for Maori); compensatory education provision (Department of Education, 1970); mainstreaming of Maori schools (transferred to state Board control from 1969); a selection of Maori cultural elements into the curriculum (Maori arts and crafts); change of focus from considerations of inputs to equality of outcomes; and increased implementation of Maori medium education have shown, according to Chapple, Jefferies & Walker (1997), that "the education gap in participation and performance between Maori and non-Maori is multidimensional. Maori as a group perform less well on average than the rest of society on almost all measurable dimensions" (p. x). Everything seems to have been tried, according to the system, yet equality of performance between Maori and non-Maori is just as critical an issue today as it was several generations ago.

If there has been a glimmer of hope, then the last of these policy initiatives—implementation of Maori medium education—has offered it. Even that statement needs qualification. The pressure for increased Maori medium education has arisen from Maori sources and not the system itself; yet the system is charged with the responsibility of educating "all" children to the best of their abilities. Maori communities have over a long period made claims to the establishment to include their language, knowledge, history and practices into the curriculum.[9] None of this is new but how can it have taken so long for the system to respond positively to such overpowering good sense? We might suppose that Western knowledge and Maori experience were treated as a hierarchy with the former taken as superior to the latter. As Dewey (in Jackson, 1999) has pointed out, "Western thought has systematically built its structures of social inequality out of this simplistic and spurious dichotomy between reason and experience and we are deeply influenced by it which is why so many educated Westerners believe that their ability to reason, to analyse, and to know endows them with an ability to evaluate, assess, and make decisions on behalf of those who allegedly lack these rational skills and are moved merely by emotion, appetite and instinct."

Munz will surely be aware that texts on Maori educational research and its methodologies are non-existent outside the two recent publications by Bishop (1996) and Smith (1999). The only other research text in this field I am aware of is by Royal (1992), and it focuses specifically on researching tribal histories and traditions. Yet Munz still thinks it is advisable to take a long knife to a readable, scholarly and useful text on the field of research. I wonder why? Not even Smith would be too upset with some of his claims, but to what end should they be defended? Is the university facing a philosophical threat? Is research conducted by indigenous researchers on indigenous peoples causing them even greater harm than hitherto? Or is it that indigenous researchers are creating knowledge that is useful in their fields and are making a difference?

Linda Smith clearly follows a different intellectual tradition from Munz, that of being value explicit, and as a social scientist there are many who advocate this principle as a necessary moral as well as methodological stance. One who accepts this view is the internationally acclaimed linguistic scholar Skutnabb-Kangas (1981, p. xiii) who said, "The only kind of objectivity one can aim for is to attempt to describe as openly as possible one's own position and the criteria one has adopted, instead of appearing to be neutral. . . . " I would go further and say that only those with an intellectual commitment to a discipline and no responsibility beyond the university can afford to espouse a value neutral position on research. Of course, this does not mean such researchers are neutral; what they do is claim that they are objective and again, by another feat of magic, suppose that objectivity is to be preferred to subjectivity. The crucial method for achieving objectivity is to create distance, but social science research is about people: how does one become objective without becoming detached? Detachment is the problem, not objectivity or subjectivity. At least two mystifications seem necessary in the process of prioritising objectivity: firstly, creating a set of concepts, a language that is so abstract that only other research initiates can understand it; and/or, secondly, applying complex mathematical formula to statistical data that must be studied in postgraduate courses before anyone can use them and, even then, not without the appropriate textbook.

Munz also makes it seem that at least two of his international peers, Foucault and Said, are deluded, like Smith. They are champions of the "other" and their interpretations of history or "historiography" as Foucault would have it, are "discourses," as ways of talking, thinking or representing a particular subject or topic that produces meaningful knowledge. Ransom (1997, p. x) argues that "Foucault is a philosopher of difference, a theorist and champion of excluded voices and suppressed identities." I cannot see Smith being disturbed by this description of Foucault, indeed, that is most likely to be the reason she, and a large number of others, find his work emancipatory. As to the issue of "othering," Munz claims that the acquisition of knowledge about a people (for example, indigenous people) through people telling their own stories is "nothing less than emotional politics." Acquisition is not the passive, humanitarian notion Munz would have us believe. A multitude of barbs is revealed when it comes to analysing Western scholarly acquisition of indigenous knowledge, and much of this fits under the definition of colonialism and imperialism, despite Munz's views to the contrary.

AN EDUCATION "TO BE MAORI"

The need to evoke new "gods" is more critical today for Maori than it has ever been. However, it is foolish to believe that after about 150 years of cultural imperialism Maori are seeking a return to the ancient atua (gods) for their salvation. For every one who is, there are a thousand who are not; fundamentalism is possible everywhere. The new "gods" include secular reasoning, scientific objectivity and literacy, and an ecologically sustainable vision of our society and planet. It is about asserting what O'Sullivan (1999, p. 225) describes as "a relational totality" and what Maori have always believed to be the primal matrix, whakapapa/genealogy.

If Maori were ever in doubt that they would get a fair deal in New Zealand society, the last almost two decades have completely removed any uncertainty about that. The "gaps" between "haves" and "have nots," between "rich" and "poor," between "those who succeed" and "those who fail," and between "Pakeha" and "Maori" have continued to increase despite a series of what Popper calls "piecemeal interventions" from governments over generations. According to a report from the Ministry of Maori Development (2000, p. 12), six critical factors affect the rate at which Maori economic development can expand. These are: fewer skilled managers, a low capital base, over-reliance on primary commodity exports, less familiarity with information technology, fewer skilled workers and multiple-owned land. Maori are marginalised to the extent that they suffer severely in terms of each of these factors. The report shows significant disparities between Maori and non-Maori in a variety of economic sectors such as employment and income, participation in knowledge-based industries, the percentage of Maori students who leave schools with no formal qualifications, rates of home ownership, and household income distribution, to name but a few.

If there is an emerging educational vision among Maori, it is the desire for an education that enhances what it means to be Maori; so simple and yet so profound. The sentiment behind the vision is encapsulated in the proverb:

He iti pou kapua, ka ngaro; Ka huna tini whetu i te rangi.

(Though a cloud may be small it is sufficient to obscure many stars in the sky)[10]

Henare (1995) uses the French statement "plus être" (to be more) rather than "plus avoir" (to have more) as the crucial idea behind the current "Maori renaissance." Maori would argue that this notion is closer to what they would aspire to as a people than the latter which could be argued is more the inheritance of Pakeha society, of Western civilisation, of "developed" nations, of industrialised, modernised, capitalist societies. This does not mean that Maori lack an acquisitive inclination since that is patently not true, as tribalism, disputes over territory and traditional quarrels over boundaries often attest. It is more because of the concept of cultural identity and the loss of language, religion and the symbolic significance of land that the need to "be more" takes on a priority. The need is deeply rooted in their recent history of being a colonised people. Maori now have comparatively little arable land, their language and knowledge are at a critical stage in terms of survival, and they, as a people, are so thoroughly perplexed in their apparent inability to sustain themselves as a viable entity within the nation state that having more of anything is like temptation for "forbidden" fruits. These fruits are available to Maori, so it seems, only as long as they accept the hegemony[11] of Pakeha culture.

What Maori really want and need are those fruits that originate in Te Moana-nui-a-Kiwa, the Pacific Ocean and in Aotearoa, New Zealand. These are the fruits that belong to them and which they have been systematically denied for at least 150 years. This is what it means for Maori today when they assert "we want to be more Maori." They want to know their language (te reo Maori). They want their traditional institutions to flourish (the marae, for example). They are hungry to learn about their ancient history as well as their interpretations of colonial history. They are aware their ancestors keenly sought much that belonged to European civilisation; they want to honour that desire with at least the same amount of vigour as their tupuna (ancestors) demonstrated. They want to maintain those aesthetics that derive from the Maori world that make them unique in the world. More than anything else, they do not want to be limited in any way, in terms of where and how they regain these fruits.

With the advent of te kohanga reo (language nests, schools for early childhood), kura kaupapa Maori (Maori philosophy and language immersion primary schools), whare kura (Maori philosophy and language immersion secondary schools) and wananga (Maori tertiary institutions),[12] one could be bemused and bewildered by the way the all-powerful education system has turned its back on providing "adequate" resources[13] for the sorts of initiatives I have suggested in the paragraph above. Pakeha teachers and a significant

proportion of Maori teachers have habitually steered away from doing anything that was too seriously Maori. Most have been content to do something like talking about the Maori creation stories, visiting a marae (traditional Maori institution), putting down a hangi (traditional cooking method), teaching some well rehearsed waiata (song/poetry) and the odd haka (posture dance), studying "traditional" Maori ways, and introducing a few greetings and commands in the Maori language. But very few indeed have done anything remotely Maori that progressed beyond the kindergarten level.

New Zealanders in general might benefit from a deeper cultural understanding of their country, but whether they do or not is not the primary concern of this article. Maori want a deeper understanding of their country in every way possible because to know one's own land intimately is to know oneself. They want the education system to facilitate that desire. Euripides aptly expressed the negation of that desire in 431 BC:

> There is no greater sorrow on Earth than the loss of one's own native land.[14]

The excuse of the majority for this lack of progression is "fear": fear of getting it wrong, fear of making a mistake, fear of making fools of themselves and fear of offending Maori. The reason for minimal progress is more sinister and is aligned with ignorance and arrogance rather than fear. The only reason these so-called fears persist is because the majority of Pakeha do not value Maori knowledge and culture themselves; they therefore only consider Maori knowledge and culture to be of exotic interest, as peripheral activities, and a distraction from the main agenda, which in today's world seems to be the identification of the New Zealander in the global market. Politicians will send Maori cultural groups overseas to accompany them in marketing some economic exchange because Maori indigeneity is a "brand" that is uniquely New Zealand. Of course, Maori groups do not have to accept being patronised, but if you are offered a trip overseas paid for by the tax payer to do "what comes naturally" and to be feted by international hosts, it seems petulant to refuse on the grounds that your own leadership is exploiting you.

The kaupapa Maori initiatives mentioned above have received substantial public moneys over the almost 20 years of their existence. Nevertheless they are still seriously under-resourced compared with mainstream institutions. The resourcing has not kept pace with the demand. Millions of dollars have been spent and te kohanga reo and the other kaupapa Maori intiatives have blossomed. Politicians and officials have been able to say with hands over hearts that they have been supporting the movement and can prove it. Governments have instituted legislation to enable the creation of kaupapa Maori institutions as well as the protection of their specific educational philosophy, Te Aho Matua. The Ministry of Education has been formally involved in negotiated partnerships with iwi/tribal groups to help create educational capacity at the family, community and regional levels. The Education Review Office has been working with Kura Kaupapa Maori to find a review methodology that sits comfortably with the kura while still fulfilling the Review Office obligations to the Crown. The Ministry of Maori Development has responsibilities to monitor the performance of government departments and agencies in the delivery of services to Maori. These are all highly important activities and contribute hugely to the success of the kaupapa Maori movement.

IS JUSTICE POSSIBLE?

Early childhood institutions, primary schools, secondary schools and even universities can say, "We will put up a 'Maori option'," but if it is not of a high enough standard or does not have sufficient Maori content, the message to Maori students is, "Then go to one of these other institutions (kohanga reo, wananga etc.) that does offer what you want." This all sounds plausible and reasonable, but there are at least two fundamental problems that I can see. Firstly, there are not enough of these "other" institutions around, that is, there is an access problem. Secondly, this re-direction of Maori clients suggests that the system-in-general, usually referred to as "mainstream," has only minimal responsibility for nurturing Maori history, language, arts and crafts, knowledge, customs and so on—there is an accountability problem. The quantity of Maori content in the curriculum is determined by what Pakeha deem to be sufficient for the population at large, that is, Pakeha society.

Maori, like all other New Zealanders, have as much right to an education from the system in general as they have to any alternative such as Montessori, Catholic schools, integrated or private schools, or wharekura. Twenty years after the establishment of kohanga reo, most Maori students, by far, still tend to be enrolled in mainstream institutions. Most of those students, it could be argued, choose to be there; it is not a decision by default, although that would be an argument difficult to prove or disprove without empirical research. This point is the crux of the matter in deciding how mainstream educational institutions might respond to contemporary developments in Maori education.

A fundamental premise of this article, then, is that the epistemological foundations of the educational enterprise in New Zealand must, necessarily, incorporate the "traditions" of Maori as well as Pakeha New Zealand. Without at least these two epistemologies and methodologies in education, we have the privileging of one culture over another. As the subordinate minority, Maori are historically and economically marginalised and as a result experience the ongoing colonisation of their culture. It is not realistic to suggest that the dual epistemologies called for should be equal since the Maori population at the time of the 1996 Census was 14.5% (523,400 people) of the total New Zealand population of 3.62 million people. At that time 83.1% of Maori were urban dwellers, 37% of them under the age of 15 compared with 20% of the non-Maori population (Ministry of Maori Development, 2000, pp. 12–13). The dualism argued for should be based on basic principles of justice, which according to Strike (1982, pp. 227–228) must be grounded in what it means to be a person. Strike elaborates by referring to Rawls's justice as fairness.[15] What Rawls calls the "difference principle" reads in part: "Social and economic inequalities are to be arranged so that they are to the greatest benefit of the least advantaged." The principle requires inequalities to work to the benefit of all, particularly the least advantaged members of society. As an example, increasing the volume of Maori language, knowledge, values and so on into the mainstream education system will likely advantage Maori in the short term but will not disadvantage non-Maori in the long term even though there could be resistance at the time of initiation.

The fact that all who call themselves New Zealanders today arrived on these shores on a waka, whether that was on a canoe (the "Tainui" from Hawaiki), a settler ship, (the "Tory" from England) or a plane (a Boeing 747 from Samoa) does not alter the fact that when the colonising nation arrived here, Maori were already inhabiting the whole of the country. The fact that the British were from a culture technologically more advanced than the Maori is, in social justice terms, immaterial to that prior fact. The suggestion that the British were a more enlightened nineteenth century colonising nation than some of the other European countries is immaterial.

The fact that the British considered the Maori culturally superior to others such as the Australian aboriginal is immaterial. The only thing that is material is that the British took over Aotearoa, made it New Zealand and shaped it in their own image as though those who were resident did not matter. The education system, especially through the compulsory years of schooling, must do much better in incorporating a Maori knowledge base through pedagogies based on Maori aspirations. This paper has focused only on the first of these agendas, a Maori knowledge base within an appropriate context.

TOWARDS A THEORY OF SCHOOLING

What is needed in mainstream education, certainly for the compulsory sector, is a theory of schooling. To develop a theory of schooling we will also need theories of knowledge, of pedagogy, of child development, of learning, of assessment and evaluation, of the curriculum, and of community relations. None of this is easy to do but one would expect that a system of schooling that has been centralised, universal and compulsory since 1877 would have a coherent philosophy of education tucked away in a text book somewhere. I suppose kura kaupapa Maori, being a relatively new option, could be expected to have such a theory about itself and indeed they do; Te Aho Matua is the name they give their philosophy and it is a theory of kaupapa Maori schooling.

In considering a "theory of knowledge," or a "theory of pedagogy" etc., a consideration of the deep conceptual structures is called for.[16] In a simple version of systems theory, for example, inputs like ecological factors (geographical area, parental choice and teacher-pupil ratios), school processes (academic emphasis, rewards and punishments, staff stability and expertise), and intake factors (socio-economic status and ethnicity) must be empirically related to school outcomes such as academic attainments, ability to converse and communicate in the Maori language, attendance, participation, acceptable behaviour, enhanced job prospects and so on. To make an empirical distinction between school "outcomes" (those factors in the experience of pupils that are thought of as the effect or outcome of going to school) and what was done or needed to "cause" these effects, an explicit "theory of schooling" has to be developed. Otherwise the "factors" that are abstracted cannot be said to represent in some faithful way the reality of school.

The reality of schooling as experienced by Maori makes schooling for the majority of them a fundamentally flawed experience to the degree that accusations of educational malpractice (Baugh, 1999) are not over-statements of their reality.

CONCLUSION

What I have to say has an historical dimension but is more about today and tomorrow than about yesterday. The discussion of the development of the Maori medium in the education system has a particular focus on the environment surrounding the emergence of the TKR, which prompted the development of kura kaupapa Maori, which in turn led to the creation of wharekura, and the re-emergence of wananga. The transition was far from being smooth and, indeed, was fraught with frustration and at times despair. The current debate revolves around the strengthening of Maori education in both mainstream and kaupapa Maori. The idea of governance issues and the notion of a Maori Education Authority are the most recent developments, but are little more than the manifestation of the continued frustration of Maori to influence the system in a way which gives them an advantage.

A constant thread throughout these developments is a "politicisation process" where

questions of "representation," "legitimation" and "voice" are countered by the rhetoric of a conservative backlash arguing issues of "separation," "control" and "authority."

The existing education system will never work in the real interests of Maori so long as the central philosophical assumptions of the education system remain entrenched in the Western tradition. The kura and wananga developments are premised on the belief that "Maori have the right to be Maori," that the existing education system will not deliver on that belief to the extent that the majority of Maori in the system will fail to gain an education, and that the only path to redress past and present injustices is to develop a "separate" system. The focus of the kaupapa Maori initiatives keeps the debate on Maori terms and is both an educational and a political agenda. The majority of Maori students remain in "mainstream" institutions; the introduction of at least two epistemological traditions into schools, it has been argued, can make a difference in the performance of all students in the New Zealand education system.

NOTES

1. Maori are the indigenous people of New Zealand. Maori is both singular and plural as well as being the name of their traditional language. Pakeha is the term Maori use to describe European New Zealanders who originate from the first colonizing settlers who came mainly from England and Scotland. The term Pakeha is becoming generic among the white population in describing themselves rather than European or New Zealander, although the latter term is common among both Maori and Pakeha who travel overseas and wish to distinguish themselves from the English, Scots, Americans etc.

2. See Durie (1994, pp. 45–46). The Act outlawed "every person who gathers Maoris around him by practising on their superstition or credulity, or who misleads or attempts to mislead any Maori by professing or pretending to possess

supernatural powers in the treatment or cure of any disease or in the foretelling of future events."

3. See Donzelot (1980, pp. 93–94) for the way in which the family has been used historically as an object of social policy and intervention.

4. For a useful critique of Popper's brand of manicheanism, see Freeman, 1975.

5. The Wellington Evening Post, 13 March 2000 ran the headline "Review faults Vic's Maori dept." and the story-line, "Low morale and internal tensions among staff . . . have been attributed to the difficulties of trying to uphold two disparate cultural traditions."

6. See Manning, 1999.

7. Webster refers to the Maori Renaissance as a "series of distinguishable social movements (which) began in the economic recession of the late 1960s, in the context of the first major unemployment New Zealand had known since the Depression" (p. 29). The social movements have been marked by ideas like ethnic mobilisation, self identification, ethnic politics, language revitalisation and the rebirth of ideologies of traditionalism. Each one of these ideas has spawned a number of on-the-ground activist "struggles" most initiated by Maori but many also supported by Pakeha.

8. See Arnstein in Cunningham (1999) for an interesting tool for assessing the inter-related issues of participation and control.

9. See historical texts on Maori education such as Barrington & Beaglehole, 1974; Jenkins & Matthews, 1995; and Simon, 1998.

10. Marangaiparoa (a Maori chief) came to the assistance of Ngati Raukawa (a Tainui tribe) when they were very hard pressed. The latter were appalled at the small number of their allies, whereupon Marangai spoke these words. (Whakatauki - Proverbs, undated).

11. I am using the concept of hegemony as used by Gramsci to mean the exercise of a special kind of power - the power to frame alternatives and contain opportunities, to win and shape consent so that the granting of legitimacy to the dominant group appears not only spontaneous but also natural and normal. See Clarke et al. (1982, p. 38) in Hall & Jefferson (eds).

12. The Te Kohanga Reo (TKR) movement began in 1982 in which volunteers who were fluent speakers of Maori, mostly middle-aged and elderly, assembled in their villages and homes to speak only or primarily the Maori language with their pre-schoolers. This was the beginning of the Maori language immersion movement. Most of the speakers were lay people who were familiar with Maori cultural values and practices, and they instituted their own philosophical ways of operating—what is now commonly referred to as "kaupapa Maori." Within a few short years, over 500 such kohanga reo (language nests) had sprung up around the country. As these children moved into primary schools, pressure went on the compulsory sector to create Maori language immersion classes then schools. The first kura kaupapa Maori school was established by a group of Maori parents and elders in 1985 and operated outside the Education Act because no such school was defined in legislation. By 1998, 59 such schools are situated around the country, with a further 121 schools offering either immersion or bilingual Maori/English programs. More recently, some kura kaupapa Maori (9) have extended their classes to offer secondary education through immersion Maori and following a kaupapa Maori. These schools are designated wharekura. The first tertiary level kaupapa Maori institution was established in 1978 (Te Wananga o Raukawa) and a further two have emerged, while another three wananga have been established as tertiary private training establishments (see Ministry of Education, 1999).

13. By "adequate resources," I mean resources sufficient in quality and quantity to turn a potential into a reality and this requires a lot more than just money. Resources include decision-making powers, political will, access to influential persons, flexible work schedules, time, expertise, sound communications, and the capacity to affect other people in a direction which is compatible with their own wishes or preferences. See Rogers, 1974.

14. United Nations High Commission for Refugees, 1991.

15. See Rawls, 1971. This is far too complex a work to discuss in detail here, but an appreciation of his arguments is critical in understanding any liberal education system such as New Zealand's current system.

16. I have borrowed liberally from Michael Young (1983, pp. 29–34) and his critique of Fifteen thousand hours for this section.

REFERENCES

Adams, P. (1977). *Fatal necessity; British intervention in New Zealand 1830–1847*. Auckland/Oxford: Auckland/Oxford University Press.

Barrington, J.M., & Beaglehole, T.H. (1974). Maori schools in a changing society—An historical review. Wellington: NZCER.

Baugh, J. (1999). *Out of the mouths of slaves—African American language and educational malpractice*. Austin: University of Texas Press.

Best, Elsdon (1973). *Tuhoe, children of the mist*. Wellington: A.H. & A.W. Reed (originally printed 1925).

Bishop, R. (1996). *Collaborative research stories: whakawhanaungatanga*. Palmerston North: Dunmore Press.

Carr, W., & Kemmis, S. (1986). *Becoming critical: Knowing through action research*. Deakin University.

Chapple, S., Jefferies, R., & Walker, R. (1997). Maori participation and performance in education—A literature review and research program. Report for the Ministry of Education, May. Wellington: New Zealand Institute of Economic Research.

Clarke, J., Hall, S., Jefferson, T., & Roberts, B. (1982). Subcultures, cultures and class. In S. Hall, B. Stuart, & T. Jefferson (Eds.), *Resistance through rituals—Youth subcultures in post-war Britain*. London: Hutchinson in Association with the Centre for Contemporary Cultural Studies: University of Birmingham.

Cunningham, C. (1999). A framework for addressing Maori knowledge in research, science and technology. A discussion paper prepared for the Ministry of Research, Science and Technology (June).

Department of Education. (1972). Language programmes for Maori children. Wellington.

Donzelot, J. (1980). *The policing of families—Welfare versus the state*. London: Hutchinson.

Durie, M. (1994). *Whaiora—Maori health development*. Auckland: Oxford University Press.

Freeman, M. (1975). Sociology and utopia: some reflections on the social philosophy of Karl Popper. *British Journal of Sociology, 26*(1), 20–33.

Guba, Egon E., & Lincoln, Y.S. (1991). What is the constructivist paradigm? In D.S. Anderson & B.J. Biddle (Eds.), *Knowledge for policy: Improving education through research* (pp. 158–170). London: Falmer Press.

Hargreaves, A., & Fullan, M. (1998). What's worth fighting for out there? Ontario Public School Teachers' Federation. An Affiliate of the Ontario Teachers' Federation.

Henare, M. (1995). Te Tiriti, te tangata, te whanau: the Treaty, the human person, the family. In International Year of the Family, Rights and responsibilities. Papers from the International Year of the Family Symposium on Rights and Responsibilities of the Family, Wellington, 14–16 October.

Holmes, B. (1981). *Comparative education: Some considerations of method*. London: George Allen & Unwin.

Jackson, M. (1999). Refugee experience, displacement, and the critique of cultural fundamentalism. *Sites*, 37, 3–16

Jenkins, K., & Matthews, K.M. (1995). Hukarere and the politics of Maori girls' schooling, 1875–1995. Hukarere Board of Trustees with Te Whanau o Hukarere.

Keesing, F.M. (1928). *The changing Maori*. London: Thomas Avery & Sons.

Kincheloe, J.L., Slattery, P., & Steinberg, S.R. (2000). *Contextualising teaching*. New York: Longman.

Kuhn, T. (1962). *The structure of scientific revolutions*. Chicago: University of Chicago Press.

Manning, R. (1999). History never repeats itself? Colonial historical trends confront National Administrative Guidelines. *New Zealand Annual Review of Education*, 9, 63–81. In I. Livingstone (Ed.), School of Education, Victoria University of Wellington.

Mazrui, A. (1986). *The Africans—a triple heritage*. London: BBC Publications.

Ministerial Advisory Committee on a Maori Perspective for the Department of Social Welfare (1986). Puao-Te-Ata-Tu (Day Break)—Appendix.

Ministry of Education (1999). Nga Haeata Matauranga—Annual Report on Maori

Education 98/99 and Direction for 2000. Wellington: Ministry of Education.

Ministry of Maori Development (2000). Maori in the New Zealand Economy. 2nd edn. (June). Wellington.

Moorehead, A. (1979). *The fatal impact—An account of the invasion of the South Pacific 1767–1840*. Harmondsworth: Penguin Books in association with Hamish Hamilton.

Munz, P. (1999). Open and closed research. *New Zealand Books—A review, 9*(5), 6.

O'Sullivan, E. (1999). *Transformative learning: educational vision for the 21st century*. London: Zed Books.

Popper, K. (1977/1945). *The open society and its enemies*. Vol. 2. The high tide of prophecy: Hegel, Marx, and the aftermath. London & Henley: Routledge & Kegan Paul.

Ransom, J.S. (1997). *Foucault's discipline: the politics of subjectivity*. Duke University Press.

Rawls, J. (1971). *A theory of justice*. Cambridge, Mass: Harvard University Press.

Rogers, M.F. (1974). Instrumental and infra-resources: The bases of power. *The American Journal of Sociology, 79*(6), 1418–1433

Royal, Te Ahukaramu C. (1992). *Te haurapa: an introduction to researching tribal histories and traditions*. Wellington: Bridget Williams Books Ltd. and Historical Branch, Department of Internal Affairs.

Simon, J. (Ed.) (1998). *Nga kura Maori—The Native Schools' system 1867–1969*. Auckland: Auckland University Press.

Skutnabb-Kangas, T. (1981). Bilingualism or not: the education of minorities. *Multilingual Matters*.

Smith, G.H. (1992). Tane-nui-a-Rangi's legacy . . . Propping up the sky—Kaupapa Maori as resistance and intervention. Paper presented at NZARE/AARE Joint Conference, Deakin University, Australia, 20 November.

Smith, L.T. (1999). *Decolonising methodologies: research and indigenous peoples*. London and New York: Zed Books.

Spindler, G.D. (Ed.) (1963). Education in a transforming American culture. In *Education and culture—Anthropological approaches*. New York: Holt, Rinehart & Winston.

Stanfield, John H. (1985). The ethnocentric basis of social science knowledge production. *Review of Research in Education, 12*, 387–415, Ch. 10. E.W. Gordon (Ed.). American Educational Research Association.

Strike, K.A. (1982). *Educational policy and the just society*. Chicago: University of Illinois Press.

Tahana, A.W. (1980). A critical analysis of some studies of Maori schooling. Unpublished M.A. Thesis, Education Department, University of Auckland.

Trochim, W.M.K. (1999). *The research methods knowledge base* (2nd ed.). New York: Cornell University.

United Nations High Commission for Refugees (1991). *Images of exile*. United Nations Organisation.

Waitangi Tribunal (1986). Finding of the Waitangi Tribunal relating to Te Reo Maori and a claim lodged by Huirangi Waikerepuru and Nga Kaiwhakapümau i Te Reo Inc. Soc. Wellington: Waitangi Tribunal.

Wallace, A.F.C. (1973). Schools in revolutionary and conservative societies. In F.A.J. Ianni & E. Storey (Eds.), *Cultural relevance and educational issues—Readings in anthropology and education*. New York: Little, Brown & Co.

Webster, S. (1998). *Patrons of Maori culture—Power, theory and ideology in the Maori renaissance*. Dunedin: University of Orago Press.

Weiss, Carol H. (1991). The many meanings of research utilisation. In Anderson and Biddle (pp. 173–182). See above.

Willinsky, J. (1998). The educational politics of identity and category. *Interchange, 29*(4), 385–402

Young, Michael F.D. (1983). A case study of the limitations of policy research. In B. Tizard et al. *Fifteen thousand hours—Secondary schools and their effect on children*. London: University of London School of Education.

Wally Penetito is a Maori New Zealander of the Tainui confederation of tribes. He has taught in primary schools, been an advisor to schools on the education of Maori children, been a senior manager in the public service, and as an academic for the last four years expects to complete his Ph.D. this year on the "Sociology of Maori Education."

Wally Penetito est un néo-Zélandais Maori de la confédération des tribus Tainui. Il a été professeur du primaire, conseiller en éducation des enfants Maori auprès des écoles, cadre supérieur dans la fonction publique, et après avoir repris ses études depuis quatre ans, il espère terminer cette année son doctorat, intitulé "Sociology of Maori Education."

Reading 2.8

Naming the "Outsider Within"

Homophobic Pejoratives and the Verbal Abuse of Lesbian, Gay, and Bisexual High-School Pupils

CRISPIN THURLOW

INTRODUCTION

It is a disturbing fact that homophobic verbal abuse is rife in many parts of the world, and runs largely unchecked in high schools (Epstein, 1994; Unks, 1995; Kitzinger, 1996; Fontaine, 1997). In the U.K., this has recently been borne out again by a series of surveys commissioned by Stonewall[1] which report that as many as 93 per cent of young gay, lesbian and bisexual people who are "out" at school suffer verbal abuse, but that as few as

Reprinted with permission from Elsevier Science from the *Journal of Adolescence*, 24, Crispin Thurlow, Naming the "Outsider Within," pp. 25–38, 2001.

6 per cent of high schools have any policy to deal specifically with homophobic bullying (Mason and Palmer, 1996; Douglas *et al.*, 1997; Stonewall, 1999). Not surprisingly, writers concerned with young lesbian, gay and bisexual high-schoolers describe them as an "invisible" minority and one of the most significant "at risk" groups of adolescents (Savin-Williams, 1990; Mac an Ghaill, 1994; O'Connor, 1995; Harris, 1997). Watney (1993 in Redman 1994:133) even goes as far as describing their institutional neglect as "nothing less than State-sanctioned child abuse."

The Effects of Homophobic Bullying and Verbal Abuse

Concerned with the long-term, detrimental effects of homophobic bullying on mental health and social development, Rivers (1996 in Douglas *et al.*, 1997) has found that name-calling sits at the top of the list of a range of abusive practices reported by lesbians and gay men. Nayak and Kelly (1996) too have found this to be the most common form of homophobic bullying in schools. Certainly, not all homophobic name-calling is intentionally directed at young gay and lesbian pupils; for example, researchers have consistently found that terms such as "gay" and "poof" are often used to refer to anything deemed unmasculine, non-normative or "uncool" (Armstrong, 1997; Cameron, 1997; Duncan, 1999). Regardless of the object or intention, however, the perpetual degradation of these terms as hate-words pollutes the social-psychological environment in which young bisexual, gay and lesbian people must live.

Whether young people are out, coming out, or slowly and privately awakening to their homosexuality, the stigmatizing effects of homophobia on self-esteem are inescapable. Quite simply, "homophobic content becomes internalized and often causes protracted

dysphoria and feelings of self-contempt—the juxtaposition of homosexual desire and acculturated self-criticism is inimical to healthy psychological development" (Maylong, 1981 in Savin-Williams, 1990: 177). The threat is therefore one of profound social and psychological alienation, rendering the "invisibility" two-fold as these young people cease also to exist even within, and for, themselves.

Adolescent Pejorative Slang and the Naming of Other

Abusive naming practices are indexical of social attitudes and mark delineations, whether latent or explicit, of ingroup and outgroup. Naming others is an indispensable contrastive resource for proclaiming identity—establishing who one is and who one is not (Valentine, 1998). Nowhere is this more evident than in adolescence, when the value of peer status is at a premium, and as young people rework the foundations of their unique, life-long project of identity construction. Like adults, language is the primary tool they use to constitute not only Self but also social categories and relations (cf., Brown *et al.*, 1994; Eckert and McConnell-Ginet, 1995). What is more, with its own conservative micro-politics (Johnson and Epstein 1994: 224) the school environment merely exacerbates this contrastive impulse. In his recent ethnography, Duncan (1999) sets the scene: "In the norm-bound social confines of the school and classroom, the comparative and competitive ethnic propagates an informal peer rivalry: the rush begins to stake a claim on being normal." Of course, one of the ways this is achieved is through the continual, vocal branding of Other.

The use of taboo slang can simultaneously mark one out as different or rebellious by breaking social norms or showing disrespect for authority, and can be used to reinforce group membership through verbal displays of shared knowledge and interests. According to de Klerk (1997), it is this very combination of distinguishing and bounding functions that makes slang and swear words an attractive linguistic resource for teenagers especially. Sutton (1995) and Garrett *et al.* (2003) also attest to the unusually high prevalence of pejorative slang among teenagers. The naming of Other is an ineluctable part of social identity development. Unfortunately, however, as Valentine (1998:2–1) notes, "names are also ascribed, and can be forced on recipients against their will . . . unpleasant nicknames, focusing on deviations from the normal and "right," can stick to you, and can hurt."

In spite of being such a common, everyday occurrence, there are surprisingly few instances in the literature where writers deal as explicitly with abusive naming practices as, say, Lees (1983), Risch (1987) or Sutton (1995). What writing exists has also tended to focus on sexist or racist pejorative labelling. With the exception of Dynes (1990), Armstrong (1997), and Valentine (1998), one is hard-pushed to find writers dealing exclusively with homophobic pejoratives and certainly not in early adolescence. In fact, while writers such as Eckert and McConnell-Ginet (1995) have explored in great detail the (less "colourful") social labelling practices of adolescents, one of the only relevant adolescent studies in the area of taboo slang is de Klerk (1997). Even though she uses a relatively small sample and considers teenage expletives rather than nominal or adjectival pejoratives (i.e. name-calling), de Klerk's study offers a useful backdrop for the current study.

The Aims of the Current Study

As part of a much larger investigation into metacommunication and communication awareness in early adolescence, the current study sought to establish the prevalence of homophobic verbal abuse reported by young

people themselves, and the quality they attached to this kind of abusive language. As such, the study was not about the world constructed by young gay and lesbian people themselves; instead it explored just one example of the way in which their life-world is constructed for them—or, more correctly, destructively constructed as a bad place to be. In a sense, then, the aim was to put a figure, however crude, on this particular aspect of the experience of young gay, lesbian and bisexual people.

METHOD

Sample

A total of 377 Year 9 pupils (Age = 14–15) were drawn from a convenience sample of five co-educational high schools in either of two major Welsh and English cities.[2] There were almost equal numbers of boys ($n = 191$, 51%) and girls ($n = 186$, 49%). In terms of ethnic heritage, about a third ($n = 118$, 31%) of the participants described themselves as coming from ethnic minority backgrounds (that is, they preferred to describe themselves in terms such as Black, Muslim, Asian or Somalian, rather than English/Welsh, White, or Christian).

Procedure

At the end of a much larger questionnaire considering various aspects of metacommunication and communication awareness, and in a question attracting a 100 per cent response rate, participants were simply asked the following: "What words do people at school use for slagging someone off? Write down as many words as you can."[3]

The participants were encouraged not to be shy and were reminded that their answers were confidential and anonymous. They were told that they could write down anything and everything they could think of but, to encourage individual responses, that they were not allowed to say the words out loud, suggesting that, "Although not everyone uses these words, or necessarily likes them, there are still things we hear about us all the time." Any teachers present while the questionnaire was administered respected the strict confidentiality of this exercise.

Having written down as may items as they wanted, participants were then given a second instruction: "Now put a tick next to the ones you think are the worst ones." ("Worst" was characterized for them as being "heavy-duty," "most offensive" or "most offensive" or "really bad.") In this way, they were required not only to report as many pejoratives as they knew (not necessarily used), but also to express an attitude towards them by rating those which they considered to be especially pejorative or taboo—that is, carrying the sense of their being either antisocial or immoral, or both.

Analysis

All the items reported were transcribed and then assigned to semantic categories on the basis of their primary lexical content. (For studies using similar strategies with adolescent word lists, see Sutton, 1995; de Klerk, 1997; Garrett et al., 2003). Together with a small group of colleagues and with reference to several dictionaries of contemporary slang (e.g. Partridge, 1991; Thorne, 1996), the author identified the eight basic categories into which most of the items appeared to fall, with a ninth category for those items falling into none of the first eight:

1. Homophobic (e.g. queer, poof, giner, lesbian);[4]
2. Racist (e.g. nigger, Paki, Somalian);
3. Top-5 (i.e. cunt, wanker, motherfucker, bastard, and all fuck derivatives);[5]
4. Sexist (e.g. slag, slut, whore, cow, bitch, slapper);

5. Phallocentric (e.g. dickhead, prick, sheepshagger);
6. Scatological (e.g. shit, arse-wipe, turd, scatty);
7. Others—Social-Personalty (e.g. loner, said, pompous, stupid);
8. Others—Physicality (e.g. fat, ugly, smelly);
9. Uncategorized (e.g. jackass, dustbinman/woman, paedophile, and other unknown, local items not found in the dictionaries).

Each pejorative item was then assigned to one of these nine categories, as well as counting separately the number of items marked as "worst" in each category. All imperative or expletive items (e.g. *fuck off* and *fuck!*) which were neither nominal nor adjectival (e.g. *fucker* and *you're fucked up*) were omitted.

A clear system of guidelines was established for consistently assigning items to categories. Each item was counted only once whether it was a single-word item (*shit*) or a compound item (*shitface* or *stupid shit*). Categories were ranked in order of research priority so that items were assigned first on the basis of their homophobic or racist content (e.g. *queer bastard* assigned to the category "Homophobic" even though it contained a Top-5 reference; similarly, *Black bastard* assigned to "Racist" and not "Top-5"). All other Top-5 items (i.e. *bastard, stupid bastard, ugly bastard,* etc.) then took precedence over Sexist items which were assigned before Scatological items, Phallocentric items, and so one.

Following the same guidelines, an SPSS-generated random sample of 15 per cent of participants' responses was also categorized by a second independent rater. Strong inter-rater reliability (Scott's pi of 97.75%—see Krippendorf, 1980) further confirmed the consistency of the categorization protocol.

RESULTS

Overall, a total of nearly 6000 ($n = 5956$) individual pejorative items were reported by

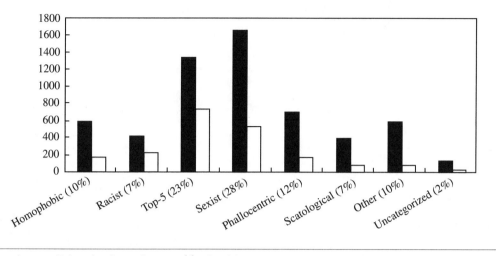

Figure 1   Pejorative Items Reported by Participants

Note: Number of items reported (black bar) and number rated "worst" (white bar) per category. Figures in brackets indicate percentage of total items reported (*n* = 5956).

participants, about a third of which (*n* = 2111, 31%) were rated as "worst." Figure 1 shows how these items were distributed according to the nine categories.

In spite of having such a wealth of information available for analysis and discussion, the focus here is kept on the occurrence of homophobic items only, albeit with limited reference to racist items and the overall patterns of reporting according to school, sex and ethnic heritage. Table 1 presents a summary of the results reported here, showing means, standard deviations, percentage counts and significant between-group differences for the average number of items reported and rated "worst." (For the straightforward purposes of the current analysis, a series of ANOVAs and *t*-tests was used.) A detailed breakdown of the range of homophobic pejoratives reported is given in Table 2.

Homophobic items accounts for 10 per cent of all the items reported (*n* = 590), which was very much smaller than the number of sexist items offered (28%), but significantly more than racist items (7%) ($t_{(376)}$ = 3.796,

$p < 0.001$). This proportion of all the items reported is strikingly large, especially given that looser analytic categories like Scatalogical, Others—Social-Personality, and Others—Physicality accommodated a wide range of common, socially generic abusive labels.[6] The homophobic items, by contrast, exclusively indexed a single group. Most notably, these items also appeared to be especially vitriolic, with nearly 10 per cent of them occurring as compounds with Top-5 words such as *fucker, cunt,* and *twat.* These "transferred derogatory labels" (Wood, 1984) have the reciprocal effect of intensifying the homophobic insult. Although the common alliterative form *Black bastard* was predominant within racist/Top-5 compounds, racist items were at least 60 per cent less likely to appear as compounds in the same way as homophobic items.

In spite of containing so many Top-5 taboo words, only 28 per cent of the homophobic items were rated as "worst." This compares noticeably with racist items where 55 per cent were rated as "worst."

Table 1   Summary of Mean Results Together with 2-tailed Significance of the Differences
Between Groups (where appropriate)

	Mean Reported Items (SD)		Mean Number of Items Rated "Worst" (as percent of items reported by group)		Between-Group Differences: Number of Items Reported/ Number of Items Rated as "Worst"
Total Items	15.79	(8.19)	5.59	(35)	
School					
School A	15.84	(6.84)	4. 94	(31)	
School B	17.56	(6.69)	6.87	(39)	No significant difference
School C	17.45	(7.19)	6.39	(37)	*No significant difference*
School D	16.04	(10.29)	5.57	(35)	
School E	11.35	(7.93)	3.61	(32)	
Sex					
Girls	14.47	(6.14)	5.47	(38)	$t_{(324)} = 3.154, p = 0.002$
Boys	17.09	(9.62)	5.72	(34)	*No significant difference*
Ethnic heritage					
Ethnic majority	16.15	(7.98)	5.58	(35)	No significant difference
Ethnic minority	15.02	(8.61)	5.64	(38)	*No significant difference*
Homophobic items	1.57	(1.86)	0.44	(28)	
School					
School A	1.94	(2.08)	0.57	(29)	
School B	1.55	(1.83)	0.46	(30)	No significant difference
School C	1.72	(1.87)	0.46	(28)	*No significant difference*
School D	1.41	(1.91)	0.39	(27)	
School E	1.25	(1.65)	0.32	(26)	
Sex					
Girls	0.95	(1.38)	0.23	(24)	$t_{(332)} = 6.763, p < 0.001$
Boys	2.27	(2.07)	0.63	(29)	$t_{(309)} = 4.096, p < 0.001$
Ethnic heritage					
Ethnic majority	1.74	(1.93)	0.45	(26)	$t_{(261)} = 2.844, p < 0.005$
Ethnic minority	1.19	(1.65)	.040	(34)	$t_{(375)} = 0.491, p > 0.1$
Racist Items					
Ethnic heritage					
Ethnic majority	0.92	(1.35)	.049	(54)	$t_{(154)} = 2.707, p < 0.01$
Ethnic minority	1.54	(2.34)	0.87	(57)	$t_{(159)} = 2.432, p < 0.05$
Sex					
Girls	.08	(1.41)	0.49	(57	$t_{(342)} = 2.668, p < 0.01$
Boys	1.35	(2.00)	0.73	(54)	$t_{(355)} = 1.906, p = 0.057$

A paired-sample comparison of the mean difference between the percentage of homophobic items ($\mu = 28$) and the percentage of racist items ($\mu = 55$) rated "worst," confirmed a highly significant difference between participants attitudes towards homophobic and racist pejoratives ($t_{(376)} = 7.385, p < 0.001$).

Where racist items were rated on a par with Top-5 items as highly taboo ($\mu = 55$), homophobic items were, proportionally speaking, not regarded as being nearly as serious.

The only significant between-group difference found in the overall reporting of pejoratives was that boys reported significantly more

Table 2   Breakdown of Total Homophobic Items Reported (n = 589)

Items	Comments
Gay	Also gaylord, gay-boy, etc.
Queer	*Queer, gay, bender,* etc. compounds with Top-5 and other category items (*n* = 54) such as *twat* (7), *bastard* (19), *cunt* (7) *fucker/fucking* (6), as well as various items such as *queerish motherfucker, queer prostitute, your dad is a bender, your dad is queer, your dad sucks dick, you're so ugly you pay gay men to have sex with you.*
Bent/bender	
Cocksucker	Also knobsucker, you suck dick (from boys)
Homo/sexual	
Poof/poofter	
Ginger	
Rent boy/hustler	
Battyman/boy	(one school only)
Faggot	
Pansy	
All others	e.g., *Shit-stabber, knob-jockey, bum-bandit, bum-basher, bum boy, arse-bandit, bugger, turd-burglar, shirt-lifter, basher, knobjock*
Lesbian	
Lez/lezzo	
Fanny-basher	Includes fanny-licker (from girls)
Dyke	

items than girls ($t_{(324)}$ = 3.154, p = 0.002), although there was no overall difference in the extent to which boys and girls rated items as "worst." Similarly, one-way ANOVAs revealed no significant overall differences between the reporting or rating of items in terms of school. Nor were there ethnic heritage differences.

As far as homophobic items were concerned, there were again no significant overall differences in the reporting or rating of items by the different schools or in terms of ethnic heritage. Once again, however, boys reported significantly more items than girls ($t_{(332)}$ = 6.763, p < 0.001), with girls reporting just under a third (*n* = 176) of the total of homophobic items. In this instance, boys also rated homophobic items as significantly taboo than girls ($t_{(309)}$ = 4.096, p < 0.001). Ethnic majority participants reported significantly more homophobic items than their ethnic minority peers ($t_{(261)}$ = 2.844, p < 0.005).

Finally, for further comparative purposes, it was found that significantly more racist items were reported *and* rated as "worst" by ethnic minority than ethnic majority participants ($t_{(154)}$ = 2.707, p < 0.01; $t_{(159)}$ = 2.432, p < 0.05). Overall, boys reported significantly more racist items than girls ($t_{(342)}$ = 2.668, p < 0.01) and, although not statistically significant, girls tended to rate racist items more highly (i.e. as taboo) ($t_{(355)}$ = 1.906, p = 0.057).

DISCUSSION

. . . degrading homosexuality in public contexts serves to maintain the invisibility of homosexuals . . . [and] usage of this kind of language, therefore, by disregarding the hurt that it may cause to some, indicates how unimportant the feelings of these people are (Armstrong, 1997:362).

In terms of overall reporting, the results of the current study were consistent across the five schools which would suggest that the responses of these young people were reasonably representative of many young people this age in the U.K. Furthermore, since the reporting of homophobic pejoratives also held across schools, it is likely that this too was fairly representative. As such, homophobic references are strikingly represented in young people's reports of abusive naming practices and yet clearly not regarded as especially offensive. Even though these participants' reporting of pejoratives did not mean that they necessarily used them themselves, it does confirm that such words are in use. Furthermore, without making claims for the regularity or rate of occurrence, it is not unreasonable to expect that incidence of their reporting reflects the incidence of their use. With apparently little concern for their antisocial ramifications, homophobic pejoratives, many of them vitriolic, constitute one of the most predominant categories of abusive language among young adolescents.

Of the large and varied repertoire of homophobic pejoratives reported, and as other writers (see introduction) have found, the most common of these was "*gay*" (along with "*gaylord*" and "*gayboy*"). In spite of its being one of the playground weapons of preference, this is ironically the very word that many young homosexual people will more than likely be choosing to use to describe themselves. Together with various derivatives and qualifiers, the other most commonly reported homophobic pejoratives were "*queer*," "*bent*," "*cocksucker*," "*poof*" and "*homosexual*"—once again, even the most supposedly "neutral" of terms, "*homosexual*," is considered a suitable resource for slagging someone off. Evidently, to rephrase Cameron (1995 in Romaine, 199:309), in the mouths of homophobes, language can always be homophobic.

The homophobic pejoratives listed were also some of the most vitriolic. Male homophobic items included the expected, hostile collection of reductive, stereotypic sexualizations (e.g. "*shit-stabber*," "*shirt-lifter*" and "*bum-boy*"). In fact, the vast majority of all the homophobic items reported referred to male homosexuality; comparatively few (only 14%) specifically female homophobic pejoratives were reported, with "*lesbian*" being the most common of these. Interestingly, Sutton (1995) too reports no female homophobic items in her study of "ugly names" for women. This absence is possibly in keeping with the relative paucity of such terms more generally, and very likely related to broader issues of gendered inequality such as the even greater marginalization (or "silencing") of lesbians (Dynes, 1990; Hughes, 1998).

More consistently than any other category of abusive names in the study, homophobic items also appeared in conjunction with the first most taboo items ("*cunt*," "*wanker*," "*motherfucker*," "*bastard*" and "*fuck/ing*"). On their own, these highly taboo items were, not surprisingly, rated by participants a some of the "worst" words to be used at school (together with racist terms—discussed shortly). However, consistent with their overall low rating, homophobic pejoratives were still regarded as relatively inoffensive—in spite of being qualified with these highly taboo items.

Verbal Derogation and Outgroup Evaluation

Whatever their reported attitude to homophobic words themselves, it cannot be assumed that this is necessarily indicative of young people's attitudes towards the social group which these words apparently describe. It should be remembered that a word like "*gay*" can often be used loosely to describe anything undesirable such as a lack of interest in sport, academic success or a lack of aggression (Redman, 1994; Duncan, 1999). Even though, in the current study, specifically negative words were asked for, many supposedly pejorative words can also, depending on their context, be used with "variable force" (Garrett *et al.*, 2003) to describe someone negatively or positively (e.g. when teasing). What is more, members of the social group references by homophobic verbal abuse often really are invisible in the way that overt tokens such as skin colour or religious practice confirm ethnic minority status. As such, unlike racist pejoratives, homophobic pejoratives often have a less clearly, less deliberately identified relation to their target. Notwithstanding this, as Valentine (1998:10–2) says, "a name may be an utter fabrication, constructed out of falsehoods, and yet be a potent source of discriminatory identification and practice." It may well be that homophobic pejoratives are not always used with serious intent, but perhaps this is exactly where their vitriol lies: used with such carefreeness (or, rather, carelessness), young people are seemingly unaware of the damage their words cause. After all, they reason, these are not bad words—not like racist words. Homophobic pejoratives are certainly hurtful, though, if you *are* homosexual.

With their vernacular repertoire inevitably representing existing stereotypes and outgroup evaluations, the attitudes of young people towards the use of homophobic words may, at the very least, be used as something of a social-distance yardstick (cf. Eckert and McConnell-Ginnet, 1995; de Klerk, 1997; Garrett *et al.*, 2003). This becomes apparent when comparing the ratings of racist and homophobic pejoratives. Racist pejoratives were clearly regarded as especially taboo—proportionally speaking, as offensive as even some of the most taboo (i.e. Top-5) items. The intention with this comparison is not be drawn into a futile, and politically counter-productive, comparison of the plight of oppressed minorities—not least because the divisions are always only artificial and belie the inevitable complexity of

the situation (see Mac an Ghaill, 1994). Nonetheless, what these young people's responses do confirm is a relative, and widely shared, disregard for the feelings of lesbian, gay and bisexual people. As Unks (1995:3) comments, "Picking on persons because of their ethnicity, class, religion, gender, or race is essentially taboo behaviour, but adults and children alike are given licence to torment and harm people because of their sexuality." In fact, it has been the case for some time now that even the accusation of racism is itself regarded as a serious pejorative (van Dijk, 1987).

Ultimately, it is the intersection between young high schoolers' understanding and evaluation of these words and the shared values in wider circulation that is of real interest—in particular, differences between their socially inculcated sensitivities to, say, sexism, homophobia and racism, and the particular sexual and social politics of the playground. School communicative practices simultaneously have locally distinctive features and reflect the influence of broader societal and historical norms and values (Eckert and McConnell-Ginet, 1995). To an extent, this school-society interplay can also be seen in the different reporting and rating of homophobic pejoratives by boys and girls in the current study.

Sex Differences and Gendered Naming Practices

There is no doubt that girls do use abusive language and that traditional gender stereotypes have long since changed (Risch, 1987; Sutton, 1995; de Klerk, 1997). Although not reporting as many as the boys and granted that this is no guarantee of actual use, what is interesting here is that such a number of homophobic items were reported by the girls. It is also noteworthy that the vast majority of these terms referred to male homosexuality. In her study of women's derogatory terms for men, Risch (1987) found that almost 300 participants reported not a single homophobic item. Whether this represents a shifting sociolinguistic pattern of use is unclear. As is true of all slang (cf., Hughes, 1998), both Risch (1987) and Waksler (1997) have commented specifically on the shifting patterns of use (in terms of both user and subject matter) with previously gendered slang.

Notwithstanding their use of abusive language, girls and women are nonetheless thought to be more politically tolerant than boys and especially with regards homosexuality (Sotelo, 1999). Certainly, in the current study, it was the girls who also showed a tendency towards greater sensitivity for racist pejoratives. What was notable, however, was that the girls did not rate homophobic items as seriously as the boys. Given the preponderence of male homosexual terms, this may have much to do with the relative "vulnerability" of recipients to different categories of abusive names, and be in keeping with shifting priorities for social categorization/comparison (see Turner and Giles, 1981). For example, just as girls have a heightened sensitivity to sexist slurs (Lees, 1983), the ethnic minority participants in the current study showed a greater sensitivity to racist terms—these two groups no doubt appreciate better than others just how damaging and hurtful these terms can be. In other words, it may be that the girls in the current study were rating homophobic items less seriously because, unlike the boys, they are simply not as susceptible to the gendered slur which these words seemingly entail.

With all its connotations of masculinity and toughness, boys stereotypically use more abusive (swearing) language (de Klerk, 1997); they also like to foster this reputation and be seen to report more swear words (cf., Sutton, 1995). The boys in this study were certainly no different, reporting more pejoratives overall and, in some cases, more than willingly. That they reported so many more of the homophobic words is also not surprising (cf., Wood,

1984; Sutton, 1995; Armstrong, 1997; Cameron, 1997). This is even less so when one also considers that, particularly amongst boys, homophobia is often considered "natural" by both teachers and pupils (Nayak and Kehily, 1996). Duncan (1999) has recently commented on "the centrality of sexual reputation for desired social status" amongst boys in high school education. It is perhaps for this reason, therefore, that boys showed themselves to be more sensitive to homophobic slurs. Perversely, even though they are more prone to using homophobic verbal abuse, they are very aware how reputation-damaging these pejoratives can be. Having said which, this concern has little to do with the feelings and sensitivities of gay, lesbian and bisexual people. On the contrary, they fear being the recipient of such abuse precisely because they regard these people so poorly.

Context, Meaning, and the Power of Language

The current study admittedly adopts a largely formalist approach to language—which is to say, it examines language removed from its natural context (Schiffrin, 1994). There is, therefore, a certain "artificiality" to the strings of words listed by these young people, in as much as they reflect passive (i.e. reported) use rather than active (i.e. recorded) use or actual linguistic behaviour (de Klerk, 1997). Without immediate contextual information such as the nature of the relationship of the interlocutors, the likely motivation for using a pejorative, the vocal force with which it is uttered, and so on, one can never be absolutely sure of the seriousness of intent or the accuracy of the accusation. Although relating to comments already made here, this certainly raises issues which would be better revealed in a more ethnographic study. Such a study might also be able to examine more precisely the frequency of homophobic verbal abuse in terms of the regularity and rate of occurrence.

Notwithstanding the question of context, it is established opinion within Language and Communication Research and elsewhere that words are not simply neutral containers of meaning or mere reflections of social "reality." Although commonly misunderstood and contested by reactionaries (invariably resorting to the notion of political correctness" as both rhetorical weapon and war cry), language is unquestionably complicitous in the reproduction of social inequalities and power relations.[7] It is not surprising, then, that homophobic language is a major psychological stressor in the lives of young bisexual, gay and lesbian people (D'Augelli, 1996) and one of the key objectives in creating a safer school environment for them (Treadway and Yoakum, 1992). As Armstrong (1997:327) argues, language can be "violent, exclusionary and coercive." This kind of homophobic verbal abuse reported here and elsewhere is surely hate-speech as harmful as any other (cf., Whillock and Slayden, 1995; Leets, 1999) and deserves an appropriate response.

None of which is to deny the structural or institutionalized face of homophobia. Redman (1994:148) quite rightly points out that, "to combat homophobia, it will not be enough to tell pupils that "*poof*" is an unacceptable word." In the U.K., the most obvious example of structural homophobia in education is the notorious Section 28 of the 1988 Local Government Act which has often stifled what little willingness there has been to support young bisexual, lesbian and gay pupils (Douglas *et al.*, 1997). Nonetheless, within the context of a comprehensive approach to homophobia in schools, language change offers a crucial line of attack: "organizing to bring about change is not a futile activity, whereas waiting for "the language" to change itself is" (Cameron, 1998:13). Whether this

change is discussed through critical language education (see Clark and Ivanic, 1999) or sex(uality) education, it is ultimately the encoding of a presumed heterosexuality into language and other social practices that is the problem, and the primary focus really should be on the attitudes and reactions of the abusers not the abused (Savin-Williams, 1990; Johnson and Epstein, 1994, D'Augelli, 1996; Kitzinger, 1996).

CONCLUSION

It is not surprising to know that homophobia abounds in schools. Even the U.K. government has not very tentatively acknowledged this problem (DfEE, 1999:4–29), while, in the U.S.A., legal precedents have now been set which oblige state schools to protect young lesbian and gay people (see Logue, 1997). What is disturbing, however, is to find just how predominant homophobic pejoratives actually are—also to be reminded how aggressive they can be—and the relative disregard young people attach to this genre of derogation.

According to Stonewall's (1999) recent report on homophobic bullying, as many as 73 per cent of adults they surveyed had already known that they were lesbian, gay or bisexual when they were at high school. These, then, are the predecessors of the young gay, lesbian, and bisexual people currently in our high schools, the "outsiders within" (Valentine, 1998:3.3) who suffer daily verbal abuse not actually regarded as abuse.

Sticks and stones may be more likely to break their bones but the relentless, careless use of homophobic pejoratives will most certainly continue to compromise the psychological health of young homosexual and bisexual people by insidiously constructing their sexuality as something wrong, dangerous or shameworthy.

NOTES

1.   Stonewall describes itself as the "national civil rights group working for legal equality and social justice for lesbians, gay men and bisexuals" in the U.K.

2.   Four of the schools were in the same Welsh city, the fifth in a large English city. As percentages of the total sample used, the schools constituted 13, 21, 26, 18 and 19 per cent, respectively.

3.   According to Chambers 21st Century Dictionary (Robinson and Davidson, 1996: 1315) *to slag someone off* means "to criticize or deride someone harshly or to speak disparagingly about them" and derives from *slag* as a "layer of waste material from coal mining or the smelting process." It was very important that this question was phrased in a way that was meaningful to these participants.

4.   A definition for what constitutes "homophobic" is supplied by Armstrong (1997: 328): "any adaptation and extension of terms referring to homosexuals that can be interpreted as derogatory in the sense that the quality, action, attribute, or individual to which the term refers is being devalued."

5.   The Top-5 category was created, predicting that these commonly regarded taboo items would be reported frequently and rated much more highly than other items; as such, it was felt, they warranted a category of their own against which others might be compared later.

6.   The mean number of homophobic items reported was also confirmed as significantly ($p < 0.001$) higher than the mean items reported in each of these three categories.

7. Within the field of language and gender, this argument has been recently and clearly covered by Cameron (1998), Romaine (1999) and Talbot (1998).

REFERENCES

Armstrong, J. D. (1997). Homophobic slang as coercive discourse among college students. In *Queerly Phrased: Language, Gender and Sexuality.* A Livia and K. Hall (Eds). New York: Oxford University Press.

Brown, B., Mory, M. S. and Kinney, D. (1994). Casting adolescent crowds in a relational perspective: Caricature, channel, and context. In *Personal Relationships During Adolescence,* R. Montemayor, G. Adams and T. Gullotta (Eds). Thousand Oaks, CA: Sage.

Cameron, D. (1998). Introduction: why is langue a feminist issue?. In *The Feminist Critique of Language: a reader,* D. Cameron (Ed.). London: Routledge.

Cameron, D. (1997). Performing gender identity: young men's talk and the construction of heterosexual masculinity. In *Language and Masculinity,* S. Johnson and U. Meinhof (Eds). Oxford: Blackwell.

D'Augelli, A. R. (1996). Enhancing the development of lesbian, gay, and bisexual youth. In *Preventing heterosexism and homophobia.* E. D. Rothblum and L. A. Bond (Eds). Thousand Oaks, CA: Sage.

De Klerk, V. (1997). The role of expletives in the construction of masculinity. In *Language and masculinity,* S. Johnson and U. H. Meinhof (Eds). Oxford: Blackwell.

DfEE (1999). *Circular 10/99: Social Inclusion: Pupil Support.* Available (10/09/99) at: <http://www.dfee.gov.uk/circulars/10–99/10–99.htm.>

Douglas, N., Warwick, I., Kemp, S. and Whitty, G. (1997). *Playing it Safe: Responses of Secondary School Teachers to Lesbian, Gay and Bisexual Pupils, Bullying, HIV and AIDS Education and Section 28.* London: Health Education Research Unit, Institute of Education, University of London.

Duncan, N. (1999). Secondary schooling and homophobia. Paper presented at the *International Association for the Study of Sexuality, Culture and Society Conference,* Manchester Metropolitan University, Manchester, 21–24 July.

Dynes, W. R. (Ed.). (1990). *Encyclopedia of Homosexuality.* Chicago: Garland.

Eckert, P. and McConnell-Ginet, S. (1995). Constructing meaning, constructing selves: snapshots of language, gender and class from Belten High. In *Gender Articulated: Language and the Socially Constructed Self.* K. Hall and M. Bucholtz (Eds). New York: Routledge.

Elliott, M. and Kilpatrick, J. (1994). *How to Stop Bullying: A KIDSCAPE Guide to Training.* London: KIDSCAPE.

Epstein, D. (Ed.), (1994). *Challenging Lesbian and Gay Inequalities in Education.* Buckingham: Open University Press.

Fontaine, J. H. (1997). The sound of silence: public school response to the needs of gay and lesbian youth. In *School Experiences of Gay and Lesbian Youth,* M. B. Harris (Ed.). New York: The Harrington Press.

Garrett, P., Coupland, N. & Williams, A. (2003). Adolescents' lexical repertoires of peer evaluations: "boring prats" and "English snobs.' In A. Jaworksi, N. Coupland and D. Galasiński (Eds), *Metalanguage: Social and ideological perspectives.* Berlin: Mouton de Gruyter.

Harris, M. B. (Ed.). (1997). *School Experiences of Gay and Lesbian Youth.* New York: The Harrington Press.

Hughes, G. (1998). *Swearing: a Social History of Foul Language, Oaths and Profanity in English.* London: Penguin.

Johnson, R. and Epstein, D. (1994). *On the straight and narrow. In Challenging Lesbian and Gay Inequalities in Education,* D. Epstein (Ed.). Buckingham: Open University Press.

Kitzinger, C. (1996). Speaking of oppression: psychology, politics, and the languge of power. In *Preventing heterosexism and homophobia.* E. D. Rothblum and L. A. Bond (Eds). Thousand Oaks, CA: Sage.

Krippendorf, K. (1980). *Content Analysis: an Introduction to its Methodology.* Newbury Park, CA: Sage.

Lees, S. (1983). How boys slag off girls. *New Society, 13,* 51–53.

Leets, L. (1999). When word wound: another look at racist speech. Paper presented at the *49th Annual ICA Conference.* San Francisco, CA.

Logue, P. M. (1997). Lamda Legal Education & Defense Fund: Near $1 Million Settlement Raises Standard for Protection of Gay Youth. Available (22/01/00) at http://www.lambdale-gal.org/cgi-bin/pages/documents/record?record=56.

Mac an Ghaill, M. (1994). (In)visibility: sexuality, race and masculinity in the school context. In *Challenging Lesbian and Gay Inequalities in Education.* D. Epstein (Ed.). Buckingham: Open University Press.

Mason, A. and Palmer, A. (1996). *Queer Bashing: a National Survey of Hate Crimes Against Lesbians and Gay Men.* London: Stonewall.

Nayak, A. and Kehily, M. J. (1996). Playing it straight: masculinities, homophobias and schooling. *Journal of Gender Studies, 5*(2), 211–230.

O'Connor, A. (1995). Breaking the silence: Writing about gay, lesbian, and bisexual teenagers. In *The Gay Teen: Educational Practice and Theory for Lesbian, Gay, and Bisexual Adolescents,* G. Unks (Ed.). New York: Routledge.

Partridge, E. (1991). *A Dictionary of Slang and Unconventional English.* London: Routledge & Kegan Paul.

Redman, P. (1994). Shifting ground: rethinking sexuality education. In *Challenging Lesbian and Gay Inequalities in Education,* D. Epstein (Ed.). Buckingham: Open University Press.

Risch, B. (1987). Women's derogatory terms for men: that's right, "dirty" words. *Language in Society, 16,* 353–358.

Robinson, M. and Davidson, G. (Eds). (1996). *Chambers 21st Century Dictionary.* Edinburgh: Chambers.

Romaine, S. (1999). Communicating Gender. Mahwah, NJ: Lawrence Erlbaum.

Savin-Williams, R. C. (1990). *Gay and Lesbian Youth: Expressions of Identity.* New York: Hemisphere Publishing.

Schiffrin, D. (1994). *Approaches to Discourse.* Oxford: Blackwell.

Sotelo, M. J. (1999). Gender differences in political tolerance among adolescents. *Journal of Gender Studies, 8*(2), 211–217.

Stonewall. (1999, 21 April). Stonewall News: 77% of Gay Pupils Suffer Homophobic Bullying. Available (03/06/99) at <http:www.stonewall.org.uk/news>

Sutton, L. A. (1995). Bitches and skankly hobags: the place of women in contemporary slang. In *Gender Articulated: Language and the Socially Constructed Self,* K. Hall and M. Bucholtz (Eds). New York: Routledge.

Talbot, M. M. (1998). *Language and Gender: an Introduction.* Cambridge: Polity Press.

Thorne, T. (1996). *Dictionary of contemporary slang*. London: Bloomsbury.

Treadway, L. and Yoakam, J. (1992). Creating a safer environment for lesbian and gay students. *Journal of School Health, 62*(7), 352–357.

Turner, J. C. and Giles, H. (Eds). (1981). *Intergroup behaviour*. Oxford: Basil Blackwell.

Unks, G. (Ed.). (1995). *The Gay Teen: Educational Practice and Theory for Lesbian, Gay, and Bisexual Adolescents*. New York: Routledge.

Valentine, J. (1998). Naming the Other: Power, Politeness and the Inflation of Euphemisms. *Sociological Research Online, 3*(4). Available (02/07/99) at http://www.socresonline.org.uk/socresonline/3/4/7.html.

Van Dijk, T. A. (1987). *Communicating Racism: Ethnic Prejudice in Thought and Talk*. Newbury Park, CA: Sage.

Waksler, R. (1995). She's a mensch and he's a bitch: neutralizing gender in the 90s. *English Today, 11*(2), 3–6.

Whillock, R. K. and Slayden, D. (Eds). (1995). *Hate Speech*. Thousand Oaks, CA: Sage.

Wood, J. (1984). Groping towards sexism: boys' sex talk. In *Gender and Generation*, A. McRobbie and M. Nava (Eds). Basingstoke: Macmillian Education.

Crispin Thurlow, a registered psychologist, received his Ph.D. from the University of Wales and was a lecturer in the Centre for Language & Communication at Cardiff University. Currently, he is an Assistant Professor in the Department of Communication at the University of Washington. He is associate editor of the journal *Language and Intercultural Communication*.

PART III

Identities

Identity is an area of intercultural communication studies that focuses on the ways in which our identities are initially imagined and constructed and how those identities are subsequently reinforced and reinvented. There are parts of our identity over which we have little or no control—gender, sexual orientation, skin color, and place of birth, for example. To varying extents, we do have some control over other parts, such as the language we speak, the religion we profess or the denial of any faith, and the country or nation we affirm. The meanings we associate with these aspects of identities are influenced by schools, the media, and everyday encounters with others. Of course, each one of us has multiple identities. In some contexts, one identity may be in the forefront. At work, for example, our professional identity may be how others think of us and we think of ourselves at that time. That, of course, is our choice. In other contexts, we are not given that choice, as others may think of us and relate to us based on only one aspect of our identity. Sometimes that is gender, sexual orientation, or skin color.

In the first reading in this section, my long-time friend and colleague Dolores Tanno and I explore the concept of othering as it relates to identity. In general, othering is the process of the more powerful group creating and naming another group as less worthy typically based on some single aspect of identity. It is through othering that the "us" creates the "them." Our concern in intercultural research is that the social sciences so often involves the privileged researching and representing others, such as women, lesbians and gays, and Latino/a.

In "Gender Differences in Communication: An Intercultural Experience," Becky Michele Mulvaney discusses how communication based on gender identity can be understood from the perspective of intercultural communication.

Acculturation is the process of an immigrant learning and adopting the norms and values of a new host culture. In that process, the immigrant looses part of one national identity and adopts a new national identity. In an autobiographical account, Flora Keshishian describes her experiences as a descendent of Christian Armenians of Iranian nationality coping with a new life in the United States far from family and friends in Iran.

National identity is blurred on the borders of nations. Tarla Rai Peterson and her colleagues studied the discourse of women living on the Mexico-U.S. border as they talk about human health and the area's natural environment. They demonstrate that, partially because of these pressing concerns, the women have constructed a border identity.

At one time the metaphor used to describe the Internet was the "frontier." One characteristic of a frontier is that it is a space where the rules and laws have yet been applied. In that sense, it was a "free" space yet to be defined. Richard D. Pineda in "Nuestro Espacio Cyber: The Internet as Expressive Space for Latina/os in the United States" suggests that the Internet frontier medium is one where the traditional ethnic identities, language oppression, and mass media monopolization can be challenged.

Corporate advertising that is segmented by audience is often based on single identity characteristics such as ethnicity. Because advertisers believe that segmented marketing is more profitable, advertisers have developed demographic information and consumption patterns based on characteristics such as ethnicity. In "Nike's Communication with Black Audiences," Ketra L. Armstrong analyzes Nike's advertisements. Her analysis is based in symbolic interactionism, which is based on the assumptions that communication occurs through the creation of shared significant symbols and that the self is constructed through communication.

Part of the academic othering that Professor Tanno and I are concerned about is the empowered academic researcher imposing constructs and interpretations on others. In "Toward Theorizing Japanese Interpersonal Communication Competence from a Non-Western Perspective," Akira Miyahara raises the question of whether Western-developed constructs of communication competence apply in other cultures and argues that theories of Japanese communication competence should be based in the social, political, and economic surrounds of Japanese culture. As an example, the last reading in the section by Kiyoko Suedo describes the differences in the concept of *face* in Chinese and Japanese cultures and how that identity difference affects communication.

The readings in this section address many questions of identity, but particularly multiple identities and the power of some to impose identity on others. Postethnicity is a term used to affirm an individual's right to define one's self in any way one chooses. The readings in this section suggest that that right has yet to be realized.

Reading 3.1

Decoding Domination, Encoding Self-Determination

Intercultural Communication Research Processes

FRED E. JANDT

DOLORES V. TANNO

Where we hope to land (and where we do land), though only for a fleeting moment, is a "there" which we thought of little and knew of even less.

—Zygmunt Bauman,
Postmodern Ethics

BRIEF HISTORY OF THE CONCEPT OF OTHER

In his article "The Rhetoric of Othering," Riggins (1997) writes, "The term *Other* as a category of speculative thought can be traced at least as far back in time as Plato who used it to represent the relationship between an observer (the Self) and an observed (the Other)" (p. 3). Between Plato and Riggins is found the story of observation and interpretation that has led to descriptions of and judgments about indigenous populations at colonizers, travelers, and researchers sought new lands, new experiences, and new understanding, respectively.

The foundations of this story are based on written descriptions by colonialists who followed the voyages of Columbus as well as later expeditions to the Western hemisphere and the Pacific. These descriptions are found in post-Renaissance travel journals in which are recorded perceptions of indigenous populations; these perceptions have been characterized as imperialistic by several scholars (see, for example, Ani, 1994; Obeyesekere, 1992; Pratt, 1985, 1986, 1992; Vidich & Lyman, 1994). In examining the works of these scholars, we sought some understanding of how imperialism can, arguably, be characterized in two ways: perceptual imperialism and discursive imperialism.

Perceptual Imperialism

Perceptual imperialism is the process of observing and interpreting information about cultural Others through an underlying set of ideas based not so much on reality as on myth. Perhaps the best way to explain this is by using anthropologist Ganath Obeyesekere's arguments about myth, which he articulates in his book, *The Apotheosis of Captain Cook: European Mythmaking in the Pacific* (1992). This book is Obeyesekere's response to anthropologist Marshall Sahlins's (1981, 1982, 1985, 1989, 1995) claim that Captain Cook was deified by Hawaiian "savages." The foundation of Obeyesekere's counternarrative is mythmaking and myth models; he argues that "scholars assume [mythmaking] to be primarily an activity of non-Western societies, [but it] is equally prolific in European thought" (Obeyesekere, 1992, p. 10). Contrary to accepted thinking, mythos has not been eradicated by logos; it merely has hidden behind logos. From these "hidden" myths come myth models, and one of the most enduring myth models in Western culture, Obeyesekere argues, is the Western civilizer as a god to the savages. Obeyesekere uses Todorov's (1984) *The Conquest of America* to show the parallel between Cook's perceptions of the Hawaiians and the Spanish Conquistadors' perceptions of the Aztecs. In both cases, indigenous peoples were perceived as savage and animal-like, to be civilized or domesticated, or exterminated with impunity if they showed resistance.

Obeyesekere is not Hawaiian; he is Sri Lankan. But he argues that as a Sri Lankan he does not fall under the spell of Western thinking and the European myth models, which assume a "prelogical or childlike native" and a logical, superior European (1992, p. 16). Thus he is arguably more able to discern the bias underlying both the myth of the "savage" and the myth of the European god that informs interpretations of Cook.

Among many who would agree with Obeyesekere's arguments, two voices stand out. The first voice belongs to African American anthropologist Marimba Ani. In her book, *Yurugu: An African-Centered Critique of European Cultural Thought and Behavior* (1994), Ani argues that a European ideology of supremacy depends on a negative image of Other. European *utamaroho* (the spirit life of a culture or the collective personality of its members) is positive "in terms of normative European behavior . . . and functional in terms of European goals" (p. 279). But the positive aspect of this self-image is possible only because it is played out against "a composite of all those things that represent lack of value" (p. 279), that is, the negative Other image. Ani emphasizes that "culture is ideological" because it possesses force and power and because "behind its deceptive heterogeneity lies a monolithic essence" (p. 4). In juxtaposing the positive self (European) with the negative Other (indigenous peoples), Ani provides another perspective of myth models.

The second voice belongs to Mary Louise Pratt (1992). In *Imperial Eyes: Travel Writing and Transculturation*, Pratt argues that natives have often been portrayed as capable of being dominated. She uses the ideas of "contact zone" and "anticonquest" to explain this portrayal. The contact zone, that "space of colonial encounters" is a space replete with "coercion, radical inequality, and intractable conflict" where the trajectories of previously separated persons interact (p. 6). This zone calls out the strategies of "anticonquest," which Pratt defines as

> strategies of representation whereby European bourgeois subjects seek to secure their innocence in the same moment as they assert European hegemony. . . . The main protagonist of the anti-conquest is a figure I sometimes call the "seeing-man," an admittedly unfriendly label for the European male

subject of European landscape discourse—he whose imperial eyes passively look out and possess. (p. 7)

The European myth model, then, rests on dichotomous relationships: European god/indigenous savage, positive European self/negative indigenous other, and innocent European conqueror/subdued indigenous peoples.

By its nature, a contact zone brings change. In the context of the relationship between European and Other, Hösle (1992) argues, both are inevitably changed. For the European, change is wrought when the mind is forced to question and challenge the monopolistic claim on legitimacy and truth in order to account for the multiplicity of races, cultures, and civilizations. This is a change at a cognitive level. For the Other, the change is often at the level of cultural as well as physical death; contact brings destruction as, for example, the case of Mesoamerican and Andean cultural deaths and the physical deaths of Native Americans through disease and violence.

Discursive Imperialism

Discursive imperialism is language marked by "self-interest, in-group favoritism, and ethnocentrism" (van Dijk, 1993, p. 160). Discursive imperialism is also language and texts marked by domination (Clifford & Marcus, 1986). We turn to Obeyesekere for examples of discursive imperialism as he traces the process of the apotheosis of Cook. He describes the "language game" that at once deifies Cook (and by extension, Europeans) and savages the native (p. 121). In his examination of ship journals, Obeyesekere finds the following references to Cook: "They [the Hawaiians] venerated [Cook] almost to adoration" (p. 121); they looked upon Cook as a "kind of superior being" (p. 122); they

honored him "like a god" (p. 142); "as far as related to the person of Captain Cook, they seemed approaching to adoration" (p. 121).

Who, really, created "Cook as god"? It was the god, the positive self, the innocent conqueror, the same entity that, in those same journals, created the indigenous as the savage, the negative Other, the subdued native. Cook christened their land Savage Island "because of the conduct and aspect [physical appearance] of these Islands," a shipmate called the land "an Inhospitable and Savage Isle;" other ship journal entries referred to the "insolent behavior" of the natives (Obeyesekere, 1992, p. 13).

That domination and oppression coexist is a given, but what is it in the oppressor that leads to oppression? Praham (1998) provides one explanation. Oppressors are motivated by fear, ignorance or blindness or both, loss, and a need for significance. What is it that is feared to be lost? It is the paradigm used to make sense of their world and their existence within it. Pratt (1992) provides elaboration on this paradigm. Simultaneous with hegemonic practice is the desire to safeguard innocence. The innocence is part of what Pratt calls "planetary consciousness" that systematizes the world in a specific way using Eurocentric "knowledge-making apparatus" (p. 29) such as "classificatory schemes of natural history . . . in relation to the vernacular peasant knowledges they sought to displace" (p. 5). Arguing that it would be difficult to find a more "explicit attempt to 'naturalize' the myth of European superiority" (p. 32), Pratt offers as proof Linnaeus's classification of the six variety of *homo sapiens;* the European variety is unquestionably of an exceedingly finer and higher rank. His classification process is an attempt to make order out of chaos, but it is a particular type of order that is required. Once encoded, in print or culture or both, the order becomes authoritative and planetary consciousness is born.

In a different way, Ani makes approximately the same argument for why oppression exists. The mind of the oppressor wants to "control the universe . . . so that the unknown becomes known; [and] the disordered becomes ordered" (p. 514).

Such planetary consciousness created a sense of domination that contributed to a very unequal relationship between observer and observed. This universal consciousness has impact even unto this day on peoples and on the processes by which we try to understand cultural Others.

ACADEMIC UNDERSTANDINGS OF OTHER

Clearly, past observations of the Other have had inherent limitations borne of both perceptual and discursive imperialism. More current manifestations are found in the processes by which we gain knowledge of cultural Others. In the context of intercultural communication studies, that relationship is increasingly being examined (see, for example, Engnell, 1995; Shome, 1996; Starosta, 1984; Tanno & Jandt, 1994). In the context of the above discussion of perceptual and discursive imperialistic processes, we have briefly examined three areas of study, specifically, gender studies, sexual orientation studies, and Latino studies. We paid special attention to how these groups of Others have decoded the domination and begun to encode self-determination into the research process.

Decoding Domination

In contemporary times as in colonial times, cultural Others have not been defined according to who they are but rather who they are not. In colonial times, indigenous peoples were defined as "not civilized," "not Western," "not developed." In more contemporary times, women have been defined as "not

male," male homosexuals have been defined as "not heterosexual" and lesbians as "nonexistent," and Latina/o and other ethnicities as "not White." The idea of the negative self (juxtaposed against the positive self) is addressed by Ani as we noted above, but it is also addressed by Kenneth Burke (1966), less in the context of oppression and more in the context of nature of being. Nevertheless, Burke's concept of the negative is helpful in trying to understand discursive imperialism. "Language and the negative 'invented' man [women]," Burke argues (p. 9), and "the negative begins not as a resource of definition or information, but as a command" (p. 10). Mark McPhail (1991) offers another perspective on the negative; in our attempt to excavate the assumptions of hegemonic discourse, he argues, we engage in complicitous behavior. That is, our critical discourse mirrors the discourses we critique, most particularly in the use of negative language. McPhail then calls for more affirmative language.

The research story within the three areas of study we examined suggest that movement to affirming language is difficult, at least as a first step. In seems necessary to first confront the question, "How did we get to this place of Other?" before addressing how to "formulate a discourse devoid of domination." (McPhail, 1991, p. 12).

In *The Second Sex*, Simone de Beauvoir (1974) explained the situation of women as Other because she is *not man*. Who, then, is she? If man is the free, determining being who defines the meaning of his own existence, woman is the being whose meaning is defined for her. In this way, woman has historically been "commanded" to be object and excluded, shunned, disadvantaged, underprivileged, rejected, and marginalized. She, in fact, is made Other. In particular, woman has historically been made Other in the word of academia. Scholarship by women has often been negatively cast as "implicity or explicitly 'derivative'" through such descriptions as not "original," not "innovative," not "creative" (Carroll, 1992, pp. 353, 356), notwithstanding the accepted fact that all scholarship is derivative (to wit: seeing further while standing on the shoulders of giants). The persistence of feminist scholars, however, has provided different insights into the "nature of knowledge, . . . [of] multiple realities . . . , of difference, of dominance, and the politics of research" (Kramarae & Spender, 1992, p. 2). These insights have paved the path for Others who wish to decode domination and encode self-determination.

For example, during the first half of the twentieth century, sexual orientation studies were conducted almost exclusively by psychiatrists who adhered to one of two paradigms. The first was the mental illness paradigm (Harry & DeVall, 1978) and the second was the deviant paradigm (Hooker, 1957, 1965; Simon, 1989; Weinberg & Williams, 1975). These paradigms clearly contributed to a labeling of homosexuals as "not sane" and "not normal." In "Paradoxical Views of 'Homosexuality' in the Rhetoric of Social Scientists," Chesebro (1980) argued that homosexuals have been rhetorically created as Other because they are *not heterosexual*. Who, then, are they? They are the negative self, the degenerate, the fallen, the immoral. Indeed, during the first half of the twentieth century, to be homosexual was to be classified as mentally ill (Harry & DeVall, 1978) or deviant (Humphreys, 1970; Weinberg & Williams, 1975). In 1973, the American Psychiatric Association removed homosexuality from its official nomenclature of mental disorders (*Diagnostic and Statistical Manual,* III, 1991), but that did not have the effect of removing homosexuals from the realm of Other.

Another example is found in the context of Latino studies. In "The Complexity of Mexican American Identity," Delgado (1994) addresses the issue of Latinos as Others because they are *not White*. Who, then, are they? The problem with the concept of Other in the context of Latino studies, Delgado argues, is that reductionist explanation of this cultural groups "implicates an effacement of the cultural, religious, national, linguistic and racial differences of Latinos existing in the Americas" (p. 83). From the beginning, Other in Latino studies encompassed duality or multiplicity or both. Not only were they *not White*, but they were also *not monolithic*. Duality/multiplicity issues in the context of Latino studies arise from bilinguality, religious multiplicity, and multiple labels, all of which result in multiple Otherness. Perhaps the most important difference is bilinguality, that is, seeing reality through two linguistic lenses. Guillermo Gomez-Peña (1993) addresses multiple Otherness when he writes, "My identity . . . is not a monolith but a kaleidoscope . . . [which] contains a multiplicity of voices, each speaking from a different part of my self" (p. 21). Gomez-Peña relates this multiple Otherness to postmodernism as a way of life: "Most Anglo-Americans have to learn postmodernism as theory because their cultural experience is not marked by growing within and across multiple cultural strata" (p. 18). Far from being "mere" postmodern theory, this multiplicity is a quintessential feature of the Latino/a's ethnic experience.

Octavio Paz (1961) has described this quintessential feature as "a somersault between two lives" (p. 56); Ilan Staváns (1995) describes it, in the context of religion, as a conglomerate of Spanish Catholicism and Aztec, Mayan, Incan, and African beliefs and practices. Delgado (1994) argues this quintessential feature is misunderstood and thus the first tendency when pursuing understanding of the Latino/a community is the simplistic reduction of categories, that is, attempting to make multiplicity monolithic. In the context of labeling, Tanno (1997) argues that multiple labels are a fact of daily life.

The decoding of domination in the study of cultural Others unearthed a predominance of the language of *not*. To erase the negative self, to recover the positive self, became a research imperative.

Encoding Self-Determination

Within the three areas of study discussed in this article, the journey from the existential "Who am I?" to the existential cultural "I am a particular Other" has had remarkable parallels in gender, sexual orientation, and Latino/a studies. There has been a proclamation of the positive aspects of difference, of arguments for the richness of subjective experiences as sources of data and of appreciation for the importance of, even necessity for, diversity.

Postmodern feminists have, for the most part, encouraged an appreciation of difference. But, while conventional feminism focused on the differences between female and male, later postmodern feminists focused also on differences based on class and race/ethnicity within women's culture (Anzaldua, 1990; Anzaldua & Moraga, 1981; hooks, 1984). bell hooks (1984), for example, claims that feminism has been one dimensional, reflecting as it did the plight of college-educated, White, American females but purporting to speak for the generalized Other. hooks further argues that privileged feminists did not and perhaps have not yet fully understood the interrelatedness of sex, race, and class in defining and giving meaning to the Other. Like hooks, Minh-Ha (1992) has pointed out the exclusive nature of conventional feminist thought and argues for inclusiveness. Oleson (2000) adds her voice to the cry for inclusiveness by asking that feminist thought reach out to the third world. This emphasis on appreciating difference and on inviting inclusivity is one way in which the Other begins to encode self-determination. It is the members of the culture, in this case women, who begin to find their voices and,

joining the choir, speak or sing their positive selves.

Another way to encode self-determination is through label appropriation. Label appropriation is the process of taking the negative label used by outsiders, redefining that label positively, and assertively using that label as an act of self-determination. "Feminist" and "gay" and more recently "queer" and "Chicano" were all transformed from the negative connotations often attributed by those outside the community to positive, transformative labels embraced by those within the community. Larry Gross (1993) has pointed out that the preponderance of this labeling rhetoric, both within the community and externally, reflects an essentialist position and has a clear political utility in efforts to gain legal protections (Epstein, 1990; Miller, 1998; Smith & Windes, 1997). This process of identifying the positive aspects of self is ongoing; Fuss (1991) argues this is "less a matter of final discovery, than a matter of perpetual invention" (p. 7). Label appropriation, then, becomes one positive response to the existential question, "Who am I?"

IMPACT ON THE RESEARCH PROCESS

What has been the impact on the research process of decoding domination and encoding self-determination? One impact has been critical examination of what should be the proper roles of the studier and the studied.

Who Studies Whom?

Stanfield (1994) has argued that paradigms guide theory construction, methodological strategizing, data interpretation, and knowledge dissemination. As we examined the development of Other in these three areas of study, we noted an unspoken paradigm at work in the traditional research process. This paradigm is a type of academic "imperialism"—sometimes explicit, sometimes implicit—that underlies attempts to study groups of cultural Others. The essence of academic imperialism in multicultural research is found in descriptions of early interactions between explorers and indigenous peoples as a relationship between the nonrational being and the superior European. But this relationship is also made manifest in the currently acceptable relationship between the powerless studied and the powerful studier.

An example is provided by Obbo (1990), who identifies herself as an African and Ugandan. Her cultural identification is important because Africa has frequently been the studied Other. In her own study of Westerners, she writes,

> Westerners, both academics and others, have responded to my fieldwork in their home countries in ways that reveal their discomfort when the accustomed power relationships between anthropologist and "native" are reversed. The fieldnotes of a non-Westerner studying Americans upsets and makes them anxious because they feel that their culture is on the line. (p. 291)

When the other is studied, it's science; when the Other is studier, it's threatening.

What is the origin of this seemingly "natural" notion of who studies whom? In part it is that social scientific research processes have been modeled after the physical science paradigm that has highlighted objectivity. Other criticisms of the physical science model aside, it is surprising that social scientific processes have failed to keep up with changing perceptions in the physical sciences about the relationship of observer and observed. Perhaps the most significant change has been the recognition that both observer and observed are changed by the process of observation. It was not always thus.

Newtonian science, for example, assumed a physical world independent of an observer, and Newtonian physics assumed that particles and waves and energy and mass were separate realities. Rejecting this view, Planck developed quantum theory, popularized by Einstein's explanation of photoelectric effect, which led to a new paradigm. As that new paradigm applied to electrons, Planck explained all that could be known about an electron was its statistically described wave function, except when it was being *directly observed.*

Regarding the process of observation in physics, Darling (1996) quotes physicist John Wheeler:

> Nothing is more important about the quantum principle than this, that it destroys the concept of the world as "sitting out there" with the observer safely separated from it by a 20 centimeter slab of plate glass. Even to observe so minuscule an object as an electron, he must shatter the glass. He must reach in. He must install his chosen measuring equipment. The measurement changes the state of the electron. The universe will never afterward be the same. To describe what has happened, one has to cross out the old word "observer" and put in its place the new word "participator." In some strange sense the universe is a participatory universe. (Darling, p. 131)

More recently, researchers in Israel constructed a device that allowed them to observe individual electrons passing through two very small adjacent openings in a barrier. They conclude that, when unwatched, electrons pass through the openings as a wave producing an interference pattern that can be observed afterward. However, when observed the electrons behave as particles. They offer this as proof that observing a physical process affects the reality of that process.

What previously had been assumed to be a concrete, objective world, then, cannot even be said to exist outside of the subjective act of observation. Observation, as physicist Bohr

(1963) defined it, is a conscious registering of an event in the mind. Quantum physics has demonstrated that observation is a mandatory requirement for making reality tangible, and in so doing, also has demonstrated that at its most fundamental level, discreteness is no longer a tenable way of viewing the universe. Everything is meaningful only in its relationship to the rest of the cosmos.

In quantum physics the act of observation creates discreteness and, further, observations can be both contradictory and true. Most importantly, quantum physics makes it clear that the observer is not independent of the observed; the observed is in some sense "created" or changed or both by the act of observation.

In the context of social science, observation of the Other has been primarily for the purpose of developing knowledge; but in ways we have not yet fully considered, that knowledge has affected the identity of both observer and observed. In a different context and certainly ahead of his time, George Herbert Mead's (1934) views of matter, space, time, and relativity are similar to those of modern theoretical physics. The development of identity through observations of self and Other is the core of Mead's theory of self as a perceptual object. Mead saw social acts as transactions between interdependent people. But interdependence and social act had a mutual effect, culminating in a common perspective. In Mead's understanding, persons formed perceptions of self by visualizing that self from the standpoint of others. Central to this understanding is an implicit understanding of the relationship between observer and observed.

This subjective stance of the observer has been articulated by several communication scholars. As early as 1983, Wander attached morality to words in the context of ideological criticism as proof of the necessity to concede the "reality of alternative world-views" and the need to "create a better world" (p. 18). In so doing, he gave rise to the notion that political interest, not neutrality, is what gave ideology its "robust common-sense" (p. 1) and propelled criticism beyond "actions implied" to "interests represented" (p. 18). In 2000, Kincheloe and McLaren offered a postmodern view of critical race theory, and arguments therefrom, that neither the development of theory nor the analysis of data are neutral processes; that critical theory "promotes a politics of difference that refuses to pathologize or exoticize the Other" (p. 296); and that researchers must engage in self-reflection. Yet, with relatively few exceptions, these provocative and well-meaning ideas have not often been acted out in studies of cultural Others.

The good news, however, is that those exceptions can be found, some within the rhetorical context, others within the intercultural context. Within the rhetorical context, Asante and Atwater (1986), understanding the power of discourse, articulated three characteristics of hierarchical discourse: controlling the "rhetorical territory through definition," creating the "self-perpetuating ritual" that determines who knows/understands "truth," and "stifling of opposing discourse" (p. 174). Neither language not its creators and users are neutral and objective. Beginning from this assumption, Lee (1993) has proposed the need "to change research priorities and build a critical science grounded in real social problems— contradictions experienced by ordinary people in everyday life" (pp. 222–223). At the heart of Lee's conception of the critical stance is the problem of definition, or, more accurately, the definition of the problem. There is not "the definition" but rather "one among many definitions" of any problem, Lee argues (p. 222). Multiple definitions yield a more accurate picture of the problem simply because they give voice to all who feel its effects. Multiple definitions presumably also yield more just and compelling solutions. In a lesson learned from quantum physics, there may, in fact, be contradictory solutions that may be equally viable.

In the intercultural communication context, Delgado (1995) assesses *El Plan Espiritual de Aztlan* and *El Plan de Santa Barbara,* two key documents of the Chicano movement. Delgado concludes that the ideological aspects of these documents called out to Mexican Americans to become political, vocal, and effective agents of action. In the process—key to Delgado's conclusion is the emphasis on *process,* arguing that people are "more process than phenomenon"—people are transformed into agents of their own change (p. 453).

With relatively few exceptions (for example, see Gonzales, 1989; Hegde, 1998; Lee, 1993; Shome, 1996) these provocative and well-grounded ideas have not often been acted out in studies of cultural Others. Clearly, the process of understanding cultural Others raises questions of voice, authority, and authorship (Roof & Wiegman, 1995; Strine, 1997; Tanno & Jandt, 1994). Within the academy, speaking for others across race, culture, sexuality, and power is increasingly being questioned. Underlying this questioning posture is the recognition that a researcher's social identity has an impact on the meaning and truth of what is said. Privileged persons (researchers) who speak for the multicultural Other can potentially increase or reinforce oppression. When Others speak for themselves, it is an ontological and political act of empowerment that also has the potential to provide a richer, truer understanding of their culture.

For pragmatic as well as methodological reasons, many researchers have begun to study those cultures with which they identify. Researchers who are members of the group being studied tend to focus on questions relevant to that particular cultural group, questions that had received little or no attention from "outsider" research. Within the gender context, for example, feminist researchers focused on issues such as rape, date rape, mothering, single parenting, sexual harassment, lesbianism, eating disorders, and problems in the workplace. Gay/lesbian researchers focused their research on such issues as gay images in media, coming out, gays in the military, homophobia, gay relationships, gay parenting, and marriage (see, for example, Weston, 1991; queer theorists questioned the validity of categories imposed by others (Fuss, 1991); Sedgwick, 1991; Warner, 1993). Latino/Latina researchers focused on concerns such as educational opportunities, drop-out rates, political voice, and Chicana feminist issues.

At the methodological level, what changes does this portend for the research process? Historically, the research process has designated the researcher as being the center of the process, the center from which flowed research questions, interpretations, explanations, conclusions, and predictions. Specific ways by which these occurred included considering objective and quantitative tests more meaningful than subjective and experiential knowledge, and making traditional research processes the standard form of reference imposed on studies of Others (Reinharz, 1992a, 1992b).

But as the Other has become more involved in studying his or her own community or culture or both, the research process has begun to change. There has evolved a desire to create a research process that is "different, better . . . and emancipating" (Bleier, 1986, p. vii). The result has been the development of alternative methods of study; the predominance of insider researchers studying their own communities; and a decrease of the power imbalance between the observer and the observed. In addition, within the context of gender, sexual orientation, and ethnicity studies, subjective and experiential knowledges have been elevated to higher levels of credibility as sources of data for understanding. Increasingly, the researcher is more often an "insider," a member of the group being studied. An active researcher, Padilla (1985) argues, should understand that to study the concept of Latino (and we would add, of gender and sexual orientation) requires "both personal and intellectual reasons" and should incorporate one's "own practical experience" (p. vii).

In *Feminist Methods of Social Research*, Reinharz lists such "new" methodologies as grounded theory, conscientization, participatory research, and phenomenology (Reinharz, 1992a, 1992b). These new processes tend to empower both observed and observer because the observed are invited to help define the research and the observer shares the social reality or the lifestyles or both of those being studied. Further, these methodologies often eliminate the distinction between the life of the researcher and the subject matter of the research (see, for example, Bowles & Duelli-Klein, 1983; Keller, 1985; Stanley & Wise, 1983) and address ways by which both researched and researcher can benefit (Cameron, Frazer, Harvey, Rampton, & Richardson, 1992). These new methodologies have evolved because of perceptions that traditional social science has been too oppressive and exclusive and too reinforcing of power imbalances.

This reexamination of research processes in multicultural contexts is ongoing in an effort to develop research processes that flow from the cultural context and that provide a balance of power between observer and observed. We offer an extended illustration of the reexamination process of decoding domination and encoding self-determination.

DECOLONIZING METHODS

Serendipitously, while on sabbatical leave to New Zealand, one of the authors discovered Linda Tuhiwai Smith's *Decolonizing Methodologies: Research and Indigenous Peoples*

(1999). This book is the story of a Maori who confronts the question "Who am I?" both as a Maori and as a researcher. In the course of seeking answers, Tuhiwai Smith also writes the story of a research process developed from the point of view of the Other. In ways we could not have anticipated, Tuhiwai Smith's story becomes the case study illustrating all that we discuss above. Hers is an especially revealing example since she provides arguments for, and a model of, a research process that take into account the point of view of the culture being studied. We follow Tuhiwai Smith's story as she traces the path from past to present research—that is, from European-based to Maori-based research—and as she scripts a different role for researcher and researched, a different set of research questions, and a different process of knowing. In so doing, she exemplifies the decoding of domination and encoding of self-determination.

Decoding Maori Domination

Tuhiwai Smith begins her story of cultural identity,

> The past, our stories local and global, the present, our communities, cultures, languages and social practices—all may be spaces of marginalization, but they have also become spaces of resistance and hope. (p. 4)

Within these spaces of resistance and hope are found the stirrings of "Who am I?" Claiming a need for "recovery of ourselves" and for self-determination, Tuhiwai Smith engages in what she describes as "researching back," the process of using established tools of power—in this case, the research with its attendant formal rules and scientific paradigms. The reclamation of self begins by digging deep into the research process. Wherefrom does the power of research emanate? What are the values, motives, and assumptions that have supported the relative ease with which indigenous identity has historically been erased and re-created by the powerful observer/researcher? Tuhiwai Smith's story of recovering identity is no different than that told by countless Others. Tuhiwai Smith cites bell hooks, Michel Foucault, and Salman Rushdie, capturing their stories by pinpointing their foci for achieving self-determination: hook's "talking back," Foucault's "formulas of domination," and Rushdie's "Empire writes back to the center." Thus, "research back" takes Tuhiwai Smith on a path that, hopefully, will become well-trod.

Collectively, these and similar stories suggest that recovery of identity requires battle. This is a curious notion, doing battle to appropriate what should be most fundamentally ours—the most intimate, most personal, most deeply inculcated aspect of being—our identity! Perhaps this recovery process might be described as searching for and bringing together many fragments of identity: the me I define; the me defined by others; or the me I have not yet come to know because my customs, or languages, or histories have been removed or mandated away. Tuhiwai Smith makes clear that colonization and fragmentation are indistinguishable one from the other for all indigenous peoples. The marginalization and isolation of cultural groups has, in our time, been defined as a *manifestation* of postmodernism with its attendant characteristic of anomie. But all colonized, oppressed, and marginalized groups have instead been *foreshadowers* of fragmentation because they have always known anomie and always had their identities wrested from them (Gomez-Peña, 1993; Tanno, 1997). So Tuhiwai Smith reaches out for her identity and asserts she is *not* merely a colonized Other; she is Maori or *tangata whenua*. Her fight, like those of women, Latinos, and gay/lesbians described above, is against the research forces that

have given her (and other Maori) an unfamiliar identity without her permissions or her participation.

Tuhiwai Smith struggles with the meaning and impact of negation. Citing Albert Memmi's (1991) concept of a "series of negations," Tuhiwai Smith offers the following partial list: "not civilized"; "not literate" (p. 28); incapable of inventing, creating, or imagining; and perhaps most incredibly, "not fully human" (p. 25). Examining the meaning of "indigenous" in which is captured the history, assumptions, and terminology of Other, Tuhiwai Smith argues, "The Other has been constituted with a name, a face, a particular identity, namely *indigenous peoples*" (p. 2). The label (and therefore the faces and identities) have never been positive, and it is therefore not surprising that "indigenous" is seen as equivalent to "problem" (p. 90).

More specifically, the negative connotations of the word "indigenous" are manifested in a history of being renamed by outsiders: "For many of the world's indigenous communities, there are prior terms by which they have named themselves" (p. 6). Her culture is but one example. Maori-named Aotearoa was renamed New Zealand by the Europeans; a self-defined culture of many tribes (*iwi, hapu,* etc.) was labeled, under European rule, one tribe called Maori. Thus, being indigenous was the equivalent of being not merely different but also problematic, unimportant, and incapable of self-determination.

Encoding Self-Determination

For Tuhiwai Smith, self-determination begins with definition. She advocates for the use of "indigenous peoples" to replace "indigenous." The phrase captures the *collective* struggle of those around the world who share colonizing experiences (of both lands and cultures) "by a colonizing society that has come to dominate and determine the shape and quality of their lives" (p. 7). After "researching back" to analyze the impact of imperialism on labels and on processes of gaining knowledge, she researches forward; that is, she makes arguments for insider research, describes indigenous projects, and develops an indigenous research agenda and process, which she describes as the *Kaupapa Maori* research process.

In *Kaupapa Maori*, both agenda and process are embedded in the idea that indigenous peoples are self-determining in all aspects of their lives. More than that, both are offered as one manifestation of a social movement by indigenous peoples throughout the world who have too long been explained by outsiders and have been offered no opportunity to explain themselves. In this way, Tuhiwai Smith, on behalf of the Maori, joins the ranks of women, gays/lesbians, Latinos/as and various Others as they, too, find ways to resist being explained exclusively by outsiders.

Tuhiwai Smith also advocates "international mobilization," that is, "establishing or reestablishing, in some cases, international linkages or relations with other indigenous communities" (p. 112) to develop agendas for action. Tuhiwai Smith chooses as her action forum the research process, which begins with a research agenda that is, in essence, a reconstruction of prior indigenous processes, beliefs, and rituals since the research agenda "necessarily involves the process of transformation, of decolonization, of healing and of mobilization as peoples" (p. 116). The Maori research agenda is based on a metaphor of ocean tides, with the ocean as giver of life and tides designating the ebb and flow of being. This, Tuhiwai Smith writes, is in direct contrast to the static rigidity of European-based research processes yielding static, rigid concepts of Other that end up frozen over time in print. The ebb and flow of being for the Others include survival, recovery, development, and self-determination and these cannot happen

without the elements of healing, spirit, and restoration. The incorporation of these elements marks the fundamental difference between Maori-based research and European-based research because they serve to promote indigenous research agendas that are "much too politically interested rather than neutral and objective" (p. 117). At the same time, these elements capture the holistic needs of the Maori that hopefully lead to holistic knowledge about them. Tuhiwai Smith writes,

> *Kaupapa Maori* research is an attempt to retrieve space to convince Maori people of the value of research for Maori; . . . to convince the various, fragmented but powerful research communities of the need for greater Maori involvement in research; . . . and to develop approaches and ways of carrying out research which take into account, without being limited by, the legacies of previous research. (p. 183)

Along with the new research agenda, Tuhiwai Smith prescribes a culturally based code of conduct for Maori researchers that merits listing in its entirely:

1. *Aroha ki te tangata* (a respect for people)
2. *Kanohi kinea* (the seen face, that is presenting yourself to people face to face)
3. *Titiro, whakarongo . . . korero* (look, listen . . . speak)
4. *Manaaki ki te tangata* (share and host people, be generous)
5. *Kia tupato* (be cautious)
6. *Kaua e takahia te mana o te tangata* (do not trample over the *mana* [our standing in our own eyes] of people)
7. *Kaua e mahaki* (do not flaunt your knowledge) (p. 120)

These capture the elements of healing, spirit, and restoration that inform the research agenda as well as the research process described below. They also add up to an ethical code of research conduct for Maori researcher specifically, but seem to us to be universal enough to apply to all researchers of indigenous peoples as well as groups of peoples who traditionally have been objects of study rather than participants in research.

In establishing her research agenda, Tuhiwai Smith remembers the impact of labeling and engages "quite deliberately in naming the world according to an indigenous world view": for example, "*Kaupapa Maori* research" rather than "methodology" because it privileges indigenous values and practices, "community research" rather than "field research" because the former connotes "more intimate, human, self-defined space" and the latter connotes an "out there where people may or may not be" (pp. 125–127). In addition, "process" is more important than "outcome" because process promotes healing, recovery, and self-determination. Emphasis on process is directly related to such questions as: Whose knowledge is it? How and whom does that knowledge benefit? (Questions of these type have informed the work of various communication scholars [Bishop, 1992; Broome, 1991; Shome, 1996; Tanno & Jandt, 1994], but it is still the case that these studies remain the exception rather than the norm.)

Tuhiwai Smith (1999) makes the argument that *Kaupapa Maori* is a more culturally safe process because it invites the involvement of elders at the same time it satisfies the rigors of research (p. 184).

Underlying both the definitions and the preferred labeling of components of the research process is the concept of *uhanau* (extended family) as an organizational structure for research. *Uhanau* assumes not only the involvement of cultural elders but also the recognition by the researcher of his or her connection to the cultural community. In the final analysis, Tuhiwai Smith says,

> When indigenous peoples become the researchers and not merely the researched,

the activity of research is transformed. Questions are framed differently, priorities are ranked differently, problems are defined differently, people participate on different terms. (1999, p. 193)

The transformation of which Tuhiwai Smith (1999) speaks is one of recovery of personal identity, of coming to terms with the concept of difference and deciding whether or how to embrace it, and of the scripting of alternative roles for researcher and researched. In these ways, her story parallels the research stories of women, gay/lesbian, and Latino/a communities as they have attempted to be their own agents of understanding. Tuhiwai Smith's story is distinct from the stories told by these three groups because she speaks for a culture as well as a nation. Her story becomes an illustration of how traditional hierarchical discourse can be dismantled and made new from an alternative viewpoint. Her "decolonizing methodology" was developed by taking "control over the rhetorical territory" (Asante & Atwater, 1986), relabeling and redefining the language of research according to the cultural assumptions and values of the Maori.

SUMMARY/IMPLICATIONS

Across disciplines (including communication studies, as has been noted throughout this essay) more and more researchers/critics have been willing to reflect on their role in the research process (Brettel, 1993; Cameron et al., 1992; Huspeck & Radford, 1997; Pratt, 1992; Reinharz, 1992a, 1992b; Roof & Wiegman, 1995; Rose, 1990). This reflexive turn often begins with an examination of the hegemony embedded in the research process and in the language of making someone an Other. This is most explicitly found in early travel journals (Pratt, 1985, 1986, 1992) and in nature writing but implicitly present in current attempts to study cultural groups.

Increasingly, cultural Others are becoming more educated about the processes by which their cultures are studied. Tuhiwai Smith represents but one example; Rogelia Pe-Pua (1989) represents another. Pe-Pua describes *Pagtatanong-Tanong,* a Philippines method that rests on the principle of equal status between researched and researcher. In addition, *Pagtatanong-Tanong* conforms to the norms of the group being researched. The primary assumption underlying this indigenous research process is that the "level of interaction between the researcher and the informant influences the quality of data obtained" (Pe-Pua, p. 147).

The implication of these examples and those discussed throughout this article (women, gays/lesbians, Latinos) is that the cultural Others are increasingly becoming more active in the pursuit of knowledge about themselves. In the process of decoding domination and encoding self-determination, Others have critically examined processes of research, particularly the relationship between observer and observed. They have found them not in keeping with their world view and have proceeded to develop new research language and agendas.

REFERENCES

American Psychiatric Association. (1991). *Diagnostic and statistical manual of mental disorders.* (3rd ed.). Washington, DC: Author.

Ani, M. (1994). *Yurugu: An African-centered critique of European cultural thought and behavior.* Trenton, NJ: Africa World Press.

Anzaldua, G. (Ed.). (1990). *Making faces, making soul.* San Francisco: Aunt Lute Books.

Anzaldua, G., & Moraga, C. (Eds.). (1981). *This bridge called my back* (2nd ed.). New York: Kitchen Table Women of Color Press.

Asante, M. K., & Atwater, D. B. (1986). The rhetorical condition as symbolic structure in discourse. *Communication Quarterly, 34,* 170–177.

Bishop, R. (1992, July). Toward a paradigm for participant-driven empowering research in a bi-cultural context. Paper presented at the Summer Workshop for the Development of Intercultural Coursework at Colleges and Universities, East-West Center, Honolulu.

Bleier, R. (Ed.). (1986). *Feminist approaches to science.* Elmsford, NY: Pergamon.

Bohr, N. (1963). *Essays, 1958–1962, on atomic physics and human knowledge.* New York: John Wiley.

Bowles, G., & Duelli-Klein, R. (Eds.). (1983). *Theories of women's studies.* Boston: Routledge and Kegan Paul.

Brettel, C. (Ed.). (1993). *When they read what we write: The politics of ethnography.* Westport, CT: Bergin & Garvey.

Broome, B. (1991). Building shared meaning: Implications of a relational approach to empathy for teaching intercultural communication. *Communication Education, 40,* 235–249.

Burke, K. (1966). *Language as symbolic action: Essays on life, literature, and method.* Berkeley: University of California Press.

Cameron, D., Frazer, E., Harvey, P., Rampton, M.B.H., & Richardson, K. (1992). *Researching language.* New York: Routledge.

Carroll, B. (1992). Originality and creativity: Rituals of inclusion and exclusion. In C. Kramarae & D. Spender (Eds.), *The knowledge explosion: Generations of feminist scholarship* (pp. 353–361). New York: Athene Series.

Chesebro, J. W. (1980). Paradoxical views of "homosexuality" in the rhetoric of social science: A fantasy theme analysis. *Quarterly Journal of Speech, 66,* 127–139.

Clifford, J., & Marcus, G. E. (Eds.). (1986). *Writing culture: The poetics and politics of ethnography.* Berkeley: University of California Press.

Darling, D. (1996). *Zen physics.* New York: HarperCollins.

de Beauvoir, S. (1974). *The second sex* (H. M. Parshley, Trans.). New York: Vintage Books.

Delgado, F. P. (1994). The complexity of Mexican American identity: A reply to Hecht, Sedano, and Ribeau and Mirande and Tanno. *International Journal of Intercultural Relations, 18,* 77–85.

Delgado, F. P. (1995). Chicano movement rhetoric: An ideographic interpretation. *Communication Quarterly, 43,* 446–454.

Engnell, R. A. (1995). The spiritual potential of otherness in film: The interplay of scene and narrative. *Critical Studies in Mass Communication, 12,* 241–262.

Epstein, S. (1990). Gay politics, ethnic identity: The limits of social constructionism. In E. Stein (Ed.), *Forms of desire: Sexual orientation and the social constructionist controversy* (pp. 239–293). New York: Garland.

Fuss, D. (Ed.). (1991). *Inside/out.* New York: Routledge.

Gomez-Peña, G. (1993). *Warrior for gringostroika.* St. Paul, MN: Graywolf Press.

Gonzalez, A. (1989). Participation at WMEX-FM: Interventional rhetoric of Ohio Mexican Americans. *Western Journal of Speech Communication, 53,* 398–410.

Gross, L. (1993). *Contested closets: The politics and ethics of outing.* Minneapolis, MN: University of Minnesota Press.

Harry, J., & DeVall, W. B. (1978). *The social organization of gay males.* New York: Praeger.

Hegde, R. (1998). Swinging the trapeze: The negotiation of identity among Asian Indian immigrant women in the United States. In D. Tanno & A. Gonzalez (Eds.), *Communication and identity across cultures* (pp. 34–55). Thousand Oaks, CA: Sage.

Hooker, E. (1957). The adjustment of the male overt homosexual. *Journal of Projective Techniques,* 17–31.

Hooker, E. (1965). Male homosexuals and their worlds. In J. Marmor (Ed.), *Sexual inversion: The multiple roots of homosexuality* (pp. 83–107). New York: Basic Books.

hooks, b. (1984). *Feminist theory: From margin to center.* Boston: South End Press.

Hösle, V. (1992). The third world as a philosophical problem. *Social Research, 59,* 227–262.

Humphreys, L. (1970). *Tearoom trade.* Chicago: Aldine.

Huspeck, H. & Radford, G. P. (Eds.). (1997). *Transgressing discourses: Communication and the voice of the other.* Albany, NY: State University of New York Press.

Keller, E. F. (1985). *Reflections on gender and science.* New Haven, CT: Yale University Press.

Kincheloe, J. L., & McLaren, P. L. (2000). Rethinking critical theory and qualitative research. In N. Denzin & Y. Lincoln (Eds.), *Handbook of qualitative research* (2nd ed., pp. 279–313). Thousand Oaks, CA: Sage.

Kramarae, C., & Spender, D. (Eds.). (1992). *The knowledge explosion: Generations of feminist scholarship.* New York: Athene Series.

Lee, W.-S. (1993). Social scientists as ideological critics. *Western Journal of Communication, 57,* 221–232.

McPhail, M. (1991). Complicity: The theory of negative difference. *Howard Journal of Communications, 3,* 1–13.

Mead, G. H. (1934). *Mind, self, and society.* Chicago: University of Chicago Press.

Memmi, A. (1991). *The colonizer and the colonized.* Boston: Beacon Press.

Miller, D. H. (1998). *Freedom to differ: The shaping of the gay and lesbian struggle for civil rights.* New York: New York University Press.

Minh-Ha, T. T. (1992). *Framer framed.* New York: Routledge.

Obbo, C. (1990). Adventures with fieldnotes. In R. Sanjek (Ed.), *Fieldnotes: The makings of anthropology* (pp. 290–302). Ithaca, London: Cornell University Press.

Obeyesekere, G. (1992). *The apotheosis of Captain Cook: European mythmaking in the Pacific.* Princeton, NJ: Princeton University Press.

Oleson, V. L. (2000). Feminisms and qualitative research at and into the millennium. In N. Denzin & Y. Lincoln (Eds.), *Handbook of qualitative research* (2nd ed., pp. 215–155). Thousand Oaks, CA: Sage.

Padilla, F. (1985). *Latino ethnic consciousness.* Notre Dame, IN: University of Notre Dame Press.

Paz, O. (1961). *The labyrinth of solitude* (L. Kemp, Trans.). New York: Grove.

Pe-Pua, R. (1989). Pagtatanong-Tanong: A cross-cultural research method. *International Journal of Intercultural Relations, 13,* 147–163.

Praham, T. (1998, March 5–6). Beyond intolerance: The gap between imposition and acceptance. Presented at the CSU Statewide Conference on Intercultural Studies, Burbank, CA.

Pratt, M. L. (1985). Scratches on the face of the country. In H. Gates (Ed.), *"Race," writing, and difference* (pp. 138–162). Chicago: University of Chicago Press.

Pratt, M. L. (1986). Fieldwork in common places. In J. Clifford & G. E. Marcus (Eds.), *Writing culture: The poetics and politics of ethnography.* Berkeley: University of California Press.

Pratt, M. L. (1992). *Imperial eyes: Travel writing and transculturation.* New York: Routledge.

Reinharz, S. (1992a). *Feminist methods in social research.* New York: Oxford University Press.

Reinharz, S. (1992b). The principles of feminist research. In C. Kramarae & D. Spender (Eds.), *The knowledge explosion* (pp. 423–437). New York: Teacher College Press.

Riggins, S. H. (Ed.). (1997). *The language and politics of exclusion.* Thousand Oaks, CA: Sage.

Roof, J., & Wiegman, R. (Eds.). (1995). *Who can speak? Authority and critical identity.* Chicago: University of Illinois Press.

Rose, D. (1990). *Living the ethnographic life.* Newbury Park, CA: Sage.

Sahlins, M. (1981). *Historical metaphors and mythical realities: Structure in the early history of the Sandwich Islands kingdom.* Ann Arbor: University of Michigan Press.

Sahlins, M. (1982). The apotheosis of Captain Cook. In M. Izard & P. Smith (Eds.), *Between belief and transgressions: Structuralist essays in religion, history and myth* (pp. 73–102). Chicago: University of Chicago Press.

Sahlins, M. (1985). *Islands of history.* Chicago: University of Chicago Press.

Sahlins, M. (1989). Captain Cook in Hawaii. *Journal of the Polynesian Society, 98,* 371–423.

Sahlins, M. (1995). *How "natives" think.* Chicago: University of Chicago Press.

Sedgwick, E. (1991). *The epistemology of the closet.* Berkeley: University of California Press.

Shome, R. (1996). Postcolonialism interventions in the rhetorical canon: An Other view. *Communication Theory, 6,* 40–59.

Simon, W. (1989). Commentary on the status of sex research: The postmodernisation of sex. *Journal of Psychology and Human Sexuality, 2,* 9–37.

Smith, R. R., & Windes, R. R. (1997). The progay and antigay issue culture: Interpretation, influence and dissent. *Quarterly Journal of Speech, 83,* 28–48.

Stanfield, J. H., II. (1994). Ethnic modeling in qualitative research. In N. K. Denzin & Y. S. Lincoln (Eds.), *Handbook of qualitative research* (pp. 175–188. Thousand Oaks, CA: Sage.

Stanley, L., & Wise, S. (1983). *Breaking out: Feminist consciousness and feminist research.* Boston: Routledge and Kegan Paul.

Starosta, W. J. (1984). On intercultural rhetoric. In W. B. Gudykunst & Y. Y. Kim (Eds.), *Methods for intercultural communication research* (pp. 229–238). Beverly Hills, CA: Sage.

Stavans, I. (1995). *The Hispanic condition.* New York: HarperCollins.

Strine, M. S. (1997). Deconstructing identity in/and difference: Voices "under erasure." *Western Journal of Communication, 61,* 448–459.

Tanno, D. V. (1997). Names, narratives, and the evolution of ethnic identity. In A. Gonzalez, M. Houston, & V. Chen (Eds.), *Our voices: Essays in culture, ethnicity, and communication* (2nd ed., pp. 28–32). Los Angeles: Roxbury.

Tanno, D. V., & Jandt, F. E. (1994). Redefining the Other in multicultural research. The *Howard Journal of Communications, 5,* 36–45.

Todorov, T. (1984). *The conquest of America* (R. Howard, Trans.). New York: Harper and Row.

Tuhiwai Smith, L. (1999). *Decolonizing methodologies: Research and indigenous peoples.* London, New York: Zed Books Ltd.

van Dijk, T. A. (1993). *Elite discourse and racism.* Newbury Park, CA: Sage.

Vidich, A. J., & Lyman, S. M. (1994). Qualitative methods: Their history in sociology and anthropology. In N. K. Denzin & Y. S. Lincoln (Eds.), *Handbook of qualitative research* (pp. 23–59). Thousand Oaks, CA: Sage.

Wander, P. (1983). The ideological turn in modern criticism. *Central States Speech Journal, 34*, 1–18.

Warner, M. (Ed.). (1993). *Fear of a queer planet.* Minneapolis: University of Minnesota Press.

Weinberg, M., & Williams, C. (1975). Gay baths and the social organization of impersonal sex. *Social Problems, 23*, 124–136.

Weston, K. (1991). *Families we choose: Lesbian, gay, kinship.* New York: Columbia University Press.

Fred E. Jandt is professor of communication at California State University, San Bernardino, and author of *An Introduction to Intercultural Communities: Identities in a Global Community*, 4th edition, 2004, a text published by Sage.

Dolores V. Tanno is a professor in the Hank Greenspun School of Communication, University of Nevada in Las Vegas.

Reading 3.2

Gender Differences in Communication

An Intercultural Experience

BECKY MICHELE MULVANEY

INTRODUCTION

A catalog which recently arrived at my house advertises T-shirts and bumper stickers popularizing the words of feminist scholars Cheris Kramarae & Paula Treichler: "Feminism is the radical notion that women are people."[1]

Indeed, sometimes I think we've spent the last two millennia making that notion acceptable. Now, as the 20th century ends, we may be at the point of completing a first step for women—that first step has been a difficult, long-term struggle toward acceptance of women as people.

Yet history demonstrates that legal personhood does not necessarily result in comparable/equal treatment. That is, women, like so many other groups, have gained legal rights only to face less institutional, perhaps more subtle but insidious forms of discrimination. In this time when political, educational, and social discussions center on issues of diversity and of creating a constructive, multicultural society, it may be helpful to examine problems in communication between the genders as a cultural issue. This is not the only, the right, or the best way of examining gender and communication, but it does offer an alternative framework for analysis, one that perhaps defuses the potential for offensive and/or defensive posturing when discussing gender.

Hence, in this presentation I argue that it is both useful and appropriate to view gender communication as a form of intercultural communication. First, I offer a brief primer on gender differences in communication with primary emphasis on examples that illustrate how gender is both an influence on and a product of communication. In short, this discussion highlights the primary role played by communication in gender issues. Second, I offer descriptions of some salient elements of intercultural communication and I illustrate how gender communication is a form of intercultural communication. Finally, I will apply advice on how to develop effective intercultural communication skills to the situation of gender communication. During our discussion period, I hope that you, the audience (the true experts on gender communication issues and the librarian) will provide examples of problems and/or possible solutions related directly to the practicing librarian.

OVERVIEW ON GENDER AND COMMUNICATION

Two assumptions from communication theory (both classical and contemporary theories) help situate my overview on gender and communication. First, communication is epistemic. That is, communication is the medium by which we come to know things (Protagoras argued that absolute truth was inaccessible to humans; hence, truth had to be established by human standards [doxa]. Similarly, contemporary rhetorical theorists argue that truth is socially constructed through language and other symbol systems).[2] For example, it was through scientific discourse (rhetoric) that people came to view the universe as earth-centered. Human acceptance of this narrative was so strong that Galileo, in positing that the universe is sun-centered, was placed under house arrest.

My second assumption about communication is that it is axiological. That is, communication is value-laden. Virtually all communication theorists agree that language is subjective. All communication makes claims and takes stances. And some theorists, such as Weaver, Eubanks, and Winterowd would argue that no language is neutral.[3] Indeed, any use of communication exhibits an attitude, and an attitude implies an act, and all human actions have moral consequences. Hence, communication entails moral repsonsibility. The significance of communication practices in shaping our lives is no less important in the arena of gender and communication. In fact, Laurie Arliss argues that "communication is thought to be, at once, the process by which we learn to be male or female, and the product of our attempts to behave sex appropriately."[4] In describing feminist criticism, rhetorical critic Sonja Foss posits that "Its focus is on a fundamental element of human life—gender— and it is dramatically changing the form and content of knowledge about rhetoric."[5] That is, gender is both an influence on and a product of communication. Let me provide a few illustrations.

From a very early age, males and females are taught different linguistic practices.

Communicative behaviors that are acceptable for boys, for example, may be considered completely inappropriate for girls. Hence, the body of research on women and language reveals that women experience linguistic discrimination in two ways: in the way they are taught to use language, and in the way general language usage treats them.[6] So, for example, women reflect their role in the social order by adopting linguistic practices such as using tag questions, qualifiers, and fillers to soften their messages. Likewise, traditionally women were identified by their association with men, and we know that occupational titles indicated which jobs were "for men" and which were "for women." While much of this has changed today, our society retains a tendency to imply that maleness, after all, is the standard for normalcy (a female physician may still be referred to as a "woman doctor," and while a female committee chair may be called the "chair" or the "chairperson," a male in that role will more likely be called "chairman").[7] What we are taught about gender, then, is reflected in our language usage.

Communicative practices not only reflect notions about gender, but they also create cultural concepts of gender. Message sources privileged by society as legitimate knowledge generators create a web of socially compelling discourses. Thus, religious, mythic, philosophic, and scientific discourses teach us, among other things, about society's values and rules related to gender. It is no accident, then, that American myths focus on the active male and the supporting female, or that Plato defined women as "lesser men," or that Aristotle described women as "a deformity, a misbegotten male," or that St. Thomas Aquinas argued that god should not have created women, or that craniologists of the nineteenth century argued that women's smaller heads justified their subordinate position in society (thus initiating all the "pretty little head" rhetoric about women), or that Freud believed women had "little sense of justice," and so on.[8]

The rhetorical force of myths in constructing powerful worldviews is, frankly, awesome. As Edward Said explained:

> There are no innocent, no unideological myths, just as there are no "natural" myths. Every myth is a manufactured object, and it is the inherent bad faith of a myth to seem, or rather to pretend, to be a fact.[9]

Similarly, religious myths seem to be especially potent narrative forms of rhetoric. Religion "legitimates so effectively because it relates the precarious reality constructions of empirical societies with ultimate reality."[10] All these privileged discourses, I would argue, create a web of meaning, a socially constructed worldview that historically has excluded or made secondary the experience of certain groups of people.

In addition, mass mediated messages offer the most contemporary, powerful, technologically and rhetorically sophisticated strategies for shaping cultural reality. The beauty, diet, and advertising industries are the most obvious, best researched examples of contemporary, self-conscious myth-makers who control cultural concepts (and acceptable images) of gender (of what it takes and means to be male or female, masculine or feminine).[11] Consider the myriad of mass mediated communication forms available now, as we enter the twenty-first century—from the now simplistic printing press to the information superhighway and beyond. The opportunities for generating (and receiving) mass mediated messages is staggering. So too is the opportunity for abuse.

Communication, then, is of central concern when addressing gender issues. Rhetorical messages in large part determine what we consider knowledge, what knowledge we privilege, and what values we espouse. Furthermore, the role of culture in communication practices directs us to an intercultural perspective on gender and communication.

INTERCULTURAL COMMUNICATION

Intercultural communication, defined by Richard Porter and Larry Samovar as occurring "whenever a message producer is a member of one culture and a message receiver is a member of another," has been of interest to communication scholars since the 1960s.[12] Literature on intercultural communication often includes discussion of subcultures ("a racial, ethnic, regional, economic, or social community exhibiting characteristic patterns of behavior sufficient to distinguish it from others within an embracing culture or society") or cocultures (an alternative term for subcultures adopted by Judy Pearson so as not to imply inferiority in relation to the dominant society).[13] Pearson defines co-cultures as "groups of persons united by a common element who live in a culture operating within a dominant culture."[14] Communication practices by and about women clearly fit definitions of both subcultures and co-cultures. Furthermore, communication between the sub or co-culture and the dominant culture represents a form of intercultural communication. Scholars in this area often begin their discussions by identifying the main characteristics of intercultural communication. For example, Samovar and Porter identify what they call the "constituent parts of intercultural communication."[15] Dorothy Penington calls such elements "significant cultural components."[16] For the purposes of illustration, I will describe three elements of intercultural communication common to most discussions. Then, I will provide examples from gender communication to demonstrate how the intercultural communication framework is useful to us.

Worldview, language, and nonverbal communication (particularly the use of space and/or time) are often identified as important elements of intercultural communication. Worldview refers to a "culture's orientation toward such things as God, humanity, nature, the universe, and the other philosophical issues that are concerned with the concept of being."[17] An example often used is a comparison between Euro-American and Native American relationships to nature. While the Native American views the human relationship to nature as one of unity (being at one with nature), the Euro-American views the world as human-centered. Rhetorical forms such as religious, philosophical, and scientific discourses work to create a coherent world view for a culture.

Language is another significant element of intercultural communication.

Language is the medium through which a culture expresses its world view. . . . Like culture in general, language is learned and it serves to convey thoughts; in addition it transmits values, beliefs, perceptions, norms, and so on.[18]

The importance of language to intercultural communication is most obvious when cultures speak different languages. Yet, differences in meaning across culture can be just as significant when each culture uses the same language. If a British native tells her American friend to put the bags in the boot, the American may not know to place them in the trunk of the car. While this is an obvious example, Porter and Samovar point out that

Objects, events, experiences, and feelings have a particular label or name solely because a community of people have arbitrarily decided to so name them.

Language serves both as a mechanism for communication and as a guide to social reality.[19]

Finally, nonverbal communicative behavior, such as concepts of time or the use of space, differ widely from culture to culture. For example, proxemics, the study of "the way in which people use space as a part of interpersonal communication," recognizes that "people of different cultures do have different ways in which they relate to one another spatially."[20] Furthermore, the use of space helps define social relationships and social hierarchies.[21] A father traditionally sits at the head of the table in Western cultures, thus signifying his primary role in patriarchal societies. Similarly, we all know that a supervisor will exhibit a more relaxed posture than a subordinate, or that Arabs stand very close when conversing. Worldview, language usage, and proxemics are three constituents of intercultural communication which we can easily apply to communication between the genders (I believe other constituents could easily be applied as well, but I will focus on three typical elements due to time constraints).

Gender Communication as Intercultural Communication

The constituents of intercultural communication as identified by scholars such as Porter, Samovar, and Penington are points at which significant differences may occur in communication patterns, habits, and traditions across cultures. Occurrences of differences at these points suggest we are dealing with intercultural communication. Differences in worldview, language usage, and proxemics between the genders are three points of difference which suggest that gender communication is a form of intercultural communication.

Although explanations vary widely, many feminist scholars have described the female worldview as significantly different from the male worldview. Carol Gilligan, arguing from a psychological perspective, states that "female identity revolves around interconnectedness and relationship." Conversely, she argues that male identity "stresses separation

and independence."[22] And many feminist scholars, in examining the current and historical roles of women in religion, have resurrected religious practices which predate Judeo-Christian traditions and which better speak to notions of spirituality that reflect female experiences. Hence, in describing ancient goddess religions as well as contemporary practices of them, scholars note that in goddess mythology the goddess is the world (instead of a mythology which places god above or apart from the world).[23] Goddess metaphysics, if you will, creates a worldview in which the earth and nature are respected, not dominated. So, differences between female and male worldviews, like differences between Asian and American worldviews or European and Native American worldviews, may significantly affect communication.

In fact, it is difficult to discuss differences in worldviews without talking about language, since our view of the world is expressed through language and other symbol systems. Deborah Tannen, in her book *You Just Don't Understand: Women and Men in Communication*, argues that "communication between men and women can be like cross cultural communication, prey to a clash of conversational styles."[24] This is due, at least in part, to differences in the way men and women generally look at the world. Therefore, it is no coincidence that women see talk as the essence of a relationship while men use talk to exert control, preserve independence, and enhance status.[25] The ways in which concepts of social relationships (and their accompanying communication patterns) differ between genders are parallel to gender differences in worldview.

Language also reflects differences in social status between genders. Research on gender and language reveals that female language strategies invariably emulate the subordinate, nonaggressive role of women in Western society. And, language about women does no better, as suggested earlier in this paper. Differences in language usage and worldview are woven together and difficult to separate. And, nonverbal behavior is another form of "language" which demonstrates differences between men and women. Our earlier example of proxemics offers considerable evidence that gender communication is a form of intercultural communication.

"Space is a primary means by which a culture designates who is important, who has privilege."[26] Differences in the amount of space given to and taken by women and men reflect societal gender roles. So, women are less likely than men to have their own private space within the family home. And, in the workplace, employees in the traditionally female role, secretary, generally have a smaller space than the employee in the traditionally male role, executive.[27] Responses to invasion of space also differ between men and women. While men may respond aggressively, women tend to yield space rather than challenge the intruder.[28] These are but a few examples of the ways in which differences in communication between the genders fit categories of primary elements in intercultural communication. The point is that these differences can create problems in communication. Julia Wood devotes a whole chapter of her book *Gendered Lives* to the ways in which these problems are manifest in the educational system. We might assume too that the same problems are likely to visit the university library as well. An abridged list of the concerns Woods discusses includes issues familiar to us all: lack of female role models, curricular content which misrepresents white men as standard and renders women invisible, biased communication in the classroom (in both student-faculty and student-counselor communication women are not taken seriously).[29]

Woods, at the end of her chapter on gender and communication in the school setting, calls for programs which would increase sensitivity

to gender.[30] But she fails to provide specific advice. By looking at these problems via the intercultural communication perspective, we can outline specific behaviors which may improve communication between genders.

Guidelines for Improving Communication Between the Genders

In intercultural communication, identifying problem areas can also help us learn to avoid them. These problem areas can be applied to gender communication as well. Laray Barna identifies six stumbling blocks in intercultural communication: (1) assumed similarity, (2) language, (3) nonverbal misinterpretations, (4) preconceptions and stereotypes, (5) tendency to evaluate, and (6) high anxiety.[31]

This last stumbling block, high anxiety, occurs when people are completely separated from their own culture, and usually does not apply to gender communication (except, perhaps, in overtly abusive situations or highly sex-segregated societies). Awareness of the other five stumbling blocks, however, can be useful in improving our gender communication.

By learning not to assume that men and women are the same, we can become more sensitive to the fact that men and women's values and goals may differ, and generally their verbal and nonverbal language will vary as well. Conversely, awareness of societal preconceptions and stereotypes which portray the other sex as "different," or "opposite," can help us avoid such stereotypes. That is, although there may be cultural differences between the sexes, it is not productive to assume that all men love sports anymore than it is contructive to assume that all Irish consume extraordinary amounts of alcohol.

The tendency to evaluate another's culture as inferior to our own is perhaps the most difficult stumbling block to avoid, especially when applying it to gender communication. So, instead of becoming annoyed by a male's aggressive communication style, we should recognize that it is a style which is as much a part of his identity as an ethnic cuisine or a religious tradition is part of a culture. The task in improving intercultural communication is awareness and respect rather than evaluation.

CONCLUSION

In this presentation, I hope to have offered an overview of the signicant role communication plays in contemporary gender issues. Furthermore, the communication perspective allows us to examine gender communication as a form of intercultural communication. Guidelines from the discipline of intercultural communication, I believe, may be useful in improving gender communication in the library setting. I hope that in our discussion period we may explore some of the ways in which the librarian may apply these guidelines.

NOTES

1. Northern Sun Merchandising: Products For The Progressive (Minneapolis, Minn., Spring/Summer, 1994). Kramarae and Treichler are communication scholars best known for writing *A Feminist Dictionary* (London: Pandora Press, 1985).

2. See Ann Gill, *Rhetoric and Human Understanding* (Prospect Heights, Ill.: Waveland, 1994), pp. 45, 95–99; 109–201.

3. Gill, pp. 51–52; Ross W. Winterowd, *Rhetoric: A Synthesis* (New York: Holt, Rinehart, & Winston, 1968), p. 1; Richard Weaver, "Language is Sermonic," in *The Rhetoric of Western Thought,* eds. James Golden, et al (Dubuque, IA: Kendall/Hunt, 1976), pp. 147–154.

4. Laurie P. Arliss, *Gender Communication* (Englewood Cliffs, NJ: Prentice Hall, 1991), p. 10.

5. Sonja K. Foss, *Rhetorical Criticism: Exploration and Practice* (Prospect Heights, Ill.: Waveland, 1989), p. 151.

6. See Robin Lakoff's groundbreaking book *Language and Women's Place* (New York:

Harper & Row, 1975). See also a review of more recent research in Arliss, pp. 12–26.

7. Arliss, pp. 32–33.

8. Plato, *Republic, Book V,* quoted in Martha Lee Osborne, ed., *Women in Western Thought* (New York: Random House, 1979), pp. 15–16. Aristotle, *Metaphysics,* quoted in Rosalind Miles, *The Women's History of the World* (Topsfield, MA: Salem House, 1989), p. 57. *Aquinas, Summa Theologica,* quoted in Osborne, p. 68. Carol Tavris and Carol Wade, *The Longest War: Sex Differences in Perspective* (San Diego: Harcourt Brace Jovanovich, 1984), p. 14. Excerpt from Freud's letter to Martha Bernays, quoted in Miles, p. 222.

9. Edward Said, "Orientalism and The October War: The Shattered Myths," in *Arabs in America, Myths and Realities*, eds. Baha abu-Laban & Faith T. Zeadey (Illinois: The Medina University Press, 1986), p. 83.

10. Peter Berger and Hansfried Kellner, *Sociology Reinterpreted: An Essay on Method and Vocation* (New York: Anchor Books, 1981), pp. 84–90.

11. See, for example, Naomi Wolf, *The Beauty Myth* (New York: William Morrow, 1991), and Jean Kilbourne, *Killing Us Softly: Advertising's Image of Women* (Cambridge Documentary Films, Inc., 1979).

12. Richard Porter and Larry Samovar, "Approaching Intercultural Communication," in *Intercultural Communication: A Reader,* 4th ed., eds. Samovar and Porter (Belmont, CA: Wadsworth, 1985), p. 15.

13. Porter and Samovar, p. 20.

14. Judy Cornelia Pearson and Paul Edward Nelson, *Understanding and Sharing: An Introduction to Speech Communication,* 6th ed. (WCB Brown & Benchmark, 1994), p. 192.

15. Porter and Samovar (p. 24) identify the following "constituent parts": perception (including beliefs, values, attitudes, worldview, and social organization), verbal processes (including verbal language and patterns of thought), and nonverbal processes (including nonverbal behavior in general as well as concepts of time and use of space).

16. Dorothy L. Penington, "Intercultural Communication," in Larry A. Samovar and Richard E. Porter, eds., *Intercultural Communication:*

A Reader, 4th ed. (Belmont, CA: Wadsworth, 1985), pp. 31–36. Penington includes in her list of components the following: existential worldview, cosmology, ontology, language, symbol systems, schemas, beliefs, attitudes, values, temporality, space (proxemics), religion, myths, expressive forms, social relationships, communication networks, and interpolative patterns.

17. Porter and Samovar, p. 26.

18. Penington, p. 33.

19. Porter and Samovar, p. 27.

20. Porter and Samovar, p. 29.

21. Porter and Samovar, p. 29.

22. Diana K. Ivy and Phil Backlund, *Exploring GenderSpeak: Personal Effectiveness in Gender Communication* (New York: McGraw-Hill, 1994), p. 57.

23. Starhawk, *The Spiral Dance: The Rebirth of the Ancient Religion of the Great Goddess* (San Francisco: Harper & Row, 1979), pp. 1–16. See also, Carol P. Christ, "Why Women Need the Goddess: Phenomenological, Psychological, and Political Reflections," in Women and Values: Readings in Recent Feminist Philosophy, ed. Marilyn Pearsall (Belmont, CA: Wadsworth, 1986), pp. 211–219.

24. Deborah Tannen, *You Just Don't Understand: Women and Men in Communication* (New York: William Morrow, 1990), p. 42.

25. Julia T. Wood, *Gendered Lives: Communication, Gender, and Culture* (Belmont, CA: Wadsworth, 1994), pp. 141–143.

26. Wood, p. 160.

27. Wood, p. 161.

28. Wood, p. 162.

29. Wood, pp. 206–229.

30. Wood, pp. 227–228.

31. Laray M. Barna, "Stumbling Blocks in Intercultural Communication," in *Intercultural Communication: A Reader* , 4th ed., eds. Larry A. Samovar & Richard E. Porter (Belmont, CA: Wadsworth, 1985), pp. 330–338.

REFERENCES

Arliss, Laurie P. *Gender Communication*. Englewood Cliffs, NJ: Prentice Hall, 1991.

Barna, LaRay M. "Stumbling Blocks in Intercultural Communication." In *Intercultural Communication: A Reader*. 4th Ed. Eds. Larry A. Samovar & Richard E. Porter. Belmont, CA: Wadsworth, 1985, pp. 330–338.

Berger, Peter, and Hansfried Kellner. *Sociology Reinterpreted: An Essay on Method and Vocation* . New York: Anchor Books, 1981.

Christ, Carol P. "Why Women Need the Goddess: Phenomenological, Psychological, and Political Reflections." In *Women and Values: Readings in Recent Feminist Philosophy* . Ed. Marilyn Pearsall. Belmont, CA: Wadsworth, 1986, pp. 211–219.

Daly, Mary. *Beyond God The Father: Toward a Philosophy of Women's Liberation*. Boston: Beacon Press, 1973.

Eakins, Barbara, and Gene Eakins. *Sex Differences in Human Communication*. Boston: Houghton Mifflin, 1978.

Foss, Sonja K. *Rhetorical Criticism: Exploration and Practice*. Prospect Heights, Ill.: Waveland, 1989.

Gill, Ann. *Rhetoric and Human Understanding*. Prospect Heights, Ill.: Waveland, 1994.

Gilligan, Carol. *In a Different Voice: Psychological Theory and Women's Development*. Cambridge, MA: Harvard Univ. Press, 1982.

Hall, Edward T. *Beyond Culture*. New York: Doubleday, 1976.

Ivy, Diana K., and Phil Backlund. *Exploring GenderSpeak: Personal Effectiveness in Gender Communication*. New York: McGraw-Hill, 1994.

Key, Mary Ritchie. *Male/Female Language*. Metuchen, NJ: Scarecrow Press, 1975.

Kilbourne, Jean. *Killing Us Softly: Advertising's Image of Women*. Cambridge Documentary Films, Inc., 1979.

Kim, Y.Y., and W.B. Gudykunst, eds. *Theories in Intercultural Communication*. Newbury Park, CA: Sage, 1988.

Lakoff, Robin. *Language and Woman's Place*. New York: Harper & Row, 1975.

Miles, Rosalind. *The Women's History of The World*. Topsfield, MA: Salem House, 1989.

Northern Sun Merchandising: Products For Progressives. Minneapolis, MN., Spring/Summer, 1994.

Osborne, Martha Lee, ed. *Women in Western Thought*. New York: Random House, 1979.

Pearson, Judy Cornelia. *Gender and Communication.* Dubuque, IA: William C Brown, 1985.

Pearson, Judy Cornelia, and Paul Edward Nelson. *Understanding & Sharing: An Introduction to Speech Communication.* 6th Ed. Madison, WS: WCB Brown & Benchmark, 1994.

Penington, Dorothy L. "Intercultural Communication." *In Intercultural Communication: A Reader.* 4th ed. Eds. Larry A. Samovar & Richard E. Porter. Belmont, CA: Wadsworth, 1985, pp. 30–39.

Porter, Richard E., and Larry A. Samovar. "Approaching Intercultural Communication." In *Intercultural Communication: A Reader.* 4th ed. Eds. Larry A. Samovar & Richard E. Porter. Belmont, CA: Wadsworth, 1985, pp. 15–30.

Said, Edward W. "Orientalism and The October War: The Shattered Myths." In *Arabs in America, Myths and Realities.* Eds. Baha abu-Laban & Faith T. Zeadey. Illinois: Medina University Press, 1986, pp. 83–112.

Samovar, Larry A., and Richard E. Porter. *Intercultural Communication: A Reader.* 4th Ed. Belmont, CA: Wadsworth, 1985.

Spender, Dale. *Man Made Language.* Boston: Routledge & Kegan Paul, 1980.

Starhawk. *The Spiral Dance: The Rebirth of the Ancient Religion of the Great Goddess.* San Francisco: Harper & Row, 1979.

Tannen, Deborah. *You Just Don't Understand: Women and Men in Conversation.* New York: William Morrow, 1990.

Tavris, Carol, and Carol Wade. *The Longest War: Sex Differences in Perspective.* San Diego: Harcourt Brace Jovanovich, 1983.

Thorne, Barrie, and Nancy Henley, eds. *Language and Sex: Difference and Dominance.* Rowley, Mass: Newbury House, 1975.

Weaver, Richard. "Language is Sermonic." In *The Rhetoric of Western Thought.* Eds. James Golden, et al. Dubuque, IA: Kendall/Hunt, 1976, pp. 147–154.

Winterowd, Ross W. *Rhetoric: A Synthesis.* New York: Holt, Rinehart, & Winston, 1968.

Wolf, Naomi. *The Beauty Myth.* New York: William Morrow, 1991.

Wood, Julia T. *Gendered Lives: Communication, Gender, and Culture.* Belmont, CA: Wadsworth, 1994.

Becky Michele Mulvaney is with the Department of Communication, Florida Atlantic University, in Boca Raton, Florida, USA.

Reading 3.3

Acculturation, Communication, and the U.S. Mass Media
The Experience of an Iranian Immigrant

FLORA KESHISHIAN

Close to half a million international students are studying in U.S. universities (Davis, 1997/1998, p. vii). Although many will stay, all will be challenged profoundly by their relations with this society. International students, unlike other immigrants, are expected to return. Yet many international students, like other immigrants choose, and are sometimes forced, to remain. Research on acculturation generally falls in two large areas. In the first area of research, scholars such as Adelman (1988), Adler (1987), Berry (1990), Gudykunst (1988), Kim (1982, 1994), Lysgaard (1955), and Padilla (1980) examine acculturation in general and as it takes place among all immigrant groups. Other scholars concentrate on acculturation as it occurs among international students in particular.[1] For example, Loomis (1948) and Forstat (1951) examine this group's adjustment difficulties while Sellitz, Christ, Havel, and Cook (1963) discuss international students' academic, linguistic, and sociocultural problems.

Still other researchers, including Bock (1970), Furnham and Bochner (1986), and Oberg (1960), discuss "culture shock," or the reaction to a rootlessness immigrants usually experience as they try to adapt to their host culture.

In the second area of research, a number of scholars have investigated the influence of the mass media on acculturation. For example, Kapoor and Williams (1979), Kim, Lee, and Jeong (1982), Walker (1993), and Yang (1988) report that the mass media facilitate immigrants' adaptation to their host culture. Numerous studies identify media stereotypes of ethnic or racial groups (see, for example, Woll and Miller, 1987, for a bibliography), suggesting that these images influence intercultural communication (p. 20). Examining the relationship between media messages and interpersonal communication, Miller (1982, 1988) suggests that stereotypes limit the adaptation function of the mass media, and Kim (1979) concludes that interpersonal channels have a greater function than the mass media.

Through different theories, models, and methodologies all of these scholars have provided a better understanding of the complex process of acculturation. However, studies that are predominantly quantitative and science driven do not give us an entire picture of reality: They do not tell us much about the painful feelings and emotions the immigrant may experience or the negative long-lasting consequences media stereotypes may evoke against the immigrant. Intercultural communication theory and research also needs a body of qualitative work such as autobiographical or experiential studies that would bring us the voices of the immigrants. Such studies will help us more vividly see the complexities and subtleties of acculturation as well as the "construction scars" (Geertz, 1988, p. 29) to which any group might be subjected. In sum, experiential research can be "a complement to theory-driven approaches in intercultural communication" (Gonzales, Houston, and Chen, 1994, p. xv) by serving as "a passage between theory and practice" (Pagano, 1991, p. 193).

To provide a closer picture of the acculturation process, this research study takes an autobiographical approach. By venturing my own experience as an international student in New York in the late 1970s, I have tried to provide an insider's view of the complex process of adapting to a host culture and the role communication plays in, and the negative impact the mass media can have on that adaptation. Media can play a contradictory role on an immigrant's acculturation: As social and cultural agents they can facilitate the process, but they can also impede it by personalizing international relations. In the case of many Iranians who migrated to the United States around the time of the 1979 revolution, media characterizations and personal stereotyping were traumatizing.

Iran is a multicultural society composed of many religious, ethnic, and national groups. These include Persians, Kurds, Afghans,

Bakhtyaris, Baluchis, Turks, and Turkamans; and non-Muslim groups such as Zoroastrians, Baha'is, Arabs, Jews, Assyrians, and Armenians (Abrahamian, 1982). I am Armenian by ethnicity, a descendent of Christian Armenians who emigrated to Iran in the fifteenth century, and Iranian by nationality. I came to the United States as a student in August 1978, a few months prior to the development of the mass movement that would overthrow the Shah's regime in Iran. I became a permanent resident in 1994.

PROCEDURES

This research study is qualitative. Qualitative research has significantly attracted scholars internationally (Jensen, 1991). Some scholars have found this method particularly useful in their research studies because of its "explanatory power" (p. 1), especially for questions that cannot be explained by numbers alone.

This study is also autobiographical. Autobiography (also referred as personal experience, introspective, or life story) is one of the several methodologies employed in qualitative research (see Denzin and Lincoln, 1994, p. 2). Although academic disciplines generally have resisted qualitative methodologies such as autobiography (p. 4), it is not uncommon in social sciences (see Onley, 1980; Pilling, 1981; Plummer, 1983). However, the autobiographical approach has become particularly valued by the work of feminist scholars. Brodzkit and Schenck (1988); Iles (1992); Morbeck, Galloway, and Zihlman (1997); Smith (1987, 1993); Smith and Watson (1992); and Personal Narratives Group (1989) are among those feminist scholars who have shown us that one individual's story represents the stories of many, as is reflected in the title of Sommer's (1988) article, "Not Just a Personal Story: Women's Testimonies and the Plural Self."

One of the key strengths of autobiographical research, as Iles (1992) points out, is its capacity to "synthesize, blend, and transcend the realms of the public and the private" (p. ix). bell hooks (1989) stresses the revelation of self-reflexive writing and the critical link between the private and public selves. She claims that it is "in those private spaces . . . that we are most wounded, and broken" and that, "the public reality and institutional structures of domination make the private space for oppression and exploitation concrete—real" (p. 2). She also asserts that, "remembering makes us subjects in history. It is dangerous to forget" (hooks, 1982, p. 54).

Cultural critic Richard Rodriguez (1982) too has spoken to the value of autobiographical writing because it reveals a relationship between the private and the public. He believes that the writing of private experiences does good both to its writer and reader. He claims that:

> By rendering feelings in words that a stranger can understand—words that belong to the public, this Other—the young diarist no longer need feel all alone or eccentric. His feelings are public intelligibility. . . . By finding public words to describe one's feeling . . . [o]ne names what was previously only darkly felt. (Rodriguez, 1982, p. 187)

These scholars eloquently and persuasively have shown the value of autobiographical research in demonstrating that private is public, or personal is political. But such a revelation was possible by making personal experiences into public knowledge. It is in this spirit that I am writing this paper. By making public my understanding of what I had felt in private, I intend to shed light on the crucial role communication and the mass media play in acculturation—a path walked by all immigrants.

LANGUAGE BARRIER

According to Coelho (as cited in James, 1992, p. 92), "education abroad is a major developmental and psychological transition in a foreign student's life." One of the special difficulties international students, like most immigrants, face when they enter a new culture is language (see, for example, Deutsch and Won, 1963; Sales, 1990). Although this may not be true of those who stay within their own ethnic communities in the host culture, it can be a significant problem for students who leave this community for an education outside of it (see, for example, Mahdavi-Harsini, as cited in James, 1992). It certainly was for me. Despite my English studies in Iran, I went through a rough time before I felt comfortable with English. Not being confident in the use of the language can make the smallest incident become the biggest concern.

I vividly remember the frustration I experienced in my first communication course. I sat with about 300 other students in a big lecture hall, straining to understand the professor and trying to take notes—in English. Since I often failed to understand the words, I jotted down guesses in Armenian (my primary language) or Persian/Farsi (my second language). At times, when I could not make translations rapidly, I drew corresponding pictures to help me later remember the lecture. At home, I studied my incomprehensible notes and read the text a few times to grasp the ideas. Studying and successfully passing a course required much more time and energy of me that it did of the English-speaking students.

In class, I was often confused and distracted not only by the spoken language, but, perhaps more importantly, by the students' nonverbal communication, such as their appearances and the way they interacted with one another and with the teacher. For example, I was often shocked to see students walk to class in shorts, stretch their legs facing the professor, walk in late, slamming the door behind them, or display intimate behaviors toward one another publicly. I could not understand how they

would keep talking even after the professor had walked in.

I found myself even more frustrated when I had ideas and questions but hesitated to speak. I hesitated to speak because I was afraid I would be ridiculed for having an accent and because I was afraid I could not make myself understood. The only student I felt comfortable speaking with was an Armenian woman from Lebanon who shared her notes with me in Armenian. I often cried out of frustration and was afraid I would fail my courses. I felt I had become incapacitated by my limited ability to use the language.

The language barrier, lack of familiarity with other aspects of the "U.S. culture,"[2] worries about the hassle of renewing a student visa and of obtaining a work permit, and homesickness, always homesickness, made me believe that I was losing my mind. I just could not fit in; I felt more and more alienated. It was as though I were being driven from my past to a present in which I believe I did not belong. I needed something that would connect my past with the present, something that could give me a sense of identity and belonging—a bridge, perhaps, that would help me gradually give up some aspects of my past cultures to make room for acquired aspects of the U.S. culture.

To establish this tie, I sought connections with various networks. I joined Iranian and Armenian student organizations on campus. I spent long hours with Persian and other Armenians in the Student Union—a hangout for international groups of students who all talked in their native languages. These ethnic gatherings may seem to outsiders as being solely a dividing force and an obstacle to the immigrant's adaptation to the host culture, but also they can play a vital acculturating role in the social realm of the student's life (see, for example, de A. eSa, as cited in James, 1992, p. 95).

Clearly, we were all experiencing the shock of displacement without even recognizing it.

These ethnic interactions eased this shock by helping us feel that we belonged. We discussed, jokingly or with curiosity, our confusions about the U.S. culture, exchanged information about home, helped each other with homework (mostly in our native languages), criticized the unfamiliar, reminisced about the familiar past and told each other inside jokes. In this way, we assured one another that we were all going through similar problems and that we belonged to what I call an "on-campus Iran." This contact gave us moral support and helped us feel somewhat safe and secure and not completely out of place. Interestingly, we never told one another directly how lonely each of us felt, perhaps because we had not been taught in our own cultures to focus on ourselves. Perhaps we did not even realize we were lonely. Perhaps we feared that by acknowledging our loneliness to one another we would be admitting also that we could not fit in, and that would be painful. By gathering together we, in essence, indicated to each other that we were all in the same boat. These gatherings made our transition a little less difficult.

Little by little we became more familiar with the U.S. culture and acquired a better command of the English language. We even sprinkled our native conversations with English words, in part to prove that we were no longer complete strangers in the United States. As time went by, I made American friends who helped me clarify some of my confusion about my unfamiliar surroundings.[3] Once I learned to live with the reality of displacement, I depended less on these international student groups until I stopped going to them altogether. These gatherings had helped me survive.

ETHNIC SUPPORT SYSTEMS

In addition to the on-campus Iran, I discovered a number of Iranian/Armenian restaurants,

grocery stores, bookstores, and media such as newspapers, radio, and cable television stations, which I will call "off-campus Iran." Unlike on-campus Iran, which was small, school-oriented, and transitional, off-campus Iran was bigger, more familiar, and seemed more permanent. It functioned as a home away from home, particularly for those Armenians/Iranians who stayed within their own ethnic community. Although many others depended on this quasi-Iran to live their daily lives (to shop, dine, read, or watch the news, and to be entertained), I participated in it during my nostalgic moments. I was happy to know that it was there when I needed it.

Although these two quasi-Irans reduced my homesickness and gave me a sense of belonging, they were not enough. I needed also a family tie. I had of course been in touch with my family since I had left home. However, as I became more homesick, I contacted them more often through letters, photographs, family audio cassettes, and phone calls. These contacts were indispensable. I would check my mailbox several times a day, or tune my ears to the phone, desperately waiting to hear from my family. Through letters they told me about themselves and about home and reminded me how proud they were of me and how much they loved or missed me. These beautiful words seemed so permanent in writing. Occasionally, they surprised me with photographs. These photographs, which I still look at every now and then, confirmed the existence of the family I was a part of, of a reality that seemed so far away. As Sontag (1977) has suggested, photographs "enlarge a reality that is felt to be shrunk, hollowed out, perishable, remote" (p. 163). On occasions we exchanged family audio cassettes. On one of these tapes, my mother sang a song in Armenian that she used to sing to me when I was a little girl. As I listened to her taped voice, I remembered my childhood—when I would lie down, put my head on her lap, and

listen to her sing softly until I fell asleep. Closing my eyes and listening to the same soothing voice after so many years felt both comforting and tormenting.

Once I found a job, I was able to telephone my family. I found these telephone conversations instantly gratifying. Moreover, as I spoke to them I could hear the joy or sorrow in their voices and pictured them in the familiar house where I grew up. The distance between us seemed somehow shorter. These commonplace media of communication indeed helped me keep my sanity. They helped me feel I was not cut off from my past. They helped me create the family tie I needed to survive.

I realized the significance of these letters, photographs, and other means of communication in everyday life, especially when I could not use them during the social upheaval in Iran which lead to the fall of the Pahlavi regime in February 1979. With the outbreak of the revolution, the telephone lines between Iran and the United States were disconnected and the mail became unreliable. We constantly discussed the situation at home in our gatherings at on-campus Iran. I would desperately ask my relatives and friends here for some news about home. My worries increased when, in September 1980, Iraq invaded Iran, which ushered in the eight-year war between the two countries. I had continuous nightmares that my house in Tehran was hit by long-range missiles launched by the Iraqi army, and that my parents were in trouble. Only after the new government was in place could I contact home to get some news about my family.

THE "HOSTAGE CRISIS" AND THE U.S. MASS MEDIA

Despite these difficulties, acculturation was going relatively smoothly until November 4, 1979, when some student followers of Ayatollah Ruhollah Khomeini (the religious leader of the country following the revolution)

took 53 Americans hostage in Tehran. U.S. government relations with Iran changed as a result of the "hostage crisis." This incident also drastically affected my life as a soon-to-be permanent resident in the United States in the same way it affected the lives of many other Iranians. Once again, I could not telephone my family because there were no open telephone lines between the United States and Iran. The situation also had slowed down the mail, just as I had experienced during the outbreak of the revolution. I was again practically cut off from home.

My worries and frustration soon gave way to terror. I was terrified because the U.S. government had not only changed overnight its relationship to the Iranian government, but also to its Iranian residents in the United States. According to Ansari (1988), "In a manner reminiscent of the experiences of the Japanese Americans in the 1940s, Iranians in the United States became scapegoats and suffered harassment and covert discrimination, mainly because of their national heritage" (p. 120). I will never forget that as an Iranian during this period I had to go to the immigration office to prove that I was not involved in any political activities, that I was here legally; and that I could support myself financially. Without such proof, I was subject to deportation. It was isolating, humiliating, and painful to be scrutinized as a suspect. How was I supposed to trust, much less to adapt to, a host culture that distrusted me? It was difficult enough to survive on my own away from home, but it was much more difficult to worry about a possible deportation in the midst of my studies. At the same time, I was expected to adapt to the host culture and was being pushed away by it. The hostage incident slowed down the adaptation process I had so arduously begun.

The setback, however, was not because of the hostage incident alone, or because of the lack of news from home, or because of the immigration law passed specifically against Iranians living in the United States. More importantly, it was because of the manner in which the U.S. media, particularly television, presented the event. Mass media of the host society are important elements in immigrants' acculturation (see Gudykunst and Kim, 1997, p. 345). Whereas television had helped improve my English and had acquainted me with the U.S. culture, it now reflected a picture of Iran which hurt. I was no longer concerned about my so-called internal or personal problems, the language barrier, and my confusion about the school environment. I now had to worry about an external or public issue that drew the nation's if not the entire world's attention. The hostage incident "provoked considerable anti-Iranian reaction among native [born] Americans, a feeling almost nonexistent in the mid-1970s" (Ansari, 1988, p. 120).

The seeds of these negative sentiments against Iran had been planted already by the U.S. mass media during the Iranian revolution (see Sreberny-Mohammadi, 1995). There are those who have argued that the U.S. mass media "have never been mere entertainment" (Woll and Miller, 1987, p. 21) but have been used to serve ideological purposes (Schiller, 1976) and to function as "adjuncts of government" (Chomsky, 1989). Before the revolution, when the United States and Iran had favorable relations, the U.S. press hardly mentioned Iran (see Dorman and Farhang, 1987); and, when it did, the coverage was usually in the context of either U.S. arms sales to the Shah's government or issues related to Iranian oil (Larson, 1986, p. 116).

With the outbreak of the revolution, however, Iran suddenly became news; but the mass media failed to provide comprehensive news coverage of the situation (see Dorman and Omeed, 1979); Dorman and Farhang, 1987; Mowlana, 1984; Said, 1980; Sreberny-Mohammadi, 1995). Instead of clearly

discussing the socio-politico-economic forces that led to the revolution, the U.S. press made the situation in Iran look like a recurrence of a crusader's war, Islam versus Christianity, reducing the revolution to the "peculiarities of Islam" (Said, 1980). Television certainly proved to be the effective medium to convey these "peculiarities." No effort was made to explain the historical development of the revolution or the anti-U.S. sentiments in Iran. Day after day, I desperately watched television to get some news about home, but all I saw was a picture of Khomeini with other *mullahs* (Muslim religious leaders), masses shouting anti-U.S. slogans, and women covered with *chador* (veils).

In and of themselves these images were not problematic because they do represent parts of Iranian culture. But the association that the American public had made, because of the way the media had presented these images, was problematic. These negative perceptions were further intensified by references to Iranian leaders as "antimodern," "fundamentalist," and "irrational"; and referred to the people in Iran as "religious fanatics," "leftist-backed," and "backward." Thus, as Said has commented, "for however much the Iranian had gained his or her freedom from the shah and the U.S., he or she still appeared on American TV screens as part of a large anonymous mob, deindividualized, dehumanized—and *ruled again* as a result" (Said, 1980, p. 29).

Because of the hostage incident, Iran became *the* focus of the U.S. mass media. It, in fact, gave birth to ABC's (Ted Koppel's) *Nightline,* not that this program explained the situation any better. Several case studies have demonstrated how limited and incomprehensible a picture the U.S. mass media presented to the public (see, for example, Altheide, 1985; Larson, 1986; Mowlana, 1984; Sreberny-Mohammadi, 1995). What was a relatively positive, though still stereotypical and over-simplified, prerevolution and prehostage image of Iran—hospitality, Persian carpets, oil, caviar—vanished. Iran suddenly was portrayed as the United States's primary enemy and a new source of instability in the Near East, replacing the defunct "Soviet threat." Day after day I saw on television a picture of blindfolded hostages, Khomeini waving to Iranians, and masses of Iranians shouting "Death to America!" In addition to being "religious fanatics" and "backward," we were also referred to as "crazy," "stubborn," and "terrorists."

For 444 days I watched these pictures and heard these labels. For 444 days I watched a picture of the blindfolded hostages, even when television had no news about them, and felt increasingly isolated. The image the U.S. media portrayed of my homeland was so negative and alienating that it began to even make *me* wonder whether I still belonged to the Iranian culture. While I had needed connection to my family through the media (the telephone, audio-cassette, and so on) and needed the support of Armenian/Iranian community here, I later needed to become completely accepted by my host culture. But now television dashed that expectation. Television stereotyping created in me a feeling of alienation that was worse that the one I had already gone through. Worse because although I had begun to separate myself from my Armenian/Iranian culture, I had not yet become totally comfortable with the U.S. culture. I belonged neither to the past nor to the present. It seemed I had no place to go.

Because I understood and liked Iranian culture and had a knowledge of Iran's past political-economic relationship with the United States, I could not accept totally the way television presented the hostage incident. Yet these televised pictures and words affected me; every time I thought about Iran, they popped into my head.[4] Those hostage-era televised pictures and words were so strong that they would even disrupt the comforting

memories I tried to retrieve out of homesickness or as I read letters from my family.

If those pictures and words were powerful enough to have such an impact on me, how much of an impact must they have had on U.S. citizens, particularly those who had hardly any familiarity with Iran until November 4, 1979? As Gumpert and Cathcart (1982) point out, "our awareness and knowledge of other countries is dependent heavily upon our contact with media images of foreigners" (p. 348). Lippmann (1922) considers media stereotypes as the most pervasive factors that govern perception. Television was *the* medium that introduced them to Iran, and I was convinced that the image it had portrayed of Iranians was the image held by the U.S. citizens and that they would treat me accordingly. Indeed, Gudykunst and Kim (1997) argue that the mass media, particularly the new media, affect the public emotional mood about target groups, leading to social segregation and discrimination (p. 350). Shortly after the hostages had been taken in Iran, I saw a passenger on the bus who was wearing a button that read, "Nuke Iran!"

Also, a friend and professor once bluntly told me how he felt about Iran, as if I had no identity with it. He said that if he had the money and power, he would buy the most sophisticated guns to rescue the U.S. hostages in Tehran, shooting those who were holding them hostage. I understood his anger, but I also felt quite alienated by his remark and other discriminatory behaviors in the society.

Although one's perception is largely subjective, my fears and concerns were not quite a creation of my mind; I was indeed responding to a negative emotional mood that had been created against Iran/Iranians and that was being communicated to me explicitly and implicitly. After all, our understandings, meanings, and perceptions largely are influenced by communication with others, which in turn helps to construct our reality. During the

hostage period, I heard stories about Iranian immigrants who had been attacked—a woman who had been raped and, in another incident, a few men who had been beaten in a bar—because they were Iranians. These incidents affected me to a point where I no longer felt comfortable identifying myself as Iranian, and I was not alone in feeling this way. According to Ansari (1988), "the anti-Iranian reaction was so widespread that it forced Iranian-Americans to misrepresent their ethnic identity" (p. 120). When asked about my nationality, I often told people I was Armenian. I did not lie to them because I am Armenian by ethnicity. But, sadly, I did leave out the Iranian part of my identity, even though Iran is the country where I was born and grew up. I found it too isolating to associate myself with the image I knew people would have as soon as they heard the word Iran.

Although the news media dropped Iran as a subject once the hostages were released, the negative image of Iran had not been washed from the public mind. In reportage of an earthquake that erupted in northwest Iran in 1990, more than a decade after the hostage incident, *The New York Times* and *The Washington Post* still used some of the hostage-era stereotypes to report on the disaster (Keshishian, 1997). Even though, within a few years of the hostage incident, I had felt that friends, colleagues, and neighbors had accepted me into the U.S. culture, when faced with my ethnic identity/nationality, they chose to ignore it. Years after the hostage incident, when I told them that I came from Iran, I often got reactions such as: "O, Eye-ran. Things are pretty crazy there." Or, "You don't look like a person who would be able to live there." At times, some of my coworkers jokingly commented or told me how they felt about Iran and Iranians. They admitted that they usually associate Iran and Iranians with "chaos," "oppressed women," and "terrorism," adding that I should not take this oversimplified view personally, nor should I blame them because this is "what we have learned from television." When they did recognize the Iranian part of my identity, they suggested that I deny it. A former professor of mine once recommended, only part in jest, that I introduce myself as Persian,[5] instead of Iranian, because "it sounds nicer and less threatening."

For a long time I felt alienated by these remarks. Even though the U.S. culture is part of who I am today, Iranian culture, too, remains a part of me just as Armenian culture does. Because of those remarks, I was convinced that only the Western part of me was accepted by U.S. citizens. Apparently, an Iranian friend of mine shared my feelings. She told me that, sometime in 1989, in a college orientation meeting, the chair of her department had introduced her as an "international professor" because introducing her as Iranian, in the chair's words, "would be counterproductive to the department." My friend got the message to hide her identity to be accepted by her host culture.

I did not blame my colleagues or others for having those stereotypes about Iranians, although I hoped they would at least question them. The negative media image of Iran more or less still remains in the United States, and it probably will take another incident to change it. The incident does not have to be political. In fact, during the 1998 World Cup Soccer games, one of the events was between Iran and the United States. Because the sport had brought the two countries together, a question repeatedly brought up in the U.S. news was whether this game would improve the image of Iran in the United States if not the relationship between the two countries. Although it is possible that a sports game could play a role in changing the image of Iran in the United States, it would probably take a more substantial factor to erase the lingering stereotypes from the hostage era.

Thus it remains sad and dangerous that Iran's entire history and culture, as well as the political and economic factors that had led to the revolution and the hostage taking, were summed up in a few oversimplified pictures and words. It is sad and dangerous that instead of the media offering a true understanding of a country's unique politico-economic situation and examining the incident in a global and historical context and thereby allowing the audience to learn from it, the U.S. mass media gave the public a one-dimensional picture. What the public was offered were slogans and caricatures that further colored those stereotypical messages, which were easy to recognize and easy to remember, and which have, for the most part, remained in the mind of the public. Those images still persist. Sometime in 1997, enthused I told a former colleague and professor that I hoped to take students to Iran once the soured relations between the U.S. and Iran improve. He laughed hysterically at my comment and, in a joking manner, asked, "Is this going to be a one way trip?" In June 1999, another former colleague and dean, said as a "joke," that I should threaten the Provost with some "Iranian terrorists" if I am denied a tenure-track position. These so-called jokes were an indication to me that these former colleagues never went beyond their hostage-era stereotypes to get to know me as an individual. These discriminatory comments and attitudes are not limited to everyday conversations or workplace. In August 1999, once the U.S. Immigration officer knew I had just returned from Iran, he sent me to a special line for interrogation. Insinuating that I might be a terrorist, the officer asked me several questions before he let me enter the country. To an immigrant, these behaviors often signal a lack of trust and are likely to breed mistrust, leaving little room for effective intercultural communication.

So, what do we learn as a result of my experiences that has significance for intercultural communication theory and research? This autobiographic account points to the negative role of media on acculturation. It shows that media stereotypes can really hurt and have long-lasting impact: They affect the immigrant's self-concept, slow down her or his acculturation, breed mistrust, cause poor intercultural communication, and facilitate discrimination, leading to an unhealthy society. Oversimplified mediated images hurt people not only domestically and within one multicultural society but also on an international level, "fueling cross-national misunderstanding, mistrust, and conflict" (Sreberny-Mohammdi, 1995, p. 442) and influencing foreign policy (Cohen, 1963; Shaheen, 1985).

My experience with the U.S. media was not unique. Other immigrants such as German Americans during World War I and Japanese Americans in World War II also were vilified by popular media. But then telecommunications had not yet been honed into its current method of applied sciences—a difference that makes a difference. Because of the continuing global politico-economic changes, more and more people with diverse cultural backgrounds will emigrate to different countries, including the United States. No multicultural country can succeed in creating a healthy society if it uses, encourages, or tolerates stereotypes of immigrants.

Intercultural communication theory and research may not be able to change the mass media's agenda, which is to follow the official line of the State Department. However, it can encourage more research examining the relationship between stereotypes and social discrimination, one of the consequences of stereotyping the findings of this study implies. Intercultural communication theory and research also can encourage autobiographical and other experiential studies to help the immigrant realize that what he or she is experiencing is to some extent natural. Autobiographical texts have a unique capacity to empower the immigrant and the public in general:

[They] carry a potential influence on the society and add richness, depth and discernment to the public discourse. Honoring the autobiographical voice . . .–especially when that voice has been marginalized or ignored—functions to destabilize monolithic, abstract and thereby distorted portraits of time and space. (Pinar and Pautz, 1998, p. 69)

By making these private voices public knowledge, intercultural communication theory and research can help to increase public awareness and compassion. Empowered by knowledge and equipped with compassion, the public will be encouraged to organize with a rational plan, such as using the growing diversity of media sources, especially the Internet, for international dialogue. Thus informed, the public will be more likely also to question the brutalizing images that the mass media, especially network television, use to flatten and wash out the features of the international landscape for political, economic, and ideological purposes.

NOTES

1. Gregory James (1992) provides a comprehensive survey of research on international students in "Overseas students in the United States: The quest for socio-cultural and linguistic models."

2. I use this term to refer to the dominant cultural elements in the United States that have been most influential in education, law, politics, and the economy.

3. In his article "A Communication Approach to the Acculturation Process: A Study of Korean Immigrants in Chicago," Kim (1987) emphasized the importance of contact between immigrants and the members of dominant culture; and Sales (1990), in her article, "Language Use in a New Country: The Experience of Soviet Émigré in Boston," argues that immigrants need to have contact with members of both their ethnic community and the host culture.

4. These televised pictures continued to haunt me until the summer of 1997, when I went back to Iran for the first time in 19 years and returned with many comforting, positive pictures with which to replace them.

5. The word Persia is the Western label for the word *Pars,* or *Fars,* and refers to one of the many ethnic groups in Iran that controls the estate and whose language is the official language in the country.

REFERENCES

Abrahamian, E. (1982). *Iran between two revolutions.* Princeton, NJ: Princeton University Press.

Adelman, M. B. (1988). Cross-cultural adjustment: A theoretical perspective on social support. *International Journal of Intercultural Issues, 12,* 183–204.

Adler, P. (1987). Culture shock and the cross-cultural learning experience. In L. Luce and E. Smith (Eds.), *Toward Internationalism* (pp. 24–35). Cambridge, MA: Newbury.

Altheide, D. L. (1985). Impact of format and ideology on TV news coverage of Iran. *Journalism Quarterly, 62,* 346–351.

Ansari, A. (1988*). Iranian immigrants in the United States: A case study of dual marginality.* Millwood, NY: Associated Faculty.

Berry, J. (1990). Psychological acculturation: Understanding individuals moving between cultures. In R. Brislin (Ed.), *Applied cross-cultural psychology* (pp. 232–253). Newbury Park, CA: Sage.

Bock, P. (Ed.). (1970). *Culture shock: A reader in modern anthropology.* New York: Knopf.

Brodzkit, B., & Schenck, C. (Eds.). (1988*). Life lines: Theorizing women's autobiography.* Ithaca, NY: Cornell University Press.

Chomsky, N. (1989). *Necessary illusions: Thought control in democratic societies.* Boston, MA: South End Press.

Cohen, B. C. (1963). *The press and foreign policy.* Princeton, NJ: Princeton University Press.

Davis, T. M. (Ed.) (1997/1998). *Open doors.* New York: Institute of International Education.

Denzin, N. K., & Lincoln, Y. S. (Eds.). (1994). *Handbook of qualitative research.* Thousand Oaks, CA: Sage.

Deutsch, S. E., & Won, G. Y. M. (1963). Some factors in the adjustment of foreign nationals in the U. S. *International Journal of Intercultural Issues, 19,* 115–122.

Dorman, W. A. & Farhang, M. (1987). *The U.S. press and Iran: Foreign policy and the journalism of deference.* Berkeley, CA: University of California Press.

Dorman, W. A., & Omeed, E. (1979). Reporting Iran the Shah's way. *Columbia Journalism Review,* 27–33.

Forstat, R. (1951). Adjustment problems of international students. *Sociology and Social Research, 36,* 25–30.

Furnham, A., & Bochner, S. (1986). *Culture shock: Psychological reactions to unfamiliar environments.* London: Methuen.

Geertz, C. (1988). *Works and lives: The anthropologist as author.* Stanford, CA: Stanford University Press.

Gonzalez, A., Houston, M., & Chen, V. (1994). *Our voices: Essays in culture, ethnicity, and communication.* Los Angeles, CA: Roxbury.

Gudykunst, W. (1988). Uncertainty and anxiety. In Y. Kim and W. Gudykunst (Eds.), *Theories in intercultural communication* (pp. 123–156). Newbury Park, CA: Sage.

Gudykunst, W., & Kim, Y. Y. (1997). *Communicating with strangers: An approach to intercultural communication.* New York: McGraw-Hill.

Gumpert, G., & Cathcart, R. (1982). Media stereotyping: Images of the foreigner. In L. A. Samovar & R. E. Porter (Eds). *Intercultural communication: A reader* (3rd ed., pp. 348–353). Belmont, CA: Wadsworth.

hooks, b. (1982). Narratives of struggle. In P. Mariani (Ed.), *Critical fictions: The politics of imaginative writing* (pp. 3–61). Seattle, WA: Bay.

hooks, b. (1989). *Talking back: Thinking feminist, thinking black.* Boston, MA: South End Press.

Iles, T. (Ed.). (1992). *All sides of the subject: Women and biography.* New York: Teachers College Press.

James, G. (1992). Overseas students in the United States: The quest for socio-cultural and linguistic models. *American Studies International, 30,* 89–108.

Jensen, K. B. (1991). Introduction: The qualitative turn. In K. B. Jensen and N. W. Jankowski (Eds.), *A handbook of qualitative methodologies for mass communication research* (pp. 1–11). New York: Routledge.

Kapoor, S., & Williams, W. (1979, May). Acculturation of foreign students by television. Paper presented at the International Communication Association convention, Philadelphia, PA.

Keshishian, F. (1997). Political bias and nonpolitical news: A content analysis of an American and Iranian earthquake in *The New York Times* and *The Washington Post. Critical Studies in Mass Communication, 14,* 332–343.

Kim, J., Lee, B., & Jeong, W. (1982, July). Uses of mass media in acculturation. Paper presented at the Association for Education in Journalism convention. Athens, OH.

Kim, Y. Y. (1979a). Mass media and acculturation. Paper presented at the Eastern Communication Association convention. Philadelphia, PA.

Kim, Y. Y. (1982). Communication and acculturation. In L. A. Samovar & R. E. Porter (Eds.), *Intercultural communication: A reader* (pp. 359–372). Belmont, CA: Wadsworth.

Kim, Y. Y. (1987). A communication approach to the acculturation process: A study of Korean immigrants in Chicago. *International Journal of Intercultural Relations, 2,* 197–224.

Kim, Y. Y. (1994). Adaptation to a new culture. In L. A. Samovar & R. E. Porter (Eds.), *Intercultural communication: A reader* (pp. 392–405). Belmont, CA: Wadsworth.

Larson, J. F. (1986). Television and U. S. foreign policy: The case of the Iran hostage crisis. *Journal of Communication, 36,* 108–130.

Lippmann, W. (1922). *Public opinion.* New York: Macmillan.

Loomis, C. P. (1948). Acculturation of foreign students in the U.S. *Applied Anthropology, 7,* 17–34.

Lysgaard, S. (1955). Adjustment in a foreign society: Norwegian Fulbright grantees visiting the United States. *International Social Science Bulletin 7,* 45–51.

Miller, G. R. (1982). A neglected connection: Mass media exposure and interpersonal communication competency. In G. Gumpert & R. Cathcart (Eds.), *Intermedia: Interpersonal communication in a mediated world* (2nd ed., pp. 49–56). New York: Oxford University Press.

Miller, G. R. (1988). Media messages and information processing in interpersonal communication. In B. Ruben (Ed.), *Information and behavior,* Vol. 2. New Brunswick, NJ: Transaction.

Morbeck, E., Galloway, A., & Zihlman, L. A. (Eds.). (1997*). The evolving female: A life-history perspective.* Princeton University Press.

Mowlana, H. (1984). The role of the media in the U.S.-Iranian conflict. In A. Arno & W. Dissanayake (Eds.). *The news media in national and international conflict* (pp. 71–93). Boulder, CO: Westwood.

Oberg, K. (1960). Culture shock: Adjustment to new cultural environments. *Practical Anthropology, 7,* 170–179.

Onley, J. (1980). *Autobiography: Essays theoretical and critical.* Princeton, NJ: Princeton University Press.

Padilla, A. M. (Ed.). (1980). *Acculturation: Theory, models and some new findings.* Washington, DC: Westview.

Pagano, J. (1991). Moral fictions: The dilemma of theory and practice. In C. Witherell & N. Noddings (Eds.), *Stories lives tell: Narrative and dialogue in education* (pp. 193–206). New York: Teachers College, Columbia University Press.

Personal Narratives Group (Ed.). (1989). *Interpreting women's lives: Feminist theory and personal narratives.* Bloomington, IN: Indiana University Press.

Pilling, J. (1981). *Autobiography and imagination: Studies in self-scrutiny.* London: Routledge & Keagan Paul.

Pinas, W. F., & Pautz, A. E. (1998). Construction scars: Autobiographical voices in biography. In C. Kridel (Ed.). *Writing educational biography: Explorations in qualitative research* (pp. 61–72). New York: Garland.

Plummer, K. (1983). *Documents of life: An introduction to the problems and literature of a humanistic method.* London: George Allen & Unwin.

Rodriguez, R. (1982). *Hunger of memory: The education of Richard Rodriguez*. New York: Bantam.

Said, E. W. (1980). Iran. *Columbia Journalism Review, 81*, 23–33.

Sales, A. L. (1990). Language use in a new country: The experience of Soviet émigré in Boston. *The Howard Journal of Communications, 2*, 192–212.

Schiller, H. I. (1976). *Communication and cultural domination*. New York: M. E. Sharpe.

Sellitz, C., Christ, J. R., Havel, J., & Cook, S. W. (1963). *Attitudes and social relations of foreign students in the United States*. Minneapolis, MN: University of Minneapolis Press.

Shaheen, J. G. (1985). Media coverage of the Middle East: Perception and foreign policy. *Annals of American Academy of Political and Social Science, 482*, 160–175.

Smith, S. (1987). *A poetics of women's autobiography: Marginalizing the fiction of self-representation*. Bloomington, IN: Indiana University Press.

Smith, S. (1993). *Subjectivity, identity, and the body: Women's autobiographical practices in the twentieth century*. Bloomington, IN: Indiana University Press.

Smith S., & Watson, J. (Eds.). (1992). *De-colonizing the subject: The politics of gender in women's autobiography*. Minneapolis, MN: Minnesota University Press.

Sommer, D. (1988). Not just a personal story: Women's testimonies and the plural self. In B. Brodzkit & C. Schenck (Eds.). *Life lines: Theorizing women's autobiography* (pp. 107–130). Ithaca, NY: Cornell University Press.

Sontag, S. (1977). *On photography*. New York: Delta.

Sreberny-Mohammadi, A. (1995). Global news media cover the world. In J. Downing, A. Mohammadi, & A. Sreberny-Mahammadi (Eds.), *Questioning the media: A critical introduction* (pp. 429–443). Thousand Oaks, CA: Sage.

Walker, D. (1993). *The role of the mass media in the adaptation of Haitian immigrants in Miami*. Unpublished doctoral dissertation. Indiana University, Bloomington, IN.

Woll, A. L., & Miller, R. M. (1987). *Ethnic and racial images in American film and television: Historical essays and bibliography*. New York: Garland.

Yang, S. (1988). *The role of the mass media in immigrants' political socialization*. Unpublished doctoral dissertation, Stanford University, Stanford, CA.

Flora Keshishian is with the Department of Media Studies, Queen College of the City University of New York.

Reading 3.4

Reconfiguring Borders

Health-Care Providers and Practical
Environmentalism in Cameron County, Texas

TARLA RAI PETERSON

SUSAN J. GILBERTZ

KATHI GROENENDYK

JAY TODD

GARY E. VARNER

This essay explores the attempts of female health practitioners to communicate the connections between human health and the natural environment in Cameron County, Texas. Flew and colleagues (1999) argue that globalization has brought an increase in competition for cheap labor, the depletion of natural resources, and cultural penetration from the West. They suggest it may also, however, open new possibilities for positive exchanges. Few people are as ideally positioned to examine this phenomenon as are the residents of Cameron County, the southernmost county in the United States. Their experiences in the borderlands offer a unique opportunity for gaining understanding from both a local and global perspective.

Gloria Anzaldúa (1983, 1987, 1990) envisions the possibility of moving along a continuum from geographical borderlands to *mestiza* consciousness, a perspective ideally suited to a world in which everyone lives in metaphorical borderlands. Following an overview of critical aspects of Anzaldúa's theory of borderlands, we explain our research method and offer a brief description of life in Cameron County. The bulk of the essay is devoted to a discussion of discourse elicited from women who have become involved in an anguished conflict over the connections between environmental pollution and human health in Cameron County. Their talk provides a nuanced analysis of the interconnections between the people and the environment that sustains them while it enriches our understanding of how communication practices contribute to the social construction of a border consciousness.

LIVING IN CAMERON COUNTY

Cameron County, Texas, is the southernmost county on the border between the United States

Reprinted with permission from *Women's Studies Quarterly*, Volume XXIX, Nos. 1 & 2, 2002, pp. 51–63.

and Mexico. For retirees coming from all over the United States and Canada, it is a paradise of western desert, northern coastal, and tropical plants (Jahrsdoerfer and Leslie 1988). Neotropical mammals, snakes, lizards, and salamanders and at least twenty-one bird species reach the northern limits of their range here. The Texas tortoise, long-billed curlew, and an unusual hypersaline-tolerant oyster population inhabit the tidal flats. About seven hundred vertebrate species have been identified in this region. The U.S. Fish and Wildlife Service maintains two traditionally bounded wildlife refuges (Santa Ana and Laguna Atascosa), and a refuge consisting of fifty small tracts (Lower Rio Grande Valley) in the region. Santa Ana provides habitat for more endangered species than any other wildlife refuge in the United States; Laguna Atascosa was the location of the most recent ocelot and jaguarundi sightings in the United States; and Lower Rio Grande Valley provides the beginnings of a wildlife corridor. Since the 1920s, however, more than 95 percent of the Lower Rio Grande Valley's native brushland has been cleared for development, and the rate shows no sign of slowing (Jahrsdoerfer and Leslie 1988).

Cameron County is in the United States, but a guided nature walk through Santa Ana goes a long way toward dispelling the myth that political borders are impermeable. Our guide explained calmly that the damp undershorts we saw hooked in the thornbushes probably belonged to someone who had waded the river earlier that morning. Apparently it is common to wade across in the morning, change into dry clothing, and then either remain for a few days or return the same evening via the bridge. Neither people nor toxic substances respect the border. Instead, Cameron County residents drink water and breathe air that contains pollutants over which the United States government has no jurisdiction.

The crossing between Matamoros and Brownsville buzzes with around-the-clock activity. Some times are busier than others, and depending on their motivation, people assiduously avoid or seek out those times. Noisy lines of semitrailers in varying states of repair belch diesel fumes. The downtown bridge has a festive air. U. S. residents wander across, fishing in their pockets for spare change to pay the toll. They return laden with tequila, vanilla, and trinkets for friends. Mexican residents return from Brownsville laden with bags bulging with the inexpensive groceries for which the United States is famous. Some eschew the bridge, preferring less-public routes. Those eager for U.S. dollars find work around Brownsville, usually in the fields. Green cards are relatively easy to obtain, but they are not guaranteed. When holders of questionable cards are exposed to unsafe levels of pesticides and herbicides they cannot complain to a government agency. Instead some of them appear unaffected, others get sick, and still others die.

Cameron County's average weekly wage in 1992 was $362.00 (TDH-CDC 1992). People move in and out rapidly, and many avoid the census. The Brownsville Independent School District, which is the county's largest employer, is overwhelmed with a steady flow of new immigrants (Selby 1994). Compared with those of the rest of the United States, Cameron County residents have larger-than-average families and smaller-than-average incomes. Education levels are lower, while chronic disease rates are higher. Brownsville, the county seat, lies directly across the border from Matamoros, Tamaulipas, Mexico. Brownsville is Cameron County's major population center, with at least 112,000 documented residents (TDH-CDC 1992).

Maquiladora industries clustered in automotive, electrical, electronic, furniture, ceramics, textile, and chemical production promised to rescue Cameron County from its economic malaise more than a decade ago. The chemical industry has been, and is predicted to continue as, the fastest-growing segment (Texas Center 1990). *Maquiladoras* often failed to meet legal requirements for returning hazardous waste to the United States. For example, a review of Texas Water Commission records from January 1987 through June 1989 disclosed that only thirty-three of the approximately six hundred companies operating during that time returned waste from Mexican *maquiladoras* (Texas Center 1990). Since NAFTA, the plants are no longer referred to as *maquiladoras,* but they remain in business, and responsibility for international environment regulation remains uncertain.

CO-CONSTRUCTION OF THE BORDER, HUMAN HEALTH, AND THE ENVIRONMENT

Cameron County became a media star in 1991 after a nurse informed the Texas Department of Health (TDH) that three anencephalic infants had been born in Brownsville within a thirty-six-hour period (for a detailed account of media coverage, see Groenendyk 1994). When TDH officials investigated, they discovered that six anencephalic infants had been born in the same hospital between 27 March and 21 May 1991. In the anencephalic fetus, the anterior end of the neural tube fails to close, resulting in either partial or complete absence of the brain. Anencephaly occurs during the first sixteen to twenty-six days of pregnancy, and babies who are born with this condition die within a few hours (TDH-CDC 1992). Because national rates suggest that fewer than two cases per year should occur in Cameron County, the TDH contacted the Centers for Disease Control (CDC) in Atlanta, Georgia. The two organizations immediately launched an investigation of neural-tube defects reported in Cameron County during the past three years (TDH-CDC 1992). The final report was inconclusive. On the basis of recent studies of neutral-tube disorders in China, it recommended that TDH provide folic acid supplements to women of childbearing age. The only strong correlation found in the investigation was a previously established positive relationship between low socioeconomic status and the occurrence of neural-tube defects (TDH-CDC 1992). Local medical personnel, including the nurse who had made the initial telephone call, were enraged by the report's apparent minimization of their plight.

Our goal in conducting the interviews for this project was to produce a text that would enable us to understand how these women negotiated their orientation toward the earth and other humans. Because we wanted to know whether our informants considered the natural environment to be an important dimension of their lives, as well as how they characterized it, the interview protocol was designed to encourage participants to tell the stories they chose to tell, with minimal outside direction (for a detailed description of techniques used to select interviewees, conduct interviews, and analyze interview transcripts see Peterson 1997). We obtained appointments for initial interviews by telephone contact. If the person was willing to participate, a convenient time and location for the interview was arranged. We initially contacted some of the women as part of another project designed to learn how Cameron County residents conceptualized "sustainable development." Most of our interviewees representing the medical profession happened to be women. We talked with physicians, nurses, midwives, a clinic manager, and an herbalist. All of them lived and worked in Cameron County, in addition to volunteering with various nongovernmental organizations. Their ages ranged from early twenties to early sixties. Their ethnicity was mixed, and some found it impossible to define. All were fluent in English. All but two were equally comfortable conversing in Spanish. All interviews were conducted in English, however, because none of the interviewers was fluent in Spanish.

We traveled to Cameron County several times, where we conducted interviews in locations ranging from hospital waiting rooms to private offices and herb gardens. Our interviewees determined the length of the interviews, with the shortest interviews taking thirty minutes and the longest more than two hours. Over the course of approximately one year, we conducted additional interviews with all but one informant, and spent additional time in less-formal activities with all informants. We used field notes taken while visiting Cameron County, proceedings and notes from public meetings, reports prepared by government and nongovernment organizations, and newspaper and magazine articles to contextualize our interviews and other observations.

The paradox of the border seeped into everyone's talk, whether they were longtime residents or recent transplants. The same people who claimed that the border defined their lives insisted in the next breath that it existed only in the minds of distant bureaucrats. Their discourse suggests that rather than being nonexistent, the border has become a hyperreality that creates a unique culture, alienating its members from the other nation's citizens and bonding them to each other. As Anzaldúa (1987) writes, "The U.S.-Mexican border *es una herida abierta* [an open wound] where the Third World grates against the first and bleeds. And before a scab forms it hemorrhages again, the lifeblood of two worlds merging to form a third country—a border culture."(3)

All our participants stressed the interrelated concepts of border culture, complexity, and growth. They were alternatively proud of, or shamed by, their status as residents of a borderland, with its accompanying poverty, growth, migration, and cultural diversity. They also discussed the complexity of development, focusing on the complex relationship between natural and social systems. They spoke frequently of the chaotic nature of life in

Cameron County, claiming that planning initiatives often failed because organizers were ignorant of life in a borderland. The border also exacerbated difficulties associated with human population growth. Many blamed uncontrolled growth for degradation of both human and environmental health.

Narratives drawn from our participants' discourse indicate a sophisticated understanding of the complexity involved in living on the border. Everyone agreed that more knowledge was needed to cope with complex environmental problems. Most saw knowledge as developing out of some combination of science, education, and experience. Those who talked about science viewed it as potentially helpful, but often harmful as used. Those who discussed education explained that it needed to be contextualized within local experience. Preferences for managing complex natural systems ranged from aggressive micro-management to a completely "natural" approach. The range of preferences for managing human health was less broad, with even "natural" medicine applied in a very directed manner. The overall perception of growth was negative, although participants split over the valuation of industrial growth. Some labeled new manufacturing industry as positive because it expanded the region's economy. They were ambivalent, however, about whether industrial growth led to a net profit because it also increased the region's rate of human population growth, which meant that the recently expanded economy had to be shared among more people. They indicated that the number of people without the means to pay for needed infrastructure increased faster than the number of those with means. Others found only harm in the country's industrial growth. None of our interviewees viewed the region's human population growth as a positive feature. Many had seen local and regional planning efforts overwhelmed by rampant increases in human population. Much of this discussion was related explicitly to border issues. All were involved in binational health-care efforts, environmental plans, or education initiatives. Everyone described life in Cameron County as a process of negotiating border culture, complexity, and growth.

The women who shared their time with us were all involved to some degree in one of two organizations devoted to exploring the connections between the natural environment and human health.[1] Two worked at the Casa de Colores, and three were founding members of the One Border Foundation. Others volunteered whatever time they could.

Casa de Colores is a converted farmhouse on a collective farm located in the southern corner of Cameron County. Patty Niño manages the farm and directs courses in midwifery in the converted bedrooms on the second floor. Her associate, whose name we were never sure of, teaches the section on herbal treatments and manages the aboriginal art museum on the first floor. During most of our visits to Cameron County we boarded at the Casa. We first saw Patty trundling a huge wheelbarrow overflowing with some sort of grassy material, crowned with a grinning toddler. The road ended at a substantial two-story farmhouse. This one was accented with brilliant shades of pink and purple. As we stepped tentatively from our rental car, the toddler slid from her perch and ran to face us. We stared at each other until Patty and her wheelbarrow arrived. Patty spoke to her daughter in Spanish, and translated for our benefit. Then we met the museum curator. That evening, we had our fist lesson in herbal medicine from Gloria. The next time we spoke, her name was Dolores and she demonstrated a dance form we had never seen before.

Niño became a midwife because she wanted "to present that traditional birthing experience that belongs to a family." Midwifery provided her with a means for redirecting a society she feared was becoming increasingly alienated from the earth. She explained that "it's important for all communities to retain that understanding that our natural resources, all the raw materials come from the earth; that everything is made within the mother" (I1, R2). Niño assists women, particularly those who do not read or write in English, to register with the Texas Midwifery Board so that they are able to practice their craft legally. She also provides educational programs for migrant workers who have signed up to produce organic food on the cooperative farm. Niño claimed her choices were based on "valuing the earth and trying to tread lightly. Water is one of the four elements. It's sacred. The air is another element that is also sacred. And it feels really bad to me that people can violate those elemental things. So I ally myself with the people who are concerned that the health effects are going to continue" (I1, R32). Although we did not realize it at the time, Niño mentioned most of the other women we would eventually interview.

Ramirez established the One Border Foundation because the TDH-CDC study convinced her that without local control, human-health research conducted in the Lower Rio Grande Valley would ignore environmental issues that were critical to human health in the region. After efforts to cooperative with TDH and CDC failed, she attempted to sponsor independent research through the Brownsville Community Health Center but discovered that the center was barred from certain activities because of its status as a federal grantee. In addition, the clinic relies on local support to obtain alternative funding necessitated by cuts in federal support. When Ramirez proposed that the clinic should sponsor further research on anencephaly, "those who are a part of the chamber of commerce, the Economic Development Foundation, and county officials and city officials were concerned that we were going to create such a ruckus with the research that the ability to bring in new industry and tourism was going to be killed." Because the clinic "couldn't afford to kill those relationships" she decided to establish a "separate non-profit organization" (I1, R13).

Steiner, the nurse who had filed the original anencephaly report, also serves on the board. Participation in anencephaly research, even when supported by One Border rather than by the clinic, angers some residents. Steiner described an incident that occurred in a "health committee at the chamber of commerce." The chair turned to her and asked, "If they have to do the study on anencephaly why don't they do it somewhere else? Can't they do it in Hidalgo County? They need to do it elsewhere." She rolled her eyes, then added, "And this is a *health* committee!" (I1, R33, emphasis in original).

Steiner has spent hours going through hospital records searching for answers to the connections between environmental and human health. "We share so much," she declared, "we need to look at how we can work with Matamoros . . . because if you don't, you always are gonna be in a third world country. We're always gonna be dealing with that, because we're only bringing half the people up" (I2, R23).

When Brownsville's mayor repeatedly described anencephaly as "a Hispanic disease" (Terrell 1992), Steiner wondered, "Are the genetics a part of the transformation of an environmental issue?" (I1, R28). She argued that although Hispanic populations in Mexico and South America have a higher rate of anencephaly than the U.S. population, this could be caused by environmental factors as easily as by genetics. Steiner pointed out that even if neural-tube defect rates from Mexico City provided a valid comparison, the conclusion that the victims' Hispanic heritage caused the higher rates did not necessarily follow. "Mexico City is not the cleanest city in the world either," she charged. Rather, "It's one of the worst environmental areas in the world" (I1, R29–30). "Maybe it's a lot of

different causes that are happening; but let's find out what they are," she urged. "Let's don't just say, "Oh, Hispanic. You're similar to Mexico City. That's the reason'" (I1, R31).

Maria Salazar, another nurse who volunteers with One Border, indicated that the only aspect of the situation that was "caused" by the high proportion of Hispanics in the population was the choice not to conduct extensive environmental monitoring. One factor that prevented environmental monitoring was cost. "If this anencephaly problem had happened in Austin, they would certainly pour a lot of money in there," Salazar asserted, but the study was done at minimal cost "because it's on the border" (I1, R16).

Salazar explained that a border existence had ironic consequences. Both people and natural resources move between Matamoros and Brownsville with relative freedom. "A lot of people from the States go to Mexico for their health care," she explained, because they "like the care in Mexico better." Others use Mexico's socialized medical system because they "don't have any money" to pay for care in the United States. Conversely, those who cannot "access the care there . . . come over here, [and] a lot of, umm, pregnant ladies would come and deliver over here so that a child would be an American citizen. And you know, if I was pregnant, and I could get across, I'd do it too. I'd do that for my child" (Salvador I2, R101–2). All this means that greater resources were needed on the border—the no-man's-land claimed by neither Mexico nor the United States.

Susan Ramirez, a nurse at a local hospital, had grown up in Brownsville, married a Mexican national, raised her children near Tampico, Mexico, then returned to Brownsville. She works with One Border, as well as with several local environmental improvement organizations. She characterized the border culture as equally alien from both Mexico and the United States, noting, "We're part of the

United States that's true; but we're kind of in a little line; a division line that's a little bit of Mexico, a little bit of the United States. This is kind of a no-man's-land. And . . . for a while it was a forgotten land where people just kind of ignored us" (I1, R7).

She focused much of her conversation on living conditions among new immigrants. "You walk outside . . . their little shack," she explained, "and from about here to where that door is they will have an outhouse. And any time we have a lot of rain, the water level rises and the whole property is polluted" (I1, R13). Local businesspeople, she maintained, have ignored this segment of the county's population because "it's not convenient that they have to be talking about the health problems here" (I1, R22). Others have said, "Don't let them in schools. Y'know you've gotta get strict. You've gotta . . . build a wall. If you have to, arm it." Ramirez characterized her own perspective as more compatible with those who believe they have to "do something over there [in Mexico], . . . because that sort of thing [the wall] is not going to work" (I1, R228). Ramirez opposed NAFTA, but hoped it might remove existing obstacles to binational health-care initiatives. She believes that binational health-care initiatives offer the only motivation that might be powerful enough to encourage Mexico and the United States to begin working together to protect the environment.

Ramirez emphasized the significant interconnections between human health and the broader environment. She claimed that "if we get a cleaner environment, we'll probably have less health issue problems" (I2, R52). Later, she elaborated on this claim: "It's all interconnected; any way you look at it. It affects environment. Environment affects health. . . . All these things are interconnected" (I2, R307). Because she sees social and natural systems as intertwined, she believes that "it has to be more of a holistic approach to this [health]

problem. . . . We've got to talk to people from the agricultural department. We've got to talk to other people who are doing some great things that we're not even aware of—that we could probably help with in some way" (I2, R266). She used a simply analogy to illustrate the attitude of local businesspeople who refused to see the connection between industrial pollution and human health: "I mean you put two and two together and it becomes four for us [health care professionals]. But other people [local boosters], it's not convenient, it becomes a five" (I1, R22).

Rosa Gomez explained her primary interest in Cameron County's development as a desire to sustain life in a county, where "you have the Third World grasping at the First" (I2, R23). Gomez, who is a pediatrician, explained that she had become politically active in environmental issues because the TDH-CDC study convinced her that without local control, research conducted in the Lower Rio Grande Valley would not serve the needs of border residents. She was not impressed by claims of scientific objectivity. "Why is it okay to include the guy from the public utilities board who says that the water inflow valve to Brownsville, Texas, is nowhere near the *maquiladoras* [in the final report of the TDH-CDC study]," asked Gomez, "and it's not okay to include my statement, standing in front of the inflow valve, pointing at a *maquiladora,* saying, "That's a *maquiladora.* This is the water intake valve'" (I1, R15). She accused TDH and CDC using the precepts of epidemiology to further "their interests . . . in claiming the public, first and foremost." She argued that they were frightened of conducting an "investigation that might turn up some answers that may be hard to deliver" (I1, R15). Gomez resigned from her position as medical director at a local clinic when a member of its board of directors demanded that she refrain from participating in One Border-sponsored projects.

STRADDLING THE BORDER

Anzaldúa uses the physical U.S.-Mexican border as a metaphor for life. She argues that the most significant feature of borderlands is disorientation caused by the constant clash of different cultures, which is the result of arbitrary boundaries (1987). "Living on borders and in margins, keeping intact one's shifting and multiple identity and integrity, is like trying to swim in a new element" (1987, preface). The need to compartmentalize the self is a characteristic of the dominant culture that is particularly problematic for those at the borders (1983, 205). Anzaldúa argues that the requirement for border residents to choose one of their multiple identities from which to speak probably constitutes the most powerful means of silencing (1990, xxiii). She recognizes that border inhabitants are complicit in their own silencing. She writes, "I have so internalized the borderland conflict that sometimes I feel like one cancels out the other and we are zero, nothing, no one" (1987, 63). The ensuing struggle out of nothingness entails a painful effort to create a *mestiza* consciousness. Despite the disorientation and pain, Anzaldúa insists, "There is an exhilaration in being a participant in the further evolution of humankind, in being worked on. I have the sense that certain faculties ... and dormant areas of consciousness are being activated, awakened" (1987, preface).

The new consciousness energizes the border resident because it "comes from a continual creative motion that keeps breaking down the unitary aspect" of cultural paradigms. It enables a person to balance at the edge "where phenomena tend to collide. It is where the possibility of uniting all that is separate occurs" (1990, 379). Only those who internalize the borderland metaphor can "be a crossroads" for an increasingly globalized society (1987, 124). Residents of Cameron County, Texas, have opportunities to experience multiple cultures beset with contradictory versions of reality, each day. Their sense of perspective and flexibility can suggest new possibilities for integrating concerns for human and environmental health.

Our participants' discourse can help us understand how communication enables people to negotiate what it means to live in a borderland. They describe environmental issues as bounded by border culture, complexity, and growth. They articulate considerable hostility toward interest groups they think have ignored these issues. At the same time, they express a desire to develop cooperative links among previously hostile groups of local residents. Although their discourse contains numerous statements we could critique as essentialist, patriarchal, and neotraditional, we are not motivated toward such a critique. Instead, we find their power contagious.

These women have taken advantage of chaotic border conditions to reject the sanitized account of development offered by technological experts. They offer an alternative narrative of life in Cameron County, negotiated through their own experience. They do not reject all notions of professional expertise. Instead, they offer a locally grounded perspective from which both residents and outside "experts" can invent a new understanding in order to achieve more community-validated environmental protection practices for the future.

Their most fundamental demand is that they be afforded more significant opportunities to participate in policy decisions that affect their own lives. Our interviewees illustrate the sophisticated understanding of social problems possessed by many members of the lay public and their refusal to substitute a political boundary for an ecological one. They are not unaware of the difficulties involved in pursuing environmental policy at an international level. They refuse, however, to use these difficulties as an excuse to ignore fundamental problems. The Rio Grande forms a nucleus around which their region revolves. They insist that pursuing conflicting environmental policies on the river's northern and southern banks is irrational.

All borders are dangerous. Social structures are most vulnerable at their margins, because the very existence of a margin suggests another possible structure. The women of One Border and Casa de Colores pose a threat to traditional development patterns at multiple levels. Primarily, they threaten to redirect public attention to the southernmost county in Texas, which exists on the physical margins of both the United States and Mexico. In any culture, living on the border differs dramatically from living in the center. As boundary spanners, our participants pose unique threats to the social system, for "the most dangerous pollution is for anything which has once emerged gaining reentry" (Douglas 1984, 123). Our informants insist on repeatedly violating this taboo. They transgress external boundaries in their insistence that environmental and human health concerns require binational initiatives. They transgress internal boundaries when they claim that knowledge gained through mundane experience, supplemented with their ethical and religious beliefs, provides more appropriate guidelines for development than do economics and technology. They argue that the rhetoric of economics and technology has perpetuated the logic of relegating pollutant production to the border. The border, however, is their center, if a center exists. Their rejection of the status quo threatens to disrupt both internal social relations and relations between U.S. and Mexican interests. Their demand to be allowed a place at the table when policy is discussed is an attempt to reclaim the border as their center.

Maria Salazar's words at the conclusion of her second interview illustrate both the immediate and general utility of the border consciousness these women have developed. "I was never a fighter before," she said. "I mean I was just kind of real meek." She took a deep breath, then finished her statement: "But I think we need to be strong so I don't care what they think about me. I'll do whatever it takes" (I2, R147).

NOTE

1. Because our participants remain active residents of their community, we have used pseudonyms to protect anonymity. Interview excerpts are referenced to differentiate between the first and second interviews (I1/I2), and to indicate the response within that interview (R#).

REFERENCES

Anzaldúa, Glria. 1983. "La Prieta." In Gloria Anzaldúa and Cherrie Moraga, eds., *This Bridge Called My Back: Writins by Radical Women of Color*, pp. 198–209. New York: Kitchen Table Press.

———. 1987. *Borderlands/La Fronters: The New Mestiza*. San Francisco: Aunt Lute Books.

———. 1990. *Making Face, Making Soul/Haciendo Caras: Creative and Critical Perspectives by Feminists of Color*. San Francisco: Aunt Lute Books.

Douglas, Mary. 1984. *Purity and Danger: An Analysis of the Concepts of Pollution and Taboo*. Boston: Routledge and Kegan Paul.

Flew, Fiona, Barbara Bagilhole, Jean Carabine, Natalie Fenton, Celia Kitzinger, Ruth Lister, and Sue Wilkinson. 1999. "Introduction: Local Feminisms, Global Futures." *Women's Studies International Forum* 22:393–403.

Groenendyk, Kathi. 1994. *Covering the Story: A Rhetorical Analysis of Brownsville's Television Newscoverage*. Master's thesis, Texas A&M University.

Jahrsdoerfer, Sonja J., and David M. Leslie, Jr. 1988. *Tamaulepan Brushland of the Lower Rio Grand Valley of South Texas: Description, Human Impacts, and Management Options*. Washington, D.C.: U.S. Department of the Interior, Fish and Wildlife Service.

Peterson, Tarla Rai. 1997. *Sharing the Earth: The Rhetoric of Sustainable Development*. Columbia: University of South Carolina Press.

Selby, Gardner. 2 October 1994. "People Want Words Turned into Deeds." *Houston Post,* A4.

TDH-CDC (Texas Department of Health-Centers for Disease Control). 1992. "An Investigation of a Cluster of Neural Tube Defects in Cameron County, Texas," July. Austin: Texas Department of Health, and Atlanta: The Centers for Disease Control

Terrell, Gaynell. 20 August 1992. "Tackling the Mystery That Matters: Anencephalic Births Stir Mixed Feelings at Border." *Houston Post,* A8.

Texas Center for Policy Studies. 1990. *Overview of Environmental Issues Associated with* Maquiladora *Development along the Texas-Mexico Border.* Austin: Texas Center for Policy Studies.

Tarla Rai Peterson is an assistant professor in the Department of Communication at the University of Utah.

Susan J. Gilbertz and **Gary E. Varner** study and teach environmental communication and ethics at Texas A&M University.

Kathi Groenendyk is an assistant professor of communication arts and sciences at Calvin College.

Jay Todd studies and teaches communication skills at the Texas Department of Health.

Reading 3.5

Nuestro Espacio Cyber

The Internet as Expressive Space for Latina/os in the United States

RICHARD D. PINEDA

The Latina/o community is in the midst of a major demographic shift upwards. Along with this population growth, there has been an explosion of Latina/os across the spectrum of popular culture. However, lack of access to mass-media outlets and social

Nuestro Espacio Cyber, Richard D. Pineda, *Free Speech Yearbook, 38,* 2001, 116–126. Used by permission of the National Communication Association.

constructions in mainstream society pose obstacles to Latina/o freedom of expression. Meanwhile, the internet is evolving into a powerful platform for communication and freedom of speech. By developing a stronger Latina/o presence on-line, it may be possible to channel the power of the internet as a vehicle for empowerment, expression and freedom of speech.

Demographic changes in the United States effect a wide spectrum of social and political issues. While predictions for a surge in the growth of the Latina/o community were originally expected to peak closer to 2005, the most recent census data suggest a much more rapid timeframe. With a 60% increase in the Latina/o population in the United States in the last ten years, the size of the community is now on par with the African-American community and likely to outpace the overall size of the African-American community in the next several years (Booth A-04, Branch-Brioso A1, Holmes & Chapman 1A, Kettle 11). As Torres and Katsiaficas explain, the increasing Latina/o population is "closely intertwined with transnational economic forces that are restructuring and reshaping once familiar local, regional, national and international landscapes" (1). Popular culture, more than any other area, has been quick to capitalize on this trend and as a result, mass media outlets are paying greater attention to Latina/os. However, as demographics influence attention and create space for Latina/os in majority culture, little attention has been directed to how Latina/os themselves are capitalizing on new venues of free speech and expression.

While the Constitution offers protection for expression on the part of its citizens, there is no guarantee of free forums to engage in the right to free speech. Attempts to regulate equal and reciprocal access in other mass media outlets, the Federal Communication Commission's Fairness Doctrine for example, have failed to survive constitutional challenge

(Newborne 279). More importantly, as the dimension of public awareness and participation changes at the start of the new millennium, mass media is beginning to evolve past existing structures like community as the conduit for information, social participation, and empowerment. Mass media outlets available for Latina/o expression have been dominated traditionally by a corporate culture that favors a majority-based homogeneity. When attempts have been made to open expressive space for minorities, a dominant, binary racial dichotomy has impeded fruitful discourse from taking root. The dichotomy paints race in the United States as solely defined by two racial groups, Black and White, with other people of color left at the periphery of the discussion (Perea 361; Delgado 375). Even in geographic areas where there are large Laina/o communities, the opportunities to capitalize on avenues of expressive speech are still far and few between. Amidst this struggle to empower free speech, a technological revolution has occurred in cyberspace that might provide direction and space for Latina/os. Hill and Hughes, surveying the growing body of literature on the internet, explain the information superhighway provides, "the promise of nearly unlimited information delivered to your modem . . . the promise of a better democracy" (2). A significant reason for this development is the provision of space open for free dialogue and discourse. As Drucker and Gumpert suggest, "communication requires location," and "space should be regarded as a medium of communication" (25). The internet is the newest space for free speech and participation in an increasingly complex, technological world.

This article examines the internet as a vehicle for Latina/o communication, empowerment, and as a space for free expression by Latina/os. The first section examines the binary race paradigm and the effect of language on Latina/os and free expression. The second focuses on the shape of mass media in the United States and the status of openness for Latina/o participation and expression. The role of the internet as a platform for expression and change is then discussed. The last section speculates on how Latina/os can and are using the internet to challenge the binary race dichotomy, language oppression, and mass media monopolization.

RACIAL DICHOTOMIES AND EXPRESSION

Race is a challenging subject in contemporary society, especially when it comes to expression and participation. As the United States moves into a new century the concept of identification and the rise of "multiculturalism" are inextricably linked. Expression is a critical tool of identity for minorities not only to strengthen internal, community bonds but also to foster a sustainable niche in the larger community.

Identity and culture have received increased attention in the media and from academics, politicians and social activists. From the Latina/o perspective, these moves are long overdue, especially as a way to overcome society's desire to over-homogenize minority groups into familiar and distinct racial classifications. The diversification of cultures in the United States continues to be hampered by a binary racial dichotomy. If race relations continue to center on a Black/White dichotomy, Perea argues that voice, presence, and history are lost (360). The loss of voice crushes Latina/o power of expression and trivializes the rights of free speech. Rather than shift to a diversified, cultural perspective, the country exists around laws and societal rules geared to account for the differences between black and white. Social praxis as well as laws governing free speech and expression have been codified along these lines. The civil rights movement in particular, with marches and mass rallies, helped create

powerful expressive space for African Americans. Additionally, the civil rights movement provided another impetus for the rise of strong African American leaders who were able to act as opinion leaders and mobilize the movement. Even when there were tensions across the spectrum of African Americans, these voices were more consistent and able to open space that still has never been possible in the Latina/o community. The energy of the civil rights movement spilled over to Latina/os, especially with the rise of the Chicano Movement (Johnson & Martinez 1147–1148). Unfortunately, recognition and acceptance of the movement was short lived. The voice of African Americans, albeit not always prominent, has anchored one end of the race dichotomy ever since.

When laws also function to serve Latina/o or other minorities' interests, it is a limited series of protections. It is easy to castigate binary race issues as solely theoretical, but questioning the assumptions behind the existing dichotomy is essential to defining a new Latina/o presence. Espinoza makes an important point that justifies the Latina/o perspective: "Multi-identity is not an accepted concept in dominant discourse. That discourse is about being 'for us or against us . . .'" (p. 17). Understanding and communicating personal identity, however, often requires the expression of multiple and distinct defining categories and the recognition of a unifying concept, in this case the individual person.

The race dialogue that occurs in contemporary society is based upon a dichotomy between black and white. The binary paradigm has great effect on the evolution of race relations in the United States and influences the ability of both critical inquiry and discourse to advance to new levels. The paradigm that currently exists defines issue relevancy. Such a balance controls fact gathering and investigation to the point that research is focused on understanding the facts and circumstances that are relevant to the paradigm. The resulting construction funnels the creation of expressive space that places Latina/os outside of the dominant paradigm and thus marginalizes the entire group. Furthermore, it limits the access to expressive space for self-empowerment and tends to privilege stereotypes and generalizations about Latina/os while limiting the ability to challenge those misrepresentations.

Interestingly, the very use of "Latina/o" offers a positive position to unify many individual, national origin groups. The term comes from Latino Americanos and refers to anyone from the countries in Central and South America, the Spanish-speaking Caribbean, indigenous groups, and people from the United States that are either descendents or immigrants from these areas. This umbrella term comes from inside Latina/o communities and not from the government or other authorities. The nature of identity politics means contention is nearly always present in any discussion as Gimenez notes, " . . . the unique American meaning of the umbrella labels . . . reflect compromises within the US political scene and are incomprehensible to visitors and new arrived immigrants from Latin America and Spain" (168).

The purpose here is not to address the assumptions of every national origin group that falls under the rubric of Latina/o or to gloss over the disparities that exist in their group identification, but rather to justify the use of Latina/o as the identifying term. A multidimensional consideration is necessary when discussing Latina/os, especially since Latina/os have many common connections. Focusing on the incorporation of these dimensions moves us past the binary paradigm of existing racial constructions, making it possible to move from essentializing to developing a better, more engaging view of Latina/os. It also provides a mechanism from which to embrace the diversity of Latina/o culture. Empowering free

speech embraces a more complex notion of voice potentially interconnecting vast geographic distances. Recognition of the multitude of cultural influences means that the importance of the heritage and cultural development of Latina/os remains at the forefront of the discussion on expressive space. Part of the reason why expressive space is so important is because it represents the ability to share this legacy with others and champion ideals to strengthen the bonds between Latina/o groups, other minorities, and the majority culture. Freedom of speech and voice helps energize this goal and acts as a conduit for voices throughout the Latina/o community.

Another issue of equal importance to the nature of expression and Latina/o participation in American society is the use of language. English is the unofficial language of the United States, however with the spread of multiculturalism many more languages are now being spoken across the country.

Language is the foundation of expression and as the drive for English Only legislation surges, so do limits to minority expression and participation. Silencing language weakens the strength of expression by undercutting the depth and power of ideas. Perea argues that the English Only policies are thinly veiled, racist attacks on minorities, driven by "American nativism in modern form," and a desire to maintain homogeneity (568). Spanish is one of the easiest targets of the English Only movement. Recent history in California highlights state sponsored attempts to legislate a language into exile, in order to ensure a common future (Navarrette 563). While many Latina/os speak English, there is a substantial portion of the population that still speaks Spanish as the primary language. Additionally many speak both languages and are able to code switch, or move fluently between English and Spanish in the same conversation or in different conversations. These strategies to shift to English as the only language in the United States hardly seem feasible, but more importantly signal a challenger to the legitimacy of Latina/o voice and expression.

Public expression and speech in the United States cannot be limited to only one language, especially if that results in the wholesale exclusion of a growing minority population. Not only does the English Only movement stifle voice in its truest form, but also it reinforces a value hierarchy that says only certain people are worthy of being extended the right to free speech and expression. Moreover mass media also operates in one language making it harder for Spanish speakers to receive information or understand issues. Even with bilingual speakers there are a limited number of outlets that cover both languages in any sort of format. The internet, therefore, is important allowing expressive space for the fusion of languages while allowing for the use of Spanish Only conversations, information channels and even socially active discourse.

SHIFTING PATTERNS OF MEDIA PARTICIPATION

The rise of Latina/o culture and the acceptance of its pop icons might not signal a change in the ideology of a country that has consistently created obstacles to minority identity. Vinson alludes to the dilemma that faces this new cultural occurrence, " . . . being Latino is carrying less racial and ethnic significance than ever before. While the breakthrough has improved the overall position of Latinos in U.S. culture, it also threatens to diminish some of the main factors that have made Latinos so historically important—their cultural complexity and internal differences" (p. G3).

There are two sides to this tale of identity and cultural awareness, the one that Vinson documents and the one represented here. There is much to be said about gaining media attention and focus, especially if it is a way to undo past injustices. The difficulty is that the new media explosion is new only in the United States and really only for those people who do not live in racially diverse areas. As Torres and Katsiaficas explain, the demographic shift favoring Latina/os has been building for some time and reflects change in immunization patterns and development of ethnic enclaves across the United States (1).

The Ricky Martinization of pop music has been in effect for almost twelve years and perhaps signals a great problem about dominant media control and societal acceptance. That is to say there have been Latina/o artists and performers accomplishing great success in the Spanish-speaking communities, which means they fall outside of the radar of majority households and are generally considered too exotic. Only recently has this process of cultural acceptance started to change. The new attention on Latina/os has not been orchestrated internally as part of a grassroots effort. In fact, it seems like most of the social movements connected to Latina/os have been slow in terms of capturing and harnessing the power behind all of this positive sentiment.

Some might argue the recent wave of pop culture developments suggests a reversal of fortune. These examples are still ensconced in the existing corporate framework and hardly provide a free and expressive base for empowerment. Neuborne notes that in the United States, mass media power has been concentrated into approximately ten integrated companies, a substantial decrease from the thirty-plus companies in 1983 (27). At worst, the empowerment notion is constructed around material and marketing devices thought up by these media corporations. Escalante explains, "Chicano/Latino-owned media must often struggle and make do with far fewer resources," unlike their counterparts in the mainstream media (135). Latina/o owned mass media outlets cannot effectively transmit the messages that can be important to bind and celebrate a culture. Rather, the focus of these enterprises is limited to self-survival with minimal attention to expansion. Even where there are successful ventures in Latina/o mass media, it is rare for the outlets to be seen across a wide spectrum or outside of Latina/o communities.

Unfortunately, trade-off comes in accepting a new set of stereotypes and generalizations about the cultures that make up the new Latina/o era. The acceptance in society also brings a whole host of problems, as Leland and Chambers explain:

> Like other immigrant groups, Latinos in the second and third generations begin to absorb the worst of America: poorer health and diet, higher delinquency and dropout rates, more divorce and domestic abuse ... The longer families have been in the United States, the better the kids speak English and the higher their self-esteem. But they also do less homework, have lower GPAs and lower aspirations ... Children's superior English skills may upset the family order. Also, second and third generation Latinos, who grow up with higher expectations than their immigrant parents, may be less resilient when they encounter discrimination. (p. 52)

Rather than celebrate the strength of mixed cultures, many in the Latina/o community have fallen into the trap of majority America; celebrate all of a culture or none of the culture. Not only does this diminish the value of a multicultural experience, but is has negative consequences for expression and acts as resistance to social change. Rather than revel in the power of community and the strength of diversity in Latina/o communities, often times this social capital is lost in the struggle to achieve parity with mainstream America.

THE RISE OF THE INTERNET GENERATION

Relative to issues raised earlier in this article, it is imperative to address concerns of general racial inclusion vis-à-vis discussing the "digital divide" as well as to highlight the current direction of Latina/o participation online. Understanding the participation dimension will help clarify the argument for greater promotion of Latina/o expression in cyberspace. The internet is a unique platform for exercising the First Amendment right of free speech. The Supreme Court has made this abundantly clear by striking down the Communication Decency Act in its decision in *Reno v. American Civil Liberties Union*. Siegel explains the rhetoric of Justice Stevens's opinion, "strongly suggests, if not explicitly holds, that cyberspace communication deserves the same undiluted amount of First Amendment protection accorded to print media" (142). Indeed, the procedural protections offered by the Supreme Court are part of the growing recognition that the internet is not only an undeniable fact of life now, but that it is a powerful tool. Hill and Hughes qualify the status of the internet by noting its impact on change: " ... the internet will fundamentally alter the political landscape of the United States if not the entire world ... [the] political and societal change are the effect, and the internet is and will be the cause" (181). The free flow of ideas through free media helps foster democracy and participation.

The gatekeepers and media monopolies described earlier have locked out Latina/o voices. Levinson makes a distinction about the internet relative to mass media that is important to consider given the existing participation and representation of Latina/os: "The problem with the gatekeeper—whether unavoidable in the case of mass media or optional in the case of online publication—is that it cuts off the flow of ideas before the intended recipients, the readers, have a chance to select them." (134)

The development of the internet has opened up a new spectrum of information sharing and technological interconnectedness. Much about the internet's function in society is still unknown, given its unique nature and dynamic nature. Despite the success of email and cyber commerce, debate over internet use and expectations of accomplishment has only just begun. One thing is certain however; the increase of technology is shifting greater control to what Matthews calls "non-state actors" any individual or group entity not directly connected to the government, adding, " ... [They] are empowered both in relative terms and absolutely" (64). Valauskas continues by explaining the comments made at an early Web conference in Paris by one of the original internet developers Tim Berners-Lee "the really important work on the internet happens at the scale where small groups interact to solve specific problems, to explore new issues and organize ideas together" (2).

Furthermore, the most important area where defining and expressing voice is political empowerment. Pop culture icons and celebrities may be important, but unless that social capital is translated into political power, it will be impossible to advance minority causes. All too often popular culture is seen as the sole space for expression of minority voice. The internet is a crucial tool by which Latina/os can organize, share information and strive to connect to political organizations. Negroponte argues that the four largest benefits of the internet are that it is, "decentralizing, globalizing, harmonizing, and empowering," factors especially important for the Latina/o community (229). There is space on the internet for individuals to champion ideas that can bring cohesion or a direct attention to a common goal for their group. Expression that is this powerful for an individual has the potential to increase greater participation for larger groups. Evans explains the internet has an effect of "cross-pollination" on thinking and diversity noting that the experience of interacting with, "people from socioeconomic, educational, cultural, national, or generation backgrounds different from our own can provide us with thoughts or manners of expression that interrupt and transform our own" (4).

Branwyn identifies a new internet-based media, what he calls "sociomedia," which acts as a tool born of social interaction to breakdown "old relationships between media producers and consumers" (288). Socioresponsive interaction means that groups can use focal points such as identity and culture to define new agendas for expression and participation. Even if that participation is limited to online discourse, it is still revolutionary due to the more open nature of the medium. Slevin affirms this notion of participation:

> After all, it offers an opportunity for a more positive and critical approach to finding ways of developing the freedom of individuals to use the internet to participate in engagements which ... emphasize the responsibility that individuals and groups have for the ideas they hold and the practices in which they engage (47).

Recent developments in politics and social justice suggest the internet is being utilized to reach out more and spread important messages and call for action. Lau notes the new attention politicians are paying to web sites crafted for minority interest, is coming at a time when more minorities are going on-line and focusing a great deal of attention on "building virtual communities" (p. 6). The 2000 presidential election and the Gore and Bush campaigns have respectively targeted their messages to the Spanish-speaking Latina/o population on their web pages and in their campaigns.

LATINA/OS, GENERATION Ñ.COM, AND INTERNET EMPOWERMENT

The internet is not a panacea for minorities seeking redress from social oppression and a space for political expression. The internet is also not the only place that minorities can rally for empowerment and build greater community cohesion. However, the internet holds promise as a unique platform from which to evolve expressive spaces and gain, "access to the tools of signification" (Colby 125). The value of free expression is trumped if there is no way to capitalize on its power. This final section examines the notion of defining a new community for Latina/os in cyberspace, drawing on the power of individuals in the community, and the search for greater empowerment through the use of web sites and networking on the internet.

Much attention has been paid to the growing gap between those that have access and understand how to navigate the internet and those lacking even the simplest access to cyberspace. The "digital divide" is often described in meta-terms with developed, Western nations identified as the privileged segment of technology users. Developing nations fall on the diminishing side of the balance. The chasm is easily transposed to the domestic front in the United States, where minorities fall on the lower end of the divide.

With greater political attention focused on the status of minorities relative to technological advances, the politicization of the divide has garnered more attention in recent years. A 1999 study by the United States Department of Commerce detailed the divide in terms of ethnicity in the United States and shared statistical data that suggested minorities were "falling through the Net," in terms of computer ownership and participation in cyberspace (Horn and Woodall A-01). The report fueled an already growing sense of disillusion on the part of minorities that the digital divide was far outpacing their ability to actively participate in cyberspace. Certainly, one of the most common arguments made against empowerment and expression vis-à-vis the internet is that technology is insular and there are few opportunities for minorities to gain access.

The best answer to this line of argument is found in more recent studies. The latest research on Latina/o internet participation suggests that not only are Latina/os gaining ground on computer ownership and internet participation, but also they are doing it faster than any other minority group and even faster than white households (Allbritton 7; Hafner G6; Hoffman 11; Varoga 77). This data also suggests that the technology boom in the Latina/o community is anchored with the youth. This is important for several reasons; first, it means that the internet will be part of the heritage of the younger members of the Latina/o community and will inevitability continue as more of the population seeks higher levels of education or specialized work training. Second, because the internet is becoming an important cultural and social phenomenon, it is more likely the younger members of the Latina/o community will be interested in learning more about participating online. Finally, as interest grows with younger Latina/os, there is a better chance their excitement will spark interest on the part of other family members. Bridging the generational gap in the Latina/o community is a job best suited to begin with the youth and move vertically, rather than to expect information to trickle from the older generation downward. Albritton contends that online participation will increase to eventually encompass two-thirds of Latina/o households by 2005 (7).

Latina/os represent values, languages, cultures, and identities across a global spectrum stretching from South America to the Caribbean through the United States and beyond. The only existing medium that comes close to embracing those distinct flavors is the internet. Some may argue that television has been able to close gaps in social expression and provide for Latina/o representation, but as discussed earlier the nature of mass media and use of one language naturally limit Latina/o expression, representation and participation. It is possible to relish the distinction of being Latina/o online more than ever, because so many qualities can be shared and discussed and focused into sources of empowerment. There is growing potential to ease past the issues that have lead to disenfranchised groups like Latina/os, as Negroponte explains; "The harmonizing effect of being digital is already apparent as previously partitioned disciplines and enterprises find themselves collaborating, not competing. A previously missing common language emerges, allowing people to understand across boundaries" (230). Slevin continues by articulating the nature of the trust mechanism that the internet helps bring to encourage expression; "On an unprecedented level, the internet is presenting individuals and organizations with new opportunities for responsive action by allowing them to display their integrity and maintain and build up the trust of others in their actions" (47). The internet also helps create space in the "actual" or offline world through the recognition of virtual identity. Evans explains the premise behind this internet effect:

> We recognize, in other words, that the online voices have both a virtual and actual dimension. Because the virtual dimension exists always as the "other side" of its manifest content, it cannot exist in separation from this content: its being is to give rise to, to actualize itself as, this content or posting. It is a source that cannot be separated from what it produces, a voice that would disappear without its articulations. (6)

The internet offers a base from which to empower ideas and information that does not require as many resources as with other mass media. With proliferating Latina/o use of the internet and rising numbers of Latina/o web sites such as Picosito.com and quepasa.com it is easier than ever to establish web space. Similarly, these web sites have established chat rooms and space online for discussions to take place on issues related to political, economic and social concerns, that members of the Latina/o community face. These chat rooms are conducted in English and Spanish and help provide comfortable settings for conversations and dialogue to take place. A number of Latina/o social activists, political organizations and think tanks, such as the League of United Latin American Citizens (LULAC), the National Caucus of La Raza (NCLR) and the Tomas Rivera Policy Institute (TRPI), have established themselves with web pages online. Not only does the presence of these entities legitimize the internet for Latina/o voice, but also they act as evidence that the medium can be commodified for expressive space. The LULAC web site offers a wide range of information including in-depth access to political issues, scholarship and educational opportunities, as well as hyperlinks to other sites of interest to Latina/os. politicomagazine.com is an excellent site that collects articles and press information relative to Latina/o political and socioeconomic interests as well as commentary and opinion pieces from a wide range of Latina/o journalists.

The monopolization of media and its limitation on expressive space is also challenged through the internet. Latina/o writers and performers are experiencing a renaissance in terms of exposure through web sites and with advanced video and audio technology. Creative contributions can be aimed at other Latina/os without relying on the existing corporate structure. Latina/o writers can express themselves through commentary and creative writing at sites such as Elander.com and political satire appears on sites like Pocho.com. Latina/o political cartoons are even starting to proliferate on sites like Cartoonista.com. These web sites are additional examples of the power of the internet. For Latina/o groups there are limited opportunities for cultural expression in printed media and the nature of periodicals limits the breadth of content, so these sites are able to challenge those assumptions and overcome logistical obstacles.

Some contend that commercial interests shatter private space by forecasting a "collision course with free speech interests" online (Samoriski 93). The internet has inevitably faced its share of entrepreneurs, but the risk of commercialization should not appear to deter increased Latina/o participation.

A number of the Latina/o social activist, political organization and think tank web sites in existence now are operated without the intrusion of commercial interests. Even with a commercial presence online, it is hard to argue that individuals cannot move past the allure of hyper-consumerism to engage in the process of expression and empowerment. Perhaps the most important element of this commercialization process is the chance that Latina/os can find economic opportunities that could help improve their situation. If Latina/o businesses can target a Latina/o consumer base this is also useful to empowering a community. Even if Latina/os just want to communicate with others in a different language or embrace their commonalities, commercialism is a minor hindrance and not an unbreakable obstacle. Kang discusses the importance of this association among like-minded individuals as a stepping-stone to greater possibilities:

> Perhaps commonalities underlying cyber-communities could act as foundation for cooperation. To facilitate communities based on common interests, experiences, and fates, powerful search engines, enable individuals to locate others with similar profiles or similar conversational interests. In these communities based on commonalities, people share stories, ask questions, provide answers, and give advice (1171).

The presence of Latina/o enclaves across the United States signifies strong community growth. If Latina/os can extend these communities online they will be able to achieve inter-connectivity among multiple communities. Stronger communities make for greater discourse, greater celebration of similarities, and fuel the empowerment necessary for achieving expressive space. There is a concern about the strength of the change brought on by the internet, especially if the change sparks ethnic separatism or reifies cultural boundaries. Selnow offers an optimistic vision of the internet and its effect on change through the spread of information and dialogue:

> Quite possibly [the internet] will send audiences in many directions, and by tugging at separate audience threads, fray the cloth of the national agenda. We are particularly vulnerable to such a thing. We are the most pluralistic nation on earth, and while we may look ragtag at times to the rest of the world, we have sustained a sober-minded unity that is in itself remarkable. Can the internet challenge that? Yes, it can, given that information has been the nation's binding agent, particularly through a century of expanding diversity (xxxi).

The internet is unlike any other expressive space available to Latina/os today. It offers infinite space to develop a new perspective on identity and a place from which to challenge the existing order of identity politics in the United States. Tapping into resources online removes obstacles that exist in the form of corporate ownership and especially is limitations based on language. The use of multiple languages and even mixed languages can open expressive pathways for Latina/os that may have been culturally constraining previously. Expression is valuable if many individuals can share their perspective and build on each other's ideas and agendas. The internet can focus Latina/o efforts to empower expression by connecting them with powerful organizations, political lobbies, politicians and each other. No longer will activists in different parts of the country be uninformed about each other's activities. With the internet it is possible to report political change that directly effects Latina/os and not rely on mediating factors to alter or diminish the message. In the case of the 2000 presidential election, politicians are even appealing to Latina/os to vote and become active participants in the American political dialogue. Latina/os in the United States are living in remarkable times.

CONCLUSION

The internet continues to experience growing pains and may never fully evolve to the point that theorists have predicted. However, the nature of communication has forever been altered because of the internet and its wide range of tools and applications. Several issues deserve greater attention in future research on Latina/o participation on the internet: first, access is growing to favor Latina/o participation; however there needs to be more focus on the empowerment process to stimulate Latina/os seeking access. The information superhighway is only effective if people can find the appropriate on-ramp. Second, while race is an ever present issue in American society attention should not wane from better understanding the binary racial dichotomy that exists and its effect on racial discourse, especially from the Latina/o perspective. As the demographics of the United States change it is imperative to reconstruct the vision of racial relations and find ways to incorporate technology to empower change and fuel discourse that can benefit free expression. Expressive space crafted on the internet by Latina/os can be a powerful way to capture the spirit of expression and free speech that was instrumental for the empowerment and advancement of African-Americans during the Civil Rights movement. Rather than just marching on Washington D.C., an internet-based movement led by Latina/os can spur movements around the country and possibly unify a base of political and social support. Finally, future research can cultivate new researchers and help diversity Latina/o scholarship across academic disciplines. The value of expressive space for academics and social scientists is especially important in a community where there might not be a premium placed on educational opportunities and educational experience. As the technology becomes more accessible there is a challenge to share more information and empower the Latina/o community to participate online and take advantage of the expressive space and their First Amendment right of free speech.

REFERENCES

Aguilera, Elizabeth. "Latin-Oriented Web Sites Sitting on the Tip of Iceberg," *Denver Post* 24 May 2000, F-12.

Allbritton, Chris. "Race Matters: Ethnic Web Sites Bring Diversity to the Internet." *Daily News* 13 Aug. 2000, 7.

Booth, Michael. "U.S. Census Confirms Minorities" Surge Whites at 69%, but Diversity Flourishing," *Denver Post* 13 March 2001, A-04.

Branch-Brioso, Karen. "Minorities Fueled Growth in Last Decade, Census Says." *St. Louis Post-Dispatch* 13 Mar. 2001, A1.

Branwyn, Gareth. *Jamming the Media: A Citizen's Guide.* San Francisco: Chronicle Books, 1997.

Colby, Dean. "Conceptualizing the "Digital Divide': Closing the "Gap' by Creating a Postmodern Network That Distributes the Productive Power of Speech." *Communication Law and Policy 123* (2001) 123–173.

Crawford, James. "Hold Your Tongue." *The Latino Condition: A Critical Reader.* Eds. Richard Delagdo and Jean Stefancic. New York: New York University Press, 1998, 559–562.

Delgado, Richard. "The Black/White Binary: How Does it Work?" *The Latino Condition: A Critical Reader.* Eds. Richard Delagdo & Jean Stefancic. New York: New York University Press, 1998, 369–375.

Drucker, Susan & Gary Gumpert. "Public Spaces and the Right of Association." *Free Speech Yearbook 36* (1998): 25–37.

Evans, Fred. "Cyberspace and the Concept of Democracy." First Monday 5.10 (2000). 3 October 2000 (www.firstmonday.org/issues/issue5–10/evans/index.html).

Gimenez, Martha. "Latino Politics–Class Struggles: Reflections on the Future of Latino Politics." *Latino Social Movements: Historical and Theoretical Perspectives.* Eds. Rodolfo Torres & George Katsiaficas. New York: Routledge, 1999. 165–180.

Hafner, Katie. "Hispanics are Narrowing the Digital Divide." *New York Times* 6 Apr. 2000, G6.

Hill, Kevin & John Hughes. *Cyberpolitics: Citizens Activism in the Age of the Internet.* Boudler: Rowman and Littlefied Publishers, 1998.

Hoffman, Lisa. "Internet Use Among Hispanics Increases 68%." *Detroit News* 27 Apr. 2000, 11.

Holmes, Charles & Dan Chapman. "Census Confirms Surge in Minorities." *Atlantic Journal and Constitution* 13 March 2001, 1A.

Horn, Patricia & Martha Woodall. "Digital Divide Widens U.S. Racial, Economic Gap Growing with the Internet." *Denver Post* 9 July 1999, A-01.

Johnson, Kevin & George Martinez. "Mapping Intellectual/Political Foundations and Future Self Critical Directions: Crossover Dreams: The Roots of LatCrit Theory in Chicana/o Studies Activism and Scholarship." *University of Miami Law Review* 1143 (1999) 1143–1175.

Kang, Jerry. "Cyber-race." *Harvard Law Review* 113–1131 (2000) 1135+.

Kettle, Martin. "Latinos Outgrowing Black Americans." *The Guardian* 8 Mar. 2001, 11.

Leland, John & Veronica Chambers. "Generation n [~ over n]." *Newsweek* 12 July 1999, 52.

Levinson, Paul. *The Soft Edge.* London: Routledge, 1997.

Matthews, Jessica. "Information Revolution." *Foreign Policy* 119 (2000): 63–65.

Navarrette, Ruben. "A Bilingual-Education Initiative as a Prop 187 in Disguise?" *The Latino Condition: A Critical Reader.* Eds. Richard Delgado and Jean Stefanic. New York: New York University Press, 1998. 563–565.

Negroponte, Nicholas. *Being Digital.* New York: Vintage Books, 1995.

Neuborne, John. "Panel Three: Media Concentration and Democracy: Commentary." *Annual Survey of American Law* 277 (2000): 277–282.

Perea, Juan. "The Black/White Binary Paradigm of Race." *The Latino Condition: A Critical Reader.* Eds. Richard Delgado & Jean Stefanic. New York: New York University Press, 1998, 359–368.

"American Languages, Cultural Pluralism, and Official English." *The Latino Condition: A Critical Reader.* Eds. Richard Delgago & Jean Stefanic. New York: New York University Press. 1998. 566–573.

Rheingold, Howard. *Virtual Reality.* New York: Simon and Schuster, 1991.

Romney, Lee. "Computer Ownership Surges Among Latino Households." *Los Angeles Times* 12 Apr. 2000, C3.

Samorski, Jan. "Private Spaces and Public Interests: Internet Navigation, Commercialization and the Fleecing of Democracy." *Communication Law and Policy* 5–93 (2000): 93+.

Selnow, Gary. *Electronic Whistle Stops: The Impact of the Internet on American Politics.* Westport: Prager, 1998.

Siegel, Paul. "The Supreme Court and Freedom of Speech." *Free Speech Yearbook* 36 (1998): 134–147.

Slevin, James. *The Internet and Society.* Cambridge: Policy Press, 2000.

Solis, Dianne. "Hispanics Embrace Cyberspace." *Denver Post* 3 Apr. 2000, C-01.

Torres, Rodolfo & George Katsiaficas. Introduction. *Latino Social Movements: Historical and Theoretical Perspectives.* By Torres & Katsiaficas. New York: Routledge, 1999, 1–10.

Valauskas, Edward. "Lex Networkia: Understanding the Internet Community." *First Monday* 1.4 (1996). 3 October 2000 (http://www.firstmonday.org/issues/issue4/valauskas/).

Varoga, Craig. "Candidate with Hearing and Speech Difficulties, Minorities and the Net." *Campaigns and Elections* May 2000: 77.

Vinson III, Ben. "Are Latinos Breaking the Sound Barriere?" *San Diego Union-Tribune* 14 Nov. 1999, G3.

———

Richard D. Pineda received his Ph.D. from Wayne State University. He is an assistant professor in the department of communication studies at California State University, San Bernardino.

Reading 3.6

Nike's Communication With Black Audiences

KETRA L. ARMSTRONG

A SOCIOLOGICAL ANALYSIS
OF ADVERTISING EFFECTIVENESS
VIA SYMBOLIC INTERACTIONISM

An increase in the size and resources of the Black consumer market has prompted many organizations to increase their understanding of the challenges of devising marketing communications to appeal to Black consumers. The influence of culture on communication strategies aimed at ethnic groups has long been realized by marketers and advertising professionals. However, what remains a challenge is the means of adapting an effective (yet non-offensive) culturally-based approach of marketing communication. Given the salience of sport to Blacks, this is a challenge that sport organizations should also address as they devise ways of advertising and communicating sport products and services to Black consumers. This article will employ the tenets of symbolic interactionism, to analyze Nike's advertisements as vehicles to communicate with Black audiences.

In light of the growing sociological and economic importance of African American (used interchangeably with Black) consumers in the marketplace, many organizations have begun to increase their understanding of how to communicate with them effectively to facilitate a favorable marketing exchange (Mallory, 1992). One approach of marketing to Black consumers is premised on the notion that communications are most effective when their elements (i.e., the channel or medium used to transmit the information, the content of the message, the icons and symbols used to convey the message, values portrayed in the message) refer to African American culture (Hecht, Collier, & Ribeau, 1993; Pitts, Whalen, O'Keefe, & Murray, 1989; Rossman, 1994; Simpson, 1992). "Communication is meaningful because of the culture that frames it . . . all communication exists in a cultural context" (Hecht et al., 1993, p. 1). As a result, marketing communications have been carefully designed to contain promotional messages with content that is relevant to Black consumers and presented in a culturally appropriate manner. More than $700 million was spent in 1 year on advertisements targeted to African Americans (Mabry, 1989).

Ketra L. Armstrong, *Journal of Sport & Social Issues*, pp. 266-287. Copyright © Sage Publications, Inc. Reprinted by permission.

"African-American culture is constituted through communicative forms such as the use of code switching from Black English to Mainstream American English, an assertive, stylized communication manner, and rituals such as 'playing the dozens' and 'jiving' (Hecht et al., 1993, p. 19). Communications become a critical vehicle whereby African Americans construct their social worlds, create, interpret, validate, and substantiate their cultural identities (Hecht et al., 1993). "Culture is thus constituted and created through systematic and patterned communication that is interpreted through a shared code" (Hecht et al., 1993, p. 21). Although Blacks may be reached by mainstream media, many of them respond more favorably to culturally-based communications that acknowledge their heritage and respect their culture. In fact, many Blacks often ignore messages that are perceived to be irrelevant to them personally or void of appeal to their culture or reference group. What is noteworthy for marketers to understand is that a multiplier effect is created when Black consumers see a Black lifestyle in a print or television advertisement at the same time they see a general market advertisement for the same product in mainstream media (Boggart, 1990; Rossman, 1994).

Sport organizations are not exempt from responding to the importance of Blacks in the marketplace and should therefore increase their understanding of how culture influences effective sport marketing communication strategies. For the sport industry (at large) to improve its marketing and communication efforts to secure Black consumers, it must also understand the sociocultural implications for doing so. For sport to continue to grow and prosper as a business entity (i.e., maximizing the usage of its products and services among consumers who have the interest and resources to do so), sport organizations must (a) develop an understanding and appreciation of the functional and symbolic usefulness of their products and services to certain target markets and (b) devise appropriate channels by which to communicate the salient product market features to the desired markets. Herein lies the focus of this study.

SPORT ADVERTISING

Advertising is one vehicle marketers use to convey information about their products. It includes verbal and nonverbal cues, images, and printed and spoken words (Mullins, Hardy, & Sutton, 1993; Stotlar, 1993). Advertising is defined as "paid, nonpersonal communication through various media by business firms, non-profit organizations, and individuals who are identified in the advertising message and hope to inform or persuade members of a particular audience" (Boone & Kurtz, 1992, p. 532). Advertising is usually constructed around a message that has been designed to build an audience and promote an increase in sales (Shilbury, Quick, & Westerbeek, 1998). It mainly includes media such as the newspapers, television, radio, magazines, billboards, videotapes, and video screens whose objective is to place the product or service in a favorable position with high visibility (Boone & Kurtz, 1992; Stotlar, 1993).

The essence of advertising is effective communication with the desired target market. Effective communication is largely dependent upon shared values and should include signs and symbols (verbal and nonverbal) to convey meaning. Shimp (1997) defined meaning as "the perceptions (thoughts) and affective reactions (feelings) to a stimuli evoked within a person when presented with a sign such as a brand, or other consumption object in a particular context" (p. 109). Thus, meanings are subjective and are the internal responses elicited by external stimuli. Because each individual has a cultural software that imparts on their thoughts and behaviors that defines meaning in their lives, persuasive communications such as advertisements should therefore acknowledge the influence of culture on the effectiveness of communicating with members of different ethnic groups.

Advertising is often carefully crafted to be a conduit of culturally transmitted meanings. It works as a potential method of meaning transfer by bringing the consumer good and a representation of the culturally constituted world together within one comprehensive frame (Shilbury et al., 1998). Some organizations devise specific advertisements with messages for particular ethnic groups, communicating with them in a culturally-attuned manner (i.e., targeted marketing communications). Others try to find a universal or common (cultural) denominator among the masses and use it as communication technique (i.e., mass marketing communications). Regardless of the approach, persuasive communications that ignore the influence culture are rarely successful. When consumers are exposed to advertisements that contain elements that are drawn from their culturally constituted world, they process the information and are actively involved in assigning meaning to the advertised product (Shimp, 1997). Oftentimes, advertisements use verbal and pictorial symbols with overtones of meaning that are not directly related to the product (Boggart, 1990). Because a brand represents the core product and the perceptions consumers have about the product and its unique added-value (Shilbury et al., 1998), the symbolic nonproduct attributes also play a pivotal role in conveying meanings. Furthermore (in addition to addressing product and nonproduct attributes), some advertisements employ cues that are symbolic in communicating something about the buyers as consumers of the product being advertised. Thus, the overall objective of advertising is to position a brand of a product or service favorably by allowing the consumers to form mental links with the brand and internalize the symbols received in hopes

of eliciting positive cognitive and behavioral responses.

As suggested by Altheide and Snow (1991), sport is rife with elements that subject it to media formats and media logic. Sport events are very entertaining, and they have a massive appeal. Because they provide an effective medium for reaching large audiences, they are quite popular electronic and print communications vehicles for networks and advertisers. The impact television has had on sports (e.g., the changing of rules to make games more entertaining and faster paced, setting the time that games will be played to promote optimal prime time ratings) has created a price war for advertising during sporting events. Sponsors pay well in excess of $1 million to secure 15 to 30-second features during major professional sport events such as the Super Bowl, and more than $200,000 for popular collegiate sports events. Because of the magnitude of international sport events such as the Olympics, a substantial amount of money is required to obtain advertising rights. Also, networks pay a bundle to televise major sporting events. For example, CBS paid $3.5 billion to televise the 1992 and 1994 Winter Olympics, the 1990 National Football League Championships, and Major League Baseball Championships, and NBC paid $400 million to broadcast the 1994 Barcelona Games (Gorman & Calhoun, 1994). In addition to the use of electronic media such as television, advertisers also use sport as a communication vehicle in the print media. The increasing number of culturally-based magazines and newspapers make them viable vehicles whereby advertisers can target messages to specific cultural/ethnic groups.

Notwithstanding the popularity of sport, the advent of electronic technology (remote controls, split screens, picture in a picture, etc.) has made zapping (the means by which viewers change the channels to avoid watching a commercial) a critical challenge to television advertisements. The amount of clutter in magazines and newspapers has also limited the effectiveness of print advertisements, making them susceptible to being rapidly scanned by the readers. Although advertisers cannot prevent zapping or scanning from occurring, they can infuse their advertisements with elements to ensure that viewers are motivated to watch their commercials and read their printed messages. It is therefore imperative that advertisers understand what product market features and communications strategies will be attractive to their target audience.

BLACKS' SPORT MEDIA CONSUMPTION

According to a report by Humphrey ("Black Spending Power," 1998), Black power is on the rise in the marketplace, making them an important segment to advertisers. The Black population is growing at a rate of 14%, compared with a 9% growth rate for the nation as a whole. Shimp (1997) suggests that the Black population is expected to reach 39 million by 2010. Humphrey ("Black Spending Power," 1998) reports that Black spending power is also growing faster than the national average and is projected to increase from $308 billion in 1990 to $533 billion in 1999 (reflecting approximately a 73% increase in less than one decade, compared with the national increase of approximately 57%). Humphrey's ("Black Spending Power," 1998) study forecasted that Black consumers will account for 8.2% of the total buying power in 1999 (compared with the 7.4% they accounted for in 1990). The study concluded that capturing Black consumers can make the difference between many businesses making a profit or suffering a loss.

Not only is the Black consumer market a sizable market, but it is one that places much significance on sports. Research has indicated that sports are more salient to Blacks than to Whites. Blacks are more likely than Whites to incorporate sport into their daily lives and

to be more strongly affected by the sport outcome involving a favorite team or athlete (Rudman, 1986). Spreitzer and Snyder (1990) also revealed that Blacks were also more involved in sports than Whites in their operationalization of passive sport involvement as a measure of the following seven dimensions: watching sports on television, listening to sports on the radio, reading the sport pages of the newspaper, watching/listening to sport news on radio or television, reading sport books, reading sport magazines, and talking about sports with friends. Black men scored higher than White men (60% and 40%, respectively), and Black women scored higher than White women (27% and 14%, respectively) (Spreitzer & Snyder, 1990). Sachs and Abraham (1979) reported that the sport of basketball, in particular, was more salient to and had a more symbolic meaning to the Black culture than to Whites.

Advertisers and corporations who are seeking to use sport as a vehicle to communicate with Black consumers must be mindful of Blacks' noteworthy media habits. Blacks (a) (particularly Black females) watch more television than the general population, and the shows they watch are more apt to be those about Black people; (b) listen to the radio approximately 3.5 hours daily, which is about 30 minutes longer than White listeners; (c) prefer Black-owned radio stations and listen to AM stations more than Whites do; (d) can be reached with some general magazine publications, but prefer to read Black magazines; and (e) are more affected by advertising than Whites are, particularly when the advertisements contain elements that reflect their lifestyles (Boone & Kurtz, 1992; Hawkins, Best, & Coney, 1992; Johnson, 1995; Shimp, 1997).

With regard to Blacks' viewership of televised sport events, Blacks comprised 14.6% of the viewing audience of postseason professional basketball games, 12.1% of the viewing audience for postseason college basketball games, 10.2% of the viewing audience of professional baseball games, 12.9% of the viewing audience of college baseball games, 10.2% of the viewing audience of postseason college football games, 8.3% of the viewing audience of postseason professional football games, 15.7% of the viewing audience of boxing events, 7% of the viewing audience of tennis matches, and 16.7% of the viewing audiences of track and field events (Simmons Market Research Bureau, 1994). Thus, the three most popular sports among Black television viewers are track and field, boxing, and basketball. However, the sport with perhaps the largest appeal for advertisers (given its popularity in the United States) is basketball. Also, the sport of basketball was the most popular sport to watch on television for the subscribers of the Black magazines that were included in Simmons's 1994 Market Research Study. For example, postseason professional basketball was watched by 17.8% of *Jet* subscribers, 17.7% of *Ebony* subscribers, and 16.1% of *Essence* subscribers. Postseason college basketball was watched by 13.9% of *Jet* subscribers, 13.8% of *Essence* subscribers, and 13.3% of *Ebony* subscribers. Thus, basketball appears to be a popular sport for the print and electronic media consumption of Black consumers.

THEORETICAL FRAMEWORK

"Ethnicity and culture become the frames through which we view African American communication to understand their experience of social reality and articulate their perspectives on appropriate and effective communication" (Hecht et al., 1993, p. 15). Therefore, to examine effective means of communicating with Black consumers, it is imperative that the theoretical underpinning employed allows for a manifestation of the effects of African American culture.

Hecht et al. (1994) presented some sensitizing constructs that are critical to a basic understanding of communication effectiveness. They referred to sensitizing constructs as the elements that enable people to create ethnic culture and identity and to reinforce commonalities. The sensitizing constructs they deemed important were core symbols (symbols of cultural beliefs, views, central ideas, and expressed behaviors that are identified through recurrent patterns that are verbal and nonverbal) that depict their interpretation of "what is," prescriptions (evaluative aspects and notions of what should be), whether communication is problematic (because of the transient nature of multiple identities and assigning multiple meanings and interpretations), code (broad system of beliefs, values, and images of the ideal reflected in language patterns), conversation (a patterned representation of a people's experience involving exchange of rituals), and community (a grouping of persons where communality is derived from shared identity).

Hecht et al.'s (1994) sensitizing constructs are embedded in the theory of symbolic interactionism. Symbolic interactionism is a sociological perspective influenced by Blumer, with foundations in pragmatism (an interest in how individuals make practical adjustments to their surroundings). It is based on the following three premises: (a) Human beings act toward things on the basis of the meanings that the things have for them, (b) the meaning of the things arises out of the social interaction one has with others, and (c) the meanings of things are handled in and modified through an interpretive process used by the person in dealing with the things he or she encounters. Symbolic interactionism asks the question, "What common set of symbols and understandings have emerged to give meaning to people's interactions?" (Hewitt, 1994; Patton, 1990).

Symbolic interactionism was also influenced by the works of the behaviorist George

Herbert Mead: the mind, body, and conduct interconnectedness in influencing behavior. Self is the central object in symbolic interactionism. During encounters, the central object being negotiated is self. Symbolic interactionists acknowledge the multiple realities of the self as an object and they are concerned with the influence of a person's own conception of self and others' appraisal of that self, on conduct. In addition, they explore whether people orient their conduct to expectations of others in order to have their identities confirmed or be positively evaluated. Symbolic interactionism posits that the self (which includes self-image, self-esteem, and personal and social identity) is a powerful motivator for human behavior, communication, and interaction (Hewitt, 1994). Advertisements that seek to convey cultural meanings must consider the impact of self and its role in ascribing meanings and formulating responses to advertising stimuli.

Symbolic interactionism is perspective oriented (allows for the participants' frame of reference to be employed), self referent (allows participants to rely on and refer to themselves in the process of an encounter/interaction via their self-concept, self-image, and personal and social identities), negotiable (allows participants to negotiate the encounter/interaction), relational (it acknowledges participants' relations to others), and it is processual in that it allows the participants to become involved in a process of social and cognitive exchanges (Prus, 1989). The tenets of symbolic interaction (which also subsume the sensitizing constructs mentioned by Hecht et al., 1993) are necessary for understanding African American communication. As such, they collectively offer an appropriate perspective from which to evaluate the effectiveness of advertisements in their attempts to communicate meanings to Black audiences, allowing them to establish and maintain a sense of identity and affiliation with the product/service being endorsed.

PURPOSE OF STUDY

Because research suggests that sports in general and basketball in particular are salient to the Black culture, basketball appears to be a viable vehicle whereby sport advertisers may communicate with Black audiences. As such, sport marketers should note the premise (logic), grammar/packaging/contextualization, and overall presentation and delivery of the messages contained in electronic and print advertisements associated with the sport of basketball that Black consumers may be exposed to. Thus, the purpose of this study was to examine the advertisements that used basketball as a communication tool and were placed in mediums that had high visibility among Black consumers. This study sought to examine the manner in which one sport organization, Nike, Inc., communicated with Black consumers from the sociological backdrop of symbolic interactionism.

METHODOLOGY

The methodology of symbolic interactionism is naturalistic, descriptive, and interpretive. Symbolic interactionism seeks to study symbolic interaction in the natural settings of the everyday world (Hewitt, 1994; Patton, 1990). The languages, meanings, actions, and voices of ordinary people as conveyed in their verbs and nouns of the world they are experiencing are captured in the works of symbolic interactionists. Preferred methodology of symbolic interaction inquiry includes participant observation, life stories, ethnographies, and thickly contextualized interaction episodes. Thick description is the goal, as symbolic interactionists seek to uncover and illuminate the phenomenon under investigation (Hewitt, 1994; Patton, 1990).

Using the 1994 Simmons Market Research Study as a backdrop, methodology was employed to enable the researchers to analyze and provide contextualizations of the meanings portrayed and interaction episodes depicted in Nike advertisements. To examine Nike's use of electronic media, a total of five different commercials that aired during the Saturday and Sunday games of the 1994 NBA playoffs were videotaped. For an examination of Nike's usage of print media, random issues of Black magazines (*Essence, Jet, Ebony,* and *Black Enterprise*) were surveyed to locate different Nike advertisements. Data for the print analysis were found in a 1992 and a 1993 issue of *Black Enterprise* magazine. The television commercials were recorded and transcribed, whereas the magazine advertisements were photocopied then transcribed. Each transcription was then coded by three independent African American researchers. The researchers performed a qualitative content analysis using a coding sheet to assess the premise of the message, the grammar/packaging/contextualization of the message, and the overall style of presentation and delivery of the message as suggested by symbolic interactionism. To establish coder reliability, the researchers combined their analyses and discussed any discrepancies before arriving at a consensus for each category. The objectives of the methodology were to examine the intentions of Nike as the communicator, as well as the speculative effects on Black consumers as the receivers of the communication.

DATA

Following is a transcript of the electronic (television commercials) and print (magazine) advertisements examined for this study.

Electronic Media:
Television Commercial 1

The commercial setting begins with Dennis Rodman (a Black male professional basketball player for the San Antonio Spurs) walking into a barber shop. The Nike logo flashes across the screen, and music is playing. The setting quickly flashes to Rodman being inside the barber shop sitting in a chair to get his hair done. The people in the barber shop are Dennis Rodman, Tim Hardaway (a Black male professional basketball player with the Golden State Warriors), David Robinson (a Black male professional basketball player also with the San Antonio Spurs), and a Black lady who is preparing to cut Rodman's hair. As Rodman begins to talk, the viewers are shown a television with a live flashback of him playing (the commercial allows the viewers to see Rodman in real life action). The camera then zooms in on the shoes Rodman is wearing (which are Nike's). He begins, "I wanna go out there and test it, you know? The money don't mean anything to me, you know? I can go out there and play for free." Hardaway replies, "See he got them two rings, that's what it is." Laughter is heard in the background along with "yeah that's what it is." Hardaway repeats louder, "Them two rings!" Robinson adds, "Yeah they can't do nothing to him now!" Hardaway jumps in, "Before he had them two rings he was like . . [gesturing humbleness]." The group responds with laughter and hand gestures. Rodman replies, "Aw them rings don't mean anything really." Hardaway interrupts, "Oh them rings don't mean nothin'?" Rodman replies, "Naw they're a part of history." Hardaway continues, "[Well] can I have one?" Rodman is speechless initially, yet replies with a smile "Oh no, no!" The people in the barber shop burst into laughter as they jive and joke with Rodman. The Nike logo flashes across the screen and the commercial goes off.

Electronic Media:
Television Commercial 2

The commercial setting begins with David Robinson (as mentioned in the previous commercial) walking down a sidewalk with George Gervin (a Black man who was formerly a professional all-star basketball player for the San Antonio Spurs, and their current assistant coach). They are laughing and smiling as they are about to enter a barber shop. Music is playing as they are walking along. The audience sees flashes on a television screen of Gervin playing basketball in the NBA. Then the viewers see Gervin sitting in the barber shop spinning a basketball on his fingertips. The people in the barber shop include Tim Hardaway (as previously mentioned), Robinson, Gervin, a Black barber, and a couple of other Black men. Hardaway opens up, "1977, butterfly collar" (the camera focuses on a poster of Gervin in a silk warm-up suit with a butterfly collar and "ICE" inscribed on it, hanging on the wall of the barber shop). "Walk outside with that on in San Antonio now, and you'll burn up!" The people in the shop respond with laughter and hand/body gesturing. The footage of Gervin shooting his finger roll appears on the television (in the barber shop). Hardaway continues, "George, tell us about that finger roll from the free throw line." Gervin responds, "Oh yeah, that was my patented, that was my patented shot. One thing I could do was finger roll." The people in the shop respond with an outburst of laughter, the viewers then see footage on the television screen in the barber shop of Gery in performing a finger-roll shot in an actual NBA game. The camera then gets a total picture of all of the men in the barber shop. The Nike logo flashes across the screen, and the commercial goes off.

Electronic Media:
Television Commercial 3

Charles Barkley (a Black male professional basketball player with the Phoenix Suns) appears on the screen with a black background (the picture is in black and white). A clipping from a newspaper appears on the

split screen to the side of Barkley, and he begins to read:

> Teens Held in Death of Four Year Old. Phoenix—Two teenagers were charged with second degree murder for the April drive by shooting of a four year old girl. The girl was in her living room getting ready for bed when a bullet pierced the front window and struck her in the head. She died instantly. This murder marks the 10th homicide in Phoenix this year involving juveniles.

Appearing on the screen is 1–800–929-P.L.A.Y. paid for by Nike. A voice-over is heard saying: "Participate in the lives of America's youths." Barkley comments, "if not now, when?" The commercial then goes off. While Barkley was reading, he was continuously shaking his head in disbelief as he was emotionally bothered by this incident and related occurrences.

Electronic Media:
Television Commercial 4

The setting of this commercial begins with Chris Weber (a Black rookie professional male basketball player with the Golden State Warriors) walking into a barber shop. The Nike logo flashes across the screen as the music to a hit rhythm and blues song of the past, "Strawberry Letter 23," is playing in the background. The commercial immediately flashes to Weber being on the inside of a barber shop, sitting in the chair to get his hair done. Weber says, "The first person I ever dunked on was LaJuane Pounds, Detroit, Michigan! And he used to talk about my mother, talk about my shoes, my shorts . . . (the commercial flashes to Weber shooting baskets outside on a playground) . . . so I dunked on him! and I said nah! there! there you go! nah! nah!! and by that time they had gone down and scored a lay-up" (the camera flashes back to him sitting in the chair in the barber shop reflecting). "But that's all I remember from that game!" The people in the barber shop laugh. The only other visible person is the Black lady who is doing Weber's hair. The camera flashes on the Nike shoes Weber is wearing and footage of Weber dunking appears on the television in the barber shop. Weber continues, "He was the only kid who used to dog me and talk about me—but I wonder where he is now? Cause I wanna just say I dunked on 'em!" (Another footage of Weber dunking in an NBA game appears on the television in the barber shop.) Weber sits in the chair smiling. A voice, presumably that of Tim Hardaway, says, "He's probably bragging in the parks, he dunked on me, man Chris Weber dunked on me." Weber repeats, "He's bragging yeah, he dunked on me!" The commercial goes off.

Electronic Media:
Television Commercial 5

A rhythm and blues song "Express Yourself" is playing. The commercial opens up with two Black male youngsters peeking into the window of a barber shop. The commercial then flashes to the inside of the barber shop. One Black male who was sitting in the barber shop with a small Nerf basketball in his hand (Person 1) says, "Did you see Chris dunk on Barkley?" At this time the camera shows footage of Weber on the television in the barber shop coming down the court in an NBA game. At the bottom of the television in the barber shop is the Nike logo and an advertisement for a local radio station (K-FUNK 1450 AM). A flash of the Nike shoes Weber is wearing appears on the screen. A second person replies (Person 2), "Naw, I didn't see it." Person 1 replies, "Well, it went something like this" (he gets out of his chair to demonstrate what happened). Weber interrupts, "Here, put this cape on [Weber hands Person 1 the cover that was on him to prevent hair from covering

him to use as a cape], because I was super man!" Person 1 replies, "Oh yeah you were" (as Weber puts the cape around him). The camera flashes to footage of Weber playing in the NBA on the television in the barber shop. Person 1 gets up to demonstrate how Weber dunked on Barkley, Weber assumes the role of Barkley. Person 1 says, "Okay, catch it like this [footage of Weber catching the ball in an actual game against Phoenix's Barkley appears on the television] around the back" [footage of Weber taking the ball around his back flashes on the screen]. "Barkley comes over here to try to block it" (Weber and Person 1 imitate the action while footage of the actual move appears on the television). Weber (in his Barkley imitation) replies, "Wait, he's too high—he's too high!" Then Person 1 dunks the Neff ball in the basketball hoop in the barber shop. The actual footage of Weber dunking on Barkley appears on the television. Person 1 asks Weber, "Then what did Barkley say?" Weber replies, "He said I don't believe in role models, but uh, you mine." The place erupts in laughter and high five gestures and handshakes. The Nike logo flashes across the screen as Weber and Person 1 engage in a brotherly embrace, and the commercial goes off. Throughout the commercial, the words of the rhythm and blues song "Express Yourself" are heard.

Print Media:
Magazine Advertisement 1

The advertisement is in color. It features a silhouette of two youngsters playing basketball, presumably on a dilapidated playground court. Vertically, along the left side of the picture, appears the following script:

My dad's a gangster. My dad's a father. My dad runs around. My dad runs 4 miles a day. My dad says women are only good for one thing. My dad says Black women are living jewels. My dad sent me money. My dad sent for me. My dad says school's for fools. My dad says knowledge is power. Like father, like son? Scold him. Mold him. Love him. Don't let him quit. If he's third string, go to his games, anyway. If he can't hit a curve ball, don't sweat him. If he's not doing well in school, give him hell. If he can recite a rap, word for word, he can memorize a history lesson, date for date. Be there for him. And he'll be there for his brother. JUST DO IT. NIKE. (The Nike logo appears at the bottom left corner of the advertisement.)

Print Media:
Magazine Advertisement 2

This advertisement is in color. It features a huge view of the top of a dilapidated rim, one that has pieces of a net attached to it with different types of tape. The setting is one of a local playground, in a not-so-affluent neighborhood. Appearing vertically along the right side of the rim is the following script:

Goals. Some are realistic. Some aren't. You gotta bust your butt to find out. One thing's for sure. Life preys on one dimensional players. Those who put everything in one basket. It's not fair. But you realize, it's not your ball. So you've set many goals. Earn a Ph.D. Finish a marathon. Write a screenplay. Own an N.F.L. team. Run for President. Yeah, you're shooting for the stars. But that's cool. If you don't make one, you take what you've learned and alter your shot. JUST DO IT. (The Nike logo appears in the upper left corner of the advertisement.)

ANALYSIS/DISCUSSION

The content of the advertisements was analyzed according to the following three domains: the premise (logic) of the message, the grammar/packaging/contextualization of the message, and the overall style of message presentation and delivery.

Premise/Logic of the Messages

The premise of the Nike advertisements included in this study represented the historical and mythological foundation for Nike, Inc. Nike is the winged goddess of victory in the Greek mythology. Her domain was Olympus, where she sat at the side of Zeus, the ruler of the Olympic pantheon. A mystical presence, characterizing victorious encounters, Nike presided over history's earliest battlefields. A Greek would say "when we go to battle and win we say it is Nike" (Nike Publications, 1993). A swoosh is Nike's symbol of performance excellence. As such, the media logic in the advertisements reflects their slogan of "Just Do It." The "Just Do It" mentality was conveyed in the manner in which the advertisements spoke to the social ills plaguing America and the means by which people may overcome them with the support of and through interactions with their significant others (i.e., reference group, community). The logic of the Nike advertisements emanated from the premise of symbolic interactionism: meanings in their advertisements arose out of social interaction and human emotions and experiences. This was depicted in the interaction episodes displayed in the casual behavior of the men in the barber shops in the television commercials as they interacted to celebrate the accomplishment portrayed. This logic was also conveyed in the words of the print advertisements such as,

Like father, like son..., mold him scold him, don't let him quit.... If he's third string, go to his games anyway.... If he can recite a rap word for word, he can memorize a history lesson date for date.... Life preys on one dimensional players.... Those who put everything in one basket. It's not fair. But you realize, it's not your ball. . . you take what you've learned and alter your shot.

Be it winning two NBA world championship rings, having a distinctive stylish move such as a patented finger roll, taking an active role to stop teen violence, remembering getting even in a nonviolent, sport-related manner with a bully or someone who picked on you, dunking a basketball over a very proliferate athlete to establish yourself and your turf, setting goals, or looking out for sons or brothers, Nike advertisements rewarded athletic prowess, yet also contained messages of hope and encouragement to overcoming social, physical, and psychological barriers that may seem insurmountable. Thus, the premise of the Nike advertisements posited Nike as a brand that goes far beyond its functional product attributes (in athletic excellence), but also has some symbolic usefulness to Black consumers as it endorses and celebrates nuances, emotions, and interactions that occur within the African American culture.

Grammar/Packaging/ Contextualization of the Messages

A language is critical to group membership and contact with the group via abstract and concrete objects (Hewitt, 1994). Effective grammar must contain a language that is appropriate for the intended audience. The grammar and means by which Nike advertisements contextualized the language in which they communicated meanings and messages to their audiences were contained in a number of core symbols included in the advertisements. The conversational pattern of expression was perhaps one Blacks could relate to because they included patterned verbal and nonverbal representations of the Black participants' experiences. The participants in the commercials spoke to the audience in slang, jive-talking, with their codes, and with their jargon

to "express themselves" (which was the title of one of the rhythm and blues songs playing in the background). Such an inclusion of rhythm and blues music was another strategic ploy, given that music is also a critical context for communication and many Blacks have an affinity to rhythm and blues music in particular. Also, in one of the barber shop scenes, the viewers saw an advertisement for an AM radio station (which was also strategically placed given Blacks' listening habits of AM radio stations). The exchange of rituals and nonverbal gestures depicted in the commercials such as handshakes, hugs, high fives, body gestures, and so forth that the participants engaged in conveyed a special meaning and were also a critical part of the language being spoken. The print advertisements were also packaged to speak a language containing the grammar and reflections of some of the elements of inner-city life as depicted in the silhouettes of dilapidated playground basketball facilities and equipment. The grammar in the print advertisements was culturally constructed and presented in a dichotomous manner.

> My dad's a gangster. My dad's a father. My dad runs around. My dad runs 4 miles a day. My dad says women are only good for one thing. My dad says Black women are living jewels . . . . If he can't hit a curve ball, don't sweat him. If he's not doing well in school, give him hell . . . . Yeah, you're shooting for the stars, but that's cool.

Both the electronic and print advertisements contained a number of core symbols, codes, and conversations that were an integral part of the packaging of the message being communicated. Perhaps they served as sensitizing constructs, and allowed for the creation of cultural identities and the reinforcement of commonalities as the Black participants communicated with one another (in the electronic advertisements) and as Black readers were being spoken to (by the printed advertisements).

Thus, the grammar/packaging/contextualization of Nike advertisements was constructed with an appeal to some aspects of African American culture.

Overall Style of Message Presentation and Delivery

The Nike advertisements did not present blatant product endorsements. The placement of its logo/brand symbol was secondary to the interactions and symbolic settings captured and portrayed in their advertisements. The focus of the Nike advertisements was on the culture of the participants in the commercials and social interactions they (as consumers of Nike products) engaged in. The theme of each advertisement was conveyed through human interaction, experience, and emotion. Although the advertisements allowed for the participants' frame of reference to be conveyed (i.e., perspective-oriented), they also may have allowed Black consumers to engage in self-referencing techniques because they could either see themselves or significant others in the settings portrayed. The advertisements were also processual, in that they drew the audience into the message (i.e., with live footage of the actual NBA games) and enabled them to be a part of the interaction episodes. Contributing to the processual nature of the Nike advertisements was the circular, fast-paced motion in which the commercials were produced and the print messages were written. The verbal and visual inflections of the advertisements allowed for the audience to naturally be a part of the setting. The commercial action and flow of the text allowed for spontaneous expressions because they did not have a very rigid or structured format. For example, the electronic advertisements began with a scene depicting the athlete entering the barber shop, then flashed back to the athlete competing in a real basketball game, then came back to the barber shop. This format was also depicted in the flow of the text of the printed ads: "My dad sent me money. My dad sent for me. My dad says school's for fools. My dad says knowledge is power . . . . Earn a Ph.D. Finish a marathon. Write a screenplay. Own an N.F.L. team." The action/message jumped from idea to idea and from person to person, fostering a contagion effect of communication which fostered interaction among the viewers and readers.

Perhaps the most critical element of the Nike advertisements in communicating with Black audiences, however, was their relational characteristic. The frame of reference for Nike advertisements is not only the immediate situations or individual circumstances, but rather a collective community that many Black consumers may relate to. Hewitt (1994) refers to the collective community as the set of real or imaginary others with whom the person feels a sense of similarity and common purpose. Marketers often utilize the reference group influence, and Nike marketing was no exception. The Nike advertisements contained real-world settings that did not have to be manipulated or artificially contrived or reproduced for television or magazines (i.e., hanging out in a barber shop, or playground basketball). The advertisements also contained real people speaking to an audience rather than at them. Even though Nike employed professional Black male athletes as their spokespeople, the athletes were portrayed in such a manner that reduced their celebrity status and made them believable people (i.e., barber shop patrons), as opposed to larger-than-life or privileged characters. Thus, the overall style of the presentation and delivery of the messages were constructed in a manner that contained characteristics that symbolic interactionism would posit as appealing to many Black consumers.

It has often been said that people will always tune into television/radio station WIIFM (What's in it for Me). Because of their relevance to African American culture, the emotional content of the Nike advertisements may become a salient product market feature (speaking volumes to the African American culture) that will capture the attention of Black consumers thereby preventing commercial zapping and magazine scanning. The meanings of the messages were modified and interpreted through the code, conversation, presentation, and style of the advertisements that may be appealing to the Black culture. Thus, it appears that Nike's electronic and print advertisements contain the sensitizing constructs as mentioned by Prus (1989), Hecht et al. (1993), and the tenets of symbolic interaction to create relevant and symbolic meanings that are conveyed via plots, language/dialogues, messages, images, people, and interactions that are drawn from the culturally constituted world of many Black consumers. In so doing, Nike has created advertisements that are very symbolic in their nonproduct attributes. Such symbolism may result in the association of culturally-salient meanings being a perceived attribute of the Nike product being endorsed. The swoosh, therefore, may be an external stimulus that represents the total packaging of the Nike experience that evokes a positive feeling (i.e., cultural affect) within Black consumers.

CONCLUSION

Measuring the effectiveness of advertising may be ascertained from an economic or sociological perspective. The economical assessment of effectiveness is based on the increase in sales that result from exposure to an advertisement. This method is problematic in that it is largely based on sales. If the objective of the campaign is not directly one of sales (for example, one of image enhancement) this approach is not befitting. Also, difficulty arises in measuring sales due to the time lag that may occur between exposure to an advertisement and actual purchase of the product or service (Mullins et al., 1993). Although somewhat simplistic, this study adopted a sociological approach in analyzing the content of the selected Nike basketball advertisements, with regards to the means in which they contained the characteristics that were descriptive of the tenets of symbolic interactionism that may enhance communication effectiveness. One major limitation of this approach is the subjective nature of conducting a content analysis. Nonetheless, the methodology employed did allow for a cursory evaluation of Nike's attempt/ability to communicate with Black consumers. Of course, merely including culturally salient elements in a communication is by no means a guarantee that viewers who culturally identify with them will respond in a favorable manner. However, research (Pitts et al., 1989) has revealed that Black consumers do respond favorably to advertisements that are culturally targeted to them. More systematic investigations are needed but (nonetheless) based on the premises of symbolic interactionism, Nike has packaged and presented its advertisements in a culturally appropriate manner that perhaps may promote optimal communication with Black consumers. As mentioned at the outset of this article, effective communication is largely dependent on shared values and meanings conveyed in symbolic verbal and nonverbal signs and symbols. Nike advertisements contain such symbolic features and also communicate something symbolic about its consumers.

Schudson (1986) contends that advertising does not really change people's minds about a product, rather it is most effective when it celebrates the product, reinforcing existing attitudes. Nike advertisements do just that because they are drawn from the naturally occurring culturally constituted worlds of their consumers. In addition to the content of the message that may heighten viewer's interest in an advertisement, a person's conception of self is a driving motivational force (Hewitt, 1994) and may have grave implications in determining the effectiveness of the advertisement. From a symbolic interactionist perspective, Nike has been effective in including a number of sensitizing constructs that convey cultural meaning and may tap into the self-concept and consciousness of Black consumers, allowing them opportunities to relate, refer, establish, and maintain positive identities through the symbols used and images created and communicated via the Nike electronic and print advertisements.

Perhaps Nike's effectiveness in communicating with Black consumers contributed to Blacks' patronage of Nike products. Whereas Operation PUSH (People United to Serve Humanity, a Chicago-based civil rights organization) reported that Black purchases constituted 30% or $669 million of Nike sales, Nike reported that minorities accounted for only 13.6% or $303 million of its sales (Woodard, 1990). Operation PUSH claimed that Nike had a poor record of hiring Blacks at the executive level and had limited investment in the Black communities. But even during its race-oriented controversy, Nike experienced a 42% increase in sales (Grimm, 1990). So, it must be noted that Nike has received its share of charges for not being culturally sensitive to (and even being a bit exploitative of) the Black culture as a result of their intense, effective marketing efforts that are attractive to and reflective of Black lifestyles. Nike refuted the attacks and increased its hiring of Black employees (including at the executive level), its engagement in cause-related/social marketing activities, and its investments in the Black youth and in Black communities via projects such as inner-city boys' and girls' clubs, United Negro College Fund, Urban League, and education oriented basketball camps (Grimm, 1990).

Nike is not the only sport entity that has employed a cultural approach of marketing communications. For example, the National Basketball Association has advertisements that are rife with elements reflective of African American culture that may be a response to Blacks' affinity to basketball. Also, Major League Baseball (MLB) launched a commercial advertisement that featured Black rhythm and blues singer Aretha Franklin and rapper L.L. Cool J endorsing MLB. MLB also placed some print advertisements celebrating Blacks' contribution to baseball in a number of popular Black magazines such as *Ebony*. The National Football League also had a commercial advertisement depicting some young Black male youths playing football on inner-city playgrounds. Major League Soccer (MLS) also employed the talents of popular Black musicians in their commercial advertisement that featured rhythm and blues rap group Run D.M.C. promoting the MLS. Each of these ventures illustrates the need for sport organizations to address the cultural implications of communicating with Black audiences.

Advertising is a critical facet of marketing. When people buy products, they are also purchasing experiences that often become an extension of their psychosocial selves. Because of the increased cultural diversity America is undergoing, sport marketers and advertisers must be cognizant of the challenges of presenting advertisements to consumers who do not want to give up their racial, cultural, and ethnic uniqueness in their consumptions and purchase behaviors, but instead want their identities validated and their uniqueness acknowledged and respected (Wilson & Gutierrez, 1985). Thus, advertisements (along with other elements of the marketing promotional and communications mix) should be carefully crafted to speak to the intended audiences in a culturally appropriate manner, highlighting the functional and symbolic usefulness of the product to the consumers. Nike has apparently sought to communicate with Black consumers by focusing their advertisements on human interaction and emotion, with an inherent social/cultural message accompanied by a peripheral product endorsement. Yet, care must be taken to convey messages that are not exploitative, but instead that promote the establishment of long-term positive relationships with consumers.

Learning how to devise messages to appeal to the uniqueness of ethnic markets (as well as to youth, women, senior citizens, etc.) without being culturally insensitive, exploitive, or offensive is something that sport organizations must master as they seek to expand and diversify their consumer bases in an ever-increasing culturally diverse environment. The theory of symbolic interactionism may assist in such regard by providing a lens through which marketing activities may be examined. Successful advertising strategies require a knowledge of the consumer, knowledge of the product, and communications that symbolically connect the two. Although Nike may forever be at the forefront of controversy regarding its marketing practices, their advertisements provide an illustration of the importance of understanding and applying a sociological grounding to the construction of marketing communications. In this regard, Nike knows how to "Just Do It!"

REFERENCES

Altheide, D. L., & Snow, R. P. (1991). *Media worlds in the post journalism era.* New York: de Gruyter.

Black spending power on rise, survey reports. (1998, July 30). *Columbus Dispatch,* pp. 1B-2B.

Boggart, L. (1990). *Strategies in advertising: Matching media and messages to markets and motivations* (2nd ed.). Chicago, IL: NTC Business Books.

Boone, L. E., & Kurtz, D. L. (1992). *Contemporary marketing* (7th ed.). Orlando: Dryden.

Gorman, J., & Calhoun, K. (1994). *The name of the game: A business of sports.* New York: John Wiley.

Grimm, M. (1990, August 19). PUSH comes to shove as Nike defends its image. *Adweek,* p. 6.

Hawkins, D. I., Best, R. J., & Coney, 1c A. (1992). *Consumer behavior: Implications for marketing strategy* (5th ed.). Homewood, IL: Irwin.

Hecht, M. L., Collier, M. J., & Ribeau, S. A. (1993). *African American communication: Ethnic identity and cultural interpretation, language and languages behavior* (Vol. 2). Newbury Park, CA: Sage.

Hewitt, J. P. (1994). *Self and society: A symbolic interactionist social psychology* (6th ed.). Needham Heights, MA: Simon and Schuster.

Johnson, P. (1995). Black radio's role in sports promotion: Sports, scholarships, and sponsorships. *Journal of Sport & Social Issues, 19*(4), 397–414.

Mabry, M. (1989, August 14). A long way from Aunt Jemima. *Newsweek,* pp. 34–35.

Mallory, M. (1992, March 23). Waking up to a major market. *Business Week,* p. 70.

Mullins, B., Hardy, S., & Sutton, W. (1993). *Sport Marketing.* Champaign, IL: Human Kinetics.

Nike Publications. (1993). *Informational packet: Participate in the lives of America's youth.* Beaverton, OR: Author.

Patton, M. Q. (1990). *Qualitative evaluation and research methods.* Newbury Park, CA: Sage.

Pitts, R. E., Whalen, D. J., O'Keefe, R., & Murray, V. (1989). Black and White responses to culturally targeted television commercials: A values based approach. *Psychology and Marketing, 6*(4), 311–328.

Prus, R. C. (1989). *Pursuing customers.* Newbury Park, CA: Sage.

Rossman, M. L. (1994). *Multicultural marketing: Selling to a diverse America.* New York: American Management Association.

Rudman, W. (1986). The sport mystique in Black culture. *Sociology of Sport Journal, 3,* 305–319.

Sachs, M. L., & Abraham, A. (1979). Playground basketball: A qualitative, field examination. *Journal of Sport Behavior, 2,* 27–36.

Schudson, M. (1986). *Advertising, the uneasy persuasion: Its dubious impact on American society.* New York: Basic Books.

Shilbury, D., Quick, S., & Westerbeek, H. (1998). *Strategic sport marketing.* St. Leonards, NSW Australia: Allen & Unwin.

Shimp, T. A. (1997). *Advertising, promotion, and supplemental aspects of integrated marketing* communications (4th ed.). Orlando, FL: Dryden.

Simmons Market Research Bureau, Inc. (1994). Study of media and markets. *Sports and Leisure, 10*(9), 278–300.

Simpson, J. (1992,August 31). Buying Black. *Time,* pp. 52–53.

Spreitzer, E., & Snyder, E. (1990). Sports within the Black subculture: A matter of social class or distinctive subculture. *Journal of Sport & Social Issues, 14*(1), 48–58.

Stotlar, D. K. (1993). *Successful sport marketing.* Dubuque, IA: Brown & Benchmark.

Wilson, C. C. II, & Gutierrez, F. (1985). *Minorities and media: Diversity and the end of mass communication.* Newbury Park, CA: Sage.

Woodard, W. M. (1990, November). It's more than just the shoes. *Black Enterprise,* p. 17.

Ketra L. Armstrong, Ph.D., is an assistant professor of sport management at The Ohio State University. Her research interest centers on sociocultural implications of marketing sport.

Reading 3.7

Toward Theorizing Japanese Interpersonal Communication Competence From a Non-Western Perspective

AKIRA MIYAHARA

I. INTRODUCTION

Now that a new millennium has been ushered in, academic disciplines that deal with human behavior have also welcomed an era pregnant with new and challenging tasks whose outcomes are hoped to increase global and profound understanding of people's social practices across cultural boundaries. An entire issue of the *Journal of Cross-Cultural Psychology,* 31

First published in *American Communication Journal,* Vol. 3, Issue 3, May, 2000. Reprinted with permission.

(2000) was dedicated to the discussion of problems entailed in Western-based research concepts and methods thus far employed, and alternatives necessary for better cross-cultural understanding. Only with such understanding is it possible to bring about mutually satisfactory international political, economic, and cultural exchanges. Given such an overwhelming goal, an urgent objective the field of human communication, intercultural communication in particular, faces is to establish a meaningful framework for inquiries. It is to serve the inquirers as well as practitioners as a framework within which symbolic behaviors of people of diverse cultural backgrounds can be accounted for without distorting their interpretations and evaluations in any way biased toward a particular culture.

While Asian, or more broadly non-Western people's social behaviors have been largely left to speculations, and often labeled "mysterious," and "deviant," some ethnographic details have been uncovered in respect to Japan (Markus & Kitayama, 1998). Japanese people's communicative behavior has been researched intensively in the last decade or two, and consequently many characteristics "peculiar to" Japanese have been identified (for summary, see, for example, Gudykunst, 1993). To illustrate, Japanese have been described as being low in self-disclosure, both verbally (Barnlund, 1975, 1989), and nonverbally (Engebretson & Fullmer, 1970; Sussman & Rosenfeld, 1982), transmitting messages in a high-context mode (e.g., Hall, 1976; Neustupny, 1987; Ting-Toomey, 1985), and communicatively apprehensive (Klopf, 1984; Neulip & Hazelton, 1985). Most of these attributes have been ascribed to the Japanese people's collectivistic orientations (e.g., Gudykunst & Ting-Toomey, 1988; Triandis et al, 1988).

Another line of research on Japanese interpersonal communication has been growing out of the practical need for the Japanese people, particularly those in younger generations, to acquire and develop effective social skills for meaningful and satisfactory personal relationships. In the pursuit of the country's economic and technological advancement, Japanese people's educational and social needs may have been left behind as secondary concerns. As a result, the Japanese in various age groups are said to be troubled with their daily interpersonal relations in a wide range of contexts: family, school, work, health care, etc. A set of knowledge, motivations, and skills, i.e., communication competence, that will help improve the quality of human relationships among Japanese is urgently needed. Outcomes of cross-cultural comparisons between Japanese and U.S. Americans, for instance, may contribute to better understanding of each other's social attributes, and consequently practical and more importantly, culturally meaningful and feasible solutions to Japanese people's ineffective communication may be suggested. Before we can reach that goal, however, some meta-theoretical issues concerning the cross-cultural research need to be raised and carefully considered.

The purpose of this paper is to discuss and challenge several meta-theoretical issues that concern cross-cultural comparisons of Japanese and Western people's interpersonal behavior. It aims to pinpoint some obstacles in the way of conceptualizing the Japanese people's communication characteristics in an attempt to build a culture-specific theory of interpersonal communication competence for Japanese. Finally some alternative methods of cross-cultural communication research in place of pencil-and-paper surveys, using the homogeneous population (i.e., college students) will be discussed.

II. CULTURAL FILTERS IN CROSS-CULTURAL RESEARCH

Since the Morrison article (1972), in which the author claimed that people in Japan (labeled "a rhetorical vacuum") lacked persuasive skills due to the absence of a Western rhetorical tradition, scholars inspired by the heavily ethnocentric claim have conducted research in an attempt to unveil the "peculiarities" of Japanese communication. Despite their conscious attempts to characterize the Asian people's social practices, however, the scholars relied almost exclusively on theoretical concepts and methods of inquiry developed by the Western, primarily U.S. researchers. This practice was to a large extent inevitable, as systematic and scientific knowledge of inquiry was far more readily available in the U.S. scholarship of communication. The paucity of culture-specific studies may be partly ascribed to the absence of a paradigm to account for the social behaviors demonstrated by the Japanese (Hamaguchi, 1990).

When researchers note cultural diversity, they record and report their observations and possible reasons for the observed differences. These observations and interpretations are necessarily biased and bound by their individual belief systems that are shaped and influenced by their institutional, psychological, social, and religious orientations, i.e., culture (Kim, Park, & Park, 2000). Most of the observations, analyses and interpretations of the Japanese people's social behavior so far have been conducted and reported by Western scholars. While some Japanese scholars have joined efforts with their Western associates and also initiated their own to clarify the characteristics of Japanese communication behavior, they have employed approaches developed and tested on the Western, primarily U. S. soil.

It is, therefore, important to remember that "findings" obtained by a researcher on one group of people's social and psychological attributes are inevitably filtered through the researcher's cultural framework. Just as an individual behavior is influenced by, and therefore a manifestation of his/her culture, the person observing that behavior is also influenced by the cultural framework within which he/she was raised, educated, and trained. We see the world less "as it is" and more "as we are." Depending on the experiences we have had, the habits that we have acquired, we see events differently (Triandis, 1994, p. 13). Ho (1998), asserting the value of indigenous approach to people's psychological attributes, states that the conceptualization of psychological phenomena is a psychological phenomenon in itself and is, therefore, subject to investigation (p. 91). Singelis (2000) echoes this, stating that "all social psychology is cultural" (p. 76).

Ho (1998) goes on to say that much of Western psychology may be irrelevant or inapplicable in Asia. Western ideological presuppositions, such as individualism, are alien to the Asian ethos. Thus, a reliance on Western psychology can only lead to an incomplete, even distorted, understanding of Asia or of Asians. Moreover, the wholesale importation of Western psychology into Asia represents a form of cultural imperialism that perpetuates the colonization of the mind. To an alarming degree, Asians are now confronted by stereotypes about themselves generated not only by Western researchers but also by Asian researchers relying on imported, mainly American, psychology (p. 89). Such a tendency is clearly observed in the research on communication competence conducted by both U.S. and Japanese scholars.

Most studies on communication competence have been undertaken and many related concepts have been developed and tested by U.S. researchers (Spitzberg & Cupach, 1984, 1989) as well as Japanese researchers educated in the U.S. (e.g., Barnlund & Yoshioka, 1990; Gudykunst & Nishida, 1986; Hirokawa & Miyahara, 1986). It is not simply the researchers' nationalities that really matter, but their culturally conditioned perceptual filters that influence their observations and interpretations of social behavior. The consequence is that the findings reported and behavioral suggestions presented by a researcher may or may not be applicable to the people observed who do not share the same cultural attributes with the researcher.

"Assertiveness," for instance, an important communication skill regarded as conducive to the perception of interpersonal competence in the U.S. culture, runs counter to traditional Japanese values of "not standing out" but "adapting to natural and social environments." In a strong conformist society such as Japan, presenting one's feelings to others, which in turn may risk the harmony among people, is a communication behavior difficult to practice. Clearly asserting one's own points certainly does not serve an individual as a motive to behave in an interpersonal situation. To the contrary, not stating clearly what one has in mind is a sign of strength, maturity and social competence in the Asian culture, and thus may need to be added to a "competency list" for the Japanese.

The remainder of the paper addresses some specific meta-theoretical issues involved in cross-cultural research on interpersonal communication competence between Japanese and people of Western cultural attributes.

III. META-THEORETICAL ISSUES IN STUDYING NON-WESTERN MODES OF COMMUNICATION

Applied to Japanese people's communication competence research, issues involved in cross-cultural studies are boiled down to differences in ontological and epistemological/phenomenological orientations between people in the West and those with a Japanese cultural framework. More specifically, Japanese people in general are brought up in a culture that values a collectivistic or interdependent self orientation, and "being" mode of thinking, rather than individualistic or independent self orientation and doing mode that are prevalent

in most Western cultures. There is much danger, therefore, in using Western theories and concepts, e.g., communication apprehension, self-disclosure, assertiveness, and persuasion to account for and improve relationships among Japanese.

Ontological Issues

As most "scientific" studies on human behavior have been undertaken and theories and concepts have been developed in European American cultural framework, it is not surprising that the basic units of analyses and constructs employed to account for people's behavior are also influenced by the Western cultural orientation. The meaning of an "individual," for instance, is undoubtedly adopted from the Western perspective and it has been assumed to have the same meaning for people across cultural boundaries. In recent years some psychologists (e.g., Hamaguchi, 1983; Ho, 1998; Kim, Park, & Kim, 2000; Markus & Kitayama, 1991; Singelis, 2000) have strongly argued that the meaning people assign to being a person varies from culture to culture.

Ho (1998) illustrates this point by saying that such constructs as actor, ego, self, and personality reflect an individualistic conception of human existence characteristic of the West. Face, relational orientation, and relational identity, on the other hand, reflect a relational conception characteristic of many Asian cultures. The concept of the "individual" is an example that demonstrates the culture-bound nature of what is seemingly universal. The individualism-collectivism dichotomy has long been considered a powerful concept to characterize people's social and behavioral orientation. Markus and Kitayama (1991) developed the concepts of independent and interdependent self-construals, and evidence has been reported that cultural differences between collectivism and individualism are systematically reflected in the differences on the individual level, interdependent and independent self-construals, respectively (Kim, et al, 1996).

A person is regarded as being independent when he/she looks to his/her internal and individual characteristics, attributes and goals as primary regulators of behavior. For a person with an interdependent view of self, on the other hand, the self is connected to others, and becomes most meaningful and complete when it is cast in the appropriate social relationships with others. The person's desire to maintain harmony and appropriateness in relationships with others serves as a primary regulator of his/her behavior.

There have been several Japanese sociologists, psychologists and psychiatrists (e.g., Doi, 1971; Hamaguchi, 1977, 1983; Kimura, 1989; Miyanaga, 1991) who have argued that Japanese people's notion of self is different from its Western counterpart. The concept of "self" among Japanese derives not so much from the individual, as it does from a relationship between the individual and others. Depending on who the other is, and what type of relationship he/she has with others, each individual needs to adjust the communication goals and behaviors.

Hamaguchi (1983), developing the concept of kanjinshugi (interpersonalism or contextualism), argues that since collectivism as opposed to individualism regards a general collectivity of people as an analytical point of departure, such a Western-derived dichotomy fails to account for the Japanese social behavior. In Japan the fundamental form of human existence is neither the individual nor the group but rather contextual. Interpersonalism as a perspective transcends the dualism, and it is defined by mutual dependence, mutual trust and human relation in itself. This raises an important ontological issue in conducting cross-cultural research in the area of interpersonal communication competence.

Co-dependence, although not an entirely novel concept, but used to identify pathological individuals such as "adult children" has been regarded as an appropriate term to describe many Japanese youngsters. Co-dependent individuals, whether they are pathological or not, are those whose very existence and content of characters are determined only through their dependence upon and interactions with people around them. A model of "interpersonal competence" for such people would naturally have to be developed from a different starting point other than an individual. Contextualism, or interpersonalism, appears to be a more reasonable alternative, although quite difficult to operationalize as a research concept.

Regardless of the label attached to people according to their self-orientations, it goes without saying that they utilize communication strategies and tactics in order to achieve personal and relational goals, although in different manners and to different degrees. The motive for achievement is said to vary depending on how an individual is construed. Singelis (2000) asserts that achievement motivation in the West has been rooted in the idea that the goal is self-realization. In collectivist cultures, achievement motivation includes others whose boundaries are not distinct from the self. This is to say that the motivation to achieve in these cultures includes the self and others. When one's group succeeds the success accrues to the self, and, similarly, when the self succeeds, so does the group (p. 81). Given the ontological difference between individuals with independent and interdependent self-construals, the meanings and values that people attach to what appears to be the same communication behavior greatly vary. Several specific examples follow to illustrate the cross-cultural variation.

Most communication theories are based on the assumption that people seek cognitive consistencies in social situations; e.g., balance theory (Heider, 1958). Although people regardless of their cultural frameworks are believed to have the tendency toward cognitive consistency as a marker of human rationality, the notion of consistency may be culturally relative. An adjustment of communication goal and behavior according to the contextual and relational features, may be regarded as an inconsistency and an ineffective social behavior by a person of independent self-construal. A predominant feature of the self in European-American contexts, Kim (1999) argues, is the persistent need for consistency and stability. The desire for a consistent self is tied to the notion that the self is whole, stable, and integrated rather than fragmented and distributed. Such attributes as honesty, straightforwardness, integrity, and clarity in communicating one's feelings are important components of communication competence (Spitzberg & Cupach, 1984). Behavior that changes with the situation is more likely to be regarded as waffling, hypocritical, or even pathological than as flexible or responsive (Markus & Kitayama, 1998).

People with interdependent self-construal, on the other hand, often sacrifice consistency for the sake of interpersonal accommodation. This gives rise to the wide array of communication goals, and means to reach them. Showing sensitivities to others and adjusting their communication tactics accordingly is a sign of maturity, as it helps the Japanese gain approval by others. In the interdependent culture such as Japan, notions like awase (accommodation) (Mushakoji, 1976), manipulation of honne-tatemae (real intentions and facade) (Gudykunst & Nishida, 1993), deliberate use of ambiguity (Okabe, 1987), and self-restraint (Takai & Ota, 1994) are some of the strategies that contribute to smooth interpersonal interactions.

Tsujimura (1987) cites four characteristics of Japanese communication that help them relate to one another in a competent manner: ishin-denshin (communication without language), taciturnity or passivity, indirect communication

and respect for reverberation, and sensitivity toward kuuki (the constraint of mood). All these characteristics are ascribed to Japanese people's interdependent views on self. A person who is able to observe subtle, social norms associated with these attributes is regarded as mature and competent. In addition, Kim (1999) observes that while the outcomes of communication apprehension and avoidance are considered to be solely negative in the Western communication apprehension framework, it may possibly be a sign of sensitivity to the social context for a person with an interdependent view of self. The low level of motivation for verbal communication may stem from the strength of one's idealized role-identity in interaction, and the sensitivity toward the others' evaluations of the individual. "A generalized sensitivity to others' evaluations and 'fitting in' is one of the central characteristics of the interdependent self" (p. 10), which is more highly valued in many collectivistic Asian cultures including Japan.

Self-disclosure is another Western concept that is often utilized as a measure for communication competence. It serves a person as a vehicle for initiating and developing interpersonal relationships (Altman & Taylor, 1973), and an appropriate level of self-disclosure is expected to help a person maintain mental health (Cozby, 1973). How an individual goes about disclosing oneself and how he/she values it varies depending on how the self is construed. In the European-American context, if a person wants to be perceived as competent and successful, boasting (positive self-disclosure) appears to be a better strategy than disclosing negatively.

In Japanese culture the inclination to self-criticize (negative self-disclosure) may be a way to affirm the identity of the self as interdependent. This is a display of the individual's willingness to engage in the process of self-improvement that may be accomplished only by maintaining harmonious relationships with others—an important element of the interdependent, Japanese sense of well-being (Kim, 1999). Using the amount and quality of self-disclosure judged as appropriate in Western cultures such as U.S. as sole indicators of communication competence for people from different cultures, therefore, is likely to lead to falsified descriptions of their communication behavior and its effects.

The "self" is an organized and culturally relative framework that functions as a guide to what a person perceives, how he/she attaches meanings to stimuli, and how he/she associates and communicates with others. If the notion of self is different across cultures, then the different ontological orientation necessarily values differently the verbal and nonverbal communication tactics, and more profoundly people's predispositions toward the communication behaviors. Many communication concepts and theories, developed and validated in the West where independent self-construal prevails, would not be justifiably applied to people in many Asian cultures where more interdependent self-construal predominates. What has been accepted as universally meaningful and effective communication strategies and styles may only be indigenously so in the West. More divergent social practices, many of which have been discarded as ineffective, may indeed contribute to perceptions and practices of communication competence in Asian human relationships.

Epistemological/Phenomenological Issues

Closely associated with the distinctive views on self (independent and interdependent) is how an individual creates and attaches meanings to social phenomena. Kim et al. (2000) assert that our social lives are based on the firm belief that we can understand, assess, and use the concepts of agency, intentions, and motives with a high degree of reliability and validity (p. 71). This is the epistemological

perspective that is prevalent in much of Western mode of thinking, and it is often referred to as "science." Kim et al. (2000) go on to argue that in order for researchers in cross-cultural psychology to reach accurate understanding of the psychological phenomena in the respective cultures, indigenous psychological approach merits some attention. It points out, among other important issues, that people are recognized as interactive and proactive agents of their own actions rather than instinctive and reactive. How an individual is construed, then, has an important affect on how he/she looks to the causal relationship between what and how he/she communicates and what as a consequence takes place interpersonally.

The Western theories of communication competence and the related concepts are based on the assumption that an individual is the agent of social phenomena. People judge human activity in terms of purposes, motives, acts of will, decisions, doubts, hesitations, thoughts, hopes, fears, and desires. Human consciousness, agency, meaning, and goals are considered central explanatory constructs. It is the individual who is capable of and responsible for accurately observing and interpreting his/her as well as others' communicative behavior, and modifying them, if necessary, to reach personal and relational goals.

In this mode of thinking the individual is considered to be the architect of order and coherence through personal control and mastery (Kim, 1999, 20). In this view an individual's behavior based upon his/her internal characteristics is the causal agent of an observed environmental change, including human relationships around him/her. The vocabulary and grammar of the English language reflect this phenomenological mode: A person "builds," "maintains," "develops," "repairs," and "breaks up" a relationship. Everything that happens to the relationship is a direct consequence of the actions of those involved in it. This internal locus of control has been regarded as more desirable than external locus of control in the West.

In a culture where relationality (i.e., being a part, belonging, and improving the fit between what one does and what is expected) is valued, a human is not considered to be a direct agent responsible for social phenomena. The Asian self is construed as "a connected, fluid, flexible, committed being who is bound to others," as opposed to "a bounded, coherent, stable, autonomous, free entity" (Markus & Kitayama, 1998). Not having a solid and universal pattern of behavior that is applicable to and practical across the social situations is valued as merit rather than a deficiency in such cultures.

Since the self is experienced as interdependent with others, hence social structures and interpersonal frameworks and contexts provide idiosyncratic meanings and requirements, a person must carefully sense and feel the patterns of behavior appropriate in the given context. Such situational knowledge and adequate behavioral repertory necessary in a wide range of situations, coupled with the person's sensitivity to situational elements and flexibility, are difficult to obtain. A person must acquire through trial-and-error processes effective and appropriate communication skills, i.e., communication competence. Markus and Kitayama (1998) state that an appropriate, authentic, and mature personality is developed by being finely attuned to the expectations of others. It is a painstakingly long process, and thus people in Japan often use the word "naru" (being or becoming) in describing the improvement of virtually all human abilities including walking, running, swimming, riding a bicycle, and communicating. Japan has been characterized as a "being culture" as opposed to a "doing culture" that predominates much of the West.

The importance of contextual knowledge and sensitivity in Japanese interpersonal communication has been pointed out by several Japanese writers (e.g., Befu, 1989; Hamaguchi, 1983, 1990). In arguing the need for developing culture specific concepts for research on Japanese people's social practices, Hamaguchi (1983) coined the term kanjin-shugi (interpersonalism) to characterize the Japanese people's notion of self that varies rather dramatically from situation to situation. They are expected to feel the mood or air of each interpersonal situation, and improvise appropriate social behaviors depending upon the reading of the contextual features. Given such a norm, using straightforward, frank and consistent relational tactics across the situations, ability valued in the Western theory of communication competence, would be labeled as "lacking sensitivity and delicacy."

"Assertiveness" is a good example to illustrate how divergent meanings and values are associated with it, depending upon the way self is construed. Assertive people stand up for their rights, expressing freely their thoughts, feelings, and beliefs directly and honestly (Lange & Jakubowski, 1976). These attributes are regarded as elements of interpersonal competence, at least by people who view themselves as independent. These people are described as adventurous, confident, and willing or even eager to accept change in their environment, typical of the "doing" mode.

Nonassertive people, on the other hand, are characterized as inhibited, submissive, self-deprecating, self-denying, and conforming, which all contribute to the perception of communication incompetence. These people would be regarded in the independent culture as incapable of devising, deciding on, and actually implementing proper actions when necessary. Given the "being" mode, however, such non-assertive, timid, and tentative behavior would be regarded as a sign of sensitivity toward others as well as the overall social context. Kim (1999) argues that it would be imprudent to generalize the description of the high vs. low argumentative individuals (based on studies using subjects from the U.S.) to people belonging to other cultures. The outcome and perceptions of assertiveness are mostly based on research involving predominantly Anglo-Saxon subjects in the United States whose self-identity is autonomous and bounded.

People in culture where careful and often times subtle social behavior based on contextual knowledge and sensitivity is important, would necessarily be reserved and tentative in their interpersonal behavior. While such behavior may be labeled "incompetent" or "socially deficient," in an individualist society, it would help the person in a collectivist culture establish and maintain harmony with others, thus contributing to the perception of communication competence. Descriptions and evaluations associated with assertiveness in one culture do not apply to another where people construe themselves in a different manner. The single Western view of the self that sees sensitivity to social contexts as a deficit is an ethnocentric preoccupation.

IV. METHODOLOGICAL CONCERNS AND FUTURE DIRECTIONS FOR NON-WESTERN THEORIES OF COMMUNICATION COMPETENCE

Given the fundamental psychological differences such as ontological orientations and epistemological/phenomenological views between people in different cultures (e.g., Japanese and U.S. Americans), research tools necessarily need to be modified in examining the nature and effects of people's social behavior. Cross-cultural psychology, a fairly new discipline in social science, carries out research to verify the universality of existing theories. The features of the discipline illustrate the nature and complexity of, and possible contribution it can make to the general understanding of people's communicative behavior. The research takes into account cultural variables as possible causes of influence on people's behavior. This approach is classified either as an etic or emic approach. The former approach aims to test and verify the universality of psychological theories that have been developed in one culture, i.e., the West.

Kim et al. (2000) observe that there has been an implicit assumption that one's own culture is a standard by which other cultures are judged. Each culture, however, should be understood from its own frame of reference: from its ecological, historical, and cultural context. This approach represents an emic approach in psychology. Although existing psychological theories and concepts are assumed to be objective, value free, and universal, in reality they are deeply enmeshed with Euro-American values that champion rational, liberal, individualistic ideals. As such they can be characterized as imposed etics or pseudoetics, and not true universals (pp. 63–64).

Befu (1989), a Japanese anthropologist, arguing about the distinction between and characteristics of etic and emic analyses in cross-cultural research, states that "an etic analysis merely provides a tool by which one can arrive at emic understanding. By itself, etic analysis is not the objective or goal in learning about other societies or in cross-cultural research" (p. 327). This claim readily applies to the inquiry into people's communicative behavior. In order to understand the functioning of a communication tactic such as self-disclosure, the researcher needs to analyze its relation to other social attributes which function within the culture–the individual self-orientation, social structure, historical context, etc. It is only by seeing the social behavior from such a holistic perspective, that we can hope to understand the Japanese interpersonal communication in the emic sense. Thus, analysis of a given unit or event is meaningful only if it is done in the context of the larger system of which it is a part, for it is the larger system which gives the unit its peculiar shape and texture. When a given unit is surgically removed from the organic whole of which it is an integral and systemic part, as is often done for the purposes of cross-cultural comparison, it ceases to be a meaningful unit (Befu, 1989, pp. 327–8).

If research were to be conducted on Japanese people's perceptions of communication competence, using the concept of self-disclosure, for example, much background research on social and psychological aspects surrounding the communication behavior needs to be done prior to cross-cultural comparisons. The Japanese people's global as well as idiosyncratic and contextual objectives concerning the communication behavior, their perceptions of situational constraints, and also historical trends that influence their perceptions of self-disclosure must be all carefully studied.

The method of survey, typically a questionnaire, that has been traditionally used in cross-cultural comparisons of communication behavior also needs to be carefully re-considered. Questionnaires have often been administered to very homogeneous and most easily accessible populations, i.e., college students. We can never ask exactly the same questions no matter how carefully the questionnaire is developed and translated into another language. Befu (1989) argues that among many cross-cultural researchers there is a strong belief that the problem of cultural uniqueness as manifested in emic concepts can be overcome by improving translation.

Gudykunst and Ting-Toomey (1988) argue that sufficient equivalence must be established across cultures when conducting cross-cultural research. Equivalence refers to: 1 functional equivalence (goals and objectives that a communication strategy is expected to accomplish), 2 conceptual equivalence (meaning attached to specific strategies), 3 linguistic equivalence (translation of survey and interview questions), 4 metric equivalence, and

5 sample equivalence. An important question is whether the unit of analysis (an individual) in cross-cultural communication research is equivalent. Instead of arguing the validity of a questionnaire, and reliability of the items included in it, for example, we must be concerned about whether an individual is the best source to provide the information necessary.

While in Western social science the individual is assumed to be the basic building block of the society, an individual with an interdependent self-construal might not be the equivalent in non-Western culture. Hamaguchi (1977) argues that the analysis of social phenomena in Japan should not start from the concept of the individual, but instead should begin with relationships between persons because that is how the Japanese conceptualize social phenomena. He claims it is not a scientific (etic) tool of analysis, but an ethnocentric, Western, emic concept misapplied to other cultures as if it were an etic concept.

A person with an interdependent construal of self is expected to view a self-in-relation to others as an important guide for his/her behavior. Striving for one's own goals, constructing and maintaining internal locus of control, and expressing one's self directly are important skills for a person with an independent self construal. For a person with an interdependent self construal, on the other hand, "fitting in" with the group, acting in an appropriate fashion, and expressing oneself indirectly are some of the skills expected to contribute to communication competence.

Given these divergent expectations, research on the nature of interpersonal communication competence for an interdependent individual must begin with a different set of axioms. To illustrate, different aspects of the interdependent person are expected to guide his/her behavior depending on the situation. Having a wide array of social behaviors, coupled with flexibility, then would be an important component of interpersonal competence.

Direct observation of the individual's behavior in multiple situations may be an appropriate alternative to a questionnaire containing a single hypothetical situation and relying on the use of language and its meaning (that is, verbal testimony of informants) as data to deal with. Research instruments need to be contextualized and episodic, and they should allow individuals to provide their own expertise (Kim, et al, 2000, p. 71).

Some evidence has been reported that indicates Japanese people's contextual adjustment of social behavior (Cousins, 1989). Depending on the people with whom they interact (e.g., ingroups or outgroups, people of different or the same age, sex, occupation, etc.), the degrees to which their interdependent and independent self-construals guide their behavior vary. A number of writers (e.g., Gudykunst, Guzley, & Ota, 1993; Markus & Kitayama, 1991) emphasize that everyone, regardless of the culture, has both an independent and interdependent construal of the self. It is a matter of which self-construal predominates, and what social elements determine the degree to which it influences one's behavior.

Another methodological concern in social sciences is a question of consistency between a response to the questionnaire and actual behavior in the given context. A gap, if any, between a perception of what one says he/she would do in a situation and what the person actually ends up doing, may be larger for an interdependent individual. Numerous aspects such as situational factors, other people participating in the situation, and the person's reading of them are intertwined with one another in a complex manner. Such complexity renders a pencil-and-paper survey method inadequate and inappropriate.

Still another methodological issue in cross-cultural research in communication competence is the source of information, i.e., the participants in the survey. College students have been used in literally thousands of studies in social sciences as informants due to their easy access and homogeneity. Limited experience in actual social situations may have affected the content of their responses, thus rendering the findings unrepresentative of the respective cultures. Use of non-student data, preferably comparative analyses between different groups of subjects, and longitudinal survey of the same subjects may provide interesting and important information on people's communication behavior in the non-Western culture.

Befu (1989) asserts that both emic and etic approaches to inquiries into the nature and effects of Japanese social practices and customs can yield significant results. If used properly, and in an integrative manner, they would help deepen our understanding of Japan as well as contribute to building social theory. Japan is one Asian culture that has been studied intensively. Close examinations of how well Western theories can account for the people's social behavior and how they fail to do so will help social scientists understand the unique power and limitations of cross-cultural research.

V. CONCLUSION

Although the notion of communication competence, as is currently conceptualized by Western researchers, may be meaningful and useful to the people in U.S. culture, how or even whether it is practiced at all in non-Western cultures is an important question. Imposing a set of notions accepted in one culture to another, is likely to cause serious problems. While there is a desperate need for a theoretically meaningful set of knowledge and practical skills to help Japanese become competent communicators, research findings in communication so far have been generally biased toward Western, and primarily U.S. cultural values. The methods of research, mostly quantitative and hypothetico-deductive, have been borrowed from the Western academic tradition.

Asian constructs such as amae (Japanese concept that describes dependence upon another's benevolence), and woori (an inclusive group in Korea) reflect the relational nature of human existence. Using them in theory building may free the behavioral sciences from their current over-reliance on Western constructs such as actor, ego, and self rooted in individualism (Ho, 1998, pp. 99–100). A relational analysis requires consideration of how relationships are culturally defined before attempting to interpret the behavior of individuals. It entails making explicit the normative expectations and behavioral rules implicit in social relations. The strategic units of analysis are not the individual or the situation alone but person-in-relations (focusing on a person in different relational contexts) and persons-in-relation (focusing on persons interacting within a relational context).

More holistic analysis of Japanese interpersonal communication is necessary by taking into accounts such factors as contexts within which the communication takes place. Overall social, political, and economic surrounds of the Japanese society that influence people's perceptions of norms, rules and competence must be taken into account for a more meaningful and useful approach to theorizing interpersonal communication competence for Japanese.

REFERENCES

Altman, I., & Taylor, D. (1973). *Social penetration processes.* New York: Holt, Reinhart, and Winston.

Barnlund, D. (1975). *The public and private self in Japan and the United States.* Tokyo: Simul Press.

Barnlund, D. (1989). *Communication styles of Japanese and Americans.* Belmont, CA: Wadsworth.

Barnlund, D., & Yoshioka, M. (1990). Apologies: Japanese and American styles. *International Journal of Intercultural Relations, 14,* 193–205.

Befu. H. (1989). The emic-etic distinction and its significance for Japanese studies. In Y. Sugimoto & R. E. Mouer (Eds.), *Constructs for understanding Japan* (pp. 323–343). London: Kegan Paul International.

Cousins, S. D. (1989). Culture and self-perception in Japan and the United States. *Journal of Personality and Social Psychology, 56,* 124–131.

Cozby, P. C. (1973). Self-disclosure: A literature review. *Psychological Bulletin, 79,* 73–91.

Doi, T. (1971). *Amae no kozo* (The anatomy of dependence). Tokyo: Koubundo.

Engebretson, D., & Fullmer, D. (1970). Cross-cultural differences in territoriality; Interaction differences of native Japanese, Hawaii Japanese, and American Caucasians. *Journal of Cross-Cultural Psychology, 1,* 261–269.

Gudykunst, W. B. (1993). Approaches to the study of communication in Japan and the United States. In W. B. Gudykunst (Ed.), *Communication in Japan and the United States* (pp. 18–50). Albany, NY: SUNY Press.

Gudykunst, W. B., Guzley, R.M., & Ota, H. (1993). Issues for future research on communication in Japan and the United States. In W. B. Gudykunst (Ed.), *Communication in Japan and the United States* (pp. 291–322). Albany, NY: SUNY Press.

Gudykunst, W. B., & Nishida, T. (1993). Interpersonal and intergroup communication in Japan and the United States. In W. B. Gudykunst (Ed.), *Communication in Japan and the United States.* Albany, NY: SUNY Press.

Gudykunst, W. B., & Nishida, T. (1994). *Bridging Japanese/North American differences.* Thousand Oaks, CA: Sage.

Gudykunst, W. B., & Ting-Toomey, S. (1988). *Culture and interpersonal communication.* Newbury Park, CA: Sage.

Hall, E. T. (1976). *Beyond culture.* New York: Doubleday.

Hamaguchi, E. (1977). *Nihonjin rashisa no saihakken* (Rediscovering the essence of Japan). Tokyo: Nihon Keizan Shinbunsha.

Hamaguchi, E. (1983). *Kanjin-shugi no shakai Nihon* (Japan, society of contextual men). Tokyo: Touyou Keizai.

Hamaguchi, E. (1990). *Nihon kenkyu no aratanaru paradaimu* (A new paradigm for Japanese studies). In T. Umehara (Ed.), Nihon towa nan nano ka (What is Japan?). Tokyo: NHK Books.

Heider, F. (1958). *The psychology of interpersonal relations.* New York: John Wiley.

Hirokawa, R., & Miyahara, A. (1986). A comparison of influence strategies utilized by managers in American and Japanese organizations. *Communication Quarterly, 34,* 250–265.

Ho, D. Y. (1998). Indigenous psychologies: Asian perspectives. *Journal of Cross-Cultural Psychology, 29,* 88–103.

Kim, M. (May 1999). Non-Western perspectives on human communication: Implications for theory. Paper presented at the Annual Conference of the International Communication Association, San Francisco, CA.

Kim, M., Hunter, J. E., Miyahara, A., Horvath, A. M., Bresnahan, M., & Yoon, H. (1996). Individual vs. culture-level dimensions of individualism and collectivism; Effects on preferred conversational styles. *Communication Monographs, 63,* 29–49.

Kim, U., Park, Y., & Park, D. (2000). The challenge of cross-cultural psychology: The role of the indigenous psychologies. *Journal of Cross-Cultural Psychology, 31,* 63–75.

Kimura, B. (1989). *Hito to hito no aida* (Between people). Tokyo: Koubunsha.

Klopf, D. W. (1984). Cross-cultural apprehension research: A summary of Pacific Basin studies. In J. A. Daly & J. C. McCroskey (Eds.), *Avoiding communication: Shyness, reticence, and communication apprehension.* Beverly Hills, CA: Sage.

Lange, A., & Jakubowski, P. (1976). *Responsible assertive behavior.* Champaign, IL: Research Press.

Markus, H. R., & Kitayama, S. (1991). Culture and the self: Implications for cognition, emotion, and motivation. *Psychological Review, 98,* 224–253.

Markus, H. R., & Kitayama, S. (1998). The cultural psychology of personality. *Journal of Cross-Cultural Psychology, 29,* 63–87.

Miyanaga, K. (1991). *The creative edge: Individualism in Japan.* New Brunswick, NJ: Transaction.

Morrison, J. (1972). The absence of a rhetorical tradition in Japanese culture. *Western Speech, 36,* 89–102.

Mushakoji, K. (1976). The cultural premises of Japanese diplomacy. In Japan Center for International Exchange (Ed.), *The silent power: Japan's identity and world role.* Tokyo: Simul Press.

Neulip, J., & Hazelton, V. (1985). A cross-cultural comparison of Japanese and American persuasive strategy selection. *International Journal of Intercultural Relations, 9,* 389–404.

Neustupny, J. V. (1987). *Communicating with the Japanese.* Tokyo: Japan Times.

Okabe, K. (1987). Indirect speech acts of the Japanese. In D. L. Kincaid (Ed.), *Communication theory: Eastern and Western perspectives.* San Diego, CA: Academic Press.

Singelis, T. M. (2000). Some thoughts on the future of cross-cultural social psychology. *Journal of Cross-Cultural Psychology, 31,* 76–91.

Spitzberg, B., & Cupach, W. (1984). *Interpersonal communication competence.* Beverly Hills, CA: Sage.

Sussman, N., & Rosenfeld, H. (1982). Influence of culture, language, and sex on conversational distance. *Journal of Personality and Social Psychology, 42,* 66–74.

Takai, J., & Ota, H. (1994). Assessing Japanese interpersonal communication competence. *The Japanese Journal of Experimental Social Psychology, 33,* 224–236.

Ting-Toomey, S. (1985). Toward a theory of conflict and culture. In W. B. Gudykunst, L. P. Stewart, & S. Ting-Toomey (Eds.), *Communication, culture, and organizational processes.* Beverly Hills, CA: Sage.

Triandis, H. C. (1994). *Culture and social behavior.* New York, McGraw-Hill.

Triandis, H. C., Bontempo, R., Villareal, M., Asai, M., & Lucca, N. (1988). Individualism-collectivism: Cross-cultural perspectives on self-ingroup relationships. *Journal of Personality and Social Psychology, 54,* 323–338.

Tsujimura, A. (1982). Some characteristics of
the Japanese way of communication. In D. L.
Kincaid (Ed.), *Communication theory: Eastern
and Western perspectives* (pp. 115–126).
San Diego, CA: Academic Press.

Akira Miyahara is associated with Seinan
Gakuin University in Japan.

Reading 3.8

Differences in the Perception of Face

Chinese Mien-Tzu *and Japanese* Metsu[1]

KIYOKO SUEDO

Face is the public self-image that people want to present within a given social framework. Goffman (1967) defines face as "an image of self delineated in terms of approved social attributes" (p. 5). Social interactions are based on facework, or the interpersonal work one does to save one's own and the other's face. Even when an interlocutor loses face, we not only defend our own face but also protects others' face, helping them by using facework (Goffman, 1955, 1959, 1967). Brown and Levinson (1978) further developed

Goffman's notion of face and presented two additional foci. One, *positive face,* is the basic claim over the projected self-image to be approved by others. The other, *negative face,* is the basic claim to territories, personal reserves, and rights to nondistraction.

Although face is considered a universal construct in human interaction, Ting-Toomey (1988) argues that face needs and facework depend on cultural contexts. Focusing on each, she presents a cross-cultural analysis of facework in resolving conflicts within the

Reprinted with permission from *World Communication*, Vol. 24, No. 1, pp. 23–31.

Triandis's (1988) individualistic versus collectivistic culture dimension. According to Ting-Toomey (1988), in individualistic cultures such as the United States, where one tries to keep one's personal rights or autonomy, negative-face needs are greater than positive-face needs. In collectivistic cultures such as Asian countries, however, where one tries to gain approval of others, positive-face needs are greater than negative-face needs. Thus, in resolving conflicts, people in individualistic cultures are more likely to engage in direct communication styles, while people in collectivistic cultures are more likely to engage in indirect communication styles. Sueda and Wiseman (1992) conducted a comparative study of communicative strategies in an embarrassing situation that supported the Ting-Toomey's theory.

A review of the literature suggests that there are cultural differences in the orientation of positive or negative face. However, discussing face needs only within the individualistic versus collectivistic culture dimension may be too simplistic; the degree of positive-face needs may differ in different countries with collectivistic culture. Likewise, within the same individualistic culture, the degree of negative-face Chinese and Japanese share the same Chinese characters (*kanji*), to refer to one category of face *mien-tzu*[2] or *mentsu,* there may be construct differences in their perception.

In this study, Chinese and Japanese were targeted for comparison for two reasons. First, both cultures are often used as examples of collectivistic cultures, and similarities between the two cultures are more frequently discussed than differences. The two cultures are also likely to be considered as "relatives" within this simplistic framework. Second, although some researchers study differences in the perception between Chinese *mien-tzu* and Japanese *mentsu* (e.g., Lin, 1992; Mori, 1989; Nakajima, 1990), the research was not empirical. Thus the purpose of this study is two-fold:

to explore differences in the perception between Chinese *mien-tzu* and Japanese *mentsu;* and to identify how such differences in the perception affect communication between people from the two cultures.

MIEN-TZU AND *MENTSU*

The concept of face is Chinese in origin[3] and includes two aspects, *lien* and *mien-tzu. Lien* represents the confidence of society in the integrity of the ego's moral character while *mien-tzu* represents a reputation achieved through success and ostentation (Bond & Hwang, 1986). *Mien-tzu* and *lien* are different in the sense that the former needs an audience for the loss and the latter does not (Bond & Lee, 1981). That is, *mien-tzu* can be won or lost only when the audience approves or denies. *Lien* can be lost without having an audience present. This study focuses on the former aspect, *mien-tzu,* as it always derives from social interactions (Ho, 1976).

The word, *mien-tzu,* is frequently used in the Chinese language. Research suggests that it plays an important role in explaining Chinese communication styles and the rules for establishing interpersonal relationships (Bond & Hwang, 1986; Ding, 1988; Lin, 1992; Hu & Grove, 1991; Kong, 1988; Nakajima, 1990; Uchiyama, 1991; Yang, 1986). According to Ding (1988), Chinese people value *mien-tzu* no matter how rich or poor or high or low in status one is. Saving *mien-tzu* is important not only for satisfying oneself, but also for respecting others' *mien-tzu* in return. That is, saving *mien-tzu* is necessary for smooth interpersonal relationships in China. Kong (1988) states that one's *mien-tzu* is also important for all members of the clan and family that one belongs to.

Historical analyses of the Chinese concept of *mien-tzu* explain how it differs from the Japanese *samurai* or warriors' honor or Western European knights' honor. In Japan and Western Europe, honor is not centered around societal fame but around an individual's dignity under feudal systems. However, in China, since 200 B.C., society has not been governed by soldiers but by civilians, and their sense of honor was different from Japan's and Western Europe's. Chinese society did not put as high a value on a warrior's honor as Japanese society did, but rather on individual and family reputation.

With the increase of interaction with the Chinese, the word *mien-tzu* was introduced to Japan and read as *mentsu*. According to Soeda (1993), *mentsu* was not as serious as warriors' honor, for which warriors could die. Because *mentsu* is but one criterion for an individual's reputation in the community in daily life, Soeda describes it as "little honor" and warriors' honor as "big honor." *Mentsu* or "little honor" became prevalent with the decline of the warrior class.

Uchiyama (1991) presents a noteworthy difference in the perception between *mien-tzu* and *mentsu*. He suggest that Chinese *mien-tzu* becomes crucial where it concerns material profits or benefits, while the Japanese *mentsu* is not as concerned about material profits. This may be related with the Chinese way of establishing and keeping interpersonal relationships. Chinese people build a close-knit relationship within the same extended family, clan, or neighborhood. This human network is called *guanxi* (connection). People try to get economic or social resources through the informal social structure of *guanxi* rather than through the formal economic structure (Matsudo, 1989; Nakajima, 1990; Sonoda, 1991a). The greater the reputation one or one's family has, the greater the likelihood that one will succeed in the competition for limited resources. Thus, *mien-tzu* is a reputation gained by success that also assures one's future privilege.

Another difference is that while Chinese *mien-tzu* evaluates the individual, Japanese *mentsu* evaluates not only the individual but also the entire group or community to which the individual belongs (Inoue, 1977), Kindaichi (cited in Inoue, 1977) illustrates this by using one episode of *Konjiklyasha* (The Usurer), a Japanese literary work written by Ozaki (1961).[4] In the episode, the hero, *Kanichi* proposes to *Miya* not by stating how much he loves her. Instead, he tried to persuade her by mentioning that not only himself but also his friends at school will lose *mentsu* if she does not accept his proposal, because his friends also wish their marriage and have encouraged him. In this context, saving *mentsu* seems to be the hero's purpose and even supercedes his own will to marry *Miya*. This shows that one's value is not only attained by membership in a group but also by the society's evaluation of that group.

A review of the literature examining the different historical, social, and economic circumstances implies that there may exist qualitative differences in the perception between Chinese *mien-tzu* and Japanese *mentsu*.

METHODOLOGY

This study explores qualitative differences in the perception between *mien-tzu* and *mentsu*. The author examined the previous qualitative research concerning the differences in the perception of face between North Americans and Japanese (Cole, 1989; Imahori & Cupach, 1994), and on cultural conflicts between Japanese and Chinese in the business setting (Sonoda, 1994). Noting that previous research contributed either to tackling the points which a quantitative study might easily miss, or to drawing hypotheses for further study, the author conducted a series of in-depth interviews from December, 1992, to January, 1994.

Most of the interviewees belong to educational organizations. The interviewees consisted of (1) 17 Japanese who lived in the People's Republic of China;[5] (2) 11 Chinese from the People's Republic of China living in Japan;[6] (3) two Japanese who have been teaching Chinese students for over ten years, and (4) an American living in Japan who has lived in the People's Republic of China. All interviews were conducted in Japanese, except for the American interview which was conducted in English. The original set of interviewees consisted of categories 1 and 2. However, as the Chinese language ability of some participants in category 1 was limited, their interpersonal relationship with Chinese people may have remained superficial in nature. Thus, the participants in category 3 were added as interviewees. The American was added because the author considered him to be an objective observer of both Chinese and Japanese cultural aspects.

The Japanese interviewees consisted of 9 females and 10 males, with ages ranging from 21 to 52 ($\overline{X}$ = 42.1). The length of stay in China of category 1 Japanese ranged from six months to three years ($\overline{X}$ = 11 months). The Chinese interviewees consist of five females and six males, with ages ranging from 27 to 34 ($\overline{X}$ = 31.6). Except for one from Shanghai, their home cities were northern regions: three from Dalian, three from Beijing, two from Shenyang, one from Harbin, and one from Xi'an. One Japanese teacher in Category 2 was 46 years old, while the other's age was not available. The average years of teaching Japanese was 16 1/2 years. The American was a 32-year-old male who studied in Guilin for one year as an exchange student. Excluding interviewees' biographical data, the interview questions involved the following four points in interacting with Chinese/Japanese:

1. incidents where they felt their *mentsu/mien-tzu* was hurt;
2. incidents where they felt they hurt the other *mien-tzu/mentsu*;
3. incidents where they felt the other party had a strong sense of *mien-tzu/mentsu*; and
4. tips not to hurt the other's *mien-tzu/mentsu*.

The author tried to allow flexibility by being responsive and asking about new items as they came up. The time spent in each interview was from one to three hours; the average was 1.8 hours. Each interview was tape recorded and transcribed.

The data were analyzed via *KJ method* (Kawakita, 1967, 1970). This analytical method goes along with the inductive nature of this study. Every item from the interview was written down on one card each. The data from the Chinese participants were gathered in a pile and separated from the pile of the data from Japanese participants. Within each pile, similar cards were gathered and placed in small groups, and a name was given that best described the feature of each group. This process was repeated until the data were divided into several groups.

RESULTS

The first part of this section reports the characteristics of Chinese *mien-tzu* identified by both Japanese and Chinese interviewees. The second part reports the characteristics of Japanese *mentsu* identified by both Japanese and Chinese interviewees.

Finding 1: The Chinese perception of *mien-tzu* concerns economic ability or ostentation for economic ability.

This is illustrated by the Chinese tendency to prepare gorgeous gifts for their relatives or close friends. The first Japanese interviewee (J1) noted:

J1: Some of them even ask for a loan from their friends in order to buy many fancy gifts for their relatives and family members.

A parallel comment was made by the first Chinese interviewee (C1):

C1: Just a token of our feeling does not work. The important thing is how expensive and gorgeous the souvenirs are. You cannot show your feeling with inexpensive gifts, and it is bad for your *mien-tzu*.

This finding is also illustrated in the way of socialization:

J1: Chinese try to make themselves look rich. It does not matter who is the host or hostess. When I was in graduate school, my Chinese classmates never let me pay when we ate out together.

J2: When I happened to meet my students in the bus, they never let me pay for the bus. I said to them, "In Japan, students never pay for their teachers." Then they said, "We are in China."

Again, there are parallel comments.

C1: We prepare many dishes for our guests. If our guests finish all we served, we are embarrassed wondering if we served too little or if we were thought to be stingy.

C2: Japanese friends hardly ever offer anybody their cigarettes. We never forget to offer ours. Also, whenever I go out to eat with Japanese friends, they go Dutch and collect money in front of the cashier. I am very embarrassed by that. In China, somebody would pay first and split the bill later, or somebody else would pay next time.

When Chinese interviewees feel that, as Chinese, they are viewed as "poor" by Japanese, they feel their *mien-tzu* is hurt.

C3: A Chinese friend of mine is hated by other Chinese friends because she is tight with money and proves our "being poor" to our Japanese teacher by saying "Living in Tokyo costs a lot."

C1: Sometimes a women's organization in our community holds a bazaar. But Chinese generally hate second-hand clothes.

Finding 2: Chinese *mien-tzu* concerns social evaluation of one's competence.

The Chinese are trained from childhood to save one's own and family's *mien-tzu* by being competent.

J2: In China, it is very interesting that primary school students always wear a red scarf. It seems that wearing a red scarf means "good students."

C3: There is a system called *Shao Nian Xian Feng Dui*[7] in primary school in China. "Good students" can enter *Shao Nian Xian Feng Dui* and are given a red scarf. Parents are proud of their children if their children are given a red scarf early, while it is detrimental to their *mien-tzu* if their children are never given a red scarf.

Entering a university assures the Chinese a first step to being an elite, and passing or failing in the entrance examination is crucial to their *mien-tzu*.

C1: A friend of mine finally passed a university entrance examination this year. She did not let me know that she went to an evening adult school until then, because those who enter a technical school or vocational school could not make high enough scores to go to a university.

C4: In China, if you cannot go to a university, you are considered "no good." You cannot enter a good company.

C5: Once they enter a university, Chinese consider themselves smart. They even think that they do not need to study hard. If they study but do poorly on the exams, they are so embarrassed, but they do not blame themselves but somebody else.

For the Chinese, nobody should point out others' "incompetency" in public.

J3: When I taught Japanese language, one student whispered in Japanese, "I do not understand." Thus, I explained for him once more. When the class was over, I asked him, "Do you understand now?" He replied bluntly, "Of course, that was a simple thing." I was a little upset.

C5: I do not mind being scolded by a teacher personally but I am terribly embarrassed when I am scolded in public.

Nothing in China is considered as a joke if it concerns "incompetency." This is illustrated in the comments made by the American (A1) and the third Chinese interviewee.

A1: When I was teaching English, I had my Chinese students do role-plays. I assigned a role to one of my close friends because I expected her to give an appropriate response, but she did not. Then, I tried to tease her by saying, "You are a lazy student" in front of everyone. She took it seriously and would not speak to me for days.

C3: Many Japanese people have a stereotypical idea that all the Chinese people ride bikes. I cannot. One day in a seminar, when we introduced ourselves, one of my close Japanese friends tried to tease me and said something about my not being able to ride a bike. I know she was just trying to tease me, but I was really upset.

Finding 3: Chinese *mien-tzu* is especially crucial for relationships with relatives and close friends.

J1: One of my female Chinese students let her husband's brother and his friends stay in their small apartment for a month. She ruined her health because she had to study for school, take care of the guests and work part-time. She said that she had to do this because of her husband's *mien-tzu*.

C1: When our relatives visit us in Japan, our first priority is playing host to them. Otherwise, our parents would lose *mien-tzu*.

Finding 4: Studying abroad honors one's *mien-tzu*.

Just as with entering a university, studying abroad honors their *mien-tzu*, and the Chinese are patient in achieving their goals.

C4: Everybody envies you if you get a chance to study abroad. Studying abroad means you have ability, money or connections. Thus, you are expected to return to China with either a degree, enough money to start a business, or a good job.

C6: Some of my Chinese friends tolerate their physical labor in Japan to get something. In China, there is a clear demarcation between a blue-color job and a white-color job. And they would be too embarrassed to take that kind of job at home.

Thus, some of them will not return to China if they have not achieved their goal.

J4: One of my male Chinese students visited China for the summer. He was so shocked to find his former colleagues being promoted to higher positions. After graduating from a good university, he worked for a foreign-affiliated company and had his own secretary and company car. But now, he earns little money in Japan working part-time at a restaurant. After returning to Japan, he was depressed and did not attend class for a while. He said, "Why did I come to Japan, anyway?"

C3: My husband was allowed a scholarship and studied in Osaka for two years. He could neither get a Master's degree nor could he save money, and he simply returned to China with empty hands. People surrounding us criticized him and asked him, "Why did you come back to China?"

Finding 5: Chinese are reluctant to apologize or speak highly of others because doing so is detrimental to their own *mien-tzu*.

First, they never admit "they cannot do" something.

J5: When I lived in a faculty apartment in China, I often poured hot water into the bath tub and the water stopped running when the bath tub was half full. I talked to the apartment manager but he tried to escape from being accused by joking. He never said, "I cannot help you."

Second, they never apologize.

C7: When quarrelling, we never apologize even if we realize that we are wrong. Apologies are detrimental to our *mien-tzu*.

C1: Chinese seldom make a compliment to others. Even when they do, they do so only on the surface. At heart, they never think highly of others. If you speak too highly of others, you will be thought less of for that.

C1: My Chinese friend and I received a Master's degree from the same department at the same time. She knows that I am now in a doctor's program, but she never congratulated me. She acts as if she chose not to go for a doctor's program by saying, "I got tired of school."

Finding 6: Everybody's *mien-tzu* should be respected.

The comments of a Japanese interviewee illustrate how every Chinese has equal rights to claim his/her *mien-tzu*.

J5: Whenever the janitor came to my room to clean and found me helping my students with their studies, she looked happy. That is because the only thing she had to do in such a case was to leave me the vacuum cleaner. I supposed that she did not enjoy her job

particularly, and I decided that I would clean my room myself and asked the apartment manager not to hand her my room key. Then I heard that she was very upset about my request and said, "That almost sounds like I did something wrong!"

Finding 7: The importance of another *mien-tzu* depends on whether or not others will bring them benefits.

J6: My Chinese friend who is in a doctor's program sometimes listens to my advice and sometimes not. When a matter is directly related to their immediate benefits, for example, when he is publishing his paper in an academic journal, he listens to me. But, for other things, for example, when I given him advice about his research methodology, he cannot see an immediate benefit and ignores my advice.

Japanese *Metsu*

Finding 8: Japanese *mentsu* focuses on one's own social status, as well as how others value their social status.

J7: One of my Chinese students asked me to find a part-time job for him, and I asked many people and finally found one for him. But he took a better offer than mine and rejected my offer. If he had been Japanese, he would have taken my offer and tried to save my face.

C7: My adviser was upset when I asked another professor for advice. It seems that he did not want anybody to think that he was not good enough.

C8: When I went out for a drink with my adviser, he started talking about my Japanese colleague. I did not mean to criticize him but I said honestly what I thought about his research. Then my adviser looked very upset and said, "You are not in a position to criticize him."

Finding 9: Japanese *mentsu* has a hierarchy.

In Japan the need to save one's own and the other's *mentsu* varies depending on one's relative social status.

C1: In Japan, when I make my superiors lose *mentsu,* I am considered a terrible person no matter how wrong they are. But if my superiors make me lose *mentsu,* they are not considered as terrible.

C9: As Japanese social structure is vertical, with Japanese, I should be more aware of the other's *mentsu* than with Chinese. As a matter of fact, I am very much concerned with saving my adviser's *mentsu.* I always think over how and what I say whenever I consult him.

Finding 10: Japanese *mentsu* concerns personal appearance.

C1: Comparing Japanese and Chinese, Chinese stick to academic achievements more than Japanese. But Japanese have a strong sense of *mentsu* about personal appearance. They are very much concerned about how nicely they are dressed, and they judge people by clothes, which is not the case with Chinese.

Finding 11: To interact with the Japanese smoothly, you have to preserve Japan *mentsu* by making compliments.

C1: One of the secrets to get along with Japanese is to make compliments. That way, you can save their *mentsu.*

Finding 12: Even if a joke concerns someone's incompetency, it may not necessarily be threatening to *mentsu.*

A1: Suppose I try to tease a Japanese student and say "you are a lazy student," the person and the entire class will laugh and let it pass. As they know I am teasing, my comment will not hurt the person's *mentsu.* For them, acting differently or becoming the center of people's attention is more uncomfortable than being teased.

ANALYSIS

Based on the interviews, *mien-tzu* and *mentsu* differ in terms of both perception and the potential such perceptual differences have for conflict.

Differences in the Perception

In reviewing the findings, several differences in the perception between Chinese *mien-tzu* and Japanese *mentsu* become clear. First, as Finding 6 indicates, everyone has equal rights to protect one's own *mien-tzu* in Chinese culture, which supports Ding's (1988) notion that Chinese *mien-tzu* does not concern one's social status. As J5's comment illustrates, the janitor was very upset because she thought that she was taken as having done something wrong. This is a dishonorable things for her and she needs to protect her own *mien-tzu.* On the other hand, as C1's comment under Finding 9 indicates, one's needs for saving *mien-tzu* depends on one's relative status in Japanese culture.

Second, from examining Findings 3 and 9, it appears that the importance of *mentsu* is crucial in Japanese vertical relationships. Chinese *mien-tzu,* however, is crucial between people of close relationship. The findings relate to Sonoda's (1991b) argument that Chinese *mien-tzu* is not of importance in a vertical relationship. When interacting with somebody of a higher status than oneself, one accepts the other's criticism or suggestion quite naturally; however, when interacting with somebody in the same class, status or group, one becomes very competitive and tried to save one's own *mien-tzu.*

Third, while Chinese *mien-tzu* concerns actual advantages and benefits, Japanese *mentsu* is not necessarily related to substantial advantages or benefits. For example, under a different interpretation, J5's comment under Finding 6 can also be classified under Finding 7 as it illustrates Uchiyama's (1991) notion that Chinese *mien-tzu* concerns actual advantages and benefits. In looking at the episode this way, the janitor was upset because she lost not only all the privileges by cleaning that particular room (for example, whenever the foreign residents in the apartment move or return to their own countries, she was allowed to keep whatever was left in the room), but also the privilege of being assigned to clean other rooms. Japanese *mentsu* is not necessarily related to profits. For example, as J7's comment under Finding 8 illustrates, the Japanese interviewee was upset because his Chinese student took another job although he had asked the Japanese interviewee to find him a job first. This situation was made worse in light of the fact that the offer was given by a professor who constantly helped the Chinese student. The Chinese student did not realize that by not accepting the job, he was harming the Japanese advisor's *mentsu*. He was more concerned with the benefits of the job. In another example of C7's comments, the Chinese student asked a second professor for advice, thinking it acceptable because his original advisor would not lose anything material by that request.

Fourth, the author asked the Chinese interviewees for an opinion about J7's comment under Finding 8. One answered, "It does not matter whom you ask first or which offer comes first. What matters is the importance of the relationship with the person who makes an offer." Another answered, "Generally, I think that Chinese go for better conditions no matter who offers the job or when the job is offered. We do not think it that bad to reject the offer of the person who we asked first." On this matter, there is a difference in the perception between Chinese *mien-tzu* and

Japanese *mentsu*. When Chinese are concerned about another's *mentsu*, they consider the importance of *guanxi*, or the relationship with others, as well as the benefits that the others may bring them. This is implied in C9's comment in Finding 9, which illustrates that the importance of one's own and the other's *mentsu* in Japanese society varies depending on one's relative social status. This comment also is related to Finding 7 in which the Chinese doctoral candidate seemed to believe his success in getting a doctor's degree depended on his relationship with his adviser. Thus, he may be strongly concerned about saving his adviser's *mentsu*.

Finally, while Chinese *mien-tzu* is strongly related to one's economic ability or capability, Japanese *mentsu* is related to one's social status and the other's concern for one's social status or *suji* (the proper way that things are done). As C7's comment under Finding 8 indicates, the adviser felt upset because it seemed to him that the Chinese student thought he was not a good enough advisor.

Based on this analysis, positive-face needs, or whether or not one's behavior is considered appropriate in one's social framework, is strong in Japanese society relative to Chinese society, while negative-face needs, or one's basic claim to territories, is strong in Chinese society relative to Japanese society.

Communication Conflicts

There are several cases where communication conflicts occur between people from the two cultures because of differences in the perception of *mien-tzu* and *mentsu*. First, the Chinese concept of *mien-tzu* seems to concern how one's reputation is affected by others when the interaction involves economic means or ability. If that is not recognized by Japanese, communication conflicts can occur. For example, as shown in C2's comment under Finding 1, a Chinese may feel embarrassed to follow the "go-Dutch" system of their Japanese friends.[8] In addition, as A1 and C3's observations under Finding 2 demonstrate, even a joke is never taken as a joke by the Chinese when the topic concerns one's lack of ability or when it is stated in public. Friendly insults between people who are close (Knapp, 1984) may make the Chinese feel uncomfortable or embarrassed.

Second, as Finding 5 indicates the reason why the Chinese are reluctant to say "I cannot" or "I do not know" or to apologize may be because they believe their doing so is very embarrassing. However, when the Japanese do not realize this, they may easily conclude that "Chinese people always make excuses or justify themselves" or that "Chinese never blame themselves." Thus, mutual understanding between the Chinese and Japanese may be hard to achieve.

Finally, those Chinese who study in Japan are often too embarrassed to return to China unless they acquire a college degree or save enough money to start a business at home. However, this Chinese attitude may make the Japanese in the academic field lose *mentsu* because it seems to them that these Chinese students in Japan do not necessarily like studying but use their degrees as a means of getting promoted at home. Thus, Chinese *mien-tzu* conflicts with Japanese *mentsu* needs.

FUTURE DIRECTIONS

The Chinese perception of *mien-tzu* may be related more to negative than positive face in the sense that the perception of *mien-tzu* is related to one's competence and economic ability. The Japanese perception of *mentsu* may be related more to positive than negative face in the sense that the perception of *mentsu* concerns how appropriate one's behavior is within one's social framework and how appropriately one is treated by others. This study demonstrates that the existing analysis

with the dichotomy of individualistic versus collectivistic cultures is not enough; it suggests great differences in values and perceptions within the Asian culture.

Recently, Japanese scholars (e.g., Okuda & Tajima, 1991; Sukigara & Suzuki, 1992) reported cultural conflicts between the Japanese people as hosts and foreign workers and students from Asian countries. Before interpreting these cultural conflicts as merely Japanese ethnocentrism or value differences, this study suggests the importance of realizing possible differences in the perception of words and concepts between Japanese and people from other Asian countries.

This study has several limitations. First, the People's Republic of China is a huge country. There are regional differences in customs (Lin, 1990) and the degree of economic development (Ohwada, 1989). Thus, there may be differences in value. Several Chinese interviewees noted a tendency among the Northern Chinese to value *mien-tzu* more highly when compared to Southern Chinese. Second, the Chinese interviewees had a cultural sophistication about the Japanese culture which may not represent the average Chinese, who does not know anything about Japanese culture. All of the regions where the Japanese interviewees stayed in the People's Republic of China were northern regions, so the experiences they had are limited in scope. Third, the Chinese interviewees were top elites at home,[9] and they may be quite different from the average Chinese. Fourth, there may be generational differences in value between younger and older Chinese or Japanese. Finally, as a researcher, the author tried to create a rapport with each interviewee. However, how much in-depth information was obtained depended on how much the interviewees were willing to disclose themselves. Future research is needed to understand the perception of Japanese *mentsu* with the people from other Asian counties.

NOTES

1. A portion of the data of this paper was published in Sueda (1993) in the *Annual Review of Sociology* No. 6.

2. Although there are several ways to describe the construct, *mien-tzu* seems to be closest to the sound in Chinese.

3. Researchers have found the origin of face in both Western and Eastern cultures to be Chinese (Ting-Toomey, et al., 1991).

4. Ozaki published "The Usurer" (*Konjikiyasha*) between 1897 and 1902 in a major newspaper, however reference is made to the one published in a book.

5. Japanese who had experienced staying in countries such as the Republic of China, Hong Kong, Malaysia, Singapore, and Indonesia are considered to have had contact with Chinese culture; however, this study is limited to those who stayed in the People's Republic of China.

6. This study focuses on Chinese people from the People's Republic of China. The author is aware of regional differences with the PRC and does not have any intention to generalize about the "Chinese" in this study.

7. Chinese children enter a primary school when they are six or seven and automatically become a member of *Shao Nian Xian Feng Dui,* which is a preparatory organization for the Communist Party. In the past, only "good" students were registered as members of the organization. Above *Shao Nian Xian Feng Dui,* there is another organization, *Gong Chan Zhu Yi Qing Nian Tuan* or *Gong Qing Tuan.* Only "good" young people over fifteen are allowed to enter this organization (Lin, 1990).

8. One of the Chinese interviewees noted, "Because of the present trend toward a free economy system in China, people have become more money-conscious. So, people may accept a "go-Dutch" system."

9. All of the Chinese interviewees had completed their undergraduate degrees at home before coming to Japan. Only 1.5% receive a college education in the PRC (Kojima, 1989); those who go to a university are elites at home.

REFERENCES

Bond, M. H., & Hwang, K. (1986). The social psychology of Chinese people. In M. H. Bond (Ed.), *The psychology of the Chinese people* (pp. 213–266). London, U.K.: Oxford University Press.

Bond, M. H., & Lee, P. W. H. (1981). Face-saving in Chinese culture: A discussion and experimental study of Hong Kong students. In A. Y. C. King & R. P. L. Lee (Eds.), *Social life and development in Hong Kong* (pp. 288–305). Hong Kong: The Chinese University Press.

Brown, P. & Levinson, S. (1978). Universals in language use: Politeness phenomena. In E. N. Goody (Ed.), *Questions and politeness: Strategies in social interaction* (pp. 56–289). New York, NY: Cambridge University Press.

Cole, M. (1989, November). A cross-cultural inquiry into the meaning of face in the Japanese and the United States cultures. Paper presented at the Speech Communication Association Convention, San Francisco, CA.

Ding, X. (1988). *Chuhgokujin no seikatsu tetsugaku—Tohhohsensho 11* [Chinese philosophy for everyday life—Tohhoh Library Vol. 11]. Tokyo, Japan: Tohhohsensho.

Goffman, E. (1955). On face-work: An analysis of ritual elements in social interaction. *Psychiatry 18,* 213–231.

Goffman, E. (1959). *The presentation of self in everyday life.* Garden City, NY: Doubleday & Co.

Goffman, E. (1967). *Interaction ritual: Essays on face-to-face behavior.* Chicago, IL: Aldine Publishing Co.

Ho, D. Y. F. (1976). On the concept of face. *American Journal of Sociology, 81,* 867–884.

Hu, W. & Grove, C. L. (1991). *Encountering the Chinese.* Yarmouth, ME: Intercultural Press.

Imahori, T., & Cupach, W. R. (1994). A cross-cultural comparison of the interpretation and management of face: U. S. Americans and Japanese responses to embarrassing predicaments. *International Journal of Intercultural Relations, 18,* 193–219.

Inoue, T. (1977). *"Sekentei" no kohzoh.* [The structure of the reference group]. Tokyo, Japan: NHK Books.

Kawakita, J. (1967). *Hassohhoh*. [The KJ method of analyzing the data]. Tokyo, Japan: Chuhohkohronsha.

Kawakita, J. (1970). *Zoku hassohhoh*. [The KJ method of analyzing the data, part II]. Tokyo, Japan: Chuhohkohronsha.

Knapp, M. (1984). *Interpersonal communication and human relationships*. Boston, MA: Allyn & Bacon.

Kojima, R. (1990). *Tohkei* [Statistical data]. In S. Uno, K. Nomura, K. Yamauchi, S. Kojima, M. Takeuchi, & T. Okabe (Eds.), *Iwanamikohza gendai chuhgoku 3-kan: Shizukana shakaihendoh* (pp. 361–389). Tokyo, Japan: Iwanamishoten.

Kong, J. (1988). *Chuhgokujin to tsukiau hoh* [Tips for interacting with Chinese people]. Tokyo, Japan: Gakuseisha.

Lin, S. (1990). *Ryuhgakusei ga kataru Chuhgoku no rimen* [The hidden side of China illustrated by a Chinese student]. Tokyo, Japan: Gakuseisha.

Lin, Y. (1992). *Waga chuhgokuronshoh* [An analysis of China and its people]. Tokyo, Japan: Kohga.

Matsudo, Y. (1989). *Kazoku no hendoh to shakai* [Changes in family and society]. In S. Uno, K. Nomura, K. Yamauchi, R. Kojima, M. Takeuchi, & T. Okabe (Eds.), *Iwanamikohza gendai chuhgoku 3-kan: Shizukana shakaihendoh* (pp. 87–111). Tokyo, Japan: Iwanamishoten.

Mori, M. (1989). *Chuhgoku bunka to Nihon bunka* [Chinese culture and Japanese culture]. Kyoto, Japan: Jinmonshoin.

Nakajima, M. (1990). *Chuhgokujin to Nihonjinkoko ga ohchigai* [Major differences between Chinese and Japanese]. Tokyo, Japan: Bungeishunjuh.

Ohwada, T. (1989). Kakudaisuru chuhgoku no keizai kakusa [Growing regional differences in economic development]. In S. Uno, K. Nomura, K. Yamauchi, R. Kojima, M. Takeuchi, & T. Okabe (Eds.), *Iwanamikohza gendai chuhgoku 3-kan: Shizukana shakaihendoh* (pp. 239–262). Tokyo, Japan: Iwanamishoten.

Okuda, M. & Tajima, J. (Eds.) (1991). *Ikebukuro no Ajiakei gaikokujin: Shakaigakuteki jitai hohkoku* [Foreigners from Asian countries in Ikebukuro: A report on a sociological empirical study]. Tokyo: Mekon.

Ozaki, K. (1961). Konjikiyasha. [The usurer]. In *Gendai nihonbungaku zenshuh* [Contemporary Japanese Literature] 4, (pp. 5–162). Tokyo, Japan: Chikumashoboh.

Soeda, Y. (1993). *Nihonbunka shiron*. [A preliminary analysis of Japanese culture]. Tokyo, Japan: Shinyohsha.

Sonoda, S. (1991a). *Kankeishugi toshiteno chuhgoku* [Chinese Guanxism]. In K. Nomura, M. Takahashi, & K. Tsuji (Eds.), Motto shiritai chuhgoku II: shakai-bunka hen 9 pp. 40–56). Tokyo, Japan: Kohbundoh.

Sonoda, S. (1991b). *Kotonaru shiten* [A different perspective]. In Ibunka to komyunikeshon 9 pp. 63–104). Tokyo, Japan: Nihonhyohronsha.

Sonoda, S. (1994). Growth process of Japanese ventures in China. *China Newsletter, 3*, 8–11.

Sueda, K. (1993). *Chuhgokujin ga motsu mentsu no gainen to nihonjin tono komyunikeshon* [Chinese perception of face (*mien-tzu*) and its influence on communicating with the Japanese]. The Annual Review of Sociology 6, 191–202.

Sueda, K. & Wiseman, R. (1992). Embarrassment remediation Japan and the United States. *International Journal of Intercultural Communication 16*, 159–173.

Sukigara, J. & Suzuki, A. (Eds.) (1992). *Anata wa Nihon ga suki desu ka* [Do you like Japan?: Voices from Chinese students in Japan]. Tokyo, Japan: Kohga.

Ting-Toomey, S. (1988). Intercultural conflict styles. In Y. Y. Kim & W. B. Gudykunst (Eds.), *Theories in Intercultural Communication* (pp. 213–235). Newbury Park, CA: Sage Publications.

Ting-Toomey, S. Trubisky, P., Bruschke, J., Nadamitsu, Y., Sakai, J., Nishida, T., & Baker, J. (1991, Feburary). Face and culture: Toward the development of a facework taxonomy. Paper presented at the Western States Communication Association, Phoenix, AZ.

Triandis, H. C. (1988). Collectivism vs. individualism: A reconceptualization of a basic concept in cross-cultural psychology. In C. Bagly & G. Verma (Eds.), *Personality, cognition and* values: *Cross-cultural perspectives of childhood & adolescence* (pp. 60–95). New York: NY: St. Martin's Press.

Uchiyama, K. (1991). *Chuhgokujin no seikatsu fuhkei—Tohhohsensho 3* [The lifestyle of the Chinese people—Tohhoh Library Vol. 3], Tokyo, Japan: Tohhohshoten.

Yang, K. (1986). Chinese personality and its change. In M. H. Bond (Ed.), *The psychology of the Chinese people* (pp. 106–160). London, U.K.: Oxford University Press.

Kiyoko Sueda is an assistant professor of communication at Hokusei Gakuen University in Japan.

PART IV

Living Together in Peace

How many people have been murdered because of identity—nationality, religion, ethnicity, gender, sexual orientation, and the like? There is no known answer to this question. It is one for speculation. How many people have been killed in wars fought over similar issues? How many millions? One important focus of intercultural communication is how we can live together in peace *and with justice* on this planet. This section is devoted to this issue.

The first two readings establish a rhetorical and philosophical basis, and the third, a legal basis. The final readings are reports of applications at attempts at peace-making in multicultural settings.

William J. Starosta has been a major contributor to the development of the academic study of intercultural communication. He was the founder of *The Howard Journal of Communications*. In the piece "On Intercultural Rhetoric" published in 1984, he argues that cultures promote their own existence because they allow their supporters to survive in a difficult world. His analysis is based on the assumption that rhetoric is divisive and that intercultural exchanges do not necessarily achieve mutual satisfaction.

Ram Adhar Mall is a professor of philosophy and president of the international Society of Intercultural Philosophy. In "The Concept of an Intercultural Philosophy," he discusses the issue of specific philosophies found in individual cultures and what would be required for universal philosophy.

In "Women's Rights as Human Rights— Rules, Realities and the Role of Culture: A Formula for Reform," Berta Esperanza Hernandez-Truyol, a law professor at St. John's University School of Law, argues that the institutionalized invisibility of women in the global sphere must be addressed if we are to transform the content and meaning of human rights.

The first of the three application readings is by Paul Wehr and John Paul Lederach, both recognized scholars in the field of mediation and peacemaking. In the United States, mediation is practiced as a process in which a neutral third party assists disputing parties in reaching a mutually agreeable solution. In "Mediating Conflict in Central America," the authors show how that process was adapted to local cultures in a Central American dispute. And in "Islamic Mediation Techniques for Middle East Conficts," George Irani discusses how the mediation process must be adapted to disputes there.

And, finally, Kjell Skyllstad in "Creating a Culture of Peace: The Performing Arts in Interethnic Negotiations," discusses projects involving music, dance, and peace.

Reading 4.1

On Intercultural Rhetoric

WILLIAM J. STAROSTA

This chapter is self-reflexive. It constitutes a dialectically secured position about the flaws that inhere in arguing too unremittingly a dialectically secured position. That this chapter could even have been written is a paradox—the subject of this analysis remains invisible to the untrained eye and, like an enthymeme or an iceberg, lies mainly beneath the surface of one's culture.

Richard Weaver, in an essay on "The Cultural Role of Rhetoric," tells of an "agnostic dialectician" who chose not to temper truth with restraint and taste.[1] Weaver's antihero and the present author alike may "put off" the reader by telling painful truths that the reader would prefer to overlook. Alike, too, both may be ignored without a full hearing-reading. This alone would underscore the point of the analysis, that even the best ideas must be tempered by realism and humility, especially across cultures.

Cultures, because they succeed in allowing their adherents to survive in a difficult world, are self-promoting. The present analysis offers eleven propositions to explain and to extend this premise. Three set a foundation; five trace the implications of this premise for the intercultural rhetorician; and three more tell of the consequences of the practice of intercultural rhetoric that flow inexorably from a successful rhetorical effort. I do not pursue, for the moment, implications of the propositions for all rhetoric, *sui generis*. Nor do I succumb to the temptation to remove culture as a key variable, choosing instead to maintain that a difference in magnitude at some point becomes a difference in kind.

The stridency of this analysis should not deter the reader from venturing further. It is proposed that the essay be subjected by the reader to tests offered for truth by Chaim Perelman: The reader should enter into a pact with the author to discover the absolute worth of a dialectically secured position, arguing points only so long as it is sensible to do so.[2] Defensiveness should be put aside, even when cultural truisms are under attack. The resulting verities, if not truth, should be sufficient as knowledge, at least until some day we learn better.

FOUNDATION PROPOSITIONS

Rhetoric unsettles. Though writers remind us that intercultural interaction can synergistically create ideas that dwarf those they replace in value,[3] actual interaction more often confuses and distorts old ideas than transfigures them. Whatever potential for constructive synthesis may inhere in intercultural interaction, that potential is least often realized in "rhetorical" intercultural discourse, that is, that interaction that initially places cultural interactants into set sender and receive roles as a result of programmatic expectation, colonial relationship, or an active notion of cultural hierarchy.

By definition, such rhetoric cannot hope to achieve a mutually satisfying end product. The rhetorician, that is, that interactant moved by a sense of "purpose" such as fostering innovation, promoting a product, reform, or the like, is a modern-day Socrates, the "agnostic dialectician" of Richard Weaver's formulation: He or she conceives of a good in terms suitable to her or his own cultural aspirations, but then refuses to adapt these "ideas" to cultural realities. She or he argues from constitutive, not operational definitions, with resultant success posing a menace to the other society. The ideas of health, growth, salvation, social uplift, and so on are not and cannot be readily translated into other-cultural forms.

Three basic propositions establish the foundation for this position:

(1) *The cultural is the incompletely understood.* Even the simplest of the world's cultures is complex. Cultural anthropologists wisely opt to view cultures through "as if" perspectives, a lesson often lost on sojourners and functionaries who come to believe that they "know" a culture as it is.

Do we understand even our own culture very fully at a conscious level? An argument has been made[4] that we recognize some assumptions of a stranger's culture when we interact across cultures more quickly than we record our own beliefs and assumptions. What we see in the other is a perversion of our own cultural traits, especially in those instances where the other fails to parallel our own. Our image of *both* cultures is incomplete, as we perceptually fill in or delete expected details. Often, we are left with a "mirror image" view of other cultures.

Once we have noted "difference" in another culture, we proceed to assign affect to our cognitions, that is, to voice an attitude about artifacts of the other culture. Interculturalists wisely ask us to wait before assigning values to such cognitions, to learn from, appreciate, savor such differences; but they record case after case of ethnocentrism, devaluation of the other by valuation of one's own. A typical pattern of dealing with difference is to treat it with apprehensive, fear, ridicule, prejudice, suspicion, xenophobia, and ultimately hostility. A typical writer in this area talks of "differences that make a difference," in this regard.[5]

To appreciate a thing, one must truly understand it. Thus, while I am sympathetic to the call of Harms or Prosser for "interunderstanding" between cultures, non-semanticians find means to this happy end to be missing. Understanding recedes into one's cultural heritage; it is multifaceted and unique, never unitary. The meaning given an event by an extracultural observer is a poor cousin, an abridgment, of the actual cultural meaning,[6] and to that extent a surrogate for the meaning. This substitute meaning provided by the outsider varies in sense, affect, familiarity, experiential equivalence, and in intuitive "fit" as experienced by the native. This is a truism, terming the alien "the alien," with all the negative connotations of that term. The "strange" becomes the "estranged," viewed from a distance, never wholly shared. Consubstantiality is illusory.

(2) *The province of intercultural rhetoric is externalities.* As identity is the stuff of intuition, the shared is the substance of dialogue. Remaining for rhetoric is the reconciliation of

variant visions, accounts, and outlooks, which have not been reduced to a single cultural account.

Doubtless, dialectic attempts to compile elements of the true and to place them into an ideal formulation. In practice, "elements of the true" are based upon the perceptions of good of one or the other culture. As this point, argument begins to try to reconcile differences between the positions held by the interactants.[7] But the veil of culture falls between the variant accounts, leaving advocates unconvinced. Plural "truths" are adducible, each being held as natural and complete; the "conversion" of either disputant tears the victim from his or her cultural moorings. Though the "good" rhetorician should consult the crystal of dialectic in search of "good reasons," culture refracts the derived image of truth.

A given national tradition contains a panoply of life styles. Diversity of culture, whether termed a subculture, ethnic group, tribe, community, or some other name, is a given. But national diversity, even the multiversity of India or China, is shaped with reference to a common national experience. Unless we someday enter an era of true internationalism, few persons will respond to the call to act as "fellow travelers of space ship earth" in the way that they would respond to supposed needs of the motherland or fatherland. Warrants for drawing conclusions that seem to be automatically valid *within* a nation are called into question *between* nations.[8] The truism of one nation become an argument for another.

By definition, the foreigner's ideas are externalities; granting the validity of Proposition 1, they can be nothing else. Outsiders come with idea(l)s, some more and some less appropriate to self-defined needs, but all equally alien. Intercultural communication, and all the more rhetoric, uses an inapplicable standard of assessment instead of an authentic one. Given the tendency to evaluate alien objects of cognition already described above, the "external" is normally taken to be the "incorrect."

(3) *Intercultural rhetoric redefines "need" in terms of an external exigence.* To the extent that rhetoric within a culture adapts to an existing pervasive moral order, to that same extent rhetoric without a culture, but seeking a point of entry is likely to violate a culture's axiology. The way a person lives is prima facie a solution to life's requirements, or he or she could not continue to exist as the subject of this analysis.

It might appear that the definition of "needs" would be more stable between cultures than that of beliefs, assumptions, epistemic structures, or attitudes. But the foreign imputation that one "needs" salvation or powdered baby formula and that "survival" requires advanced technology or the Marxist ideology calls into question the validity of one's culturally derived, self-evident truths for others. "Privacy" might be a need for one culture, but not for another. The definition of need that is sanctified interculturally is that defined for big budgets, big cities, big media, and big powers.

An environment is partly a thing of the mind,[9] a mentalistic, Burkeian terministic screen. By adding a new partition or category to the mental landscape, the intercultural rhetorician seeks to "improve" the environment. Local explanations are replaced with "better" ones, and aliens are asked to blend into more "correct" world views. Intercultural rhetoric, if not all intercultural communication, scorns the proximate in its search for explanations and predictions. "Emic" accounts are subordinated to "etic" ones. An internal account cannot be treated as a valid standard of judgment, lest the rhetor's own world view disintegrate. What for one culture is a "world view" is, for another, an "exigence seeking remedy."[10]

IMPLICATIONS FOR THE INTERCULTURAL RHETORICIAN

Given the accuracy, in many cases, of the above propositions, the analysis now proceeds to look at the intrinsic and inescapable nature of intercultural rhetoric as practiced. Five new propositions are the basis of this treatment:

(4) *Intercultural rhetoric is extractionist.* Despite any attempt to meet the alien on his or her own cultural terms, that is, to "identify" with that person's cultural perspective, the intercultural rhetorician "extracts" the native from the setting to the extent that a result is achieved.[11] Suggestions that a rhetor "empathize" or practice "homophily" with a native, so better to convert her,[12] are rather like the expression of "understanding" by a loan shark; in both cases, the purpose served is that of the lender, and the borrower remains famished. The "debt" is inevitably repaid in the currency of the lender-rhetorician. Though the terms of repayment can be softened, they are not removed.

Nor can this be otherwise. The outsider has an end in mind, for good or ill, which can never be completely culturally compatible with the perspective of the native. If that end is even partially achieved, the native shifts from her or his original position in a direction dictated by externalities. The rhetor retains a sense of purpose, and Joseph Kraft's "identificationism"[13] becomes but a strategy or ploy toward the realization of the rhetor's purpose. Abandonment of that purpose would entail the denial of one's own agencies and institutions—hardly an acceptable result in view of the strength of purpose indicated by the seeking out of the alien culture for enlightenment in the first place. Though one may protest that it is better to be converted to new ways by flattery than by force, the underlying proposition still applies.

(5) *Intercultural rhetoric substitutes intercultural world views for intracultural ones.*

Whereas fellow feeling was earlier defined by nation-state or clan, and foreign perspectives were prima facie inappropriate, intercultural rhetoric reorients the recipient along new cultural axes. Another world, be it socialist, technological, Christian, or some other, provides a fresh basis of identity for the message recipient. The partially understood, seemingly the perfected, is the new font of wisdom and standard of ultimate reference, that is, the "ultimate term" in a pantheon of terms. Just as the rhetorician only partially understood the culture of the receiver, so too does the cultural convert pay homage to an altered vision of the innovation. It is by this process that incidental or extraneous features of the innovation, the English medium or foreign birth and schooling, become viewed as integral parts of the innovation: the medium becomes confused, in part, for the message. This "para-message" takes on unexpected forms, unless the rhetor is particularly sensitive to feedback. The misapprehension of the message represents a "third cultural" perspective, true neither to one nor to the other culture of its genesis, yet a caricature of both. Message feedback, being subject to the same limitations as the message itself, is better suited to *recognizing* than to *correcting* discrepancies.

The altered perspective replicates itself. That it could take its form *ever* in just this manner attests to its viability for others of the culture. The result is Protestantism that includes representations of God as a necessary means of worship, traditional village functionaries who ministrate to foreign messengers, or the creation of a class of rival power-seekers and malcontents who undermine traditional structures of governance and who substitute foreign trappings for substance.

(6) *Success reinforces the rhetor.* Now that the idea has been "proven" within one setting, it appears efficacious for another, mutatis mutandis. The innovation was predestined to

succeed, and will do so again elsewhere. Corollary propositions for multinational rhetoricians include:

(a) the agency's dialect remains intact as a dogma, and permits only cosmetic changes from setting to setting;

(b) innovation flows along lines of technological intrusion;

(c) the innovation flow is unidirectional;

(d) ideas flow from "big" to "small" media;

(e) rhetoric diffuses from more- to less-inclusive world views by means of perceptual "filling in";

(f) ideas flow from greater to lesser entities, for example, from large nations to small, from city to village; and

(g) ideas diffuse from greater population centers to lesser.

The certitude of one's correctness forces one's dialectic upon others. Because of the above gradients, the impact of new ideas is felt first among the socially disaffected, heightening the salience of existing social divisions. Existing divisions, moreover, decree acceptance of certain appeals by one group but not by another.[14] Extractionist rhetoric stands to intensify subnational division and social disparity.

(7) *Distinctions of materiality-nonmateriality become meaningless.* Terms come to constitute the new reality, and attitudes toward terms. A bit of new technology or a facilitative belief alike transmute one's world view. Diffusionists like Rogers and Shoemaker needlessly distinguish between the diffusion of "things" and "ideas" since the two are ultimately inseparable. Things, as artifacts of the environment in which they were spawned, carry gratuitous ideas that, in turn, call for the importation of missing parts of the context of their birth. The process is self-perpetuating. Material/nonmaterial distinctions rapidly are rendered *im*material.

(8) *Intercultural rhetoric inherently exploits.* One's actions reflect one's attitudes and

intentions, at an unconscious if not at a conscious level.[15] In proposing that another culture change, one sets in motion a process that will sever a native from her or his culture. She or he will be estranged, transformed, divided, and rendered an antagonist toward his or her culture.

Small matter that one attempts to "empathize" with native conditions; one maintains the change emphasis of the rhetorician. And identificationist-extractionist distinctions dissolve into matters of strategy, not substance. Both aim to create that "frame of reference" within which things or new ideas can take root.[16] Intercultural rhetoric, in its endorsement of the alien and the nonproximate, shows seeds of discord in a soil that is devoid of natural defenses against the germinated sprout. The intercultural rhetor, in a work, "sows the wind and reaps the whirlwind."[17]

SOCIETAL CONSEQUENCES OF INTERCULTURAL RHETORIC

The final three propositions detail the consequences of rhetorical disaffection for the society of importation. That these propositions overlap ideas already advanced is inevitable. The following analysis extends lines of analysis already introduced to their likely consequences:

(9) *Extractionist rhetoric breeds cultural disharmony.* When one psychologically, physically, or existentially removes a native from her or his cultural setting in order to modify the preference of that native, the result is the alienation of that person from the native setting. Successful inculcation of external ideas requires the disparagement of historically "correct" cultural solutions. What earlier was viewed as natural is now scorned as a mistaken orthodoxy; what flourished historically must now, in part, be supplanted. Culture, representing a complete and interrelated system for survival, is challenged, if every so slightly, by each work of the extractionist.

The socially disaffected are the most amenable to conversion to a new practice. Their support by outside sources increases their net influence and grants them power to spread disaffection, disorder, disharmony, discontent. They are cultural estrangement incarnate, rhetorical tools at work in the fashioning of further rhetorical tools, that is, estranged estrangers. They are transplanted genes in the social body, busily working in the creation of others like themselves.

(10) *Intercultural rhetoric erodes diversity.* New Media themselves supplant existing traditions; the force of technology is modern. McLuhan is correct at least insofar as he posits the interaction of one's media and one's personality. The force of the influence of one's characteristic media can be further detailed:

One's cultural inventory stresses both quantity and quality of experience. Some matters are believed firmly and uniquely by any culture, beliefs that must be constantly reinforced by the workings of the precepts of oral tradition. But, especially in the case of younger members of society and for others less prone to join the inner social dialogue, *quantity* of ideas replaces *quality* in determining correctness and cultural "fit." In place of reality testing by means of direct sensate experience or the instruction of an influential known person, certain persons taste of reality via outside, remote sources. These sources, by their nature, assume a common orchestration, with differences between them paling before their points of commonality. For reasons well understood by a generation of media scholars, media modernize. This *is* their message: that remote strangers have a more valid perspective on life than those closer and more familiar. The need to discuss things with others, "social utility," furnishes a persuasion, a "rhetoric-in-being." Technology and rhetoric become one.

(11) *Intercultural rhetoric stresses the here-and-now.* Intercultural rhetoric broadens the range of abstractions at the command of the receiver.[18] It telescopes centuries of tradition into a word such as "tribalism" or "paganism," and dismisses age-old practices with a glib dyslogism. Intercultural rhetoric, more than any *intra*cultural force, champions frustrations and raises expectations. Soon the fruits of change, the promises of rhetoric become the expected reward for the "faithful" and the neoorthodox, and constraints to achievement of these rewards become viewed as part of a conspiracy of "traditionalists." Present circumstance is too bitter a reality to taste, and too disappointing to accept. It must be viewed as "becoming," if not yet "arrived," with apology being offered for the persistence of present form and circumstance.

Teleology is truth. History assumes a force of momentum that drives inexorably toward the fashioning of a utopia, one that usually has been realized elsewhere, and is just over the horizon. Schramm's "future orientation," his "new reality just over the hill,"[19] becomes an obsession, a perverse commentary on present circumstance. Reality is logologically twisted to ignore the thrashing of reality in favor of a projected placid future. Converts apologize for their present intolerable situation, but promise that change is near. Whereas, at the start of this analysis, circumstance controlled rhetorical expression, rhetoric now comes to dictate the meaning of circumstance. One's rhetoric no longer indexes reality; it shapes it. One comes to live a propaganda.

SUMMARY AND CONCLUSION

The above analysis was suggested to me in a reading of Weaver's "Cultural Role of Rhetoric," in which Socrates was said to argue for ideal solutions for a society that had not yet even formulated a problem. This, I take to be the role of many innovation agents who await the opportunity to bulldoze McLuhan's global village.

My reasoning carries me from a view of culture that is fairly stable and immune to outside influence, through a stage where a few persons listen to outside voices, through a further stage where these individuals constitute a channel to reach others, to an end stage where change is routine, and mechanical voices call the tune. The irony of this process is that, by definition, the "answers" from the outside forces cannot be truly suited to needs. McLuhan's "mechanical bride" will leave the victim waiting alone at the alter.

The above analysis appears to be iconoclast, wholly negative, without much hope for intercultural rhetoric. This is an impression that is partially warranted, in the absence of the detailing of better versions of rhetoric; of cases where rhetoric across cultures truly responded to objectively defined need; to demonstration of ways to make feedback corrective of the flaws of the original communication process; and a piece-by-piece sifting of traditional rhetorical tools to discover which will most faithfully objectify the message and place it within the phenomenal structures of the recipient culture without disrupting other features of the culture.

Some of the above propositions are offered without apparent substantiation. The reason for this is that to limit the application of findings to international education, religious conversion, international marketing, birth control campaigns, technical assistance, or some other arena would needlessly limit the analysis. The analysis applies to most, if not all, cases of intercultural rhetoric, and the reader may seek refutation in any area imaginable.

The above analysis may seem unduly critical of interculturalists. It is not. In fact, out of scores of economists, industrialist, and international agency functionaries, it is primarily among interculturalists that questions such as these have been raised as matters of ethical entitlement. Without the interculturalist to expound upon the more acute problems of passing messages between cultures, no theory of intercultural consumer rights and sender responsibilities will ever be formulated. To this end, I offer these observations.

NOTES

1. The reader should be familiar with Richard M. Weaver, "The Cultural Role of Rhetoric," in *Visions of Order* (Baton Rouge: Louisiana State University Press, 1964), since it will be the subject of a parallel throughout this chapter.

2. Chaim Perelman and L. Obrechts-Tyteca, *The New Rhetoric,* trans. J. Wilkenson and P. Weaver (South Bend, IN: Notre Dame Press, 1969), argue that only by this means will argument ever cease.

3. See, for example, L. S. Harms, *Intercultural Communication* (New York: Harper & Row, 1973); and Casmir's commentary in Fred L. Casmir, ed., *Intercultural and International Communication* (Washington, DC: University Press of America, 1978).

4. Those who subscribe to a "contrast culture methodology" make the argument that we know others little, and ourselves almost not at all. Edward T. Hall, *Beyond Culture* (New York: Vintage, 1976); and Edward C. Stewart, "Outline of Intercultural Communication," in Casmir, pp. 271–272, detail this position and methodology.

5. Jon A. Blubaugh and Dorothy L. Pennington, *Crossing Difference . . . Interracial Communication* (Columbus, OH: Charles E. Merrill, 1976), pp. 2–9.

6. The problem of furnishing a context for meaning that was studied by I.A. Richards, *The Philosophy of Rhetoric,* (New York: Oxford University Press, 1936), is complicated further by cultural diversity. The "abridgment of contexts" found in intercultural interaction, therefore, must serve to introduce questionable meanings and connotations.

7. Though, as Perelman claims, argument proceeds from "intellectual contact" in the attempt to gain "the adherence of minds," such an outcome seems unlikely even after the "contact of minds" between holders of distinctive dialectical

positions that were fostered by separate cultural traditions.

8. Stephen L. Toulmin, *The Uses of Argument* (New York: Cambridge University Press, 1958), differentiates between arguments that *use* a warrant and those that *establish* one. Truisms, the arguments that *use* warrants, can be found, it would appear, only *within* a culture. This may be the implicit reasoning behind the treatment of cultural non sequitars by John C. Condon and Fathi Yousef, *An Introduction to Intercultural Communication* (Indianapolis: Bobbs-Merrill, 1975), pp. 213–216.

9. See Harry C. Triandis, "Subjective Culture and Interpersonal Communication and Action," in *International and Intercultural Communication Annual, I,* ed. F. Casmir (New York: Speech Communication Association, 1974), pp. 17–23, for a discussion of this mentalistic environment.

10. Lloyd Bitzer, "The Rhetorical Situation," *Philosophy and Rhetoric, I* (January, 1968), pp. 1–14.

11. Charles H. Kraft, "Worldview in Intercultural Communication," in Casmir, 1983, p. 422.

12. For example, Carley H. Dodd, "Homophily and Heterophily in Diffusion of Innovations: A Cross-Cultural Analysis in an African Setting," Speech Communication Association convention, 1973, on ways of use empathy for mission work in Ghana.

13. Kraft, p. 422.

14. Kenneth Burke, among many writers, discusses a condition where "we's and they's" come to be at odds over extracultural distinctions. Marshall Singer's "perceptual definition" of cultures parallels this analysis. Sociolinguist Joshua Fishman also relates ways through which "symbolic elaboration" can "ideologize" cultural practices. See Fishman et al., eds., *Language Problems of Developing Nations* (New York: John Wiley, 1968), pp. 40–41; Burke, *A Grammer of Motives,* (Cleveland: Meridian Books, 1962), p. 440, and *Language as Symbolic Action* (Berkeley: University of California Press, 1966), p. 52; and Marshall Singer, "Culture: A Perceptual Approach," in L. Samovar and R. E. Porter, eds., *Intercultural Communication: A Reader,* 2nd ed. (Belmont, CA: Wadsworth, 1976), pp. 110–118.

15. Burke develops this idea with reference to "unconscious" rhetoric in *Language as Symbolic Action* and elsewhere.

16. Kraft, p. 421.

17. Michael H. Prosser, *Sow the Wind and Reap the Whirlwind: Heads of State Address the United Nations* 2 volumes, (New York: William Morrow, 1970), adopts this biblical metaphor.

18. William J. Starosta, "Roots for an Older Rhetoric: On Rhetorical Effectiveness in the Third World," *Western Journal of Speech Communication, 43* (Fall 1979), pp. 278–287.

19. Wilbur Schramm, *Mass Media and National Development* (Stanford, CA: Stanford University Press, 1964); and Y. V. L. Rao, *Communication and Development* (Minneapolis: University of Minnesota Press, 1966), pp. 70–74.

William J. Starosta is founder of *The Howard Journal of Communications* and has written on matters of rhetoric, culture and interethnic communication for over 30 years. He currently serves as Rhetoric and Intercultural Communication Coordinator for Howard University's doctoral program.

Reading 4.2

The Concept of an Intercultural Philosophy

RAM ADHAR MALL
TRANSLATED FROM THE
GERMAN BY MICHAEL KIMMEL

INTRODUCTORY REMARKS

There is no pure own culture just as there is no pure other culture. The same is true for philosophy. The ramifications of culture are intricate and can be traced back into the past almost endlessly. In spite of its often conspicuous ambiguity the concept of culture stands for, both, a theoretical and a practical frame of orientation. An essential property of culture is the formation of a specific lasting way of life within the human interaction with nature and other cultures. Just as all human beings are endowed with human dignity by virtue of being human, all cultures are of equal value, even if undeniable differences exist, which let us differentiate but which must not be treated as discriminatory. Philosophy is a product of culture and every culture carried philosophy within it, be it implicated in the poetic or the mythological. It is just as true that there are different philosophies (both, intra- and interculturally) as it is a fact that these philosophies are the outcome of philosophical thought.

The intercultural project of doing philosophy does not privilege either the one or the other, but it calls for a mediation between the particularity of the individual philosophies and the generality of the one and universal philosophy. One possible response to the question of philosophy's origin is to see it as a part of cultural heritage. A second response is to see it as a dispositional prerequisite of the condition of the *anthropos*. Philosophy as a metaphysical need is a part of this disposition. It is true that the differing philosophical schools of thought set different accents and correspondingly come to distinct definitions of philosophy. In itself, this is not unphilosophical. However, what proves detrimental to a philosophical discourse is absolutizing a particular view.

It was with good reason that the ancillary role of philosophy has been lamented in the Christian Middle Ages, but a merely scientistic liberation, that sees its task in analyzing, explaining and accounting for theories with an origin predominantly in the natural sciences,

Reprinted with permission from polylog: Forum for Intercultural Philosophizing 1.1 (2000). Online: http://www.polylog.org/them/1.1/fcs4-en.htm. Used by permission of polylog e.V.

again renders philosophy the handmaid of the sciences.

The view that claims philosophy to be a purely theoretical matter is not supported by the history of philosophy. Pierre HADOT, VOELCKE, DOMANSKI and others have born out philosophy's nature as a precept for life in the history of European philosophy. With the emergence of Christianity philosophy was pushed back as an independent way of life, since the Christian religion would not accord another way of life a status as equally beatifying and redeeming.

The answer to the question as to when two entities (cultures, philosophies, religions) are radically distinct and when they are only different is: They are different in the sense of constituting two instances of a generic concept. In other words, they are differing cultures, philosophies, and religions. However, they would be radically distinct, if they were different even as cultures, philosophies, and religions. In that case, it would be impossible to categorize them in the same generic concept. Such radical differences, if they existed, could not be articulated in the first place. Even counter-arguments are called arguments, however contrary and contradictory they may be. Consequently, what we have here is a general, yet overlapping and analogic concept, which manifest itself concretely in its exemplars just as in the common generic-concept. Thus the justification of this adjectives: European, Indian, Chinese, etc.

At its most simple, the intercultural perspective is not different from the intracultural view; it is also within a specific culture that various epistemological, ethical, and political models exist. It is the intercultural perspective, though, that enlarges and diversifies the range of models, and it points to principal similarities and enlightening differences. Hence, the intercultural perspective frees us from the constraints of our cultural viewpoint.

On Intercultural
Analogic Hermeneutics

The present day communication between cultures, philosophies, religions, and political world-views is of a wholly different quality than it was in the past. The renewed call upon Asia, Africa, and Latin America by Europe, and upon Europe by Asia, Africa, and Latin America is characterized by a specific situation, in which the non-European continents take part in a conversation with voices of their own.

This new kind of communication is characterized by a four-dimensional hermeneutical dialectic. First of all this is about an understanding of Europe by Europe. The inner disparities notwithstanding, Europe has—largely under the influence of factors exterior to philosophy—presented itself to non-Europeans in a unitary image. Secondly, there is a European effort to understand the non-European cultures, religions, and philosophies. The institutionalized scientific fields of oriental studies and cultural anthropology bear witness to that. Thirdly, there are the non-European cultural spheres (Kulturkreise), who now also present the way they see themselves, rather than leaving it to others. Fourthly, there is the understanding of Europe as present in the non-European cultures. This situation raises the question as to who understands whom, why and how in the best way. It may come as a surprise to Europe that in our day Europe itself has become interpretable.

In this way, the existing hermeneutic situation calls for a hermeneutic philosophy that is open-minded enough to acknowledge the fact of embedding within a tradition, including that of the own viewpoint. An interculturally oriented hermeneutic philosophy must meet the requirement of being a philosophy for which neither the world that we must come to terms with nor the concepts, methods, conceptions, and systems, which we develop in this course, constitute historically immutable a priori qualities.

A hermeneutic which promotes the identity model to paradigmatic status merely duplicates the understanding of oneself in the attempt to understand the foreign Other. It attempts to modify the Other in its substance, in order to let it become an echo of itself. Those who define truth in exclusivistic terms of the own tradition and the own tradition in terms of truth are guilty of begging the question and put intercultural communication at risk. According to this model, understanding is always tied to some sort of violence.

Therefore, the maxim of an intercultural hermeneutic is to be: The willingness to understand and the wish to be understood go together and constitute the two sides of a single hermeneutic coin. Where everything is subordinated to the wish to be understood, the Other is not acknowledged or taken seriously in its own right. In this sense, missionaries and some anthropologists studied foreign languages like Chinese or Sanskrit with much effort, less to understand the foreign people than to be understood by them. Admittedly, in understanding the Other the hermeneutic circle cannot be completely avoided, but then it must not be dogmatized, as if one were but its prisoner.

Of the three hermeneutical models to follow intercultural philosophy advocates the third. The models are as follows:

1. The identity model adopts the self-understanding of a culture, philosophy, or religion as exclusive paradigm and lends an overly strict sense to the otherwise correct phenomenological insight that the unknown must be understood within the mode of the known. This hermeneutic is guided by identity-philosophy's fiction of a complete commensurability. In an applied fashion this means that only a Buddhist can understand a Buddhist, only a Christian can understand a Christian, only a Platonist, a Platonist, and a Hegelian a Hegelian. Because

the Platonist does not exist, this hermeneutic reduces itself to absurdity.

2. The hermeneutic of the total difference absolutizes the differences and subscribes to a fiction of total incommensurability. While the fiction of complete commensurability leaves intercultural understanding a farce, the fiction of complete incommensurability renders mutual understanding impossible.

3. The "analogic hermeneutic," which is espoused by intercultural philosophy, is not reductionist and steers clear of both outlined fictions. It sets out from the existing overlaps, which are present for numerous reasons. It is only them that enable communication and translation in the first place. These overlaps can range from the anthropological to the political field.

The otherness of the other is made accessible without reducing or neglecting it. The strong striving toward identity in modernity and the equally strong thesis of difference of postmodernism lose their sting. It is only the overlaps that permit a mutual interpretation. These overlaps are produced, they are not autonomous. They are embedded into life and depend on contexts of origin, methods, insights, values, interests, and interpretations. The overlaps constitute commonalities that can be established and argued on an empirical ground beyond all ontologizing. I am fully in accord with DILTHEY when he says: *"Interpretation would be impossible, if the life-expressions were of completely foreign nature. It would not be necessary, if nothing were foreign to them."*

Furthermore, the analogic hermeneutic contends that one understands and can understand what one is not, cannot be, or does not want to be. Understanding, in the spirit of an analogic hermeneutic, does not insist on understanding in the sense of being persuasive and convincing, but also allows us to understand that, which we need not necessarily have in advance. The outer limit of any hermeneutic, including the phenomenological brand, lies at the outer limit of the process of constitution. All intentions of understanding are preceded by the analogic Other as the origin of what has to be understood; the analogic Other, however, cannot be constituted completely. It is only given to a good to create in his own image.

The hermeneutic subject of the analogic hermeneutic is not a subject apart from the empirical, cultural, historical; instead, it is the same subject, but with the intercultural attitude permitting it to be translocally located. Such a hermeneutic subject being a meditative-reflexive agent has no particular language as native tongue. It is perpetually being accompanied by the consciousness that each concrete subject could just as well have been another. The naivete of the merely mundane subject resides in the incapacity to perceive the own vantage point as one among many. The super-ordinate attitude of the hermeneutic subject enables us to perceive vantage points as such, including our own, thereby testifying to the required openness and tolerance.[2]

ON A DEFINITION OF INTERCULTURAL PHILOSOPHY

What Intercultural Philosophy Is Not

First, intercultural philosophy is not the name of a particular philosophical convention, be it European or non-European. Secondly, intercultural philosophy is, in spite of the necessary centers of the various philosophical traditions (origins of philosophy), located, but trans-locally so. Thirdly, intercultural philosophy is not an eclecticism of various philosophical traditions, as can still be found in such accounts of the history of philosophy that take pride in compiling compendium-volumes.

Fourthly, intercultural philosophy is not a mere abstraction that is self-defining and

pinned down by means of formal logic. Neither is it, fifthly, a mere reaction or auxiliary construct in view of the de facto pluralism of the philosophical arena in the modern word-context of cultures. In other words, intercultural philosophy must not be reduced to a political construct born of mere necessity.

Sixthly, the intent of intercultural philosophy is also not to aestheticize in a romantically enthusiastic and amateurishly-exotic fascination with the extra-European. The aim of intercommunication between cultures is too crucial for this. Seventhly, intercultural philosophy is not the locus of compensation, i.e. an attempt to find in the other that of which you are deficient. With such intent, prejudice and ignorance have given rise to the contrastive designations of European philosophy vs. Asian wisdom (*philosophia* and *philousia*). Eighthly, intercultural philosophy is no offshoot of post-modernity, even if it endorses and supports it.

Ninthly, intercultural philosophy is no trans-cultural philosophy, as far as this term is meant to refer to a fixed pivotal point, an entity exterior to or above the manifold philosophical traditions. That is one of the reasons for which we prefer the prefix "inter" to the prefix "trans." Moreover, the prefix "trans" is already semantically overloaded and has been frequently exploited in philosophy and theology. The prefix "inter" points to an interstitial space that can be observed and experienced, and that is analogically extended almost in the sense of WITTGENSTEIN's family resemblance. In my view, the only meaning of the prefix "trans" that corresponds and does justice to the orientation of intercultural philosophy is that of an attitude not positioned outside cultures or philosophies, but within these and going along with these. One could almost speak of a family resemblance between this and the transcendental reduction of HUSSERL's philosophy, which is an attitude equaling religious conversion.

It is perplexing that, while European philosophers accuse Indian philosophy of being too religious, theologians consider Indian religion as being too philosophic. It remains to be hoped for that a conceptual clarification in the spirit of intercultural philosophy will resolve this seeming contradiction. Those who stand at the intersection of different cultures and live from translating and transposing life-forms and language games, experience under the skin how pressing, difficult, and necessary a conversation between cultures is.

What Intercultural Philosophy Is

First, intercultural philosophy identifies a mental and philosophic attitude, which accompanies all specific cultural configurations of the *philosophia perennis* like a shadow and prevents these from absolutizing themselves. Methodologically it proceeds in such a manner that it does not privilege any conceptual system without cause, and that it aims at harmonizing concepts. In this way it can contribute substantially to a liberating discourse. It is a home-made misgiving to believe that intercultural philosophy would deconstruct the concepts of truth, culture, religion, and philosophy. What this misgiving makes evident, though, is the extremely relativistic and totalizing use that was made and is in part still being made of these terms.

Thirdly and consequently, intercultural philosophy indicates a conflict in tandem with a claim. It is a conflict because the long-neglected cultures of philosophy, that have been misunderstood and oppressed due to ignorance, arrogance, and various factors external to philosophy, sue for equal rights in today's world-content of philosophy. It sets a claim because the non-European philosophies and cultures want to offer solutions by reflecting problem-settings that are particular to them. Fourthly, it follows that intercultural philosophy constitutes an emancipative process. With regard to this process we must bear in mind that it is not about emancipation in the sense of the intra-European Age of Enlightenment, but about an act of emancipation of non- and extra-European thought from its one-sided images that came into being in Europe centuries and even millennia ago.

Fifthly, intercultural philosophy means accepting the necessity to conceptualize and share the history of philosophy anew from the foundations upwards. The universality of philosophical rationality emerges in various philosophical traditions, while at the same time transcending these. Sixthly, intercultural philosophy means a conception of philosophy, which makes heard the omnipresent aspect within philosophia perennis in many races, cultures and tongues. Thereby intercultural philosophy forestalls the tendency of several philosophies, cultures, religions, and political outlooks to spread globally. The uniformity of the hardware of the European technological formation must not be allowed to incorporate the healthy plurality of cultural softwares. "Westernization" is not automatically equivalent to "Europeanization." One is almost tempted to speak of a myth of "Europeanizing humanity."

Seventhly, intercultural philosophy advocates unity without uniformity. The transcultural nature of the formal, technological, and scientific conceptual apparatus should not be mistaken for the spirit of interculturality. Eighthly, it is part of the nature inherent in intercultural philosophy to promote a sense of modesty with regard to the own epistemological, methodological, metaphysical, ethico-moral, political, and religious access to the regulative One of many names.

In the absence of a universally acceptable Archimedean-point intercultural philosophy ninthly treats the various philosophies as different, but not radically distinct points to the True Philosophy. In intercultural philosophy the nature of philosophy is determined more with regard to the philosophers' questions than to their answers. This applies both intra- and interculturally. Speaking of the one European, Indian, or Chinese philosophy in a singularizing way idealizes in a reductionist fashion and takes a part for the whole.

Tenth, intercultural philosophy thereby aims at a transformation of philosophy to take it beyond its mono-cultural centeredness. Eleventh, intercultural philosophy is the condition for making a discipline of comparative philosophy possible, since the latter remains in a state of isolated parallelism without the former. Twelfth, intercultural philosophy thus frames a model of philosophy that accepts that the concept of philosophy is generally applicable, while it gives the plurality of philosophical centers and origins their legitimate due. Thirteenth, intercultural philosophy brings to the fore the historically contingent nature of a practice in philosophical historiography to the effect that an inquiry into all non-European philosophies is undertaken only from the perspective of European philosophy. To show that the converse is just as possible and legitimate is one of the objectives of intercultural philosophy.

It is a historical contingency that there exists an Orientalism but no Occidentalism. Fourteenth, intercultural philosophy is aware of the eurocentrism in Western Orientalism and highly appreciates the merits of SAID, but it does not wish to throw out the baby with the bathwater. It aims at an intercultural discourse that leaves the old constellation of the Orient-Occident dichotomy behind, that speaks in favor of centers, but opposes centrism.

Intercultural philosophy knows a four-fold perspective: one philosophical, one theological, one political, and one pedagogical. From a philosophical viewpoint intercultural philosophy indicates that it is wrong to define philosophical truth exclusively through a particular tradition and a particular tradition through philosophical truth. From a religious viewpoint inter-religiousness is another name for

interculturality. The one *religio perennis (sanatana dharma)* also comes in various theological guises. Inter-religiousness is no religion of its own that one could belong to. It is a sensibility that makes us open and tolerant. In addition to that, it helps us prevail over the temptations of fundamentalism.

From the political viewpoint interculturality is another name for a pluralist-democratic and republican conviction, that does not exclusively accord political truth to any particular groups, class, or party. The pedagogical perspective, which in a respect is the most crucial, amounts to the practical attempt to learn and teach, meaning in thought and action, from kindergarten to university the views of the other three perspectives. Only in this way it is possible to provide against fundamentalisms, where-ever they may arise; as soon as they dominate the arena of political practice pedagogy comes too late. Ernst CASSIRER's analysis of symbolic forms endows the philosophy of intercultural orientation with the indispensable flexibility to safeguard against the dangerous sway over the dynamic ideas and structures of philosophies, cultures, and religions in an artificial and uniform fashion.

THE ISSUE OF TRANSLATION

It can be felt under the skin by whoever lives in more than one language and is forced to find orientation in more than one culture and philosophy that philosophical truth, despite the metonymical exchange of names, shifts back and forth and releases us from the overly narrow constraints of the purely philological. Linguistic proficiency is a necessary but not sufficient precondition for the mastery of everyday matters.

It is undisputed that the process of transposing is a troublesome thing and never succeeds in producing total congruence, be it on the inter- or intracultural level. Nevertheless, this is generally the case irrespective of whether we translate the Greek *logos* as the Latin *ratio*, as the Christian God-Father, as the German *Vernunft*, as the English term *reason*, or in expressions of other languages. To be sure, a similar translation is even more difficult and problematic in the intercultural field because of the greater differences of the language- and culture-spheres. Yet, the differences between the three towns of Athens, Rome, and Jerusalem were no less considerable in the beginning.

The European history of thought testified to the fact that there has been translation and comparison in the European sphere of culture and thought from the beginning onwards. And this was well justified and conducive to living. The conceptual apparatus of Greek philosophy was put into service of Christian philosophy.

In the Asian area the Sanskrit term *dhyana* (meditation, concentration, contemplation) has completed a similar journey—resulting in the Chinese *chan* and Japanese *zenna* or *zen*. Both examples show that translations and transpositions were practiced in both cultural spheres. This practice seems to be based on the theoretical conviction that things and concepts need to be named by language, but do not completely collapse in them in a way that leaves no remainder.

In his *Conversation with a Japanese* HEIDEGGER writes that *"the name and that which it names come from European thought, from philosophy."* Thereby HEIDEGGER conveys the view that not only the name of philosophy (which is correct), but also its subject-matter is Greek and European (which is wrong). HEIDEGGER, who is said to have read LAOZI (Lao Tse) over and over again, should have perceived that Dao does not exhaust itself in the name "Dao." Making philosophy a European destiny constricts its universality in an uncalled-for fashion. In this respect LOEWITH believed HEIDEGGER's basic conviction to have been that *Sein* (Being) has a predilection for the Graeco-European

spirit.[4] Such a belief, regardless if it is European or not, is detrimental to the impartiality of philosophical truth.

In the absence of the interculturally oriented attitude one cannot possess the necessary distance to one's own tradition, no matter how well informed about a foreign culture one is. Max MÜLLER, the world-famous Indologist to whom India owes a great deal of gratitude, in a sense applies the Hegelian metaphor of age-levels in an effort to depict the philosophy and religion of India as not yet fully mature. This evolutionistic schema attributes an almost a priori and ab ovo status to cultures. The following words of Max MÜLLER presuppose the old Euro-centric view: *"People do not yet see the full importance of the Veda in an historical study of religion. The bridge of thoughts [. . .] that spans the whole history of the Aryan world has the first arch in the Veda, its last in Kant's Critique. While in the Veda we may study the childhood, we may study in Kant's Critique of Pure Reason the perfect manhood of Aryan mind."*(5)

LOGIC AND ETHICS FROM AN INTERCULTURAL POINT OF VIEW

As exemplification of intercultural philosophy I would like to venture a brief cultural comparison of philosophy in the fields of logic and ethics.

Logic in India and Europe

Adjectives like Indian, Chinese, European, etc. are justified because their designatum may also be designated by other adjectives. The universality of logic is not lost on us if we speak of, say, Indian logic, devoid of its generic meaning.

WITTGENSTEIN answered his self-addressed inquiry into the common denominator of different language games by stating that they all follow rules. In what—we may ask—does the shared and overlapping aspect of the superordinate concept of logic consist? The theory of inference lies at the heart of logical thought. Therefore, logic from an intercultural point of view is the endeavor to provide arguments for inferences. These patterns of argument can diverse, both interculturally and intraculturally.

In his authoritative work *Formale Logik* Bochenski writes: *"Formal logic was, as far as we know, created in two and only in two cultural spheres: in the Occidental and the Indian."*[6] My arguments with respect to logic in an intercultural perspective attempt to show a few principal similarities and remarkable differences, for example as regards syllogism, the principle of contradiction, the question of validity, etc.

In India logic has also developed from the methodology of discussion and disputation (*sambhasa, jalpa, vitanda, tarka*). A good example for a methodology of discussion (*tarka-sastra*) can be found in a discussion to become famous in world literature between the monk NAGASANA and the Graeco-Bactrian King MENANDROS, reigning around 150 B.C. in Afghanistan and the North of India, who professed philosophical and religious interests and had received training in the art of discussion and debate. The text in question called *The Questions of Milinda* goes as follows:

The king spoke: Venerable Nagasana, wilt thou continue to discuss with me?"

"If thou, great king, wilt discuss in the language of the scholarly man, I will discuss with thou. But if thou mean'st to discuss in the language of the king, then I will not discuss with thou."

"How, venerable Nagasana, do wise men discuss?"

"In a discussion among wise men, o great king, there is winding motion that rises and descends by way of convincing and conceding; distinctions and counter-distinctions are made. Yet, the wise men are not befallen by anger."

"But how, then, do kings discuss?"

"If kings assert a claim in a discussion and somebody refutes the claim they order punishment to be inflicted on this person."[7]

These statements and arguments of the Buddhist monk-philosopher apparently exhibit a number of similarities with Socratic-Platonic dialogues and thinkers. In *Menon* 75 c-d SOCRATES expounds the integrity, who are not only intent on gaining a victory. Openness and self-moderation are the same virtues that NAGASANA attaches importance to. In addition to that, NAGASANA, in his way, puts forward the conditions of the possibility of a "domination-free discussion" and of "communicative action" (HABERMAS).

The Indian theory of syllogism (*anu-mana-sastra*) can be traced back to various models of discussion that are present in the Indian tradition of philosophy. Indian epistemology differentiates between two main types of knowledge: the direct type (*pratyaksa/ aparoksa*) and the indirect type (*paroksa*). Among the six means of knowledge, which are perception (*pratyaksa*), inference (*anu-mana*), reliable word (*sabda*), analogy (*upamana*), hypothesis (*arthapatti*), and the not-realization of the source of knowledge (*anupalabdhi*), perception is the only direct means to acquire knowledge.

Inference stands for a recognition that follows another. If you see smoke you infer that there is fire. This step of inference is firstly a source of knowledge and secondly a way of argumentation. Thus, two functions, one epistemological, the other logical, are conceptually fused into one here.

The object of the inferred idea is not given to the sense organs. We see the smoke, but not the fire; we perceive a smile, but not the joy. The Indian theory of syllogism keeps two forms of inference apart: inference for a subject (*svarthanu-mana*) and inference for the others (*parathanumana*). The first form principally amounts to a process of epistemogenesis with a more psychological bent. This syllogism generally contains three propositions (which are comparable to the Aristotelian):

Wherever there is smoke, there is also fire.
There is smoke on that mountain.
Hence, there is fire there.

Inference as a way of argument to convince others, on the other hand, contains five propositions. This five-part syllogism looks as follows:

1. Thesis (*pratijña*): On that mountain there is fire.
2. Reason (*hetu*): Because there is smoke.
3. Evidence (*udaharana*): Whenever there is smoke there is fire, as for example in the kitchen.
4. Application (*upanaya*): There is smoke over that mountain and smoke is always accompanied by fire.
5. Conclusion (*nigamana*): Consequently, there is fire on that mountain.

This five-part syllogism may seem unnecessarily lengthy, logically cumbersome, and not formal enough when compared to the three-part one. Yet, in didactic or pedagogic respect it makes good sense. These two forms of the syllogism may be transposed into one another. The three-part Aristotelian syllogism is amenable to a reformulation in five parts:

1. Thesis: Socrates is mortal.
2. Reason: Because he is human.
3. Example: Whoever is a human being is mortal, for example Pythagoras.
4. Application: Socrates is a human being, and being human invariably goes with being mortal.
5. Conclusion: Therefore Socrates is mortal.

In addition to the empirical and inductive reasoning, which results from the repeated observation that where there is smoke there is fire, where there is none there is no fire, and where fire is absent smoke is absent as well, the invariant relation (*vyapti*) between the mediating concept of smoke and the topical concept of fire is assumed to be constitute and permanent. There is even mention of the perception of general properties and relations. In the act of perceiving a cow there is a simultaneous perception of the general quality of cow-ness. The technical term for this is *samanya-laksana-pratyaksa*. Here a comparison with Aristotelian intuitive perception may be launched.

The Indian theories of negation (*abhava*), of dialectic thought, and of doubt are further topics from the field of logic that are amenable to presentation from an intercultural perspective. The category of doubt, for example, stands for a recognition (*samxaya-jñana*) occurring when there are two contradictory opinions with regard to one subject-matter. Doubt is neither true nor false. Contrary to most European views, doubt in Indian thought is not necessarily an impeding force to action. It is possible that philosophical doubt does not constrain our actions. Yet, doubt leads to action if the risk incurred in the action is not overly great.

Principal Affinities and Instructive Differences

The differences may seem to be of purely terminological or superficial nature. Yet, this is not the case. Even in logical thought the intercultural perspective can suggest lines of inquiry that pertain to the anthropological status of human beings as such. However, while these differences continue to exist, they must not be seen as deficiencies.

While the Aristotelian syllogism is, as a rule, of deductive and formal nature, the Indian syllogism remains in active contact with epistemological and psychological factors. The notion of formal validity is also important for Indian logical thought, but not at the expense of the material aspect of our inferences. The presence of the step of evidence in the Indian syllogism makes this clear. We may surmise that this is the reason why Indian logic has, despite its existing dispositions, never developed a purely formal logic. From an intercultural point of view we may raise the question what is understood, realized, and given due appreciation once the formal validity is recognized. Is it not the if-then structure of inferences that makes Europeans immortal, given that all men are immortal and that Europeans are human beings? Is this a matter of inference (*anumana*) in the sense of a realization or a matter of formal argumentation (*tarka*) without any material insights? All these are questions of interest.

The primacy of perception in Indian thought may the reason why this though shows limited interest in purely formal matters. In the metaphysical and logical thought of Europe we quite often find the idea of pure possibility. Empirical matters cannot be the reason for this. It may have been modeled on the Judeo-Christian tradition with its notion of creation from the nothingness. Even in Leibnizian thought innumerable possible worlds precede the one real (best?) world. Such a thought is, on the whole, alien to Indian thought, since potential states (*yogata*) can be envisaged after realities have been given to us. The two modes of potentiality and impossibility presuppose our encountering reality. Thus, Indian logic remains more intensionalistic than a class-logic.

Furthermore, Indian logic does not consider psychologism to lead us astray. Instead it attempts a rapprochement of logic, psychology, and epistemology. Logic is embedded into the greater context of life.[8] Thereby Indian logic avoids mere formalism and Platonism of forms.

In the West Asian thought has frequently been accused of not accepting the principle of contradiction. However, the actual state of affairs is considerably more intricate. A cannot be, at the same time, A and not-A. This is being accepted by ARISTOTLE and Buddhist logic alike. However, it is justified differently. For Aristotle the self-identity of A was at peril. For the Buddhists there is no such thing as an identical A.

The logic of Jainism does not challenge the validity of the principle of contradiction, but its unconditional validity. The principle is valid only if the same place, the same time, and the same respect are presupposed. The seven-step predicate-logic (*saptabhangi-naya*) of the Jainas make it equally evident that a multivalent logic is more in accordance with Indian thought.

The principles of causality and contradiction as well as the categories of order and-chaos are subject to a reappraisal if we accept that in Chinese thought Dao stands for a principle of order, which relativizes the weight of the generic notion of these principles. The Chinese can sidestep the principle of contradiction by referring to the principle of harmonious unification (*ho*) pertaining to the balance of the greater nature. The renowned sinologist GRANET advances a highly interesting explanation why the Chinese lack a sense of formal syllogism.

"Of what value would a syllogistic inference be for a way of thinking that refuses to deprive space and time of their concrete nature? How can one claim that Socrates, being human, also is mortal? Is it to be taken for granted that in future times and in other locations humans will die? What can be claimed, however, is that Confucius is dead and consequently I will also die, since there is little hope that somebody deserves a longer life than the greatest of sages."[9]

This may strike some of us as peculiar. The principal question from an intercultural point of view is this: What is logical consistency and how do we comprehend it? May it not be the case that we have two kinds of consistency, one of formal-logic orientation and one of ethico-moral orientation? Being formally valid is more culture-independent than being semantically true.[10]

Epistemological modesty and philosophical restraint are therefore further ethically and politically relevant consequences of philosophical thinking from an intercultural point of view.

Ethics in Cultural Comparison

Ethics makes every effort to approximate the state of things as they are to the state as they should be. In this respect there is neither complete agreement about how things are nor about how they should be. Even the ideas about how to perfect the self and the world diverge, both inter- and intraculturally. In his book Pragmatism—*An Open Question* Hilary PUTNAM posits that philosophy's central concern is how one should live. *"We value tolerance and pluralism, but we are disturbed by epistemological skepticism which came with this tolerance and pluralism."*[11]

One of the central questions in ethics is that how values by which we are led are anchored. The moorings can be of humanist or theological nature. In opposition to theocentric and anthropocentric models Chinese "Universism" propounds that man is embedded in his way into the greater balance of nature and should not expect any privileged position. Heaven does not weep, heaven does not laugh, as LAOZI says. The supporting structure of the whole cosmos is more primeval, powerful, and encompassing than that of the history of mankind. In this context the question of man's privileged position gets another meaning.

Ethico-moral thought frequently starts from the assumption that the good should be rewarded. The various religions and philosophies provide different rationales for this. KANT for example posits the immortality of the soul and the existence of God, in order to guarantee that this connection of goodness and reward is established. In Indian thought,

e.g. Buddhism, the Karma-principle is invoked to achieve this connection. In theologically oriented ethical thought it is God's will that is responsible for this. It is difficult to draw a demarcating line between theology and philosophy here.

We can see that overlapping ethico-moral beliefs receive different philosophical rationales. Principles of universal ethics must neither be formally nor power-politically legitimized if they are to be interculturally effective. It is not the idea to find a universally valid ethical standard that is unreasonable, but the view that this has been found in a particular philosophy, religion, or culture is fundamentalist. The idea of human rights is also not proper to a single culture. Today we know that the numerous inscriptions of the Buddhist king ASHOKA of the 3rd century B.C. contain human rights in spirit and in letter. The human being as such must be—at least in principle—capable of recognizing and acknowledging the universal validity of human rights, even if he has been deluded by various ideologies into violating these rights.

WINDELBAND, who speaks very highly of Chinese culture, denies that it has discovered the universal ethical principle. According to him Chinese thought also lacks the revealed religious truth. Almost in an Hegelian euphoria, WINDELBAND goes so far as to approve of the European conquest and mission with all its negative consequences for the following reason: *"With this approval we would only sanction a brutal right-makes-might, if we were not of the conviction that the victorious society represents the higher values."*[12]

THE TASK OF INTERCULTURAL PHILOSOPHY

The intercultural view has made evident that there is no such thing as an absolute claim of the One, if one does not privilege one place, time, language, religion, or philosophy out of prejudice or ignorance. The conceptual and substantive clarification of intercultural philosophy has furthermore shown that the history of philosophy is itself an inexhaustible reservoir of diverging interpretations. In this way the history of philosophy is a hermeneutic location. What follows is that there cannot be a merely a priori determination of philosophy and culture that is ascertained per definitionem.

Those who would consider the term "intercultural philosophy" vague for lack of accurate criteria forget that in identifying cultures, philosophies, religions, and political *Weltanschaungen* a certain amount of embedding in tradition and personal decision cannot be denied. If one expects general acceptance and unanimity, one puts excessive demands on them. In the competition of philosophical arguments the philosophical dispositions and ways of socialization also play a role that is partly even decision.[13]

All ethico-moral and political models revolved around the improvement of relations between man and fellow man, respectively between man and nature. The question keeps emerging whether the external changes do not merely constitute the necessary, but not the sufficient conditions for the intended improvements.

The current globalization of technical formations admittedly manifests itself as a process of universalizing in the hardware aspects of the human condition, yet the ethico-moral software aspects of cultures lag behind and get stuck in their tracks. This may be the reason for the tremendous bustle going on to establish a link between ethics and other sciences.

The intercultural orientation, which believes in on the reciprocity of the inner core and outer skin of human nature, escapes any kind of evanescence and one-sidedness in creating an image of man. Such an attitude makes an intercultural discourse possible without any fear of losing one's self in the other and

without any attempt to incorporate the other. LEVINAS writes: *"Occidental philosophy coincides with the disclosure of the Other. The Other, which manifests itself as Being loses its otherness in that process. From the beginning on philosophy is spellbound by the horror of the Other than remains an Other in an insurmountable allergy."*[14]

Mirce ELIADE has raised the interesting question relevant to the present day when the Asian spirit did not gain a foothold in Europe as opposed to the Graeco-Latin culture. With reference to Europe's discovery of the Sanskrit language, the Upanishads, and Buddhism at the end of the 18th and in the 19th century Eliade speaks of a second and unsuccessful Renaissance. For ELIADE the main reason for the abortive attempt is to be seen in the fact that the second Renaissance, unlike the first, remained a matter for the Orientalists, while being scarcely noticed by the philosophers, theologians, men of letters, artists, and historians, unless in a romantic idealization of the Asian spirit.

If it is the case that we stand at the threshold to a "third Renaissance" in the present day "world-eon" (SCHELER) to technological formation and renewed encounter of cultures, and there is considerable evidence for this, this is not the Orientalists' merit, but rather a result of the non-European cultures being historically present in the present global situation. If this third Renaissance is granted success we are all called upon to make the necessary contribution of our own position in the spirit of interculturality. It is to be desired that the intercultural outlook will help us in that.

The intercultural view does not reject the existence of centers, it only rejects centrisms of all brands. No culture, whether Asian, European, African, or Latin-American can remain wholly confined in its own tradition without seeming provincial.

Intercultural philosophy is a fundamentally novel orientation and, at the same time, a constitutive element and the aim of doing philosophy from an intercultural point of view. The theory of intercultural philosophy that has been laid out here posits an overlapping and universal, but a-locally located rationality of the *philosophia perennis*. This amounts to a change of paradigm, which lets, both, the theoretical and the practical branches of philosophy see, teach, and do research from an intercultural viewpoint. It is a matter of a new historiography of philosophy. In his article *The Human Being in the Eon of Conciliation* SCHELER speaks of a "Cosmopolitan philosophy" and writes *"that national spirits are called upon to complement each other in all cultural matters, and to complement each other irreplaceably."*[15]

Prior to any kind of comparativist approach, regardless in whichever discipline it is situated, it is therefore imperative to adopt the culture of interculturality, in order to create the conditions for a possible philosophical conversation conducted in mutual respect and tolerance. Comparative philosophy goes blind without the intercultural philosophical orientation; intercultural philosophy goes lame without comparative philosophy. They both belong together.

NOTES

1. W. Dilthey: *Gesammelte Werke.* Bd. 7 Göttingen 1973, 225.

2. Cf. R. A. MALL: *Philosophie im Vergleich der Kulturen. Interkulturelle Philosophie—eine neue Orientierung.* Darmstadt 1955, 91ff.

3. M. HEIDEGGER: *Unterwegs zur Sprache.* Pfullingen 1960, 86.

4. Cf. K. LÖWITH: *Geschichtliche Abhandlungen.* Stuttgart 1960, 175.

5. Quoted in: K. ROY: *Hermeneutics. East and West.* Calcutta 1993, 67.

6. J. M. BOCHENSKI: *Formale Logik.* Freibug/Br. 1956, 13.

7. J. MEHLIG (Hg.): *Weisheit des alten Indien.* Bd. 2. Leipzig 1987, 347f.

8. In his lectures of Göttinger on logic, MISCH tries to anchor the logical in the general context of life. Cf. G. MISCH: *Der Aufbau der Logik auf dem Boden der Philosophie des Lebens.* Freiburg/Br. 1994.

9. M. GRANET: *Das chinesische Denken.* Frankfurt/M. 1985, 255.

10. Vgl. R. A. MALL: *Was konstituiert philosophische Argumente?* Bremen 1996 (*Bremer Philosophica 1996/1*).

11. H. PUTNAM: *Pragmatismus—eine offene Frage.* Frankfurt/M. 1995, 10.

12. W. WINDELBAND: "Vom Prinzip der Moral" (1983). In: DERS.: *Präludien, Aufsätze und Reden zu Philosophie und ihrer Geschichte.* 2 Bde. Tübinger 1919, 176.

13. Vgl. R. A. MALL: *Was konstituiert philosophische Argumente?* Bremen 1996 (*Bremer Philosophica 1996/1*).

14. E. LEVINAS: *Die Spur des Anderen.* Freiburg/Br. 1983, 211.

15. M. SCHELER: *Gesammelte Werke.* Bd. 5. Bern 1954, 386. Hervorhebung durch den Verfasser.

Ram Adhar Mall is professor of philosophy at the Universities of Bremen and Munich. He is president of the International Society of Intercultural Philosophy.

Reading 4.3

Women's Rights as Human Rights— Rules, Realities and the Role of Culture
A Formula for Reform

BERTA ESPERANZA HERNANDEZ-TRUYOL

> From the first dawn of life unto the grave,
> Poor womankind's in every state a slave.
>
> * * *
>
> We will our rights in learning's world maintain;
> Wilt's empire now shall know a female reign.[1]

Beijing, China. Tuesday, September 5, 1995. Beijing International Conference Center (BICC). The afternoon plenary of the United Nations Fourth World Conference on Women: Equality, Peace, Development is about to start in a hall too small to seat everyone who wants to be there. Other than places for some of the delegates from each attending State, space is limited and in high demand. A lucky few lined up for hours to get a ticket; many ended up negotiating prime space in front of one of several TV screens strategically located throughout the building. A hushed silence fell in the hall and in the areas surrounding the TV screens. The introduction: Hillary Rodham Clinton, First Lady of the United States of America. She speaks on women, children, poverty, education, health, and economic and political participation. She gets into a rhythm as she softly makes her point: "If there is one message that echoes forth from this conference, it is that human rights are women's rights—And women's rights are human rights." Emphasizing her message, she gives detailed examples—"it is a violation of human rights when babies are denied food, or drowned, or suffocated, or their spines broken, simply because they are born girls." She continues—"it is a violation of human rights" when women and girls are subject to: violence, even in their own homes; female genital mutilation; bride-burning; girl-killing; rape, sometimes as a tactic or prize of war; forced abortion; forced sterilization and

Reprinted with permission from *Brooklyn Journal of International Law*, 1996, 21 Brooklyn J. Int'l L. 605.

the usual litany of abuses that are, regrettably, all too common and all too well known. The silence is broken, first by nervous and gradually empowered applause which fills the building—inside and outside the hall.[2]

I. INTRODUCTION

Imagine, as we go into the 21st century, needing support for such a simple statement: that over half of the world, meaning women, are indeed humans and have human rights. This apparently revolutionary concept has resulted in a powerful, emerging movement in the international human rights arena which urges the recognition and acknowledgement of women's rights as human rights. This movement was clearly embraced by First Lady Hillary Rodham Clinton (and many other world leaders) in China in September 1995, with her declaration that "human rights are women's rights. . . . and women's rights are human rights." The catalysts at the core of this global initiative to recognize and promote women's rights as human rights are the correlative needs to eradicate the institutionalized invisibility of women in the global sphere, to craft a means to implement existing rights to benefit women's lives, and to develop, expand, and transform the content and meaning of such rights to reflect women's realities and compel women's equality. This article explores the roles played by rules of law and by the conflation of economic, social, political, religious, cultural, and historic realities in the marginalization of women in the international, regional, and domestic spheres worldwide. Its centerpiece is a proposed analytical model deconstructing and reconfiguring the human rights framework to ensure that women's rights that exist in theory become reality.

The United Nations Human Development Report 1995 states the shocking, but all-too-well known fact quite plainly: "In no society today do women enjoy the same opportunities as men." Recognizing the second-class status of women in societies around the world and the dangers of the marginalization that results, this article, as the title suggests, reviews and analyzes the rules that exist and the realities that persist. It proposes reform in the context of cultural, religious, and traditional norms and practices. Part II describes the general setting that provided the impetus for women around the world to unite and demand their rights as human beings. Part III reviews the international human rights construct to establish that, as a matter of paper rights, women are, or should be, protected under existing norms. Part IV reveals that the reality of the conditions and status of women worldwide is a far cry from the equality mandated by the rules. This section includes an assessment of some gender-specific practices, some of which are justified by culture, history, and tradition, as well as a scrutiny of various substantive provisions of the body of human rights documents to show that women are, indeed, not equal in their enjoyment of, or protection by, established international norms. In Part V, this piece explores the role of culture in analyzing the nature and obligations of compliance with articulated human rights. Finally, Part VI designs a methodology that reconstructs the existing approach to rights to ensure, facilitate, and safeguard women's enjoyment of the full range of human rights.

To be sure, the analytical methodology proposed is not necessarily limited to a scrutiny of gender issues. Indeed, it cannot be limited to gender because gender is not, and cannot be, a monolithic category. Gender cannot be considered essential or viewed in isolation. Women's personhood is also indivisible from racial, ethnic, cultural, and other aspects of their identity. Women speak in different tongues and experience life in different ways. It is, thus, with a multiple perspective or multi-dimensionality analysis that this article addresses women's rights as human rights.

II. THE GLOBAL SETTING

Notwithstanding roadblocks in law and life, women have refused to accept, and indeed have fought strongly against, their imposed invisibility and silence. Throughout time, women have made unrelenting efforts to raise their voices, urge their perspectives, and demand that their needs be met. Women have been at the forefront of this human rights drive, presenting their separate realities and insisting that issues affecting them because of their sex be deemed an integral part of the human rights construct.

The traditional exclusion of women from the articulation, development, implementation, and enforcement of human rights has rendered gender issues invisible, and consequently has shielded gender-based abuses from much needed scrutiny. For example, the flawed public/private dichotomy historically interfered with the recognition of wrongs inflicted on women because of their sex such as domestic violence, which now is acknowledged as a violation of domestic, regional, and international rights, including, among others, the right to security of the person. This false public/private dichotomy, in the name of the "rule of law," has ghettoized women's interests and conspired to deny equal status to women.

The exclusion of women from the enjoyment of human rights exists in all three of the so-called generations of human rights–first (civil and political), second (economic, social, and cultural), and third (solidarity). Thus, international norms must be reconceptualized to reach issues that concern individuals such as sexual harassment, gender-based violence, reproductive freedom, education, and the right to vote, as well as issues that pertain to states, governments, and intergovernmental organizations, such as economic policies and structural adjustment programs. The incorporation of the multiplicity of women's voices and concerns into the rights discourse is essential to effect this reformulation of rights. Scholars, representatives (at the national, international, intergovernmental, and non-governmental levels), and activists in various fields must work together, utilizing an interdisciplinary approach to the rights construct, to implement existing rights in a fashion that includes and protects women. Only such an approach will develop, expand, and transform the content and meaning of human rights in a manner that will reflect women's realities and include women's diverse perspectives.

The proposed analytical model takes a necessary, and appropriate, multidimensional perspective. The current construct which defines rights and prohibitions with a single-issue focus is ill-equipped as an analytical tool to evaluate diverse and indivisible women's issues. Further, the multidimensional perspective incorporates a culturally sensitive analysis that embraces the realities and voices of women from different cultures, religions and traditions to ensure that the new international human rights construct is indeed egalitarian in both principle and application.

Although these concerns and issues are not new, it is only now that women have gained access to domestic and international arenas—both formal and informal—that the gender dimensions of human rights norms are being explored and that a feminist critique of international law is emerging. Despite the infancy of this "women's rights are human rights" movement, there are some who have already begun to dispute the need for any focus on international women's human rights. These critics suggest that such discourse is inappropriate and unnecessary because international human rights norms include women as human beings, and sex, meaning female, as a protected class. Thus, the proper emphasis is on all people, not just women. Predictably, critics of the feminist methodology take the formalistic, simplistic approach that a focus on women's human rights is misplaced because international, regional, and domestic instruments facially mandate gender equality.

This analysis is defective for various reasons, not the least of which is that it would be inconceivable to challenge a concern about the rights of people belonging to a racial, religious or indigenous group on the grounds that they are simply people too. Further, such criticisms are problematic as a "reality check" on women's everyday lives empirically and reveal the historic invisibility and silencing of women in the rights discourse and the present global status and condition of women as second-class citizens.

Focusing on women's rights as human rights in the international forum is not only proper but also imperative. The breadth and depth of issues pertinent to women's human rights reflect existing problems in the world at large. Gender is a particularly well-suited point of reference for the reconstruction of the flawed, monocular scheme precisely because it encompasses vital and often ignored issues of race, ethnicity, nationality, culture, language, color, religion, ability (physical and mental), socioeconomic class, and sexuality.

Another reason to concentrate on gender is that it affords a sharp focus within the macrocosm of international law. Virtually every society—and its structural, political, social, cultural, and religious systems—evidences some form of gender discrimination or subjugation. Sex inequality is a global reality. Indeed, its prevalence gives female subordination and marginalization the appearance not only of inevitability but also of normativity.

Significantly, a woman-centered analysis will prevent those in the United States, as well as in other western States, from considering gender problems and concerns as existing only in "other places" such as Third World states, or states with non-western-based traditions, perspectives and outlooks. One example of the universality of sex inequality is the feminization of poverty—a global reality that neither can be ignored nor disputed. Other factors that freely interact to perpetuate gender subordination and disparity are persistent discriminatory employment practices, inequitable social-structural relationships, and gender-based violence—daily facts of life for women. The concept of "women as wombs" is also a pervasive worldwide phenomenon and is central to the universal failure to recognize the plethora of issues attendant to women's health, which include, but are not limited to, bearing children. Most important, the concept of women's health must be redefined beyond "sick" or "medicalized" needs to include matters of well-being such as education (schooling, in general and health, including reproductive issues, in particular), economic self determination, political participation, environmental safety, and personal security, to name a few.

Issues relating to reproductive freedoms highlight the critical importance of approaching rights as indivisible and reveal the weakness of the normative single-right approach as under-inclusive. It lends itself to a critique from a feminist perspective, from a cross-cultural perspective, including considerations of race, ethnicity, and religion, as well as from a multidisciplinary perspective, be it anthropological, medical, epidemiological, and/or lay fact-finding. When dealing with women's issues, both domestically and internationally, it is vital to employ a multidimensional strategy that integrates the indivisibility of rights and incorporates the manifold concerns of women in any particular situation.

The value of such an approach is that it mandates a global outlook. Perhaps it is just human nature to notice problems in someone else's backyard before noticing those in our own. However, the truth is that we all live in glass houses (or at least in a house with a glass ceiling), and it is only appropriate that we learn to turn our eyes to our own backyards.

To understand and eventually resolve women's issues and problems worldwide, we must discipline ourselves to see global concerns from myriad perspectives including not only gender, but also the intersection of gender with, and the indivisibility of gender from, race, ethnicity, nationality, culture, language, color, religion, physical and mental ability, socio-economic class, and sexuality.

It is in this context that this article addresses the notions of international women's human rights. Although women's involvement in this arena is a relative novelty, the success of women already can be felt. The impact of women's voices and perspectives is evident in the changes made concerning reproductive freedom issues, issues of domestic violence, and issues of gender-based violence in times of armed conflict. The work continues on issues of work, education, and self-determination.

III. THE RULES

Initially, women achieved global visibility not within the formal international system itself, but by creating an informal track running parallel to the formal system. This parallel track was necessary because women were excluded from all aspects and levels of official international structures and policy-making. Grass roots activism by individual women and through the work of non-governmental organizations (NGOs) created a bridge to the formalistic/traditional international framework. This parallel system met with unprecedented success, as evidenced in Rio, Vienna, Cairo, and Beijing. Such actions initiated the reconstitution of the rights construct to meet women's real needs, effect women's self-determination, and ensure women's visibility in the global sphere at all levels—locally, statewide, and internationally. These efforts significantly have transformed the concept of women's rights as human rights.

The formal notion that sex equality is central to human rights dates to 1945 when the United Nations Charter (U.N. Charter), among other things, "reaffirmed . . . the equal rights of men and women" and stated as one of its purposes the achievement of international cooperation "in promoting and encouraging respect for human rights and fundamental freedoms . . . without distinction as to . . . sex . . . ." In February 1946, after the U.N. Charter's adoption, the Economic and Social Council (ECOSOC) created the Commission on Human Rights (UNCHR). The UNCHR's agenda was embodied in a body of human rights documents that constitute the foundation of international human rights norms: the Universal Declaration of Human Rights (Declaration or Universal Declaration), adopted in 1948, and two international covenants that were adopted in 1966 and entered into force in 1976—the International Covenant on Civil and Political Rights (ICCPR) and the International Covenant on Economic, Social and Cultural Rights (Economic Covenant). Significantly, all three of these instruments expressly provide for sex equality.

It is important to point out that various other instruments, some substantive in perspective and some regional in scope, have expanded and strengthened this human rights foundation. For example, three regional instruments aimed at the protection of human rights—the European Convention for the Protection of Human Rights and Fundamental Freedoms (European Convention), the American Convention on Human Rights (American Convention), and the African Charter on Human and Peoples' Rights (African Charter)—all expressly provide for sex equality.

In addition, two classification-specific instruments, one focusing on race—the International Convention on the Elimination of All Forms of Racial Discrimination (Race Convention), and the other on sex—the

Convention of the Elimination of all Forms of Discrimination against Women (Women's Convention)—also expressly mandate gender equality. In fact, the Women's Convention throughout expressly articulates the goal of establishing equality for women in all spheres, ranging from the public to the private, including health, education, and political participation, among many others. Through activism, women have become a force in the discourse about and development of international norms, and new meaning has been brought to basic notions of sex equality and human rights.

For example, in the reproductive freedom area, women's rights activists have transformed the concept of reproductive rights from the narrow concept of women's health in maternity and childbirth (which stereotypes "women as wombs"), to a holistic view coalescing a great amalgam of rights including first, second, and third generation human rights. These generations of rights are all promised by, and included in, the documents that constitute the foundation of international human rights norms, i.e., the Universal Declaration, the ICCPR, and the Economic Covenant, as well as various other international, regional, and conference documents such as the Women's Convention, the Race Convention, the American Convention, the African Charter, the European Convention, the Cairo Programme of Action, the Social Summit Declaration and Programme of Action, and the Beijing Platform for Action for the Fourth World Conference on Women. These instruments provide for the protection of rights to privacy, health, equality and non-discrimination, education, religion, travel, family life, decision-making regarding the number of children and their spacing, information, life, liberty, security of the person, integrity of the person, freedom from torture, freedom from slavery, political participation, free assembly and association, work, enjoyment of the benefits of scientific progress,

development, environment, peace, democracy, self-determination, and solidarity, to name various of the rights pertinent to the protection of women's international status and condition as human beings.

By addressing these substantive rules first, this article takes an easy route. Without exception, the international instruments that define human rights expressly mandate sex equality and prohibit discrimination on the basis of sex. With such clear formal pronouncements requiring gender equity, it is intriguing, but given the historical context not all that surprising, that gender inequality persists. As the following section will show, despite the rules that the lofty aspirational goals of equality have fallen far short of expectations and obligations creating a large schism exists between women's "paper" rights and the realities of their everyday lives.

IV. WOMEN'S REALITIES

Ironically, the first place where women's voices must be raised and their presence made visible is in the very same formal rules' constructs discussed above. The international instruments that define human rights—the U.N. Charter, the Universal Declaration, the ICCPR, the Economic Covenant, regional instruments, and substantive human rights instruments such as the Women's Convention and the Race Convention, facially provide protections on the basis of sex. However, the implementation of these human rights documents must be reformulated to protect in practice. Women's articulated rights must be translated to compel real, not virtual, equality.

Unlike theory, the reality for women has been that, until the Women's Convention, and Vienna, Cairo, Copenhagen and Beijing, in both the formal context and in the parallel track, women's voices and perspectives were absent from the international human rights discourse and structure. Women were not present when the rules were being crafted and thus the rules were not made by women for women or with women in mind. Consequently, women's problems, issues, and concerns were not central to the rights framework. The invisibility of women as rule-makers led to the inevitable, surreal struggle to assert simply that women are human beings too, and thus entitled to the rights and freedoms contained in international human rights norms.

It is important to emphasize the significance of the Women's Convention which, by focusing on gender issues, places women's interests and concerns at center stage. This treaty articulates the goal of establishing equality for all women in all aspects of public and private life, including health, education, and political participation. The Women's Convention, by taking a holistic approach to women's rights and lives, is a testament to the indivisibility of rights and the humanity of women.

In reviewing the realities of women's lives worldwide in the context of international women's human rights, two distressing facts surface. First, the rules are, at best, imperfect and, at worst, venal in effecting women's exclusion—silencing women's voices and rendering them invisible. Second, as far as universally enjoying human rights—women simply do not. This is as true in the West as it is in the East, and in the North as it is in the South. The condition of women, as evidenced by the on-going tragedies in Bosnia, Haiti, and Rwanda—where women have been pillaged and raped as instruments or prizes of war—illustrates that women are a long way from being universally respected or heard, let alone safe.

Significantly, this is not a woman's reality solely in times of war. One need not go to Bosnia or even to war for evidence of women's inequality. One need only look at the realities of everyday life. The United Nations, no bastion of gender equality, confirms the persistent and prevailing gender disparities in its description of women as the "largest excluded group in the world." This sad truth of women's subordinate status is borne out regardless of which statistics are considered: employment, economics, personal autonomy, education, political participation, health or personal security (i.e., freedom from violence)—all matters that are critical to women's enjoyment of their international human rights and freedoms. Notwithstanding the existing "paper rights," the universal fact is that women are routinely subjected to torture, starvation, terrorism, humiliation, mutilation, rape, multiple birth and other maternity-related health risks, economic duress, and sexual exploitation, simply because of their sex. Recurrently, these inflictions on women because of their sex are justified or explained by culture and tradition: genital mutilation, female infanticide, bride burning, foot-binding, slavery, face-hiding, wife-beating, honor-killing, forced pregnancy, forced abortion, and multiple, early and closely spaced, child-bearing and birthing, to name but a few. These practices, that some accept without protest because they are based on sex, would be inconceivable to justify if they were instead predicated upon another protected classification, such as race (although until recently culture and tradition were used to justify racial discrimination, including apartheid and slavery). Yet, all these practices, individually and collectively, interfere with women's general well-being and perpetuate women's second-class status and conditions.

In fact, the United States Department of State (another institution whose crowning glory is certainly not gender equality), recognizes "the problem of rampant discrimination against women," and the resulting myriad human rights violations women suffer simply because of their sex. Women worldwide are rendered invisible and silenced by being killed, physically abused into submission, and even starved.

In addition to such direct physical abuses, women's human rights and freedoms are further imperiled by the systematic denial of their political, economic, social, civil, and other legal rights which purportedly ensure women's full participation in the cultural and political life of the state. Even as we approach the 21st century in today's world, some women are still silenced by exclusion from such basic activities as voting, traveling, and testifying in court. In addition, women are shut out from economic discourse by being forbidden to inherit and own property, and routinely are denied access to education, remunerated employment, and health care. Girls and women have their nutritional needs and food denied because of their sex. Moreover, in a cruel twist, women even are denied custody of the children they have borne, simply because of their sex. All of these practices and policies, physical and mental roadblocks to women's ability to achieve equality and enjoy their human rights, are often justified by culture. These limitations, exclusions, and denials maintain the status quo and ensure that women remain ill-equipped to assert, let alone vindicate, their rights. Considering that the rules formally mandate gender equality, these facts of life demonstrate that there is a serious void between the rules of human rights and the realities of women's lives, with both conspiring to marginalize and subordinate women.

It is indeed ironic that the discrepancy between the paper rights and the everyday realities can be explained, in part, by a review of the very rules that purport to protect women. Notwithstanding the sex equity/equality rhetoric of the instruments, a scrutiny of some provisions indicates that in the rules themselves sex, meaning female, is a leading indicator of inequality. In fact, many articles in human rights documents expressly exclude sex as a basis of protecting first, second, and third generation rights, many of which affect women's well-being. This existing rights framework creates at least the effect of excluding women, and at worst the intent to exclude women from equal participation in, and enjoyment of, internationally accepted rights and freedoms. These exclusions, purposeful or not, render women invisible and silent in the human rights world, making sex less important than other protected classifications.

For example, notwithstanding the ICCPR's express protection of gender equality, Article 20 provides that "any advocacy of national, racial or religious hatred that constitutes incitement to discrimination, hostility or violence shall be prohibited by law." On its face, Article 20 does not proscribe advocacy of hatred based on sex. Does such omission signify that advocacy of gender-based "hatred that constitutes incitement to discrimination, hostility or violence" is acceptable, or even appropriate? Certainly, canons of construction support and even urge such a conclusion. Moreover, the logical inference of Article 20 is that discrimination, hostility or violence based on sex is not as venal or heinous as ethnicity-based, race-based or religion-based hatred. This message is powerful and frightening, given the prevalence of violence against women, especially when combined with some of the cultural pretexts.

Similarly, the Economic Covenant falls short of providing full protection based on sex. In Article 13, parties to the Covenant recognize and agree that education:

> shall be directed to the full development of the human personality and the sense of its dignity, and shall strengthen the respect for human rights and fundamental freedoms. . . . And shall enable all persons to participate effectively in a free society, promote understanding, tolerance and friendship among all nations racial, ethnic, or religious groups, and further the activities of the United Nations for the maintenance of peace.

In a paragraph that explicitly enumerates the classes protected, gender again stands out because of its absence. This omission in Article 13 signifies that exclusion from participation in a free society on the basis of sex is not only acceptable but the rule of law. This exclusion of sex is significant because of the paramount importance of education to women's self-determination, overall well-being, and particularly to the attainment of human rights.

Not surprisingly, the regional instruments are similarly flawed. For example, the American Convention effects an exclusion almost identical to that found in Article 20 of the ICCPR. The African Charter excludes sex in its prohibition of mass expulsions, making gender-based expulsions, at best, not as bad as other expulsions such as those based on nationality, race, ethnicity or religion, and, at worst, acceptable in the name of law. This is particularly distressing because women and their children comprise 70–80% of the world's refugees. Significantly, refugee women as displaced persons whose status disadvantages them, are denied their human rights and freedoms in the very sphere where they need the most protection.

Finally, the Race Convention commits a similar though more egregious faux pas: it excludes sex in making reference to a provision of the Universal Declaration that includes sex. This exclusion demonstrates that sex, meaning female, is so inconsequential that it can be deleted even from where it exists.

These provisions that exclude sex as a basis of protection of certain rights are particularly troubling in light of canons of construction. Both common law and the Vienna Convention on the Law of Treaties mandate that when a general provision and a specific provision conflict, the specific or detailed provision shall prevail. Using such rules of construction, the drafters effectively excised sex-based protections from certain substantive provisions in the instruments themselves, even if the lofty preambular language included sex as a protected classification. While in theory this can be attributed to, at best, sloppy drafting, in the real world of rights advocacy it means a loss of rights and perpetuation of subordination based on sex.

The realities of women's lives, as handicapped by an insensitive legal framework, entrench the invisibility, silence, and exclusion of women from the international fora at the rule-making, rule-interpreting, and rule/rights-enforcing levels. This exclusion imperils women's holistic well-being and denies full personhood on the basis of sex. For instance:

- While the rules protect against discrimination based on sex, the reality is virtual starvation of the girl child and female infanticide.
- While the rules protect the right to life, the reality is maternal mortality because of too-early, multiple, and closely spaced pregnancies and a lack of health services during pregnancy and childbirth.
- While the rules prohibit genocide, the reality is the rape of women and girls for ethnic cleansing and/or as prizes of war.
- While the rules prohibit torture, the reality sees brides burned and others raped.
- While the rules guarantee women's bodily integrity and equality, the reality sees women as wombs and as war booty.

The juxtaposition of rules and realities is ample evidence of the limitation, implausibility, and inefficacy of the traditional, unidimensional approach to achieving international protection of women's human rights and freedoms. Women's exclusion from the rights construct at all levels has meant loss and denial of rights and the perpetuation of subordination of women derived from and influenced by gender-based stereotypes, customs, and tradition. Women's rights advocates must work towards the adoption of a multidimensional, multiple-perspective human rights approach that recognizes rights affecting women as indivisible from, and integral to, the existing rights construct. The reconfigured model also must accommodate women's diverse experiences, including those informed by race, ethnicity, nationality, culture, language, color, religion, socio-economic class, and sexuality.

For example, one of the problems the world must face, in light of the Bosnian, Haitian, and Rwandan tragedies, is that a gender-based genocide construct does not exist. This limited view of the rules renders women who have been repeatedly and brutally raped, and those who have been forcibly impregnated, invisible in the legal world. Rape in se is a horror, but it is not recognized as such. Rather, in order to condemn this largely female-victim crime it must be placed in the largely male construct of torture—the proverbial round peg in a square hole. The prohibition against rape formally must be articulated as a separate offense against the law of nations so that there can be no question that it is a heinous and inhuman crime whatever the context, be it global war or the neighborhood bar.

Steps must be taken to remedy the existing gaps between rules and realities. Part VI proposes a model that considers women's concerns at all stages: rule-making, rule-interpreting, and rule/rights-enforcing. However, first it is important to examine the role of culture in the existing rights construct.

V. THE ROLE OF CULTURE

Cultural views of gender have created, facilitated, and perpetuated the schism between paper rights and the realities of women's lives. Throughout time, a myth of equality has permitted subordination of women at all levels of their existence under the guise of a benevolent and inclusive rule of law. Indeed, even in those rare instances when practices that effect the subordination of women are conceded to be human rights violations, victims often have no relief.

The fundamental problem is that international law, like other social institutions, has evolved as normative. This "norm" is the well-entrenched perspective by which all is analyzed and measured: a white, Western/Northern European, Judeo-Christian, heterosexual, propertied, educated, male ideology. This concept of "normal" represents the group that historically has controlled, and still controls, the power structure which then "protects" or in some cases colonizes its subordinates by conferring rights that exist only as this ruling class chooses to define them.

Governments endorse such a myopic perspective and, in fact, accept and promote it as the rule of law. Certainly, only in this framework can an ability such as childbearing be labeled a disability simply because the normatives cannot do it. Is it a wonder then that the focus on women's rights, particularly their bodily integrity and health rights in areas of sexuality and reproduction, is a relative novelty?

One chilling example of the facilitating role of normativity in the manipulation of women is government interference with individuals' reproductive freedom to effect a state population policy. This meddling wholly disregards that health, reproductive, and sexual rights and freedoms belong not to governments but to individuals. It is individuals who should be able to exercise such rights in light of their particular circumstances which, of course, may include socio-economic, religious, and cultural considerations, but are free from state encroachment upon, interference with, or regulation of such rights and freedoms. Nevertheless, world history is replete with examples of governments' exploitation of women's fertility to increase or decrease the population in order to meet perceived state needs.

For example, although the then-Soviet Union decriminalized abortion in the 1920s, the government reversed its policy in the mid-1930s to compensate for the loss of population anticipated in expectation of a World War. Yet, in 1955, in post-Stalinist Russia, abortion again was decriminalized. Similarly, the devastating effects of World War II on the population prompted many Eastern European states to outlaw abortion in the hopes of increasing population to re-establish the labor force and rebuild armies.

Even Adolf Hitler, shortly after rising to power, criminalized abortion and instituted an anti-abortion policy in order to increase the population of the state, a policy that resulted in many more abortionists being criminally charged. Indeed, during World War II, German tribunals could impose the death penalty for illegal abortions. However, in Hitler's Germany, the charged abortionists could use as a defense that the woman was Jewish—termination of a Jewish fetus did not violate the proscription against abortion. More recently, the government of Germany has sought to encourage births by offering payments of approximately $650 for each child.

Governments also have used abortion laws to reduce population. For example, India and China, two countries with serious overpopulation problems, have instituted coercive abortion policies as an integral part of the state's program to control population growth. Because these societies maintain a preference for boy children, reproductive technologies have been used for sex selection purposes, although recently, both India and China have passed laws to prohibit this practice. State coercive reproduction policies, as well as the private use of technology for sex-selection objectives, not only perpetuate the subordination of women and the stereotype of "women as wombs," but also severely affect women's well-being by, among other things, infringing upon their exercise and enjoyment of guaranteed international human rights. Thus, government regulation of fertility must be scrutinized and exposed as a calculated attempt to control

women's bodies in violation of their individual human rights and freedoms.

In this context, serious consideration must be given to the notion of cultural relativism. As will be discussed, culture is, or can be, used both to perpetuate women's subordination in the name of tradition, or to subordinate non-dominant cultures in the name of law. Culture can be but a smoke screen to prevent dealing with and recognizing historic oppression of women and their subjection to the prevailing normative culture.

Especially in an extreme case such as female genital mutilation (FGM), a practice recently condemned by the Committee on the Elimination of Discrimination Against Women (CEDAW) recommendations and the Cairo Programme of Action, a holistic women's well-being approach mandates abolition of such a practice. Otherwise, as far as controlling deleterious "health" effects of FGM, all that arguably would be required for its legitimacy is an antiseptic setting, notwithstanding its many long-term disadvantages to women, including interfering with their health, safety, bodily integrity, and sexuality.

The question of cultural relativism squarely presents a challenge to the notion of the universality of human rights. Some cultural relativists would have the human rights structure itself be limited, rather than enriched, by culture. They would posit that treatment of an individual that comports to local traditions is non-reviewable under universal human rights norms because the tradition itself is the defining factor of what is right and what is a right in a given locality.

This position is contrary to the lessons learned from slavery, the Holocaust, and contemporary tragedies such as Bosnia. Certainly, if governments could exterminate entire groups of people in the name of culture, human rights would be but a faded dream. A plethora of recent events have focused attention on practices ranging greatly in their nature and effects such as FGM, caning as a form of punishment, the imposition of the death penalty (especially on minors), the wearing of a veil, the cutting off of a hand for stealing, to name a few that some argue are wholly unacceptable as violative of human rights norms, but that others justify in the name of culture, religion, and tradition. The relativists' rejection of value judgments—ironically, a value judgment in itself—is simply flawed. This article opposes such a hands-off approach which, interestingly, tends to be most vehemently employed when the rights of women are at stake, such as the right to property ownership, integrity of the body, self-determination, or enfranchisement. This skewed strand of relativism appears to be simply pretextual—an excuse to keep women under the proverbial thumb of patriarchy in the name of culture, religion or tradition. Like racism, sexism in the name of culture is no less sexism than sexism for sport. Why is it, we should ask ourselves, that when women are deprived of rights simply because of their sex, the justifications of culture, religion or tradition are so readily acceptable and defensible?

This article, of course, does not constitute, nor should it be read or interpreted to constitute, a blanket rejection of culture, religion or tradition. Rather, it advocates cultural pluralism as an objective in any human rights discourse. Ethnocentric, culturally-biased notions of right and wrong should be evaluated in the context of appreciation for and recognition of other world views. Personal decisions should be exercised by the individual herself, not by institutional fiat, and the individual should be free to believe in, follow, or observe cultural, religious or traditional practices or not. This, too, has its limits, as no one would argue that torture or genocide should, or could, ever be justified in the name of culture. Further, an individual's right might well be illusory vis á vis societal and familial pressures and expectations. Certainly social ostracism, rejection or

even punishment for failure to submit to a practice might well negate, if not vitiate, the individual's free will and exercise of her rights, including the right to self-determination.

International human rights theory supports the concept of the universality of rights. Indeed, while human rights documents consistently address culture as a basis upon which protections must be afforded, not one cites to culture as the grounds upon which protected rights may be abridged. Rather, many of these documents support the conclusion that some aspects of culture, particularly those justified solely by status, particularly sex, must cede to universal human rights. For example, the African Charter on the Rights and Welfare of the African Child expressly balances rights and culture and requires member states of the Organization of African Unity to "abolish customs and practices harmful to the welfare, normal growth and development of the child and in particular:

(a) those customs and practices prejudicial to the health or life of the child, and
(b) those customs and practices discriminatory to the child on the grounds of sex or other status."

Similarly, the Women's Convention squarely confronts the possibility of the misuse of culture as a pretext to discriminate and urges states parties "to take all appropriate measures, including legislation, to modify or abolish existing laws, regulations, customs and practices which constitute discrimination against women." Further, the Women's Convention requires that states parties "take all appropriate measures: (a) to modify the social and cultural patterns of conduct of men and women, with a view to achieving the elimination of prejudices and customary and all other practices which are based on the idea of the inferiority or the superiority of either of the sexes or on stereotyped roles for men and women. . . ."

This rejection of cultural relativity is not intended to give a sweeping endorsement to the concept of universality as it has been applied under the present "normative" construct. As one activist keenly observed, "one of the biggest problems with universality as it has existed in the past is that in the process that led to universal articulation, a lot of people did not participate." Hence, this article proposes an analytical model that respects this critique. The issue in this perspective of universality is not about colonizing by way of a Western imposition of moral or ethical views. Rather, it exposes the present construct as flawed for failure to consider perspectives of insiders and outsiders. This problem is resolved in the proposed model, in part, by ensuring that culture—meaning the customs, practices and rituals of a particular group as well as the ideas, beliefs, and values underlying them which define the roles and status of the people in a given community and shape their way of life—is included as part of the analysis in the context of an amalgam of indivisible rights.

Indeed, this author rejects and eschews the normative analytical construct that dichotomizes cultural relativism and universality of rights without so much as a consideration of possible alternative methodologies. In the model proposed here, observations, findings, and judgments have to be fluid, not carved in stone. Only such an approach can accommodate modern societies, diverse peoples, and the rule of law. As science, religion, technology, communications, medicine, anthropology and, yes, even the law, grow and evolve, our way of looking at tradition, social conditions, medical progress, technological changes, and the nature and status of rights also should grow and evolve.

The inviolability and indivisibility of human rights must be the foundation for all analyses. It would be as absurd to suggest that there is no difference between and among cultures as it would be to suggest that genocide and torture are not universal wrongs. Thus, human rights cannot and should not be excised from or exorcised of culture. In this context, however, acts and practices that harm an individual's physical or mental well-being unequivocally and irreversibly, even in the name of culture, are simply wrong. Indeed, denial of equality to women on cultural, religious and traditional grounds appears to create a "Catch 22" situation: if an obligation to eliminate barriers to women's equality can be limited by the status quo—such as culture, religion and/or tradition—and the status quo has at its core entrenched and institutionalized inequality on the basis of sex, then equality can never be achieved, being shielded by the law that purports to mandate it.

This certainly is not to say or to suggest that there are no cultural considerations or accommodations to be made when dealing with human rights. Quite the contrary, factors such as race, nationality, ethnicity, etc., are integral to the human rights construct. However, there is a distinction to be made between considering or accommodating cultural customs and using culture as a pretext to deny the integrity and dignity of individuals on the basis of sex. These rights—to culture, religion, tradition—are rights of the individual that governments should neither impose upon nor abridge in the name of the law. In other words, international human rights scholars, activists and representatives should neither use culture as a shield to protect practices that violate women's human rights, nor use human rights norms as a sword, a weapon of subjugation, colonialism and moral imperialism, to oppress other communities and ways of life.

VI. REFORM

This article proposes, and in this part develops, a theoretical and analytical construct that effects much needed reform in the international human rights arena to render women visible and raise women's voices, all women's voices, so that human rights can be women's rights too. In order to bridge the gap between the rules and the realities, the proposal urges the adoption of a theoretical construct that uses communication theory, legitimacy theory, and critical feminist/race theory as applied to international human rights law in a multidisciplinary, multidimensional context. The model requires that the following three inquiries be made at each stage of the rule-making process. First, the gender question: are there any gender implications of the proposed lawmaking; second, the women's question: a non-essentialist, multidimensional evaluation of the impact of the lawmaking on women; third, the culture question: an analysis of the cultural implications of the lawmaking.

The common thread of each inquiry, of course, is to make women visible and raise their voices so that their needs are met and their rights are respected. The basic tenet of the communication theory incorporated into this methodology is the recognition that communications are at the root of law-making. Although the ultimate lawmaking function may be relegated to specialized institutions, these institutions as well as the process of creating, interpreting, and enforcing the laws, must include and integrate the views of those about whom the law is concerned and for whom the law creates expectations as to future behavior. In this view, it is essential to focus on raising women's voices and including women's perspectives with a critical feminist/race conceptualization at all stages of the formal and informal international prescriptive processes: rule-making, rule-interpreting and rule/rights-enforcing. To achieve this end, it stands to reason that representation of women, by women, is highly desirable, if not a legal and moral imperative.

Similarly, the proposed model incorporates concepts from Professor Franck's legitimacy theory which is based on the premise that the legitimacy of a government is dependent upon having the consent of the governed and respect for the opinion of the people. In this regard, the government, to be legitimate, must ascertain the opinions and desires of the people, including women, by asking the articulated questions at each stage of the lawmaking process. Once prescribed, a government must follow the rule of law, an integral part of which is providing for and securing individual rights.

Moreover, the critical feminist/race dimension (like the communications and legitimacy theories) would also require women's participation. Only with women's presence and perspectives in the process of government and governing, will women's concerns and issues become an integral part of, and incorporated into, the global agenda. It is significant that the failure to ask the pertinent questions concerning gender, women, and culture is largely due to the exclusion of women from the global communication process which makes, interprets, and enforces international legal norms. Without women in the roles of commissioners, rapporteurs, committee members, commission members, U.N. and international agency representatives, activists, citizens, and scholars, women's thoughts and feelings, rights, needs, realities, and perspectives will not be expressed or addressed. Without women's input, the normatives will retain a monopoly on, and power over, false-truth images.

Inquiry 1: The Gender Question—Are there any gender implications of the rules or practices that otherwise appear neutral or objective? In human rights considerations, this question will ascertain whether (and which) women's rights are involved. Women must be among the inquirers as well as the inquired.

Inquiry 2: The Women's Question—What will the implications of the rule or practice, as interpreted and enforced, be on the real lives of women, and how will women be disadvantaged? It is imperative to conduct this inquiry in a non-essentialist manner with a multidimensional, holistic perspective. In order to avoid, and institutionally eschew essentialism, the methodology requires the inquiry to address the conflation of gender and other aspects of a woman's personhood, such as race, ethnicity, class, ability, and sexual orientation, both to evidence and to account for the indivisibility of rights. The methodology also must ensure that any identified causal links between gender and a particular outcome are accurate and relevant to the issue being considered.

To be sure, such articulation of the women's question is over-simplified. In its proper application, it must take into account the multiplicity of coexisting factors and issues—the multidimensionality of women's lives. Thus, the inquiries need to be taken factor by factor, issue by issue, not simply creating dichotomies, but permitting consideration of combinations, permutations, and implications of rules and practices for women, who by their status constitute anywhere from one to manifold "deviations" from the norm. Thus, the proposed women's questions, effectively a series of communications in which women participate in the process of governance both as inquirers and as the inquired, will better facilitate a proper landscape for making a reality of women's paper rights.

Recent events are evidence that women have slowly but surely started this process. In Vienna, the "Women's Issues" NGOs were recognized as the most effective of all groups, both official and unofficial, attending the conference. They made women's voices heard and women's realities visible, effecting the establishment of women's rights as an official part of the human rights agenda. The same is true for the ICPD—women again organized, galvanized, and were heard. Such efforts to present and evaluate women's issues from a multidimensionality and interdisciplinary perspective require an analysis of cultural relativity.

Inquiry 3: The Culture Question—What are the cultural considerations driving the practices and rules? To evaluate any perceived or claimed cultural conflict between a practice and a universal human right, the model proposes applying a balancing test which includes aspects of the communication, legitimacy and critical feminist/race theories. First, one must obtain information about the cultural practice from both an "insider's" and an "outsider's" perspective, the insider being the proponent or practitioner of the cultural practice; the outsider being the normativo/a asserting the conflict. In addition, in light of the challenged practice, the human rights norm must also be examined from both an insider and an outsider perspective, the insider here being the proponent of the human rights principle and critic of the culture.

In this context, particular attention to cultural practices is necessary so that they may be carefully protected from the improper imposition of outsiders' ideologies. However, culture must not be used as a smoke screen to prevent recognizing and dealing with the historic oppression of women and their universal, cross-cultural subordination. In examining a cultural practice that appears to disadvantage only women, or have a disproportionately burdensome impact on women, the cost of violating the human rights norm must be weighed against the benefit of the cultural practice. One should commence by asking at least these questions: What is the origin and value of the cultural practice?; What is its level of significance to the culture and within the community?; What is its level of intrusion on a protected individual right?; and How significant is the human rights norm to the international community? The inquiry must be further contextualized by addressing the following: the nature of the practice being challenged, who is challenging the practice (i.e., an insider versus an outsider), the challengers' motives for opposing the practice, and the claimed harmful outcomes of the practice.

In this regard, we must recognize that a broad range of practices exists. At one end of the spectrum are rituals such as ear-piercing female infants, a practice that arguably has no detrimental lifelong effect on women's human rights and freedoms, including health. At the other end of the spectrum are practices such as FGM, female infanticide, and reproductive controls, such as forced pregnancies or forced abortions—both equally troubling, all of which have dramatic and harmful life-long effects on women's reproductive and sexual health rights and freedoms both in se and as indivisible parts of a plethora of rights critical to women's existence, well-being and full personhood, including life, health, privacy, family life, economic self-determination, political participation, education, and equality.

Significantly, it is imperative that for any analysis of cultural practices to be valid, it must be conducted from the perspective of both "insiders" and "outsiders." For example, industrial state feminists need to think seriously about how certain practices could be explained to others. Consider, for example, the glass ceiling phenomenon, the feminization of poverty, the denial to mothers of welfare benefits if they have more children than a state thinks they should, while fathers (many of whom do not support the mothers or the children) are not part of the "welfare reform" equation. Of course, there are extremes, such as FGM, where the age at the time of the procedure is, or could or should be, a critical issue. This raises the interesting question of whether analysis of the practice could or should depend on whether the genital surgery was delayed until an appropriate age of consent. Would "consent" make the practice an elected procedure and thus not a violation of the rights to bodily integrity? In such cases, the answer would have to include considerations of individual free will and self-determination. Is the problem solved by, as some recently have suggested, performing the procedure in

an antiseptic hospital setting? What about other elected cosmetic surgeries that carry serious physical and mental health risks, such as breast augmentation? Even if none of these practices is acceptable, the methodological question remains: how does the human rights community inform a group that certain practices violate human rights norms. For example, what is the appropriate way to inform certain communities, for example American Indians that domestic violence is unacceptable conduct and not private business as usual.

It is clear that there are no easy answers to the cultural inquiry. However, there are questions that can be raised and examined to start the process of communication that will eventually, and hopefully, lead to a multidimensional and culturally sensitive perspective. This proposed process represents a major leap forward in ensuring the protection of women's human rights.

VII. CONCLUSION

The proposed methodology, with its expansive and extensive role for women, will better facilitate an inclusive global setting for addressing women's issues, resolving women's problems, and effecting women's greater participation in a process that is central to their dignity and status as women and as human beings. In this context, the role and propriety of government regulation must be scrutinized as part of the overall inquiry. Take for example reproductive freedom controls. Ostensibly, such controls are intended to protect a nascent form of life, or some other allegedly appropriate government interest. A look at the history of reproductive freedom regulations, however, spins a different tale of manipulation of women's bodies for improper purposes.

One of the critical differences in the human rights world today is the growing number of NGOs whose focus and concerns are women's rights. These NGOs have spoken loudly and clearly on women's issues, insisting that women be included in the process and successfully planting women firmly in the international rights landscape. This process was successfully started in Vienna and has continued in the ICPD, at the Social Summit, and in Beijing, despite large obstacles. However, women's initiatives must not stop at NGO membership, but must reach all women—in their everyday lives, of having babies, working for no pay, making less money than men even when they are paid, and suffering personal abuse to their bodies and dignity simply because of their sex.

In looking at this constituency, a central concern is whether "when human rights deprivations occur, can victims or others bring complaints to appropriate transnational decision makers for remedy?" To be sure, various international covenants and declarations provide for the right of individual petition. However, this process is far removed and remote from many women's realities. The implementation of women's human rights must extend beyond paper to involve local groups and grassroots organizations in not only the process of taking complaints but in taking appropriate action as well (with the support and assistance of transnational legal institutions) in order to provide real, rather than theoretical, remedies. This is particularly true in seeking redress for so-called culturally justified practices, about which local groups are the most informed and aware. The formalistic concepts of complaints must be expanded to include more informal structures to ensure that women are visible and their voices heard. These changes are at the heart of the proposed reform.

The outcome sought from this process is the enjoyment by women of their human rights. This requires the development, expansion, and transformation of the content and meaning of articulated human rights norms so that they include, and apply to, the reality of women's lives. It is important to challenge unlawful deprivations; it is imperative to mobilize a continuing consensus; it is vital that the rules are interpreted and enforced for the protection and fulfillment of women's human rights. The methodology urged in this article seeks to facilitate the creation and the realization of a holistic, non-essentialist, multidimensional construct in which women are not, and indeed cannot be, marginalized or subordinated. It focuses on the inclusion of all women in a system that defines and defends women's rights as human rights, and thus protects and promotes the well-being, integrity, and international human rights and freedoms of women worldwide.

NOTES

1. Sarah Egerton, The Emulation (1703), quoted in *The Oxford Dictionary of Quotations* 267 (Angela Partington ed., 4th ed. 1992).

2. See First Lady Hillary Rodham Clinton, Remarks to the United Nations Fourth World Conference on Women Plenary Session 6–7. (Sept. 5–6, 1995) (copy on file with the Brooklyn Journal of International Law) (hereinafter Fourth World Conference on Women).

Berta Esperanza Hernandez-Truyol is a professor of Law, St. John's University School of Law.

Reading 4.4

Mediating Conflict in Central America

PAUL WEHR
JOHN PAUL LEDERACH

ANALYTICAL APPROACH

A regional process of conflict resolution has recently evolved in Central America the principal framework for which has been the Esquipulas II agreement of 1987. In this paper we analyze mediation within Esquipulas, first from a region-wide perspective, then as it has been used to moderate and resolve conflicts within Nicaragua. How mediation has been applied in this historical case may have implications for how students and practitioners of third party intervention conceive of the role of mediator.

We begin with a discussion of mediation as a theoretical concept and how our analysis of the Esquipulas case and our personal involvement in Nicaraguan mediation has influenced our conceptualization of the role of intermediary. We develop the concept of the Insider-Partial as a mediator type. We then proceed to discuss the development of mediation within Esquipulas as an historical *process* that moves through time, and produces, responds to and transforms events. Process implies action and in mediation third parties act to move conflict toward settlement. Since mediators create this

process, who they are and what they do is necessarily of concern to this paper. Oscar Arias Sanchez, for example, has been a key mediator-negotiator in Esquipulas.

We go on to examine the Esquipulas mediation in terms of the *structure* it has created for conflict resolution—the rules, agenda, principles, timelines and organizations fashioned to move conflictants toward settlement. The principle of simultaneity of implementation (Hopmann, 1988) and the commissions for carrying it out illustrate the structure of Esquipulas mediation.

We next discuss the Esquipulas mediation as *context*, the larger environment influencing third party efforts. Conflict research has addressed the importance of the immediate mediation setting for inducing settlement. Just as important is the wider context or environment influencing the conflict toward or away from resolution. In the case of Esquipulas, that context appears to have been of special import. The change of US presidential administrations and the presence of international volunteers and nongovernmental organizations are noteworthy examples of contextual determinants of mediation success in Nicaragua.

Reprinted by permission of Sage Publications Ltd from Paul Wehr and John Paul Lederach, Mediating Conflict in Central America, *Journal of Peace Research,* © International Peace Research Institute, Oslo, PRIO, 1991.

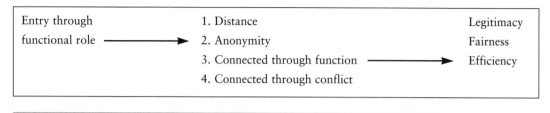

Figure 1   Neutrality-based Model

Our paper concludes with a discussion of some theoretical and practical implications of the outsider-neutral and insider-partial mediator roles illustrated by Esquipulas mediation. Our major recommendations are for a more inclusive set of mediator types and more systematic selection of mediators to reflect that range. Mediators, we conclude, must become more aware of the influence of context on mediation outcomes and how it can be made more supportive of mediation efforts.

CONCEPTS OF MEDIATION

Our concept of mediation has been very much influenced by our on-site involvement as observer and practitioner in Central American conflict resolution. One of us spent a year as mediator of one of the two major conflicts in the Nicaraguan civil war. The role of mediator has been characterized in numerous ways in the mediation literature, reflecting the various levels at which mediators work and the quite different personalities, skills, attributes and positions they bring to their work. Our experience in Central America leads us to add to those characterizations a model of mediation we see as having particular relevance for third party intervention in developing nations. We will first discuss some of those roles and definitions of mediation, then how our concept relates to them and how it could expand the concept of mediation.

The Outsider-Neutral

One common conceptualization of mediation roots the mediator's effectiveness in *externality* (coming from outside the conflict situation) and *neutrality* (having no connection or commitment to either side in the conflict). In the North American field of intergroup and interpersonal conflict management, for example, mediation is commonly defined as a rather narrow, formal activity in which an impartial, neutral third party facilitates direct negotiation. Mediator neutrality is reinforced by their coming from outside the conflict, facilitating settlement, then leaving. In North America this distance of mediator from disputants is heavily emphasized. Mediators are referred to as "third party neutrals." Ethics codes bind mediators to that principle. Mediators' neutrality protects the legitimacy and authority that are created primarily through their professional role, position and function—a rational-legal type of authority as Weber (1922/1957) described it. This neutrality-based intervener is what we call the Outsider-Neutral.

The outsider-neutrals maintain distance from the disputants (see Fig. 1). They are chosen because they have no connection with either side that will affect the outcome and are thereby judged to be unbiased. Outsider-neutrals are connected to disputants through the conflict alone, relating to them only during the mediation process in ways relevant to the function of mediation. Only small parts of the lives of conflict parties and interveners intersect: those related to the conflict.

According to this view, the assurance of neutrality in mediation creates the necessary perception of mediator legitimacy, professionalism and fairness. The mediator works to present a neutral self, to perform credibly in a way that defines the situation in which the mediation/negotiation performance takes place as neutral and impartial (Goffman, 1959). Neutrality and impartiality are defined negatively, in terms of what the mediator is *not*. The third party is *not connected* to either disputant, is *not biased* toward either side, has *no investment* in any outcome except settlement and does *not expect any special reward from either side* (Moore, 1986, pp. 15–16).

The International Mediator

International mediation is conceived with much greater breadth and diversity than is the North American view of intergroup and interpersonal mediation. The complexity of international and intercultural disputes calls forth perhaps a greater variety of mediator roles. And so we find the mediator-broker (Touval, 1982) and the mediator-conciliator (Yarrow, 1978) among many others. Each conceptualization emphasizes a different role played or function performed by international third parties. Touval's able discussion of the different mediator roles and conceptualizations suggests that the concept of international mediator remains somewhat open. There are other terms that from our review of the third party literature appear similarly imprecise. Neutrality, for example, is on occasion to be translated as even-handedness, or even balance, as in Yarrow's characterization of Quaker conciliation as "balanced partiality."

Theorists generally do not see mediator neutrality and impartiality as requisites for successful international mediation. In fact in some cases mediator connectedness and bias prove to facilitate settlement. We do find in the theory, however, a strong assumption of the importance of externality for mediation success. The successful mediator must intervene from outside the *conflict* situation.

The Insider-Partial

We suggest an additional mediator role (one that may be particular to more traditional societies) whose effectiveness depends neither on externality nor neutrality but on quite the opposite attributes—internality and partiality. We further suggest from our observations of Central American mediation, that the insider-partial mediator complements quite usefully those interveners who bring neutrality from outside the conflict situation.

The insider-partial is the "mediator from within the conflict," whose acceptability to the conflictants is rooted not in distance from the conflict or objectivity regarding the issues, but rather in connectedness and trusted relationships with the conflict parties. The trust comes partly from the fact that the mediators do not leave the postnegotiation situation. They are part of it and must live with the consequences of their work. They must continue to relate to conflictants who have trusted their commitment to a just and durable settlement. Such a mediator is more likely to develop out of more traditional cultural settings where primary, face-to-face relations continue to characterize political, economic and social exchange, and where tradition has been less eroded by modernity.

In a recent ethnographic study, Lederach (1988) found that neutrality is not what Central Americans seek for help in resolving conflict. They look primarily for trust, *confianza*. In the *confianza* model (see Fig. 2), authority to mediate is vested in the third party through a personal relationship with the disputant(s), rather than by a secondary role

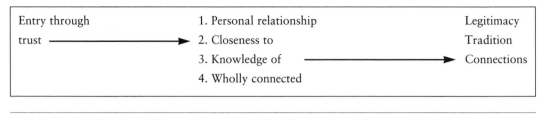

Figure 2   Confianza-based Model

such as external intervener. This is what Weber (1922/1957) called traditional authority.

Trust-based mediation assumes accumulated, sometimes intimate knowledge shared by helper and helped. One who can "deposit *confianza*" in another knows that person well. They are connected in many ways, not just through a limited service performed. As Simmel wrote, "the more we have in common with another as whole persons, the more easily will our totality be involved in every single relation to him [sic]" (1950, p. 44). In just that sense, the insider-partial does not relate with the conflictants simply through an intervention. Their trust relationship permits them to resolve the conflict together.

With respect to trust, the insider-partial is not the polar opposite of other models. Personal trust is always a concern in selecting any mediator. But with insider-partials it is the *primary* criterion for selection. They are recognized above all as having the trust of all sides. Unlike the outsider-neutral chosen for the absence of connection with disputants, the insider-partial is selected precisely for positive connections and attributes, *for what they are and do:* they *are close to, known by, with and for each side.* This *confianza* ensures sincerity, openness and revelation and is a channel through which negotiation is initiated and pursued.

We propose, then, to add the insider-partial to the taxonomy of types and roles of international mediators. Its potential for useful combination with outsider-neutrals and other

types will, we trust, become apparent as we show how several of them were combined in Esquipulas mediation.

The Esquipulas Process

Esquipulas is the most recent of a series of historical efforts to resolve interstate conflict and promote regional integration in Central America: the Central American Confederation, 1823–38; the Central American Court of Justice, 1907–17; a regional federation all but ratified in 1923; the Central American Common Market from 1960 onward. There have been counterforces as well: border conflicts such as the 1969 so-called Soccer War between El Salvador and Honduras; the Filibuster Wars of the nineteenth century; military governments that have favored national over regional identity. When the Sandinista movement overthrew the Somoza regime in 1979, such counterforces were holding in check the region's long-standing desire for self-determination.

The Sandinista revolution radically altered social and political conflict throughout Central America, most of all within Nicaragua itself. There it moderated though did not eliminate class conflict, but it created two new conflicts. First, the Sandinistas' effort to integrate by force the Atlantic Coast peoples into a revolutionary state stimulated armed resistance in the East. Second, the Sandinistas' Marxist ideological approach to governance and nation-building encouraged defections from their own ranks. Many of these dissidents became, along with Somozista elements, the raw material for a US-organized Contra insurgency after 1982. The more conservative elements in Nicaraguan society, led by the Catholic hierarchy and those of the upper class who had remained, came to oppose Sandinista policies and to give some support to the Contra movement.

The Nicaraguan revolution became increasingly militarized with the aid and involvement of the USSR and Cuba. The US-sponsored military buildups in El Salvador and Honduras completed the prospect of a region headed toward the abyss. As the Contra activity expanded into Honduras and Costa Rica it inevitably drew those nations into the Nicaraguan conflict. This transformation of national conflicts into a regional superpower confrontation moved neighboring states such as Mexico to initiate formal peace-making efforts.

Contadora

Contadora, begun in January 1983 by Panama, Mexico, Venezuela and Colombia, was an experiment in collective mediation. Its goal was to detach Central American conflicts from large US-Soviet competition and to shift them from military to political and diplomatic levels. The Contadora Group, consulting with a Central American Group (presidents of Guatemala, El Salvador, Nicaragua, Costa Rica, Honduras) and a Contadora Support Group (Peru, Brazil, Argentina, Uruguay) had produced a draft treaty by 1986. The draft was a blueprint for demilitarizing Central American conflicts and resolving them through negotiation.

Contadora reached an impasse in mid-1986. Honduras, under pressure from the Reagan Administration with its growing military presence there, declined to sign the treaty (Buvollen, 1989a). The USA had alternately

ignored and criticized Contadora while pursuing its military options throughout the region. The USA was, therefore, simultaneously subverting the Contadora process diplomatically (Bagley, 1987) and intensifying the conflicts Contadora sought to moderate.

While Contadora fell short of its objectives, viewed within the larger peace process it was considerably more productive than would appear. Contadora created bases on which Esquipulas could build. It provided a consultative history and frame work, and a comprehensive and accurate diagnosis of the region's conflicts. Most important, perhaps, it was an example of Central American regional independence. Contadora happened not only without but *in spite of* US policy.

Actually, we find much of Contadora in Esquipulas. Eight Contadora documents are acknowledged as precedents in the Esquipulas treaty (Gomariz, 1988, p. 355). Contadora states have subsequently participated in both the International Verification and Support Commission and the UN Observer Group—Central America peace-keeping force. It appears to us, then, that Esquipulas was not a break with Contadora, as some (Robinson, 1988) may see it, but a continuation of it within an exclusively Central American framework.

While Esquipulas built upon Contadora, it was also motivated by the latter's failures. One such stimulus was the refusal of Honduras to sign the Contadora Act, a failure which led to Congressional resumption of military aid to the Contra insurgents. That alarming development motivated Oscar Arias Sanchez, newly elected president of Costa Rica to make a new initiative. Arias had been involved in the final Contadora consultations. With a four-year term before him in the region's most stable political system, he had many of the resources needed by an international intermediary (Young, 1967).

Arias set to work simplifying negotiation objectives. Contadora's preoccupation with security issues had produced proposals too complex to work. Arias set aside security as a temporarily insoluble problem. He circulated a simple draft agreement among his fellow presidents. Ortega excepted. His success at simplification is suggested by the comparative lengths of the "Acta de Contadora" (pp. 22) and the Esquipulas agreement (pp. 6).

The Time Path

By February 1987, Arias was receiving encouragement from his presidential counterparts. That was met over subsequent months with increasing opposition from the Reagan Administration. Its release of the "Wright-Reagan Plan" two days before the August Central American Group summit meeting was perceived by the group as an attempt to undercut the peace process. Hopmann (1988) credits that perception with motivating the five presidents to sign the agreement. They were also urged to sign by certain members of the US Congress. With the signing of "Procedimiento para Establecer la Paz Firme y Duradera en Centroamerica" (Gomariz, 1988, pp. 355–361), a frame work was created for mediated negotiation both among the signatory governments and between them and their respective insurgent opponents.

The agreement set objectives and prescribed specific measures: *demilitarization* of conflict through ceasefires, refusal of support for and use of territory by insurgents; *national reconciliation* through negotiated settlements, amnesty for insurgents, repatriation of refugees; *democratization* of political systems through free and open elections, ending states of emergency protection of human rights; *continuing regional consultation* through periodic summits and a parliament. Subsequent summits assessed interim progress, adjusted timetables, invited third party participation and renegotiated agreements. The San Jose meeting (1988), for example, led to a

Sandinista ceasefire and negotiations with the Contras. The San Salvador summit (1989) produced agreement on Nicaraguan elections and Contra demobilization and repatriation. The Tela agreement (1989) firmed up the demobilization schedule and its supervision by the International Commission for Verification and Support. The Montelimar summit (1990) ratified and reinforced the new Nicaraguan transition and Contra demobilization agreements that guided both the transfer of power from the Sandinistas and Contra disarmament.

By April, 1990, Nicaragua, Guatemala and El Salvador all had national reconciliation commissions in place and operating. In Nicaragua, the peace process had produced some striking precedents: an internationally supervised election and a peaceful transfer of power, the transformation of a revolutionary government into a reasonably loyal opposition; a procedure for disarming and reintegrating insurgents into civilian life. In Nicaragua, the Esquipulas process had been faithful to the intentions if not the implementation timetable of the agreement. Elsewhere in Central America, however, Esquipulas had produced no real peace.

Leaders in the Process

Three of the Esquipulas participants were responsible for getting it to work: Oscar Arias of Costa Rica through his orchestration and mediation; Vinicio Cerezo of Guatemala through his organizing and hosting of the initial summit, his insistence that Nicaragua be included as a full participant, and his subsequent role as its reliable supporter within the group; and Daniel Ortega of Nicaragua through his negotiating flexibility and important concessions at key points.

Arias was a central figure as a mediator-negotiator. Since Costa Rica was already in compliance with "Procedimiento," he had a special status in the group. He appeared to combine the exogenous and endogenous approaches to conflict management (Bercovitch, 1984). Arias's secure tenure in Costa Rica and his status as Nobel Laureate were resources to be drawn on. He used a number of obvious intermediary tactics (Robinson, 1988): early private confrontation of Ortega on the need for Nicaraguan flexibility; building momentum toward agreement to enlist a reluctant Honduras; using deadlines and timing of meetings to preclude US subversion— all to produce the Esquipulas II agreement.

The Esquipulas Structure

Three principles determined the structure for implementing the agreement (Hopmann, 1988): *simultaneity* (eliminating the "who goes first" problem—a thorny one with respect to Contra demobilization and elections); *calendarization* ("who does what by which dates"); and *transparency* ("how we how that they are doing it"). Commissions were created to apply those principles: a region-wide Commission for Verification and Support; a National Commission of Reconciliation in each nation; subnational Conciliation Commissions were necessary (see Fig. 3). Commission members were selected for their moral leadership, for useful connections they had with the conflicting parties, and for their experience as intermediaries. They illustrated the connected, trusted insider-partial third party. These commissions came to use outsider-neutral mediators as well and were in turn used by them. We next examine how the Esquipulas structure was used rather successfully in Nicaragua.

The National Reconciliation Commission

Because of its international and military impacts, the Contra-Sandinista conflict was the major concern of Esquipulas. Cardinal Obando y Bravo was chosen to head the NRC. He was not selected for his neutrality. His hostility toward the Sandinistas was well known. But his status as spiritual leader, his close connections with resistance elements, and his visibility as a national symbol all suggested his usefulness as intermediary. The two sides met under Obando's auspices early in 1988. Several months of negotiations produced the Sapoa agreement and a subsequent government ceasefire, though direct talks were then broken off by the Contras and not resumed for over a year.

Obando's mediation became more instrumental as the 1990 national elections and Contra demobilization approached. Several sets of delicate negotiations were necessary, involving at various points the Contra commanders, the verification and support commission, the Sandinista government, the UN, the OAS, the UNO opposition and, after 25 April 1990, the Chamorro government. Throughout the difficult period between the March elections and the April transfer of power, Cardinal Obando was the most visible intermediary. It is not clear how active or directive his mediation was but each time he intervened—Sapoa, Toncontin, transition negotiations—a major, durable agreement issued from the negotiation.

The Conciliation Commission

The second mediation effort involved the Sandinista government and the Atlantic Coast resistance. The Indians and Creoles had historically been isolated from the Hispanicized Pacific Coast. British and US manipulation of ethnic divisions had encouraged that isolation (Brooks, 1989; Hale, 1988). The *costenos,* therefore, had been relatively unengaged in the anti-Somoza rebellion and hardly welcomed a revolutionary Nicaragua.

Sandinista attempts to integrate the East Coast were met first with suspicion, then with resistance. The situation swiftly degenerated into armed conflict that sent 30,000 refugees into Honduras and Costa Rica and caused

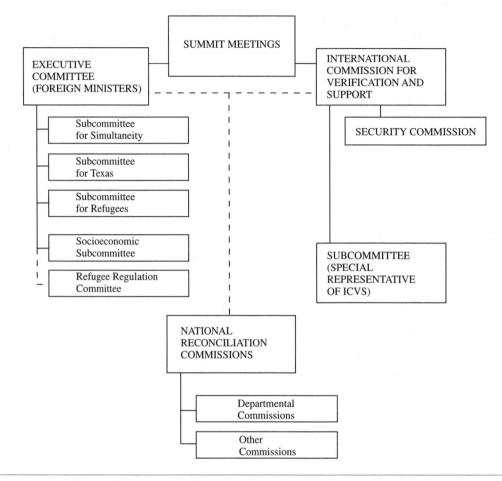

Figure 3   Esquipulas II Institutional Structure

much destruction particularly in the Miskito northeast. By 1984, realizing its past errors the Sandinista government began a two-track conciliation strategy. The first track initiated talks with Atlantic Coast leaders. These would subsequently result in a National Autonomy Commission (1984), local ceasefires, elected Peace and Autonomy Commissions (1986), the drafting of a National Autonomy Law, and its ratification by a Multi-Ethnic Assembly (1987) (Buvollen, 1989b; Sollis, 1989). This lengthy consultative process reflected the Atlantic Coast's complex ethnicity, with six groups speaking four languages. Though these groups numbered only 300,000, a tenth of Nicaragua's population, their region represented well over a third of its land area and much of its natural resource base.

Essential in this autonomy-building process were certain well-regarded persons from the East who were sympathetic to the revolution, thus trusted by both the Sandinistas and the indigenous leaders (Freeland, 1989, p. 178). Such intermediaries as Myra Cunningham and

Humberto Campbell sustained the dialogue to ultimate agreement. They are further examples of those insider-partials whose reservoir of trust and mutually recognized stature among conflictants, and cross-cutting affiliations with both sides, are so substantial as to permit a mediating function.

The second track involved Sandinista negotiations with the leaders of the armed resistance who were in exile and who had joined to form YATAMA in 1987. Their objectives were the restoration of historical Indian traditions and territorial rights, not the multi-ethnic regional independence made possible by the Autonomy Law. Esquipulas provided a new mediating structure for the Sandinista-YATAMA conflict.

Whereas the Catholic Church had an important mediating role in the Sandinista-Contra conflict, here the intermediary was the Moravian Church. It is the primary church on the Atlantic Coast just as Catholicism is dominant in the West. Rooted within the Miskitos, Ramas, Sumos and Creoles, it had the trust of the various resistance leaders and was the logical intermediary. In the early 1980s the Moravian Church, seen as antirevolutionary by the Sandinistas, had suffered greatly, losing pastors, churches, schools and hospitals in the Sandinista-Indian war. From 1983 on, however, the Moravian Provincial Board and the Sandinista government had worked to improve relations. Church leaders had facilitated ceasefires and autonomy consultations. Board members had been schoolmates of key resistance leaders and had maintained those ties.

It was not surprising, therefore, that YATAMA asked Moravian leaders to mediate Sandinista-YATAMA negotiations. The government, too, accepted the Moravians in this role, while acknowledging that they were neither neutral nor impartial. As Interior Minister Tomas Borge put it, "They are more there than here." With some balance provided

by appointees from the West, the team began mediating direct talks in January 1988. The Moravian Provincial Board, Gustavo Parajon of CEPAD (a Protestant relief organization) and member of the National Reconciliation Commission, and John Paul Lederach of the Mennonite Central Committee (another relief and development agency) were named members of this Conciliation Commission.

Throughout 1988 the Commission mediated under serious constraints. The North/CIA Contra operatives were doing all possible to inhibit a Sandinista-Indian agreement, since that would preclude a united Nicaraguan resistance. The mediators were kept on the move by CIA-funded kidnapping threats and assassination attempts against them as they went about their work. Competition among YATAMA leaders and Sandinista indecision also slowed progress, but by late 1988 agreements had been reached on 60% of the issues. Not until September 1989, however, was full agreement publicly acknowledged with the added intervention of former US president Jimmy Carter.

The Conciliation Commission mediation reflected the *confianza*-inspired, insider-partial model discussed earlier. Its success depended not on neutrality or externality but on continuing relationships of trust its members had with the conflictants. During face-to-face negotiation phases, Commission members lived side by side with YATAMA leaders. They ate and relaxed with both sides together. Their knowledge and connections were used by each side to explain its views and objectives to the other. The Commission, therefore, was much more connected to disputants than in neutrality-based mediation.

Its functions were broad rather than narrow. Its range of tasks stretched from arranging travel and daily schedules for disputants and resolving their family problems to negotiating a ceasefire in a war involving several national governments. Such a diverse mix is not beyond the scope of international third party intervention (Pruitt & Rubin, 1986), but it suggests the multidimensional role of the insider-partial rather than the narrower specialized one of the outsider-neutral. The commissioners' legitimacy as mediators came not from their distance from the conflict but from their personal connections that inspired the disputants' trust. That trust relationship with the conflict parties created safe negotiating space.

The Commission's legitimacy as third party also issued from the duration and depth of their functions. The outsider-neutral usually leaves a conflict soon after settlement. The insider-partial, the *confianza* model of mediation, implies a continuing mediator-disputant connection. The Moravians and CEPAD have continued to work with both sides in peace development ever since the 1988 ceasefire.

The Commission's multiple functions were carried out at different levels of the conflict. They worked on Peace and Autonomy Commissions, thus connecting with that process at the local level. They accompanied exiled leaders to their home villages as part of the reconciliation process. At the national level, the Commission mediated the Sandinista-YATAMA negotiation. Internationally, it worked with Nicaraguan refugees in Honduras and Costa Rica and brought East Coast exiles together from three nations to form the YATAMA negotiating team. Given these multiple and continuing conciliation functions at several levels, Commission mediators were generalists rather than specialists. Their effectiveness depended equally on *who they were* in relation to the conflictants (not who they were not) and *what they did* (not what they did not do).

Insider-partial mediation had produced a tentative settlement. But final and public agreement was facilitated by an outsider-neutral, Jimmy Carter who, as chair of the Council of Freely Elected Heads of State, had come to Nicaragua to monitor the 1990 elections for fairness and legitimacy. He offered to mediate any remaining Sandinista-YATAMA differences, maintaining that Indian leaders had to be free to return to participate in the electoral campaign.

Carter asked that YATAMA be offered the same conditions for political reintegration extended to the Contras—renounce armed struggle, participate in the political system, encourage demobilization of all armed insurgents. The sides agreed publicly to conditions earlier arrived at and within a week of the Carter-Borge meeting. Brooklyn Rivera and the other leaders were returning to Nicaragua, Carter made good use of his leverage—the Sandinistas very much wanted his certification of the elections. Timing was also working for him. The pressures of the impending election and its high visibility in the world produced disputant flexibility that was absent a year earlier. Carter went on to serve other useful third party functions, as a monitor and conciliator during the elections themselves, and in the difficult post-election transition period.

In the resolution of the Sandinista-YATAMA conflict we have seen how insider-partial and outsider-neutral intermediaries were used at different times and in different settings. The autonomy conciliation relied heavily upon those intermediaries who were trusted by both sides because they belong to both. Within Esquipulas, the Conciliation Commission pursued the Sandinista-YATAMA conflict with considerable success as "mediators from with" who had the trust of both sides. Finally, the Carter intervention broke the impasse, permitting YATAMA leaders to return, thus furthering the democratization and demilitarization goals of Esquipulas. These disparate approaches to mediation were mutually complementary. All of them required considerable trust in the mediators. The evenhanded external mediator combined with the trusted intermediaries engaged in long-term peacemaking within Nicaragua to moderate that conflict. All may well continue to intervene, for intercoastal, interethnic and interpersonal conflict in Nicaragua has no end in sight.

There is a second set of outsider-neutrals that we should mention here. These were the mediating agencies structured into the conflict through the International Commission of Verification and Support, provided for in the Esquipulas agreement but not actually created until the Tela summit of August 1989. This Commission carried out the repatriation, disarming and resettlement of Contra troops. Represented on the ICVS were the Organization of American States, the Contradora groups and the UN Observer Group—Central America with its contingent of 800 Spanish and Venezuelan peacekeeping troops. Structured into Esquipulas to validate and monitor its achievements, then, were three international governmental organizations with a major concern for the plan's success—the UN, the OAS and the Contadora Group. By June of 1990, the commission had disarmed 11,000 of 15,000 insurgents and guaranteed a peaceful Sandinista-to-opposition transfer of power, surely one of history's most successful peace-keeping operations.

The Esquipulas Context

We have presented Esquipulas mediation both as a process over time and in terms of the intermediary structures developed to implement it. A third perspective for understanding it is through its broader conflict environment. That context was created largely by actors not directly involved in the mediation.

Certainly Reagan's Contra option rapidly lost momentum in the waning of his second term. Civil wars in Central America quickly lost their East-West cast as the Reagan-Gorbachev friendship began to thaw the Cold War. Decisions in Washington and Moscow to end military aid to the Nicaraguan conflictants did much to reinforce the efforts of Esquipulas mediators.

When Reagan left office in 1989, his Central America policy team went with him. That group had labored mightily to sink Esquipulas and discredit Oscar Arias. Arias mistrusted Assistant Secretary of State Elliott Abrams. It was reported by a key Costa Rican official that he had postponed an Esquipulas summit meeting until Abrams had left office.

The US Congress influenced the mediation context both in its encouragement of Contadora through Jim Wright, Christopher Dodd and others, and by opening space for the Arias initiatives through its Iran-Contra investigations in the summer of 1986. Precisely when Contadora had stalled, those revelations exposed the deep divisions in congressional opinion over Reagan Central America policies—divisions which renewed the regional search for alternatives. It also permitted a progressive decoupling of the Sandinista-YATAMA conflict from the Contra war, a separation which made both easier to resolve. Senator Kennedy, at the request of Indian rights organizations, pressured the Sandinistas to be more flexible on the rights of the indigenous peoples. The American Indian Movement's involvement was influential though ambiguous in its consequences for settling the Sandinista-Atlantic Coast conflict.

Arias's Nobel Peace Prize gave Esquipulas new legitimacy. It heartened the mediators, renewed support in the US Congress for negotiated settlement, and further engaged European governments and publics in the peace process. The award punctuated the substantial support for both Nicaraguan development and Esquipulas that was already coming from Europe.

The United Nations came to influence the Esquipulas context more and more toward negotiated settlement. The General Assembly resolution of 27 June 1989 stimulated agreement at the Tela summit on a "Joint Plan for the Voluntary Demobilization, Repatriation and Relocation of the Nicaraguan Resistance." Subsequent UN funding and staffing of the UNOG-Central America and its peace-keeping contingent proved invaluable in disarming and reintegrating Nicaraguan insurgents. Its third party presence must be given much credit for the peaceful transfer of power in Nicaragua in 1990.

Citizen volunteers from North America and Europe were important shapers of the mediation context. They worked from both ends of the problem, at home and in the field. In the USA, peace activists influenced government policy directly toward political and diplomatic settlement and away from military confrontation. The Central American peace lobby in the US, through such groups as Friendship Cities, Witness for Peace, Sanctuary, Pledge of Resistance and CISPES helped build public and congressional support for Esquipulas.

In Central America, such peace movement organizations provided a "sympathetic third party" presence that worked to moderate conflict. Thousands of people visited and lived in Nicaragua, El Salvador and Guatemala as volunteer generalists, technical experts, human rights escorts and representatives of municipal governments and labor unions. This citizen third party presence moderated conflict, producing a more supportive mediation environment. It encouraged flexibility of Central American governments, who wished to appear reasonable and non-violent. It reduced violence through its on-site reporting of military and paramilitary action. It represented to Central Americans a larger citizen movement in North America and Europe that was pressing for policy changes and sending direct assistance to alleviate suffering. The reaction to the Contra killing of US volunteer Benjamin Linder in 1987 suggested the importance of such a presence for restraining militarization.

Many of these persons were working in Nicaragua under the auspices of bongo vernmental organizations. These NGOs had a longstanding presence in the region, responding to conflict in the usual ways of lobbying for policy changes and providing civilian war relief. But we saw emerging in the Esquipulas context a broader, more active NGO role in peace-making, notably mediation by Protestant and Catholic representatives, and secular organizations like the Carter Center in Atlanta. The Moravian Church, CEPAD and the Mennonite Central Committee provided mediators and sites. They channeled resources for the negotiation from a mediation support network including the World Council of Churches. The Moravian Church in Nicaragua has been still more broadly engaged in conflict *transformation* (Lederach, 1990)—the continuous involvement of sympathetic third parties to move a conflict from latent to overt and negotiation stages. That is a long-term effort involving empowerment of weaker parties, trust-building, conflict skills development and other requisites for transforming a conflict situation into sustainable peace.

THEORETICAL CONSIDERATIONS AND PRACTICAL IMPLICATIONS

By mid-1990, Esquipulas had been only partially successful in moving the region toward stable peace. In El Salvador and Guatemala, civil conflict and state repression continued to undermine economies and kill thousands, though there were preliminary insurgent-government negotiations underway in both cases. Critics of Esquipulas will point out that Nicaragua has been the focus for change. Conflict-producing conditions in other participating states have received little attention at Esquipulas meetings. The principle of simultaneity has not been applied in that respect.

The Nicaraguan conflicts, on the other hand, appeared to be well on their way toward successful management. An end to military confrontation, disarming and reintegration of insurgents, the end of conscription and major reductions in military forces, a classic pluralist election and peaceful transfer of power, an autonomy process for integrating Atlantic and Pacific regions. All of those achievements were reached within or with the help of Esquipulas. It may be that a conflict management model had to be developed in Nicaragua before other Esquipulas states with more deeply rooted problems with social conflict and state violence could open to the process. Time and events will tell.

Our study of Esquipulas raises some theoretical and practical issues. Should the conceptualization of mediator roles be broadened to embrace developing world variants such as the Insider-Partial? Should identification and selection of mediators be more systematically done, with greater care for drawing upon and creatively mixing the external and internal conflict moderation resources available? Should more attention be given by international mediators to modifying the wider context to be more supportive of their intervention?

Expanding the Mediator Concept

Our study suggests that the field would do well to agree on a simple, inclusive definition of mediation, differentiating the mediator roles as research and practice reveal them. We prefer to define mediation simply as third-party-facilitated negotiation, and the mediator as one(s) "who attempts to help the principals reach a voluntary agreement" (Pruitt & Rubin, 1986, p. 166). Within such a simple, inclusive definition a hundred flowers can bloom, so to speak. Esquipulas has produced some variations on the basic mediation theme that we have not found in the literature.

We have suggested the concept of the *insider-partial* to reflect a type very visible in Nicaraguan mediation. We distinguished that

from the *outsider-neutral* concept characterizing mediation in North America, and from international mediator roles which generally assume that third parties must come from outside the conflict situation. We have shown how the I-P and O-N polar opposites interacted synergistically in Nicaraguan mediation. It may be, however, that externality and neutrality are dimensions, or continua, along which every mediator falls. Those dimensions may be independent of one another, rather than interdependent as the types we suggest imply.

If the O-N and I-P types are valid, however, each bringing different strengths to the same conflict, as did Jimmy Carter and the Conciliation Commission, what practical consequences might issue from teaming them up as counterparts in a mediation? They might not work together physically, but would consult, divide up functions, coordinate interventions and the like. If these are distinct types, each of which perform different but equally important functions in mediated negotiation, that would influence the mediator selection process. In any event, it would seem useful to explore the I-P concept further. Though we have presented it here as a region-specific, culture-determined model, it might have equally useful functions in the postindustrial societies of the world.

Esquipulas suggests other additions to the range of mediator roles. We noted the way Oscar Arias appeared to act as both mediator and negotiator. He, too, was internal to the conflict situation, had the trust of all parties, yet had a status apart. The *mediator-negotiator* of Esquipulas appears to have some precedents in the Kissinger of the Yom Kippur War negotiation (Rubin, 1981) and the Walesa (1987) of Polish Solidarity, both of whom seem to have played such a dual role. If it is not a new genre, should it as least be included in the range of mediator types? Would there be a place as well for the *mediator-legitimizer* characterized by Obando y Bravo, whose role went much beyond providing good offices. The full weight of the Church's moral authority in his person appears to have legitimated such negotiation and guaranteed the implementation of its outcomes.

One question raised by such a discussion is whether mediator selection in such cases should not be more conscious and deliberate than it normally is, according to mediator functions required and persons and agencies available? If, for example, the Carter and Conciliation Commission interventions had been coordinated, each performing different, complementary functions, a year of time might have been saved. We are suggesting that the selection of mediators could and should be a more systematic and informed process.

Modifying the Mediation Context

Our study has suggested the importance of the *mediation context*—the events, persons and attitudes influencing the mediation from a distance. Time and again in Esquipulas negotiation was transformed. A striking example was the agreement of August 1989 between the Sandinista government and the United National Opposition for free and open elections. It was reached in a televised marathon negotiation reminiscent of that which legitimized Polish Solidarity in 1980 (Wehr, 1985). The Sandinista-UNO accord triggered the breakthrough three days later for the Tela agreement on Contra demobilization. The context had been transformed to permit this.

Both supportive and obstructive forces in the mediation context, while not controllable by mediators, are amenable to their influence. If the larger environment were seen as more integral to mediation success, third party interveners could map that context to identify key influentials, a preliminary step to creating more support for negotiated settlement. Could mediators have a more direct influence on

mass communicators, for example, who frame the issues, characterize the actors, present the options and largely determine whether a context encouraged or discourages mediated settlement? The mass media were exceptionally influential in the context of Nicaraguan mediation (Chomsky, 1987). Should a mediation team include someone with exclusive responsibility for mapping the context for ways to render it more supportive of the intervention?

An important mediation-supportive element in the Esquipulas context was the presence of *conflict moderators,* the "sympathetic third parties" described earlier. Conflict moderation is the third party's most important function. It is a more realistic goal than permanent resolution, which is rarely possible (Touval, 1982). Does the Esquipulas experience show the conflict moderating sympathetic third parties to be so useful in the mediation context that a conscious effort should be made to include them as a desirable component of international third party interventions?

Mediation from within the Conflict

Esquipulas has revealed to us how rich may be the indigenous resources for conflict moderation and negotiated settlement in developing areas of the world. The insider-partial, the mediator-negotiator, the mediator-legitimizer, the sympathetic third party are conflict management roles that are probably useful beyond Central America as well. The effective combining of such local resources with external third parties in Esquipulas can be seen as a contribution to the theory and practice of international third party intervention. We suspect that international mediation would be more effective were the various external and internal mediators and the moderators within the context to be systematically identified and enlisted: a deliberate citizen volunteer presence, a mixed team of outsider-neutrals and insider-partials, a resident *conflict transformation* group working on a deep-seated conflict situation.

It remains to be seen whether Esquipulas innovation in conflict management will produce positive results in other Central American states as it has in Nicaragua. Continuing involvement of the UN and other international interveners will help determine those results. Thus far, however, Esquipulas represents a major step forward in regional conflict management, a model well worth the attention of scholars and practitioners alike.

REFERENCES

Bagley, Bruce, 1987. "The Failure of Diplomacy," pp. 181–211 in Bruce Bagley, ed., *Contadora and the Diplomacy of Peace in Central America,* vol. I. Boulder, CO & London: Westview.

Bercovitch, Jacob, 1984. *Social Conflict and Third Parties: Strategies of Conflict Resolution.* Boulder, CO: Westview.

Brooks, David, 1989. "US Marines, Miskitos and the Hunt for Sandino: The Rio Coco Patrol in 1928," *Journal of Latin American Studies,* vol. 21, no. 2, May, pp. 311–342.

Buvollen, Hans Petter, 1989a. "Low-Intensity Warfare and the Peace Plan in Central America," *Bulletin of Peace Proposals,* vol. 20, no. 3, pp. 319–334.

Buvollen, Hans Petter, 1989b. "Regional Autonomy in Nicarauga: A New Approach to the Indigenous Question in Latin America," *Alternatives,* vol. 14, no. 1, January, pp. 123–132.

Chomsky, Noam, 1987. *On Power and Ideology: The Managua Lectures.* Boston, MA: South End.

Freeland, Jane, 1989. "Nationalist Revolution and Ethnic Rights: The Miskito Indians of Nicaragua's Atlantic Coast," *Third World Quarterly,* vol. 10, no. 4, pp. 166–190.

Goffman, Erving, 1959. *The Presentation of Self in Everyday Life.* Garden City: NY: Anchor Doubleday.

Gomariz, Enrique, ed., 1988. *Balance de una esperanza: Esquipulas II un año despues.* San Jose: FLACSO.

Hale, Charles, 1988. "Relaciones interetnicas y la estructura de clases en la costa atlantica de Nicarague," *Estudios Sociales Centroamericanos,* vol. 48, no. 4, September-December, pp. 71–91.

Hopmann, P. Terrence, 1988. "Negotiating Peace in Central America," *Negotiation Journal,* vol. 4, no. 4, pp. 361–380.

Lederach, John Paul, 1988. "Of Nets, Nails and *Problemas:* A Folk Vision of Conflict in Central America," unpublished PhD dissertation in sociology, University of Colorado at Boudler.

Lederach, John Paul, 1990. "Conflict Transforamtion: The Case for Peace Advocacy." Unpublished paper. Mennonite Central Committee, Akron PA, USA.

Moore, Christopher W., 1987. *The Mediation Process: Practical Strategies for Resolving Conflict.* San Francisco, CA: Jossey-Bass.

Pruitt, Dean & Jeffrey Z. Rubin, 1986. *Social Conflict.* New York: Random House.

Robinson, Linda, 1988. "Peace in Central America," *Foreign Affairs,* vol. 66, no. 3, pp. 591–613.

Rubin, Jeffrey Z., ed., 1981. *Dynamics of Third Party Intervention: Kissinger in the Middle East.* New York: Praeger.

Simmel, Georg, 1950. *The Sociology of Georg Simmel.* New York: Free Press.

Touval, Saadia, 1982. *The Peace Brokers: Mediators in the Arab-Israeli Conflict, 1948–1979.* Princeton, NJ: Princeton University Press.

Walesa, Lech, 1987. *A Way of Hope.* New York: Henry Holt.

Weber, Max, 1957. *The Theory of Social and Economic Organization.* Glencoe, IL: Free Press. [Originally published in German 1922.]

Wehr, Paul, 1985. "Conflict and Restraint: Poland 1980–1982," pp. 191–218 in Petere Wallensteen, Johan Galtung & Carlos Portales, eds., *Global Militarization.* Boulder, CO & London: Westview.

Yarrow, C. H. Mike, 1978. *Quaker Experiences in International Conciliation.* New Haven, CT: Yale University Press.

Young, Oran R., 1967. *The Intermediaries: Third Parties in International Crisis*. Princeton, NJ: Princeton University Press.

Paul Wehr is an associate professor of sociology at the University of Colorado at Boulder. His research has dealt primarily with movements for social and political change, particularly those using various types of nonviolent action.

John Paul Lederach is Professor of International Peacebuilding at the Joan B. Kroc Institute of International Peace Studies at Notre Dame University and Distinguished Scholar at Eastern Mennonite University.

Reading 4.5

Islamic Mediation Techniques for Middle East Conflicts

GEORGE E. IRANI

Many Middle Eastern scholars and practitioners trained in the United States have returned to their countries of origin ready to impart what they learned about Western conflict resolution techniques. In Lebanon, Jordan, Egypt, and other countries in the region, the teaching and practice of conflict resolution is still a novel phenomenon.

Conflict resolution is viewed by many as a false Western panacea, a program imposed from outside and thus insensitive to indigenous problems, needs, and political processes.

Indeed, many people in the Middle East view conflict resolution as a scheme concocted by the United States meant primarily to facilitate and hasten the processes of peace and

---

Reprinted with permission from www. mediate.com.

"normalization" between Israel and its Arab neighbors.[1] In assessing the applicability of Western-based conflict resolution models in non-Western societies, theoreticians and practitioners alike have begun to realize the importance of being sensitive to indigenous ways of thinking and feeling, as well as to local rituals for managing and reducing conflicts.

Middle East peacemaking has been a rather superficial phenomenon in the sense that diplomatic agreements have not "trickled down" to the grassroots. Peace treaties based solely on economic and political enticements, coercion or purely strategic considerations cannot last if they are not accompanied by a sincere, profound exploration of the underlying, emotional legacies of fear, hatred, sorrow, and mistrust resulting from decades of warfare and unending cycles of victimization and vengeance. In order to bring peace to the Middle East, policymakers must foster and encourage a dialogue that takes into consideration indigenous rituals and processes of reconciliation.

The purpose of this essay is to explore and analyze non-Western modes and rituals of conflict reduction in Arab-Islamic societies. The necessity for such a study also stems from the dearth of available works relating conflict management and resolution processes to indigenous rituals of reconciliation. There is a need to fathom the deep cultural, social, and religious roots that underlie the way Arabs behave when it comes to conflict reduction and reconciliation.

Thus, this article discusses the socioeconomic, cultural, and anthropological background in which conflicts erupt and are managed in the Middle East. Issues such as the importance of patrilineal families; the question of ethnicity; the relevance of identity; the nature of tribal and clan solidarity; the key role of patron-client relationships; and the salience of norms concerning honor and shame need to be explored in their geographical and socio-cultural context.

Religious beliefs and traditions are also relevant to conflict control and reduction, including the relevant resources in Islamic law and tradition. Different causes and types of conflicts (family, community, and state conflicts) need to be considered, as do indigenous techniques and procedures, such as wasta (patronage-mediation) and tahkeem (arbitration). The rituals of sulh (settlement) and musalaha (reconciliation) are examples of Arab-Islamic culture and values and should be looked at for insight into how to approach conflict resolution in the Middle East. Finally, there is the need to consider the implications of these issues and insights for practitioners and policymakers. To what extent is an integration of Western and non-Western models of conflict reduction and reconciliation possible?

This paper looks first at Western and non-Western approaches to conflict "resolution" and points to important cultural differences in approaching conflict management, including the role of the individual in society; attitudes towards conflict; styles of communication; expectations of mediators, understandings concerning "victimization" and "forgiveness," and the usefulness of governmental (and/or nongovernmental) programs and institutions—such as truth commissions—for "national reconciliation." The second section considers the geographical, sociological, and cultural influences on the Arab Middle East. It highlights the importance of relation ships based on family, patriarchy and gender, kinship, and clientism, and points to the continuing underlying code of honor (and its counterpart, shame) in conflict and conflict management.

The third part considers the concept of ritual and its role in conflict "control and reduction" (as opposed to conflict "resolution") and focuses on the rituals of sulh and musalaha as examples of indigenous Arab modes of settling disputes. The final section considers the implications for policymakers and practitioners and suggests an alternative approach to national reconciliation in Lebanon.

CONFLICT RESOLUTION: WESTERN AND NON-WESTERN APPROACHES

Although conflict is a human universal, the nature of conflicts and the methods of resolving conflict differ from one socio-cultural context to another. For instance, in contemporary North American contexts, conflict is commonly perceived to occur between two or more individuals acting as individuals, i.e., as free agents pursuing their own interests in various domains of life. Conflict is often perceived as a symptom of the need for change. While conflict can lead to separation, hostility, civil strife, terrorism and war, it can also stimulate dialogue, fairer and more socially just solutions. It can lead to stronger relationships and peace.[2]

The basic assumption made by Western conflict resolution theorists is that conflict can and should be fully resolved.[3] This philosophy, whereby virtually every conflict can be managed or resolved, clashes with other cultural approaches to conflict.[4] Many conflicts, regardless of their nature, may be intractable, and can evolve through phases of escalation and confrontation as well as phases of calm and a return to the status quo ante. This is why this essay adopts the idea of conflict control and reduction to depict the processes of settlement and reconciliation in the Arab-Islamic tradition.

The third basic assumption in U.S.-based conflict resolution is that conflict usually erupts because of different interpretations regarding data, issues, values, interests and relationships.[5] According to the prominent anthropologist Laura Nader:

Conflict results from competition between at least two parties. A party may be a person, a family, a lineage, or a whole community; or it may be a class of ideas, a political organization, a tribe, or a religion. Conflict is occasioned by incompatible desires or aims and by its duration may be distinguished from strife or angry disputes arising from momentary aggravations.[6]

Conflict in Western perspectives is also viewed as having a positive dimension, acting as a catharsis to redefine relationships between individuals, groups, and nations and makes it easier to find adequate settlements or possible resolutions. During the last ten years, more and more voices within the field of conflict resolution have been calling attention to the importance of acknowledgment and forgiveness in achieving lasting reconciliation among conflicting parties. Many of the world's most intractable conflicts involve age-old cycles of oppression, victimization and revenge. These conflicts, which can have dangerous and long-lasting political repercussions, are rooted in a psychological dynamic of victimization. Racism and "ethnic cleansing" are only the most dramatic manifestations of such cycles of victimization and vengeance.

One of the guiding principles of U.S.-inspired conflict management and resolution is to help individuals or groups embroiled in conflict to acknowledge one another's psychological concerns and needs so that they will be able to overcome their historic sense of victimization.[7] Victimization is a crucial concept to grasp when dealing with protracted conflicts, whether personal or political. Overcoming feelings of victimization, which, unfortunately, are endemic to the human condition, is the most important step towards healing. Usually, acts of violence (whether inflicted on an individual or a group), are the results of deep feelings of being victimized, regardless of who is the victim or victimizer.

In the case of nations and ethnic groups embroiled in conflict, acknowledgment of unhealed wounds from pain inflicted in the past facilitates the resolution of conflicts. From a Western psychological perspective, conflict usually erupts because some basic needs have not been fulfilled, such as needs for shelter, food, self-esteem, love, knowledge, and self-actualization.[8] The non-fulfillment of these needs, exacerbated by acute feelings of victimization, inevitably leads to conflict and may eventually lead to war. A first step in the process of healing, then, is the mutual acknowledgment by all parties of their emotions, viewpoints and needs. Thus, the first and most crucial skill which conflicting parties must develop is that of actively listening to each other.

Communication skills are fundamental to conflict resolution. In many cultures, the art of listening is drowned out by arguments and the never-ending struggle to get one's point across first. The opposite of listening is not ignoring; rather, it is preparing to respond. Mediators are trained to listen carefully to all parties involved in a dispute. Active listening is a method that ensures that the whole meaning of what was said is understood.

Mediation is another skill used by Western practitioners in conflict resolution. The mediator confronts two basic tasks when involved in settling a dispute. First, he or she has to encourage people to negotiate in such a way that there is an equitable outcome. Second, the mediator has to be completely neutral and place the expertise and power of decision-making in the hands of the conflicting individuals or groups themselves. In addition to mediation in conflict resolution, negotiation is another important tool in Western conflict resolution processes. "Interest-based" negotiation focuses on people's long-term interests, rather than on short-term perspectives, and does not encourage hard or soft types of bargaining (this is the case when one of the parties has to give in or compromise) which usually lead to unsatisfactory "positional" compromises.[9]

Following the collapse of various dictatorial regimes in Latin America and Central Europe (e.g., Chile, Argentina, Brazil, East Germany, Czechoslovakia and Poland), truth and justice commissions were formed to "police the past," i.e., to investigate the extent of human rights violations committed against civilians by the former military juntas and Communist parties in these countries. These efforts encouraged a healing process of atonement and remorse for past crimes which, in turn, helped citizens and governments alike to rebuild democratic institutions. A similar process recently began in South Africa following the dismantling of the apartheid regime and the election of Nelson Mandela as President of the new Republic of South Africa.

Lebanon shares some of the problems affecting societies in transition, though the country has not fully regained control of its sovereignty. In April 1994, as a contribution to the ongoing efforts at intercommunal reconciliation in post-war Lebanon, the Lebanese American University assembled on its Byblos campus a group of government officials, NGO activists, students, and lawyers, for a three-day conference entitled "Acknowledgment, Forgiveness, and Reconciliation: Alternative Approaches to Conflict Resolution in Post-War Lebanon."[10] The conference focused primarily on the psychological and interpersonal aspects of the Lebanese War, especially the politics of identity and the vicious circle of victimization and vengeance that fueled the long conflict.

Conference participants were initially uncomfortable with and suspicious of the theory and techniques of Western conflict resolution. Mixed feelings were expressed about the applicability of conflict resolution in the Lebanese social context. A Christian banker who was educated in the United States noted that conflict resolution theory was initially forged in labor management relations in the United States and that later it was applied to business and then to community relations and academia. He raised an important methodological question: "How can a theory which is supposed to be dealing with definite, programmed, institutionalized relationships deal with the unprogrammed, informal, and random relationships characteristic of social and political contexts in a totally different society?"

A Muslim academic and social activist declared that a better concept would be "conflict management" because "it is impossible completely to solve conflicts; the existence of conflicts goes together with human existence." He raised the related point that conflicts were interrelated, the resolution of one conflict was contingent upon the resolution of other conflicts. "The crisis of Lebanon and the Middle East are the best proof of what I am saying," he concluded.[11]

The conference also revealed interesting insights into Lebanese conversational culture. The National Director of the Young Women's Christian Association-Lebanon (YWCA) commented that in Lebanon, when individuals are engaged in "heart-to-heart" conversations, they often interrupt with expressions of empathy and support. "It is not like interrupting rudely. The process of the discussion shows our concern because we are a very emotional people. That is the problem: we usually talk all together. We are active talkers and active listeners!"

A further area of difficulty came to light when participants discussed the necessity, in active listening, of remaining silent when the other person is talking, especially in cases of intense argumentation. In Lebanon, remaining silent is sometimes interpreted as meek acquiescence or agreement. A government representative from the Ministry of Education stated that "in the rural areas of Lebanon, if you do not talk, it means you are dull; the more you talk, the more it is assumed you know. People want to show that they know, especially those

who go to town and come back to the village. They always talk."

The key role of third parties or mediators in disputes was also addressed. In Lebanese culture, as in Arab culture in general, the mediator is perceived as someone having all the answers and solutions. He therefore has a great deal of power and responsibility. As one participant put it: "If [the third party] does not provide the answers, he or she is not really respected or considered to be legitimate."[12] Finally, a number of conference participants expressed their expectations that conference organizers and facilitators would provide ready-made solutions to Lebanon's woes. This expectation was not unusual in the context of Lebanese culture and politics.

For several centuries, politics in Lebanon have been repeatedly penetrated by outside powers, either to foment strife or to impose solutions. The phenomenon of relying on outsiders for answers and solutions reveals some of the fundamental blind spots in Lebanese political thought: a lack of responsibility for one's actions and behaviors. At a more practical level, many Lebanese have opted to forget about the war and get on with their lives, even if the wounds and consequences of the war are still very much alive in the collective and individual Lebanese psyches.

Denial seems to be the defense mechanism of choice for many traumatized Lebanese in the wake of the long and damaging war. This behavior is not unique to the Lebanese situation. Victimization is a crucial concept to grasp when dealing with protracted conflicts, whether personal or political. Overcoming feelings of victimization (which, unfortunately, may be said to be endemic to the human condition), is the most important step towards healing.

Participants reacted to this new approach by exploring the sources of Lebanon's conflict through the psychological scars of victimization. A Lebanese woman educator, while acknowledging the value of this approach, pointed out that these conflict resolution tools in the Lebanese context are hindered by the paradox that Lebanon is a "very individualistic society, but unfortunately, we do not have individuals." She went on to explain that "in order to have conflict management or conflict resolution, you have to recognize the other. But, you do not have the other if you do not have the individual. That is why there is no reconciliation, forgiveness, and conflict resolution [in Lebanon]. The existence of the individual is essential in this process."

This trenchant observation neatly summarizes the state of society in post-war Lebanon. Rather than a cohesive group of individuals bound together by an agreed-upon set of rights and obligations, (i.e., citizens), the Lebanese instead comprise an agglomeration of competing communities, each of which requires absolute allegiance and obedience from its members. Every one of these communities feels that the others have victimized it, so the process of acknowledgment, forgiveness, and reconciliation has to begin at the community level, rather than at the individual level.

These new and challenging concepts of conflict resolution—acknowledgment, victimization, communication skills, interest-based negotiation—elicited many reactions from conference participants. The most poignant reaction came from a Lebanese woman whose husband was "disappeared" during the war and who founded the Committee of Families of Kidnapped People.[13] Commenting on victimization and how to overcome it in negotiations, she used two examples to emphasize her point:

> The first example concerns the Israeli occupation of my country. If my country began negotiations with Israel, it means that there is an intention to solve the conflict. But I do not understand why Israel is insisting on keeping me a victim because after each

negotiation session, there are more dead people in the villages of South Lebanon. I cannot understand how I will emerge from a sense of victimization if I am negotiating and paying in victims every day. It is no longer a matter of common interests, but of recognition of rights. Someone is refusing to recognize these rights to the party we are calling the victim.

The second example she gave was personal and related to the issue of the 17,000 kidnapped Lebanese whose fates are still unknown.

> The kidnapped person is a victim and so are his family members. These people have to stop being victims and maybe they even have to fight not to be victimized. But when the obstacles are still there and the kidnapper does not acknowledge any of my rights, what will my position be as a victim? How can we reach a solution if I have a right and he has an interest?

Finally, many Lebanese participants at the conference raised the issue of government accountability for crimes committed during the Lebanese War. In the case of Lebanon, the state's apparatus was noticeably absent during the long civil war. Thus, the central government and its institutions bear little, if any, direct responsibility for the atrocities committed between 1975 and 1990. Instituting war tribunals or truth and justice commissions in post-war Lebanon without some form of external, third-party intervention would undoubtedly be perceived as an affront by one community against another.[14]

THE ARAB MIDDLE EAST: THE SETTING

Geography has an impact on the ways people interact and behave for the protection of their honor and their scarce resources. The Arab

Middle East is distinguished geographically by a variety of landscapes. The Arabian Peninsula is characterized by a large desert and other arid landscapes, and a scarcity of water.

In the Levant (Syria, Lebanon, Palestine, Jordan), environmental conditions are more clement. Jordan and some areas of Palestine are semi-arid and poor in water while Lebanon and Syria are blessed with milder climates and numerous springs and rivers. Lebanon, has a rugged mountainous terrain but also a fertile valley (the Bekaa Valley) and self-sufficiency in water.

Ecological realities in the Middle East have given rise to three key modes of subsistence: nomadic, village, and urban. Although communities of pastoral nomads, village farmers, and city-dwelling merchants and artisans were historically distinct from one another, they were nonetheless economically interdependent. Their lives and interests were always in actual or potential contact, and quite often in conflict. Although pastoral nomadism has become increasingly rare as a viable mode of subsistence, due to the advent of nation-states with closed borders and the rapid, dramatic urbanization and of the region's population, nomadic peoples and their traditions have nonetheless left a very deep imprint on Middle Eastern culture, society, and politics. One anthropologist hypothesizes that the characteristic form of pastoral nomadism that developed in this semi-arid zone accounts for the strikingly similar cultural orientations found throughout the vast area of the Middle East:

> In the Near East today we find a remarkable similarity among the traditions of many people throughout a large region . . . . Islamization, the spread of a religious faith, is often offered as an explanation for this uniformity. But could Islam by itself have become so deeply-rooted among the diverse peoples of such a vast area, unless it was

somehow a response to a life experience which all of these people shared in common? . . . . Extreme arid conditions resulted in independent little herding groups dispersed across the desert and steppe. . . . This situation is reflected in the atomistic form which political alliances tended to take.[15]

Sociologically, the peoples of the Middle East remain famous for their loyal attachment to their families, distinctive rituals of hospitality and conflict mediation, and effective and flexible kin-based collectivities, such as the lineage and the tribe, which until quite recently performed most of the social, economic, and political functions of communities in the absence of centralized state governments.[16] Family in the Middle East is dominated by the powerful role patriarchy plays in decision-making.[17] The father's authority in his family is an integral part of the more general authority system. Patriarchal authority maintains not only the genealogical cohesiveness of the family but also the cohesiveness of social life. This patriarchal pattern of power is made concrete and takes shape in the primacy of the zaim (leader) of the family. The zaim controls and defends the cohesiveness of the family inside the group as well as in the relationships between the family and other families. The zaim acts as the family referee and sanctions conflicts that erupt within his family, while controlling the solidarity and support within and between family members. He acts as the family's ambassador towards outsiders. Given that every village is made up of many families, each family is headed by a zaim. The heads of each family form the assembly of the village zuama.[18]

A related element in understanding social and political behavior in the Middle East is kinship systems. Despite the creation of modern states following the collapse of colonial rule, the basic unit of identification for the individual is not the state, the ethnic group, or the professional association, but the family.

Several writers on the Arab Middle East have underlined the fact that the only nation-state in the contemporary Arab Middle East is Egypt.[19] Egypt has a homogeneous population that identifies itself first and foremost as Egyptian. The only sizeable "minority," the Copts who number around 6 million members, consider themselves as the descendants of the original population of Egypt from pharaonic times. Their allegiance is to Egypt as both government and country.

In Saudi Arabia, on the other hand, it is a family—the House of Saud—that dominates the body politic. The same applies to the various sheikdoms of the Arabian Gulf. In other countries of the Levant, namely Syria and Iraq, families from minority communities rule their respective societies.[20]

Since Lebanon obtained independence in 1943, it has been ruled by a few prominent families—both Christian and Muslim—such as the Maronite Catholic Gemayel and Chamoun families, the Sunni Es-Solh and Salam families, and the Druze Jumblatt family. As a strategy for survival, the patrilineal kinship system of the Middle East has certainly proved flexible and effective over many centuries under a variety of social, economic, and political conditions. The distinctive kinship systems and practices of the Middle East are part of the region's civilizational heritage. Kinship is implicated in nearly every aspect of life and most social institutions, including religion and morality.

Michael Meeker, a prominent anthropologist, speculates that the cultural uniformity which we now find in the arid zone does not reflect the traditions of a people bent on violence. "On the contrary, it reflects . . . a moral response to the threat of political turmoil. The process of Islamization itself can be viewed in part as a moral reaction to the problems that arose from the circumstances of Near Eastern

pastoral nomadism. . . . All over the arid zone, popular traditions can be described in terms of three cultural themes: 1) agonistic rhetoric of political association . . . , 2) humanistic religious values which center on conceptions of exemplary personal behavior, and 3) social norms of personal integrity and familial propriety which often take the form of concepts of honor. . . ."[21]

Religion also plays a very important role in affecting the individual's life in both private and public interactions. Birthplace of the three monotheistic faiths—Judaism, Christianity and Islam—the Middle East is a part of the world where religion plays a crucial symbiotic role in the individual's and community's life. The socio-cultural and historic environment that saw the birth and spread of these three religions encouraged a close relationship between the private and public in the individual's life in the Middle East.

In Judaism, the land (eretz), the people (ha'am), and the book (torah) cannot be separated. The same applies to Islam, which is a code of conduct, both temporal and spiritual. The Qur'an dictates the faithful's relations with God and people of other faith living within the framework of the Islamic umma (nation). Christianity in the Arab world is also very similar to Judaism and Islam. For example, for some Christians in Lebanon religious values are superseded by the fight for survival. Religion is used in an ethnic sense.[22]

Middle Eastern societies are defined by a variety of ethnic identities. Armenians, Kurds, Jews, Copts, Circassians, Maronites, these are but some of the minorities that dwell in the contemporary Middle East. The existence of ethnic and ethno-religious groups pre-dates the rise of Islam and the creation of modern states in the Middle East. In the Qur'an, "Peoples of the Book" (Christians and Jews) are treated as "protected peoples," dhimmis, which literally means those on the conscience (dhimma) of the Islamic community. In order to be protected, non-Muslims had to pay a tax, jizya.[23]

Under Ottoman rule, individuals living in the empire did not identify as Ottomans, Turks, Persians, or Arabs, but rather, as Muslims, Christians, Jews, and Druze. The Ottoman administration was controlled in its majority by Sunni Muslims and converts from other religions. In the Ottoman empire, Islamic tolerance of Christians and Jews was defined by the millet (nations) system. "Under the system local communities of a particular sect were autonomous in the conduct of their spiritual affairs and civil affairs relating closely to religion and community, such as church administration, marriage, inheritance, property, and education."[24]

Ethnic groups thus identified with their religious leaders more so than with any abstract notion of the state. The millet system estranged Arab Christians from political life and deepened suspicions between them and Muslims. Christians were treated as foreigners and suspected of being agents of foreign powers; their loyalty was often in doubt. After the fall of the Ottoman empire and in reaction to their plight, Middle Eastern Christians were at the forefront of the new movement for Arab nationalism, the secular movement in the Arab world, and some among them founded socialist parties, such as the Baath (renaissance) Party now in power in Syria and Iraq.

The collapse of the Soviet Union and the pervasive impact of economic globalization have had a negative impact on individuals in the Middle East. Lacking strong and legitimate governments, they have turned to their nuclear and extended families for support and mutual assistance. In addition to reactivating kinship networks, religious and ethnic affiliations, and patronage relationships, Middle Easterners have also embraced the latest inventions of modern technology such as compact discs, satellite dishes, and the World Wide Web.

A perceptive observer of Arab society, Halim Barakat, writes that "the contemporary Arab economic order is a peculiar cluster of different modes of production, all operating at once, which renders it simultaneously semi-feudal, semi-socialist, and semi-capitalist."[25] This schizophrenic nature of Middle Eastern society is also illustrated by the coexistence of religious fundamentalists and secular intellectuals, agrarian forms of production and subsidiaries of multinational corporation, and traditional practices and cosmopolitan attitudes. Following the 1967 Arab-Israeli war which led to the defeat of major Arab armies and disillusionment with the failed promises and dreams of their leadership, the peoples of the Middle East compensated for this failure and betrayal by relying on traditional sociocultural modes of survival.

Political scientist Bassam Tibi notes that "unlike the imperial and the territorial dynastic states that were familiar in Middle Eastern history, the externally imposed new pattern of the nation-state is defined as a national, not as a communal, polity. . . . In varying degrees, all states of the Middle East lack this infrastructure. . . . In most of the states of the Middle East, sovereignty is nominal. The tribal-ethnic and sectarian conflicts that the colonial powers exacerbated did not end with the attainment of independence. The newly established nation-states have failed to cope with the social and economic problems created by rapid development because they cannot provide the proper institutions to alleviate these problems. Because the nominal nation-state has not met the challenge, society has resorted to its pre-national ties as a solution, thereby preserving the framework of the patron-client relationship."[26]

Social relationships in the contemporary Middle East thus require a melting of the individual's identity and personality within the framework of his communal group. A Maronite Catholic in Lebanon belongs to his community from birth to death whether he/she likes it or not. In addition, the confessional system which is pervasive in Lebanon and other countries in the Middle East means that the individual citizen must be part of a patronage network. Although patron-client relations "play an important role in facilitating the distribution of goods and services among the population and harnessing popular support behind leaders," ties of patronage are essentially asymmetrical: perpetuating these relationships also perpetuates and reinforces the unequal power structure in the starkly stratified societies of the contemporary Middle East.

Patron-client ties ensure that people are kept "in their place: the rich and powerful maintain their dominant positions, from which they have the advantage of becoming even more rich and powerful, while the less fortunate are kept in their subordinate position of dependency, remaining virtually powerless over the decision-making processes and larger forces that shape their lives."

Clientelism and the absence of citizenship in the Western sense of the word have profound implications for reconciliation and processes of conflict reduction in the Middle East. Private justice is meted out through a network in which political and/or religious leaders determine the outcome of feuds between clans or conflicts between individuals. Ideologies of honor and shame also play a key role in this context. Most of the blood feuds in Lebanon, Jordan, and Palestine originate from incidents where family honor has been harmed. Usually, women are the direct victims of such tragedies. More and more Arab women are struggling to lessen the impact of honor crimes and fight for the abolition of this feudal tradition.[27]

RITUALS, CONFLICT CONTROL, AND CONFLICT REDUCTION

Rituals play an important role in human behavior, especially in conflict control and conflict reduction. In his entry on ritual, the prominent British anthropologist, Edmund R. Leach writes that "citations in the Oxford English Dictionary from the fourteenth century on reveal two distinct trends of common usage for the words rite (ritual), ceremony (ceremonial), and custom (customary).

On the one hand, these terms have been used interchangeably to denote any noninstinctive predictable action or series of actions that cannot be justified by a "rational" means-to-ends type of explanation." Later on, Leach writes, there is a close connection between rituals and communication behavior. "Human actions can serve to do things, that is, alter the physical state of the world (as in lighting a bonfire), or they can serve to say things. . . . Almost every human action that takes place in culturally defined surroundings is divisible in this way; it has a technical aspect which does something and an aesthetic, communicative aspect which says something."[28]

Anthony Giddens, the famous British sociologist, remarks that rituals are crucial to both the individual's emotional well-being and communal harmony and social integration:

> Without ordered ritual and collective involvement, individuals are left without structured ways of coping with tensions and anxieties. . . . Communal rites provide a focus for group solidarity at major transitions as well as allocating definite tasks for those involved. . . . Something profound is lost together with traditional forms of ritual. . . . Traditional ritual . . . connected individual action to moral frameworks and to elemental questions about human existence. The loss of ritual is also the loss of such frameworks.[29]

This very important observation brings to the fore the malaise that exists in Western society where anomie and atomistic modes of living have relegated customs and rituals to the trash heap of pre-modern, non-rational history. The individual is then left to fend for him or herself through individualistic means. In conflicts, individuals in Western societies have recourse to an attorney or a therapist. The family becomes an alien entity and alienation leads to violence and despair.

For a country coming out of 16 years of civil strife, priorities do not include training for conflict control and reduction. In Lebanon and other Arab societies, conflict resolution techniques are learned and adopted by professional groups such as businessmen or businesswomen, bankers, engineers, etc. For the rest of the population, conflict control and reduction are handled either by state-controlled courts or by traditional means.

In this context, one of the basic criticisms launched against Western conflict resolution techniques is that they are either too mechanistic or based on therapy-oriented formulas. Although Western techniques and skills are relevant and useful, they ought to be better adapted to indigenous realities.

For instance, in Lebanon, the majority of social workers are women. They are trained in Lebanon's major academic institutions: the state-controlled Lebanese University and the Jesuit-controlled Universite Saint-Joseph. Once their degree is completed, most of these graduating social workers confront the realities of Lebanese society.

In conflicts involving couples, social workers were usually approached by battered wives; husbands usually refused to deal with the social worker. The path to resolution thus went through the local religious or political zaim (leader), not through the social worker. (As was mentioned above, this is a typical pattern in patriarchal societies.)

Another issue facing social workers attempting to mediate conflicts in Lebanon was child custody matters. In Middle Eastern societies, in the case of divorce, children are kept in the custody of the father. In some instances mothers try to keep their children.

The young ones become hostages in the two-way conflict that pits their father's family against their mother. Recently, a decision was made by a Lebanese NGO to stop these training workshops.

These examples highlight the predicament of applying Western modes of conflict control and reduction in communally-based societies where patriarchy is predominant and religious values are paramount. This problem is related to the basic reality that Arab states lack citizens in the Western meaning of individuals bound to one another and the state by an agreed-upon interlocking system of rights and duties. What we have instead are individuals belonging to communities and abiding by their rules and rituals. This does not exclude the fact that many young professionals and educated men and women are struggling to establish secular societies based on individual rights and responsibilities and state accountability.

In large Arab cities, individuals involved in conflicts are more likely than are villagers to resort to the official legal system to settle their disputes. The legal system, however, is clogged and corruption is pervasive. Moreover, the interpretation of the rule of law in sectarian-based societies or societies based on tribal modes of social interaction has a different meaning. The law is usually that of the powerful and the wealthy (politicians and clergy) or heads of village clans or bedouin tribes.[30]

The rule of law also has to confront the pervasive and powerful influence of patronage and its strong emphasis on asymmetrical power relationships. For example, an individual who has committed a crime can face both the legal justice system and the tribal mode of conflict control and reduction. This situation underlines the importance of studying closely modes of reconciliation and conflict control in an Arab-Islamic environment. The observer interested in conflict control and reduction in non-Western societies has to look into the rituals that inform individual and community behavior following a crime or any other illegal action.

THE RITUALS OF
SULH AND MUSALAHA

The Middle Eastern rituals of sulh (settlement) and musalaha (reconciliation) are alternative and indigenous forms of conflict control and reduction. The sulh ritual, which is an institutionalized form of conflict management and control, has its origins in tribal and village contexts. "The sulh ritual stresses the close link between the psychological and political dimensions of communal life through its recognition that injuries between individuals and groups will fester and expand if not acknowledged, repaired, forgiven and transcended."[31]

The judicial system in Lebanon does not include sulh as part of the conflict control process. Nonetheless, sulh rituals are approved and encouraged in rural areas where state control is not very strong. The ritual of sulh is today used in the rural areas of Lebanon (the Bekaa Valley, the Hermel area in eastern Lebanon and the Akkar region of north Lebanon).[32]

In the Kingdom of Jordan the ritual of sulh is officially recognized by the Jordanian government as a legally acceptable tradition of the Bedouin tribes. In Israel, the ritual of sulh is still in use among the Palestinian citizens of Israel living in the villages of Galilee.

In some Middle Eastern societies, such as Lebanon, Jordan, and Palestine, rituals are used in private modes of conflict control and reduction. Private modes are processes not controlled by the state whereby customary, traditional steps are taken to restore justice. Sometimes, both private and official justice are invoked simultaneously in fostering reconciliation.

One such step is the process of sulh (settlement) and musalaha (reconciliation). According to Islamic Law (Shari'a), "the purpose of sulh is to end conflict and hostility among believers so that they may conduct their relationships in peace and amity. . . . In Islamic law, sulh is a form of contract ('akd), legally binding on both the individual and community levels."[33] Similar to the private sulh between two believers, "the purpose of [public] sulh is to suspend fighting between [two parties] and establish peace, called muwada'a (peace or gentle relationship), for a specific period of time."[34]

"Sulh is the best of judgments." This is how the Jordanian Bedouin tribes describe the customary process of settlement and reconciliation. The Jordanian Judge Muhammad Abu-Hassan makes a distinction between public sulh and private sulh. Public sulh is similar to a peace treaty between two countries. It usually takes place as a result of conflicts between two or more tribes which result in death and destruction affecting all the parties involved.[35]

Given the severity of life conditions in the desert, competing tribes long ago realized that sulh is a better alternative to endless cycles of vengeance. Each of the tribes then initiates a process of taking stock of its losses in human and material terms. The tribe with minimum losses compensates the tribe that suffered most, and so on.

Tradition has it that stringent conditions are set to settle the tribal conflict definitively. The most famous of these conditions is that the parties in conflict pledge to forget everything that happened and initiate new and friendly relations. The consequences and effects of public sulh apply whether the guilty party was identified or was unknown at the time of the sulh.

Private sulh takes place when both the crime and the guilty party are known. The parties may be of the same tribe or from different tribes. The purpose of private sulh is to make sure that revenge will not take place against the family of the perpetrator.

Regarding the final outcome of sulh, there are two types: total sulh and partial or conditional sulh. The former type ends all kinds of conflict between the two parties, who thenceforth decide not to hold any grudges against each other. The latter type ends the conflict between the two parties according to conditions agreed upon during the settlement process.

Here is a brief sketch of how the ritual of settlement and reconciliation is used in the Middle East. Following a murder, the family of the murderer, in order to thwart any attempt at blood revenge, calls on a delegation of mediators comprised of village elders and notables, usually called muslihs or jaha (those who have gained the esteem of the community).

The mediators initiate a process of fact-finding and questioning of the parties involved in the murder. As soon as the family of the guilty party calls for the mediators' intervention, a hodna (truce) is declared. The task of the muslihs or jaha is not to judge, punish or condemn the offending party, "but rather, to preserve the good names of both the families involved and to reaffirm the necessity of ongoing relationships within the community. The sulh ritual is not a zero-sum game."[36]

To many practitioners of sulh and musalaha, the toughest cases to settle are usually those involving blood feuds. Sometimes, a blood price is paid to the family of the victim that usually involves an amount of money, diya, set by the mediators. The diya (blood money) or an exchange of goods (sometimes the exchange includes animals, food, etc.) substitutes for the exchange of death.

The ritual process of sulh usually ends in a public ceremony of musalaha (reconciliation) performed in the village square. The families of both the victim and the guilty party line up on both sides of the road and exchange greetings and accept apologies, especially the aggrieved party.

The ceremony includes four major stages: 1) the act of reconciliation itself, 2) the two parties shake hands under the supervision of

the muslihs or jaha; 3) the family of the murderer visits the home of the victim to drink a cup of bitter coffee; and 4) the ritual concludes with a meal hosted by the family of the offender. The rituals vary in different places but the basic philosophy is based on sulh (settlement), musalaha (reconciliation), musafaha (hand-shaking), and mumalaha ("partaking of salt and bread," i.e., breaking bread together).[37]

In the first chapter of the Qur'an, the Prophet Muhammad describes the extent and limits of punishment (qisas) and retribution:

O ye who believe!
The law of equality
Is prescribed to you
In cases of murder:
The free for the free,
The slave for the slave,
The woman for the woman.
But if any remission
Is made by the brother
Of the slain, then grant
Any reasonable demand,
And compensate him
With handsome gratitude.

This is a concession
And a Mercy
From your Lord [38]

The Qur'an is a very important source to understand modes of conflict control and reconciliation in Arab-Islamic societies. The holy book of Islam calls for equity in cases of revenge and for forgiveness in cases of apology and "remission."

IMPLICATIONS FOR PRACTITIONERS AND POLICYMAKERS

The collapse of the Soviet Union and the end of superpower competition throughout the world have awakened dormant ethno-religious conflicts in many regions which can have lethal and devastating consequences. Most of these conflicts are based on centuries'-old feelings of victimization and powerlessness. Such feelings are behind the unending cycles of revenge and counter-revenge we see in Bosnia and Kosovo, Rwanda and Burundi, Sri Lanka, Northern Ireland, between Israelis and Palestinians, and in Lebanon.

Consideration of the role of power in convincing enemies to settle and resolve their conflicts, is crucial for the success or failure of reconciliation efforts. If conflict control and reduction is to succeed in the new global political order, diplomats, policymakers, and practitioners, must first rethink how power is perceived and used.

According to the political philosopher Hannah Arendt, true power has nothing to do with guns, muscles, threats or dictators:

> [P]ower is what keeps the public realm, the potential space of appearance between [people] acting and speaking, in existence. . . . Power is always . . . a power potential and not an unchangeable, measurable and reliable entity like force or strength. While strength is the natural quality of an individual seen in isolation, power springs up between people when they act together and vanishes the moment they disperse. Because of this particularity, which power shares with all potentialities that can only be actualized but never fully materialized, power is to an astonishing degree independent of material factors, either of numbers or means.[39]

This definition of power hints at its transformative, not just its coercive, capacity. Empowering victims and helping them overcome painful legacies from the past can take place through transformative reconciliation rituals such as sulh and musalaha. "Such rituals readjust individuals and communities to changing aspects of their life-worlds, thereby enabling them to complete difficult and troubling transitions as individuals and as members of a society."[40]

In a recent paper, Thomas Butler suggested that at the end of the hostilities in Bosnia and following the steps leading to acknowledgment and apology, "the act of forgiveness itself should be marked by a ritual to be prepared jointly by historians, poets, and musicians."[41] At the conclusion of the 1994 conference on "Acknowledgment, Forgiveness and Reconciliation: Alternative Approaches to Conflict Resolution in Lebanon," a suggestion was made by some participants to adapt the ritual of sulh in order to facilitate acknowledgment, apology, and forgiveness at the national, not just communal level in post-war Lebanon. Ghassan Mokheiber, a prominent Lebanese attorney who has written about traditional reconciliation rituals in Lebanon, has stated that modified processes of sulh and musalaha could play a similar role to that of truth and reconciliation commissions in Latin America and South Africa.

The Arab-Islamic rituals of reconciliation are a non-Western indigenous application of the process of acknowledgment, apology, compensation, forgiveness, and reconciliation. Through sulh and musalaha, the ritual of conflict control and reduction takes place within a communal, not a one-on-one, framework.

Here lies the importance of these rituals for conflict resolution practitioners as well as policymakers. The problem confronting Western approaches to reconciliation, is that in Middle Eastern societies in which the conceptual category of the individual does not have the same validity and importance as in Western cultures. The individual is enmeshed within his or her own group, sect, tribe, or millet. Religion continues to play a crucial role individual and collective lives.

Power in Middle Eastern societies is usually concentrated at the top of the hierarchy whether in the village zaim or government leaders (presidents, kings, military autocrats). The state itself is constructed differently from Western nation-states: the concept of national "reconciliation" must occur within entities that were artificially created after World War II. Moreover, given the absence of participatory democracy and the pervasiveness of autocratic rule, the population at large cannot be convinced of the desirability of reconciliation unless tangible benefits ensue. These fundamental realities must be taken into consideration when implementing peace processes in the Middle East.

The history of Israeli-Egyptian and Israeli-Palestinian agreements is not encouraging as far as the transformative power of reconciliation is concerned. Peace in these circumstances resulted from military persuasion and economic enticement. At the popular grassroots level, peace is perceived as an ideal imposed by a superpower's need to pacify a region of the world whose culture and values are unfathomable except through an orientalist perspective.

Returning to Hannah Arendt's definition of power, collective empowerment of the community of citizens ought to be undertaken in coordination with religious and clan leaders in urban, rural, and remote areas. Religious and traditional leaders ought to be involved in empowering their followers as long as peace is based on a sense of equity and justice. As long as Palestinians, Egyptians, Lebanese, Jordanians, Syrians, and other Arabs perceive that the "peace process" is being imposed on the Middle East without addressing age-old grievances, the harder reconciliation with Israel will be. The ritual of sulh and musalaha offers an example to follow and adapt.

NOTES

1. See Muhammad Abu-Nimer, "Conflict Resolution in an Islamic Context: Some Conceptual Questions," *Peace and Change*, Vol. 21, No.1 (January 1996), pp. 22–40.

2. The author was introduced to conflict resolution and trained to teach and apply its skills by Dr. Merle Lefkoff, an experienced facilitator based in New Mexico.

3. This world view is in line with a utilitarian philosophy which pervades intellectual debates in the United States.

4. For further details, see Paul Salem, "A Critique of Western Conflict Resolution from a non-Western Perspective," in Paul Salem, ed. *Conflict Resolution in the Arab World* (Beirut: Lebanon: American University of Beirut, 1997).

5. Western processes of conflict resolution range across a continuum that include situations in which parties have most control (communication, collaboration and negotiation) to situations where parties have least control (mediation and arbitration).

6. Laura Nader, "Conflict: Anthropological Aspects," in David L. Sills, ed. *International Encyclopedia of the Social Sciences*, Vol. 3 and 4 (New York: The MacMillan Co. and The Free Press, 1968), p. 236.

7. For further discussion of victimization and its central role in the perpetuation of conflicts, see Joseph V. Montville, "Psychoanalytic Enlightenment and the Greening of Diplomacy," in Vamik D. Volkan, Joseph V. Montville, and Demetrius A. Julius, eds., *The Psychodynamics of International Relations*, Volume II (Lexington, Masachusetts: Lexington Books, 1991).

8. See Abraham H. Maslow, *Motivation and Personality*, Third Edition (New York and London: Harper and Row, 1987).

9. In his influential book, *Getting to Yes,* Roger Fisher writes that interest-based negotiation, has four basic elements: 1)separate the people from the problem; 2) focus on interests, not positions; 3)invent options for mutual gain; and 4) insist on using objective criteria. For further details, see Roger Fisher and William Ury, *Getting to Yes: Negotiating Agreement Without Giving In,* Second Edition (New York: Penguin Books, 1991).

10. The author, together with his wife, Laurie E. King-Irani, organized the conference in Lebanon. Funded in part by the U.S. Institute of

Peace, this conference was the first organized discussion of the applicability and relevance of acknowledgment, forgiveness, and reconciliation to conflicts in Lebanon and the Middle East.

11. These comments can be found in George Emile Irani, "Acknowledgment, Forgiveness, and Reconciliation in Conflict Resolution: Perspectives from Lebanon," in George E. Irani and Laurie E. King-Irani, eds. *Lessons from Lebanon* (forthcoming).

12. ibid.

13. There are no official figures regarding the number of Lebanese kidnapped and "disappeared" during the ar. Recent figures published in some Lebanese media sources mention the number of kidnapped Lebanese o be around 17,000. Most are unaccounted for and presumed dead.

14. As of this writing, only one warlord, Dr. Samir Geagea, head of the Maronite-Christian dominated militia of the "Lebanese Forces" (now dissolved), was put on trial and is serving a life sentence in jail.

15. Michael Meeker, *Literature and Violence in North Arabia* (Cambridge, MA: Cambridge University Press, 1979), p. 7.

16. For further details see Laurie E. King-Irani, "Kinship, Class and Ethnicity: Strategies for Survival in the Contemporary Middle East," in Deborah Gerner, ed. *Understanding the Contemporary Middle East* (Lynne Rienner Publisher, 1999).

17. A thorough groundbreaking analysis on the role patriarchy plays in the Middle East can be found in Hisham Sharabi, *Neopatriarchy: A Theory of Distorted Change in Arab Society* (New York: Oxford University Press, 1988).

18. Ibid.

19. For a thorough analysis of Egyptian and Arab politics in general see the work of the Lebanese-American scholar, Fouad Ajami, *The Arab Predicament: Arab Political Thought and Practice Since 1967* (Cambridge, MA: Cambridge University Press, 1981).

20. In Iraq, Saddam Hussein and his family, from the Sunni Muslim village of Takrit in north-central Iraq, have dominated Iraqi politics since the early 1970s. The same applies to Syria, where President Hafiz al-Assad's minority Alawi community holds all reins of power. Both Saddam Hussein and Hafez al-Assad are now grooming their sons to take over power in their respective countries.

21. Meeker, op.cit. p. 19.

22. See my *The Papacy and the Middle East: The Role of the Holy See in the Arab-Israeli Conflict* (Notre Dame, IN: University of Notre Dame Press, 1989).

23. Regarding the legal status of non-Muslim minorities, see Antoine Fattal, *Le statut legal des non-Musulmans en pays d'Islam* (Beirut: Imprimerie Catholique, 1958).

24. Michael C. Hudson, *Arab Politics: The Search for Legitimacy* (New Haven, CT: Yale University Press, 1997), p. 58.

25. Halim Barakat, *The Arab World: Society, Culture, and State* (Berkeley, California: University of California Press, 1993), p. 77.

26. Bassam Tibi, "The Simultaneity of the Unsimultaneous: Old Tribes and Imposed Nation-States in the Modern Middle East," in Philip S. Khoury and Joseph Kostiner, eds., *Tribes and State Formation in the Middle East* (Berkeley, California: University of California Pres, 1990), p. 147–149.

27. See Hazem al-Ameen, "Beirut: The Arab Women's Tribunal Symbolized in an Angry Body," *Al-Hayat,* March 6, 1998, p. 24.

28. Edmund R. Leach, "Ritual" in David L. Sills, ed. *International Encyclopedia of the Social Sciences*, Vols. 3&4, (New York: The Macmillan Co. and the Free Press, 1968), pp. 520–526.

29. Anthony Giddens, *Modernity and Self-Identity: Self and Society in the Modern Age* (Palo Alto, CA: Stanford University Press, 1991), p. 204.

30. For an excellent analysis of the legal system in the Arab world see the book by Nathan J. Brown, *The Rule of Law in the Arab World* (Cambridge: Cambridge University Press, 1997).

31. Laurie E. King-Irani, "Rituals of Reconciliation and Processes of Empowerment in Post-War Lebanon," in I. William Zartman, ed. *Traditional Cures for Modern Conflicts: African Conflict Medicine,* (Boulder, CO: Lynne Rienner Publisher, 1999).

32. For further details see Nizar Hamzeh, "The Role of Hizbullah in Conflict Management Within Lebanon's Shia Community," in Paul Salem, ed. op.cit., p. 93–118.

33. M. Khadduri, "Sulh" in C.E. Bosworth, E. van Donzel, W.P. Heinrichs, and G. Lecomte, *The Encyclopedia of Islam,* Volume IX, (Leiden, Holand: Brill, 1997), p. 845–846.

34. Ibid.

35. For further details on Jordanian bedouin rituals of reconciliation see Mohammad Abu-Hassan, *Turath al Badu' al-Qada'I* (Bedouin Customary Law) (Amman, Jordan: Manshuraat Da'irat As Saqafa wa al-Funun, 1987), p. 257–259.

36. King-Irani, op.cit.

37. For further details on the basic principles of sulh as applied in the Galilee, see Elias J. Jabbour, *SULHA: Palestinian Traditional Peacemaking Process* (Shefar'Am, Israel: House of Hope Publications, 1996).

38. Surah 1:178 in *The Holy Qur'an, Text, Translation and Commentary,* Abdullah Yusuf Ali, New Revised Edition (Brentwood, MD: Amana Corporation, 1989).

39. Hannah Arendt, *The Human Condition* (Chicago: The University of Chicago Press, 1958), pp. 200–201.

40. King-Irani, op.cit.

41. Thomas Butler, "Blood Feuds and Traditional Forms of Peacebuilding in the Old Yugoslavia," Unpublished paper. Quoted by permission of the author.

George E. Irani received his Ph.D. in international relations from the University of Southern California. Betweeen 1993 and 1997 he was assistant professor at the Lebanese American University in Beirut. Currently he is a member of the core faculty at Royal Roads University (Canada).

Reading 4.6

Creating a Culture of Peace

The Performing Arts in Interethnic Negotiations

KJELL SKYLLSTAD

INTRODUCTION

What are the basics of peace education? What ignites it, what powers the process? The study of peaceful societies, societies in social balance, may give us some answers to questions we educators ask. I have found in my studies of tribal societies, mostly in South-East Asia, an

Reprinted with permission of the author.

intimate connection between artistic training and education for citizenship. Music, dance and theatre are important arenas for training in democratic participation and conflict transformation.

The cultural crises we now see unfolding may be traced to our modern societies discontinuing these vital processes of social learning. And those societies that still retain and practice the traditional techniques of promoting conflict solution through the performing arts are threatened with extinction. I am especially referring to the aboriginal peoples of Australia, South America, Asia and Africa.

Musical interaction creates social values. Two or more people create something that is greater than the sum of what they create each on their own. And sympathies are formed—strong feelings of belonging. Music making in a group brings out the social dynamics of the group. Harmonic as well as strained relationships are brought to the front. This is the very essence of chamber music. Through musical dialogues the interrelationship within the group is explored. The following is a report on three projects where interethnic music making has proved successful in promoting intercultural understanding.

A Time for
Exploring: Resonant Community

In 1988 the State Concert Agency of Norway (NORCONCERT) initiated a pilot project to probe into the possibilities of extending its school program in an intercultural direction with the intent of fulfilling the new Curricular Master Plan and assist schools in their effort to foster interracial understanding and intercultural cooperation. The project aimed at involving competent teachers from the immigrant communities together with artists from the countries of origin in presenting immigrant and refugee cultures—music, dance and performing arts.

The convincing success of this program brought about the inauguration of a three-year program involving 18 schools in the Oslo area. Six of these schools (A-schools) were to participate in an intensive arts education program concentrating on immigrant cultures. Six others (B-schools) were to participate in a regular school concert series also featuring immigrant cultures, while the six remaining (C-schools) would function as control institutions.

The following goals were formulated:

1. To spread knowledge and create understanding for the values that reside in the culture of immigrants by presenting live music and dance to children.
2. To bring out the musical resources that lie in the various immigrant groups in Norway, as well as to provide external professional support through performers from the immigrants' home countries.
3. To ease the process of integration for immigrants through multicultural interaction.

The target groups were

1. Pupils between the ages of 10-12 years old in Norwegian primary schools situated in areas with varying concentration of immigrant pupils. The same pupils were to follow the project for three years (grades four through six).
2. Families of the children involved in the trial study.

Researchers from several countries, in several independent studies, have discovered negative attitudes towards children of other races or minority cultures already in pre-school age. Prejudicial attitudes in the form of stereotypes become more pronounced with age. But it appears that the personality development in pre-adolescence gives room for more nuanced views, based on a greater interest for individual features and curiosity for other ways of living.

Based on a greater ability for identification across racial boundaries among the 10-14 year olds, a more open and friendly disposition is found in this age group. But the positive disposition does not seem to last once these children become teenagers, when peer-group pressure and the need to conform makes itself felt.

Many factors indicate that the ages 10-14 are critical years. The development towards a greater openness as a result of personal maturity may also, with appropriate influence continue into adolescence, or it may stiffen into stereotypical attitudes and negative patterns of behaviour. Once prejudicial attitudes have been internalized, they are extremely difficult to change. A standard American textbook in adolescent psychology (Cole and Hall: *Psychology of Adolescence*) states:

> Various people have attempted to reduce the amount of already measured prejudice in a given group. The logical assumption was that an intolerant person will loose his negative attitudes once he has been given adequate information about, and adequate contact with, those whom he dislikes. The matter is, however, not so simple, because prejudice rests upon emotional rather than intellectual grounds. There seems to be practically no relationship between knowledge of a feeling toward a group, and an already established prejudice is reduced only a little if at all by supplying facts to counterbalance it. Nor does more education have much effect. . . . (Cole and Hall: 1970, p. 495).

This is confirmed by van Dijk in his in-depth study *Communicating Racism*:

> Positive information, counterarguments, and basic principles of adequate interaction in multiethnic societies, are virtually absent in socialization, communication, and other instances of social information processing. This also explains why challenging ethnic prejudice is much more difficult than accepting them. This means that if recipients are already prejudiced it will not be easy to change such prejudices.

It was precisely this kind of understanding that led to the focus on a musical methodology as an important tool in fostering tolerance. The conclusion from these findings must be that preventive measures must be set before prejudicial attitudes have been firmly established. They cannot be based on the communication of information alone, but must confront the irrational and emotional bases of racist and discriminatory attitudes. Van Dijk, writes on the basis of his findings that "ethnic attitude change may require complete ideological reorientation." (Ibid., p. 328)

The idea was not primarily to present the music traditions of the immigrant communities in their "pure" form, but rather to stimulate participation in interethnic musical activities. Students of different ethnic origin were encouraged to try their hand on various percussion instruments, forming small classroom bands or ensembles, accompanying dancing and musical plays. In the larger gatherings the whole school population was invited to join in. Sometimes even parents were invited for evening performances and musical games.

Cultures from three geographical zones would be presented: Asia (first year), Africa (second year) and Latin-America (third year). Immigrant organizations, foreign embassies as well as individual artists were contacted for participation in the project, and auditions were held for musical talents in refugee centers. Countries of origin were in some cases visited to study programs of artistic education and the ways music and art function as integrative factors in the individual communities and the society at large. During these visits contacts with leading artists were established, and their teaching methods discussed. The actual content and forms of presentation were worked out in a long process of cooperation with the participant artists, who also helped in finding suitable audio-visual aids and material for a written syllabus for each cultural area.

With the cooperation of the State Film Board two videos were produced centering on the musical heritage of immigrant and refugee children and youth. These films were made available in the native languages as well (Farsi and Urdu).

Tests were given at the beginning and end of the project and evaluated. The main findings were:

1. A considerably greater increase in the A-schools (as compared to the other school models) from 1989 to 1992 in the number of pupils who report that they have no personal problems with mobbing. This is most marked with the immigrant pupils and it indicates a clear connection between the project and improved social relationships in the schools. The tendency towards better social relations and diminished ethnic conflicts in the school environment is confirmed by reports from the teachers.
2. Attitudes towards immigrants seem to have remained unchanged in the A-schools, while there was a greater degree of negative attitudes among the pupils in the B- and C-schools in 1992 than at the beginning of the project in 1989.
3. A greater number of pupils in the A-schools at the end of the project consider immigrants to be honest, law-abiding, industrious and kind, while there are fewer in the other school models.
4. Immigrant pupils in the A-schools have strengthened their self–image during the project. The teachers report that there has been a highly positive development in identity formation and activity level of immigrant pupils.

A Time for the Celebration of Differences: From "The World in the North" to the "Multicultural Asian Music Festival"

The immediate success of the project led to a new direction in the musical programming of the National Concert Association as well. Several troupes of immigrant musicians have been involved in around 1000 intercultural performances reaching half of the school population. Most of these concerts have presented music of more than one ethnic group.

In a community project in an area of racial conflict all schools and cultural organizations of the village joined forces with the visiting group in a coordinated intercultural effort. Music and dance workshops were held for several age groups from pre-school children to adults, school concerts as well as creative cooperative sessions with local folk music groups. One of the outcomes of this cooperation was a recording that turned out the number one Norwegian bestseller.

On Aug. 1st. 1992 a Norwegian Multicultural Music Center was started as a follow up of this program. It functions as a resource center in close cooperation with NORAD, the State Agency of Development and Aid especially focusing on artistic and especially music cooperation on an equal basis with developing countries in three continents, and establishing links with immigrant communities.

One of the first initiatives was the Afrobrazz project. An African and a Norwegian ensemble were invited to live together in a small Norwegian village, VŒgŒ, and develop a common musical concept for later concerts in Norway and in Africa. An important aspect of the plan was to involve all the various musical organizations of the community in the music-making, in the way the whole village is involved in festivities in a traditional African setting. The project proved to be highly successful.

Each year a World Music Festival is arranged simultaneously in all four Nordic capitals featuring immigrant and refugee musicians in concert appearances with artists from countries of origin. The festival also includes interethnic music projects in schools and kindergartens in and around the capital.

The Nordic model of the multicultural festival became the inspiration and basis for the Multicultural Festival of Asian Music, held in Colombo and Kandy, Sri Lanka. The festival was initiated by the present author, who between 1992-1995 directed a three-year scientific exchange and development program instituted between the Institute of Aesthetic Studies, Kelaniya University and the Department of Music and Theatre, University of Oslo. This festival featured ensembles from 5 Asian countries, including a mixed ensemble from Sri Lanka of Singhalese and Tamil musicians playing together. The festival was aired by Sri Lankan TV and Young Asia Television.

A Time for Peace-Zaman el Salaam

Right in the heyday of the Intifada Israeli singers often joined Israeli Palestinian and Arabic singers combining Hebrew and Arabic texts. This must be seen as some kind of protest against the official cultural policy. Since the establishment of the state of Israel in 1948, Arabic song in Israel was an extremely marginalized phenomenon. Hebrew and Arabic programmes on Israeli TV are completely separated. Since these media are government controlled, Arabic songs with strong social and political messages are never aired, not even in programmes for the Arab minority. This rejection of Oriental or Arabic music meant not only the rejection of minority cultures, but the rejection of the culture of the large part of the Jewish population, that of oriental descent. (Perelson 1998, pp. 113-128)

The first one to break this pattern was the Israeli singer Alon Olearchik, very popular in Israel, with the song "Shalom Salaam" performed together with the Arab singer Amal Murkus at the annual childrens' song festival in 1986:

Believe there is reason enough
In the world

To make peace now between people
It's time to make peace
Not tomorrow, but today

Shalom Salaam
Shalom Salaam

Another song Moshe and Mussa was written as part of an Israeli-Arab kindergarten project in Jaffa. Two children Moshe (a Jew) and Mussa (an Arab) tell of their friendship.

Moshe and Mussa two friends
Moshe and Mussa go to kindergarten
Sometimes silent, sometimes crying
Sometimes laughing, sometimes singing

By the port of the city of Jaffa
Everyone will sing this song
Shalom Aleihem, Aleykum Salaam
There's nothing like a twosome to tour the world

Another song by Uzi Khitman goes:

Here we are, you and me
And me and you
With two voices
And one song

And this is is exactly the idea that made the following event such a remarkable demonstration of the power of song. During an Intifada demonstration the well-known Israeli singer Amnon Abubbul was hit in the head by a rock hurled by a Palestinian.

Rather than thinking of revenge, he began to ponder in what ways he could contribute to bring peace. After being released from the army he found out that near his kibbutz there lived a Palestinian poet from Nazareth—Fathi Kasem. He contacted him to tell his story and share his thoughts. Together in a few days they made a peace song in Arabic—Zaman el Salaam - expressing the longing of both peoples for peace:

Like an ocean - Peace, my love, has a wide embracing soul
There are times of ebb and flow in days of struggle and sorrow
Between storms and thunder feelings burst out my love:
Time for Peace – Inshallah

There is a time from far away I long like a lone star in the sky
There are times of ebb and flow in days of struggle and sorrow
Out of the lightning the rainbow glows
and I will know the time has come
Time for Peace - Inshallah

But still there was no music. Then out in the desert Amnon heard a violin sobbing. It sounded very Arabic. It was the violin of the master musician Yair Dalal, who headed an Israeli-Palestinian orchestra. Dalal had been teacher at the Eilat Conservatory of Music and since 1992 Assistant Professor at the State Teachers College Seminar Hakibutsum. He had been teacher in oriental music at the Jewish-Arab community Center in Jafo and director of a Palestinian-Jewish childrens' orchestra at the Jerusalem Center for Music. He has been giving workshops in intercultural music methods and Middle East music traditions at the University of Oslo and Norwegian teachers colleges. This was the music he wanted for the peace song. Two days before the signing of the Cairo agreement it came out as a CD. Did it influence the negotiations? The artists had no way of finding out.

But they got a new chance. To celebrate the anniversary of the Oslo Accord famous Finnish singer Arja Sajonmaa was looking for music and heard about the song. She wanted a choir to come to Oslo to reach the emotions through poetry and song. And so it happened

that 50 Israeli and 50 Palestinian children under very difficult circumstances met on several occasions for practice in the Palestinian territories to prepare for the concert. Other Arabic and Israeli songs were learned and permanent friendships were formed. They were to sing with 100 Norwegian children - in three languages: Arabic, Hebrew and English. And they were to be accompanied by the Oslo Philharmonic Orchestra directed by the famous conductor Zubin Mehta.

Then on Sept. 13, 1994 after long unresolved negotiations in Paris and a whole night of fruitless talks in Oslo, Chairman Yassir Arafat and Israeli Foreign Minister Shimon Peres came to the concert, exhausted and disappointed. The children sang, joined by 7000 spectators in the refrain, and accompanied by Yair Dalal on the oud and violin, the Israeli-Palestinian orchestra and the Oslo Philharmonic. Before a stunned audience the former Norwegian Foreign Minister, Bjšrn Sverre Godal, announced that a peace document had been signed.

How could this happen? What potential for emotional and conceptual impact lies in a multicultural ensemble? What did the event signify for the participant musicians, the children, the live audience, the politicians and the international TV-audience who watched the performance?

The focal point of departure was a real life experience, human suffering brought about by war, by ethnic conflict—the wounded singer seeking out his enemy to make a plea for peace in poetic images. Then there was the marriage of words to music, a music born out of the experience of multi-ethnic music making, the Israeli-Palestinian orchestra performing across borders, the fruit of a long interaction. And then there was the all-important process of the rehearsals, of preparing for the performance. Jewish and Palestinian met for the first time through the medium of music. Finally there was the process of the social ritual of the performance itself. In a way it served as an initiation of the children into peacemaking, supported by key devoted artists, politicians from both sides and a huge public identifying with the children, accepting and endorsing their message.

Since the Peace concert Yair Dalal, together with the Israeli-Palestinian ensemble that formed the instrumental nucleus beside the Oslo Philharmonic as well as other interethnic groups, have been extremely active giving concert performances in many parts of the globe and issuing new recordings. I was happy to witness last August the highly successful Ethno-dance festival in an immigrant part of Tel Aviv where the various ethnic groups, mainly oriental Jews presented their music and dance together with visiting foreign artists from Asia and Europe. National dishes were served in an outdoor bazaar area where handicrafts were on display and sale. Dalal is a teacher at the Bar Ilan-University outside Tel Aviv, that recently employed 40 new teachers of Arabic and other oriental music, according to Dr. Seroussi's correspondance with me inspired by the Resonant Society project.

A Time for Sharing—
Music for a Multicultural Bosnia

In 1994 Dr. Svanibor Pettan of the Ljubljana Academy of Music came to Norway on a research assignment, supported by the Norwegian Research Council. This was after my lectures in Croatia and Slovenia on creative peace education. The main purpose was to initiate a research program on the possibilities of music intervention in the rehabilitation of refugees. Together we started a course at the Department of Music and Theatre in the University of Oslo "Music in Exile," which focused on the cultural situation in former Yugoslavia, with special emphasis on the interethnic character of Bosnian ensembles. As part of the research program the participating

Norwegian students formed, together with Bosnian refugees, a sevdalinka ensemble, Azra. The ensemble was expressly formed to perform in refugee reception centres and culture clubs with the purpose of helping the refugees living in Norway and preparing them for resettling in a multi-ethnic Bosnia of the future.

The Azra project was designed to use ethno-musicological and anthropological evidence of commonalities among the Bosnians, as an alternative to the political "general understanding" locked in the alleged differences along ethnic lines. It was to confront negative propaganda to which many refugees fall victims that people claiming different ethnic and religious affiliation, though all indigenous to Bosnia-Herzegovina, cannot live together any more. The project was designed to help Bosnian refugees during their stay in Norway and prepare them for coexistence in a multiethnic Bosnia-Herzegovina in the future.

The ensemble set out to offer to all Bosnians, regardless of their ethno-religious affiliation, a musical concept with which they could associate, and at the same time to keep public attention on Bosnia-Herzegovina and its fate, including the refugee problem.

Prior to the war, musicians of all Bosnian ethnic groups shared in the preservation, evolution and affirmation of both the rural musical traditions as well as the urban musical genres, foremost the "sevdalinka." Musical ensembles were often interethnic. The dividing lines were geographical, not ethnic. After the war a process of musical apartheid set in. Instruments that originally had been shared by all ethnic groups, were now seen to be ethnically exclusive, like the epic songs with gusle accompaniment, now claimed to be Serb only. During the siege on Sarajevo, Serbian rebels placed loudspeakers in their positions around Sarajevo blaring out such gusle songs performed by their leader, the notorious war criminal Radovan Karadzic.

The Azra ensemble, on their part, under the guidance of Dr. Pettan carefully chose Bosnian songs that were loved cross-ethnically and that had themes of a common emotional appeal: The Bosnian landscape, love and longing. The instruments were "neutral"—accordion, clarinet, flute, guitar, bass—in order to counteract the apartheid tendency mentioned. The ensemble included Norwegian songs in their repertory, so as to build bridges between the refugees and their Norwegian hosts.

The project proved successful from the very start as there seemed to be an almost insatiable demand among the refugees for the music of their homeland. Evaluation on the basis of activities during the first six months indicated positive moves toward the strengthening of Bosnian cultural identity, improved self-image and social relations. Since then the ensemble has expanded its activities, having performed on national TV in the Norwegian Theatre and in a number of Norwegian cities with very positive feedback. One should add their participation in international conferences on migration and music education and cultural support work in other European countries. The project also led to a series of interethnic music and theatre initiatives in Croatia and Slovenia.

The lessons from the past hold promise for the future: From various parts of the globe we are experiencing new efforts to incorporate the performing arts in peace education. It is important that we share these experiences and move forward in a concerted effort to realize the goal set before us: Spreading a Culture of Peace.

REFERENCES

Blacking, John. *How Musical is Man?* London 1976.

Blacking, John (Ed). *The Performing Arts,* London 1979.

Cole, Louela and Hall, Irma. *Psychology of Adolescence,* London 1970.

Council of Europe. *Training Teachers in Intercultural Education,* Strassbourg, 1986.

Dijk, Teun A van. *Communicating Racism,* Newbury Park, California, 1986, Sage.

Perelson, Inbal. Power relations in the Israeli popular music system in *Popular Music,* Vol. 17/1 1998, Cambridge University Press.

Pettan, Svanibor. Making the Refugee Experience Different. "Azra" and the Bosnians in Norway, in ed. Renata Jambresic Kirin. *War, exile, daily life: cultural perspectives,* Zagreb 1996.

Kjell Skyllstad is at the University of Oslo, Norway, Department of Music and Theatre.

PART V

Colonialization and Globalization

The Latin word *colonia* has the meaning of "farm," "landed estate," "settlement," and particularly of a public settlement of Roman citizens in a hostile or newly conquered country, such as the Roman coloniæ in Britain.

According to the *Oxford English Dictionary*, the term *colonial* means "Of, belonging to, or relating to a colony, or (spec.) the British colonies; in American history, of or belonging to the thirteen British colonies which became the United States, or to the time while they were still colonies. Now freq. derogatory." And the term *colonialism* is defined as the "the colonial system or principle. Now freq. used in the derogatory sense of an alleged policy of exploitation of backward or weak peoples by a large power." Note how the OED itself engages in othering by labeling occupied peoples as backward and weak. That itself defines what colonization has meant to peoples worldwide.

Anticolonialism became a major modern theme as dozens of European colonies in Asia and Africa became free. Anticolonial studies in academia have focused on three themes: that colonialism was a distinctively Western policy that was inflicted on the world, that the West became wealthy and the colonies impoverished, and that the descendants of colonialism are worse off than they would have been had colonialism never occurred. The first two readings in this section are from two of the leading anticolonial intellectuals—Wole Soyinka and Ashis Nandy.

Wole Soyinka was born in 1934 in western Nigeria. He received his doctorate from the University of Leeds and was a dramaturgist at the Royal Court Theatre in London. He returned to Nigeria to study African drama and literature. He has published drama, novels, and poetry deeply rooted in African culture and with a knowledge of literary legacies of European culture. The first reading in this section is Wole Soyinka's acceptance speech upon receiving the Nobel Prize for Literature.

Ashis Nandy is Senior Fellow and Director of the Center for the Study of Developing Societies and Chairperson of the Committee for Cultural Choices and Global Futures, both located in Delhi. Nandy has coauthored a number of human rights reports and is active in movements for peace, alternative sciences and technologies, and cultural survival. He is the author of the second reading in this section, "Consumerism: It's Hidden Beauties and Politics."

Mike Featherstone in the introduction to the book *Global Culture* (1990) suggests that globalization refers to the "cultural integration and cultural disintegration processes . . . that occur on a trans-national or trans-societal level" (p. 1). It might appear that globalization is a necessary response to deal with world problems of population, AIDS, and the distribution of wealth. However, the term today is more typically used to refer to the unprecedented worldwide spread of markets and democracy.

Proponents of globalization argue that economic systems are based on private property and that democratic governments improve human life. Opponents of globalization argue that because the United States has promoted both free markets and democracy throughout the world, globalization reinforces U.S. wealth and dominance and in effect has become the "new" colonization.

In the reading "Interculturalism in Singapore: Looking for the Big, Bad Other," William Peterson introduces the question of globalization to the world of the performing arts. Lalita Rajasingham in "The Impact of Universities on Globalisation" brings the concepts of technology and education into the discussion of globalization. That discussion is continued by Randy Kluver in "Globalization, Informatization, and Intercultural Communication."

The final reading is by Mohan R. Limaye, a professor of Business Communication and International Business at Boise State University. Limaye was born and raised in India. He first came to the U.S. as a Fulbright scholar and eventually became as U.S. citizen. His paper is an opinion piece originally written for his students to encourage discussion. The reading "Five Ways to Reduce the Foreign Terrorist Threat to the United States" does not address physical security, but it addresses the dangers of globalization.

REFERENCES

Featherstone, M. (1990). Global culture: An introduction. In M. Featherstone (Ed.), *Global Culture: Nationalism, globalization and modernity* (A Theory, Culture & Society special issue, pp. 1–14). London: Sage.

Reading 5.1

Nobel Lecture, December 8, 1986

WOLE SOYINKA

THIS PAST MUST
ADDRESS ITS PRESENT

A rather curious scene, unscripted, once took place in the wings of a London theatre at the same time as the scheduled performance was being presented on the actual stage, before an audience. What happened was this: an actor refused to come on stage for his allocated role. Action was suspended. A fellow actor tried to persuade him to emerge, but he stubbornly shook his head. Then a struggle ensued. The second actor had hoped that, by suddenly exposing the reluctant actor to the audience in full glare of the spotlight, he would have no choice but to rejoin the cast. And so he tried to take the delinquent actor by surprise, pulling him suddenly towards the stage. He did not fully succeed, so a brief but untidy struggle began. The unwilling actor was completely taken aback and deeply embarrassed—some of that tussle was quite visible to a part of the audience.

The performance itself, it should be explained, was an improvisation around an incident. This meant that the actors were free, within the convention of the performance, to stop, re-work any part they wished, invite members of the audience on stage, assign roles and change costumes in full view of the audience. They therefore could also dramatize their wish to have that uncooperative actor join them—which they did with gusto. That actor had indeed left the stage before the contentious scene began. He had served notice during rehearsals that he would not participate in it. In the end, he had his way, but the incident proved very troubling to him for weeks afterwards. He found himself compelled to puzzle out this clash in attitudes between himself and his fellow writers and performers. He experienced, on the one hand, an intense rage that he had been made to appear incapable of confronting a stark reality, made to appear to suffer from interpretative coyness, to seem inhibited by a cruel reality or perhaps to carry his emotional involvement with an event so far as to interfere with his professional will. Of course, he knew that it was none of these things. The truth was far simpler. Unlike his colleagues together with who m he shared, unquestionably, the same political attitude towards the event which was being represented, he found the mode of presentation at war with the ugliness it tried to convey, creating an intense disquiet about his very presence on that stage, in that place, before an audience whom he considered collectively responsible for that dehumanizing actuality.

And now let us remove some of the mystery and make that incident a little more concrete. The scene was the Royal Court Theatre, London, 1958. It was one of those Sunday nights which were given to experimentation, an innovation of that remarkable theatre manager-director, George Devine, whose creative nurturing radicalised British theatre of that period and produced later icons like John Osborne, N. F. Simpson, Edward Bond, Arnold Wesker, Harold Pinter, John Arden, etc., and even forced the then conservative British palate to sample stylistic and ideological pariahs like Samuel Beckett and Bertold Brecht. On this particular occasion, the evening was devoted to a form of "living" theatre, and the main fare was titled ELEVEN MEN DEAD AT HOLA. The actors were not all professional actors; indeed they were mostly writers who jointly created and performed these dramatic pieces. Those with a long political memory may recall what took place at Hola Camp, Kenya, during the Mau-Mau Liberation struggle. The British Colonial power believed that the Mau-Mau could be smashed by herding Kenyans into special camps, trying to separate the hard cases, the mere suspects and the potential recruits—oh, they had it all neatly worked out. One such camp was Hola Camp and the incident involved the death of eleven of the detainees who were simply beaten to death by camp officers and warders. The usual enquiry set up, and it was indeed the Report which provided the main text on which the performance was based.

We need now only to identify the reluctant actor, if you have not guessed that by now - it was none other than this speaker. I recall the occasion as vividly as actors are wont to recollect for ever and ever the frightening moment of a blackout, when the lines are not only forgotten but even the moment in the play. The role which I had been assigned was that of a camp guard, one of the killers. We were equipped with huge night-sticks and, while a narrator read the testimony of one of the guards, our task was to raise the cudgels slowly and, almost ritualistically, bring them down on the necks and shoulders of the prisoners, under orders of the white camp officers. A surreal scene. Even in rehearsals, it was clear that the end product would be a surrealist tableau. The Narrator at a lectern under a spot; a dispassionate reading, deliberately clinical, letting the stark facts reveal the states of mind of torturers and victims. A small ring of white officers, armed. One seizes a cudgel from one of the warders to demonstrate how to beat a human being without leaving visible marks. Then the innermost clump of detainees, their only weapon—non-violence. They had taken their decision to go on strike, refused to go to work unless they obtained better camp conditions. So they squatted on the ground and refused to move, locked their hands behind their knees in silent defiance. Orders were given. The inner ring of guards, the blacks, moved in, lifted the bodies by hooking their hands underneath the armpits of the detainees, carried them like toads in a state of petrification to one side, divided them in groups.

The faces of the victims are impassive; they are resolved to offer no resistance. The beatings begin: one to the left side, then the back, the arms—right, left, front, back. Rhythmically. The cudgels swing in unison. The faces of the white guards glow with professional satisfaction, their arms gesture languidly from time to time, suggesting it is time to shift to the next batch, or beat a little more severely on the neglected side. In terms of images, a fluid, near balletic scene.

Then the contrast, the earlier official version, enacting how the prisoners were supposed to have died. This claimed that the prisoners had collapsed, that they died after drinking from a poisoned water supply. So we staged that also. The prisoners filed to the water wagon, gasping with thirst. After the first two or three had drunk and commenced writhing with pain, these humane guards rushed to stop the others but no, they were already wild with thirst, fought their way past salvation and drank greedily the same source. The groans spread from one to the other, the writhing, the collapse—then agonized deaths. That was the version of the camp governors.

The motif was simple enough, the theatrical format a tried and tested one, faithful to a particular convention. What then was the problem? It was one, I believe, that affects most writers. When is playacting rebuked by reality? When is fictionalizing presumptuous? What happens after playacting? One of the remarkable properties of the particular theatrical convention I have just described is that it gives off a strong odour of perenniality, that feeling of "I have been here before." "I have been a witness to this." "The past enacts its presence." In such an instance, that sense of perenniality can serve both as exorcism, a certificate of release or indeed—especially for the audience, a soporific. We must bear in mind that at the time of presentation, and to the major part of that audience, every death of a freedom fighter was a notch on a gun, the death of a fiend, an animal, a bestial mutant, not the martyrdom of a patriot.

We know also, however, that such efforts can provoke changes, that an actualization of the statistical, journalistic footnote can arouse revulsion in the complacent mind, leading to the beginning of a commitment to change, redress. And on this occasion, angry questions had been raised in the Houses of Parliament. Liberals, humanitarians and reformists had taken up the cause of justice for the victims. Some had even travelled to Kenya to obtain details which exposed the official lie. This

profound unease, which paralysed my creative will, therefore reached beyond the audience and, finally, I traced its roots to my own feelings of assaulted humanity, and its clamour for a different form of response. It provoked a feeling of indecency about that presentation, rather like the deformed arm of a leper which is thrust at the healthy to provoke a charitable sentiment. This, I believe, was the cause of that intangible, but totally visceral rejection which thwarted the demands of my calling, rendered it inadequate and mocked the empathy of my colleagues. It was as if the inhuman totality, of which that scene was a mere fragment, was saying to us: Kindly keep your comfortable sentiment to yourselves.

Of course, I utilize that episode only as illustration of the far deeper internalised processes of the creative mind, a process that endangers the writer in two ways: he either freezes up completely, or he abandons the pen for far more direct means of contesting unacceptable reality. And again, Hola Camp provides a convenient means of approaching that aspect of my continent's reality which, for us whom it directly affronts, constitutes the greatest threat to global peace in our actual existence. For there is a gruesome appropriateness in the fact that an African, a black man should stand here today, in the same year that the progressive Prime Minister of this host country was murdered, in the same year as Samora Machel was brought down on the territory of the desperate last-ditch guardians of the theory of racial superiority which has brought so much misery to our common humanity. Whatever the facts are about Olof Palme's death, there can be no question about his life. To the racial oppression of a large sector of humanity, Olof Palme pronounced, and acted, a decisive No! Perhaps it was those who were outraged by this act of racial "treachery" who were myopic enough to imagine that the death of an individual would arrest the march of his convictions; perhaps it was simply yet another instance of the Terror Epidemic that feeds today on shock, not reason. It does not matter; an authentic conscience of the white tribe has been stilled, and the loss is both yours and mine. Samora Machel, the leader who once placed his country on a war footing against South Africa, went down in as yet mysterious circumstances. True, we are all still haunted by the Nkomati Accord which negated that earlier triumphant moment on the African collective will; nevertheless, his foes across the border have good reason to rejoice over his demise and, in that sense, his death is, ironically, a form of triumph for the black race.

Is that perhaps too stark a paradox? Then let me take you back to Hola Camp. It is cattle which are objects of the stick, or whip. So are horses, goats, donkeys etc. Their definition therefore involves being occasionally beaten to death. If, thirty years after Hola Camp, it is at all thinkable that it takes the ingenuity of the most sophisticated electronic interference to kill an African resistance fighter, the champions of racism are already admitting to themselves what they continue to deny to the world: that they, white supremacist breed, have indeed come a long way in their definition of their chosen enemy since Hola Camp. They have come an incredibly long way since Sharpeville when they shot unarmed, fleeing Africans in the back. They have come very far since 1930 when, at the first organized incident of the burning of passes, the South African blacks decided to turn Dingaan's Day, named for the defeat of the Zulu leader Dingaan, into a symbol of affirmative resistance by publicly destroying their obnoxious passes. In response to those thousands of passes burnt on Cartright Flats, the Durban police descended on the unarmed protesters killing some half dozen and wounding hundreds. They backed it up with scorched earth campaign which dispersed thousands of Africans from their normal environment,

victims of imprisonment and deportation. And even that 1930 repression was a quantum leap from that earlier, spontaneous protest against the Native Pass law in 1919, when the police merely rode down the protesters on horseback, whipped and sjamboked them, chased and harried them, like stray goats and wayward cattle, from street corner to shanty lodge. Every act of racial terror, with its vastly increasing sophistication of style and escalation in human loss, is itself an acknowledgement of improved knowledge and respect for the potential of what is feared, an acknowledgement of the sharpening tempo of triumph by the victimized.

For there was this aspect which struck me most forcibly in that attempt to recreate the crime at Hola Camp: in the various testimonies of the white officers, it stuck out, whether overtly stated or simply through their efficient detachment from the ongoing massacre. It was this: at no time did these white overseers actually experience the human "otherness" of their victims. They clearly did not experience the reality of the victims as human beings. Animals perhaps, a noxious form of vegetable life maybe, but certainly not human. I do not speak here of their colonial overlords, the ones who formulated and sustained the policy of settler colonialism, the ones who dispatched the Maxim guns and tuned the imperial bugle. They knew very well that empires existed which had to be broken, that civilizations had endured for centuries which had to be destroyed. The "sub-human" denigration for which their "civilizing mission" became the altruistic remedy, was the mere rationalizing icing on the cake of imperial greed. But yes indeed, there were the agents, those who carried out orders (like Eichmann, to draw parallels from the white continent); they—whether as bureaucrats, technicians or camp governors had no conceptual space in their heads which could be filled—except very rarely and exceptionally—by "the black as also human." It would be correct to say that this has remained the pathology of the average South African white since the turn of the last century to this moment. Here, for example is one frank admission by an enlightened, even radical mind of that country:

> It was not until my last year in school that it had occurred to me that these black people, these voteless masses, were in any way concerned with the socialism which I professed or that they had any role to play in the great social revolution which in these days seemed to be imminent. The "workers" who were destined to inherit the new world were naturally the white carpenters and bricklayers, the tramworkers and miners who were organized in their trade unions and who voted for the Labour Party. I would no more have thought of discussing politics with a native youth than of inviting him home to play with me or to a meal or asking him to join the Carnarvon Football Club. The African was on a different plane, hardly human, part of the scene as were dogs and trees and, more remotely, cows. I had no special feelings about him, not interest nor hate nor love. He just did not come into my social picture. So completely had I accepted the traditional attitudes of the time."

Yes, I believe that this self-analysis by Eddie Roux, the Afrikaaner political rebel and scientist, remains today the flat, unvarnished truth for the majority of Afrikaaners. "No special feelings, not interest nor hate nor love," the result of a complete acceptance of "traditional attitudes." That passage captures a mind's racial tabula rasa, if you like—in the first decade of this century—about the time, in short, when the Nobel series of prizes was inaugurated. But a slate, no matter how clean, cannot avoid receiving impressions once it is exposed to air—fresh or polluted. And we are now in the year 1986, that is after an entire century of direct, intimate exposure, since that confrontation, that first rejection of the dehumanizing label implicit in the Native Pass Laws.

Eddie Roux, like hundreds, even thousands of his countrymen, soon made rapid strides. His race has produced its list of martyrs in the cause of nonracialism—one remembers, still with a tinge of pain, Ruth First, destroyed by a letter bomb delivered by the long arm of Apartheid. There are others—André Brink, Abram Fischer, Helen Suzman–Breyten Breytenbach, with the scars of martyrdom still seared into their souls. Intellectuals, writers, scientists, plain working men, politicians—they come to that point where a social reality can no longer be observed as a culture on a slide beneath the microscope, nor turned into aesthetic variations on pages, canvas or the stage. The blacks of course are locked into an unambiguous condition: on this occasion I do not need to address us. We know, and we embrace our mission. It is the other that this precedent seizes the opportunity to address, and not merely those who are trapped within the confines of that doomed camp, but those who live outside, on the fringes of conscience. Those specifically, who with shameless smugness invent arcane moral propositions that enable them to plead inaction in a language of unparalleled political flatulence: Personally, I find sanctions morally repugnant. Or what shall we say of another leader for whom economic sanctions which work against an Eastern European country will not work in the Apartheid enclave of South Africa, that master of histrionics who takes to the world's airwaves to sing: "Let Poland be," but turns off his hearing aid when the world shouts: "Let Nicaragua be." But enough of these world leaders of double-talk and multiple moralities.

It is baffling to any mind that pretends to the slightest claim to rationality, it is truly and formidably baffling. Can the same terrain of phenomenal assimilation—that is, one which produced evidence of a capacity to translate empirical observations into implications of rational human conduct—can this same terrain which, over half a century ago, fifty entire years, two, three generations ago produced the Buntings, the Roux, the Douglas Woltons, Solly Sachs, the Gideon Bothas—can that same terrain, fifty, sixty, even seventy years later, be peopled by a species of humanity so ahistorical that the declaration, so clearly spelt out in 1919 at the burning of the passes, remains only a troublesome event of no enduring significance?

Some atavistic bug is at work here which defies all scientific explanation, an arrest in time within the evolutionary mandate of nature, which puts all human experience of learning to serious question! We have to ask ourselves then, what event can speak to such a breed of people? How do we reactivate that petrified cell which houses historic apprehension and development? Is it possible, perhaps, that events, gatherings such as this might help? Dare we skirt the edge of hubris and say to them: Take a good look. Provide your response. In your anxiety to prove that this moment is not possible, you had killed, maimed, silenced, tortured, exiled, debased and dehumanized hundreds of thousands encased in this very skin, crowned with such hair, proudly content with their very being? How many potential partners in the science of heart transplant have you wasted? How do we know how many black South African scientists and writers would have stood here, by now, if you had had the vision to educate the rest of the world in the value of a great multi-racial society.

Jack Cope surely sums it up in his Foreword to THE ADVERSARY WITHIN, a study of dissidence in Afrikaaner literature when he states:

Looking back from the perspective of the present, I think it can justly be said that, at the core of the matter, the Afrikaaner leaders in 1924 took the wrong turning.

Themselves the victims of imperialism in its most evil aspect, all their sufferings and enormous loss of life nevertheless failed to convey to them the obvious historical lesson. They became themselves the new imperialists. They took over from Britain the mantle of empire and colonialism. They could well have set their faces against annexation, aggression, colonial exploitation, and oppression, racial arrogance and barefaced hypocrisy, of which they had been themselves the victims. They could have opened the doors to humane ideas and civilizing processes and transformed the great territory with its incalculable resources into another New World.

Instead they deliberately set the clock back wherever they could. Taking over ten million indigenous subjects from British colonial rule, they stripped them of what limited rights they had gained over a century and tightened the screws on their subjection.

Well, perhaps the wars against Chaka and Dingaan and Diginswayo, even the Great Trek were then too fresh in your laager memory. But we are saying that over a century has passed since then, a century in which the world has leapt, in comparative tempo with the past, at least three centuries. And we have seen the potential of man and woman—of all races—contend with the most jealously guarded sovereignty of Nature and the Cosmos. In every field, both in the Humanities and Sciences, we have seen that human creativity has confronted and tempered the hostility of his environment, adapting, moderating, converting, harmonizing, and even subjugating. Triumphing over errors and resuming the surrendered fields, when man has had time to lick his wounds and listen again to the urgings of his spirit. History—distorted, opportunistic renderings of history have been cleansed and restored to truthful reality, because the traducers of the history of others have discovered that the further they advanced, the more their very progress was checked and vitiated by the lacunae they had purposefully inserted in the history of others. Self-interest dictated yet another round of revisionism—slight, niggardly concessions to begin with. But a breach had been made in the dam and an avalanche proved the logical progression. From the heart of jungles, even before the aid of high-precision cameras mounted on orbiting satellites, civilizations have resurrected, documenting their own existence with unassailable iconography and art. More amazing still, the records of the ancient voyagers, the merchant adventurers of the age when Europe did not yet require to dominate territories in order to feed its industrial mills—those objective recitals of mariners and adventurers from antiquity confirmed what the archeological remains affirmed so loudly. They spoke of living communities which regulated their own lives, which had evolved a working relationship with Nature, which ministered to their own wants and secured their future with their own genius. These narratives, uncluttered by the impure motives which needed to mystify the plain self-serving rush to dismantle independent societies for easy plundering—pointed accusing fingers unerringly in the direction of European savants, philosophers, scientists, and theorists of human evolution. Gobineau is a notorious name, but how many students of European thought today, even among us Africans, recall that several of the most revered names in European philosophy—Hegel, Locke, Montesquieu, Hume, Voltaire—an endless list—were unabashed theorists of racial superiority and denigrators of the African history and being. As for the more prominent names among the theorists of revolution and class struggle—we will draw the curtain of extenuation on their own intellectual aberration, forgiving them a little for their vision of an end to human exploitation.

In any case, the purpose is not really to indict the past, but to summon it to the attention of a suicidal, anachronistic present. To say to that mutant present: you are a child of those centuries of lies, distortion and opportunism in high places, even among the holy of holies of intellectual objectivity. But the world is growing up, while you wilfully remain a child, a stubborn, self-destructive child, with certain destructive powers, but a child nevertheless. And to say to the world, to call attention to its own historic passage of lies—as yet unabandoned by some—which sustains the evil precocity of this child. Wherein then lies the surprise that we, the victims of that intellectual dishonesty of others, demand from that world that is finally coming to itself, a measure of expiation? Demand that it rescues itself, by concrete acts, from the stigma of being the wilful parent of a monstrosity, especially as that monstrous child still draws material nourishment, breath, and human recognition from the strengths and devises of that world, with an umbilical cord which stretches across oceans, even across the cosmos via so-called programmes of technological co-operation. We are saying very simply but urgently: Sever that cord. By any name, be it Total Sanction, Boycott, Disinvestment, or whatever, sever this umbilical cord and leave this monster of a birth to atrophy and die or to rebuild itself on long-denied humane foundations. Let it collapse, shorn of its external sustenance, let it collapse of its own social disequilibrium, its economic lopsidedness, its war of attrition on its most productive labour. Let it wither like an aborted foetus of the human family if it persists in smothering the minds and sinews which constitute its authentic being.

This pariah society that is Apartheid South Africa plays many games on human intelligence. Listen to this for example. When the whole world escalated its appeal for the release of Nelson Mandela, the South African Government blandly declared that it continued to hold Nelson Mandela for the same reasons that the Allied powers continued to hold Rudolf Hess! Now a statement like that is an obvious appeal to the love of the ridiculous in everyone. Certainly it wrung a kind of satiric poem out of me—Rudolf Hess as Nelson Mandela in blackface! What else can a writer do to protect his humanity against such egregious assaults! But yet again to equate Nelson Mandela to the archcriminal Rudolf Hess is a macabre improvement on the attitude of regarding him as sub-human. It belongs on that same scale of Apartheid's self-improvement as the ratio between Sharpeville and Von Brandis Square, that near-kind, near-considerate, almost benevolent dispersal of the first Native Press rebellion.

That world which is so conveniently traduced by Apartheid thought is of course that which I so wholeheartedly embrace—and this is my choice—among several options—of the significance of my presence here. It is a world that nourishes my being, one which is so self-sufficient, so replete in all aspects of its productivity, so confident in itself and in its destiny that it experiences no fear in reaching out to others and in responding to the reach of others. It is the heartstone of our creative existence. It constitutes the prism of our world perception and this means that our sight need not be and has never been permanently turned inwards. If it were, we could not so easily understand the enemy on our doorstep, nor understand how to obtain the means to disarm it. When this society which is Apartheid South Africa indulges from time to time in appeals to the outside world that it represents the last bastion of civilization against the hordes of barbarism from its North, we can even afford an indulgent smile. It is sufficient, imagines this state, to raise the spectre of a few renegade African leaders, psychopaths and robber barons who we ourselves are victims of—whom we denounce before the world and overthrow when we are able—this Apartheid society insists to the world that its picture of the future is the reality which only its policies can erase. This is a continent which only destroys, it proclaims, it is peopled by a race which has never contributed anything positive to the world's pool of knowledge. A vacuum, that will suck into its insatiable maw the entire fruits of centuries of European civilization, then spew out the resulting mush with contempt. How strange that a society which claims to represent this endangered face of progress should itself be locked in centuries-old fantasies, blithely unaware of, or indifferent to the fact that it is the last, institutionally functioning product of archaic articles of faith in Euro-Judaic thought.

Take God and Law for example, especially the former. The black race has more than sufficient historic justification to be a little paranoid about the intrusion of alien deities into its destiny. For even today, Apartheid's mentality of the pre-ordained rests—according to its own unabashed claims, on what I can only describe as incidents in a testamentary Godism—I dare not call it Christianity. The sons of Ham on the one hand; the descendants of Shem on the other. The once pronounced, utterly immutable curse. As for Law, these supremacists base their refusal to concede the right of equal political participation to blacks on a claim that Africans have neither respect for, nor the slightest proclivity for Law—that is, for any arbitrating concept between the individual and the collective.

Even the mildest, liberal, somewhat regretful but contented apologists for Apartheid, for at least some form of Apartheid which is not Apartheid but ensures the status quo—even this ambivalent breed bases its case on this lack of the idea of Law in the black mind. I need only refer to a recent contribution to this literature in the form of an autobiography by a famous heart transplant surgeon, one who in his own scientific right has probably been a candidate for a Nobel Prize in the Sciences. Despite constant intellectual encounters on diverse levels, the sad phenomenon persists of Afrikaaner minds which, in the words of Eddie Roux, is a product of that complete acceptance of the "traditional attitudes of the time."

They have, as already acknowledged, quite "respectable" intellectual ancestors. Friedrich Wilhelm Hegel, to cite just my favourite example, found it convenient to pretend that the African had not yet developed to the level where he

> attained that realization of any substantial objective existence—as for example, God, or Law—in which the interest of man's volition is involved and in which he realizes his own being.

He continues:

> This distinction between himself as an individual and the universality of his essential being, the African in the uniform, undeveloped oneness of his existence, has not yet attained: so that the knowledge of absolute Being, an Other and a Higher than his individual self, is entirely wanting.

Futile to waste a moment refuting the banal untruthfulness of this claim, I content myself with extracting from it only a lesson which escapes, even today, those who insist that the pinnacle of man's intellectual thirst is the capacity to project this universality in the direction of a Super-Other. There is, I believe, a very healthy school of thought which not only opposes this materially, but has produced effectively structured societies which operate independently of this seductive, even productively, inspiring but extravagant fable.

Once we thus overcome the temptation to contest the denial of this feat of imaginative projection to the African, we find ourselves left only with the dispassionate exercise of examining in what areas we encounter differences between the histories of societies which, according to Hegel and company, never conceived of this Omnipotent Extrusion into Infinite Space, and those who did—be these differences in the areas of economic or artistic life, social relations or scientific attainment—in short, in all those activities which are empirically verifiable, quite different from the racial consequences of imprecations arising from that post Adam-and-Eve nudist escapade in the Old Testament.

When we do this, we come upon a curious fact. The pre-colonial history of African societies—and I refer to both Euro-Christian and Arab-Islamic colonization—indicates very clearly that African societies never at any time of their existence went to war with another over the issue of their religion. That is, at no time did the black race attempt to subjugate or forcibly convert others with any holier-than-thou evangelizing zeal. Economic and political motives, yes. But not religion. Perhaps this unnatural fact was responsible for the conclusions of Hegel—we do not know. Certainly, the bloody histories of the world's major religions, localized skirmishes of which extend even to the present, lead to a sneaking suspicion that religion, as defined by these eminent philosophers, comes to self-knowledge only through the activity of war.

When, therefore, towards the close of the Twentieth Century, that is, centuries after the Crusades and Jihads that laid waste other and one another's civilizations, fragmented ancient cohesive social relations and trampled upon the spirituality of entire peoples, smashing their cultures in obedience to the strictures of unseen gods, when today, we encounter nations whose social reasoning is guided by canonical, theological claims, we believe, on our part, that the era of darkness has never truly left the world. A state whose justification for the continuing suppression of its indigenes, indigenes who constitute the majority on that land, rests on claims to divine selection is a menace to secure global relationship in a world that thrives on nationalism as common denominator. Such a society does not, in other words, belong in this modern world. We also have our myths, but we have never employed them as a base for the subjugation of others.

We also inhabit a realistic world, however, and, for the recovery of the fullness of that world, the black race has no choice but to prepare itself and volunteer the supreme sacrifice.

In speaking of that world—both myth and reality—it is our duty, perhaps our very last peaceful duty to a doomed enemy—to remind it, and its supporters outside its boundaries, that the phenomenon of ambivalence induced by the African world has a very long history, but that most proponents of the slanderous aspects have long ago learnt to abandon the untenable. Indeed it is probably even more pertinent to remind this racist society that our African world, its cultural hoards and philosophical thought, have had concrete impacts on the racists' own forebears, have proved seminal to a number of movements and even created tributaries, both pure and polluted, among the white indigenes in their own homelands.

Such a variety of encounters and responses have been due, naturally, to profound searches for new directions in their cultural adventures, seeking solaces to counter the remorseless mechanization of their existence, indeed seeking new meanings for the mystery of life and attempting to overcome the social malaise created by the very triumphs of their own civilization. It has led to a profound respect for the African contribution to world knowledge, which did not, however, end the habitual denigration of the African world. It has created in places a near-deification of the African person—that phase in which every African had to be a prince—which yet again, was coupled with a primitive fear and loathing for the person of the African. To these paradoxical responses, the essentiality of our black being remains untouched. For the black race knows, and is content simply to know, itself. It is the European world that has sought, with the utmost zeal, to re-define itself through these encounters, even when it does appear that he is endeavouring to grant meaning to an experience of the African world.

We can make use of the example of that period of European Expressionism, a movement which saw African art, music, and dramatic rituals share the same sphere of influence as the most disparate, astonishingly incompatible collection of ideas, ideologies, and social tendencies—Freud, Karl Marx, Bakunin, Nietzsche, cocaine, and free love. What wonder then, that the spiritual and plastic presence of the Bakota, Nimba, the Yoruba, Dogon, Dan etc., should find themselves at once the inspiration and the anathematized of a delirium that was most peculiarly European, mostly Teutonic and Gallic, spanning at least four decades across the last and the present centuries. Yet the vibrant goal remained the complete liberation of man, that freeing of his yet untapped potential that would carve marble blocks for the construction of a new world, debourgeoisify existing constrictions of European thought and light the flame to forge a new fraternity throughout this brave new world. Yes, within this single movement that covered the vast spectrum of outright fascism, anarchism, and revolutionary communism, the reality that was Africa was, as always, sniffed at, delicately tested, swallowed entire, regurgitated, appropriated, extoiled, and damned in the revelatory frenzy of a continent's recreative energies.

Oscar Kokoschka for instance: for this dramatist and painter African ritualism led mainly in the direction of sadism, sexual perversion, general self-gratification. It flowed naturally into a Nietzschean apocalyptic summons, full of self-induced, ecstatic rage against society, indeed, against the world. Vassily Kadinsky on his part, responded to the principles of African art by foreseeing:

a science of art erected on a broad foundation which must be international in character insisting that

> it is interesting, but certainly not sufficient, to create an exclusively European art theory.

The science of art would then lead, according to him, to

> a comprehensive synthesis which will extend far beyond the confines of art into the realm of the oneness of the human and the "divine."

This same movement, whose centenary will be due for celebrations in European artistic capitals in the next decade or two—among several paradoxes the phenomenon of European artists of later acknowledged giant stature—Modigliani, Matisse, Gauguin, Picasso, Brancusi etc. worshipping with varying degrees of fervour, at the shrine of African and Polynesian artistic revelations, even as Johannes Becher, in his Expressionist delirium, swore to build a new world on the eradication of all plagues, including

> Negro tribes, fever, tuberculosis, venereal epidemics, intellectual psychic defects - I'll fight them, vanquish them.

And was it by coincidence that contemporaneously with this stirring manifesto, yet another German enthusiast, Leo Frobenius—with no claims whatever to being part of, or indeed having the least interest in the Expressionist movement, was able to visit Ile-Ife, the heartland and cradle of the Yoruba race and be profoundly stirred by an object of beauty, the product of the Yoruba mind and hand, a classic expression of that serene portion of the world resolution of that race, in his own words:

> Before us stood a head of marvellous beauty, wonderfully cast in antique bronze,

true to the life, incrusted with a patina of glorious dark green. This was, in very deed, the Olokun, Atlantic Africa's Poseidon.

Yet listen to what he had to write about the very people whose handiwork had lifted him into these realms of universal sublimity:

> Profoundly stirred, I stood for many minutes before the remnant of the erstwhile Lord and Ruler of the Empire of Atlantis. My companions were no less astounded. As though we have agreed to do so, we held our peace. Then I looked around and saw—the blacks—the circle of the sons of the "venerable priest," his Holiness the Oni's friends, and his intelligent officials. I was moved to silent melancholy at the thought that this assembly of degenerate and feeble-minded posterity should be the legitimate guardians of so much loveliness.

A direct invitation to a free-for-all race for dispossession, justified on the grounds of the keeper's unworthiness, it recalls other schizophrenic conditions which are mother to, for instance, the far more lethal, dark mythopoeia of Van Lvyck Louw. For though this erstwhile Nazi sympathizer would later rain maledictions on the heads of the more extreme racists of his countrymen:

> Lord, teach us to think what "own" is, Lord let us think! and then: over hate against blacks, browns, whites: over this and its cause, I dare to call down judgement.

Van Lvyck's powerful epic RAKA was guaranteed to churn up the white cesspools of these primordial fears. A work of searing, visceral impact operating on racial memory, it would feed the Afrikaaner Credo on the looming spectre of a universal barbaric recession, bearing southwards on the cloven hooves of the Fifth Horseman of the Apocalypse, the black.

There is a deep lesson for the world in the black races' capacity to forgive, one which,

I often think, has much to do with ethical precepts which spring from their world view and authentic religions, none of which is ever totally eradicated by the accretions of foreign faiths and their implicit ethnocentricism. For, not content with being a racial slanderer, one who did not hesitate to denigrate, in such uncompromisingly nihilistic terms, the ancestral fount of the black races—a belief which this ethnologist himself observed—Frobenius was also a notorious plunderer, one of a long line of European archeological raiders. The museums of Europe testify to this insatiable lust of Europe; the frustrations of the Ministries of Culture of the Third World and, of organizations like UNESCO are a continuing testimony to the tenacity, even recidivist nature of your routine receiver of stolen goods. Yet, is it not amazing that Frobenius is today still honoured by black institutions, black leaders, and scholars? That his anniversaries provide ready excuse for intellectual gatherings and symposia on the black continent, that his racist condescensions, assaults have not been permitted to obscure his contribution to their knowledge of Africa, or the role which he has played in the understanding of the phenomenon of human culture and society, even in spite of the frequent patchiness of his scholarship?

It is the same largeness of spirit which has informed the relationship today of erstwhile colonial nations, some of whom have undergone the most cruel forms of settler or plantation colonialism, where the human degradation that goes with greed and exploitation attained such levels of perversion that human ears, hands, and noses served to atone for failures in production quota. Nations which underwent the agony of wars of liberation, whose earth freshly teems with the bodies of innocent victims and unsung martyrs, live side by side today with their recent enslavers, even sharing the control of their destiny with those who, barely four or five years ago, compelled them to witness the massacre

of their kith and kin. Over and above Christian charity, they are content to rebuild, and share. This spirit of collaboration is easy to dismiss as the treacherous ploy of that special breed of leaders who settle for early compromises in order to safeguard, for their own use, the polished shoes of the departing oppressors. In many cases, the truth of this must be conceded. But we also have examples of regimes, allied to the aspirations of their masses on the black continent, which have adopted this same political philosophy. And, in any case, the final arbiters are the people themselves, from whose relationships any observations such as this obtain any validity. Let us simply content ourselves with remarking that it is a phenomenon worthy of note. There are, after all, European nations today whose memory of domination by other races remains so vivid more than two centuries after liberation, that a terrible vengeance culturally, socially, and politically is still exacted, even at this very moment, from the descendants of those erstwhile conquerors. I have visited such nations whose cruel histories under foreign domination are enshrined as icons to daily consciousness in monuments, parks, in museums and churches, in documentation, woodcuts, and photo gravures displayed under bullet-proof glass-cases but, most telling of all, in the reduction of the remnants of the conquering hordes to the degraded status of aliens on sufferance, with reduced civic rights, privileges, and social status, a barely tolerate marginality that expresses itself in the pathos of downcast faces, dropped shoulders, and apologetic encounters in those rare times when intercourse with the latterly assertive race is unavoidable. Yes, all this I have seen, and much of it has been written about and debated in international gatherings. And even while acknowledging the poetic justice of it in the abstract, one cannot help but wonder if a physical pound of flesh, excised at birth, is not a kinder act than a lifelong visitation of the sins of the father on the sons even to the tenth and twelfth generations.

Confronted with such traditions of attenuating the racial and cultural pride of these marginalized or minority peoples, the mind travels back to our own societies where such causative histories are far fresher in the memory, where the ruins of formerly thriving communities still speak eloquent accusations and the fumes still rise from the scorched earth strategies of colonial and racist myopia. Yet the streets bear the names of former oppressors, their statues and other symbols of subjugation are left to decorate their squares, the consciousness of a fully confident people having relegated them to mere decorations and roosting-places for bats and pigeons. And the libraries remain unpurged, so that new generations freely browse through the works of Frobenius, of Hume, Hegel, or Montesquieu and others without first encountering, freshly stamped on the fly-leaf: WARNING! THIS WORK IS DANGEROUS FOR YOUR RACIAL SELF-ESTEEM.

Yet these proofs of accommodation, on the grand or minuscule scale, collective, institutional, or individual, must not be taken as proof of an infinite, uncritical capacity of black patience. They constitute in their own nature, a body of tests, an accumulation of debt, an implicit offer that must be matched by concrete returns. They are the blocks in a suspended bridge begun from one end of a chasm which, whether the builders will it or not, must obey the law of matter and crash down beyond a certain point, settling definitively into the widening chasm of suspicion, frustration, and redoubled hate. On that testing ground which, for us, is Southern Africa, that medieval camp of biblical terrors, primitive suspicions, a choice must be made by all lovers of peace: either to bring it into the modern world, into a rational state of being within that spirit of human partnership, a capacity for which has been so amply demonstrated by every liberated black nation on our continent, or—to bring it abjectly to its knees by ejecting it, in every aspect, from humane recognition, so that it caves in internally, through the strategies of its embattled majority. Whatever the choice, this inhuman affront cannot be allowed to pursue our Twentieth Century conscience into the Twenty-first, that symbolic coming-of-age which peoples of all cultures appear to celebrate with rites of passage. That calendar, we know, is not universal, but time is, and so are the imperatives of time. And of those imperatives that challenge our being, our presence, and humane definition at this time, none can be considered more pervasive than the end of racism, the eradication of human inequality, and the dismantling of all their structures. The Prize is the consequent enthronement of its complement: universal suffrage, and peace.

Wole Soyinka was born in Nigeria. He received his doctorate at the University of Leeds. He has taught drama and literature at various universities in Ibadan, Lagos, and Ife and at Cambridge, Sheffield, and Yale. His dramas are based on the mythology of his own tribe, the Yoruba.

Reading 5.2

Consumerism

Its Hidden Beauties and Politics

ASHIS NANDY

THE NOVELTY OF CONSUMPTION

Consumerism is not the first choice of human beings. Nor is it a basic need. There is no evidence in contemporary psychology, anthropology or ethology that consumerism is a part of human nature, that we cannot survive without unending consumption. Not even the great champions of the free market have dared to claim that human happiness is inescapably hitched to the kind of consumption that the prosperous are encouraged to practise in the name of development today. Even much of the West, identified the world over with infinite consumption, had no genuine tradition of heavy consumption before the beginning of this century, probably not until the 1940s.

Consumption was discovered as a value and a lifestyle only about five decades ago. Previously, it had been a character trait of profligate rulers and the spoilt children of a few super-rich; now it has become a marker of social achievement and thus, a part of everyday life. People now consume stories of super-consumption through newspapers, journals and television—the way they used to read, dream, and vicariously enter the harems of Oriental potentates. Earlier, the aristocracy, when it consumed mindlessly, did not dare to advertise the fact, for it was incongruent with class status. Only the newly rich were expected to flaunt their wealth. High consumption became a marker of social status and success and a patented remedy for feelings of social inadequacy and personal inferiority.

U.S. HEGEMONY: INSTITUTIONALIZING CONSUMERISM

Perhaps no other country has become so deeply identified with consumption in our times as the United States, though some of the most powerful critiques of consumption, too, have come from that country. Perhaps the reason for both is that in no other country has consumption been so systematically institutionalized as a need in itself. A few city-states like Hong Kong and Singapore and a few small kingdoms acting as city-states, such as Dubai, have also jumped on the band-wagon of "consuming societies." These are societies where not only is consumption an end in itself, but the entire country often looks to a casual observer like a huge supermarket, and the country's political economy, if not life itself, is organized around consumption. However, the global cultural impact of such city-states is a fraction of that of the United States.

In the United States, the successful institutionalization of consumption might have come about because it is mainly a society of immigrants that has tried to build a public culture hitched to the psychological and social needs of the exiled and decultured. The institutionalization of consumption is an incidental by-product of this larger cultural process which has been going on for the last 200 years. As I have already said, consumption has anxiety-binding properties, particularly in the lives of the uprooted, the lonely and the lost in the masses.

This culture of exile also provides a clue to the unique status that the United States has begun to enjoy as everyone's second country. In pre-war Europe, Paris claimed the status, I am told, of being every European's second city. For many subjects of British and French colonies, Paris and, to an even greater extent, London had a similar status. Today, it seems that only the United States can claim that status. The size of the American market (including the market for conformity and deviance and for new faiths, ideologies and creeds) has a role to play in this. The United States is the consumer's paradise. Even dissent has a better market there than elsewhere; it is consumed more avidly and widely than almost anywhere else. Even this critique of consumption can be consumed.

QUESTIONING THE SPIRIT OF CONSUMPTION

In the 1940s, Erich Fromm coined the term "marketing orientation" to describe a personality type that included persons who sold themselves, rather than things, in the modern marketplace. He did not foresee that one day

we would have another personality type that would consider it "normal" to consume for the sake of consuming. The consuming orientation is now a hallmark of style and high fashion; there are persons and groups in the world who are famous only for their flamboyant consumption. These hyper-consumers would have put to shame the greediest of the rich before World War II.

Usually when justifying consumption, the marketers claim that it will lead to greater consumption of the physical essentials of life by the poor. Alternatively, they extol the technological growth or economic modernization that follow a consumption explosion, allegedly serving as an engine of development. It has, however, already become obvious that the kind of consumption they have in mind—or are comfortable with—has nothing to do with any such grand social vision. For once built, a culture of consumption becomes a self-perpetuating affair. As has been the case with the super-consuming rich, it becomes an end in itself. This is not unknown to the development experts; they expect consumption to lead to a consumption-oriented development and technology. I am not saying that their economic logic is faulty. I am arguing that their justification of consumption only captures a small part of the phenomenon and spirit of consumption.

To understand that spirit, one must first face the fact that to make consumption a value, human beings have to be re-engineered. The first step is to isolate or uproot a person from his or her community, traditions, and family. Instead, he or she has to be given a large, anonymous quasi-community called the nation, a more manageable set of cultural artifacts called traditions (artifacts that can be consumed in a theatre, gallery, classroom or tourist resort) and a nuclearized unit called family where the elderly and children both become either intrusions or liabilities that have to be sometimes borne but never treated on the same footing as the conjugal pair, bonded together by a commodified concept of sex.

MOVING AWAY FROM THE LONELY CONSUMER

Simultaneously, an ideological basis has to be laid for consumption. The possessive individual who, according to many European scholars, provides the very basis of modern liberal capitalism has to be redefined as the consuming individual. Simultaneously, the right to property has to be redefined as the right to consumption. And the sovereignty of this consuming individual has to be declared so that the apparent sacredness that attaches to the individual in many theories of the state, freedom and rights begins to attach to the act of and the right to consumption. Some social and political activists claim that standardized production systems are now producing standardized consumption patterns, for only such patterns now make economic sense. Many popular ideas of democracy in the global mass culture seem, on closer scrutiny, to be an attempt to protect this pattern and the particular form of individualism that goes with it. As some put it, "dollarized poverty" is now matched by dollarized wealth and dollarized individuals.

To such an individual—lonely, narcissistic, and decoupled from community ties—consumption becomes the ultimate value, a guarantor of social belongingness and status. He or she compensates for an empty social life by consuming. One is, because one consumes.

This lonely individual is the basic constituent of all projects of global marketing. Marketing is all about creating needs. Basic needs do not have to be advertised; people automatically try to meet them and are willing to work or pay for them. Advertisements become necessary to create artificial needs. Marketing is the art and science of creating such needs by linking them to basic human needs. This linkage is often not noticed. Many talk of consumerism as a form of conspiracy to cheat the ordinary, innocent citizen with the help of smart, high-pitched advertisement. Ordinary citizens are not that easily cheated. They are influenced by advertisements, but first a void has to be created in their lives, so that the magic of advertisement and its seductiveness can work on them.

Creation of that void is crucial. Only when his or her life is emptied of a deep sense of belongingness to a community, family or tradition does the atomized individual begin to seek meaning in various pseudo-solidarities, one of the most important of which, today, is the solidarity of consumers. Presidents and prime ministers in the First World are now made or unmade on the basis of threat they pose to—or the promises they offer of—mega-consumption. Consumption, or the hope of it, now gives meaning to the lives of many, however odd that may sound to a large proportion of the world. This has even produced a new internationalism which, paradoxically, relieves one from any responsibility to learn about other countries or communities. You do not have to, for others also consume, and therefore they are. They also can be known through their consumption patterns.

CONSUMABLE CULTURE?

Yet, consumerism is not anti-cultural. Being a world-view, it has a place for culture. The place is not for culture as we have known it—vibrant, unmanageable, fuzzy and often subversive to the projects called modernity and development—but for a consumable culture. Once such a culture becomes triumphant, many known entities in our world acquire new meanings. For instance, I notice remarkable and rapid changes taking place in ancient civilizations such as China and India. There are already signs that, under a consumerist dispensation, the Indianness of India may become a liability and yet, at the same time, a capital. Much effort, we may presume, will be made in the coming years to encash that Indianness as a form of commodified classicism or ethnic chic, "viewable" on the week-ends and sellable in the tourist market.

Do cultures resist consumerism? I do not really know. But I like to believe that they can hit back when threatened with extinction, whether the threat is real or imagined. Human biology can be even more aggressively resistant. A large majority of the killers in the First World have to do with over-consumption.

Worse is the fate of those ethnic groups in the First World which have not developed any skepticism towards consumption. Let us note, with a sense of alarm, that the incidence of cardiac diseases among expatriate South Asians in some of the western societies today is three times that among the native whites. Is this to be the trend for the future?

Ashis Nandy is a political psychologist and social theorist and a Fellow at the Centre for the Study of Developing Societies, New Delhi.

Reading 5.3

Interculturalism in Singapore

Looking for the Big, Bad Other

WILLIAM PETERSON

The 1996 Australasian tour of producer Michael Edgley's four million dollar *Aida* received considerable attention throughout the region. Boasting a cast of over 1,000, the Singapore production featured animals from the Singapore Zoo, a 200-tonne, 65 by 45 meter set, and a huge central pyramid that nearly grazed the ceiling of the cavernous Singapore Indoor Stadium. According to Singapore's English-language daily newspaper,

---

Reprinted with permission from *Dis/Orientations: Cultural Praxis in Theatre: Asia, Pacific, Australia.* Edited by Rachel Fensham and Peter Eckersall. Clayton, Australia: Centre for Drama and Theatre Studies, 1999. Copyright of the author.

Editor's Note: This reading was revised by William Peterson in December, 2002.

The Straits Times, producer Edgley chose to begin the international tour in Singapore because "with its Global City of the Arts initiative, [it] is determined to be a pivotal arts capital." Echoing the rhetoric of Singapore's arts administrators, he added, "No other city in my experience has such a powerful will to success in its pursuit of excellence" (Koh, 1996). The press held up the size and scale of the production as proof of Singapore's cultural greatness, while Edgley's glowing comments about the arts infrastructure provided confirmation that the country's arts policies were on the right track.

The choice of *Aida* is in itself significant, as this opera more than any other could be said to constitute a classier and more extravagant version of the "Instant Asia" cultural revues presented to Western tourists at expensive Singaporean hotels. In *Culture and Imperialism,* Edward Said singles out *Aida* as one of the monumental works of Western culture that effectively positions Asia as the exotic East. He observes, "As a visual, musical, and theatrical spectacle, *Aida* does a great many things for and in European culture, one of which is to confirm the Orient as an essentially exotic, distant, and antique place in which Europeans can mount certain shows of force" (1993: 112). Indeed, with its cavalcade of soldiers, prisoners, guards, jugglers, dancers, court attendants, and priests, the key protagonists in the event—the enslaved Ethiopian princess and the commander of the conquering Egyptian army—are almost lost in the visual splendor and human vastness of the work. Said argues that even though the story is set in North Africa, *Aida* has historically represented a kind of generic Orient to the Western audience; the pageantry and exoticism that characterizes this fictitious Orient reflects a vision of the East as a place of mystery and strangeness that is also present in many other "masterpieces" of Western high culture. Thus *Aida* could be seen as yet another work that contributes to

the view of Asia as a monolithic other, a sticking place for all that is exciting, different, sensuous, exotic, and—though unknowable—ultimately yielding and conquerable.

Certainly Singaporeans have every right to patronize an expensive[1] high culture events such as *Aida* just as Western opera-goers do. The case of *Aida* is an illustration on a grand scale of how a Western-generated view of Asia as a place of mysticism and exoticism can meet with an enthusiastic reception in an Asian country. The view of Asia offered in *Aida* is not one of a specific country or even of any of the three largest cultures that constitute contemporary Singapore (Chinese, Malay, Indian); instead the opera materializes a fictional, imaginative realm that reflects Western mythologizing about the idea of the Orient rather than the reality of any actual place. Thus the "cultured," educated, English-speaking Singaporean opera-goers watching *Aida* shares with their Western counterpart a willingness to enter into this fiction of a generic Orient.

For the Singaporean theatre practitioner working in English, there is an extent to which social, political and economic forces have all collectively contributed to an internalization of this Western gaze upon a monolithic East, complicating and even derailing existing models of interculturalism.[2] One widely circulated model proposed by Patrice Pavis (1996) assumes that "source" and "target" cultures constitute fixed points of reference in the intercultural exchange. In Singapore's case, Pavis's concepts of "source" and "target" cultures have little relevance, as the source culture may well be partially or largely derived from a view that others (i.e. Westerners) have of Asia. No theatre company in Singapore better illustrates this complex intercultural web than the Asia in Theatre Research Centre, a group formed in 1987 by the late William Teo[3]. Teo consciously modeled his group upon the intercultural explorations of Ariane Mnouchkine's Théâtre du Soleil and Peter

Brook's Paris-based International Center for Theatre Research. Throughout the 1980s and 1990s Mnouchkine and Brook were the two most visible and highly acclaimed Western directors creating Asian-influenced intercultural work. The ways in which Teo's company have absorbed the aesthetics of these two Western theatre practitioners provides a vivid illustration of cultural studies critic Rey Chow's observation that, "What confronts the Western scholar is the discomforting fact that the natives are no longer staying in their frames" (1993: 28).

Over the last two decades, Mnouchkine's Théâtre du Soleil, based at the Cartoucherie, the company's warehouse space on the outskirts of Paris, has developed a reputation for staging the works of Shakespeare using a range of Asian theatrical conventions and forms. Mnouchkine's productions of Shakespeare place his plays in a mythic dimension, a world where stylized gesture and ritual replaces psychologically-motivated acting. In her discussion of the group's work with *Richard III*, Mnouchkine observes: "We wanted to make Asian theatre a voyage of research, simply because Western theatre offers little in this way, and because realism has started to bore me" (1996: 96). According to Mnouchkine, this "research" component is a search for fundamentals:

> As far as I am concerned, the origin of theatre and my source is Asia. The West has led us towards realism, and Shakespeare is not realist. For actors who want to be explorers, the Asian tradition can be a base to work from. In Asia, the theatre seems to have stopped today, but traditions which die can give life to something elsewhere" (1996: 96).

Prior to founding the Théâtre du Soleil in 1964, Mnouchkine traveled through Japan and Indonesia (1996: 94), a trip that she remembers as "a bit hippie style" (1996: 95). Thus Mnouchkine's observations about Asian theatre would appear to stem largely from her experience as a young backpacker traveling through a few Asian countries over three decades ago. That her recollections are so old and so limited may explain her surprising ignorance of the incredible richness and diversity of performance in Asia today; indeed, for Mnouchkine to assert that theatre in Asia has "stopped" is not only culturally arrogant, but it also suggests that she is ill-informed.

Perhaps the most striking feature of Mnouchkine's Orientalist discourse however is her tendency to make sweeping statements that are expressed as if they are true of Asian culture in its many manifestations from India to Japan. Mnouchkine elaborates on avant-garde theatre icon Antonin Artaud's famous dictum that "The theatre is Oriental" (1996: 95), observing, "I know what he meant. From Asia comes what is specific to theatre, which is the perpetual metaphor which the actors produce—when they are capable of producing it. That is what we do: try to understand the metaphors that an actor can make use of" (1996: 97). Like Artaud, Mnouchkine's rhetoric suggests that Asian theatre is somehow closer to the source of pre-linguistic knowledge, unfettered by the dead-end of Western realistic theatre, thus providing Western actors with a new base from which to work. She adds, "I found in Asia such beauty in things, in gestures, a simple ceremonial quality which seems to be indispensable in the theatre. In Asia there is a perpetual formalization of every action" (1996: 97). As Indian theatre critic Rustom Bharucha has argued, interculturalism in this instance might be viewed as having been born out of a certain ennui, a reaction to aridity and the subsequent search for new sources of energy, vitality and sensuality through the importation of "rejuvenating raw materials'" (1991: 207). Here context is rendered unimportant as the "raw materials" of the East are reworked by the creative geniuses of the West.

Similarly Teo's other source of inspiration, Peter Brook, has been criticized for ignoring the Indian cultural context in his production of the epic poem, *The Mahabharata*. Brook's staging of the "poetic history of mankind" toured to six countries in 1987–88 and was acclaimed by many Western critics, but viewed more circumspectly by Indian critics such as Rustom Bharucha who argued that[4]

> If Brook truly believes that The Epic is universal, then his representation should not exclude or trivialize Indian culture, as I believe it does. One cannot agree with the premise that "*The Mahabharata* is Indian but it is universal." The "but" is misleading. *The Mahabharata*, I would counter, is universal because it is Indian. One cannot separate the culture from the text (1991: 213).

Bharucha argues that Brook's reduction of the complex, multi-layered religious and philosophical Hindu epic into a tight, narrative-driven story accessible to Western audiences results in a *Mahabharata* that has little to do with India, thus undermining the supposed universality inherent in the work.

Given the fierce criticism leveled against Mnouchkine and Brook for appropriating random aspects of Asian culture, it is perhaps surprising that an Asian group would hold the work of these practitioners in such high regard. Nevertheless, the connection between Teo's group and the work of Brook and Mnouchkine was furthered in 1992 when Georges Bigot, one of the leading actors from Mnouchkine's Théâtre du Soleil, conducted a month-long, 100-hour workshop with company actors in preparation for their 1993 production of *Macbeth*. Bigot, known for his portrayal of Prince Norodom Sihanouk in *The Terrible but Unfinished History of Norodom Sihanouk, King of Cambodia*, and his *Richard II*, came to Singapore courtesy of the French government. This cultural connection was underscored by an introductory message in the program from the French Embassy's Cultural Counselor, which cited Bigot's visit as an example of their support for the arts in Singapore, and added, "Rest assured that this will certainly not be the last time that leading French dramatic and performing personalities will be brought in to assist in the promotion of the arts in Singapore" (Asia in Theatre 1993). That the counselor chose the phrase "promotion of the arts" in revealing as it suggests that the project was not about creation so much as it was about selling a cultural image.

Bigot makes his subject position abundantly clear in an extended statement that was also printed in the program: "My inspiration comes from here, from the east." He laments the lack of interest in Asian traditions that he finds "here"—meaning here in the "East"— and observes that, "We learnt the art of theatre from here, whereas they [i.e. Asians] take inspiration from the caricature of Western theatre, mimicking the psychology and the realism" (Asia in Theatre 1993). Bigot's comments reflect the continuing tendency on the part of many Western theatre practitioners going back to Artaud in the 1930's to see all of Asia as a single entity which constitutes a monolithic "other." Given the Théâtre du Soleil's history of merely quoting the visual referents of the Asian forms they have borrowed, one wonders what he means when he suggests that "*we*"—meaning avant-garde Western practitioners like himself—"learnt the art of theatre *here*"; while his comments might lead one to believe that he had in fact apprenticed with Asian theatre practitioners "here" in Asia, in reality he means nothing of the sort. Théâtre du Soleil learned the Asian art of theatre, or what aspects they wanted from it, largely at home, in the Cartoucherie on the outskirts of Paris, and not *in situ* from masters of any of the vast array of Asian performance forms.

His dismissal of acting "here" in Asia as "mimicking the psychology and the realism" of Western theatre is equally perplexing; where, specifically, is the "Asia" of which he speaks? Is he talking about acting in Mandarin-language historical soap operas on Singaporean television? Acting in Thai folk drama *likay* performances? Or acting in a Chinese-language version of Arthur Miller's *Death of a Salesman* staged in Shanghai? That Bigot fails to understand that Asian versions of stage realism may constitute something other than "caricature" or "mimicry" is significant, as it reflects an unwillingness to look at what this Western form might mean when applied to another cultural context with performance traditions and styles of acting that differ from those of the West. Furthermore, what he may perceive as clumsy attempts at expressing "realism" and "psychology" might be read completely differently by a rice farmer in West Sumatra, an English-educated Singaporean, or a noodle seller in Hong Kong. In his condemnation of Western acting, Bigot also contributes to a recurring theme that the theatrical avant-garde in the West has been repeating for about 100 years now: namely, the insistence that realism is killing the theatre, when in fact a great deal of performance in the West throughout the Twentieth Century has had little to do with realism. Reactions against realism began the moment the form took hold in the West and they haven't stopped coming—at least not yet.

Bigot concludes this section of his narrative with the declaration, "I'm trying to bring back some of what I've learnt here," adding, "You have riches here, you have a sense of theatre" (Asia in Theatre 1993). Like Artaud, whose life was changed after witnessing a Balinese cultural show at the 1931 Exposition Coloniale in Paris, Bigot seems besotted by the exoticism of the East. What distinguishes him from Artaud, however, is that he is not content merely to use a very particular Asian performance tradition as a source of inspiration, but that he is willing and able to return the "riches" of the East to their home.

Putting aside the amazing cultural imperialism implicit in such a claim, the ultimate irony may well be that Singapore is perhaps the most highly manufactured place in all of Asia; creatively engineered by the English as a center for shipping operations in Southeast Asia, Singapore everywhere bears the imprint and the legacy of a city-state that was created for the benefit of its colonial masters. Cultures from all over Asia intermingle and exist separately in Singapore, while even the numerical majority—the Chinese—have until recently been further divided by their distinct dialect and cultural groups. Even today, many Chinese over fifty are far more likely to speak fluent Hokkien, Teochew, Cantonese, or Hakka than fluent Mandarin or English. Singapore is in many ways one of the most culturally diverse spots in Asia, in spite of the dominant influence of English culture and the English language from the early days of colonization. There is virtually no sense at all in which traditional Asian forms actually originate in Singapore; they merely ended up there. Thus Bigot's declaration that he is "bringing back" what he has learned "here" makes little sense; instead his comment reflects a remarkable ability to conflate all of the East as a site of wisdom and knowledge.

Given the one stop "Instant Asia" feel that Singapore aggressively markets overseas to potential Western tourists, it is perhaps not surprising that a Westerner might believe himself capable of guiding Singaporeans back to their Asian roots. The comments of actors who participated in the workshop further reinforce Bigot's position as Asian theatre guru. One actor, who characterizes Bigot as a "theatre genius," writes of how, "Various research [sic], with Chinese opera actors for example, has helped the troupe assemble ideas, simultaneously giving our work an Asian allure" (Asia in Theatre 1993). While it should be noted that the actor who made these remarks was Caucasian, her uncritical acceptance of the language of exoticism and consumerism is quite telling. Chinese opera, a category of performance that includes a wide range of cultural expressions in a huge range of dialects, is seemingly reduced to a commodity that can provide a work of Western dramatic literature with a kind of "Asian allure." Thus Asia has been made alluring to an Asian audience, an audience which sees the Asian part of its own identity as having a kind of "otherness" akin to the way a European might experience the exotic East on the stage in London or Paris. In this case, the "other" would appear to have "otherized" themselves.

All of the extended commentaries contained in the program for the event were in fact written by Caucasian actors, further distancing Asian Singaporeans from the process. Expatriate American actor Christina Sergeant's commentary on the workshop describes how Bigot taught them to create their characters externally, by encouraging them to put to creative use "a rack full of oversized, body disguising costumes and make-up laid out in front of lighted mirrors" (Asia in Theatre 1993). She recalls how Bigot would occasionally admonish them for not being "well dressed" when they devised costumes that were not both aesthetic *and* practical and notes that he would "rechannel" their "desire to get weird and whacky with white face and black eyeliner" by encouraging them to use "the make-up simply and economically to better project our characters." Bigot apparently also ingrained in them what he termed "the little laws of theatre" which in Sergeant's commentary are reduced to aphorisms such as "Listen to the other characters on stage," "Move, then talk," and "Play in the present" (Asia in Theatre 1993). Oddly enough, the first and last of these "little laws" sound more like American Method acting mantras than guides to avant-garde acting.

The comments of Bigot as well as those of the other actors who made statements in the program clearly place him in the role of theatrical guru. In a Singaporean context, the theatre guru is usually someone who has studied with a Western master in the context of a short workshop; the former student then returns to Singapore as a guru themselves, imparting the technique of the master to students hungry for new techniques, but short on time. Patrice Pavis speaks of the problems associated with guru, and the market-value attached to an association with a particular theatre artist or approach:

> So each individual, and sometimes each micro-group, has at its disposal a series of (de)formative experiences, patiently acquired from the relevant masters; the sum of these, often mannered and exotic, becomes their calling card. Moreover such acquisition sometimes degenerates into an exchange of cultural stereotypes, for metatheatrical amusement (1996: 15).

In Bigot's case, a Western guru would appear to have played his exotic Asian "calling card" before an Asian group, thus ultimately succeeding in exoticizing Asia for Asians.

An account of the rehearsal process for *Macbeth*, also contained in the program, makes it very clear that the production "was to be in the same style as that of Georges' and the Théâtre du Soleil—facing front, for the audience, realistic but not naturalistic." That the term "realistic" was used to characterize the style of the production seems a bit at odds with Bigot's earlier disparagement of both psychology and realism. Nevertheless, there can be no doubt that the production very much reflected the working methods and visual style of the Théâtre du Soleil. A lengthy rehearsal process of six months preceded the final staging of the work, during which time all actors had the opportunity to play any part they wished. Final casting occurred only half way through the rehearsal process. As with the Théâtre du Soleil, gestural patterns that reflected a fundamental emotional core for the character were developed during rehearsal and integrated into the action of the play; these gestural patterns, though all within the realm of ordinary human movement, were often pressed beyond the limits of realistic acting. In addition, actors went on outings to experience Chinese opera, *wayang kulit*[5], and to a farm where they witnessed the ritual slaughter of chickens for dinner, to "get a taste of killing" (Asia in Theatre 1993).

While most of the group remained in Singapore rehearsing, Teo and a few company members went to India in search of "props and inspiration" (Asia in Theatre 1993). Given the fact that Indians constitute Singapore's third largest ethnic group and that the city boasts a "Little India" which is one of the most culturally vibrant neighborhoods on the island, one might imagine that an overseas venture to India would have been superfluous. Perhaps because Singapore's Indian community is largely South Indian and Tamil-speaking, they were bypassed in favor of the culture of India's north. The account of the group's "passage to India" entitled, interestingly enough, "Passage Through India," reads a bit like a travelogue of a Western backpacker in search of enlightenment. It begins with the statement, "We built our journey around the full moon in November," and proceeds to describe a number of encounters with a range of spiritual practices that include the annual Pushkar fair, a pilgrimage that brings hundreds of thousands of Hindu pilgrims to a sacred lake near the city of Jaipur (Asia in Theatre 1993). Also visited was an ashram outside of Agra that was started by the founder of the Krishna consciousness movement, as well as the North Indian city of Dharamsala, the home of His Holiness the Dalai Lama and a world center for Tibetan Buddhism. No where in the account of the group's pilgrimage to these holy sites is there

any indication of the ways in which their experiences had an impact on the production they went to research. Indeed, there was very little that was identifiably Indian in the final production of the play, apart from a generic overlay of Indianness in some of the costuming and make-up worn by the performers.

The venue in which *Macbeth* was staged bore some similarities to Mnouchkine's Cartoucherie, a former munitions factory that the group initially occupied by squatting. Illegal occupation was not required to obtain a similar venue in Singapore, however. In 1992, with the help of Singapore's National Arts Council and the Urban Redevelopment Asociation (URA), Teo's group moved into an unoccupied warehouse on the banks of the Singapore River on Merbau Road. Like Mnouchkine's Cartoucherie, the warehouse remained fundamentally a found space, complete with rough hewn walls, moss, and bare floors. For their production of *Macbeth*, approximately half of the space was used as a public area and dressing room in which the actors and performers were free to mix before and after the show; while the other half was given over to the auditorium and stage. In the context of Singapore, where theatres are universally new, air-conditioned, and absolutely modern, Teo's choice of a warehouse was indeed quite unconventional. Sadly, the government reclaimed the space after a few years and the warehouse has subsequently been demolished.

Because Teo was committed to using "new, raw actors, not necessarily the best ones," the final production featured a diverse cast, many of whom had no significant stage experience (Asia in Theatre 1993). The cast was also quite international, prompting some critics to complain that the range of accents in the show was bewildering; the country's best known critic at the time, Hannah Pandian, found the "Scottish" accent of the young actor playing Banquo quite incomprehensible, an observation that many found amusing given that the actor playing the role, Jean-Marc Favre, speaks with a very heavy French accent. Those who followed the reception that Brook's *Mahabharata* received will recall that the range of Englishes spoken in his production was also a source of contention. Because Teo was less concerned with classical oration than the physicality and visual dimension of the work, it is not surprising that the final production was fast-paced, highly physical, presentational, and driven by dynamic and rhythmic movement patterns. The visual life of the piece was enhanced by stylized gestural patterns, elaborate costuming, and striking full-face makeup influenced by traditional Indian theatre, all of which stood in sharp contrast to the roughness of the physical environment in which the action of the play was taking place. The proximity of the actors and the audience and the spectators to each other, coupled with the heat and relatively primitive conditions inside the theatre, contributed to a sense of heightened emotion and danger. In short, it was not a *Macbeth* that most who saw are likely to easily forget. Negative criticism of the show seemed to center largely around the way in which language was used by the cast members; because many had no acting experience, and all but a few had no prior experience dealing with classical language, it is hardly surprising that to lovers of the verse, the production was found to be somewhat lacking.

For his part, Teo would probably not have cared about such criticism. Indeed for him, the process was all-important. One of his former students recalls how Teo repeatedly made the point in rehearsal that "the performance is the dessert. It is not essential" (Smith 1997). Like the Théâtre du Soleil, Teo's group has had the luxury of a long rehearsal process; however unlike Mnouchkine's company no one in the group—including Teo—made a full-time living as a theatre artist. In fact Teo's source of income at the time derived largely from his popular hair salon on fashionable Orchard

Road, at the very center of Singapore's consumer empire. It should be noted that Teo once lived in Paris, and it was there that he developed a taste for the work of the Théâtre du Soleil. Like Mnouchkine and Bigot, he states of his group that "our ideas and our point of departure comes from the ancient traditions found in Asia" (Asia in Theatre 1993). While Teo's staging of *Macbeth* was exciting, visually stimulating theatre, there is an extent to which wrapping Shakespeare's text with an overlay of ancient generic "Asianess" absolves the creators of the work from having to ask fundamental questions about the play's content and its potential relevance for contemporary Singaporean audiences.

Virtually all English-language theatre in Singapore is intercultural by neccessity. TheatreWorks is the company most strongly associated with attempts to blend Asian influences with modern technology and aspects of Western avant-garde practice, and under the leadership of Artistic Director Ong Keng Sen, it has developed a recognizable and highly syncretic house style. Their 1997 Japanese adaptation of *King Lear* (text by Kishida Rio), however, took their theatre practice in a new direction by retaining the integrity of different performance and cultural traditions by representing them simultaneously on stage; well-known Noh actor Umewaka Naohiko played the dual roles of Lear and the ghost of his wife, while Beijing opera actor Jiang Qihu enacted the role of the eldest daughter. In addition to the two actors speaking classical Japanese and the highly-inflected Mandarin of Beijing opera, additional actors performed in Malay, Thai and English.

One newspaper account that trumpeted the success of the venture with the headline, "Ong's Lear Takes Tokyo by Storm," contained the more ambivalent comments of Odajima Yuji, regarded as one of Japan's leading theatre critics. Odajima raises some interesting issues with regard to TheatreWorks's *Lear* that can be applied to other works where attempts are made to retain the integrity of each individual performance form:

> We have a symphony where everyone is working together. I would have liked to see a violin concerto instead. Since there were so many theatrical styles and languages on stage, I had expected more tension, more chaos. In that sense, I cannot call the performance a huge success. But it is certainly a very successful step toward more of this kind of theatre" (cited in Kwan 1997).

If "intercultural" implies a kind of reciprocity between elements and some kind of synthesis in the final artistic product, then TheatreWorks' production of *Lear* falls outside that category and lies instead in the realm of the "cross-cultural," where the cultural currents are placed together in the same stream, but each element retains its distinct identity. Throughout the extended press accounts of a work that constituted perhaps Singapore's most singularly ambitious work to date across the divides of culture, the "why" question was nowhere in evidence. Apart from the fact that one is able to create such theatre, what is the point of doing it? Even critic Odajima's comments about the show representing a "very successful step toward more of this kind of theatre" do not question the value or use of the form. One of the problems with a theatre practice based largely on cross-cultural borrowings or, in Teo's case, on the elusive search for sources, roots, or authenticity, is that the finished work can become so emotionally cool or technically complex that it never fundamentally engages with the culture lived and experienced by those in the audience.

Indeed, intercultural and cross-cultural work does not necessarily impart insights into cultures that are any more deep and meaningful than those offered by yet another reprise of the gargantuan grand opera *Aida*. In spite of the "authentic" pedigree of the cultural assemblages in some inter and cross-cultural work, it is not merely their placement on stage, but rather the context and politics of their embodiment that give them life in a new cultural context. Without context, the offerings continue to be made for public consumption by the rich in the world's richest nations. David Savran's comments about the implications of the consumption model in American theatre can also be applied to Singapore:

> For the liberal pluralist, America is less a melting pot than a smorgasbord. He or she takes pride in the ability to *consume* cultural difference—now understood as a commodity, a source of boundless pleasure, an expression of an exoticized Other. And yet, for him or her, access to and participation in so-called minority cultures is entirely consumerist (1995: 220).

As inter/multi/cross-culturalism becomes increasingly the basis for theatre practice throughout the developed world both East and West, it is important to question the ultimate value of this practice and who ultimately is served by it. Consumers in rich countries such as Singapore, Australia, Europe, and the U.S. are increasingly offered a continuous buffet of cultural salads that rearrange and reconstitute cultures both foreign and domestic, "authentic" and syncretic, while they remain no closer to actual engagement with the big, bad Other—even when the other may be themselves.

NOTES

1. Tickets to Aida cost S$70, S$150, and S$250.
2. For an historical perspective on the role of English language drama in Singapore see Birch (1997).
3. The original name of the company was Asia in Theatre Research Circus. The company's late Artistic Director, William Teo, noted that "we called it a circus because we would rehearse in parks, at the beach, and we didn't know where we would perform" (Tsang 1997). In the aftermath of Teo's death, in 2002 the group changed its name yet again to the more ambitious World-in-Theatre

Research Centre. In this paper, the company will be referred to by the shorter "Asia in Theatre Research," the name used at the time in which the work under consideration was produced.

4. For the substance of Bharucha's argument refer to his monographs "A View from India," in D. Williams (ed.) *Peter Brook and the Mahabharata: Critical Perspectives.* London: Routledge, 1991, 228–252; "Somebody's Other: Disorientations in the Cultural Politics of Our Times," in P. Pavis (ed.) *The Intercultural Performance Reader,* London: Routledge, 1996, 196–212; and "Peter Brook's Mahabharata: A View from India" in *Theatre and the World: Performance and the Politics of Culture,* London: Routledge, 1990, 68–87.

5. *Wayang kulit,* literally "show (or performance) leather" in Bahasa Indonesian, is known as shadow puppetry in the West.

REFERENCES

Asia in Theatre Research Circus (1993) Program for *The Tragedy of Macbeth,* 16 March-3 April, Merbau Road Warehouses, Singapore.

Bharucha, Rustom (1990) *Theatre and the World: Performance and the Politics of Culture.* London: Routledge.

— (1991) "A View from India," in D. Williams (ed.) *Peter Brook and the Mahabharata: Critical Perspectives,* London: Routledge, 228–252.

— (1996) "Somebody's Other: Disorientations in the Cultural Politics of Our Times," in P. Pavis (ed.) *The Intercultural Performance Reader,* London: Routledge, 196–212.

Birch, David (1998) "Singapore English Drama: A Historical Overview 1958–1985," in Sanjay Krishnan (ed.) *Nine Lives: Ten Years of Singapore Theatre,* Singapore: Cairnhill Arts Centre, 22–53.

Chin, Daryl (1989) "Interculturalism, Postmodernism, Pluralism," *Performing Arts Journal* 33/34: 163–175.

Chow, Rey (1993) *Writing Diaspora: Tactics of Intervention in Contemporary Cultural Studies.* Bloomington: Indiana University Press.

Kiernander, Adrian (1996) 'Introduction to Ariane Mnouchkine Interviews, "The Theatre is Oriental,"' in P. Pavis (ed.) *The Intercultural Performance Reader,* London: Routledge, 93–94.

Koh Boon Pin (1996) "Pyramids, 800 Homegrown Talents and Animals," *Singapore Straits Times* Website, 22 May.

Kwan Weng Kin (1987) "Ong's Lear takes Tokyo by storm," *Singapore Straits Times,* 12 September.

Mnouchkine, Ariane (1996) "The Theatre is Oriental," in P. Pavis (ed.) *The Intercultural Performance Reader,* London: Routledge, 95–98.

Pavis, Patrice (1996) "Introduction: Towards a Theory of Interculturalism in Theatre?" in P. Pavis (ed.) *The Intercultural Performance Reader,* London: Routledge, 1–21.

Said, Edward (1993) Culture and Imperialism, NY: Alfred A Knopf.

Savran, David (1995) "Ambivalence, Utopia, and a Queer Sort of Materialism: How Angels in America Reconstructs the Nation," *Theatre Journal* 47.2: 207–227.

Smith, Dane (1997) Personal Interview, Hamilton, New Zealand.

Tsang, Susan (1997) "If It's a Good Piece of Art, I Cry," *Singapore Straits Times Website,* 3 March 1997.

William Peterson (Associate Professor, California State University San Bernardino) helped design and initiate the theatre programs at the University of Waikato in Hamilton, New Zealand and the National University of Singapore. His many articles on theatre and politics in Singapore, Māori theatre, Australian theatre, Indonesian dance, and American performance art have appeared in a wide range of publications and reference works. He is the author of *Theater the Politics of Culture in Contemporary Singapore* (Wesleyan University Press, 2001) and he holds a Ph.D. in Dramatic Arts from the University of Texas at Austin.

Reading 5.4

The Impact of Universities on Globalisation

LALITA RAJASINGHAM

Globalisation is an old concept tracing back to Marco Polo, Magellan, Drake, and Columbus, from the thirteenth century through the nineteenth century, where long voyages that took many years were undertaken to expand territory, trade, and colonise. Explorers and conquerors then defined and shifted the prevailing knowledge paradigm according to what Michel Foucault (1970) called *zeitgeist,* an episteme—an all-encompassing body of unconscious knowledge peculiar to a particular time and place. The concept of paradigm shifts accorded with Thomas Kuhn's (1962) ideas expressed in his classic text, *The Structure of Scientific Revolutions,* which argued that "when paradigms change, the world itself changes with them" (1962:110).

Although globalisation is not new, in the latter half of the twentieth century it has distinct characteristics: shrinking and compressing of time and space. Old sailing ships and land transport to annex new territories took months, whereas information and communications technologies now instantaneously erode borders linking and connecting people more profoundly and intensely than ever before.

There is now prolific literature that examines the dimension and impact on societies of globalisation processes. New texts are embedded in the referential networks of the subject (Tehranian et al. 2002; Huntington 1993, 1996) and reflect paradigm shifts brought about by communications and information technologies in the brand new episteme of the twenty-first century. Whether in the thirteenth or twenty-first century, the engine that drives globalisation is communication and information technology. In the remote jungles of the Amazon, the deserts of Africa, the mountainous terrains of north Asia, the Antarctic people listen to the radio and watch television bringing "glimpses of heaven, visions of hell" (Sherman and Judkins 1992) changing their paradigms.

Initially, the term globalisation was used to describe an economic paradigm, a neo-liberal free market game of global monopoly that all countries are encouraged to play until it becomes the only game in the world. But, like the Monopoly board game, the rich tend to get richer and the poor—unless they have a lot of luck—get poorer with stops in jail (Tiffin and Rajasingham 2003).

Globalisation as an economic paradigm failed to take into account the ecological impact, demographic issues, the erosion of democracy, and the impact of new technologies that accompany it. It is more than a flow of money and commodities. The way globalisation is played as an economic paradigm impacts every aspect of life on a finite planet and has already gone beyond the point where people might seek to opt out. But it is too late. With the growing interdependence of people in the world comes the integration of technology, economies, and culture. New technologies, the Internet and virtual reality with their embedded hegemonic imperatives, new actors, new rules such as multilateral agreements, and intellectual property backed by enforcement mechanisms challenge national governments calling for shared values and paradigm shifts. But when paradigm change is forced on particular societies in time and place, upheaval and "clash of civilization" (Huntington, 1993) become reality. We either are the steamroller or the road, and with new multimedia technology like HyperReality, nanotechnology, and artificial intelligence (AI), the rules and elements are no longer determined solely by the human players, and we are not even certain what the rules are.

In the sixteenth century, Francis Bacon suggested that information is power.

The parameters of knowledge began to expand with paradigm shifts moving the boundaries of knowledge from metaphysical to scientific paradigms, from worldviews of Newton, Darwin, and Einstein. In a knowledge society, knowledge is capital, to be acquired, controlled, and protected.

KNOWLEDGE AND UNIVERSITIES

In his text *The Idea of a University* published in 1873, Cardinal John Newman set the ground for the discourse that defined the modern university: "A university, I should lay down, by its very name professes to teach universal knowledge" (Newman, 1996: 25).

Beck (1964) said "After centuries of intellectual effort, man has forged for himself instruments and methods of thought upon which he can rely for a solution of his problems and for an understanding of the universe around him" (1964: 17).

We associate knowledge with a university. Its research, creation, processing, and application of knowledge are the *raison d'etre* of universities in the last thousand years. But where can one find knowledge in a university? Is it in the library, in the head of an academic, in a course of study? Knowledge resides in all these. While the knowledge paradigm in the medieval university was theology based, in the modern university there is no longer a universe of knowledge as the term university might imply; rather, we tend to think of knowledge in terms of subjects offered, as science, anthropology, philosophy, or mathematics.

Like all human organisations and institutions, as the university changes with a new episteme, so too does the knowledge it teaches and researches. Not only has knowledge been broken up into a multiplicity of subjects, but it is seen differently from university to university, country to country, and language to language (Tiffin and Rajasingham 2003). Whereas medieval universities in Europe had a common language in Latin, modern universities use the written language of the nation that supports them. But even here, in the same university with the same common language, we find the same subject addressed from different perspectives in different paradigms of different subjects. Those who have studied in more than one language will resonate with the Saphir Whorf hypothesis, otherwise known as the theory of linguistic relativity, that the way we think depends on the language we think in (Whorf 1956).

The prevailing postmodern mood sees virtue in multiple knowledges on the same theme

(Lyotard 1984). The growing fragmentation and lack of consensus as to what constitutes knowledge create a context for chaos. If a language means all things to all people, it is babble. If knowledge is whatever an individual thinks it is, then there is no paradigm and no way people can communicate and cooperate in its application. If knowledge is a paradigm that varies according to the subject studied, then its wider application in society will be as confusing as letting people skilled in different versions of football play in the same game. If knowledge is a paradigm that varies according to the country or culture, then global issues can be addressed only from the perspective of that country or culture (Tiffin and Rajasingham 2003).

The Dialectic

University systems are designed for the societies they serve. In the industrial society, the university as we know it prepared for life in a nation state. Worldwide, conventional universities that long and well served the needs of the industrial society are increasingly unable to respond to the fast changing needs of the knowledge society and the increasing numbers seeking university education. Universities are transport and buildings based and dependent on fast depleting fossil fuels, are costly, bureaucratic, and slow to adapt to change. This chapter explores some trends that will help shape universities as systems that respond to the needs of a multicultural, global, networked world. What kind of university can meet it?

As we are in the process of becoming a global society operating in a global economy and the worldwide demand for lifelong learning opportunities grow, we need education that prepares us for life in a global society. We therefore need global education not instead of, but as well as, national education to, in Buckminister Fuller's words, "think global and act local."

The Horns of a Dilemma

In order to be internationally competitive and survive, societies are facing the dilemma of responding to the demands for new skills for the global knowledge society through university systems geared for the past needs of the nation state and the industrial society.

What is needed is effective, lifelong, cost-efficient, culturally appropriate instruction that can match the needs for global skills related to new knowledge paradigms delivered interactively, at the convenience of the learner. Learners, no matter where their physical location, should be able to interact with teachers, with content and with one another in synchronous and asynchronous modes, using text, words, and still and moving images. This is the virtual class on the Internet where students are equipped with global skills to solve global problems, and at the same time act local in consonance with their own cultures and social networks.

The modern university is national, taxpayer funded, in the language of the nation, and subject to national laws and mores. The interaction between teachers and learners about the application of knowledge to problems takes place in rooms in buildings and is based on transport technologies.

The means for a better way to educate more people than is possible with conventional universities strapped for resources are with us in the technologies that enable globalisation. In 1995 we published *In Search of the Virtual Class: Education in an Information Society*, which outlined the idea of a virtual university based on the Internet that could be available to anyone anywhere, addresses multiplicity of knowledge, and can be multilingual.

Education is Communications

According to Lev Vygotsky (1978), the three essential components of education are teacher, learner, and problem in a social setting where teacher helps learner to solve a problem. Education is communications, both being information-intensive activities and dependent on communications technologies to interconnect teacher, learner, problem, and knowledge. Therefore, a university is a communications system where teacher helps learner to apply knowledge to problems (Tiffin and Rajasingham 1995).

Advances in communications and information technology such as the Internet, virtual reality, and HyperReality are rapidly changing the way we learn, do business, bank, shop, and play. Societies' future in an increasingly global digital economy will depend on how its people are educated at tertiary level. As building and transport technologies increase in costs, therefore, education for the future environment based on telecommunications networked environments will be the key to survival in the new millennium, offering educational opportunities to more people than is possible in current conventional classrooms.

Worldwide, the demand for education is increasing in tandem with rapid advances in communications and information technologies. Just as roads and railways brought teachers and learners together to learn how to apply knowledge to problems in the modern university, the Internet, multimedia, virtual reality, and HyperReality are likely to provide the communications infrastructure for universities in the emerging global knowledge society. It is suggested that the future university will be based on telecommunications rather than transport, will be global, virtual, and commercial, and will use artificial intelligence (AI), virtual reality (VR), and HyperReality (HR) environments.

A university is a system through which society learns to understand and make meaning of complex civil and professional processes. The challenge for the future university will be to design global education on the Internet that addresses the needs of different cultures in curricula and approaches to learning.

However, what is needed and yet to be designed is a system through which societies can make meaning out of complex globalisation processes. Traditionally this system was the university which through the creation and dissemination of knowledge, taught students to apply knowledge to problems in culturally appropriate ways and so make meaning of their social environments. In the increasingly global economy, education is the fundamental key to wealth creation and competitiveness. Education, like communications is culture-specific, contextualised in people's beliefs, myths, symbols, protocols, meanings and values. Luke (1993) suggests, it is "as much about ideologies, identities, and values as it is about codes and skills" (p. 11).

THE UNIVERSITY IS A COMMUNICATION SYSTEM

All educational systems are communication systems, special kinds of communication systems in which teachers interact with students to help them apply knowledge to problems. This is a neo-Vygotskyan model, and by teacher and learner we mean people in these roles with relationship to each other. The teacher could be a parent or a peer as well as someone with a formal title of teacher. And it allows for the rules to be reversed at any point, as frequently happens today in a postgraduate course where a professional student might know more about a particular problem than the professor and for the moment therefore takes over the role of teacher.

The knowledge/problem axis is also relative and refers to the knowledge needed to deal with a particular problem in a particular culture and episteme. Education is where one learns how to apply the knowledge embedded in the culture to deal with the world's problems in a way that is culturally acceptable. The idea has been highlighted in Western societies in recent years with the concept of political correctness.

Once university teachers or students are engaged in research, the nature of the communication system changes. The knowledge/ problem axis remains, but the teacher student relationship is replaced by a researcher interaction with researcher axis. There may be junior and senior researchers.

At the apex of the educational system, the modern university is seen as key to supporting and, through research, strengthening the national knowledge paradigm. Universities provide the experts in court cases, government committees and commissions, and in popular debate in the media. In providing a litmus for whether or not something fits with the national paradigm, they are seen as acting as a conscience of society. This suggests that, within the national knowledge paradigm and within the university approach to querying this knowledge, there is a value system. The modern nation state is secular, its value system is one of rationalisation based upon scientific method. In this, the modern university becomes its temple.

Changing Paradigms

Where science formed the philosophical paradigm of the modern university, religion provided the philosophical paradigm of the mediaeval university. Where the scientific method was used to query knowledge in the modern university, logic was used to query it in the mediaeval university. Where the modern university shared its knowledge paradigm with the State and whilst intimately part of a process whereby the norm or dominant paradigm of the State was maintained, the mediaeval university shared the dominant paradigm of the Catholic Church until the time of the Reformation. After that, it shared the philosophy of the dominant religion of whatever state

it found itself in. Prior to the Reformation, the Catholic Church appears to have favoured the process in the university of querying the religious paradigm. Just as today's scientist believes that all questions can be resolved within the scientific paradigm, mediaeval theologists believed that whatever the problem, the application of logic would see it resolved in terms of a manifestation of God's will.

Some of these allied themselves with the ruler of the state that they were in, in effect becoming state religions. In such cases the tendency was for the universities within the state to adopt the new religious paradigm and to teach established knowledge within the philosophical structure of the dominant ideology. What was becoming the national religion supported the state ruler with such ideological ideas as a divine right and the local university in effect credited by the state religion and dependant on the state ruler for its very existence began the long process of becoming a state institution.

However, the paradigm shift between the mediaeval university and the modern university was very gradual, taking about 500 years, and this was the Dark Ages in Europe. In the wake of the Reformation, universities became teaching institutions for the passing on of established knowledge. Questioning of the religious paradigm within which they operated was a dangerous business that could lead to the stake and the inquisition. Where, to begin with, teachers in mediaeval universities were paid by their students, in the post Reformation, as they became increasingly dependent upon the state, teachers were paid by the state.

In our book *The Global Virtual University* (Tiffin and Rajasingham 2003), we suggest a dominant knowledge paradigm of a curriculum for a Global Virtual University. It is emerging at a time when the power of the nation state is in decline in many Western countries and power seems to be shifting to transnational corporations. This is reflected in the administration of many Western universities where economic rationalism could be seen as replacing scientific rationalism.

Increasingly what is taught and what is researched are determined by support from the industrial and commercial world. Basic research for the sake of research or questing for new knowledge is discouraged unless it has a source of funding outside the university. Yet this may well be more like the shift that took place in the mediaeval university with the reformation when, although power shifted from the papacy to the sovereign state, the dominant paradigm remained a theological one, and, albeit in some universities the theology had changed, it was still an ethological explanation of the world. Scientific rationalism may be modified by economic rationalism, but it is still a form of rationalism that pertains to the modern university and to the interests of those who pay for it.

A Global Virtual University

There is one way in which a global virtual university is different from any of its predecessors and that is in the technology of the communication system by which teaching and research are done. All previous university paradigms have been based upon the face-to-face communication supported by some form of reading and writing technology encompassed in some kind of rule. In this, universities, like other educational institutions, modelled themselves on the world for which they were preparing their students. Ever since there have been schools and universities, their students have gone forth to employ the skills they have learned in rooms, whether they be offices, shops, or workrooms. The virtual university will prepare people for an entirely different world. It is a world that we can hardly as yet comprehend. To respond to multiperspectives in a globalised world, the virtual university will need to be global, multilingual, and multicultural. The HyperClass is a step towards this.

The HyperClass

HyperReality is a technological platform developed by Nobiyoshi Terashima of Waseda University, Japan and is the intermeshing of physical reality and virtual reality, and human intelligence and artificial intelligence (Terashima 2001). It gives some kind of vision of a place where what you see, hear, touch, taste, and smell (but not what you swallow) may be atomic in origin or may be nothing more than bits of information mediated by computers and telecommunications whose origins may be operated by human intelligence with the natural intelligence of natural creatures or to artificial intelligence and artificial lifeforms. HyperReality is a reality in which physical reality and virtual reality symbiotically coexist. This, of course, has always been the case in universities or any other educational system that uses writing and abstract speech, but in HyperReality, the co-existence is a seamless one whereby teachers and students and what is demonstrated in a class may be real or may be virtual, and it may be difficult to distinguish between them. Objects can be manipulated and re-modelled collaboratively according to the participants in their own physical reality, their own culture, and in their own episteme.

It is not simply that the university of the future will need to teach with computers and telecommunications to prepare students for a world in which they will use such technology. It implies a different perception of reality and consequently a different perception of knowledge and problems. When we can build detailed virtual models of reality, when we can create comprehensive worlds within worlds, it becomes possible to experiment with possible alternatives for the real world at a very comprehensive level and seek to connect our inner virtual world with the physical reality of the outside world. We move towards this with genetic engineering. A research from being a study of what was and what is becomes a study of what could be. It becomes a design process.

The university of the future addresses not the needs and necessities of nation states but those concerned with curricula needs and cultural concerns of globalisation itself. It suggests the balancing of economic rationalisation with a form of global rationalisation that seeks to balance commercial forces with survival issues, and between cognitive skills and affective/humanistic skills.

For some 300 years, mediaeval universities and modern universities co-existed, often in the same buildings. If the university of the future focuses on globalisation and the virtual world and is, in itself, global and virtual, there will still need to be universities that focus on the local and the physically real. And to do this by existing in the physical world, they will still need rooms to ensure our security while we venture into the virtual world. HyperReality is a technology that makes possible the co-existence of the physically real and the virtually real and would suggest that global virtual university will co-exist in the future with the modern university.

The world's first HyperClass was held in December 2000 when a three-way link using digital image avatars was successfully made in HyperReality between Waseda University in Japan, Victoria University of Wellington in New Zealand, and the Queensland Open Learning Network in Australia. An avatar in New Zealand handed a virtual CD-ROM from Japan to an avatar in Australia, who then handed it back to the avatar in Japan, who fitted it into a virtual computer. The experiment was successfully repeated two days later. The interaction took place inside a computer-generated virtual class, where the virtual mixed with the real in the form of the three avatars, one participant in each country in attendance,

and the task was to pass a virtual object originally located on a table, from one participant to the next. The task was successfully completed as the virtual object travelled at the click of the mouse from Japan to Australia, then to New Zealand and back to Japan again.

Simple as this sounds, this experiment is the accumulation of many years of collaborative research, and its implications are profound for the future of education in a global knowledge society. A research project has been in progress since 1997 to apply HyperReality to education in a HyperClass where the intersection of virtual reality and physical reality, human intelligence and artificial intelligence makes possible a future where the people and the objects around you may be real or may be virtual and may have human intelligence or artificial intelligence.

In conventional communication systems, transport systems and buildings are the means of communication that bring teachers and students together to learn how to apply knowledge to problems. This process can now be done by the Internet, where teachers and students interact to apply knowledge to problems by telecommunications and computers. This is called a *virtual class* that seeks to replicate the fully meshed, multimediated communications systems of a conventional classroom, at different locations. A HyperClass is the interactive conjunction of a real class made of atoms with a virtual class made of bits of information.

As e-commerce, e-shopping, e-banking, and e-learning as virtual classes and virtual universities now proliferate the Internet, it is suggested that the future education will be competitive and big business.

The *HyperClass* (Tiffin and Rajasingham 2001: 110–125) describes the design and development of the technology platform that would allow students in their own physical localities to climb through the computer-generated "window" and freely intermingle in real-life space as full-bodied three-dimensional beings, from different locations in culturally appropriate ways. In this environment, teachers can be virtual and students real and *vice versa,* and both teachers and students could be virtual.

The virtual class/HyperClass paradigm at its most basic can be thought of as the critical communications systems for instruction in a knowledge society and as having a function analogous to the conventional classroom in an industrial society. Will this be the shape of future education?

The virtual class and virtual university are dependent on information technology, based on digitalisation, and the merger of computers, telecommunications, and video. This merger brings with it virtual reality, multimedia, nanotechnology, artificial intelligence, and HyperReality, providing access to a breadth of intellectual and cultural resources far greater than ever before. The dichotomy of what is physically real and what is virtually real is what Nicholas Negroponte refers to as the world of atoms and bits. We must learn to live in this dualism because it is the defining infrastructure of the knowledge society that is rapidly emerging.

Will the clusters of technologies that bring revolutionary infrastructures make possible the global virtual university, the default educational system of the knowledge society where education through our five senses will be available to anyone anywhere at any time in culturally appropriate ways?

Today's schools, colleges, and universities could not exist without the roads that make it possible for students and teachers to come together to make use of the buildings that house libraries and classrooms and support systems. Virtual schools and virtual universities are rapidly appearing on the Internet. What distinguishes them is that they use computers and telecommunications instead of buildings and transport to bring teachers, students, knowledge, and problems together in a virtual class.

A HyperClass is a class that is conducted in an environment where physical reality and virtual reality comingle in a way that becomes increasingly seamless. It is a combination of a conventional class and a virtual class. Teachers, students, knowledge, and problems can come together in a class via local transport, and they can also come together via the Internet.

The Need for the HyperClass

National education systems have come into existence over the last hundred years in response to the needs of commerce and industry in industrial societies. Today, on the Internet, commerce follows education. It is schools and universities that have pioneered the use of the Internet. It is the young that lead the way. In trying to understand cyberspace, students surf the web before their teachers.

In 1997 a group of New Zealand students joined a group of Japanese students for a seminar in the Master of Communications. The medium was videoconferencing. Both students and academics saw their counterparts in the other country as two-dimensional images on a video monitor. The seminar proceeded in a conventional manner. Academics from both countries presented papers and students asked questions. Pictures were carefully composed by video cameras and framed on the monitors in the manner of a television programme.

At one point there was a break of 15 minutes, and the videoconferencing link was left open so that the students in the two countries could communicate socially. Suddenly the communication changed. It seemed as though the video monitor had become a dormitory window through which students were leaning and chatting with frank curiosity about each other: "Hi, what's your name?" "What subjects are you taking?" "How about a date?"

There seemed to be a raw desire for a technology that would allow students to climb through that window and freely intermingle as full-bodied, three-dimensional beings. This is the basic goal of the HyperClass concept as described earlier in this chapter.

The current use of telecommunications in education—for e-mailing, bulletin boards, text chat, audiographic conferencing, generating Webpages, surfing, and videoconferencing—is a step along the road towards a virtual class that would ultimately be in distributed virtual reality on broadband fiberoptic networks; with developments in HyperReality, we suggest that the virtual class will become a HyperClass.

THE HYPERCLASS IN A GLOBAL VIRTUAL UNIVERSITY

HyperSchools, HyperColleges, and Hyper-Universities can exist in real and virtual dimensions at the same time. In so doing they will provide an intersection between the local and global dimension in education.

The universities can be in different countries and can link classes in different universities in different countries in a Hyper-University. A student could go to a conventional class in a conventional university or stay at home and use a PC and the Internet to link to a virtual class in a virtual university. A HyperClass allows a student to do both. A HyperClass exists where the virtual and real dimensions intersect in a coaction field where students and teachers in a conventional classroom can synchronously interact with students and teachers in other universities that may be in other countries.

A coaction field conceptualised by Terashima (2001: 9) is where students and teachers in a conventional classroom can synchronously interact for the purpose of learning with students and teachers in other universities, possibly in other countries. The HyperClass is where real and virtual dimensions of students and teachers intersect, providing a common

field to reconcile the learning that is local with learning that is global in order to understand the subject from multiple perspectives of other cultures than one's own (Tiffin and Rajasingham 2001: 110–125).

Participants in a HyperClass come together because of their interests in a specific subject domain, and it is suggested, therefore, that the development of HyperUniversities can be dedicated to specific disciplines, in contrast to national universities that emphasise location. Instead, the emergence of virtual universities in specific fields such as communications, nanotechnology, Chinese literature, and so on could emerge, fitting with Terashima's (2001: 8) definition of HyperWorlds as a technical environment where coaction between reality and virtual reality is based on a shared domain of knowledge.

In the HyperClass, the relationship between knowledge and problem domains suggests another important contrast to conventional classroom processes. In a conventional classroom, the application of knowledge to problems is expressed symbolically, through alphanumeric notation and two-dimensional still pictures. If the subject matter in a Hyper-Class requires no more than similar visualisation then all that is required besides the means for real and virtual students and teachers to interact is some kind of virtual display unit—a whiteboard/blackboard. Regardless of whether it is in a real classroom or a virtual class, a whiteboard that acts as a short term memory of an instructional event is one of the most basic and powerful instructional devices at a teacher's disposal and must be available in a HyperClass.

However, Tiffin and Rajasingham suggest that when problems have a real life referent in the participants' social reality, then classrooms with whiteboards may not be the best place for learning. For example, learning how to drive a car from a whiteboard or a book, or where medical students who can write an essay on a disease but cannot recognise it when a patient has it, proves the inadequacy of alphanumeric and diagrammatic instruction alone. The challenge is to transfer learning from the classrooms to real life situations. It is a problem that is seldom addressed because of the way that what is learned in a classroom is tested in a classroom and solutions to problems are examined in the way they were learned, that is, alphanumerically, rather than testing the application of knowledge to real life situations in whatever form they take, in multimediated simulated environments.

The HyperClass introduces a new dimension in education with the juxtaposition of knowledge with problems that have a referent in physical reality. But it is not easy to take someone on a field trip to a volcano or to ensure they are there when the volcano erupts in a safe way that demonstrates what volcanoes do, and so on. HyperReality that allows for object modelling can take a class to an active volcano, or the bedside of a patient in crisis while, at the same time, it can window key knowledge that students should have while they study the problem.

Basically, with HyperReality technology, objects are created in 3-D using an array of videocameras, creating a database/library of problem case studies that could include dangerous conditions. Learners could for example, drive a virtual car through a virtual reality of a specific intersection in which they could be faced with a vast array of different situations. The 3-D modelled objects can be manipulated by learners seeking solutions to their problems with the help of their teachers and peers from diverse cultural perspectives.

A significant strength of HyperReality as contrasted with virtual reality today in for example, ActiveWorlds, is that the communication process is prescribed using the shapes and designs that have already been created by someone else as computer-generated virtual reality that embed the cultures of its creators and designers. HyperReality on the other hand allows a syncretion of cultures. The content of the communication process can be designed, altered, and objects modelled by the participants can then be used to catalyse collaborative learning from multicultural perspectives. In introducing the idea of teletranslation, Minako O'Hagan suggests that it constitutes an emerging industry of global proportions that is necessary if globalisation is to work (O'Hagan 1996).

In today's education and training, students are faced with practical problems, and their comprehension of the problem domain is limited by their human perspective of time and space. For example, motorists may sense the size and speed of their vehicle in relation to that of other road users, but they cannot see the way they use the road from the perspective of the other drivers. Today's researchers conduct experiments to test the relationship between a theory and problem domain it addresses, and the process is analysed, described, and reported in text using words, numbers and diagrams. The ability to collect objects and case studies as virtual realities from multiple perspectives suggests a new methodology for research.

The creation of virtual reality simulacra of problems has many advantages over simple alphanumeric descriptions, especially because it means that everyone is looking at the same thing but from their different perspectives. The description of the HyperClass in this study reflects the inadequacy of alphanumeric representation in limited bandwidth, and that absence of visual and sensorial cues affects clear communications. To draw an analogy, it is like reading Hamlet rather than being at the performance in the Globe Theatre.

Like a conventional class, a HyperClass is essentially synchronous in nature and, like a conventional class, can readily embed asynchronous episodes during the class as well as before and after it. However, to prepare people for life in the information and knowledge society where networking is a valuable skill, the HC will need to facilitate communication at all levels, in synchronous or asynchronous mode and between virtual and real components.

To participate in a HyperClass, students and teachers will need avatars. Moving through such Internet VRML sites as WorldChat or Black Sun suggests that we have a lot to learn about communication protocols between virtual people if we are to move this kind of communication beyond the level of street graffiti. The problem was well identified when Snoopy said, "On the Internet, no one knows you are a dog."

Perhaps the most profound aspect of the teacher/learner axis in a HC is that the avatars of teachers and students may not necessarily represent human intelligence. HR is a platform for human intelligence to interact with artificial intelligence. As this is being word-processed, a little cartoon character, a wizard looking like a paper clip keeps popping up on the screen to say it sees someone is trying to write something and could it help. Someone has tried to programme a just-in-time (JITAIT) artificially intelligent teacher that follows Vygostky's ZPD model of learning. It detects that someone has a problem and comes along to try and help them apply the knowledge they need to deal with it. The fact that the device pops up when there is no problem and offers the wrong help and never turns up with useful knowledge when there is a problem does not mean that one day such wizards won't work. The idea is already there for just in time (JIT) teaching agents, especially when the instructional tasks are clear and there are strong patterns of student needs and frequently asked questions (FAQs).

Marvin Minsky (1986) first proposed the idea of small programmes called agents with a degree of autonomy, an appearance of intelligence and the ability to work collaboratively.

Interlinking agents are now being devised for office systems to look after such tasks as schedule management, email management, meeting arrangement, and workflow management (Asakura et al. 1999). A HyperClass needs to reflect the *modus operandi* of the society for which it prepares people. It makes sense to have agents who will set up a HyperClass and ensure that everyone and everything is present.

As a pedagogical system, in a HyperClass, a teacher and a learner can be virtual or real. A virtual teacher can have human intelligence (HI) or artificial intelligence (AI). Teachers and learners can communicate synchronously using speaking avatars, or asynchronously using written words. Knowledge and problems can be embodied in the teacher and the learner or they can be represented alphanumerically or in simulacra. Problems can be real; knowledge, however, is always abstract. The interaction of teachers and students over the application of knowledge to problems takes place at the level of the individual, the dyad, the group, the class, and the university.

What is a Global Curriculum?

Thus far in this chapter we have looked at the need for a global virtual university to provide the kind of professionals who address global problems in complex societies. What is needed is a curriculum for a global virtual university that incorporates what is universal in university curricula as an integrated whole, responsive not only to national needs but to global needs and issues of the first global episteme. Such a curriculum could be delivered in part from the curriculum of a global virtual university with a global perspective, and in part from society's local university with its local perspective.

In our book *The Global Virtual University*, we propose a curriculum that includes global demographics, global education, globalisation of business and commerce, global communications, globalisation of work, and so on (Tiffin and Rajasingham 2003). Further elaboration of a global curriculum, issues of accreditation, quality assurance, and trust is beyond the scope of this chapter.

There is, thankfully, one golden rule of futurology: Whatever is predicted will not come to pass, at least not in the way expected. However, without some attempt to look into the future, it will find us unprepared. Whether one of the trends I have described, some combination of them all, or something quite different emerges, I have attempted to paint a picture of what a university could be like in the near future as an environment of broadband telecommunications, artificial intelligence, HyperReality, and globalisation takes shape around us. It will be virtual not actual, global not national, and student-supported not state-supported.

Universities, however, are not knowledge factories. They are interactive communication systems, and a global virtual university would need to conform to the age-old paradigm of the university while making radical changes that are needed if there is to be a better way to respond to the demands of globalisation. It could be to the knowledge society what oil companies are to the industrial society: the engine that drives global civil society in the emerging new episteme.

REFERENCES

Asukara, T. et al. (1999). "Office work support with multiple agents." *NEC Research and Development*, 40, 3: 308–313.

Beck, F. A. G. (1964). *Greek Education*. London: Methuen and Co.

Foucault, M. (1970). *The Order of Things*. New York: Pantheon House.

Huntington, S. P. (1993). "The Clash of Civilization." *Foreign Affairs,* Summer.

— (1996). *The Clash of Civilizations and the Remaking of World Order*. New York: Simon & Schuster.

Kuhn, T. S. (1962). *The Structure of Scientific Revolutions*. Chicago: University of Chicago Press.

Luke, A. (1993). "Shaping Literacy in Schools: An Introduction." In L.Unsworth (Ed.), *Language as Social Practice in Primary School*. Melbourne: MacMillan.

Lyotard, J. (1984). *The Postmodern Condition: A report on knowledge*. Minneapolis: University of Minnesota Press.

Minsky, M. (1986). *The Society of Mind*. New York: Simon & Schuster.

Newman, J. H. (1996). *The Idea of a University*. Frank, M. Turner (Ed.). New Haven: Yale University Press.

O'Hagan, M. (1996). *The Coming Industry of Teletranslation*. Clevedon: Multilingual Matters.

Sherman, B., and Judkins, P. (1992). *Glimpses of Heaven, Visions of Hell*. Great Britain: Hodder & Stoughton.

Tehranian, M., and Chappell, D. W. (Eds.). (2002). *Dialogue of Civilizations: A New Peace Agenda for the New Millennium*. London: I. B. Tauris.

Terashima, N. (2001). "The Definition of HyperReality." In John Tiffin & Nobiyoshi Terashima (Eds.), *HyperReality: Paradigm for the Third Millennium*. London and New York: Routledge.

Tiffin, J., and Rajasingham, L. (1995). *In Search of the Virtual Class: Education in an Information Society*. London and New York: Routledge.

Tiffin, J., and Rajasingham, L. (2001). The HyperClass. In *HyperReality: The Paradigm for the Third Millennium*. John Tiffin and Nobiyoshi Terashima (Eds). London and New York: Routledge.

Tiffin, J., and Rajasingham, L. (2003). *The Global Virtual University*. London and New York: Routledge.

Vygotsky, L. (1978). *Mind in Society: The Development of Higher Psychological Processes.* Cambridge, MA: Harvard University Press.

Whorf, B. L. (1956). *Language, Thought, and Reality,* New York: Wiley.

Lalita Rajasingham, Ph.D., is Senior Lecturer and Director of the Masters and Ph.D. in Communication Studies, School of Information Management, at Victoria University of Wellington, New Zealand.

Reading 5.5

Globalization, Informatization, and Intercultural Communication

RANDY KLUVER

Globalization is not the only thing influencing events in the world today, but to the extent that there is a North Star and a worldwide shaping force, it is this system.

—*Thomas Friedman,*
The Lexus and the Olive Tree, 1999.

INTRODUCTION

Friedman's comment above serves to illustrate the profound importance assigned to the cultural and technological forces now reshaping the world. Indeed, Friedman is only one in a long line of commentators and analysts who have ascribed tremendous importance to the forces of globalization and informatization that have already redefined industries, politics,

First published in *American Communication Journal*, Vol. 3, Issue 3, May, 2000. Reprinted with permission.

and cultures, and perhaps the underlying rules of social order. Societies and communities have no choice but to participate in this "New International Information Order," but the character of their participation is shaped by specific social, cultural, economic and political conditions. This complex multi-level process of mediation between the global and the local, as an inherently communication phenomenon, promises to change not only the context, but likely the nature of intercultural communication.

But what are these forces that seem to have such a profound effect on our lives? The awesome potential of information technologies and globalization has already had a profound impact upon industries, particularly the financial markets. What are the implications of these forces for those interested in intercultural communication? Moreover, in what ways can intercultural communication theory help us to understand these forces? Is the traditional study of intercultural communication, bound as it is by the interpersonal context, even relevant to the new issues arising with globalization and informatization?

It is the purpose of this essay to explore the relevance of these globe-shaping forces to intercultural communication, and vice-versa, to identify some of the salient questions for theorists of intercultural communication that arise as a result of these forces, and finally, to identify the role of intercultural communication in providing foundations for understanding a globalized, technologized world.

GLOBALIZATION AND INFORMATIZATION

I will begin by trying to define the key terms in order to avoid the mistakes of overgeneralization or misrepresentation. Globalization has been defined in various ways, but is most typically defined in reference to the interconnectedness of political entities, economic relationships, or even computer networks. Globalization refers primarily to the ways in which economic and industrial institutions (such as industries or corporations) interact in various locations throughout the world, with primacy given to no specific geographic location. Friedman argues that "globalization involves the inexorable integration of markets, nation-states, and technologies to a degree never witnessed before" (1999, p. 7). Kennedy (1993) describes globalization in primarily economic terms, defining it as primarily integrative structures (p. 47). He further argues that globalization of economic structures means that local and national governments eventually cede control of policy to the global institutions (primarily multinational corporations, but also including non governmental, regional, or international organizations, such as the World Bank or the International Monetary Fund.)

Even though the term globalization typically refers to economic phenomenon, there are ripple effects that make the impact of globalization much broader socially and culturally. Ideas, customs, and cultural movements all follow closely after the exchange of goods across national boundaries. For example, international trade has been the vehicle by which most religions have spread, including Buddhism to East and Southeast Asia along the Silk Road, Islam to Southeast Asia, and Christianity to Eastern Europe, Central Asia, and the Americas. These changes might be marginal, such as the emergence of the "Hello, Kitty" cult around the world, or they may be profound, such as the rise of new religious, political, environmental, or cultural movements, such as the Falungong movement, one that relies almost exclusively upon electronic communications media to recruit and mobilize.

At the recent Davos Economic Forum in Switzerland, Humberto Eco differentiated between globalization as a fact and globalization as a value. Globalization as a fact is the real economic ties, institutions, and realities that underlie a new economy. Globalization as a value is the extent to which we seek further integration of markets, pools of capital, and industries, although many seem to use the term to refer not to greater economic integration, but rather cultural and social integration. Not everyone is in full support of further globalization, as is evidenced by the December, 1999 riots at the World Trade Organization in Seattle. Opponents, such as Stop WTO!, have argued that globalization creates further poverty, destroys the environment, and ultimately favors the interests of multinationals over national interests, or WTO rules encroaching on domestic regulations, as illustrated in this graphic implying incompatible interests.

By informatization, I refer to the process primarily by which information technologies, such as the world-wide web and other communication technologies, have transformed economic and social relations to such an extent that cultural and economic barriers are minimized. In his groundbreaking book, *Information Society as Post Industrial Society,* Yoneji Masuda (1981) argues that the technological innovations will provoke radical cultural and social changes that will be fundamentally different from the status quo. In the post-industrial, information-based society, knowledge, or the production of information values, will be the driving force of society, rather than industrial technologies (p. 29). Moreover, the convergence of technologies will precipitate further changes that promise to fundamentally alter the human landscape.

Wang describes the same phenomenon (1994) which she calls "informatization" as "a process of change that features (a) the use of informatization and IT [information technologies] to such and extent that they become the dominant forces in commanding economic, political, social and cultural development; and (b) unprecedented growth in the speed, quantity, and popularity of information production

and distribution" (p. 5). The UNDP estimates that the number of Internet users in mid 1999, 150 million, will grow to 700 million by 2001 (Human Development Report, 1999). This "New International Information Order" no longer allows national or regional considerations to stand in the way of the global integration of values, attitudes, and shopping brands.

Thus, informatization is the process whereby information and communication technologies shape cultural and civic discourse. This would include not just computers and the internet, but other related technologies that have as their primary characteristic the transfer of information, including more traditional media technologies, such as film, satellite television, and telecommunications. As societies and economies re-orient themselves around technologies, there are inevitable consequences.

These two concepts, globalization and informatization, thus explain different phenomena, but there is a marked overlap between their social, political, economic, and cultural functions. Although globalization ultimately refers to the integration of economic institutions, much of this integration occurs through the channels of technology.

Although international trade is not a new phenomemon, the advent of communications technologies has accelerated the pace and scope of trade. Previously, ideas and technologies took centuries to diffuse across the globe, not seconds (Sprague, 2000). With electronic communication media, however, within an instant, the most novel ideas can reach around the globe, or news of events in one continent can drastically affect financial markets around the world. On a daily basis, over one trillion dollars flows around the world on these electronic networks (Kennedy, p. 51). Conversely, globalization allows the proliferation of information technologies, and creates a world wide market and clear strategic incentives for the adoption of information technologies.

Observers of the twin forces of globalization and informatization have argued that these forces will likely have consequences far beyond the immediate economic context. Rather, they are likely to have a profound impact on the cultural and social consequences of society. Certainly, globalization has contributed to a greater global consciousness that makes political and economic issues extend far beyond their immediate borders. Human rights, the environment, and workers' rights are just a few examples of issues that have gained international, or global constituencies. Tibet's status under Chinese rule illustrates the new global reality. The Dalai Lama, for example, now has as large a following among Westerners as he does in Dharamsala. Celebrities like Richard Gere and the reincarnated lama Steven Seagal contribute their advocacy for Tibet's human rights campaign, even as the face of Tibetan Buddhism changes by the interaction (Lopez, 1997).

Masuda argues that the post-industrial society will likely have the same impact, if not more, than the industrial revolution had on eighteenth century Europe. Just as the industrial revolution ultimately contributed to an increase in urbanization, social dislocation, and the development of new economic forms, the information revolution will create a new social context, including the emergence of "information communities," participatory democracy, and a spirit of globalism. Masuda clearly predicted the convergence of technological capacities with the growth of globalization, echoing McLuhan's metaphor of a global village.

Other scholars argue that globalization and informatization are likely to diminish the concept of the nation as a political institution at all (Poster, 1999). Friedman (1999) argues that as nation-states decline in importance, multi-national corporations, nongovernmental organizations, and "superempowered individuals" such as George Soros gain influence and importance. As these non-political organizations and institutions gain importance, there are inevitable challenges to political, economic, and cultural processes.

The overall impact of these forces, however, is difficult to discern. Predictions that they would usher in a new utopia, in which demarcations of economic, political, or geographical advantage would no longer matter, have proven to be chimeric. In some ways, globalization and informatization have clear advantages for human societies, but there are just as many potential problems that arise, so that the overall impact is still merely a subject for speculation. On the positive side, globalization and informatization can empower individuals and societies to engage in international arena for economic, political, and cultural resources. Moreover, these forces allow for the greater flow of information, even from places and to people who have traditionally been sealed off from the free flow of information. North Korea's Central Daily News, for example, is just as accessible to anyone with an internet connection as is CNN. As Friedman argues, technologization has brought about a "democracy of information" (p. 53).

Moreover, there is a proliferation of information about lifestyles, religions, and cultural issues. For example, the rise of the internet allows commerce to take place from anywhere, to anywhere, and is open to anyone. Consumers around the world can buy books from a source such as Amazon.com, and never have to travel outside of their country to get access to the information previously limited to the developed world. Religious pilgrims can use live video streams to have a "virtual visit" to religious shrines, such as the Western Wall. The telecommunications and computer networks also allow for unprecedented global activism. Nonprofit activist groups such as the Ruckus Society, for example, use technological means to gather volunteers, teach about environmental and human rights activism, publicize events, and raise support through such traditional means as offering coffee mugs and T-shirts to supporters. This democratization of information increases the potential for international harmony, although it by no means guarantees it.

Information technology can also be used to empower marginalized communities, and some resources, such as the Global Knowledge partnership, engage in activities to make information technologies, including computing resources and telecommunications, as well as more low-tech media forms, available for the purposes of national and local economic development. This video clip from the World Bank argues that technological development should be used for the purposes of providing for health, agriculture, and environmental change, and ultimately, to eliminate poverty (World Bank statement on new technology, 2000). Some argue that the new forces will help to democratize regimes that must either allow information or risk losing out on economic growth, contributing to an inevitable democratization of societies. In the People's Republic of China, for example, the webwar between the government and democratic activists is usually won by the activists (US Embassy, 2000). There is no doubt that there is far greater access to various opinions, but whether or not these are accessed, and their impact if they are accessed, is still open to some debate.

On the negative side, however, these twin forces threaten to undermine centuries of tradition, local autonomy, and cultural integrity. The internet, for example, is overwhelmingly an English language medium, and those who want to participate fully with all it has to offer had best read English (Barber, 1995). In fact, a high level government panel recently recommended that Japan consider adopting English as an official language in the future (English "imperialism," 2000). Moreover, globalization establishes a global economic system in which those with the most capital are best able to capitalize on the global market, setting up what Friedman calls a "winner take all" system (1999, p. 245). Although technology levels the playing field, it does nothing to diminish the size of the competitors. The US, for example, overwhelmingly benefits from the rise of information technology, as it is the US that dominates almost all commercial sites and many, if not most, of the most profitable technology manufacturers. In addition, Westerners have clear advantages in telecommunications, as illustrated by the fact that there are more internet connections in Manhattan than in the entire African continent (World Bank statement on technology, 2000). The same access to information made possible by the internet also empowers those with devious ends, such as international terrorism or even garden variety hackers, with greater powers at their disposal to exploit or attack others.

A United Nations Development Project report in 1999 argued that globalization was indeed widening the gap between the rich and poor nations, and that the industrialized nations overwhelmingly benefit from both globalization of markets and the rising importance of information and knowledge in the new global economy. Moreover, the report estimates that English is the language of choice for 80 percent of web sites, and that 26 percent of Americans use the World Wide Web—as opposed to 3 percent of Russians, 0.4 percent of the population of South Asia and 0.2 percent for Arab states (UNDP, 1999).

Finally, one of the potentially most devastating impacts of the forces of globalization and informatization is that there is created an insidious conflict between the new global economic order and the local, or even tribal, interests. Friedman argues that this tension between the "lexus (global) and the olive tree (local)" is one of the defining characteristics of the new world. Barber (1995) characterises the dialectic between "McWorld vs. Jihad" as an inevitable point of conflict in the future, between a "McWorld tied together by communications, information, entertainment, and commerce" versus a "Jihad . . . against technology, against pop culture, and against integrated markets; against modernity itself" (1995, p. 4).

Moreover, the aggressive nature of the forces of globalization and informatization make mutual acceptance untenable. It is impossible to stand outside the globalizing world, as there are too many political, economic, social, and even technological forces pushing nations and societies in that direction. Although it might be possible for an individual to refuse to cooperate, the very nature of the globalized world makes it impossible for whole societies to stand against it and still prosper.

This brief introduction to the forces of globalization and informatization is by no means exhaustive, but it helps to raise some of the salient issues for further discussion. I will turn my attention now to the implications of these forces for international and intercultural communication theory, and give tentative expression to some of the questions that arise for theorists of intercultural communication.

As noted previously, intercultural communication theorists have often noted the globalizing forces of economic integration, tourism, migration, etc., as important forces that provide a rationale for increased intercultural communication competency. Few, however, have attempted to discern the more fundamental questions of how these forces will change the very nature of intercultural contact. (One notable exception is Chen and Starosta, 2000.) In this section, I will attempt to articulate several broad areas of questions, and articulate some important areas that merit the attention of intercultural communication theorists. I will articulate these in two broad categories, the social implications and the interpersonal implications. Given that the field of intercultural communication is typically construed as primarily interpersonal, it might seem more helpful to address these first. However, given the fact that these forces are inherently cultural and social, I think it best to begin with a discussion of the larger social and cultural implications.

GLOBALIZATION, INFORMATIZATION, AND CULTURAL CHANGE

The first broad area of questions to be addressed is that of the social and cultural implications of globalization and informatization, and the relevance to intercultural communication. These are areas that are typically not directly addressed by theories of intercultural communication, but rather more often come within the range of theorists of international communication, critical theory, or even post-colonial literary theory. However, given the force we have ascribed these trends in the contemporary world, it is critical that theorists of intercultural communication engage them, as it is the social and cultural context in which all intercultural communication arises. I will specifically discuss three critical areas that need to be addressed, our understanding of culture, the ways in which cultural change is precipitated by globalization and informatization, and their role in defining personal and communal identity.

Culture, of course, is an amorphous concept, even in the most rigorous theories of intercultural communication. Typically, it is defined as a symbolic system, which includes issues of perception, cognition, and understanding. Culture is not merely an abstract set of folk practices, nor a collection of touristy festivals. Rather, as Geertz (1973) defines it, it is a set of symbolic systems, that serve not only to define and identify the culture and social structures, but also to articulate the synthesis of two essential parts of human culture, ethos and world view. Geertz employs a very diffuse, totalistic conception of culture, that can not easily be perfunctorily articulated. Every specific act, every utterance, every thought must be understood within a much larger, much broader context.

There are certain inherent challenges that globalization, in particular, make upon our understanding of culture. One of these is a tendency to equate "culture" with "nation." Scholars and teachers speak of Russian culture, Chinese culture, or Japanese culture, for example, with little reference to the distinctions between very different groupings within a national boundary. The nation, as a political abstraction, is certainly very different from the culture, which as Geertz (1973) has described it, is primarily a system of symbols. Although scholars distinguish between co-cultures within North American boundaries, this concept is rarely applied to other nations. Within the boundaries of the Peoples' Republic of China, for example, there are approximately 80 different linguistic groupings, bound by geographical, political, and yes, even cultural distinctions. The language most often called Chinese, Mandarin, or putonghua, the official language based on the dialect of the northern region around Beijing, is the official spoken language, but to the vast majority of citizens of the nation, it is a second language. Each of the regions of China have vastly different ethos, and yet this is rarely considered in abstract pronouncements about "Chinese culture." In a globalized world, the political abstractions known as nations are becoming increasingly irrelevant, while the symbolic systems known as cultures are continually in flux. With greater access to cultural diversity from within nations, our conception of "culture" will take on narrower frames of reference.

Beyond the inherent instability of the nation alluded to earlier, does globalization force us to redefine cultural boundaries? Do globalization and informatization bring about culture convergence or divergence? Do the ties

formed by economic and technological integration increase or diminish the impact of culture on communication? How does global interaction affect one's cultural identity? When Israelis read South African websites, or when Chinese read Japanese sites, which cultural background is most significant?

This question is not easy to answer because it entails certain other fundamental questions. For example, media forms themselves are not passive entities. Cultural forms, codes, and values determine issues of media content and media design, including aesthetic, technical, and logical criterion. One has only to compare the websites of the aforementioned North Korean Central News Agency with the much more visibly dynamic Western news sites, such as CNN, to see immediate differences in perceptions of what "news" is, how it is to be presented, and the cultural, economic, and political assumptions regarding its purposes.

A related area of discussion is that of the forces of globalization and informatization in cultural change. Many theorists argue that globalization is working in a fundamentally centripetal manner, forcing homogenization and consumerism along Western lines. Observers from both traditionalist and integrationist perspectives perceive a certain convergence across cultural and national boundaries. The rise of a new class of capitalists in recently developed nations is often praised as a verification of the universality of notions of rationality, liberalism, secularism and human rights (Robison and Goodman, 1996, p. 2). In other words, a new culture is forming that transcends traditional political and geographic boundaries, that can best be defined by profession, technological expertise, or social class.

Others decry the "coca-colonization" and "McDonaldization" of the globe, and argue that the rampant global rise of consumerism ultimately will destroy traditional cultures. In a recent Chinese news publication, for example, a Chinese scholar argues that the "blind worship" of foreign consumer goods, the tendency to disparage patriotic heroes and uplift "traiterous literati," and the compromise of national dignity are all symptoms of the "dregs of colonial culture" (Li, 1999, p. 10). In other words, the globalization of China's economy, including consumer products, as well as the rise of cybercafes on Chinese streets, all indicate the evil nature of the changing circumstances.

As evidence for the claim of homogenization, analysts point to graphic indicators, such as the abundance of McDonald's restaurants around the world, such as one in Oman. Such blatant symbols of multinational power are indicative of the homogenization of traditional societies. Integrationists, on the other hand, argue that unlike previous manifestations of colonial power, there is nothing coercive about offering hamburgers to willing consumers.

This has serious implications regarding the transformation of culture. Globalization and informatization provide a context that ultimately can be at odds with traditional cultural forms. To what extent, for example, can Islam, which is rooted in the history and the language of the Arabs, survive postmodern globalization? Islam has certainly taken root in culturally diverse locales, such as Central Asia and Southeast Asia, but the globalized future presents a different set of challenges. As a world view, Islam might very well provide a welcome bed of stability in a world of change (Ahmed, 1992). As a cultural practice, however, globalization has introduced tensions into Islamic societies, such as allowing youth access to vastly different world views, creating a tension within traditional Muslim societies. For example, in the 1990's a survey indicated that Michael Jackson was more popular in Indonesia than Mohammed, and merely reporting on the survey landed an unfortunate journalist in jail (Hitching, 1996).

It is not just Muslim societies that must deal with the unknown future, however, but all societies in which tradition has played a major role in providing guidance to social life; in short, all societies. Some might well experience a backlash as illustrated by the rise of the Taliban in Afghanistan, while others find themselves in vastly changed social circumstances. In 1997, representatives of the South Korean government, undoubtedly one of the nations that had most benefited from global economic and technological change, argued before the United Nations that globalization represented a threat to cultural diversity that must be guarded against (United Nations Press Release, 1997).

If informatization and globalization have the capacity to transform culture (the yang), then they also strengthen them (the yin). There is evidence that indicates that the emerging globalized information society, rather than weakening cultural and national identity, actually strengthens traditional cultural forms. Although the web is in English, for example, the rise of technology and the globalization of commerce allows for innovation and creativity in the enhancement of nonmainstream perspectives. For example, these forces have enabled the rise of a new genre of music, Vietnamese pop music, that would not arise in a world bounded by more traditional economic structures. The overseas Vietnamese population, from geographically diverse locations such as Southern California, France, and Canada, would not likely support the rise of concert tours, recordings, and the other trappings of the entertainment industry without the linkages that can occur in a more globalized world, which allows an economy of scale necessary to make Vietnamese pop music profitable. Zhang and Hao argue that in the "age of cyberspace, the role of ethnic media in fortifying the cultural traits of ethnic immigrants is expected to be further strengthened. As a result, ethnic groups are more likely to be assimilated into the mainstream culture without losing their own cultural roots and ethnic identity."

In this sense, then, the forces of globalization and informatization have a centrifugal effect, allowing the rise of new local traditions and cultural forms. It also increases the ability of outsiders to learn more about significant cultural, religious or historical traditions without the filtering mechanisms of more traditional media. Whereas most local bookstores, for example, carry but a handful of histories of non-Western societies, web access allows one to explore the histories, politics, economics and societies of the most inaccessible regions.

Perhaps the most succinct way of addressing these questions is to distinguish levels of integration and polarization. At the economic and technological levels, there is certainly integration. Local industries can no longer afford to not be vulnerable to international competition, and must position themselves within a global context. The anti-WTO protests in Seattle were inherently about the conflict between global trade realities in conflict with local regulation in areas such as genetically modified foods. Moreover, anyone with access to the technology can gain information about and from any part of the globe. At the level of individual identity, however, informatization and globalization allows a myriad of possibilities for the individual to make radically different choices than previously possible; in other words, these twin forces allow, and even encourage, polarization.

This leads us to the third critical issue for scholars of intercultural communication, which relates to how individuals define their local and communal identity. At the personal level, one's individual ethos can be ever more narrowly defined, providing the potential for a further polarization (or "tribalization," to use Barber's term) of personal identity. There are at least three aspects to this argument. First, rather than seeing oneself as essentially a citizen of a nation or a local community, people are more free to define themselves along narrower conceptions of identity and commitment, either

ethnic, religious, or ideological affiliation. In this sense, the more global we become, the more provincial our attitudes can become. We are no longer forced into a certain homogeneity of lifestyle, belief, or social knowledge, but we are also no longer forced to work through issues with our neighbors.

Second, by gaining access to vast amounts of information, one is no longer dependent upon the village for knowledge and/or affirmation. For example, communication technologies allow citizens of nations in which religious conversion is illegal access to inconceivable amounts of information about other global faiths, radically revamping what has historically been one of the most significant intercultural communication encounters, religious missions, and making a true independence of thought possible. Christian mission organizations, such as Campus Crusade for Christ, are already beginning to build extensive web sites with clearly evangelistic intent. Conversely, Islam, Buddhism, Taoism, Hinduism, and various other faiths all appear on the web, lending themselves not only to easy propagation, but also to reinvention. This has both liberating as well as debilitating aspects, because if one can more easily define herself outside of the boundaries of the local community, she can no longer rely as fully upon the local community for support. Ultimately, whether a cyber-neighbor is as reliable as a physical neighbor is but mere speculation.

Moreover, communication by electronic channels is ultimately affected by the media itself, producing potentially irrevocable distortion. Jacques Ellul argued decades ago, for example, that the technologies of modern life are ultimately destructive when applied to certain kinds of messages, such as religion (1965). In his discussion of communication technologies, which Ellul argues are a form of the totalizing system of propaganda, he argues that "Christianity disseminated by such means is not Christianity" (p. 230). Further, he argues that when the church uses the means of ideological indoctrination to propagate the faith, it might reach the masses, influence collective opinions, and "even leads many people to accept what seems to be Christianity. But in doing that the church becomes a false church" (p. 230). So although the information systems that permeate the modern world allow for a greater dissemination of information, there remains the danger of the dehumanization of that information, and the social context that makes the information relevant.

And finally, the fact that globalization and informatization allow, even encourage, one to adopt new perspectives and identities, allows one to make superficial commitments to a new identity. Students who have access to marginal (and marginalized) belief systems by access to the web, for example, might come to see themselves as adherents, with little or understanding of the larger history and body of beliefs that constitutes the larger community of believers. This superficial identification with "the other" can disrupt social unity at a great cost, and yet not provide any compensatory alliances or social unions. It is one thing to convert to a new faith when in the midst of an encouraging body of support, it is another altogether when one is, in all critical aspects, removed from any sources of social support.

In summary, the cultural and social changes accompanied by globalization and informatization have clear relevance to theorists in intercultural communication in at least three key ways. The conception of culture, the ways in which cultural change is precipitated by these trends, and the role of these forces in defining personal identity and social unity are all important issues of discussion for communication scholars, as they provide the foundational assumptions for our interpretation of the processes of intercultural communication.

GLOBALIZATION, INFORMATIZATION, AND INTERCULTURAL COMMUNICATION

It should be evident by now that the trends of globalization and informatization have important implications at the foundational level for intercultural communication theory, namely, our very understanding of culture, society, and communication. I will now turn attention to some critical questions concerning the impact and role of globalization and informatization on intercultural communication practice and behavior. I will introduce only three issues, certainly not an exhaustive list, but enough to demonstrate the necessity of further research in this area. Specifically, I will raise the issues of the impact of culture on computer-mediated communication and other communication issues, the effectiveness of communication technologies to actually fulfill some of the political and social promises made for them, and the role of intercultural communication skills for professional success.

Intercultural communication has traditionally been discussed in primarily interpersonal behavior, although not exclusively so. Informatization, however, forces us to consider the ways in which culture influences the successful transmission of messages in radically different channels than traditionally conceived. The influence of culture on communication behavior is central to our field of study, and by any account, telecommunications, cyberspace, and other emerging media forms are becoming increasingly popular modes of communication. Although there is an emerging literature on technology as a communication form and computer-mediated communication (Jackson, 1997), even prompting an on-line journal, as of this writing there has been little, if any, substantive analysis of the impact of the new media form across cultural boundaries. Does a Japanese youth, for example, respond to CNN.com the same way that a Pakistani would? Since there are inherent cultural issues associated with any form of communication, what complicating factors are raised by the advent of communication technologies?

This issue could significantly affect how intercultural communication is taught. Some of the key concepts associated with intercultural communication, such as the distinction between high and low context cultures, are problematic when applied to new communication contexts. Since high context cultures are those where there is a greater social knowledge, and communication is typically less explicit, can persons from a high context background rely on the same subtle nonverbal cues and situational variables when using the internet or email, for example? How is high context culture messaging transformed when there is an absence of nonverbal cues, environmental and situational variables, and at best imprecise manifestations of status and hierarchy? Does this force high-context communication to become low context? Is communication across cultures made easier across technological channels, since the ever troublesome nonverbal cues that complicate much interpersonal intercultural communication lose their importance? What new nonverbal cues arise in electronic communication? What constitutes communication competence in the new context? The number of issues associated with this line of inquiry is endless, and could radically alter how we think about, and teach, intercultural communication skills and theory.

A second significant issue associated with the convergence of global values, technology, and communication is the ability of technologies to truly fulfill the promises made for it, both in the encouragement of intercultural interaction as well as its effectiveness in the development of new political, social, or cultural movements.

Certainly, the potential for further interaction with people from diverse cultural backgrounds increases with the availability of technology, but do people typically seek out diversity when interacting with technologies,

or do they interact primarily with people much like themselves? UN Secretary General Kofi Annan, for example, argued that "we in the United Nations are convinced that communications technology has a great democratizing power waiting to be harnessed to our global struggle for peace and development. The quantity and quality of available information is changing dramatically every day, in every country, in every corner of the world. Citizens are gaining greater access to information, too. And the spread of information is making accountability and transparency facts of life for any government" (United Nations, 1998).

Although these expectations reveal a potential for communication that can bring together a critical mass for political or social change, it is not clear that it is sufficient to do so. During 1989's Tiananmen demonstrations, for example, Chinese students and scholars residing in North America and Europe made use of all available means of communication to support the pro-democracy movement, including fax machines and email, and many of the networks developed during that period continue to this day in web presence, such as the Support Democracy in China page or Amnesty International's web site. The effectiveness of web presence as a persuasion device, moreover, has not been established. Does the presence of Tibetan Buddhism on the web, for example, encourage the growth of the religion? To what extent is the religion re-invented when introduced by means of technology?

A final area of inquiry related to these issues is the manner in which intercultural communication skills enable greater effectiveness in personal and professional life, in a globalized and technologized social context. One of the characteristics emerging from globalization and informatization is the rising dominance of a new "knowledge class," which is defined as a class that is supported solely by its participation in the new information industries, with little reliance upon traditional manufacturing or production industries, including agriculture. Peter Drucker argues that "the acquisition and distribution of formal knowledge may come to occupy the place in the politics of the knowledge society which the acquisition and distribution of property and income have occupied in our politics over the two or three centuries that we have come to call the Age of Capitalism."

By extension, it is communication skills, both in sending and receiving, that determines how well an individual, an organization, an industry, or a nation, does in acquiring and applying knowledge, thus broadening the chances for success. Certainly, the ability to effectively negotiate the inherent cultural issues in communication becomes more of a competitive edge in a global world. It is likely that this new knowledge class will see a convergence of certain skills, attitudes, and world views, unbounded by traditional national or cultural boundaries. Stock brokers in Japan are likely to have more in common with their counterparts in Germany and the US than they are with their own grandparents.

However, "knowledge" is an inherently relativistic concept (Breen, 1997). As Drucker (1994) argues, "the knowledge of the knowledge society, precisely because it is knowledge only when applied in action, derives its rank and standing from the situation. In other words, what is knowledge in one situation, such as fluency in Korean for the American executive posted to Seoul, is only information, and not very relevant information at that, when the same executive a few years later has to think through his company's market strategy for Korea." Drucker's argument is that the distinction between information and knowledge becomes all the more pressing, even as the shifting contours of the global world are likely to turn once vital knowledge into mere information. Participants in the global system are likely to find themselves ever and always pursuing new knowledge, and never arrive at a place where they know everything they need for success in most situations.

SUMMARY AND CONCLUSIONS

My goal in this essay has been to provide some initial probes into the role of the trends of informatization and globalization in intercultural communication. Of course, some of the issues that seem important today will no doubt fade into insignificance in the near future, while as yet-unheard-of issues will arise to take their place. Nevertheless, given the transforming effects of globalization and informatization in the social and cultural worlds, it is imperative for scholars of intercultural communication to begin to understand how these forces will affect not only the foundational theoretical assumptions of our scholarship, but also the significant impact of these trends on the actual practice of intercultural communication.

I would like to conclude with a brief comment about the role that scholars of intercultural communication can play in developing a theoretical framework which might serve to facilitate future understanding of these issues. Scholars and theorists of intercultural communication, perhaps more than any other discipline, are in a privileged position, as traditional disciplinary frameworks are insufficient to deal with the new realities. The twin forces of globalization and informatization can perhaps be best explained from within a framework provided by intercultural communication theorists, as from its earliest days the discipline has been concerned with the development of global consciousness, the overcoming of the conceptual and behavioral defaults provided by culture, and how communication changes individuals. It is thus likely that intercultural communication scholars can best provide a critical schema for understanding "culture" in the new world. Communication theorists have long understood that culture is inherently a symbolic system, and that it is thus a close scrutiny of the nature of symbols, their transformation, and their impact that best prepares one to understand the ways in which these forces shape and alter our symbolic understandings of our lives. Moreover, it is from within this framework that we are perhaps best suited to document and analyze the salient issues of communication consumption in a cross-cultural, cross-national, wired world.

REFERENCES

Ahmed, A. S. (1992). Postmodernism and Islam: Predicament and Promise. London: Routledge.

Barber, B. (1995). Jihad vs. McWorld: how globalism and tribalism are reshaping the world. New York: Random House.

Breen, M. (1997). Information does not equal knowledge. Journal of Computer Mediated Communication, 3 (3).

Chen, G. and Starosta, W. (2000). Communication and global society. New York: Peter Lang.

Drucker, P. (1994, November). The age of social transformation. The Atlantic Monthly, 274. (5). 53–80.

Ellul, J. (1965). Propaganda: the formation of men's attitudes. New York: Knopf.

"English "imperialism:" the Japanese have more to gain than lose by learning the language. (2000, April 7). Asiaweek, 26. (13). 21.

Friedman, T. (1999). The lexus and the olive tree: understanding globalization. New York: Farrar, Straus, Giroux.

Geertz, C. (1973). The interpretation of cultures. New York: Basic Books.

Geertz, C. (1983). Local knowledge: further essays in interpretive anthropology. New York: Basic Books.

Hitching, B. (1996) McDonalds, Minarets, and Modernity: The anatomy of the emerging secular Muslim world Sevenoaks, Kent, UK: Spear Publishing.

Jackson, M. (1997)Assessing the structure of communication on the world wide web. Journal of Computer Mediated Communication, 3, 1.

Kennedy, P. (1993). Preparing for the twenty-first century. New York: Random House.

Li. Z. (1999). Contention on the issue of "colonial culture." Chinese Sociology and Anthropology, 31, 4, 8–14.

Lopez, D. (1998). Prisoners of Shangri-la: Tibetan buddhism and the west. Chicago: University of Chicago Press.

Masuda, Y. (1982) Information Society as Post-Industrial Society. Bethesda, MD: World Future Society.

Poster, M. (1999). National identities and communications technologies. The Information Society,15 (4), 235–240.

Robison, R. and Goodman, D. S. G. (Eds.). (1996). The New rich in Asia: mobile phones, McDonald's, and middle-class revolution. London and New York: Routledge.

Sprague, J. (2000, February 18). Asia's worldly past: everything old is new again. Asiaweek, 26. (6).

United Nations. (1997, October 22). World must reap benefits of globalization without eroding cultural diversity, Republic of Korea tells second committee. United Nations press release GA/EF/2770. New York.

United Nations. (1998, March 24). Secretary General says communications technology has great democratizing power waiting to be harnessed to global struggle for peace and development. United Nations Press Release SG/SM/6502 SAG/4. New York.

United Nations Development Program. (1999). Human Development Report, 1999. New York.

US Embassy report, (2000, January). China's Internet "Information Skirmish." Beijing.

Wang, G. (1994). Treading different paths: informatization in Asian nations. Norwood, NJ: Ablex.

World Bank, (2000). Statement on Global Knowledge. New York.

World Bank, (2000). Statement on New Technology. New York .

Zhang, K. and Hao, X. (1999) The Internet and Ethnic Press: A Study of Electronic Chinese Publications. The Information Society, 15 (1). pp. 21–30.

Randy Kluver is a part of the Information and Communication Management Programme, National University of Singapore.

Reading 5.6

Five Ways to Reduce the Foreign Terrorist Threat to the United States

MOHAN R. LIMAYE

Nobody or no measures can guarantee total security. If the United States, however, implements the following five courses of action, it will in my judgment reduce its external terrorist threat to a large extent:

1. Pursue genuine attempts to promote democracy in those areas of the world where presently authoritarian or dictatorial regimes rule.
2. Be a good, well-behaved citizen in the world community of nations.
3. Call its troops home from abroad. In other words, close down its military bases on foreign soil.
4. Serve as a model of human rights protection for other nations by protecting human rights here at home.
5. Share its wealth with the poorest nations of the world, just because it has more.

INTRODUCTION

I write this essay to provide a largely non-American viewpoint, one educated Third-World perspective on this topic. I'm a naturalized U.S. citizen, who has spent the first 30 years of his life in India and over 37 years in the U.S. This opinion piece, like an op-ed page, could serve as a springboard for discussion not only at an institution of higher education but at other forums as well. Since this is not a scholarly paper, every statement is not supported by empirical evidence, nor is there a bibliography at the end as academic papers do.

Though the envy and love-hate syndrome of the world for the successes and wealth of the United States explain to a certain extent the resentment toward it felt by the people and governments of some countries, that is not the whole story. Thinking that this envy *wholly* accounts for the 9–11–2001 terrorist attack will lead to delusion or complacency and hence a lack of incentive to reform or revisit the U.S. foreign policy. That is why I'm not emphasizing the envy factor in my analysis below.

Another caveat needs to be mentioned at the outset of this paper: I'm using the term U.S. to stand for the government of the United States. I'm occasionally employing the term

The author acknowledges with gratitude the various suggestions made by Professors Jerry LaCava and Peter Lichtenstein, and my students (who will remain anonymous) at Boise State University and Professor Gerald J. Alred of the University of Wisconsin-Milwaukee.

"Americans" almost interchangeably with American administrations, thus blurring the distinction between a people and their government. I'm, however, aware of the distinction and of the fact that governments, even in democracies, do not necessarily reflect the opinions of all the people and that they pursue policy options at odds with the beliefs of some of their own populace.

At times in this essay, I may sound harsh in my criticism of the U.S. policies, but it is leveled to improve or correct the actions taken by the U.S. so that the threat of terrorism would diminish. I'm not suggesting that other countries are better than the U.S. On the contrary, I firmly believe that no other nation is morally superior to the United States. But my critique is aimed at making America better than other nations and, consequently, safer than it has felt in the aftermath of 9–11–2001.

After that harrowing event, the United States is understandably preoccupied with imminent and long-term threat to its security. Presently, U.S. government agencies are taking measures of the kind that any competent and watchful law enforcement departments anywhere would take for protection from short-term dangers. But the long-term threat will not diminish just through "police" or "detective" measures. I believe that *strategic policy* actions are necessary for reduction in the long-term threat to the U.S. from foreign terrorists. I, therefore, suggest that the United States implement the five above-mentioned courses of action to meet its objective of security risk reduction.

[1] Pursue genuine attempts to promote democracy in those areas of the world where presently authoritarian or dictatorial regimes rule.

Though the U.S. is the first modern democracy born out of a revolution, it has lacked fervor to spread democracy elsewhere. In the 20th century, for instance, it has been cool toward the independence struggles of former colonies. India gained its freedom from the British and became a democracy without U.S. intervention. In fact, the U.S. sided with the French in Indochina (today's Laos, Cambodia, and Vietnam), the Dutch in Indonesia, and the British in East Africa (today's Kenya, Uganda, and Tanzania) when the people in these countries were fighting to gain their independence. In WWI and WWII, one could argue America was fighting to save, not democracy, but the colonial rulers like the British, French, Dutch, etc., who were trying to hold on to their empires. In recent times, during the Cold War, the U.S. became addicted to propping up dictators as long as they were perceived to be anti-communist. Most of the leaders (even though democratically elected) that the U.S. saw as left-leaning were eliminated (examples: There is considerable evidence that Iran's Mussadegh in 1953 and Chile's Allende in 1973 were assassinated with covert help from the CIA). Right-wing dictators, however, were supported by the U.S. even when they were hated by the populace: the Shah of Iran, Marcos of the Philippines, and Suharto of Indonesia come to mind.

The United States needs to stop supporting such autocratic leaders if it wants to be universally perceived as the "leader of the free world." Some short sighted U.S. leaders encouraged Iraq's Saddam Hussein (during the Iran-Iraq war) and created the Taliban with active support from Pakistan under the excuse of creating a force to fight against the Soviet Union in the 1980s. Little did they see that they were creating a "fundamentalist" monster that would bite the moderate world. The lesson to be drawn from these activities is that purity of means cannot be sacrificed even for laudable ends. We treat Saudi Arabia and Pakistan, two authoritarian regimes that have been breeding grounds for terrorism, as our friends and clients. By supporting such regimes, the U.S. makes enemies of those around the globe who are repressed seemingly with its blessings. Wouldn't most Americans have been proud (including me) if the U.S. had invaded Afghanistan to free the women of that country repressed under the Taliban regime long before 9–11–01, and encouraged genuine democracy there? *If the U.S. is going to intervene in foreign countries at all* (which, incidentally, I do not approve), it should be done for just and ethical causes, not for greed, to ensure cheap oil supply, or to support U.S. multinational corporations' interests abroad. The world is thus dismayed when it sees, on the one hand, the U.S. supporting various despots while preaching democracy, on the other.

Thomas L. Friedman, a *New York Times* political commentator, in an article "Where Freedom Reigns" (August 14, 2002) emphasizes his point that, in a democracy like India, Muslims have not resorted to violence because they have legitimate ways open to voice their grievances and get them resolved. He, therefore, asserts that "the U.S. is so wrong not to press for democratization in the Arab and Muslim worlds. Is it an accident that India has the largest Muslim minority in the world, with plenty of economic grievances, yet not a single Indian Muslim was found in Al Queda?"

One wonders whether the U.S. deems it safer to have despots around that it can control and bribe than take chances with democracies (as in India, Western Europe and, recently, in Indonesia and Latin America) that it may not be able to predict and control. Like other nations, the U.S. seeks stability and peace because they are good for business and general prosperity. Though many methods (for instance, bribery and force) exist to achieve these goals, the U.S. may find that promoting genuine democracy will in the long term prove to be a more effective method to ensure lasting peace and security worldwide.

[2] Be a good, well -behaved citizen in the world community of nations.

What being a well-behaved citizen of the world entails for the United States is (a) not to be unilateral in its actions and decisions toward other countries but respect the wishes of the world as reflected in the United Nations and (b) not use that world body only when it serves the U.S. will. Several examples of the U.S. ignoring or rejecting world opinion can be cited: the Kyoto (Japan) accord on global warming, the issue of reparation for slavery which came up at the U.N. conference on racism and various other forms of discrimination, threats by the United States to stop or reduce payment of its dues to the United Nations, labeling nations at odds with its positions as evil or irresponsible, turning a blind eye to the tribal atrocities in Africa, and demanding exemption for its military officers from the jurisdiction of a currently-planned International War Crimes Court. As the French say, these behaviors are the symptoms of a "hyper" power.

Some Americans ask, "Why is the U.S. measured by a higher standard than the rest of the world?" The answer invariably is: Because the U.S. sets itself up as God, judging and rewarding or punishing other countries based solely on its verdict, nations all over the world expect the U.S. to be like the unerring God and evaluate its actions in that light with standards higher than they would judge themselves by. If American belief in its exceptionalism makes the U.S. claim to be the greatest country on earth, a New Jerusalem, its intentions and behaviors are bound to invite exceptional criteria and high moral standards. Since Ronald Reagan's presidency, the U.S. has forgotten a modest stance necessary for a learner. The U.S. seems to give the impression that the world has nothing to teach it. It presumably exemplifies the expression, "Power corrupts and absolute power corrupts absolutely." The Pew attitude survey, reported widely in the press in late December 2002, concluded that positive feelings toward the U.S. have declined in many countries of the world.

In general, many Americans have a very low tolerance for criticism. The present U.S.

administration, in particular, seems to prefer a monologue. It would rather not hear what the rest of the world has to say. For example, Iraq believes that it has a more defensible claim to Kuwait than the U.S. had to Hawaii. With a few exceptions, even the U.S. media do not report other countries' reactions. Only the British are heard because they have been following the leader (the United States) faithfully for the last at least one hundred years. But even the British have lately exhibited signs of nervousness: British Prime Minister Tony Blair warned Bush to "listen" to the international community's fears about an increasingly uncompromising stance taken by his (Bush's) administration regarding Iraq. "It (chaos) can come from the world splitting into rival poles of power; the U.S. in one corner; anti-U.S. forces in another. It can come from pent-up feelings of injustice and alienation, from divisions between the world's richer and its poorer nations" (*Dawn*, 1–9-2003). In this speech, Blair further counseled the U.S. to show that "the desire to work with others" is in its own interest too.

Some more indications of what the rest of the world thinks about U.S. unilateralism and imperial attitudes occurred in 2001 when the United States was not offered a seat on the UN Human Rights Commission. Also, the political parties that protested against the U.S. approach to the Iraq issue gained more seats in Germany's national assembly in the recent (October 2002) German elections. To me, the current U.S. positions and actions are helping radicalize even those elements in the world that have been traditionally moderate. The U.S. is looking for an enemy without, while in fact the enemy is within—U.S. imperial attitudes and arrogance of wealth and power. Even though American imperial ambitions today aren't territorial, they still bring up fear and animosity in many parts of the world.

[3] Call its troops home from abroad. In other words, close down its military bases on foreign soil.

Since the demise of the Soviet Union, the U.S. has favored a uni-polar world with itself as its military, economic, and cultural center. The United States keeps a huge arsenal of weapons of mass destruction and does not itself pass the Comprehensive Test Ban Treaty (CTBT) while pressuring other nations to sign the CTBT as well as the Nuclear Non-Proliferation Treaty (NPT). This seems like an ironic twist to the saying "Do unto others what you would have done to you." (Ask others to do what you don't want to do.) The U.S. defense budget, moreover, is 40% of the entire world's budget for defense. The U.S. has been spending (since the presidency of Ronald Reagan) around $300 billion a year on its defense. Its defense budget is more than the total of 15 next-on-the-list nations' defense budgets. The U.S. hawks would however maintain that, to police the world and punish the axis of evil, even higher allocations of funds are necessary.

It has been suggested that the U.S. military presence all over the world is paradoxically in keeping with the isolationist tendencies present throughout American history. It is one way to keep at arm's length America's potential enemies and even to eliminate them before they have a chance to enter the United States. There may be some truth to this theory.

That's why the U.S. maintains military bases almost on all continents. But now that the Soviet Union is no more, some countries resent the presence of U.S. troops in their midst as an affront to their sovereignty. Even though the *governments* of some nations may not protest the U.S. military presence in their midst very vigorously because of the economic benefits accrued, the *citizens* in many of these countries are often not happy about the client-state position their countries have to endure. Witness the loud protests staged by South Koreans in January 2003 against the U.S. military presence in the demilitarized zone. Similarly, many even moderate Middle

Eastern Arabs (according to three surveys recently conducted by Al Jazeera, a Middle Eastern television channel) are in favor of the removal of American troops from Saudi Arabia. The Philippines, for instance, had the U.S.-maintained Clark and Subic Bay bases removed from their country, but many bases elsewhere (in Okinawa, Japan, for example) are resented not just because they are inadequately monitored or policed but also because they serve as reminders of America's imperial role in the world. In my judgment, closing down these bases and bringing our men and women home will go a long way toward calming foreigners' nerves and reducing terrorist potential which feeds on such resentment. Let other nations be left to protect their own sovereignty. Closing down American bases abroad may appear to some Americans to weaken or jeopardize the U.S. position in the world. However, paradoxically, in my judgment, it will strengthen U.S. security through the removal of this irritant "colonial" symbol from around the world, now that the Soviet Union, the other empire, no longer exists. I'd suggest that the U.S. deploy its military power only at the request of the United Nations. The five nations' (Britain, China, France, Russia, and the U.S.) veto monopoly in the UN Security Council would, however, continue to jar with the sensibilities of other weaker nations.

[4] Serve as a model of human rights protection for other nations by protecting human rights here at home.

Outright killing or incarceration of hundreds of people during peacetime is not the only kind of violation of human rights. There are also other subtler but very demeaning forms of human rights violations. Dictatorships can be accused of the more obvious crimes against human rights, such as gassing its citizens, sudden and unexplained disappearance of dissenters, and long jail sentences without fair trials. But the U.S., a civilized

democracy, can be rightfully accused of several violations of human rights of the insidious kind not only in its past but right now. The real issue is how you define "human rights." The outrageous acts, like the ones mentioned above, are classified universally as the most abhorrent kinds of human rights violations. But I propose that the situations of the types listed below should also be labeled as human rights violations in a wealthy democracy like that of the United States: lack of healthcare insurance for over 40 million Americans, mismanagement and non-accounting of $100 billion worth of trust funds held on behalf of Native Americans for which the Secretary of the Interior has been chastised by a federal judge, and millions of people in despair induced by poverty, drugs, and resource-starved inner city schools. In America we value the rights to life, liberty, and the pursuit of happiness. But how can there be a right to life when health care is denied to many millions of citizens? Similarly, how can there be freedom or liberty for a large number of people when they have no money to exercise any choice? And how can the very poor in America pursue happiness when happiness is tied to material possessions?

As an example of my broadened definition of human rights, let me cite another case: Thousands of American missionaries have been targeting the poor of the world (through bribery and covert coercion) who do not have the means to resist attempts at conversion directed toward them. Exploiting people's poverty for conversion purposes through helping them "monetarily" and thus putting them under obligation is, in my estimation, one of the most disgusting forms of human rights violation. Evangelical churches and their congregations in the United States in the meanwhile are congratulating themselves for a (noble!) job well done. These conversions are taking place not because of the superiority of the (Christian or, for that matter, Islamic) dogma and philosophy but because these missionaries are armed with wealth to distribute to the needy, mainly in the Third World. What's even more revolting to me is how the new converts are surreptitiously encouraged to transfer their loyalties from their country of origin or birth to the country of the donors. As a native of India, I have a direct experience of watching Christianized tribes in Northeast India clamoring for secession from India and for sovereign nationhood for themselves. The U.S. must share the blame along with the other nations from where the proselytizers come. Delinking the material help these missionaries provide from their evangelism or zeal for conversion will soothe many people around the world who are incensed by such unfair conversion attempts.

Finally, the statistics of one young black male out of every four being currently incarcerated in U.S. jails is not flattering to the United States's record on human rights. In 2001 the Associated Press released a report under the caption "Black voters' ballots invalidated more often." The story referred to an analysis which concluded that "black voters disproportionately are denied their votes in elections, either by accident or design" (*The Idaho Statesman*, April 6, 2001). I suppose that the irregularities in the U.S. general (Presidential) elections of 2000 may have prompted the study.

[5] Share its wealth with the poorest nations of the world, just because it has more.

Though the terrorists who attacked the United States on 9–11–2001 did not come from the poor nations of the earth, the benign neglect demonstrated by the U.S. toward the poor of this earth does neither induce warm nor positive feelings for the United States. Poverty has often led to radicalism, which in turn can lead to terrorism. It's therefore in the interest of the United States to empower the people of the developing world by pumping productive resources there. Of course,

monitoring where the resources go ought to be an integral part of this aid. More hope for the poorest of this earth through wealth creation and its equitable distribution means less attraction for them to join terrorist organizations. It is fashionable in the U.S. to blame socialist policies, corrupt officials, red tape, and greedy dictatorships for the poverty of the Third World countries. Very rarely, however, is it admitted that the very scant allocations of resources by the rich countries for the poor is the main reason why the poor have remained poor. The wealthy will always say that you can't solve problems by throwing money at them. The poor, however, never say such things. They will gladly trade places with the rich. The world problem is, in fact, merely a macrocosm of the inequitable distribution of wealth within the United States itself.

It is unfortunate that the wealthiest nation in the world should act in such an insensitive and stingy manner. Since Reagan's presidency, the generous spirit of (post-WWII) Marshal Plan is dead in the United States. Of all the industrialized advanced nations of the world, the U.S. gives out the least foreign aid (excluding military aid) in terms of the percentage of its gross domestic product (GDP). Education, nutrition, freedom from disease, and infrastructure are the dire needs of the Third World today; and the United States, along with the other wealthy nations of the world, has the ability to remedy these wants, if it finds the will or readiness to part with only a small fraction of its GDP to leverage it for the enrichment of the lives of millions of people in the poorest regions of the world.

An ironic part of this issue of poverty alleviation is that most Americans call themselves Christian. The hypocrisy and contradiction of this claim would be palpable or evident for anybody who interprets a "Christian" as someone who believes in Christ (as the Savior) and is committed to following in his path. Everything Christ said and did (as the Bible tells us) was *against* greed and accumulation of wealth and *for* helping those in need. The parable of the Prodigal Son, Christ's reference to a camel more easily passing through the eye of a needle than a rich man entering into the kingdom of God, or the story of his turning water into wine (just enough for the guests, not for hoarding until the price of wine went up), etc. provide some evidence for my belief that capitalist America is really anti-Christ since Jesus's sayings and deeds are inconvenient for those who would rather hold on to their wealth than distribute it. Incidentally, it's easier to proclaim "In God we trust" because none can challenge convenient assertions such as "Wealth is a sign of God's favor," as Reformation Protestants did.

I also need to expand upon the latter part of my fifth course of action, "Share its wealth . . . *just because it has more*." I say "just because it (the United States) has more" deliberately for it lays to rest or circumvents the arguments of many neo-classical economists, such as America's wealth is not at the expense of other nations, or the poor deserve to be poor because of their "lack of character," or there will always be poor people (and poor countries), or the poor will squander the money, or inequitable wealth distribution is, in fact, good (for whomever!).

CONCLUSION

I believe that these measures, separately and together, will result in a noticeable reduction of terrorism directed at the United States. The first measure, promoting democracy, will give people a voice. They will also have no reason to blame the U.S. for supporting and protecting unpopular dictators. The second measure, acting like a good citizen among nations, will reduce the resentment felt for the bully as well as the consequent desire to retaliate. The third action, calling troops home, will allow America not to be perceived as an empire. The

fourth American action, serving as a model for human rights, will create admiration for the U.S. And the fifth action, sharing wealth, will let the world see the United States as following in the path of Christ, not as a worshipper of Mammon, the god of wealth.

Though I'm an optimist, I do not see much chance for positive change in the United States. There are two reasons for my doubts: First, as long as the U.S. government and a majority of citizens see the cause of terrorism as purely external, they will be only concentrating on violent means and the instruments of war directed outwardly against the world. There will be little movement toward changing U.S. policies. Second, the three most significant national institutions that need to be introspective and self-evaluative—the school, the church and the media—have not, in my judgment, seen the need to change. For example, American churches (more or less) tow the line of the wealthy few, instead of condemning rampant greed and capitalism run amuck. The school teaches whitewashed American history and strives to produce hyper-patriotic, occupationally trained citizenry rather than encouraging independent thinking and fearless inquiry. The media, with a few exceptions, follow submissively the lead of the U.S. government and the so-called think tanks in matters of foreign policy rather than questioning the assumptions and conflicts of interest behind that policy.

A question may arise at this point: What can average American citizens do to improve the situation? For one thing, they can elect candidates to the national legislature and the presidency who believe in the program of action I'm suggesting in this essay. For the second, they could keep questioning the motives of those who are pursuing the present shortsighted policies. For the third, they should write to their legislators and to the media to express their dissatisfaction with the status quo and demand positive change. For the fourth, they could organize meetings, marches, and debates to awaken public conscience and awareness about the fact that the interests of a few are jeopardizing the wellness and security of a whole nation.

To my knowledge, very few American public figures—thinkers, opinion shapers, or political leaders—have recommended such a far-reaching and comprehensive program of action as I recommend here to reduce the post 9–11–2001 security problem of the United States. No amount of money can buy security for any nation. I am, however, convinced that the measures I suggest here will go a long way toward making the United States more safe and secure than it has felt since that tragic and gruesome event. In the bargain, the U.S. will also create and enhance a positive and endearing image for itself around the world.

Mohan R. Limaye (Ph.D., University of Wisconsin–Milwaukee), a Fulbright scholar from India, retired from Boise State University in January 2003. He has taught and researched in the areas of intercultural business communication, workforce diversity, democracy, and global business.

Index